Dryden's Handbook of Individual Therapy

Dryden's Handbook of Individual Therapy

fifth edition

edited by
Windy Dryden

Los Angeles | London | New Delhi
Singapore | Washington DC

Editorial arrangement, Preface, Chapter 14 and
Appendix 1 © Windy Dryden 2007
Chapter 1 © Colin Feltham
Chapter 2 © Alessandra Lemma
Chapter 3 © Cassie Cooper
Chapter 4 © Ann Casement
Chapter 5 © Jenny Warner and
    Gerhard Baumer
Chapter 6 © Brian Thorne
Chapter 7 © Fay Fransella, Peggy
    Dalton and Grant Weselby

Chapter 8 © Emmy van Deurzen
Chapter 9 © Malcolm Parlett and Juliet Denham
Chapter 10 © Keith Tudor and Robin Hobbes
Chapter 11 © Mark Dunn
Chapter 12 © Stirling Moorey
Chapter 13 © David Richards
Chapter 15 © Bill O'Connell
Chapter 16 © Martin Payne
Chapter 17 © Henry Hollanders
Chapter 18 © Michael Barkham
Chapter 19 © Mark Aveline

Previous editions have been published as *Individual Therapy in Britian*
(1984) and *Individual Therapy: A Handbook* (1990), and *Handbook of
Individual Therapy* (1996, 2002)

This edition published 2007
Reprinted 2010

SAGE Publications Ltd
1 Oliver's Yard
55 City Road
London EC1Y 1SP

SAGE Publications Inc.
2455 Teller Road
Thousand Oaks, California 91320

SAGE Publications India Pvt Ltd
B1/I I Mohan Cooperative Industrial Area
Mathura Road, New Delhi 110 044
India

SAGE Publications Asia-Pacific Pte Ltd
33 Pekin Street #02-01
Far East Square
Singapore 048763

British Library Cataloguing in Publication data

A catalogue record for this book is available from
the British Library

ISBN 978-1-4129-2237-1
ISBN 978-1-4129-2238-8 (pbk)

Library of Congress Control Number available

Typeset by C&M Digitals (P) Ltd, Chennai, India
Printed in Great Britain by the MPG Books Group
Printed on paper from sustainable resources

Mixed Sources
Product group from well-managed
forests and other controlled sources
www.fsc.org Cert no. SA-COC-1565
© 1996 Forest Stewardship Council

For Louise

Contents

Preface

The first edition of this handbook was published in 1984 and attempted to fill a gap in the market at that time by having British authors write on well-established approaches to individual therapy for a British readership. The three subsequent editions published at six-year intervals carried on this tradition. In this, the fifth edition, the most successful elements of the previous editions have again been retained. Contributors of chapters detailing specific therapeutic approaches were once again asked to keep to a common structure (Appendix 1) in writing their chapters (Chapters 2–17), there is a chapter placing therapy in a cultural social context (Chapter 1) and chapters are included on research and training as they pertain to individual therapy (Chapters 18–19).

As before, I have sought feedback on the previous edition and have included chapters on solution-focused therapy, narrative therapy and integrative and eclectic approaches. All other chapters have been updated or completely rewritten and each has a new case example.

I welcome feedback on this handbook and hope that readers will once again join me in thanking all the contributors for a job very well done.

Windy Dryden, London

The Editor

Windy Dryden is Professor of Psychotherapeutic Studies, Goldsmiths College, University of London. He is a Fellow of the British Psychological Society and of the British Association of Counselling and Psychotherapy. He began his training in REBT in 1977 and became the first Briton to be accredited as an REBT therapist by the Albert Ellis Institute. In 1981, Windy spent a six months sabbatical at the Center for Cognitive Therapy, University of Pennsylvania, one of the first British psychologists to do an extended training in Cognitive Therapy. He is a Fellow of the Albert Ellis Institute and a Founding Fellow of the Academy of Cognitive Therapy.

While his primary therapeutic orientation is REBT, Windy has been very much influenced by his cognitive therapy colleagues and by the working alliance theory of Ed Bordin. His research interests are in the historical and theoretical roots of REBT (with Arthur Still) and the phenomenology of hurt, the study of which is informed by REBT theory.

Windy is perhaps best known for his voluminous writings in REBT/CBT and the wider field of counselling and psychotherapy. To date he has authored or edited over 160 books, making him probably the most prolific book writer and editor currently alive in the field today. He has also edited 17 book series including the best selling Counselling in Action series.

Windy was the founding editor of the *British Journal of Cognitive Psychotherapy* in 1982 which later merged with the *Cognitive Behaviorist* to become *the Journal of Cognitive Psychotherapy: An International Quarterly*. Windy was co-founding editor of this journal with E. Thomas Dowd. In 2003, Windy became the editor of the *Journal of Rational-Emotive and Cognitive-Behavior Therapy*.

List of Contributors

Dr Mark Aveline retired from his NHS post in 2002 and is now Emeritus Consultant in Psychotherapy and Psychiatry with Nottinghamshire Healthcare NHS Trust. He is also Honorary Professor of Counselling and Psychotherapy at Leicester University and was President of the Society for Psychotherapy Research during 2003–4.

Michael Barkham is Professor of Clinical and Counselling Psychology and Director of the Psychological Therapies Research Centre at the University of Leeds and visiting professor at the Universities of Sheffield and Northumbria and Newcastle. He is a Fellow of the British Psychological Society, a past UK President of the UK chapter of the Society for Psychotherapy Research, and currently joint editor of the *British Journal of Clinical Psychology*. He has published widely on psychotherapy process and outcome and has a major interest in building a practice-based evidence for the psychological therapies.

Gerhard Baumer studied psychology and trained as an Adlerian Psychotherapist in Berlin. He has been working in private practice for 26 years and writes articles, gives lectures and runs workshops regularly in Germany and England. He is an international Adlerian trainer and a co-chairman of ICASSI. He has co-authored a chapter in S. Palmer (ed.) *Introduction to Counselling and Psychotherapy* (Sage, 2000).

Ann Casement is a training analyst at the Association of Jungian Analysts, London, which she represents on the Executive Committee of the International Association for Analytical Psychology. She is a licensed New York State Psychoanalyst. She also contributes articles and book reviews to *The Economist* and professional journals.

Cassie Cooper is a practising Kleinian trained Psychoanalytic Psychotherapist and Counselling Psychologist with a strong interest in Attachment Theory. She is a founder member and Fellow of The British Association for Counselling and Psychotherapy and an active member of The United Kingdom Council for Psychotherapy. She has contributed chapters in 12 text books on psychotherapy and counselling, some of which are now translated into Italian and German. The former Head of a University Diploma Course in Counselling, she continues to work full time as a psychotherapist and supervisor in the South London area, plus acting as consultant to Carlton TV on counselling issues. Her recently completed Doctorate was entitled Cult Membership as a Disorder of Attachment.

Peggy Dalton is a Fellow of the Royal College of Speech and Language Therapists and a PCP Psychotherapist, working with both children and adults. She is a member of PCP Education and Training, involved in course development, teaching and supervision. Her writing includes *A Psychology for Living* with Gavin Dunnett (2nd edn; Whurr, 2005) and *Counselling People with Communication Problems* (Sage, 1994).

Juliet Denham is a Teaching and Supervising Member of the Gestalt Psychotherapy and Training Institute and part of the training team at Manchester Gestalt Centre. She works in Birmingham and Shropshire as an individual and group therapist and supervisor and teaches in several training centres in Britain and Europe.

Emmy van Deurzen is an existential psychotherapist, counselling psychologist and supervisor and Director of Dilemma Consultancy Limited (www.dilemmas. org). She was the founder of Regent's College School of Psychotherapy and Counselling and of the New School of Psychotherapy and Counselling which she now directs. She is Professor of Psychotherapy with Schiller International University and Honorary Professor with the University of Sheffield, where she co-directs the Centre for the Study of Conflict and Reconciliation. She is the author of a number of books on existential psychotherapy, which have been translated into a variety of languages. Her latest book is *Psychotherapy and the Quest for Happiness* (Sage, 2007).

Mark Dunn, Consultant Psychotherapist. Mark trained as a psychotherapist at Guys Hospital and specialises in CAT. He teaches psychotherapy and is an experienced clinical practitioner and supervisor in a range of therapeutic models. He retired from the NHS in 2004 and leads a private psychotherapy clinic. In addition he works with the Metropolitan Police and other organisations in coaching, employee assistance and executive support roles. He can be contacted at: mark@bridgepsych.com and www.bridgepsych.com.

Colin Feltham, is Professor of Critical Counselling Studies, Sheffield Hallam University and Course Leader for the MA Professional Development in Counselling and Psychotherapy. His publications include the *Dictionary of Counselling* (2nd edn, with Windy Dryden; Whurr, 2004), *Problems Are Us* (Braiswick, 2004) and *What's Wrong with Us?: The Anthropathology Thesis* (Wiley, forthcoming).

Fay Fransella is Founder of the Centre for Personal Construct Psychology at the University of Hertfordshire; Reader Emeritus in Clinical Psychology, University of London; and visiting Professor of Personal Construct Psychology at the

University of Hertfordshire. Her books include *Personal Construct Counselling in Action* (with Peggy Dalton, 2nd edn; Sage, 2000) and as editor *Essential Practitioner's Handbook of Personal Construct Psychology* (Wiley, 2005).

Robin Hobbes is a Teaching and Supervising Transactional Analyst. The former chair of the British Institute of Transactional Analysis he now chairs the Institute's clinical Sub-Committee. He co-directs Elan training – a psychotherapy and counselling training centre in Manchester.

Henry Hollanders founded and directed the Professional Doctorate in Counselling at the University of Manchester where he was a lecturer for 20 years prior to his partial retirement in 2006. He continues to lecture on counselling and psychotherapy at the University as well as supervising PhD and Professional Doctorate students. He has a counselling and psychotherapy practice based in Manchester and in Pendle in Lancashire.

Caroline Kitcatt is a person-centred counsellor, trainer and supervisor. She is the Centre Director of the Norwich Centre for Personal and Professional Development and the Managing Director of Norwich Centre Projects Ltd. She is an associate tutor on the Post-Graduate Diploma in Counselling at the University of East Anglia.

Dr Alessandra Lemma is a psychoanalyst and psychoanalytic psychotherapist. She works as a Consultant Clinical Psychologist in the Adolescent Department at the Tavistock Clinic and in private practice. She is the author of several books on psychology and psychotherapy: *Starving to Live: The Paradox of Anorexia Nervosa* (Central Publishing, 1994), *Invitation to Psychodynamic Psychology* (Whurr, 1995), *Introduction to Psychopathology* (Sage, 1996), *Humour on the Couch* (Whurr, 2000); *Introduction to the Practice of Psychoanalytic Psychotherapy* (Wiley, 2003), *The Perversion of Loss: Psychoanalytic Perspectives on Trauma* (ed. with S. Levy; Whurr, 2004).

Dr Stirling Moorey is Consultant Psychiatrist in CBT and Head of Psychotherapy for the South London and Maudsley NHS Trust. He trains psychiatrists and other professionals in CBT. He is currently researching the efficacy of CBT in palliative care and is co-author of *Cognitive Behaviour Therapy for People with Cancer* (with S. Greer; Oxford University Press, 2002).

Bill O'Connell is currently the Director of Training with Focus on Solutions Limited, a company specializing in the delivery of training in the solution-focused approach. Until 2003 he was a Senior Lecturer at the University of Birmingham where he headed the MA in Solution-Focused Therapy programme. He is a Fellow of the BACP and an accredited counsellor. He has a background in social work and youth work. He is the author of *Solution Focused Therapy* (Sage, 1998), *Solution Focused Stress Counselling* (Continuum/Sage, 2001) and co-editor with Dr Stephen Palmer of the *Handbook of Solution Focused Therapy* (Sage, 2003). E-mail: focusonsolutions@btconnect.com.

Malcolm Parlett is a teaching and supervising member (and co-founder) of the Gestalt Psychotherapy and Training Institute and a psychotherapist and organizational consultant in private practice. In 2006 he retired from being Editor of the *British Gestalt Journal* and Visiting Professor of Gestalt Psychotherapy at the University of Derby. He is the author of many chapters and papers about Gestalt therapy.

Martin Payne counsels in Primary Care in Norwich. Initially a person-centred counsellor, he more recently undertook training in Narrative Therapy with Michael White. His publications include articles for *Context, Counselling* and the *British Journal of Guidance and Counselling*, and *Narrative Therapy: an Introduction for Counsellors* (2nd edn; Sage, 2006).

David Richards, Professor of Mental Health at the University of York, develops, measures and tests new ways of organising low-intensity treatments for people with mental health problems in primary care. He is at the forefront of efforts to improve access to treatment for those suffering from common emotional distress.

Brian Thorne is Emeritus Professor of Counselling at the University of East Anglia, Norwich and a Co-founder of the Norwich Centre. He has contributed substantially to the professional literature and his autobiography, *Love's Embrace*, has recently been published (PCCS Books, 2005).

Keith Tudor is a qualified and registered psychotherapist with a practice in Sheffield where he is a founding Director of Temenos. He is a Teaching and Supervising Transactional Analyst. He is the author/editor of seven books in the field of psychotherapy and mental health, the editor of a series of books on *Advancing Theory in Therapy* (published by Routledge), and an Honorary Fellow in the School of Health, Liverpool John Moores University.

Jenny Warner was a Speech and Language Therapy Manager in the NHS and an Adlerian therapist, family counsellor, supervisor and international trainer. She is now retired. She has written chapters in S. Palmer (ed.) *Introduction to Counselling and Psychotherapy* (Sage, 2000, 2006) and C. Feltham and I. Horton (eds) *Handbook of Counselling and Psychotherapy* (Sage, 2000).

Grant Weselby is a chartered Clinical Psychologist based in a Community Mental Health Team. Within this role he applies PCP clinically as well as providing input to the local PCP Foundation Training Course.

Individual Therapy in Context

Colin Feltham

The fine-grained, moment-by-moment reality of what is referred to as psychotherapy and counselling (hereafter simply 'therapy') happens most commonly between two individuals, in private. Not only is it private then but confidential later, so that relatively little of the actual phenomena of therapy, in spite of some consumers' write-ups, disguised case studies, transcribed tape-recordings and conversational analyses, find their way into publications. This book presents the theories of various mainstream therapies structured according to certain historical, conceptual, professional and clinical frameworks, along with case studies. A focus on research, training and supervision is provided in later chapters. In order to provide some wider and integrating balance, this introductory chapter looks briefly at a number of transtheoretical areas in order to contextualise this most private of activities. Whether approaching each chapter as a taster prior to deeper immersion in a particular approach, or as a student of the broad phenomenon of counselling and psychotherapy, the reader will hopefully benefit from a brief historical and critical overview of this kind.

THE NATURE OF HUMAN SUFFERING AND PSYCHOLOGICAL NEED

Some of the literature on therapy creates or sustains the impression that it arrived a little over a century ago with Freud and perhaps his immediate predecessors and contemporaries, and that not much of interest or relevance existed or is worth talking about from before that time. But quite clearly human beings have suffered and have had emotional or spiritual needs or aspirations for centuries, if not millennia, even if these have been expressed in very different ways. During that time many remedies or solutions have been practised (Bankart, 1997; Ehrenwald, 1991; Ellenberger, 1970). Today's needy or helpseeking client and trained therapist did not appear in a vacuum and we deceive ourselves if we imagine they did.

There are several reasons for including these topics. First, while psychotherapeutic theorists are asked to consider their 'image of the person' and human nature, this area of theory is arguably one of the weakest in many models of therapy, probably due to therapists' background lying in psychology rather than philosophy or historically grounded disciplines, and to their naturally prioritising urgent, practical, clinical concerns. Messer (1992) discusses therapists' 'belief structures' and 'visions of reality' and the very language used betrays a certain subjective tenor. Secondly, this weakness is not merely an intellectual inelegance but a potential pitfall for the advance of theory and clinical understanding and for the status of therapy. Thirdly, since the development of evolutionary psychology and psychotherapy over the past decade or so, relatively few writers from the ranks of different therapeutic models have kept pace with this trend (exceptions including Gilbert and Bailey, 2000; Langs, 1996; Stevens and Price, 2000). Fourthly, another weakness in most theories of therapy has been in their definitions of the scope of what they can do in relation to what clients need; in other words, a failure to define 'suffering' or deficit or, if this terminology is disliked, then an alternative nomenclature and set of explanations. Fifthly, it is doubtful whether progress can be made towards the integration of therapeutic models without a better philosophical and scientific focus on what it means to be human and to have psychological needs, if indeed any consensus can be achieved in our so-called postmodern era.

There is considerable agreement that we have existed for about 100,000 to 150,000 years in our *homo sapiens sapiens* form. Our ancestors' upright gait came about some 4 million years ago, notable increases in brain size took place about 2.5 million years ago, coinciding with significant meat-eating. Some writers have speculated on such distant events and our modern problems with birth difficulties – long, dependent and vulnerable childhoods, over-cognitivization and environmental rapaciousness. Even now, in our contemporary theoretical models of therapy, we are sometimes obliged to make judgements as to whether cognition or emotion is the primary mode of human functioning, the latter being more evident earlier in our evolution and probably having some female bias, the former arguably having connotations of emotion-suppression, control and detachment – some models urge us to think more rationally, others to feel more deeply.

Our original ancestors, probably from Africa, were hunter-gatherers who lived co-operatively in quite small groups. By some accounts, patriarchy did not become the norm until about 12,000 years ago, probably coinciding with the rise in agriculture, domestication of certain animals, the birth of civilisations, tooth decay and so on. Use of alcohol is recorded from 7,000 years ago and opium

5,000 years ago. There is ample evidence of violence and, alongside geographical expansion and technological progress, common anxieties about death. A drastic decline in the nomadic, hunter-gatherer lifestyle occurred about 4,000 years ago, coinciding roughly with the advent of the Abrahamic religions. In short, there is a recognisable human story comprising both progressive and destructive, and myth-making and knowledge-seeking elements. We have become increasingly technologized, urbanized and overpopulated (projected to rise to 8 billion by 2020) and we have obviously not overcome our warring tendencies, although many live in conditions of relative peace and prosperity.

Unless we believe that we are psychologically completely different from our remote ancestors, it is likely to be helpful to speculate about which psychological structures were laid down in prehistory that we may still incorporate and wrestle with today. Most agree that early human beings would have had to contend with the vicissitudes of food supply, climate and health, and the threats presented by predators, warring tribes and in-group conflict and sexual competition. Debate continues among anthropologists, archaeologists and paleopsychologists as to whether we enjoyed periods and places characterized by plenty and peacefulness, or so-called golden ages. Certain feminist, anarcho-primitivist and other writers regard the birth of universal human suffering as more or less coterminous with the rise of agriculture and the gradual dominance of patriarchy, early technology, domestication of animals and oppressive, hierarchical civilisation (Taylor, 2005). Arguably, in small hunter-gatherer communities, we lived largely in harmony with nature and each other, perhaps with rare exceptions. Biblical and other accounts suggest a radical change from such a benign nature towards division of labour, tribal conflict, frequent adversity and a heightened sense of mortality – but no consensus exists about this. We can, however, concede that widespread tension exists between civilisation and many of the discontented individuals within it.

All religions offer accounts of human beings losing deep contact with spiritual identity, suffering as a consequence, and needing guidance or succour. Whether certain individuals neurotically hanker for a bygone age or for lost intrauterine bliss (Freud's 'oceanic feeling') when they present for therapy is a moot point. In roughly the last 200 years, the dominance of industry and capitalism with their attendant effects on working lives is extremely significant. Those forms of unhappy servitude, or what Marx termed 'immiseration', associated with capitalist prosperity (Bunting, 2005) may or may not be compensated for by the advantages provided by medicine and technology, such as disease reduction and prevention, higher rates of successful births and greater longevity. While some argue that we now live in and need to adjust to a 'post-emotional society', others are alarmed at the loss of emotional intelligence and humanness, qualities that are of course the bread and butter of most forms of therapy.

Many now argue that there is no universal human nature at all, that we cannot speak meaningfully of *a* human nature but only of different theoretical versions, different cultures and individuals (Ashworth, 2000). Others argue that we have an all too obvious set of determined characteristics – many of them, like aggression, jealousy, greed and deception, highly negative – which parallel a range of freedoms (Pinker, 2003). Today's debates echo the unresolved nature–nurture debates of past decades. But we can say with confidence that it is in our common nature to be born, to be dependent when young, to grow, to couple, to age and die, and along the way most of us struggle and experience suffering to some extent. If, therefore, we have any shared human condition known to all 6 billion of us, it is this – that we must negotiate our way across the lifespan with whatever resources we possess, and most of us are driven to avoid suffering and maximise pleasure, as Freud wrote. Even then, none of us can avoid ageing and physical death and many have far more than their share of loss and sorrow, depending on genetic inheritance, formative experiences, life events, luck, exercise of choices, cultural and idiosyncratic factors. Kleinian and existentialist therapies take such realities on board more obviously than most other models of therapy. It is also the case that most of us define ourselves and are closely supported by families and communities; and that insufficiencies in care, abuse, shame, loss and rupture in the social domain explain the formation of many of our psychological problems.

Insofar as distinct images of human nature, or pertinent aspects of it, can be identified in the approaches outlined in this book, we might select the following: self-deception, struggle, dualism, socioteleology, trustworthiness, personal scientists, existential becoming, experiencing, OK-ness, cognitive processing, hedonism, storytelling, solution-building. Some approaches have no single clear view of human nature and many regard us as complex biosociopsychological beings. Key questions for exponents of different models of therapy include the following: To what extent is there an agreement on any essence of human nature and its problematic aspects? To what extent does each model either address this and explain how it is incorporated, or dismiss it as irrelevant, and why? Where does each model lie on the spectrum from conceiving human beings as being 'wholly determined' to 'wholly free'? To what extent is each model optimistic or pessimistic in its outlook? To what extent does each model remain open to new information from scientific or other disciplines? Significant differences in answers to these (and one would expect humanistic approaches to be somewhat more optimistic than psychoanalytic approaches, for example) indicate their implicit philosophies of human nature and potential.

RELIGIOUS, PHILOSOPHICAL, BIOLOGICAL AND PSYCHOLOGICAL THERAPIES

Archaeological evidence for psychological distress and treatment is understandably hard to come by. But it is estimated that burial rituals were taking place at least 100,000 years ago, indicating an acute awareness of death of kin and problematic psychological reactions. It has been speculated, on the basis of worldwide distribution, that schizophrenia may have arisen at least 80,000 years ago, suggesting marked behavioural differences in some individuals and perhaps ways of attempting to construe and respond to these differences. There is evidence of post-traumatic stress reactions following battle, from 4,000 years ago. Hinduism, one of the world's oldest major religions, probably began its development about 6,000 to 4,000 years ago. Religions in themselves suggest the expression of a psychological need for explanations, comfort and guidance. Evidence for primitive medical incantations dates from around 4,500 years ago. The shift from mythological and religious to medical and philosophical analyses of illness, disease and distress is gradual, with Greek philosophy appearing only around 585 BCE. Aeschylus' notion of *iatroi logoi* or healing words appeared around 500 BCE, Galen's categories of temperaments (choleric, melancholic, phlegmatic and sanguine) stem from 325 BCE, and the works of philosophers are replete with ideas that recur in our own contemporary therapeutic literature.

Christian and other religious traditions contain compassionate views and practices, including prayer for the afflicted, faith healing, laying on of hands and prescriptions for 'right living'. But very often those afflicted by mental distress and marked outward behavioural differences were dealt with punitively as they were regarded as possessed by demons. This religious interpretation started to give way around the thirteenth century CE to early concepts of madness and psychiatric institutions and later, very gradually, to humane forms of asylum. Robert Burton's monumental *The Anatomy of Melancholy* was first published in 1621 and shows the extraordinary penchant of an English writer for careful analysis of psychological distress in its many forms and suggested remedies. This 'proto-DSM' (*Diagnostic and Statistical Manual*) was necessarily filled with religious reflections and the rough science of its time but had the wisdom to include dietary and behavioural as well as insight-oriented remedies. The eighteenth century saw a wave of attempts at psychiatric classification and some (e.g. Szasz, 1988) place the roots of psychotherapy at around this time. Concepts of moral management and humane treatment can be seen in the initiatives of Samuel Tuke among others at the end of the eighteenth century. The first journal of psychology, *Mind*, made its appearance in 1876. As well as a somewhat linear movement *from* myth and religion towards scientific medicine and psychiatry over the centuries, one can also see continuing overlaps and competition.

Ellenberger (1970) traces the rise of therapy from the 'primitive psychotherapy' of the Guyanan medicine man and the use of drugs, ointments, massage and diet. He also acknowledges therapeutic work with loss of the soul, spirit intrusion, breach of taboo and sorcery across many cultures. Possession and exorcism are phenomena associated with the Christian church as well as many non-western cultures, Ellenberger making links with the 'hysterical neurosis' and attempted cures of late nineteenth century Europe. Ellenberger also lists confession, gratification of frustrated wishes, ceremonial healing, incubation, hypnosis and magical healing, and temple healing and philosophical psychotherapy as forerunners to contemporary scientific psychotherapy. Hence, we can see the seeds of today's methods in distant history – we can also see, in certain epochs, rivalry between schools of therapy or healing, as in early Greek schools of healing. Albert Ellis' (1994) repeated tribute to the stoic philosopher Epictetus (55–135 CE) demonstrates a clear link across almost 2,000 years between original stoicism and the modern, psychological, clinical therapy of rational emotive behaviour therapy and cognitive-behavioural therapy (CBT) generally. But many similar ideas are found in the teachings of the Buddha more than 500 years before Epictetus. Let us recall too that Frank's (1974) anthropologically informed study of psychotherapy acknowledged such sources as well as contemporary transcultural likenesses, arguing that certain common factors could be found universally. The superiority of western, talking therapy is easily assumed but this is being questioned by some, such as Moodley and West (2005), and arguments put forward for an integration of psychological with traditional healing methods.

Physical, medical or biological models of therapy have early roots and include herbal remedies, blood-letting, emetics, trepanning, acupuncture, neurosurgery, electroconvulsive therapy (ECT) and psychopharmacology among others. Even homeopathy must be considered a form of physical intervention. In the west, psychiatry developed as the extension of medical analysis and treatment into the domain of severe psychological or emotional problems. Psychiatric abuses and failures – unwarranted incarceration, indiscriminate and damaging use of ECT, drugs used as a 'chemical cosh' with highly negative side-effects, and crude, botched lobotomies – created much vociferous opposition from patients and formed part of the drive against the 'bio-medical model' (Breggin, 1993). Today, psychopharmacological treatment for schizophrenia and bipolar disorder, for example, is largely accepted but also strongly objected to by some groups. While a great deal of counselling and psychotherapy has been historically criticised for targeting the self-indulgent 'worried well', psychological therapy has been increasingly appropriated and boosted by those suffering from depression, anxiety and similar conditions wanting to talk in an exploratory, cathartic and social learning manner rather than (or as well as) ingesting medication. There is growing research evidence in support of the use of certain medications alongside psychological therapies and in some cases a demonstrated superiority of talking therapy (particularly CBT) over medication (Clark et al., 1994).

The prefix *psyche* comes from the Greek for breath, soul or life. The *psychological* therapies clearly did not properly begin with Freud in 1896, who regarded himself as a neurologist and his discovery, *psychoanalysis* (the 'talking cure'), as his own creation. Many, including Kirschner (1996) regard psychoanalysis as having its conceptual and inspirational origins in religious and romantic aspects of the Judeo-Christian tradition. Many of the founders of contemporary mainstream psychotherapies themselves have Judeo-Christian origins. The term *psychotherapy* appeared in 1853 but did not refer to an applied discipline necessarily drawing from psychology. *Psychology* itself appeared as a technical term in 1748 and even then had overtones associating it with 'soul'. Psychology has of course had its internal battles over identity and has moved significantly from its early insistence that it should scientifically exclude subjectivity. What we generally mean by 'psychological therapy' is an essentially talking-and-listening form of help that does not primarily utilise medical or physical means. While this could broadly include any spiritual or philosophical concepts and techniques (these are, after all, not medical or physical), it tends not to. Since psychology is promoted as a scientific discipline, clinical psychology, and latterly counselling psychology, have been advanced as applied scientific professions, in turn suggesting a superiority over earlier religious and philosophical traditions of helping people with their problems in living.

Perhaps the cumbersomeness of the five-syllable term 'psychotherapy' has encouraged its abbreviation to the colloquial term 'therapy', which is also used as a way of collapsing the problematic of 'psychotherapy and counselling' into one term. The BACP's monthly magazine *Counselling and Psychotherapy Journal* was pragmatically renamed *Therapy Today* in 2005, for example. It is hard to deny the inherent problematic of non-ambiguous names in this field (James and Palmer, 1996) but it is important to remember that its multiple roots in historical politics are partly responsible and that the continuing proliferation of theoretical models reflects this. Like it or not, the therapy field is problematically divided into competing psy-professions and therapeutic approaches.

CURRENT SOCIO-CULTURAL CONTEXTS OF THERAPY IN BRITAIN

The United Kingdom is comprised of England (population 50.1 million), Scotland (5 million), Wales (3 million) and Northern Ireland (1.7 million). (These demographic figures are for mid 2004 and taken from www.statistics. gov.uk). The average age is 38.6, with 1 in 5 under 16 and 1 in 6 over 65. Births are running at 1.77 children per woman, at an average age of 29.4. Average life expectancy is approximately 75–80, with women still outliving men, and expectancy varying quite considerably by region and income. At the 2001 census 36 million described themselves as White Christians. The minority ethnic population was 4.6 million; almost half of these live in the London area and comprise 29 per cent of all residents there. Estimates for the total gay population are 2.6–9.7 per cent (male) and 2.6–8.4 per cent (female). There are about 10 million disabled people. About 1 in 4 people are thought to experience some mental health problem in the course of a year (www.mentalhealth.org.uk). Headline health concerns in recent years include suicide, obesity, teenage pregnancy, sexually transmitted diseases, insomnia, stress and excessive or problematic nicotine and alcohol consumption; and crime has risen in spite of high levels of employment. Home ownership levels are high, as are personal debts, unemployment is low, levels of long-hours work are high, and UK citizens currently face the prospects of a raised retirement age.

Cushman's (1995) seminal text on the historical development of psychotherapy within the American context remains highly instructive but no directly comparable British text exists. Cushman's analysis problematises the rise of the peculiarly western sense of self and Rose's (1989) analysis of British trends in the rise of psychology and its influences on our sense of a private self has some resonances. Significantly, in spite of a decades–long tradition of couple counselling and group therapy, individual therapy remains by far the preferred choice. We are told by the authors of one piece of (market) research (BACP/ FF, 2004) that 21 per cent of the British population have had some form of counselling or psychotherapy and that up to 82 per cent of people would willingly have therapy if they thought they needed it. Previous estimates of the numbers experiencing therapy had been around 5 per cent at most and there may be reasons to doubt a figure as high as 21 per cent. Nevertheless, since the struggling 1970s, when counsellors and psychotherapists encountered a great deal of public and media resistance, acceptance has clearly grown. The visibility and accessibility of counsellors in many GP practices means that therapy is no longer perceived as an elitist, unaffordable or dubious activity but as potentially available and beneficial to the entire adult population. Availability has been buttressed by the presence of free counselling in many colleges and universities, employee assistance programmes and voluntary organizations such as Relate, Cruse and Mind. A gradual softening of the traditional British 'stiff upper lip' attitude may also be part of this development.

Twentieth century therapeutic provision was driven by a combination of factors: early psychoanalytic pioneers promoting their ideas via medical training, psychology and social work practice, by the needs of military returners from war suffering from post-traumatic stress, by the personnel of voluntary agencies and others exploiting American therapeutic practices and by a general enthusiasm for theories focusing on the inner life of individuals and its improvement. Britain became home to several eminent psychoanalysts, the Tavistock Clinic and Institute of Psychiatry were very influential in the dissemination of therapeutic theory and practices. Attachment theory and object relations therapy, driven by Klein, Winnicott, Bowlby, Fairbairn and others, owe much to the British empirical tradition of infant observation; and key figures like R.D. Laing promulgated original views on the limits of psychiatric treatment and the promise of talking therapy.

The sociologist Halmos is well known for his thesis that counselling arose around the 1950s as formal religion and politics were often perceived as not meeting individual needs: 'at least to some extent, the counsellors have been responsible for a revival of interest in the rehabilitation of the individual, and a loss of interest in the rehabilitation of society' (1978: 7). Perhaps the 1960s, 1970s and early 1980s were characterized by a certain secularism, hedonism and optimism (which paralleled the humanistic psychology movement), and respect for formal politics declined markedly in the 1990s and early 2000s alongside a steady turn against left-leaning politics and towards acquisitiveness. But at the same time the growing impact of feminist freedoms, the rise of multiculturalism and gradual acceptance of homosexuality made for an interestingly diverse society in which consumer demands and health reforms have combined to favour certain forms of counselling and psychotherapy (notably, CBT), as well as witnessing a growth of interest in spirituality and transpersonal therapies.

Attempts to categorise 'national character' are perilous and easily shot down, and the increasingly multicultural nature of Britain may eventually render them pointless. But traditionally the British have been portrayed variously as stoical, eccentric, enterprising, creative, tolerant, humorous, sexually inhibited and xenophobic, for example. For a considerable time, therapy was resisted in many quarters as indulgent, 'touchy-feely' (over-emotional), negatively American, and looking for, or creating, problems where none existed – stoicism was elevated over emotional expressiveness. Apart from the critique of the monolithic notion of British character associated with recent waves of immigration, a longstanding perception of psychological and behavioural differences between the English, Scottish, Welsh and Northern Irish includes stereotypes of regional toughness versus softness, drunkenness, fieriness, madness, dourness and so on. What we can say is that events as marked as 'the troubles' in Northern Ireland have shaped regional character somewhat, left peculiar psychological scars and stimulated the construction of necessarily specialised services for those afflicted by post-traumatic stress disorder (PTSD) (DHSSPS, 2002). In terms of population density, class and affluence, it remains the case that the training for and delivery of psychoanalytic therapy is concentrated in London. The concentration of particular therapeutic approaches in certain regions and cities has more to do with psychotherapeutic entrepreneurs, accidental and historical factors than with local character, need or planned services.

Can it be said that the contemporary social and psychological problems of the British have a character distinct from those of other nations? In many surveys of self-assessed happiness the UK rates highly, for example an 87 per cent level of happiness and 10th position among 50 surveyed nations (www.nationmaster.com). Yet commentators such as James (1996) have assessed Britain as a 'low serotonin society', that is, populated by depressed citizens who cannot keep pace with the heavy capitalist expectations placed on them and who sense that ever greater acquisition and pleasure-seeking does not result in satisfaction but in compromised mental health. This, however, does not explain any distinctiveness about British society, global capitalism and affluence accompanying in China, for example, rapidly increasing levels of depression and suicide; and Scandinavian gloom, a mere stereotype or not, is very familiar. Layard (2003) cites a figure of about 35 per cent for British happiness across the past 40 years but points out that we deserve to be much happier given our level of affluence compared with eastern European nationals. Dunant and Porter (1996) reported on links between increasing anxiety and technology, on rising violence, environmental anxiety, HIV/AIDS, social alienation, family breakdown, racism and the problems of youth. The suicide bombings in London in 2005 triggered significant PTSD and widespread anxiety (as well as alleged stoicism) as Londoners braced themselves for further terrorist attacks. Taken together, such depression and anxiety as national characteristics paint a gloomy picture and one that inexplicably contradicts the more optimistic happiness survey cited above. Trite though the conclusion is, we must assume that UK citizens are pulled between the kind of stoicism advocated by Furedi (2004) and frank demoralization. George Cheyne's *The English Malady*, published in 1733, celebrated for its portrayal of depression as a very common characteristic, shows that this is nothing new.

The UK has been a major importer of American therapy models, as of most other American commodities. In turn, Britain has provided inspiration for many other countries in developing their own therapy services and professions, as well as a certain positive energy devoted to professionalized therapy and links with social justice. *Psychotherapists and Counsellors for Social Responsibility* was formed in 1995 to promote the political dimension of therapy, to challenge oppression and to champion better and fairer provision of therapy. Decades ago Reich sought to integrate psychoanalytic with Marxist concepts. Adler, Horney, Fromm and others attempted to bring social conditions into the aetiological equation. In the heyday of humanistic therapy, Re-evaluation Co-Counselling had begun to promote the discharge of social as well as individual distress. Groups like *Red Therapy* sought to combine radical individual and group therapy with social action. Many Jungians in particular focused their analyses on the intrapsychic causes and threats of war. Some practitioners, largely in the urban USA, have created models of 'social therapy' using community group activities in place of individual therapy to help address problems of racism and addiction among others. For the past couple of decades many therapists have successfully drawn attention to the different psychological needs of ethnic minorities, sexual minorities, disabled people and women, all of which groups traditionally fell outside standard models of the aetiology of psychological distress and need. The movement known as critical psychology stands firmly behind such developments. The journal *Psychotherapy and Politics International,* launched in 2003, also attests to a level of commitment to address these concerns. But while these continue, a certain lack of vigour is apparent, possibly explained by the increasing success of counselling and psychotherapy in mainstream health care and their weakness politically.

Pilgrim (1997) and Smail (2005) remain highly sceptical that therapy or therapists will make any serious inroads on the extent of social distress. Recent world events, pivoting around '9/11', subsequent wars and a climate of terrorism, undermine any naïve fantasy we may have had that daily life is getting better due to therapeutic insights and treatment (Hillman and Ventura, 1992). Beyond the soft rhetoric of concern for their citizens, governments have ratcheted up their commercial and military ambitions. No connection is made between increasing worldwide depression and waiting lists for therapy, for example, and the demoralization and anxiety generated by environmental degradation, employment insecurity and war. Ritzer (2004) shows the prevalence of social problems worldwide – including population growth, inequalities in wealth distribution, ethnic conflicts, family breakdown, disease, crime and so forth – of which diagnosed mental health problems, while extremely serious, are merely one small part. What has been referred to as the 'upstream' aspect of psychological problems (social, economic and political causes) remains unaddressed by the professional bodies in the therapy field, the focus remaining, naturally but unsatisfactorily, on the downstream aspects (the impact on the well-being or otherwise of the individual). As with the question of human nature, it may be that theoreticians and trainers need to explain far better how their models of therapy might answer valid questions about the social context.

Epidemiological context

Therapy has responded to, indeed been forged by, urgent and obvious psychological distresses and needs. It has developed like many services in an *ad hoc* rather than a planned way. The awareness of any need for or creation of an epidemiology of psychological distress has therefore been slow to emerge. Clearly, it would be useful to know the extent of the problem we are dealing with on a national scale, if not to be able to predict future needs. But this is complicated by the breadth and non-specificity of the kinds of problems and concerns brought to counsellors and psychotherapists and by their not uncommon indifference to and suspicion of matters of psychodiagnosis and quantification. While the *DSM* may confidently list around 340 psychological or psychiatric disorders, counsellors and psychotherapists will dispute many or even all these. Sanders (2005), for example, gives a radical account of person-centred opposition to the 'medicalization of distress'. And many of the concerns brought to therapists do not qualify as disorders by compilers of the *DSM*. The pain of marriage breakdown, bereavement and work stress – common issues for counsellors in the voluntary sector and employee assistance programmes, for example – may well be considered 'subclinical' presentations by psychiatric colleagues.

Abernathy and Power (2002) confirm the methodological difficulties in and slow development of the field of the epidemiology of mental distress, the first rigorous UK study appearing only in the mid-1990s. This identified significant degrees of fatigue, sleep problems, irritability, worry, depression, anxiety, obsession and panic, and women as experiencing almost all these to a higher degree than men. Other surveys have identified problematic levels of alcohol abuse and suicide that have led to the short-term stepping up of specific government health policies to tackle them. Layard (2005) has identified the significance of mental distress both in terms of individual suffering and health economics and the struggle continues to have psychological distress recognised – and its treatment duly funded – on a par with physical illness. Many surveys of the benefits of counselling within companies attempt to quantify distress, its relationship with occupational inefficiency and the likely benefits of therapy in addressing it. Worldwide increases in depression are regularly publicised.

Twenty per cent of women and 14 per cent of men in the UK are considered to have some form of mental distress. While women are more often diagnosed with anxiety, depression, phobias and panic attacks (18 per cent), men are three times more disposed towards alcohol dependence and twice as disposed to drug dependence. It is thought that as many as 15 per cent of pre-school children may have mild mental health problems and 7 per cent severe mental health problems. In the 16–19 year old bracket, 6 per cent of boys and 16 per cent of girls have some form of mental health problem. In the over 65 group, 15 per cent have depression. These diagnostic labels and figures may be somewhat crude and objected to by many but they give us some indication of the scale of what potentially faces therapists and planners of mental health services. Longer term, we might speculate that prejudices against therapy provision for the young and old are now disintegrating and better age-related services must be planned, along with ethnically sensitive provision. Any significant growth in terrorist activities implies a need for increased specialized post-trauma services and so on.

The implications of epidemiological surveys, however crude, seem to have been noted belatedly by those overseeing the profession and training of counsellors and psychotherapists. While training courses have flourished, it has been apparent ('on the ground', contrary to Aldridge and Pollard, 2005) that employment for many therapists – in relation to numbers graduating each year – remains relatively scarce: full-time jobs are few, most employment is part-time and many therapists maintain quite small, part-time private practices alongside other work. Rigorously planned psychotherapy and counselling services (planned, that is, on the basis of estimates of the public's psychological needs and of numbers of clinicians needed to meet these) are to date a rarity, although clinical psychology training and provision is guided by such considerations. Almost certainly, the growth of seriousness with which evidence-based practice is taken will inevitably coincide with the development of better epidemiological estimates; and all this in turn is likely, eventually, to impinge on training numbers and theoretical models. To the best of my knowledge, no analysis of mental health problems by aetiology exists. That is to say, extraordinarily difficult though it is, if we were able even broadly to assign psychological problems to clusters of predisposing factors (e.g. biological propensity, perinatal complications, problematic parent–child interactions, early years and later life negative events, impaired life chances, expectable and unexpected losses, individual coping differences and so on), we could hypothetically design and deliver accurately personalised psychological therapy accordingly. Some such attempts have been made (Newman and Goldfried, 1996), in some cases attempting to factor in gender, but the likelihood is that much more knowledge and time are required before this becomes a significant clinical reality.

The professional and stakeholders' context

Pilgrim (2002) structured his brief history of British therapy into three phases, with the relevant professional bodies duly making their various appearances throughout this period. His categorization has psychoanalysis and behaviourism as co-existing and competing between 1920 and 1970, 'third force psychology' (the humanistic approaches), pluralism and eclecticism appearing largely after 1970, and the 'return of professional authority and its postmodern critics' after 1980. Let us set over those periods the births of the British Psychological Society (1907); British Psychoanalytic Society (1901); Medico-Psychological Association (becoming the Royal College of Psychiatrists in 1970); Alcoholics Anonymous (1935); the National Marriage Guidance Council (1938, now Relate); first Standing Conference for the Advancement of Counselling in 1970 (becoming the British Association for Counselling in 1977, to which the term 'Psychotherapy' was added in 2000); the British Association of Behavioural and Cognitive Psychotherapies (BABCP) was founded in 1972; the UK Standing Conference on Psychotherapy in 1989 (becoming the United Kingdom Council for Psychotherapy in 1993; the British Confederation of Psychotherapists, breaking away from the UKCP as the more 'purist' psychoanalytic training institutes (1991) renamed itself the British Psychoanalytic Council (BPC) in 2004.

A few key events should be picked out here. Just as Freud had to engage in a battle with the medical establishment over 'the question of lay analysis', so Rogers had to fight against the psychological establishment to launch and legitimately practise his model, a fight which partly fuelled the growth of 'counselling'. In 1971 a government report concerned about the activities of scientologists (Foster, 1971) spurred action among therapists, resulting in the publication of a call for statutory regulation (Sieghart, 1978). This process has had its ups and downs. Occasional embarrassing events, such as the comedian Bernard Manning's publicised gaining of BAC membership, the failure of the Alderdice Bill, and opposition from many within the psychotherapy world itself, have both stimulated and dogged the professionalization of therapy.

This small slice of professional history may show some of the emergence of interest groups, how interests cluster and endure, and how the politics of the 'psy-professions' operate. While some bodies represent quite wide spectrum interests (e.g. BACP and UKCP), others such as the BABCP and BPC focus on well-defined schools of practice. Some of these contain individuals and organizations as members, others represent only training institutes. Some, like the BACP, have very large memberships (approximately 23,000), while others are relatively small. Of BACP's membership, 22.7 per cent are currently accredited (around 5,500) and 83 per cent are female. The UKCP has 6,500 registered psychotherapists. The BPC has 1,300 registered psychotherapists, while the BABCP has 5,500 members. Overlapping memberships mean that it is difficult to estimate how many active therapists there are in the UK and no accurate figure is available. One crude estimate from a journalistic source had it that in 1993 there were 30,000 paid therapists, 140,000 volunteer counsellors and 140,000 people using counselling skills in their work. Aldridge and Pollard (2005) allude to 37,500 members of pertinent professional bodies, so it may be that this figure is about right. Ninety per cent of those who replied to a questionnaire sent to 20 per cent of these members reported being in paid work.

Statutory regulation of therapy has been on the agenda for many years. At the time of writing (early 2006), an interim report had been made to the Department of Health on the state of play in British training, standards, ethics and competencies in therapy (Aldridge and Pollard, 2005). Practitioner training courses numbering 570 were identified, with a variety of titles among these which the authors say 'can only cause confusion to the public' (2005: 7). The title of 'counsellor' was being used by 54 per cent of those sampled, with 26 per cent using 'psychotherapist' and others designating themselves as 'therapist', 'analyst', 'psychoanalyst' or 'hypnotherapist'. Of these 61.4 per cent work with their clients for up to 20 sessions. It is acknowledged that further work is required before the therapy field can be formally submitted to regulation via the Health Professions Council[1] and even now doubts about the whole process are being aired.

DIFFERENTLY CONCEIVED AND NAMED THERAPEUTIC APPROACHES

In Aldridge and Pollard's (2005) survey self-designated humanistic and integrative practitioners represented 57.34 per cent of those responding, 18.25 per cent analytic, 10.52 per cent cognitive, 2.4 per cent systemic and 2.25 per cent NLP/hypnotherapeutic. In a more detailed section, although still not precise, it appears that the most commonly self-identified approaches are, in order of popularity with practitioners: integrative, person-centred, psychodynamic, cognitive-behavioural, humanistic and then psychoanalytic and eclectic about equal. Each approach is in a sense a different offer of explanation and help for psychological challenges – each is a product of its time, place and creative personalities and each will have some measure of appeal, success and shelf-life. Some will in time be modified, some will become dominant and some will become obsolete. Interestingly, a large discrepancy appears to exist between practitioner preferences and evidence-based indications, and this data cannot tell us what clients' preferences are.

Broadly speaking, psychoanalysis was dominant at the turn of the twentieth century and challenged only gradually by the rise of the cognitive-behavioural and humanistic therapies from about the 1970s onwards. But we know that even within Freud's lifetime it proved impossible to develop a model that attracted consensus, with early fall-outs by Adler and Jung being legendary and many subsequent schisms following these. Historians of psychotherapy will continue to analyse such developments but we can speculate with some confidence that departures from the original Freudian model were driven by sincere differences of viewpoint and aspiration, different professional and cultural backgrounds and markedly different personalities. The development of therapy models has been neither primarily collaborative nor scientifically focused and accountable: it has largely hinged on the energy and inspiration of outstanding male figures and their professional intimates. One count has it that a mere 36 named therapeutic approaches existed in the 1950s, this increasing to 250 by 1980 and over 400 by the end of the twentieth century (Feltham, 1997). Some critical commentators suggest that the creation of so many models reflects the scientific indiscipline of a field in which, it seems, 'anything goes'; the competitive nature of the society from which most therapy models have arisen, that is, the USA; and the idiosyncrasies, proprietorial nature and fame- and profit-seeking motives of their authors.

Whatever the true picture, we have a scenario of proliferation of therapeutic models that some consider unwieldy, confusing and not credible. One text has referred to this as 'therapy wars' (Salzman and Norcross, 1990). On the other hand, the integrative movement has continued to seek common ground and rapprochement between therapies. Yet another perspective has it that many apparently different models are in fact quite similar and merely slight variations on common themes. One simplification is to speak simply of cognitive-behavioural and interpersonal models, for example. Interestingly, while one research thrust commends common relationship factors in all therapy as pivotal, another appears to underscore CBT, perhaps the least of the relationship-focused therapies, as of superior effectiveness; thus leaving us potentially confused as to the relative merits of the relationship-focused and the technique-focused therapies. Lambert (1992) has argued from evidence that a mere 15 per cent of client improvement is accounted for by techniques specific to designated therapy models. By contrast, 30 per cent is due to common factors (empathy, acceptance, warmth, etc.), 40 per cent to extratherapeutic factors (client's ego strength, helpful events and social support) and 15 per cent to placebo factors. By their very nature, distinct models of therapy do not convey a picture of this kind.

This book presents the case, as it were, for us to take seriously 15 distinct therapy models. Although nothing as crass as mud-slinging competitiveness is in evidence, an implicit difference of views exists on human nature, psychological disturbance, therapeutic techniques and style, change process and so on. Also, each purports to have some sort of original edge. Let us ask first what they have in common, and secondly on what grounds they differ. Most obviously, all these models but one (Kleinian) are mainly male-created (Laura Perls is *sometimes* credited with co-creating Gestalt therapy; and many women appear more visibly as second-generation proponents of cognitive, person-centred and other approaches). A majority stem from the initiative of one dominant founder, that is, not from lengthy, painstaking research and scientific committee-style deliberations. All but the original psychoanalytic models were created in the second half of the twentieth century. A majority of the founders have Judeo-Christian origins. All have Euro-American origins, with American predominance. All models agree on the taboo against sexual contact with clients and on confidentiality, and most on traditional professional boundaries (Tribe and Morrissey, 2005). All share the view that their approach requires rigorous training and high levels of skill. Most share the view that their model is capable of addressing a wide array of presenting concerns. Some agree on the mixed (determined and free) nature of being human but vary in their views on how free or genetically 'pre-determined' we are. All tend to see therapy as quite necessary, despite sharing the view that individuals have personal responsibility and efficacy independently of therapists.

When we turn to the differences, however, these are much larger. Some approaches (person-centred, personal construct and behaviour therapy) have psychological roots. Many have psychoanalytic affiliations or origins (Gestalt, transactional analysis and cognitive analytic therapies most obviously, after the earliest psychoanalytic models); and even the founders of models as non-psychoanalytic as cognitive therapy and rational emotive behaviour therapy have originally psychoanalytic affiliations. One (existential therapy) has a primarily philosophical affiliation. The newest, solution-focused and narrative therapies, draw from systemic and constructivist views. Some, such as Freudian, Kleinian and person-centred, are 'purist' in what they are composed of (that is, minimal integration from elsewhere) and how they are practised, while others, such as Gestalt, cognitive analytic and rational emotive behaviour therapy, have a greater integrative make-up and capacity. Some, such as cognitive and behaviour therapy, are readily researched and others far less so. They differ in typical length of treatment (compare long-term psychoanalysis with very brief behaviour therapy or solution-focused therapy, for example). They differ with regard to whether therapy is mandatory in the therapist's own professional development, Freudian, Kleinian and Jungian training most emphatically demanding this, while the more cognitive and behavioural approaches generally do not. Active or passive (client-led) style of therapy is another defining feature (compare Ellis' with Rogers' in this regard, for example), as is temporal focus – past, present or future orientation. Most psychoanalytically oriented approaches inevitably focus strongly on past patterns, for example, while existential, Gestalt and cognitive therapies tend to maintain a strong focus on current life and solution-focused therapy an orientation towards the future (see Slife, 1993).

Whether goals or symptoms are paramount (see the cognitive and behavioural therapies), as opposed to being regarded as implicit or surface features (as in most psychoanalytic and humanistic therapies), is also a key distinguishing feature. Similarly, the extent of therapeutic ambition differs. While behaviour therapy is clearly aligned with problem-assessment and goal-attainment, for example, psychoanalysis is ambivalent about specific aims (Sandler and Dreher, 1996). Freud aspired to mere 'common unhappiness', while Rogers wrote hopefully of the 'fully functioning person' and 'the person of tomorrow'. Inclusion or predominance of certain personality and technical modalities – cognition, behaviour, emotion, dreams, meaning, spirituality, etc. – also helps to define each approach. We might say that each approach is constructed and promoted on the basis of a different clinical epistemology; that is, each approach claims to know best how to understand ailing human beings and how to reduce suffering or maximise personal resourcefulness or happiness. What we cannot say is that the popularity of each model equates with theoretical elegance or clinical effectiveness. The person-centred approach, for example, ranking high with many practitioners, has often been criticised as being theoretically light and has relatively little empirical evidence to support claims to reliable positive outcomes.

In spite of decades of effort towards integrative rapprochement, no slowing down of the proliferation of therapeutic approaches is evident. Explicitly constructed integrative models such as cognitive analytic therapy have appeared since the 1970s but have unintentionally added to the sum total of therapies rather than reducing it. Integrative literature and conferences abound (Newman and Goldfried, 1996) but this is not reflected in any obvious movement towards practical convergence. Heart can be taken from the number of practitioners, however, who report practising integratively based on professional experience, clinical wisdom and responses to client needs in busy and diverse practice settings. Observers of the initiatives towards a unified profession have sometimes used the simile of 'herding cats' to highlight the difficulty of bringing together practitioners who often have fiercely defended affiliations and negative views about others. We have no rigorous analysis of who the pragmatic integrationists are and who the partisan, politically entrenched are but the attractions and indeed coming imperatives of statutory regulation may well exert some influence on the dynamics of the different approaches to therapy.

THERAPY AND ITS CRITICS

Freud had his contemporary critics such as Karl Kraus and there has been no cessation in critique during the past century. It is natural that in its original counter-cultural form psychoanalysis should have shocked and therefore stimulated some to criticism. Throughout its history and subsequently that of psychoanalytic psychotherapy, other forms of psychotherapy and counselling, this field has frequently been attacked by scientists, philosophers, theologians, psychologists, sociologists, journalists and others with reservations falling within an array of well-intentioned and well-informed views and ignorant and scathing criticisms. This is not merely an irritant for therapists but a significant aspect of the field from which much can be learned (Feltham, 1999; Samuels, 1992).

Psychotherapy and counselling are not *self-evidently* vitally necessary, scientifically justifiable, universally helpful or palatable. The validity of therapy – and of different therapeutic approaches – must be clarified to its funders and consumers. Therapists tend to enter the field as enthusiastic believers (often originally as successful clients themselves) whose belief is reinforced by investment in their own personal training therapy, immersion in self-funded training and personal economic prospects. Historically, therapy has emerged as a set of practices and specialised vocabularies in which adherents are immersed and which have been offered to a public who knows little about them. Indeed, many 'insiders' (therapists) do not have an accurate grasp of theoretical approaches other than their own and those charged with conducting public relations exercises for the professional bodies sometimes struggle to convey in accessible terms what is in fact a highly complex field. When it is said that 'therapy' works, this is shorthand for 'we believe that our (dozens of different) therapies work'. Objective research into what troubles people psychologically, why, and what best helps them, has been slow to arrive on the scene (see Chapter 18).

One of the oldest of critiques, famously championed by Hans Eysenck, is simply that therapy does not work, or has insufficient evidence to claim that it works, any better than a placebo or time itself 'works'. In fact Eysenck really meant that only behaviour therapy worked reliably and psychoanalysis and its derivatives did not. Much subsequent research has eroded the Eysenckian critique. On empirical grounds, critics have expressed scepticism about the actual existence or validity of cornerstone concepts such as the unconscious, Oedipus complex, inner child, repressed memory, actualising tendency, automatic negative thoughts, and so on. The propositions of therapists commonly derive from clinical observation and inspiration rather than rigorous experiments or philosophically robust theorising, and often do not express themselves in ways that can be readily tested and verified scientifically. Unfortunately, since so many divergent (aetiological and therapeutic) concepts exist in this field, significant and credible progress in verification is impeded.

Following his own disillusioning therapy as a trainee and his critique of Freud's seduction theory, Masson (1990) exposed many examples of neglect, malpractice and outright abuse by therapists that he used as a basis for arguing that (a) therapy itself is riddled with abuses of power and (b) this abuse is intrinsic to any asymmetrical therapeutic practice based on expertise, it is endemic and it cannot be corrected. All Masson could suggest for those suffering from mental health problems was non-specific mutual help. His critique has helped to spawn greater efforts to stress accountability and strengthen complaints procedures but, if anything, the voice of the discontented client is getting louder (Bates, 2006). Meanwhile, there is obviously little the profession can do to assuage the likes of Masson and even the anti-professionalization lobby among therapists (House, 2003) cannot satisfactorily address the implications of his total condemnation of therapy.

Another major source of critiques lies in the socioeconomic and sociocultural domain. While therapy may indeed help individuals to be somewhat happier or more personally resourceful, it cannot or will not modify the social conditions that foster unhappiness (Smail, 2005). It can be argued that the mitigating effects of therapy act positively in a ripple-like manner from individuals outwards to society; but it can equally be argued that a world of 6 billion individuals, or even a country like Britain of 60 million, facing constant, stress-inducing capitalistic pressures, will not be significantly improved by individual therapeutic efforts. Even more seriously, the energy expended on micro-remedial individual analysis and change is likely to divert attention from the need for the macro-remedial. In other words, therapy in this analysis is seen as somewhat narcissistic, undermining of social change efforts and, indeed, as ultimately futile. It is interesting that Layard (2003, 2005) portrays conditions in Britain, contra Smail, as favourable to greater happiness, given better support from CBT.

Therapy has also remained until recently quite stubbornly indifferent or even opposed to questions of multicultural spirituality or religion and religious adherents' critique of therapy as self-centred rather than community-focused and God-centred. Add to this the rising costs of training for therapy, most of which (with the exception of clinical psychology training) are met by trainees themselves, which reinforces the middle class nature of therapy provision, and it is clear that therapy is not usually a naturally active ally against poverty, racism, sexism and other domains of oppression. The charge that therapy remains Eurocentric, if not Anglocentric, is not easily dismissed. Therapists may *talk* about empowering their clients, say critics, but this is naïvety at best.

Scientific, intellectual and academic context

Psychoanalysis arose *sui generis,* even if Freud was nominally a neurologist. It developed as a practice supplemented by a theory. Arguably it has never become nor will become the natural science that Freud hoped and intended it would, in spite of some ongoing attempted linkage between psychoanalysis and neuroscience and a mooted 'neuropsychoanalysis'. While it has influenced intellectual debate and entered university departments, its influence may be more marked in departments of English and Critical Theory than in clinical or scientific departments. Nevertheless, some thriving academic units for the study of psychoanalysis and analytical psychology have been established and manage to survive academic scepticism. A small number of writers from analytical psychology (Stevens and Price, 2000), psychoanalysis (Langs, 1996) and cognitive-behavioural therapy (Gilbert and Bailey, 2000) affiliations have also shown the relevance of their approaches to an understanding of salient features of evolutionary psychology.

Counselling too arose primarily as a *practice*, its training often being provided by the voluntary sector and other non-academic institutions; and training is still provided independently and in further education. In higher education settings in the UK, counselling is taught at different academic levels and in different academic departments (usually psychology, education, social work, nursing, lifelong learning). In the academic context, counselling does not have the heavyweight identity of traditional science, social science and humanities subjects but is often regarded as a lightweight, somewhat dubious and possibly ephemeral subject. It is often perceived as a vocational *training* rather than a serious academic education. Some counsellor trainers question whether it properly belongs in universities, although since 2002 it has been included within the Universities Psychotherapy and Counselling Association. Psychoanalysis has more cachet, as has psychotherapy (although some psychotherapy training remains external to universities) and clinical psychology has solid status as a health discipline grounded in the science of psychology, and its doctoral level training lends it considerable gravity. Some courses (particularly some MAs) combine reference to both counselling and psychotherapy in their titles, which can lead to further confusion about disciplinary identities (Aldridge and Pollard, 2005). Therapy is often regarded as a minority vocational subject and/or as 'odd' in its insistence on high tutor–student contact hours, personal development groups, requirements for personal therapy and intensive supervision. It still does not have the statutory identity or career structure of allied professions like social work or nursing.

Psychology is not without its critics who regard its longstanding scientific aspirations as either pretentious or unachievable (Joynson, 1974); and some clinical psychologists like Smail (2005) regard the entire enterprise of the psychological therapies as self-serving, self-deluded and self-protective rather than liberating. Although it may be perceived as a natural source of relevant knowledge and sustenance for therapy, psychology has an ambiguous place in the theoretical development and training of counsellors and psychotherapists. Many, but by no means all founders of therapy approaches, have had a background in academic psychology; and some express a high level of ambivalence or even hostility towards it (e.g. van Deurzen-Smith, 1993). The original behaviour therapists and more recent cognitive behavioural therapists are most closely associated with the scientific psychological tradition, particularly with social learning theory. Recent positive psychologists like Seligman and Carr, advocating the 'science of happiness', are aligned with CBT, solution-focused and associated therapies. Clinical psychologists are far more likely to warm to the concept of being practitioner-scientists (Elton Wilson and Barkham, 1994). Psychoanalytic and psychodynamic therapists draw more from their own case studies and aspects of developmental psychology. Humanistic therapists create and value their own humanistic psychology with its honouring of subjectivity; and existential therapists turn to philosophy rather than psychology.

Perhaps it is natural that therapists' concentration on the individual, on the inner subjective world and aspirations of individuals and all this within the privacy of the confidential setting, means that a more powerfully developed intellectual tradition has not yet grown up around therapy. A certain ambivalence persists among many therapists as to the very nature of intellectuality and generalization, possibly linked with the psychoanalytic concept of intellectual defence mechanism. First-hand experience, emotion and intuition are often more highly prized by practitioners than conceptualization and theorizing (Norcross and Guy, 1989). The vocational and faith-like character of much therapy may also militate against what is perceived as an overly analytical and excessively generalist outlook. Relatively few texts exist making pertinent connections between therapy and philosophy, sociology and anthropology. Also, the litera- ture of counselling and psychotherapy has been slower than that in many cognate disciplines to reflect postmodernist preoccupations but this has begun to change (Lowenthal, 2003). Finally, we should remember that therapy is a rela- tive newcomer to academia and several decades may well be required before it is more solidly and confidently established as a discipline with intellectually robust dimensions.

EMERGING AND FUTURE TRENDS

Simultaneously encouraging and potentially undermining, the growth of accept- ance of psychological counselling and psychotherapy in the British NHS signals a turning point in the development of the field. Increasing job opportunities in this domain go hand in hand with an emphasis on statutory regulation and evidence-based practice. Growth of demand from the public and for evidence in support of therapy is generally accompanied by a demand for greater evidence of exactly what works best and why (Roth and Fonagy, 2005). The UK's National Institute for Clinical Excellence (NICE) requires and facilitates the col- lection of evidence and its dissemination in the form of best practice guidelines on what is considered safe and effective. This has not yet become 'dictatorial' – and indeed reassurances are given that it will not compromise practitioners' own creative autonomy – but is becoming influential. Evidence-based practice (or 'empirically supported therapy' in North America) is an international trend with certain advantages and disadvantages and, however disliked by many therapists, is unlikely to be reversed in the short-term (Feltham, 2004).

In 2005 Lord Richard Layard presented a landmark address to the Sainsbury Centre for Mental Health in London. Arguing for significantly greater funding for mental health treatment ('now our biggest social problem'), he called specif- ically for the creation of 250 new mental health centres employing an additional 10,000 therapists within 10 years. Basing his call both on careful economic esti- mates and the moral case that psychological suffering be treated as effectively as physical illness, within acceptable waiting times, Layard also detailed a per- ceived need for a specified kind of training focusing on time-limited CBT as the treatment of choice, based on available research findings. At the time of writing, the professional bodies have shown real interest but, in some cases, are con- cerned that Layard is taking a position that implicitly seriously threatens the status of psychoanalytic, humanistic and systemic-constructivist approaches and positive perceptions of them. The principle of 'absence of evidence of effective- ness' is tacitly and incorrectly taken to mean 'ineffectiveness' (*vis-à-vis* many humanistic and psychodynamic approaches) and anecdotal evidence of cognitive behaviour therapists cherry-picking clients and cases of long-term relapse following CBT are ignored or played down. Nevertheless, if taken up, Layard's proposal will be a major development in the field. 'CBT favouritism' might also act as an urgent spur to psychoanalytic and humanistic researchers and/or as catalytic in the integrative movement.

The long-running movement towards the professionalization of therapy in the form of statutory regulation is at the time of writing going through a consultation phase between the Department of Health and the major professional bodies (BPS, BACP, UKCP). Following a comprehensive mapping exercise, the current intention is that counselling and psychotherapy will be submitted to the Health Professions Council for scrutiny and eventual acceptance[1]. This will lead to a formal register of practitioners, to protection of title and other means of formalising therapy as a recognised profession. It is hoped that this may occur by 2008 or soon after and it therefore appears that the process of professionalization will have taken something like 40 years since its inception. The benefits will include a level of protection of the public, clarifying the function of therapists and their training norms. Disadvantages may include restricted creativity, increased bureaucracy and costs to practitioners, increasing academicization of training and arbitrary exclusion of some practitioners.

The early dominance of psychoanalysis and psychoanalytic models has gradually given way to the pluralism of psychological therapies available today. This proliferation is welcomed and celebrated by some as mirroring diversity, individuality and trends in postmodernism. Others, both critics and custodians of the profession, regard proliferation as a danger, a sign of lack of order. But there is no abatement in the growth of distinct therapies. Models of brief, integrative, systems and constructivist therapy in particular have been growing. Yet alongside this outward appearance of unchecked and credulity-straining multiplicity, it seems likely that many practitioners have been learning to adapt their internalized training models to the demands of their unique clients in their local settings. This is especially true of primary care counsellors who have adapted to work in multidisciplinary teams with short-term contracts with clients presenting with a range of mild to moderate psychological problems.

Another area of growth in model-building and practice adaptation connects what is broadly termed 'spirituality' with psychological therapy. Interest in clients' spiritual and religious lives and the possibility of drawing from spiritual themes to enhance therapeutic progress goes back to Jung and Assagioli, and transpersonal therapy is well established among humanistic practitioners. A combination of changing demographics (the rise of multiculturalism and increasing longevity), critiques of western therapy as too technical-rational and individual-centred, and a gradual worldwide spread of therapy is highly likely to make an impact. West (2004) uncovered prejudices against discussing the use of prayer and other spiritual practices in clinical supervision, for example, and Moodley and West (2005) present possibilities of greater integration of western with 'traditional healing' practices. While it is not surprising that Freudians have inherited Freud's extreme scepticism towards religion and scientifically grounded therapists have emphasised rationality in their work, there is a danger of becoming alienated from the client population served. Indeed Rowan (2005) believes that only those therapies that embrace but go beyond the instrumental and relational towards the transpersonal are doing justice to the whole person. Also, of some surprise in recent years has been the successful experimental integration of meditation techniques into forms of cognitive behavioural therapy such as mindfulness-based cognitive therapy and dialectical behaviour therapy.

At the more materialist, scientific and technological end, we witness continuing research into – as well as controversy over – psychopharmaceuticals, with doctors heavily subscribing anti-depressants alongside or in lieu of counselling and CBT. The trend towards prescribing medication for young people (e.g. primarily Ritalin for attention deficit and hyperactivity disorder, and antidepressants for low mood among children) has been sharply criticised. With child mental illness in 2004 running at approximately 1 in 10, advocates for medical versus psychotherapeutic responses are not in short supply. Likewise, increasing research in neuroscience can either bring out in force those in favour of identifying and remedying genetic deficits or those seizing on any evidence of links between kindly early experiences and later optimal brain development and mentally healthy behaviour (Cozolino, 2002). The expanding field of epigenetics, demonstrating how, for example, certain genes may be switched on in response to traumatic life events and such responses transmitted to subsequent generations, could well vindicate some therapeutic insights. The growth of e-mail counselling and cybertherapy – either in the form of individualised therapist responses or therapeutic computer packages (e.g. CBT programmes for depression) – is probably driven by both a fascination with technology generally and a preoccupation with costs. But it is growing and becoming refined, however many therapists may object to its apparently depersonalizing effects and undermining of traditional relationship values.

Current British government aspirations to provide additional combined early years care with extended education could well dovetail with policies centring on education in citizenship and social respect, as well as greatly extended mental health care (as advocated by Layard, 2005). At the time of writing the UK government is considering the use of CBT packages to help the unemployed regain confidence and re-enter the job market. Swelling interest in the positive psychology movement would also fit well here philosophically and clinically. Although subject to democratic and economic vicissitudes, such developments if materialised would probably be welcomed by therapists generally. However, some therapists and commentators on the therapy scene would caution against premature and uncritical hopes for universal 'happiness on the NHS' or a cradle-to-grave 'nanny state' or 'therapy state' (Furedi, 2004; Weatherill, 2004). It would be a supreme irony if the therapy movement that commenced with Freudian radicalism, reinforced by humanistic counterculturalism, spending several decades in a relative wilderness, finally culminated as a victim of its own success in becoming an unwitting instrument of government-engineered socialization. Put differently, therapy (particularly humanistic therapy) may be in danger of selling out to the values of the medically-oriented marketplace after many years of opposing it and championing the humanly subjective (Hansen, 2005). Therapy watchers will be observing with great interest to what extent the field concedes thus or continues to assert its own insights, values and pluralistic practices.

NOTE

1. Developments in late 2006 suggested this may change to a separate Psychological Professions Council (PPC). Readers are advised to consult professional body websites and newsletters for up to date status reports.

ACKNOWLEDGEMENTS

I am very grateful to Sukhdeep Khele (BACP), Mike Bowen (UKCP) and Elizabeth Reddish (BPC) for their views and data on their organization's perspective.

REFERENCES

Abernathy, J. and Power, M. (2002) 'The epidemiology of mental distress', in C. Feltham (ed.), *What's the Good of Counselling and Psychotherapy? The Benefits Explained.* London: Sage.

Aldridge, S. and Pollard, J. (2005) *Interim Report to the Department of Health on Initial Mapping Project for Psychotherapy and Counselling.* Rugby: BACP and UKCP.

Ashworth, P. (2000) *Psychology and 'Human Nature'.* Hove: Psychology Press.

BACP/FF (2004) *The Age of Therapy: Exploring Attitudes Towards and Acceptance of Counselling and Psychotherapy in Modern Britain.* London: British Association for Counselling and Psychotherapy and the Future Foundation.

Bankart, C.P. (1997) *Talking Cures: A History of Western and Eastern Psychotherapies.* Pacific Grove, CA: Brooks/Cole.

Bates, Y. (ed.) (2006) *Shouldn't I Be Feeling Better By Now? Client Views of Therapy.* Basingstoke: Palgrave.

Breggin, P. (1993) *Toxic Psychiatry: Drugs and Electroconvulsive Therapy: The Truth and the Better Alternatives.* London: HarperCollins.

Bunting, M. (2005) *Willing Slaves: How the Overwork Culture is Ruling our Lives.* London: Perennial.

Clark, D.M., Salkovskis, P.M., Hackmann, A., Middleton, H., Anastasiades, P. and Gelder, M.G. (1994) 'A comparison of cognitive therapy, applied relaxation and imipramine in the treatment of panic disorder', *British Journal of Psychiatry,* 164: 759–69.

Cozolino, L. (2002) *The Neuroscience of Psychotherapy.* New York: Norton.

Cushman, P. (1995) *Constructing the Self, Constructing America: A Cultural History of Psychotherapy.* Cambridge, MA: Perseus.

Deurzen-Smith, E. van (1993) 'Psychology and counselling', in W. Dryden (ed.), *Questions and Answers on Counselling in Action.* London: Sage.

DHSSPS (2002) *Counselling in Northern Ireland: Report of the Counselling Review.* Belfast: Department of Health, Social Services and Public Safety.

Dunant, S. and Porter, R. (1996) *The Age of Anxiety*. London: Virago.

Ehrenwald, J. (ed.) (1991) *The History of Psychotherapy*. Northvale, NJ: Aronson.

Ellenberger, H.F. (1970) *The Discovery of the Unconscious: The History and Evolution of Dynamic Psychiatry*. New York: Basic Books.

Ellis, A. (1994) *Reason and Emotion in Psychotherapy,* revised and updated edition. New York: Birch Lane Press.

Elton Wilson, J. and Barkham, M. (1994) 'A practitioner-scientist approach to psychotherapy process and out-come research', in P. Clarkson and M. Pokorny (eds), *The Handbook of Psychotherapy*. London: Routledge.

Feltham, C. (ed.) (1997) *Which Psychotherapy? Leading Exponents Explain their Differences*. London: Sage.

Feltham, C. (1999) 'Facing, understanding and learning from critiques of counselling and psychother-apy', *British Journal of Guidance and Counselling,* 27 (3): 301–11.

Feltham, C. (2004) 'Evidence-based psychotherapy and counselling in the UK: critique and alternatives', *Journal of Contemporary Psychotherapy,* 35 (1): 131–43.

Foster, J.G. (1971) *Enquiry into the Effects and Practice of Scientology*. London: HMSO.

Frank, J.D. (1974) *Persuasion and Healing: A Comparative Study of Psychotherapy* (rev. edn.). New York: Schocken.

Furedi, F. (2004) *Therapy Culture: Cultivating Vulnerability in an Uncertain Age*. London: Routledge.

Gilbert, P. and Bailey, K.G. (eds) (2000) *Genes on the Couch: Explorations in Evolutionary Psychotherapy*. London: Brunner-Routledge.

Halmos, P. (1978) *The Faith of the Counsellors*. London: Constable.

Hansen, J.T. (2005) 'The devaluation of inner subjective experiences by the counseling profession: a plea to reclaim the essence of the profession', *Journal of Counseling and Development,* 83 (4): 406–15

Hillman, J. and Ventura, M. (1992) *We've Had a Hundred Years of Psychotherapy and the World's Getting Worse*. San Francisco, CA: HarperCollins.

House, R. (2003) *Therapy Beyond Modernity: Deconstructing and Transcending Profession-Centred Therapy*. London: Karnac.

James, I. and Palmer, S. (eds) (1996) *Professional Therapeutic Titles: Myths and Realities*. Leicester: British Psychological Society.

James, O. (1996) *Britain on the Couch*. London: Arrow.

Joynson, R.B. (1974) *Psychology and Common Sense*. London: Routledge & Kegan Paul.

Kirschner, S.R. (1996) *The Religious and Romantic Origins of Psychoanalysis*. New York: Cambridge University Press.

Lambert, M.J. (1992) 'Psychotherapy outcome research: implications for integrative and eclectic prac-tice', In J.C. Norcross and M.R. Goldfried (eds), *Handbook of Psychotherapy Integration*. New York: Basic Books.

Langs, R. (1996) *The Evolution of the Emotion-Processing Mind*. London: Karnac.

Layard, R. (2003) 'Happiness: Has Social Science a Clue? Lecture 1: What is Happiness? Are We Getting Happier?' London School of Economics: Lionel Robbins Memorial Lectures 2002/03.

Layard, R. (2005) 'Therapy for all on the NHS'. Sainsbury Centre (London) Lecture, 12 September.

Lowenthal, D. (2003) *Post-Modernism for Psychotherapists: A Critical Reader*. London: Routledge.

Masson, J.M. (1990) *Against Therapy*. London: Fontana.

Messer, S.B. (1992) 'A critical examination of belief structures in integrative and eclectic psychotherapy', In J.C. Norcross and M.R. Goldfried (eds), H*andbook of Psychotherapy Integration*. New York: Basic Books. pp. 130–165.

Moodley, R. and West, W. (eds) (2005) *Integrating Traditional Healing Practices into Counseling and Psychotherapy*. Thousand Oaks, CA: Sage.

Newman, C.F. and Goldfried, M.R. (1996) 'Developments in psychotherapy integration', in W. Dryden (ed.), *Developments in Psychotherapy: Historical Perspectives*. London: Sage.

Norcross, J.C. and Guy, J.D. (1989) 'Ten therapists: the process of becoming and being', in W. Dryden (ed.), *On Becoming a Psychotherapist*. London: Routledge.

Pilgrim, D. (1997) *Psychotherapy and Society.* London: Sage.

Pilgrim, D. (2002) 'The cultural context of British psychotherapy', in W. Dryden (ed.), *Handbook of Individual Therapy* (4th edn.). London: Sage.

Pinker, S. (2003) *The Blank Slate: The Modern Denial of Human Nature.* London: Penguin.

Ritzer, G. (ed.) (2004) *Handbook of Social Problems: A Comparative International Perspective.* Thousand Oaks, CA: Sage.

Rose, N. (1989) *Governing the Soul: The Shaping of the Private Self.* London: Routledge.

Roth, A. and Fonagy, P. (2005) *What Works for Whom? A Critical Review of Psychotherapy Research* (2nd edn.). New York: Guilford.

Rowan, J. (2005) *The Future of Training in Psychotherapy and Counselling.* London: Routledge.

Salzman, N. and Norcross, J.C. (eds) (1990) *Therapy Wars: Contention and Convergence in Differing Clinical Approaches.* San Fransisco, CA: Jossey Bass.

Samuels, A. (1992) 'Foreword', in W. Dryden and C. Feltham (eds), *Psychotherapy and its Discontents.* Buckingham: Open University Press.

Sanders, P. (2005) 'Principled and strategic opposition to the medicalisation of distress and all of its apparatus', in S. Joseph and R. Worsley (eds), *Person-Centred Psychopathology: A Positive Psychology of Mental Health.* Ross-on-Wye: PCCS Books.

Sandler, J. and Dreher, A.U. (1996) *What Do Psychoanalysts Want? The Problem of Aims in Psychoanalytic Therapy.* London: Routledge.

Sieghart, P. (1978) *Statutory Regulation of Psychotherapists: a Report of a Professions Joint Working Party.* Cambridge: Plumridge.

Slife, B. D. (1993) *Time and Psychological Explanation.* Albany, NY: State University of New York Press.

Smail, D. (2005) *Power, Interest and Psychology: Elements of a Social Materialist Understanding of Distress.* Ross-on-Wye: PCCS Books.

Stevens, A. and Price, J. (2000) *Evolutionary Psychiatry: A New Beginning* (2nd edn.). London: Routledge.

Szasz, T. (1988) *The Myth of Psychotherapy.* Syracuse, NY: Syracuse University Press.

Taylor, S. (2005) *The Fall.* Winchester: O Books.

Tribe, R. and Morrissey, J. (eds) (2005) *Handbook of Professional and Ethical Practice for Psychologists, Counsellors and Psychotherapists.* London: Brunner-Routledge.

Weatherill, R. (2004) *Our Last Great Illusion: A Radical Psychoanalytical Critique of Therapy Culture.* Exeter: Imprint Academic.

West, W. (2004) *Spiritual Issues in Therapy: Relating Experience to Practice.* Basingstoke: Palgrave.

2

Psychodynamic Therapy: The Freudian Approach

Alessandra Lemma

HISTORICAL CONTEXT AND DEVELOPMENT IN BRITAIN

Historical context

From its beginnings over 100 years ago, psychoanalysis has courted as much interest as it has controversy. It remains one of the most stimulating and rich set of hypotheses about human nature and the workings of the mind. As a treatment method, it has been significantly developed by Freud's followers and dissidents. However, some of the core Freudian theories and techniques underpin the current schools of psychoanalysis.

Freud was a cultured and gifted man and, importantly, a Jew. Freud's origins and cultural background are not without significance for an understanding of the personal, social and political factors motivating and shaping the development of his ideas (Robert, 1977; Roith, 1987). However, Freud failed to make links between his own Jewish origins and his theories even though he was acutely aware of the effect of his Jewish roots on the acclaim of his ideas. Indeed, when his friend and colleague, the Swiss psychiatrist Carl Jung – the only non-Jew then affiliated to the psychoanalytic movement – left Freud's following in 1914, Freud was concerned that psychoanalysis would be considered as no more than a 'Jewish national affair'.

Freud may well have wanted to play down the Jewish connection, but this fact was at the forefront of other people's minds. In the 1930s, with the rise of the Nazis, psychoanalysis was attacked: Freud's writings, together with those of

Einstein, H. G. Wells, Thomas Mann and Proust were burned in public bonfires for their 'soul disintegrating exaggeration of the instinctual life' (Ferris, 1997). His position in Vienna became increasingly difficult. On 12 March 1938 German troops moved into Austria. On the 13th the Board of the Psycho-Analytic Society met for the last time. Freud likened their predicament to that of the rabbi Johannan ben Zakkai who fled Jerusalem after the Romans destroyed the temple and began a religious school in his place of refuge. Freud urged his colleagues to follow this example. In a strong vote of confidence the Board, before dissolving, agreed that the Society should reconstitute wherever Freud might end up.

Along with many of his colleagues Freud was forced into exile. Some fled to America, others to Palestine, Australia and South America. Others still, including Freud, found a home in Britain. Those analysts who remained in Germany practised but only under strict Nazi requirements. Classical Freudian analysis itself was deemed unacceptable. Along with Darwin, Freud was vilified for subverting the high values of fair-skinned races.

The very real persecution suffered by the psychoanalytic movement in its infancy left a deep scar. From the outset, Freud saw psychoanalysis as a cause to be defended against attack and select analytic institutes which emerged could be seen to be the 'bastions' of this defence (Kirsner, 1990). This had the unfortunate effect of keeping at bay other perspectives and related fields of enquiry, fearing their evaluation, criticism and attack.

The movement's paranoia, however, has not just been a feature of its relationship with the outside, non-analytic world. Even though the past 10 years have witnessed a greater openness, for example the current dialogue between some psychoanalysts and neuroscientists (e.g. Kaplan-Solms & Solms, 2000). It has also been a striking feature of the quality of the relationships within the psychoanalytic establishment itself amongst its own rival theoretical offspring. The history of psychoanalysis is one of schisms. Indeed, psychoanalysis is an umbrella term covering a number of theoretical schools which, whilst all originating from and honouring some of Freud's original ideas and beliefs, have since evolved very different theories about personality development and different techniques for achieving the goals of psychoanalysis as a treatment for psychological problems.

Development in Britain

The development of the British Psychoanalytic Society, established in 1913 by Ernest Jones is a very good example of the difficulties of living in a pluralistic society (Hamilton, 1996). Since its inception, three distinct groups – the Contemporary Freudians, the Kleinians and the Independents – have had to live together in one society with the unavoidable tensions associated with living in close proximity to neighbours who do not necessarily share your same point of view. To regard oneself as belonging to any one of the three groups usually reflects the training therapist's allegiance, that is, the affiliation of the person with whom the trainee undertakes their training analysis. Nowadays, however, there is far more fluidity in these groupings, allowing for a richer exchange of ideas. The actual usefulness of these groupings is also being questioned.

For the last 20 years or so the British Freudians have formally referred to their group as the Contemporary Freudians. The new name reflects the advances in thinking that have taken place since Freud's time. The Contemporary Freudians are a rather heterogeneous group of practitioners who have been influenced by both object-relational and developmental perspectives within psychoanalysis, as well as including those who lean more specifically towards contemporary Kleinian thinking. There are also a small number of older British Freudians who were trained by, and remain loyal to, Anna Freud and who would be more appropriately referred to as 'Classical Freudians'.

It is possible to obtain Freudian psychoanalysis in Britain through the Institute of Psychoanalysis or through other psychoanalytic training organizations. In the NHS, in the main, only once-weekly psychoanalytic psychotherapy is offered and this is not necessarily of an explicitly Freudian orientation. The three theoretical groups are represented in the various NHS-based psychotherapy departments in Britain, but rarely within the same department. The Kleinians and Independents are, however, more dominant in Britain in terms of numbers.

THEORETICAL ASSUMPTIONS

Image of the person

Psychoanalysis, as originally conceived by Freud, reflects back to us a rather unflattering picture: we are beings driven by sexual and aggressive urges, we are envious, rivalrous and we harbour murderous impulses even towards those we consciously say we love. Much as we might like to believe that what we see, experience and know directly accounts for all that is important in life, Freud challenged our preferred belief in conscious thought as the ultimate datum of our experience. Rather, he suggested, we are driven by conflicting thoughts, feelings and wishes that are beyond our conscious awareness, but which none the less affect our behaviour – from behind the scenes as it were.

From the very start, psychoanalysis questioned the trustworthiness of human communication. It teaches us never to trust what appears obvious; it advocates an ironic, sceptical stance towards life and our conscious intentions. This is because, Freud suggested, we are beings capable of self-deception. Our mind appears to be structured in such a way that it allows for a part to be 'in the know' while another part is not 'in the know'. Not only can we be fooled but we can also be pulled in different directions, sometimes even oblivious to who or what may be responsible for this. An experience common to all of us is that of feeling, at least some of the time, conflict within ourselves or with others in our life. The idea of *psychic conflict* is central to psychoanalysis and to its view of human nature. It was one of Freud's great insights that our emotional experiences are dynamic, that is, the outcome of conflicting forces, ideas and wishes.

The topographical model of the mind

Freud proposed two models of the mind to account for the experience of conflict. The first is known as the *topographical model* consisting of three levels of consciousness. The first level, the *conscious*, corresponds to that which we are immediately aware of, whatever we may be concentrating on at any given moment – for instance, reading this chapter. Beneath the conscious level lies the second level, the *pre-conscious*, consisting of whatever we can recall without great difficulty. That is, the pre-conscious acts as a kind of storage bin for all those memories, ideas and sense impressions, that are readily available to us, but to which we are simply not attending all the time. Beneath the pre-conscious lies the *unconscious*.

Freud used the term unconscious in three different senses. First, he used it descriptively to denote that which is not in our consciousness at any given moment but is none the less available to us. This is roughly equivalent to the pre-conscious level and is no longer a controversial notion in contemporary psychology. Cognitive neuroscience has shown that most of the working brain is non-conscious in this sense; for example, memory can be acquired without any conscious awareness, and thinking, decision making and problem solving all involve unconscious aspects (Milner et al., 1998). Even our processing of emotional experience has been shown to occur unconsciously in an automatic way. Moreover, this type of processing has been found to be qualitatively different from conscious processing at the level of the neuro-mechanisms involved (Morris et al., 1998).

Secondly, Freud used the term unconscious in a systemic sense denoting his later understanding of the unconscious not as a gradation of consciousness but as a hypothetical system or structure of the mind. Finally he used it to denote the *dynamic unconscious*, that is, a constant source of motivation that makes things happen. In this sense what is stored in the unconscious is said not only to be inaccessible but also to have ended up in the unconscious because it was repressed. The unconscious contains sexual and aggressive drives, defences, memories and feelings that have been repressed.

The pre-conscious and the conscious systems both obey the usual rules of thinking, namely they are logical, reality tested and linear in time and causality. These rules are typical of what is referred to as *secondary process thinking*. The unconscious system obeys a different set of rules typical of *primary process thinking*. In this part of our mind information is not subjected to any kind of reality testing so that mutually exclusive 'truths' may coexist and contradictions abound. Because of these properties the unconscious mind has been likened in the classical Freudian model to an infantile and primitive part of us.

The structural model of the mind

In 1923 Freud revised the topographical model and replaced it with the *structural model*. This new model conceptualized the human psyche as an interaction of three forces: the *id*, *ego* and *superego*. These could be seen to be three different agencies of our personalities each with its own agenda and set of priorities. They were said to have their own separate origins and their own highly specific role in maintaining what might be regarded as 'normal' personality functioning.

According to Freud each one of us is endowed with a specific amount of *psychic energy*. The latter notion was used by Freud to explain the workings of our mental life and was characteristic of his tendency to draw analogies between psychological and physical events. Freud believed that we invest people, objects or ideas with psychic energy. *Cathexis* refers to the amount of psychic energy which becomes attached to the mental representative of a person or object, for example to the memories, thoughts or fantasies about a person. This investment of psychic energy is an indication of the emotional importance of the person or object to the individual in question.

In the newborn infant psychic energy is bound up entirely in the id, the mass of biological drives with which we are all born. The energy of the id is divided between two types of instincts: the Life and the Death instincts. The *Life instinct* is aimed at survival and self-propagation. Into this category fall our needs for food, warmth and, above all, sex. The energy of the Life instinct, the *libido*, was considered by Freud to be the driving force permeating our entire personalities and propelling us through life. In his earliest formulations Freud spoke as though our basic drive was entirely sexual and all other aims and desires arose by some modification of our sexual drive. Among Freudian therapists nowadays the term libido has lost a great deal of its original sexual connotations and refers essentially to the idea of drive energy; that is, the energy we may invest in our pursuit of particular interests in some topic or activity or in relationship with others.

In opposition to the Life instinct stands the *Death instinct*. Discussions of the Death instinct, including Freud's, tend to be rather vague. It is clear, however, that Freud saw the human organism as instinctively drawn back to a state in which all tension would be dissipated – in short, the state of death. This instinctive attraction towards death gives rise to self-directed aggressive tendencies. However, since self-destruction is opposed and tempered by the life-preserving energy of the libido, our aggression in most instances is redirected outward against the world. Aggressive instincts are a component of what drives behaviour. Our self-preservative instinct relies on a measure of aggression to fulfil its aims. In other words, it is imperative that we do not lose sight of aggression's 'propelling function' (Perelberg, 1999), which is essential to preserve life.

The Death instinct represents Freud's broadest philosophical speculation. Amongst Contemporary Freudians therefore, few still hold on to the notion of a Death instinct and find it much more useful to talk about, and to work with, such concepts as guilt, aggression, anger or conflict with the superego. Indeed the Kleinians have developed the notion further; they talk much more of patients 'turning away from life' or 'seeking a near-death state', which are seen as derivative of the operation of the Death instinct.

The instincts of the id are essentially biological. They are not amenable to reason, logic, reality or morality. They are, in a sense, reckless. They are concerned only with one thing: the reduction of whatever tensions our organism may experience. Our innate tendency to maximize pleasure and minimize pain was referred to by Freud as the *pleasure principle*. While the id knows what it wants and needs, it is in some respects 'blind' – blind to what constitutes safe or ethical ways of getting what it needs since it takes no account of reality. To fulfil this function Freud said that the mind developed a new psychic component, the *ego*, which he believed to emerge at about six months of age. The central function of the ego is to serve as a mediator between the id and reality. In contrast to the id's pleasure principle, the ego operates on what is called the *reality principle*, the foundation of which is a concern with safety.

Freud suggested that as we grow up we take into ourselves ideas and attitudes held by others around us. Parents are said to play an important role in curbing or inhibiting the id's excesses. As children we internalize our parents' standards and values and these come together to form the *superego*. This account of the formation of the superego is an instance of what is called *introjection*. The rules, the abstract moral principles and the ideal image of who we ought to be can be thought of as a person inside us who has strong views and is always ready to criticize if our behaviour is not up to standard. This person inside us is equivalent to our superego. While most of us have some awareness of the moral rules and standards which govern our behaviour the superego is only partly conscious.

The psychosexual stages of development

Freud's belief that our sexual life begins at birth led him to describe what are referred to as the stages of psychosexual development. He argued that we all progress through a series of stages, in each of which our psyche directs its sexual energy towards a different *erogenous zone*, that is, a part of our body which is a source of pleasure. Freud first proposed the *oral* stage (0–1 years) where satisfaction is predominantly derived by the infant via the mouth, for example from sucking the nipple or the thumb. Second, is the *anal* stage (1–3 years), where gratification is derived from gaining control over withholding or eliminating faeces. Everyday observations of toddlers highlight how, as they negotiate their increasing separateness from their parents, they come to view their faeces as their own possessions which they want to hold on to or give up in their own good time. The potential for battles and conflict between parent and child, for instance over toilet training, during this period is great. It is at this stage that defecation is said to symbolize giving and withholding. Metaphorically speaking, conflicts at the anal stage are seen to pose a major dilemma for all children with regard to the need to adapt to, or to resist, parental control.

The third stage (3–5 years), the *phallic* stage, sees the child beginning to be more aware of their genitals, with consequent curiosity and anxiety about sexual differences. The phallic stage is thought to be vital to our psychological development because it is this stage that provides the backdrop to the Oedipal drama. In Greek mythology, Oedipus unknowingly kills his father and marries his mother. Likewise, according to Freud, all children during the phallic stage long to do away with the parent of the same sex and take sexual possession of the parent of the opposite sex. The notion of an Oedipal phase places desire at the core of our psychology.

The resolution of the *Oedipus complex* is believed to be crucial to our development. Freud hypothesized that at the same time as the little boy harbours his incestuous desires towards his mother he also experiences *castration anxiety* – the child's fear that his father will punish him for his forbidden wishes by cutting off the guilty organ, his penis. Lacking penises, girls appear castrated to him and the little boy fears a similar fate. Girls, on the other hand, realizing that they have been born unequipped with penises, experience the female counterpart to castration anxiety, namely *penis envy*. They are said to harbour angry feelings towards the mother for having created them without a penis. While the boy's castration anxiety is what causes him to repress his longing for his mother, the girl's penis envy impels her towards her father, desiring a child by the father – the desire for a child being understood merely as a substitute for her former desire for a penis.

With time both the boy's and the girl's Oedipal desires recede and rather than remaining at war with the same-sex parent who is experienced as a rival, both settle for *identification* with the same-sex parent, incorporating their values, standards and sexual orientation. The resolution of the Oedipus complex was therefore linked by Freud to the development of the superego.

The Oedipal phase brings into relief feelings of rivalry and competitiveness and challenges the child with the negotiation of boundaries. Rivalry which is well managed by the parents can lead to constructive preoccupations in the child with fairness and justice (Raphael-Leff, 1991). From a developmental point of view, the child's recognition of the parents as sexual partners encourages an essential relinquishment of the idea of their sole and permanent possession. It involves awareness of the differences that exist between the relationship parents can enjoy with each other as distinct from that which the child is entitled to enjoy with them.

At its core, psychoanalysis is about the vagaries of our desire, our recalcitrant renunciations and the inevitability of loss. Whichever way you look at it, someone somewhere is always missing something in the psychoanalytic drama. Freud starkly reminded us that we simply cannot have it all our own way. Relinquishment and acceptance are common currency within psychoanalysis. The hard lessons begin at birth. As reality impinges on us, frustration, disappointment, loss and longing make their entry into the chronicles of our existence. The breast – that archetypal symbol of never-ending nourishment and care – eventually dries up. These very experiences, however painful, are those which have been singled out by psychoanalysis as privileged in our development towards adaptation to the so-called real world. Freud stressed the need to develop a capacity to delay gratification, to withstand absence and loss, all of which challenge our omnipotent feelings.

Conceptualization of psychological disturbance and health

Freud popularized *neurosis*. Even though clear demarcations hold a certain appeal, especially when we are dealing with human behaviours which have the potential to threaten our need to believe in a stable and orderly world, Freud challenged such demarcations in the context of mental health. He bluntly stated that we are all, to an extent, neurotic. He believed that it was not possible to distinguish so-called 'normal' from 'neurotic' people. Where there was a difference it was held to be one of degree rather than kind. Neurotic conflict is distinguished from the conflict that Freud postulated as being common to us all not by virtue of its content; rather it is the more accentuated nature of the conflict in the neurotic person which gives rise to considerable suffering.

The notion of a dynamic unconscious is central to an understanding of neurosis because Freud (1917) held that neurosis resulted from an unconscious conflict. He argued that neurotic symptoms were born of unconscious conflict between the ego and the id and the resulting blocking or imbalance of energy flow. In addition, Freud thought that his neurotic patients were stuck somewhere in the past; their neurosis was understood to belie 'a kind of ignorance' about their emotional life. Because of fears and anxiety, neurotic individuals held on to their past, according to Freud, precluding development and change.

Freud's theory of psychosexual development is also integral to an understanding of neurosis as he argued that the conflict underlying neurosis has an essentially sexual basis. At first, Freud believed that neurosis resulted from the repression of painful memories which, once recalled, frequently revealed traumatic sexual experiences in childhood. Thereafter he came to believe that, in many cases at least, no such traumatic seductions had in fact taken place and this led to the development of the *wish theory* which stressed the role played by fantasy and desire. In this latest theory, Freud understood neurosis as resulting from repressed erotic impulses. This theory, however, proved to be something of a dead end. Indeed, in his later work, Freud emphasized far more the role of anxiety in neurosis. The experience of anxiety was seen to act as a warning signal in response to internal pressures (e.g. id wishes) or external pressures (e.g. actual trauma) on the ego. In neurotic conflict, the ego strives to keep the dangerous drive from gaining access to consciousness. This places the ego under considerable pressure and impoverishes it so that the ego fails to keep up its defensive efforts, thereby allowing the drive's discharge in the disguised form of neurotic symptoms.

In order to protect the ego from the discomfort of anxiety, *defences* are called into place. Symptoms represent therefore *compromise formations* which express in disguised form unacceptable sexual and aggressive impulses, thus allowing us to carry on with our daily lives. Neurotic symptoms could perhaps be said to be creative insofar as they represent attempted solutions to conflicts which help us to restore a measure of psychic equilibrium.

Acquisition of psychological disturbance

Freud was a committed psycho-archaeologist who thought that the excavation of the past was essential to an understanding of ourselves. He found meaning in the seemingly irrational symptoms of his hysterical patients which had puzzled physicians before him. He understood these as resulting from painful memories which had been repressed into the unconscious and were struggling for expression. Put simply, he suggested that we acquire psychological problems through forgetting what troubles us.

A central theme running throughout psychoanalytic theorizing is the importance of our early experiences, from birth onwards, and their impact on the subsequent development of our personalities and consequently on the aetiology of psychological difficulties. What happens to us as children is seen to shape our personality in a very profound way. Indeed, all psychoanalytic theories have at their root the belief that the present can be understood in light of the past. Freud's original model of development and the acquisition of psychopathology was undoubtedly a deterministic one, which suggested that all events were determined by a sequence of causes and that nothing happened by accident. In the psychological realm this means that we can trace causal links between our behaviour in the here and now and our past, early, experiences.

The Contemporary Freudian understanding of how the mind works and how we can develop emotional problems has been greatly enhanced by the work of the late Joseph Sandler and his wife Anne-Marie Sandler (1984, 1997), both Contemporary Freudians. The Sandlers suggest that we all have formative interpersonal experiences which contribute to the development of *dynamic templates* or, if you like, schemata of self–other relationships. These templates are encoded in the *implicit memory system*, which stores non-conscious knowledge of 'how to do things' and relate to others. The Sandlers refer to this as the *past unconscious*. Its contents are not directly accessible in the form of autobiographical memories. The *present unconscious*, on the other hand, refers to our here-and-now unconscious strivings and responses. Although its contents may become conscious, they are still frequently subject to censorship before being allowed entry into consciousness. Our behaviour in the present is said to function according to rules and patterns of relating to the self and others which were set down very early on in our lives. The actual experiences which contributed to these 'rules' or templates are, however, thought to be irretrievable. According to this model, psychological disturbance may result from being locked into patterns of relating – with all the associated emotional states (e.g. depression), thoughts and wishes – which are ultimately limiting to the individual's development and mental health.

Perpetuation of psychological disturbance

Freud was only too well aware of the self-defeating patterns of behaviour that seem to prevent people from resolving their psychological problems. He believed that the persistence of psychological disturbance resulted from a fixation to particular periods in the patient's past as though the patient is really unable to free themselves from it and therefore to engage with the present in a more constructive way.

However distressing a symptom or a given life situation may be, there may yet be some *secondary gain*, a kind of payoff, for the individual which helps to explain the deadlock with regard to change. The forces underlying self-defeating and self-destructive behaviour are frequently so potent that their cost in terms of personal distress does not appear to act as a powerful enough deterrent. For instance, the suffering that symptoms impose may assuage a person's unconscious guilt and their 'need to suffer', as Freud put it, or the disabling nature of symptoms may help the person to side step other situations which are likely to generate conflict. In satisfying such unconscious needs the symptoms become powerfully reinforced.

Not only do some people remain in intolerable situations, and so perpetuate their psychological difficulties, but some actually appear to be compelled to repeat the same maladaptive patterns in their lives, as if they unconsciously search for situations that can bring only unhappiness and that often represent a re-enactment of earlier relationships and dynamics. Freud called this phenomenon the *compulsion to repeat*. While all therapists would agree that this is a commonly observed pattern, there is nevertheless considerable disagreement as to how one can explain it. Freud's own view was that the compulsion to repeat reflected an individual's attempt to master anxiety, relating to an earlier period, that would otherwise be too overwhelming. This was in keeping with his views on the nature of traumatic dreams where, for instance, following an accident the person may repeatedly dream about the accident. Freud understood such repetitive dreams as attempts to master the anxiety retrospectively.

The compulsion to repeat is a fascinating phenomenon as it challenges us with the existence of behaviour whose aim appears to be ostensibly self-destructive, even if it may well represent an unconscious attempt at mastery. The evidence of self-destructive tendencies in people reveals that vast quantities of the aggressive instinct are sometimes directed inwards and Freud therefore saw the compulsion to repeat as a manifestation of the Death instinct. Indeed it was this that led him to concede that there exists in us a compulsion to repeat which overrides the pleasure principle otherwise believed to rule our instinctual life.

Change

Freud's structural model of the mind, as we have seen, suggests that we live life in a perpetual state of intrapsychic conflict generated by the opposing demands of the id, ego and superego. The experience of conflict calls into place defences so as to protect the ego from anxiety. In so doing, however, the status quo is maintained since the individual fails to confront the source of the anxiety and simply invests emotional energy in the upkeep of the defences. If the resulting anxiety is severe enough to disrupt the person's functioning and defences fail, this can precipitate a kind of breakdown which may nevertheless, paradoxically, act as a spur to change. Indeed people often present for psychological help at times of stress either when their defensive strategies have failed them, or when the conflict becomes ego-dystonic, that is, it is not associated with any second-ary gain but is experienced as wholly unpleasurable.

The early Freudians espoused a deterministic model of development which focused on what prevented people from changing, for example people's fixation at a given developmental stage, or the unconscious needs met by maintaining the status quo, thus precluding development and change. This model reflected a one-person psychology, that is, the emphasis was exclusively intrapsychic and favoured linear, causal explanations which had the appeal of simplicity. Far less attention was devoted to the much more interesting question of how people man-age to change *in spite of* any predisposing factors that increase the likelihood of psychological problems and reduce the likelihood of change.

An overemphasis on the past as a major determining influence denies the inher-ent complexity of the human condition and the many forces and influences which shape us and produce change. Moreover, a strict deterministic stance is no longer tenable, as modern physics has highlighted the problems of such a position. Events are now no longer regarded as inexorably and absolutely determined: their occur-rence is more a matter of high or low probability. Research indeed suggests that it is difficult to be very specific about the longer-term consequences of childhood events (see Lemma, 1995 for a review). This is particularly so since we all vary tremendously and people exposed to the same adverse experiences respond quite differently and show varying degrees of resilience in the face of adversity. To understand change we have to develop more complex models which allow us to take into account the influence of those experiences that can introduce change into an individual's life, such as, for example, the impact of other relationships besides those of early childhood. This has been one of the major contributions of relational, attachment-based models within psychoanalysis which have influenced the Contemporary Freudians. Nowadays, psychoanalysis espouses a two-person psychology reflecting the importance of the attachments we develop throughout life and how these can contribute to revisions and changes to the early models of relationships we develop as a result of our experiences in our families of origin. Indeed the vast majority of contemporary British analysts would comfortably label themselves as 'object-relational' in their approach, irrespective, for example, of their affiliation to the 'Freudian' group.

Even though we are not entirely determined by our past we can often trace in our own developmental histories some very interesting and meaningful relationships between the past and the present so that psychological events cannot be considered just to be haphazard. This notion, central to Freud's thinking, is at the core of the principle of *psychic determinism*: that is, in the mind nothing just happens by chance. Events in our mental life which may at first appear random or unrelated to that which preceded them are only apparently so. The notion of psychic determinism, however, does not imply a simple relationship of cause and effect in our mental life. Rather, it is generally recognized that a single event may be *overdetermined*, the end product of biological, developmental and environmental forces – all of which can contribute to psychological change or to arrests in development.

PRACTICE

Goals of therapy

Any discussion on the goals of psychotherapy exposes an inherent problem that cuts across all the schools of psychoanalysis: what psychotherapists state publicly through their theories does not necessarily reflect what they believe implicitly and therefore what they actually do in practice with patients (Sandler and Dreyer, 1996).

At the level of public theories, the stated aims of the early Freudian approach were quite clear: the therapy would bring about a discharge of affect, a *catharsis*, and the role of the therapist was to interpret instinctual wishes and fantasies that had been repressed in the unconscious and the conflict with which they were associated. The overall aim within this context was to bring the latent instinctual wish to consciousness and overcome the resistance to their acceptance.

It is a well-known fact that psychoanalytic psychotherapists shirk from using the concept of cure in their written work. This dread of 'pathological therapeutic zeal' – to use Greenson's (1967) telling phrase – has been inherited from Freud, who was no therapeutic optimist. Moreover, Freud was far less interested in psychoanalysis as a therapeutic system than as a tool for understanding both individual and society. As far as he was concerned, psychoanalysis should be valued for its contributions to a science of human being rather than for any quick results as regards personality change or the alleviation of neurotic symptoms. Freud was indeed rather pessimistic, or one could perhaps more accurately say 'realistic', about the therapeutic benefits of psychoanalysis. In a hypothetical discussion with a patient, he stated that psychoanalysis could help transform 'hysterical misery' into 'common unhappiness'. This may not sound like a very enticing outcome for the majority of people, who harbour hopes of fundamental change and happiness. But Freudian psychoanalysis espouses a very particular philosophy of life, one within which life, as we have seen, is unavoidably lived in conflict. Repression is considered integral to our survival in a social world which confronts us daily with the impracticability of living our life under the sway of the pleasure principle. The aim of psychoanalysis as therapy was not, according to Freud, the reduction of suffering but was centred on the necessity of living with one's limitations and conflicts.

The aims of psychoanalytic treatment have shifted over the years along with the changing conceptualizations of the nature of psychological problems (Steiner, 1989). When Freud at first subscribed to a model of dammed-up libido where problems arose largely as a result of sexual inhibitions, the aim of psychoanalysis was to free the patients from their inhibitions so as to allow for a discharge of the libido. At that stage, the primary aim of treatment was therefore to make the unconscious conscious.

However, along with his later structural formulation of the mind in terms of id, ego and superego, Freud emphasized the need to modify defences, to reduce the pressures from the superego so that the patient could become less frightened of the superego and to strengthen the ego: 'where id was there shall ego be', as Freud put it. He believed that the therapist and the patient's weakened ego needed to become allies against the instinctual demands of the id and the conscientious demands of the superego (Freud, 1938). Within this model, psychological problems were thus understood to result from conflict. Those therapists who still subscribe to this model aim primarily to extend, through the psychoanalytic process, the patient's knowledge of themselves, in the hope that with such knowledge – their insight – they may be able to make choices which are not exclusively ruled by neurotic needs so that new compromises and more adaptive solutions can be explored.

The aims of Contemporary Freudians reflect some of these early thoughts insofar as improvement of reality testing and the acquisition of insight are still considered important aims. Most Contemporary Freudians have, however, incorporated ideas arising from both the Kleinian and Independent traditions which have elaborated treatment aims. This trend is perhaps best reflected in the work of Joseph and Anne-Marie Sandler (1997) who view the aim of psychoanalysis as that of helping the patient achieve psychic reintegration by reclaiming parts of the self which have been split off and projected into others because they could not be otherwise managed.

Notwithstanding the integration of various strands of analytic thinking, the broad therapeutic aims reflect something of Freud's original humbleness insofar as Freudian therapists recognize that psychic conflict cannot be completely eradicated, in the same way that the transference cannot be completely resolved. Insight is aimed for but it is no longer viewed as a strict requirement, just as retrieval of repressed childhood memories is no longer the main goal. Instead, the emphasis is on bringing about intrapsychic changes which could result in an improved resolution of conflicts and hopefully expand the individual's capacity for self-reflection.

Selection criteria

In Freud's time, the selection criteria for psychoanalysis were pretty straightforward: being a classical analyst meant accepting the view that psychoanalysis
was only appropriate for those patients who suffered from neuroses, whose psychopathology was rooted in the Oedipal phase and who could reveal their infantile neurosis in the transference through the so-called *transference neurosis*.
Although there still exists a minority of therapists aligning themselves with
Freud's original views on the matter, the vast majority of Contemporary
Freudians would feel somewhat restricted by this stance. Since the 1970s, cases
of patients diagnosed as psychotic or personality disordered have been treated
more frequently by psychoanalytic psychotherapists of all persuasions.
However, perhaps it is amongst the Freudians that one is likely to find more
diverse views on this matter.

Broadly speaking, the more contemporary Freudian approach shares selection
criteria with the other schools of psychoanalysis. When assessing a patient with
a view to psychoanalytic treatment, the assessor is likely to take into account the
following:

- the patient's ability to get actively involved with the therapeutic process;
- the patient's interest in and capacity for self-reflection, however rudimentary;
- whether the patient has sufficient ego strength to withstand the inherent frustrations of the
  therapeutic relationship and to undertake self-exploration;
- whether the patient can tolerate frustration and anxiety and other strong affects without threats
  to the self (e.g. suicide), to others (e.g. violence) or to the therapy (e.g. forms of acting out);
- evidence of at least one positive relationship;
- the availability of other support systems in the patient's life.

In the NHS psychoanalytic psychotherapy is a very scarce resource, weighed
down by long waiting lists. It is usually offered to those who present with
moderate to severe difficulties which have taken a chronic course. Generally
speaking, such an approach seems most indicated when the patient presents with
problems of a characterological nature or where there are interpersonal difficulties. Nowadays, the patient's formal diagnosis, for example whether they suffer
from borderline personality disorder or manic depression, is considered less
relevant than whether the patient shows some capacity for engaging with the
therapeutic process.

The drive towards evidence-based practice has encouraged many practitioners
to use research as a guideline for which treatment works best for a given diagnostic group (Roth and Fonagy, 2006). Although this type of guidance is
immensely helpful and should be considered when formulating patients' problems and deciding on treatment interventions, there is also recognition, especially among psychoanalytic practitioners, of the limitations of such an
approach. This is because when we see a patient who presents with so-called
depression or anxiety, the individual formulation of the patient's difficulties is

probably going to be a far more reliable guide to what they need, and what help they can use, than their formal diagnosis.

When considering the suitability of a *brief psychodynamic approach* several factors need to be considered (Malan, 1979):

- There is a good history of interpersonal relationships even if conflicted.
- The patient's difficulties must lend themselves to focusing on one theme or core conflict.
- The conflict is at a neurotic, oedipal level (i.e. not indicative of borderline or pre-oedipal problems).
- During the assessment the patient responds to interpretations concerned with the identified focus.
- The patient is motivated to work with the chosen focus.
- The potential contra-indications for brief therapy (e.g. risk of impulsive behaviour), if present, are thought to be manageable.

Group psychoanalytic psychotherapy is also available: this does not identify strictly with a Freudian approach, but reflects an integration of various strands of analytic thinking. In a general sense the same criteria apply as for individual psychotherapy. However, there are some instances when a group approach may be the best treatment modality. For example, where a psychoanalytic approach is thought to be indicated, but where there is a concern about the possibility of a regressive transference (e.g. excessive dependency) or where the patient displays an intolerance of dyadic intimacy and would find the intensity of a one-to-one relationship overwhelming, a group approach might be recommended.

None of the above criteria would be sufficient in isolation to arrive at a decision; these are some of the thoughts that an assessor would have in mind, but they would always need to be considered in light of patients' problems and personal history and along with their capacities and vulnerabilities. Moreover, none of the criteria stated here have been backed up consistently by research findings; they merely reflect common clinical thinking and practice in the author's experience of working in the NHS.

Qualities of effective therapists

What makes a good Freudian therapist, as opposed to a Kleinian one for example, is not really a useful question. It is more helpful to think about what makes a good psychoanalytic psychotherapist generally speaking, as the label 'Freudian' probably adds little to our understanding of the very complex process of psychotherapy and the factors that facilitate it.

The most important qualities are *curiosity*, which fosters understanding that goes beyond the manifest meaning of what the patient tells the therapist, and *integrity* so that what the patient shares is handled sensitively and professionally with due respect for the patient's vulnerability in the context of the therapeutic relationship.

The greatest challenge for a psychoanalytic psychotherapist is to develop the capacity to monitor their own unconscious processes so as to safeguard the analytic space which exists for the patient. Ensuring that the therapist's own difficulties or frustrations do not impinge on the analytic space requires that the therapist him or herself has undergone a lengthy analysis so as to become aware of, as Freud called them, their 'blind spots'. In addition, engagement in this process hones the therapist-to-be's ear for unconscious communication as they learn to decipher their own.

A capacity for what Freud called *free-floating attention* is also needed. This denotes a capacity to be sensitively attuned and open to peripheral perceptions so as to catch the unconscious communications which are latent in the patient's material.

Aiming to maintain a *neutral stance*, a notion that we will look at further in the next section, is essential so as to allow the development of a space for thinking about problems with a patient without the encumbrance of moral dictates and judgements, though this does not mean that therapists operate without any ethical responsibilities.

Therapeutic relationship and style

The therapeutic relationship

Psychotherapy unfolds in a relational context: patient and therapist meet with both explicit and implicit aims and expectations. Both bring to the relationship their personal motivations and needs. The analytic relationship can become as complex as any intimate relationship: the patient may experience intense feelings of anger, hate, envy, love, sexual attraction and many others towards the therapist.

As Freud's understanding of the variables that facilitated change in psychoanalysis evolved, the relationship between therapist and patient gradually took centre stage. He noted affective changes in the patient's attachment to him developing in the course of treatment. These feelings were regarded as *transference* coming about as a consequence of a 'false connection'. He came to see transferences as new editions of old impulses and fantasies aroused during the process of psychoanalysis, with the therapist replacing some earlier person.

At the root of the Freudian concept of transference lies the notion that the way in which we respond to particular people in the present is under the influence of our experiences in the past. In a general sense we approach new relationships according to patterns from the past, that is, we transfer to people in the present feelings and attitudes from the past which may not be appropriate. These represent a repetition, or a displacement, of reactions which originated in regard to significant figures in early childhood. This suggests that we may have developed habitual types of reacting to other people which have become part of our personality, such as a tendency to be afraid of authority so that certain feelings and modes of being may be repeatedly triggered in situations where we are faced with authority figures.

At first Freud thought that the transference was an unwanted complication in his new technique. But he soon capitalized on his former so-called error to formulate the major pillar of psychoanalytic technique: the analysis of transference. This was further divided into the positive and the negative transference – the positive and negative feelings which the patient transfers to the analyst.

In 1909 he remarked that transference was not just an obstacle to psychoanalysis but might play a positive role as a therapeutic agent. Later he concluded that it was in fact necessary for any psychoanalytic cure. Patients who were unable to develop a transferential relationship were not thought to be treatable by psychoanalysis. Despite this, Freud also warned practitioners of the powerful erotic charge of the transference, which creates the need for a professional ethic that prevents therapists from taking advantage of the seductive potential of the therapist/patient relationship.

Classical Freudians continue to understand the transference as a repetition of an earlier relationship. Contemporary Freudians, on the other hand, suggest that the intensity of the therapist–patient relationship arouses latent emotional experiences, but what transpires between patient and therapist is understood to be a *new* experience influenced by the past, not just a repetition.

Underpinning more contemporary views of transference continues to be a basic, and all too rarely challenged, assumption that can be traced throughout psychoanalytic theorizing, namely the existence of an objective reality known by the therapist and distorted by the patient (Stolorow and Attwood, 1992). One important implication of this position, with clinical ramifications, is a view of the therapeutic relationship, and of the process of psychotherapy itself, as one in which the impact of the observer on the observed as an ever-present influence on the therapeutic dyad is minimized.

The intersubjective school of psychoanalysis has now engaged with such issues, but it is an approach that has found more favour in North America than in Britian. Mainstream discussions of the analytic relationship continue to stress the importance of analytic neutrality, anonymity and the relative unresponsiveness of the analyst.

Few would, however, dispute the centrality of a bond or alliance between patient and therapist as a sine qua non of therapeutic work. Influential reviews of the psychotherapy outcome research literature underscore the importance of interpersonal factors as prominent ingredients of change in all therapies (Lambert et al., 1986; Horvath and Luborsky, 1993; Roth and Fonagy, 2006) and the studies have very consistently found a strong relationship between the therapeutic alliance and outcome that overrides technical differences between the therapies studied (e.g. Krupnick et al., 1996).

The notion of a *therapeutic* or *treatment alliance* has its origin in Freud's writings on technique although he never designated it as a distinctive concept. Originally it was encompassed within the general concept of transference. In

1913 Freud referred to the need to establish an 'effective transference' before the full work of psychoanalysis could begin. The essential distinction made by Freud at this time was between the patient's capacity to establish a friendly rapport with the therapist on the one hand, and the emergence of revived feelings and attitudes (i.e. the transference) which could become an obstacle to therapeutic progress on the other.

Some psychoanalytic theorists have been concerned with differentiating the treatment or therapeutic alliance from transference 'proper' (Sandler et al., 1973) – a trend reflected in the work of Greenson and Wexler (1969) in the way they regard the core of the alliance as being anchored in the 'real' or 'non-transferential' relationship. Zetzel (1956) made a notable contribution to this issue, stating that the presence of a real object relationship is necessary for the therapeutic alliance to develop, and, significantly, that these conditions are necessary for the psychoanalysis itself to proceed. This reflects a more general Freudian position which proposes that a part of the patient's ego is identified with the therapist's function and aims, while another part is engaged in resistance. The therapeutic alliance reflects the operation of the so-called *observing ego* which works alongside the therapist.

Although the analysis of transference is considered nowadays to be at the heart of analytic work, as we shall see in the next section, it is also a powerful dynamic. It is believed to be part of what drives the relationship. A patient can therefore also be a transference object for the therapist and can arouse in her feelings that are inappropriate to the present relationship. *Counter-transference*, the phenomenon accounting for the therapist's reactions to her patient, has been variously defined. At first Freud used this term to denote the therapist's blind spots and own transference to the patient. Subsequent formulations broadened the concept to the inappropriate emotional responses created in the therapist by the patient's transference material and role expectations. In more contemporary, especially Kleinian usage, it denotes all of the feelings aroused in the therapist by the patient. In other words, there has been a shift from seeing counter-transference as something which interferes with technique (the Classical Freudian position) to viewing such responses by the therapist as a means of understanding the patient's unconscious communications, thereby acting as a direct guide for analytic interpretations of the current material. This latter view is now shared by many contemporary Freudians and Kleinians alive.

Style

Many myths abound about how a Freudian therapist behaves, not least of which is the idea that they say relatively little during sessions. On this, as indeed on many other variables, therapists will differ greatly along a continuum ranging from very passive/silent to very interactive. Some of the Classical Freudians are perhaps most identified with the silent end of the spectrum whereas there will be far more variability amongst the Contemporary Freudians on this question.

When we look at the pre-eminence of the interpretation of transference phenomena, it becomes possible to understand why therapists adopt a particular therapeutic style. Indeed, this emphasis is intimately linked to the analytic persona many therapists model themselves on: a relatively unobtrusive, neutral, anonymous professional who sacrifices her so-called 'normal' personality so as to receive the patient's projections, thereby providing fertile ground for the development of the transference. Therapists in training are typically encouraged to remain cordial yet aloof, and to avoid engaging in a conversational style with the patient or to disclose any personal information.

The notion of the therapist as a blank screen for the patient's projections is, however, difficult to uphold. This was Freud's (1912) own ideal as he described how the analyst should function as a 'mirror' to the patient's projections so that the reactions to the therapist could then be analysed to throw light on the patient's relationships more generally. However, the viability of the mirror-like attitude was gradually challenged (Balint and Balint, 1939; Klauber, 1986; Greenberg, 1996).

The therapist as a person is a variable that cannot and should not be ignored. Moreover, it is a variable that – even if it were possible – we need not try to eliminate as it contributes to the analytic ambience of collaborative work which provides the essential backdrop to analytic work. Patients live in a real world as well as in their phantasy world and the exchanges with the therapist's humanity involve confrontations with their limitations as much as with their strengths. In other words, an important aspect of the therapeutic relationship is that it involves a confrontation with the reality of the therapist as real person, capable of spontaneous responses and, hence, inevitably fallible. The negotiation of disappointments and frustrations with a therapist who is real, in the sense just outlined, provides a potentially mutative interpersonal experience as long as this can be worked through. Just as a therapist compromises her potential effectiveness if she remains too fully a real person with no sensitivity to the distortions of projection, she will be equally ineffective if she remains solely a 'symbolic object' (Szasz, 1963). The therapeutic situation requires of the therapist that she function as both and of the patient that he perceive the therapist as both. Being neutral should not preclude an empathic, authentic, warm attitude. This was indeed Freud's own style with his patients which he unfortunately never clearly articulated in his papers on technique, but which shines through in his case histories and in his patients' reports of their analyses with him (Couch, 1979).

Major therapeutic strategies and techniques

Free association and the use of the couch
In some key respects Freudian therapists remain true to Freud's own practice. While they were reclining back on the analytic couch, Freud encouraged his patients to share all their thoughts as they came to mind without any regard for logic or order. This was his fundamental rule and the cornerstone of his

technique: *free association*. Freud was well aware of the demand he placed on his patients and he wrote, 'In confession, the sinner tells us what he knows; in analysis the neurotic has to tell more' (1926: 289). Freud insisted on the rule of free association because he realized that whatever the seemingly plausible reasons for the appearance in his patients' conscious minds of certain thoughts or images, these were used, as it were, by deeper forces pressing for expression. In encouraging patients simply to share everything that came to mind Freud hoped to be led to their inner conflicts through their associations. Whilst free-associating, patients certainly reveal a lot about themselves, their aspirations, fears, fantasies – often far more than would be the case if the therapist asked many questions or structured the therapeutic session more. Free association is, however, an ideal towards which the patient strives but in practice it is very difficult indeed to share all the contents of our thoughts. None the less the principle of free association underpins all current psychoanalytic practice.

When patients are seen more frequently than once weekly, the use of the couch remains standard practice. Typically the therapist sits out of the patient's sight, behind the couch. This way the usual conversational style that is encouraged by face-to-face communication, with its attendant non-verbal cues, is inhibited. Lying on the couch is thought to facilitate a more free-associative style. Also, the use of the couch has probably survived over the years because it benefits not only the patient but also the therapist, who does not have to be under the patient's constant visual scrutiny. This allows the therapist to think more freely and to become more sensitively attuned to the latent communications in the patient's manifest material.

Dream interpretation

Dream interpretation, once thought to be 'the royal road to the unconscious' (Freud, 1905), is nowadays viewed as less central to Freudian analytic technique. Dreams are believed to be carriers of unconscious meaning and are interpreted as they arise, but they no longer hold the centre stage that Freud awarded them. When they are worked with, the patient is asked to associate to elements of the dream, so as to access its latent meaning. It is through an understanding of the meaning of the patient's personal associations that the dream is eventually interpreted.

Interpretation of defence and of transference

Through its use of interpretation, psychoanalysis offers the patient a scheme or system of thought which enables them to make some sense out of their distress. Strictly speaking, to interpret in the analytic sense means to make an unconscious phenomenon conscious (Greenson, 1967). Interpretations help the patient to become aware of the unconscious meaning, source or cause of their feelings, thoughts and behaviours. To arrive at an interpretation the therapist may use clarificatory questions and prompts but these are usually kept to a minimum.

While interpretations seldom immediately get rid of symptoms, they do provide valuable relief from the patient's fear of chaos and meaninglessness. They offer the patient new concepts and information which allow for meaningful connections between symptoms and experiences that may have been, up until that point, mysterious. The creation of a powerful explanatory model acts as a means of reducing tension, replacing confusion with some degree of clarity.

The term 'interpretation' may give the misleading impression that when in analysis the patient tells the therapist their thoughts and dreams and the latter simply interprets these in light of the patient's past history. This makes it sound as though the patient is a passive recipient waiting for the therapist to dispense the 'truth' or the answer which will explain psychic pain away. Rather it is the patient ideally who arrives at their own interpretations through the process of exploring how they feel. The therapist will of course at times point out certain patterns, or emphasize something the patient has said which they appear to be glossing over but that may in fact be quite significant, while at other times they may highlight inconsistencies in thoughts or feelings which reflect underlying conflicts and defensive processes. Nevertheless, the best interpretations are those that invite the patient to explore further, to become curious about their own mind and therefore to build on the interpretation with further associations.

Throughout Freud's writings and those of his followers, we find numerous references to *defences,* whose aim is to ward off conflict and the ensuing anxiety. Classical Freudian therapists still believe that one of the core tasks of psychoanalysis is to undertake an *analysis of defence and resistance*. This focus is taken up to varying degrees by Contemporary Freudian therapists. It involves the clarification, confrontation, interpretation and working through of defences and resistances as they arise in the course of psychotherapy (Greenson, 1967).

The concept of defence mechanisms refers to a process designed to avoid danger and hence anxiety which is a product of perceived danger. Defences falsify reality in order to avoid situations which are perceived as threatening to the self. In 1926, Freud revised and broadened the concept of defence, which he had previously conceived as synonymous with *repression*, and recognized repression as just one of many defence mechanisms. Repression refers to the confinement to the unconscious of thoughts, images and memories which, if allowed into consciousness, would give rise to anxiety. Sometimes certain facts may be remembered but their connection to each other or their emotional significance is repressed as, for example, when someone recounts a traumatic experience with none of the expected accompanying emotions. Conflict may then arise when the person encounters a new experience which is somehow connected with what was previously repressed. In these cases we often find a tendency on the part of the repressed and unconscious to use this new experience as an opportunity for its outlet – it finds what is called a *derivative*. Because repressed material continues to exist in the unconscious and may develop such derivatives, repression is not a once and for all occurrence; it is a process that requires a constant input of psychic energy so as to maintain it (Fenichel, 1946).

Anna Freud developed much further the concept of defences and underlined the need for analysis to address the ego's defences against conflict so as to help patients obtain a more harmonious relationship between the psychic agencies and between them and the external world. Many defence mechanisms have been highlighted by psychoanalysis (e.g. projection, reaction formation, introjection, displacement, undoing isolation, identification with the aggressor). Anna Freud's (1936) book describes the most common ones.

The cornerstone of Contemporary Freudian analytic technique, like that of other schools of psychoanalysis, is the *interpretation of transference*. The outcome of therapy is held to be related by many, if not most, Contemporary Freudians to the successful elaboration and re-evaluation of patterns of relating which become accessible through an analysis of transference phenomena, that is, the enactment in the present of implicit schemata or dynamic templates of self–other relationships (Sandler and Sandler, 1997) and their interpretation. There appears to be a continuum along which therapists broadly situate themselves on this question. This ranges from those who believe in the 'total transference' and who focus almost exclusively on the here-and-now transference interpretation, and those who draw a clear distinction between real and distorted aspects of the relationship and whose range of interventions includes so-called 'extra-transference' interpretations (Hamilton, 1996). The latter position is the one typically associated with Classical Freudians and some Contemporary Freudians.

The change process in therapy

Contemporary Freudians believe that understanding how patients construe their early experiences is more important than the unravelling of what actually happened to them in the past. The emphasis in therapy is thus on the meaning attributed to an experience rather than on the fact of the experience itself. This is in keeping with research findings which suggest that autobiographical memory is unreliable and privy to the vicissitudes of our desire – in other words, we remember what we want to remember and this is not necessarily a factually accurate picture of what actually took place (see Fonagy and Target, 1997). However, this does not mean that the reality of people's lives is ignored. Rather, the therapist's task is to listen both to what actually happened *and* to the meaning the patient ascribes to their experiences.

As we have seen, our early experiences are now thought to be encoded as procedures (i.e. how to do things and how to relate to others). This contributes to the development of templates for how relationships work and what may be expected of others and is expected of oneself. Following on from this assumption is the belief that therapeutic change results from the elaboration and re-evaluation of current models of relationships which are implicitly encoded as procedures. Change is no longer thought to flow from uncovering repressed memories, as research suggests that it is not really possible to directly access unconscious memory. Rather, change occurs through an understanding of the vicissitudes of the new relationship created between the patient and the therapist, which is informed by the past and thus gives some clues as to the model of relationships that the patient operates from.

The capacity to make explicit, and to reflect on, implicit models of how relationships work has been shown, for example, to be critical in breaking the intergenerational transmission of insecure attachment patterns (Fonagy et al., 1993). The capacity for self-reflection is a vital moderating variable which can make a difference. People who lack this capacity are those more likely to develop psychological problems later in life, especially in the context of a history of a difficult childhood. Those who have endured very traumatic childhood experiences, but who nevertheless have developed the capacity for self-reflection, are more likely to break the intergenerational cycle of transmission of destructive patterns of behaviour and of relating. 'Self-reflective function', as it is referred to, can now be experimentally measured. It describes the capacity to process emotional experience, acting as a mediating device between our experience and the outcome that is translated into behaviour. It refers to our ability to relate to ourselves as thinking and feeling beings. It involves acknowledging mixed emotions, recognizing the irrationality of some of our beliefs and desires and the frequently pressing nature of our emotional states, along with our vulnerability in the face of such experiences.

Nowadays discussions on the nature of change often, but by no means exclusively, focus on the notion of *adaptation* rather than fundamental personality change or change in psychic structures. People are not necessarily thought to 'get better' as such; rather they are said to understand themselves better so that they have more options and are able to exercise the options open to them. This, in turn, may contribute to a subjective sense of well-being and a reduction in symptoms.

Limitations of the approach

Psychoanalysis is a rich, complex and stimulating theory and application, but it does not present a unified view either of the nature of our development or of the mutative factors in psychotherapy. It has a long, antagonistic relationship to empirical research. Psychoanalysis, however, badly needs the self-correcting methodology of empirical science so as to enable it to rationally decide between the rival theories which make up the umbrella term 'psychoanalysis'. Without a research perspective the danger is that psychoanalysis will continue to be a breeding ground for fanaticism and narrow-mindedness, which has in the past lent it the appearance of a cult or religion (Szasz, 1978). Not surprisingly, the easiest target for criticism has been the behaviour of some analysts who have acted more as true believers than as genuine enquirers.

Fortunately, over the last 20 years in particular, partly as a result of a *rapprochement* between the fields of child development and psychoanalysis, there has been an upsurge in empirical studies which have tried to substantiate some core psychoanalytic assumptions. There is now also increasing interest in the factors that are related to the successful outcome of psychotherapy (Stern et al., 1998). This will hopefully pave the way for research into other mutative factors in psychotherapy beyond the interpretation of transference which has perhaps been overvalued as the key to therapeutic change in more Contemporary Freudian thinking by contrast to a more Classical Freudian approach. Which interventions are the most facilitative of change remains a key research question. It would be of interest, for example, to study further the outcome of analytic approaches that focus more systematically on the interpretation of transference as opposed to approaches which make more use of reconstructive or supportive interpretations.

Recent psychoanalytic contributions have indeed challenged the pre-eminence of transference interpretation. This challenge is presented by those theoreticians and clinicians influenced by both dynamic and systemic ideas who underscore the need for the co-construction of new contexts by the meeting of two subjectivities (Beebe and Lachmann, 1988, 1994; Sameroff, 1983; Stern et al., 1998). The underlying assumption in these accounts is that both patient and therapist contribute to the regulation of the exchange, even if their respective contributions cannot be regarded as equal. From this perspective regulation is an emergent property of the dyadic system as well as a property of the individual. Within this context there is room for a variety of interventions, other than transference interpretations, which may have mutative potential.

A view commonly held by sceptics is that psychoanalytic treatment 'seems to produce a good many more converts than cures' (Crews, 1993: 55). Until recently, this criticism has been hard to refute as there has been a dearth of outcome research evaluating the effectiveness of psychoanalytic treatments. The stereotypical response by a significant number of psychoanalytic psychotherapists to outcome research is that it is not meaningful. Indeed, the evaluation of psychotherapy is inextricably linked to individual views on science and scientific method, on the nature of 'meaningful' questions, on how far the complex phenomena of psychotherapy can be scientifically investigated and, not least, on how one defines a successful outcome, that is whether one is 'cured'. While such arguments need to be considered there are obvious scientific, moral, political and financial reasons for at least attempting to carry out outcome research. The primary advantage of outcome studies is that they place into the empirical arena the many conflicting and hyperbolic claims made about the superiority of one approach over another. Furthermore, the value of knowing the relative efficacy of alternative techniques, the differences in the range or type of outcomes produced and the process through which such outcomes are achieved, encompasses critical theoretical and practical questions.

Psychoanalytic approaches undoubtedly have a place amongst a range of psychological therapies even though they have not been evaluated as extensively as other therapeutic modalities (Roth and Fonagy, 2006). Not everyone, however, benefits from a psychoanalytic approach. It would be desirable, but not at present possible, to specify criteria regarding who is most likely to benefit. This is a question that is being researched further.

Case example

The client

Tony, a 19-year-old man, was referred by his doctor because of difficulties with managing his anger such that he tended to make impulsive decisions rather than tackle a problem. Indeed, in our first session, he told me that he had recently dropped out of university after a tutor had accused him of plagiarism. His parents had been very concerned about this behaviour and had encouraged him to get help.

Tony presented as a likeable, very articulate young man whose verbal dexterity stood in sharp contrast to his physical clumsiness. For example, on entering my room he often knocked over something or bumped into furniture. Observing him over time, I soon gained the impression that he did not comfortably inhabit his own body.

Tony was adopted as a very young baby. He described a happy early childhood but, aged seven, he had felt sidelined when his adoptive parents unexpectedly naturally conceived a baby girl. Although he related this quite factually, it was very apparent that Tony had felt devastated by the birth of his sister. His devastation seemed to centre around what I understood to be his experience of having been 'deceived' by his adoptive parents as he had believed he would be their only child.

The therapy

During the early months Tony cancelled several times, at very short notice, leaving elaborate messages for me outlining why he could not attend. The excuses he gave had one thing in common: they were all fairly implausible, if only because they repeatedly cast him in a favourable light – the good son, the helpful citizen, the trusted friend. On one occasion, for example, he had found himself caught in a trapped lift and had to help other distressed people trapped with him; on another occasion, he had stumbled across an injured animal that he had taken to the animal hospital. He would also recount somewhat implausible events from his childhood that left me feeling his whole self was precariously built on a lie.

In the first six months I found myself simply listening to Tony. I intervened very sparingly, occasionally commenting on emerging patterns of behaviour, but by no means making very full interpretations either at the level of transference or of a more reconstructive kind linking past and present. My cautious, more passive approach was informed by a number of factors. Firstly, in the early stages of any therapy, we cannot possibly know enough about the patient to make fuller interpretations in a meaningful way. Secondly, such extensive interpretations are not necessarily helpful because they can deprive the patient of an opportunity to discover himself; rather, the therapist's skill lies precisely in knowing how to titrate the extent and depth of an interpretation so that the patient can make best use of it. Finally, with Tony in particular, I noted my sense that I needed to tread carefully in response to my perception of the fragility of his defensive structures. This more low-key start allowed me to gain a picture of his internal world by paying close attention both to the content of what he was saying as well as to the emotional impact on me of what he related. In other words, I saw my role as allowing the transference to develop whilst closely monitoring my own countertransferential responses.

The tales of near-death experiences or acts of bravery placed Tony at the epicentre of some impending disaster. The sense of urgency conveyed by the stories helped me to understand Tony's desperate need to impress upon me a very particular version of himself. Tony was not deluded. He knew very well that he was lying, but as he told me the lie, he needed to believe in its truth and, crucially, he needed me to believe in it too. Rather than feeling duped or undermined as I was being offered another untruth, my countertransference was primarily one of feeling protective and sympathetic towards this young man. For this reason, I decided to accept his lying as the only way he felt he could safely communicate with me.

Eight months into the therapy Tony began to wonder about his birth mother. The time it took him to broach this subject was an indication of how the early experience of abandonment remained very painful for him. With some encouragement from me as I sensed how frightened he was to engage in any exploration of his feelings about his birth mother, he eventually mused about what she looked like. This fleeting thought was quickly followed by him saying that he 'didn't buy' the story his adoptive parents had given him when they had described his mother as a deprived, adolescent girl who had no resources to look after him. In moments of despair and rage, Tony would say that this was a 'lie'; he remained convinced that his birth mother had been no more than a 'selfish, spoilt girl' who was now living comfortably with her family and never gave him a second thought.

Six weeks before our first summer break, Tony began part time work in a bookshop. Within two weeks of starting this job, Tony started the session speaking somewhat manically about how his boss would be showing his writing to a publisher. The following week, Tony returned, in a very manic state of mind:

Patient: You won't believe this! My boss has set up lunch for me with this big publisher to discuss my writing … I'm going to have to get down to some serious work because if there's a deal, it's got to be secured quickly because it's almost August and everyone disappears then. You know what publishers are like … they're fickle … so unless something is in black and white they might change their minds and then I'll be back to square one.

Therapist: I think you may be quite worried about how fickle I am in my commitment to you if I can go away for the summer. Just as you are keen to secure a contract with this publisher, you're anxious to secure a firm place in my mind over the summer break and perhaps it feels easier to believe that I will keep 'Tony-the author' in mind more than 'Tony-the sales assistant'.

At this point I was well aware of Tony's lies and of their defensive function. Through my transference interpretation I was not directly addressing his lying; rather, I was trying to help him to make contact with his anxiety about my view of him, which I considered to be one of his core anxieties underpinning all his relationships. Taking up this dynamic in the transference, and working on it with Tony when it emerged in different guises, proved to be a key part of the work we did together. Essentially, this is what is meant when contemporary psychoanalytic therapists describe 'working in the transference'. The role of the therapist here is to monitor the moment-by-moment shifts in the patient's relationship to the therapist and to himself and to eventually interpret these to the patient.

The transference relationship was dominated by Tony's insistent need to establish an idealised relationship with me. Doubt about my intentions towards him was experienced as intolerable. I was conscious that he closely scrutinized my face as we spoke as if he was always on the look out for disapproval or criticism. I often felt the pressure of his need to control my version of him in my mind, as communicated through his lies. I understood Tony's lies primarily as attempts at creating an impressive version of himself that guaranteed, for the duration of the lie, the object's love and admiration. In the transference, the lie and its impact on me – the imperative to relate to the version of him contained in the lie – was a powerful expression of his internal struggle: how to survive in a world devoid of people whom he could trust would accept his 'true' self. Yet, by lying to me and to others he perpetuated this internal drama as he could never find out whether his 'true' self would be accepted. One of the aims of interpreting the transference was therefore to help Tony understand how he had no trust that he would be loved for himself rather than a 'made-up' version of himself.

Eventually, I directly challenged Tony about his lying, careful not to shame him in so doing. This confrontation provoked anxiety, but there was also relief that we could talk openly about his need to lie. Yet, the lying did not stop at this point. The work required that we repeatedly return to his need for lying when it emerged: this is the process of 'working through' that is so often written about. This process involved both working in the transference as well as making reconstructive interpretations that linked the patterns in the transference to his developmental history. For example, interpretations that made links between his lying to me and his experience of having been lied to by his birth mother and by his adoptive parents when they later conceived his sister.

During the typically very lengthy process of 'working through' the therapist can feel she is merely repeating what has been said before. Yet, in practice, every time we revisit an 'old' pattern in our interpretations we never do so in exactly the same way as before and often subtle nuances of meaning emerge that aid the process of change. Moreover, we know only too well that whereas something can be intellectually grasped quite quickly, connecting emotionally with what has been intellectually understood is a slower and more painstaking process.

As Tony gained confidence that he was loveable, and indeed that he was loved by his adoptive parents who actually provided a consistent source of support to him, his need to lie diminished. Once this more 'honest' state of mind dominated, Tony became more receptive to his painful feelings of loss in relation to his birth mother, which he had so far defended against. A period of depression therefore ensued as Tony struggled to come to terms with his feelings towards his birth mother. When the therapy came to a close three years after we had started working together, Tony was still contemplating whether to trace his birth mother. He felt he had made significant progress and was happier in himself. He wrote to me a year after finishing to let me have news of his progress. At that stage he was back living at home and had decided to return to education. He told me that after much deliberation he had decided not to trace his birth mother.

REFERENCES

SE refers to the *Standard Edition of the Complete Psychological Works of Sigmund Freud*, 24 vols (1955–74) ed. and trans. J. Strachey, London: Hogarth Press and the Institute for Psycho-Analysis.

Balint, A. and Balint, M. (1939) 'On transference and counter-transference', *International Journal of Psychoanalysis*, 20: 225–30.

Beebe, B. and Lachmann, F. (1988) 'The contribution of mother/infant mutual influence to the origins of self and object representations', *Psychoanalytic Psychology*, 5: 305–30.

Beebe, B. and Lachmann, F. (1994) 'Representation and internalization in infancy: three principles of salience', *Psychoanalytic Psychology*, 11: 127–65.

Couch, A. (1979) 'Therapeutic functions of the real relationship in psychoanalysis' (unpublished paper). Revised version of a paper on 'The role of the real relationship in analysis' given at the Scientific Meeting in the Boston Analytic Society, 10 January.

Crews, F. (1993) 'The unknown Freud', *New York Review of Books*, 18 November: 55–6.

Fenichel, O. (1946) *The Psychoanalytic Theory of Neurosis*. London: Routledge & Kegan Paul.

Ferris, P. (1997) *Dr Freud: A Life*. London: Random House.

Fonagy, P. and Target, M. (1997) 'Perspectives on the recovered memories debate', in J. Sandler and P. Fonagy (eds), *Recovered Memories of Abuse: True or False?* London: Karnac.

Fonagy, P., Steele, H., Moran, G., Steele, M. and Higgitt, A. (1993) 'Measuring the ghost in the nursery: an empirical study of the relation between parents' mental representations of childhood experiences and their infants' security of attachment', *Journal of the American Psychoanalytic Association*, 41: 957–89.

Freud, A. (1936) *The Ego and the Mechanisms of Defence*. London: Karnac.

Freud, S. (1905) *Three Essays on Sexuality*, Vol 7. London: Penguin.

Freud, S. (1912) 'The dynamics of transference'. *SE12*: 99–108.

Freud, S. (1917) 'Fixation to traumas in the unconscious', Vol 1. London: Penguin.

Freud, S. (1926) 'The question of lay analysis', *SE15*. London: Penguin.

Freud, S. (1938) 'An outline of psychoanalysis', Vol. 15. London: Penguin.

Greenberg, J. (1996) 'Psychoanalytic words and psychoanalytic acts', *Contemporary Psychoanalysis*, 32: 195–203.

Greenson, R. (1967) *The Technique and Practice of Psychoanalysis*. London: Hogarth Press.

Greenson, R. and Wexler, M. (1969) 'The non-transference relationship in a psychoanalytic situation', *International Journal of Psychoanalysis*, 50: 27–39.

Hamilton, V. (1996) *The Analyst's Pre-conscious*. Hilderdale, NJ: The Analytic Press.

Horvath, A. and Luborsky, L. (1993) 'The role of the therapeutic alliance in psychotherapy', *Journal of Consulting & Clinical Psychology*, 61(4): 561–73.

Kaplan-Solms, K. and Solms, M. (2000) *Clinical Studies in Neuro-Psychoanalysis*. London: Karnac.

Kirsner, D. (1990) 'Mystics and professionals in the culture of American psychoanalysis', *Free Associations*, 20: 85–104.

Klauber, J. (1986) *Difficulties in the Analytic Encounter*. London: Free Association Books & Maresfield Library.

Krupnik, J. et al. (1996) 'The role of the therapeutic alliance in psychotherapy & pharmacotherapy outcome: findings in the NIMH Collaborative Research Programme', *Journal of Consulting & Clinical Psychology*, 64: 532–9.

Lambert, M., Shapiro, D. and Bergin, A. (1986) 'The effectiveness of psychotherapy', in S. Garfield and A. Bergin (eds), *Handbook of Psychotherapy and Behavior Change*. New York: Wiley.

Lemma, A. (1995) *Invitation to Psychodynamic Psychology*. London: Whurr.

Malan, D. (1979) *Individual Psychotherapy and the Science of Psychodynamics*. Oxford: Butterworth Heinemann.

Milner, B., Squire, L. and Kandel, E. (1998) 'Cognitive neuroscience and the study of memory', *Neuron Review*, 20: 445–68.

Morris, J., Ohman, A. and Dolan, R. (1998) 'Conscious and unconscious emotional *learning* in the *human amygdala*', *Nature*, 393: 467–70.

Perelberg, R. (ed.) (1999) *Psychoanalytic Understanding of Violence and Suicide*. London: Routledge.

Raphael-Leff, J. (1991) *Psychological Processes of Childbearing*. London: Chapman & Hall.

Robert, M. (1977) *From Oedipus to Moses: Freud's Jewish Identity*. London: Routledge & Kegan Paul.

Roith, E. (1987) *The Riddle of Freud*. London: Routledge & Kegan Paul.

Roth, A. and Fonagy, P. (2006) *What Works for Whom?* London: Guilford Press.

Sameroff, A. (1983) 'Developmental systems: contexts and evolution', in W. Massey (ed.), *Massey's Handbook of Child Psychology*, Vol. 1. New York: Wiley.

Sandler J. and Dreyer, A. (1996) *What Do Analysts Want?* London: Routledge.

Sandler, J. and Sandler, A.M. (1984) 'The past unconscious, the present unconscious: an interpretation of the transference', *Psychoanalytic Enquiry*, 4: 367–99.

Sandler J. and Sandler, A.M. (1997) 'A psychoanalytic theory of repression and the unconscious', in J. Sandler and P. Fonagy (eds), *Recovered Memories of Abuse* London: Karnac Books.

Sandler, J., Holden, A. and Dare, C. (1973) *The Patient and the Analyst*. London: Karnac Books.

Steiner, J. (1989) 'The aim of psychoanalysis', *Psychoanalytic Psychotherapy*, 4(2): 109–20.

Stern, D., Sander, L., Nahum, J. et al. (1998) 'Non interpretative mechanisms in psychoanalytic therapy: there's something more than interpretation', *International Journal of Psychoanalysis*, 79(5): 903–22.

Stevens, R. (1983) *Freud and Psychoanalysis*. Milton Keynes: Open University Press.

Stolorow, R. and Attwood, G. (1992) *Contexts of Being*. Hillsdale, NJ: Analytic Press.

Szasz, T. (1963) 'The concept of transference', *International Journal of Psychoanalysis*, 44: 432–43.

Szasz, T. (1978) *The Myth of Psychotherapy*. Syracuse, NY: Syracuse University Press.

Zetzel, E. (1956) 'Current concepts of transference', *International Journal of Psychoanalysis*, 37: 369–76.

SUGGESTED FURTHER READING

Bateman, A. and Holmes, J. (1995) *Introduction to Psychoanalysis*. London: Routledge.

Bettelheim, B. (1982) *Freud and Man's Soul*. New York: Fontana.

Budd, S. and Rusbridger, R. (eds) (2005) *Introducing Psychoanalysis: Essential Themes and Topics*. London: Routledge.

Greenson, R. (1967) *The Technique and Practice of Psychoanalysis*. London: Hogarth Press.

Lemma, A. (2003) *Introduction to the Practice of Psychoanalytic Psychotherapy*. London: Wiley.

Sandler, J., Holder, A., Dare, C. and Dreher, A. (eds) (1997) *Freud's Models of the Mind: An Introduction*. London: Karnac Books.

3

Psychodynamic Therapy: The Kleinian Approach

Cassie Cooper

HISTORICAL CONTEXT AND DEVELOPMENT IN BRITAIN

Historical context

Melanie Klein born in Vienna (1882) was an 'unexpected' baby, the youngest of four children; her siblings were Emilie, Emanuel and Sidonie. Her father (Morris Reiz) was a highly orthodox Jew. Her mother (Libussa Deutsch) was the daughter of a local rabbi. In accordance with Jewish custom their marriage was arranged whilst her father was still a student at a local yeshiva (religion school).

Melanie's birth followed the turbulent period in European history which came after the Napoleonic Wars. This was the so called 'age of emancipation' for the Jewish community, when professional barriers and prejudices wavered at the onset of the new, radical political theories and philosophies.

Facilitated by new professional opportunities, Morris Reiz left his religious studies and attempted to read medicine. This became too difficult so he moved instead into dentistry. He was never a successful wage earner. The family had to struggle financially and Sidonie (their third child) died tragically at the age of eight. The family were traumatized.

Melanie's parents considered themselves intellectuals and pursued their interests in art and science. They expected their remaining children to do the same. Her father visibly indicated his preference for her sister Emilie, whilst Melanie, in turn, looked to her brother Emanuel for validation and affection. Emanuel, now a medical student, was supportive to Melanie and encouraged her education and ambition. She hoped to emulate him, to become a doctor, and studied hard at Latin and Greek, the necessary requirements for entry into a gymnasium (grammar school); she did well at school and was full of enthusiasm for the future.

The family continued to struggle financially. The health of her father and her brother declined. Eventually, Emanuel had to curtail his studies and take time off to recuperate. He was advised to travel to warmer climates, leaving Melanie to continue her studies alone. In 1900 her father died and Emanuel's health continued to deteriorate. She was now 18 years old.

Melanie had to reassess her future. The prospect of continuing her medical studies was not possible. Reluctantly, she reconsidered her position. Always attractive and courted by several friends of her brother who were proposing marriage, she selected Arthur Klein, an industrial chemist. This was a complete capitulation to the social and religious conventions of her day that found it more acceptable for a Jewish woman of her age and class to marry and have children. In 1902 at the age of 25 Emanuel died. Melanie was devastated. Life was bleak and comfortless. She married in 1903, but the birth of three children, Melitta (1904), Hans (1907) and Eric (1914), did little to lift the disappointment and disillusionment in her marriage. Arthur Klein was frequently unfaithful, restlessly seeking to move his business interests to Budapest. In 1911 despite a move from Vienna to Budapest his business developed severe financial problems. Melanie had begun to revive her interest in medicine and psychiatry. She read the works of Sigmund Freud and became attracted to Freudian theory. This offered ideas on personal development that resonated with her own feelings of bereavement, loss, disappointment and anger, and she was determined to pursue these interests.

Arthur Klein was spending more and more time away from home. Melanie arranged to meet Dr Sandor Ferenczi, a leading Hungarian analyst, a colleague and correspondent of Freud. She was his analytic patient between 1912 and 1919 while the First World War ravaged Europe.

Melanie's personal analysis stimulated her emerging ideas which focused on the application of psychoanalytic theory and interpretation to work with young children. Ferenczi encouraged her to develop techniques in which toys and play were used as the equivalent of the dream interpretation and free association which are part of the analytic process for adults.

Melanie was now able to embark on her own career. In the turbulent period which followed the war she began to specialize in the analysis of children and to establish a practice. In 1921 her first published paper, 'The development of a child' was read to the Hungarian Psychoanalytic Society. The paper received a mixed reception from the strictly Freudian group, whose understanding of the analysis of young children was minimally based on Freud's own work with 'Little Hans'.

With growing interest in her work, Dr Karl Abraham, President of the Berlin Psychoanalytic Society, invited Melanie to Berlin where she could devote herself to psychoanalytic practice and research. Melanie accepted, and moved the family to Berlin. This precipitated the end of her unhappy marriage. Arthur chose to stay in Sweden where he now had business interests, and they were divorced in 1924. The end was rancorous, with both parties arguing bitterly about the custody of their children.

In Berlin, Melanie returned to analysis with Karl Abraham. She was strongly influenced by his theories on infantile development. They became strongly attracted to each other and formed a deep attachment. Melanie blossomed, developing new techniques in her work with children which offered innovative ideas on the processes of child and adult analysis.

Karl Abraham was her admirer, her staunch supporter and advocate and his early death in 1925 (after a fatal illness) was a devastating blow. Following his death Melanie resorted to regular daily self-analysis, a process which Freud had initiated. All her later material was based on daily analysis of her own and her patients' behaviour compared, examined and interpreted one against the other. Melanie continued to develop new insights and interpretations about the early years of a child's life. Her contributions to the Berlin Society evoked a great deal of controversy, but in London, Ernest Jones, one of Freud's original pupils and his biographer (the doyen of psychoanalysts in Britain) gave support to Melanie's ideas. In 1925 she was invited to London to give a series of lectures to the British Society and to analyse Ernest Jones's children. In 1926, she was invited to stay and work permanently in London.

At this time, controversy still raged about the professional position of women in medicine, psychiatry and psychoanalysis. Melanie Klein was a divorced Jewish woman with three children in an increasingly hostile and anti-Semitic climate. After consideration of the options available to her in Berlin, Melanie agreed to stay and work in London. She was happy to do so: it was in London that her work flourished, and her very individual clinical and theoretical approach was emulated by leading British analysts. She continued to live in London writing, practising, teaching and arguing until the time of her death in 1960, aged 78.

Development in Britain

Members of the British Psychoanalytic Society are often referred to as the 'English School', to differentiate the theory and practice that was developing in London (under the influence of Melanie Klein) from that of other centres of psychoanalytic learning, notably that of the so-called 'Viennese School' developed by Sigmund Freud.

These differences were accentuated by the opinion of the British (Kleinian) analysts that the relationship of mother and baby during the first few months of life is of primary importance in the development of the individual. The English School maintained that it was possible to explore and analyse the anxieties, defences and unconscious fantasies of children as young as two years of age. The transference relationship could also be interpreted using the methods of free association and play techniques. In this context, the word 'transference' is used to depict the development of an evaluative relationship between therapist and patient which is either 'positive' (good feelings) or 'negative' (rejection and hostility).

In the early 1930s, prior to the Nazi invasion of Europe, there was an exchange of lectures (Rivière unpublished, 1936; Waelder 1937), when the London, Berlin and Viennese societies were endeavouring to clarify their different stances on this and other issues. They could not agree and so agreed to differ. When the persecution of Jews became the official policy of the Nazi Party, psychoanalysis was dubbed 'The Jewish disease'. In 1938 German and Austrian analysts, knowing that they would be persecuted and unable to practise, fled to London, and to North and South America, where institutes of psychoanalytic learning had already been established.

At this point theoretical stances and points of conflict became polarized, threatening to cause a split within the established British Society. Sigmund Freud was now living and working in London accompanied by his daughter, Anna. She became fiercely antagonistic towards Melanie Klein, whose work continued to attract a large group of analysts and psychotherapists who were applying to her for training analyses and supervision. Alix Strachey, Susan Isaacs, Donald Winnicott, Paula Herman, Joan Rivière, Ernest Jones, T.E. Money-Kyrle and Hannah Segal formed part of this group, and an increasing number of students came to work with and benefit from these new ideas. Anna Freud persevered in her venomous attacks on Melanie. The British Society was shaken. Unity was preserved only by the establishment of two separate streams for training courses within the Society: the 'Continental' School of Anna Freud and the 'English' School of Melanie Klein. Later on an independent group evolved who were able to develop their own techniques and interpretations without adherence to one school or another.

In its early days psychoanalysis was considered a 'fringe' profession which guaranteed only an uncertain income and a distinct lack of the upmarket prestige enjoyed by the predominating sphere of academic psychiatry. Most of the analysts who left Germany and Austria were attracted to the USA, where psychoanalysis is now firmly established, and they have become, financially and socially, members of the upper middle class. For many years the American School tended to be narrow and conservative in its approach to conflicting psychodynamic theories. This contrasted with the English School which in the early 1920s was substantially non-medical and contained so-called 'gifted amateurs'. It was considered to be more experimental in its approach to Freudian theories and Kleinian concepts. Psychoanalysis in England can never be regarded as intellectually complacent. This is due in part to the influence of Melanie Klein and her adherents who were able to remain constant in spite of a continuous barrage of venomous anger, humiliation, malicious gossip and rumour. Few women in the profession of psychoanalysis have aroused such ire in the male establishment.

Melanie Klein, appreciated as one of the great innovators in dynamic psychotherapy, nevertheless adhered to the concepts in psychotherapy which are basic to all psychoanalytic theories. These theories (which Farrell, 1981 simplified) were as follows:

- No item in mental life or in the way we behave is accidental. It is always the outcome of antecedent conditions.
- Mental activity and behaviour is purposeful or goal directed.
- Unconscious determinants mould and affect the way we perceive ourselves and others. These are thoughts of a primitive nature, shaped by impulses and feelings within the individual, of which they are unaware.
- Early childhood experiences are overwhelmingly important and pre-eminent over later experience.

In addition to these fundamental concepts, Melanie Klein enlarged and expanded on the hitherto unknown regions of the pre-Oedipal stage (i.e. the child's unconscious wish to be sexually united with a parent of the opposite sex, thus eliminating the other parent).

She went on to propose the following:

- that environmental factors are much less important than had previously been believed;
- that the beginnings of the superego can be identified within the first two years of life;
- that an analysis is unfinished if it fails to investigate the stages of infantile anxiety and aggressiveness in order to confront and understand them;
- that the most important drives of all are the aggressive ones.

THEORETICAL ASSUMPTIONS

Image of the person

The birth of a baby somewhere in the world will, during the next few years, signal that the population of our planet has reached 11 billion. Every minute of every day 150 babies thrust their way into life: 220,000 a day, 80 million a year, wrested supine and exhausted from the darkness of the birth canal into the glare of light. Many of these babies will go hungry and their families will starve. They will arrive unwanted, neglected, to be abandoned, abused and used. Life for them will be the days full of pain and vexation portrayed in the Bible. Life is no bowl of cherries but a series of events that have to be endured, experienced and overcome. For some it would be better not to have been born.

Kleinian theory encompasses this bleak view, but also emphasizes the fact that each human being possesses the capacity to tap into resources that rest deep in the psyche waiting to be mobilized and utilized. Kleinian theory is engaged with the primal processes of conception, pregnancy and birth, the elements of life which evolve in the foetus before it develops into a living being. Parents may bring to their newborn child their own already developed capacity for living their lives in a certain way. But the baby's persona is nebulous, split, at one moment a clear page waiting to be inscribed, at another a mass of powerful instinctual drives which focus on one aim – survival.

The foetal environment is rich in acoustic stimulation and the foetus responds to the mother's moods, her eating, drinking, breathing and heartbeats. A foetus eight weeks after conception can move its limbs and in a further eight weeks has gained sufficient strength to communicate these movements to its mother through the uterine walls. At approximately 26 weeks this tiny being can change position at will and, when poked or prodded by external examination, will attempt to avoid this contact. The baby is sensitive to pain, it winces, sometimes opening its mouth in a silent cry, responding to temperature and taste. The foetus has been observed drinking amniotic fluid and responding to its mother's food intake: sweetness which it likes and bitterness which is avoided. The foetus responds to stroking of the abdomen and gentle noise, turning its face, opening its mouth and moving its tongue. It can reach forward to obtain comfort by sucking its thumbs, fingers and toes. The ability to see, hear and feel are not senses which are magically bestowed at birth, and the foetal heartbeat resonates rapidly to the external situation of its mother. The dark encapsulated environment of the uterine world is dynamic, full of changes which respond to the outside world. The environment of the uterus changes continuously during gestation. 'Each foetus inhabits a singular world subjected to different experiences and stimulations' (Piontelli, 1992: 37).

Unlike the other mammals most closely related to our species, the human baby arrives prematurely, it is weak and helpless and seems to have poor instinctual notions of how to avoid danger or to obtain satisfaction of its vital needs. It is dependent upon others. When its caretaker (usually its mother) satisfies the baby's hunger, she is at one with it and so not experienced as a separate object. If, however, the mother is unable to satisfy the baby's needs, she (or her breast) is felt to be separate from the baby and thus becomes its first distinct psychological object. When the mother leaves the baby, two things happen. The first is that the loss or removal of the breast (or its substitute) produces anxiety in the baby. Anxiety is an affectual state that warns the baby of danger. Secondly, in order to cope with this anxiety the baby has to create a mother for itself. The feeling of satisfaction that a mother represents has to be fantasized so that the baby can conjure up in its mind the imagery and feelings of a warm breast and a good feed. These feelings when internalized become the ego, the separate area within oneself.

It seems unbelievable in the 21st century that the processes of mothering and the emphasis on early childhood experiences were of little interest to the main body of the early psychoanalysts. Today, the observations and theories of Bowlby, Winnicott and Stern are relevant to the work of every psychoanalyst.

Sigmund Freud, and those who followed him, concentrated instead upon the divisions of mind that affect the human condition. Human beings are born under one law but bound unremittingly to another. Each individual, at birth, is unique but faces a headlong incursion into a world which is an arena for the orders, wishes, desires, fantasies and commands of other people. A world which is racked by the tortured patterns of humankind's laws, prohibitions, aggression and culture.

Melanie Klein and Karl Abraham pioneered the importance of the 'pre-Oedipal' layers of personality development. The connections between the ego and the impulses, the drives and the body feelings and their relationship to the outside world (represented by the touch and feel of a parent's hands) are the two poles of Klein's basic model of the neonate. She maintained that the baby brings into the world two main conflicting impulses: love and hate. Love is the manifestation of the life drive. Hate, destructiveness and envy are the emanations of the death drive. These innate feelings are constantly at war with each other. The neonate tries to deal with these conflicts.

A tiny body struggling to cope with conflicting impulses, a body with sensations which are constantly threatened by the need to gratify overwhelming desires, and which, in a very short space of time, has to develop mature mechanisms for dealing with them. The baby meets a world which is both satisfying and frustrating. It exists from the moment it seeks and finds its mother's breast or its substitute, then gradually the world becomes more complicated as it seeks and finds again its father.

During the early months of life it must be supposed that the baby can make no distinction between itself as a personal entity and the bewildering world of light and darkness which surrounds it. At this stage the baby can only experience them as objects. Its mother's nipple, a good feed, a soft cot or the touch of a hand that gives it pleasure are experienced as good objects, while something that gives pain, like hunger, wet, cold or discomfort, and particularly absences, can easily be converted into experiences that are bad.

To the baby, hunger is a frightening situation; it is not able to understand the meaning of time, of patience, the tolerance of frustration. It cannot appreciate that these situations are of a temporary nature, and will soon be followed by a feeling of pleasurable relief as the warm milk goes down. A small change in the immediate situation can change feelings of anger and discomfort into blissful gratification. It follows then that the baby is able to love and hate one and the same object in rapid succession. There are no qualifications. It is all or nothing at all, good or bad.

Conceptualization of psychological disturbance and health

Hanna Segal explains: 'In interpreting projection one indicates to the patient that he/she is attributing to another person a characteristic which is in fact their own' (1973: 121). The therapist is endeavouring to make the patient aware of the motives that lie behind the projection and the constricting distortions that can be conjured up, distorting one's view of the object and oneself. If one's own aggressive sexuality is projected on to the sexual activity of parents, the sexual intercourse of parental figures could then be perceived as cruel or sexually dangerous. This could inhibit the development of one's own sexuality in later life.

Introjection and projection

In a paper 'Notes on some schizoid mechanisms' (1952a), which was read to the British Society in 1946, Melanie Klein introduced the concepts of ego splitting and projective identification and later she related these concepts to the onset of psychosis. It was her view that anxiety was a predominant factor in psychosis since our earliest anxieties (in infancy) are psychotic in content. 'The normal development of infants,' she wrote, 'can be regarded as a combination of processes by which anxieties of a psychotic nature are bound, worked through and modified' (Klein, 1952a: 81). This was more complicated than the theory of projection described by Freud. An understanding of the processes of introjection and projection are of major importance since in the therapeutic process we can find parallels for all these situations. Every human being will go through phases in life in which they return to or experience relationships which were unsatisfactory in their past.

For every human being the outer world and its impact, and the kind of experiences they live through, the objects they come into contact with, are not only dealt with externally but are taken into the self to become part of their inner world, an entity inside the body. As we *introject* these new experiences into our personalities, we take on the concept that we can truly rely on ourselves. An enduring self-image and increased self-esteem can be facilitated by this form of introjection.

Where this can go awry relates to the relative strength or weakness of a person's ego and the supportive nurturing processes which do or do not accompany one throughout life. If, for example, we admire someone else to such an extent that we endow this other person with abilities and characteristics (good or bad) that we wish to emulate and identify with them to such an extent that we endeavour to live as they do, taking into ourselves the image and behaviour of another being, we fail to take responsibility for our own future development.

Projection goes on simultaneously. It is a manifestation of a person's ability to project on to other people those aggressive and envious feelings (predominantly those of aggression) which by the very nature of their 'badness' must be passed on by projection or, alternatively, carefully repressed. An example of this process is where the patient attempts to arouse in the therapist feelings that he or she finds impossible to tolerate but which the patient unconsciously wishes to express – using the therapist as a means of communication – evacuating unpleasant, dangerous and guilt-ridden thoughts and attempting to take over the mind of another.

It is important to understand that although projection is a general term used in other analytical theories, *projective identification* is a strictly Kleinian concept which is held, by Kleinian therapists, to be responsible for severe difficulties in both establishing one's identity and feeling secure enough to establish other outward-looking relationships. The term 'projective identification' covers a complex clinical event: one person who does not wish to own his or her feelings of love and hate manipulatively induces another into experiencing them; with consequent visible changes of affect in behaviour of both people concerned, bringing pressure to bear on the therapist, sometimes subtly, sometimes powerfully causing them to act out in a manner which reflects the patient's own projections.

It is a difficult and complicated concept to understand as it deals – in the main – with the subjective experience of a therapist and the use to which the therapist is put in being unwittingly drawn into the patient's fantasy world. For example, a patient may deal with the deprived part of his or her own childhood by idealizing the parenting process in therapy. This can in turn deprive the patient of future resourcefulness, but may also trigger off in the therapist a mutual longing for the closeness and dependence of parenthood. Inevitably the therapist must respond to these pressures, however imperceptibly they intrude.

This process highlights the internal world built up in the child and adult alike, which is partially a reflection of the external one. This two-way process continues throughout every stage of our lives, zigging and zagging, interacting and modifying itself in the course of maturation but never losing its importance in relation to the world around us. The judgement of reality is never quite free from the influence of the boiling mercury of our internal world.

Meltzer (1979) considers the concept of projective identification to be one of Melanie Klein's greatest contributions to psychoanalysis: 'A concrete conception of the inner world ... a theatre where meaning can be generated'. Bion (1988) has led the way to considerable developments in techniques in distinguishing between normal and pathological projective identification. Bion's formulation of a container/contained model illustrates how projective identification can be an essential expression of the experiences that a patient cannot capture in the spoken word.

Melanie Klein did not really consider herself to be a theoretician; she saw herself as a face worker describing these phenomena as and when she observed them, with an awareness that one may get it wrong and an emphasis on the constant need for supervision to avoid the hazard of confusing one's personal feelings with those of a patient.

Basic ideas from Freud and Bion enter into Klein's theories. We can identify with our own hatred (at times) of reality and thinking, which are the precursor to the ego's loss of reality in psychosis. We can resonate to the psychotic's unmodified primitive anxieties and their use of the defences of projection and introjection in a desperate search for a cure. Bion in his 1957 paper 'The differentiation of the psychotic from the non-psychotic personalities', comments:

> The differentiation of the psychotic from the non-psychotic personality depends on a minute splitting of all that part of the personality that is concerned with awareness of internal and external reality, and the expulsion of these fragments so that they enter into or engulf their objects. (Bion, 1988: 43)

Splitting

In Our Adult World and its Roots in Infancy   Melanie Klein (1960) described the situation which arise when the projected bad objects (representations of the child's own ferocious and aggressive impulses) rebound on it. The situation of a young mother who tries to please a baby who is literally biting the hand that feeds it, is a case in point. Children may refuse food and scream even when they are desperately hungry, kick and push when they mostly long for a caress. These stages, which thankfully are largely outgrown in the process of normal development, can be identified with the delusional sense of persecution sometimes found in the paranoid adult. A residual persecutory element can always be found in the sense of guilt which is central to all civilizations. Since the infant continues to need a good mother, indeed its life depends upon it – by splitting the two aspects and clinging only to the good one like a rubber ring in a swimming pool, it has evolved for the time being a means of staying alive. Without this loving object to keep it buoyant the child would sink beneath the surface of a hostile world which would engulf it.

Melanie Klein's view was that, in the early years of life, the objects that surrounded the infant were not seen and understood in visual terms. This included a wide range of 'objects' – parents, siblings, blankets, food, bathing, cots, prams, toys, etc. These would be construed only as they were experienced as good or bad. Klein took this further and became concerned with the splitting of aspects of the ego itself into good and conversely bad parts. In later life, these split-off parts could become more obsessional, leading to a fragmentation of the self. Klein linked this fragmentation to the onset of schizophrenia. Here the patient has carried this process of splitting to the extreme, splitting each split yet further into a multifarious and bewildering group of repressions and concessions that in the end become chaos.

Greed and envy

In a paper 'Notes on some schizoid mechanisms' Klein (1952a) singled out greed and envy as two very disturbing factors, relating them first to the child's dominant relationship with the mother and later with relationships to other members of the family, and eventually she extended them to the individual's cycle of life.

Greed is exacerbated by anxiety, the anxiety of being deprived, the need to take all one can from the mother and from the family. A greedy infant may enjoy what it has for the time being, but this feeling is soon replaced by the feeling of being robbed by others of all that it needs in the way of food, love, attention or any other gratification. The baby who is greedy for love and attention is also afraid that it is unable to give these to others, and this in turn exacerbates its own situation. The baby needs everything, it can spare nothing and therefore what can it reasonably expect to receive from others? If an infant is relatively unable to tolerate frustration and anxiety on its own, serious difficulties can arise if the mother is unable, through depression or environmental problems, to provide consolation and mediation.

The infant can then experience murderous feelings towards this seemingly ungiving mother. In seeking to destroy that which is needed for its own survival, the infant is experiencing ambivalent feelings – one moment contemplating murder, the next, suicide. Caught up in a vicious cycle, the need to attack or withdraw produces panicky feelings of being trapped, unpleasant claustrophobic feelings which are replicated in later life.

Envy is a spoiling pursuit. If milk, love and attention are being withheld for one reason or another, then the loved object must be withholding it and keeping it for their own use. Suspicion is the basis of envy. If the baby cannot have what it desires there is a strong urge to spoil the very object of desire so that no one can enjoy it. This spoiling quality can result in a disturbed relationship with the mother, who cannot now supply an unspoilt satisfaction. Envious attacks give rise to greater anxiety – particularly when these attacks are directed towards the mother. It is difficult to acknowledge what has been done – the baby's fear is that it has gone too far but it is resentful of attempts which may be offered to facilitate, to make reparation. It is only when there is such a breakdown of the natural protective forces that one notices how distorted the relationship between mother and child can become, exacerbating the post-natal situation and leading to the depressive illness to which some women are liable.

Melanie Klein enlarged on these problems, stating quite firmly that the aggressive envy experienced in infancy can inhibit the development of good object relations, i.e. the child's ability to develop an intense and personal relationship with other objects (such as toys) which they may treat as alive, lovable, able to give love in return, needing sympathy or producing anger, and able to develop personalities which could be seen to be alive. This in its turn can affect the growth of the capacity to love. 'Throughout my work I have attributed fundamental importance to the infant's first object relations – the relation to the mother's breast and to the mother – and we have drawn the conclusion that, if this primal object which is introjected, takes root in the ego with relative security, the basis for a satisfactory development can be laid' (Klein, 1957: 389).

Projective identification

Projective identification illustrates most clearly the links between human instinct, fantasy, and the mechanisms of defence. Sexual desires, aggressive impulses, can be satiated by fantasy. Fantasy can be as pleasurable and as explicit as we wish to make it, and it is also a safety net – it contains and holds those bad parts of our inner self. The use of fantasy is obvious in literature, in science, in art and in all activities of everyday life.

One aspect of murderous fantasy is the rivalry which results from the male child's desire for the mother: his rivalry with his father and all the sexual fantasies that can be linked to this. The Oedipus complex, which is described in Chapter 2, on Freudian therapy, is rooted in the baby's suspicions of the father who takes the mother's love and attention away from him. The same applies to the female child, for whom the relationship to the mother and to all women is always of supreme importance.

Klein, however, placed her emphasis on earlier and more primitive stages as precursors of the Oedipus complex. She argued that these Oedipal feelings were identifiable in the baby at the age of six months and were the result of the projection of infantile fantasies of rage and aggression on to the parent. Whilst continuing to support Freud's tripartite differentiation of the psychic apparatus into ego, id and superego, she went on to claim that each of these areas of the psyche was identifiable almost from the day of birth.

The term 'projective identification' (as defined by Klein) has become one of the most popular of all her concepts. It has been accepted (albeit grudgingly) throughout the psychoanalytic world. However, there is still considerable controversy over its definition. The controversy focuses on the difference between projection and projective identification. To simplify matters 'projective identification' is best kept as a general concept broad enough to include both cases in which the recipients are emotionally affected and those in which they are not. The motives which lie at the root of projective identification are the wishes: to control the object, to acquire its attributes, to evacuate bad qualities, to protect good qualities and to avoid separation.

The paranoid-schizoid position

Klein's conception of the paranoid schizoid position as a constellation of anxieties, defences and object relationships, characteristic of infancy, has been a major source of inspiration to her colleagues. Work on the psychotic aspects of normal patients has confirmed Klein's delineation of the anxieties and defences of the paranoid-schizoid position, especially the defences of splitting, projective identification, fragmentation and idealization.

The paranoid-schizoid position is distinguished by the characteristic persecutory anxiety of threat to the individual. This is distinct from the threat to the object (the anxiety characteristic of the depressive position). The paranoid-schizoid position is easily identifiable in earliest infancy when at the beginning of life the child builds up its inner world of the self and others, but it is not confined to early childhood development and continues throughout the life of an individual, fluctuating constantly with the depressive position.

Because of the strength of these early primitive feelings, an infant will initially experience two separate feelings about its primary object (i.e. its mother or caregiver). At one level there is the need to idealize this person, and this conflicts with moments when the loved one is experienced as horrendous. The world is experienced as light and dark, good and bad, distorted by fluctuating moods of pleasure and pain and conflicting needs and desires.

The infant lives in a constricted world peopled by individuals who are experienced as good or bad. These are the early distortions which Klein described as the paranoid position. It is with difficulty and depression that the infant grows, realizing that life is a mixture of good and bad; that those we idealize are vulnerable and can let us down. The mother we idealize as the source of comfort, nourishment and support can at the same time be the one who is the centre of attack and hatred by the loving and hating ego: a split in which good experiences predominate over bad ones. In normal development, this process is a necessary precondition for true integration in childhood, adolescence and adult life.

If, however, for any reason this process is disturbed, many pathological changes can occur. When anxiety, hostility and envious feelings become overwhelming, projective identification takes on another dimension. If there is no tidy split between the good and the bad, fragmentation takes place. The object of anger is split into tiny fragments, each one containing a small but violently hostile part of the ego. This is damaging to the development of the ego and in its attempts to relieve itself of the pain of disintegration a vicious circle can be established in which the very painfulness of confronting reality brings with it increased feelings of persecution. Reality is then distorted by bizarre objects and enormous hostility, which frighten and threaten the depleted ego.

A successful negotiation of the paranoid-schizoid anxieties experienced in the early months of the infant's development leads to a gradual organization of its universe. Splitting, projection and introjection combine to help sort out perceptions and emotions and to separate the good from the bad. From the beginning the tendency is towards integration as well as splitting. When these integrative processes become more stable and continual, a new phase of development occurs. This is how Klein describes the move to the depressive position.

The depressive position
The depressive position begins when the baby begins to recognize its mother. In the early months of life the baby is concerned with the integration of the sights, sounds and stimuli, both pleasant and unpleasant, with which it is surrounded. Out of this dreamlike world sufficient integration is achieved for the baby to experience its mother as a whole object – not a succession of parts. She is no longer breasts that can feed, hands that can hold, a voice that can soothe, facial grimaces that either please or frighten, but a complete entity on her own, separate, divided from the baby – someone who can choose to hold it close or stay away, can kiss or neglect or abuse her child. This gradual understanding of the separation process, this gradual awakening to the fact that it is one and the same person who is the container of both good and bad feelings, is then transposed internally to the baby. The infant is as separate from her as she is from it, and can both love and hate its mother.

Its previous fears of being the frail object of destruction extend subtly to an inner knowledge that it too can destroy the one person it loves and needs for survival. The anxiety has changed from a paranoid to a depressive one. In acknowledging the very existence of a separate being, the baby becomes exposed to the fear that it has made the cut. Aggression has destroyed the cord which linked the baby to the mother, leaving the child with feelings of unutterable guilt, sadness and deprivation, a hurt that can never be healed, a pain that can never be assuaged.

In the depressive situation, the baby has to deal not only with a destroyed breast and mother but also with the influx of Oedipal envy and jealousy. These processes involve intense conflict, which is associated with the work of mourning and which always results in anxiety and mental pain. In the Kleinian view, mental pain is pain: it hurts, and mere gratification does not make it go away. Separation is painful, is experienced as a kind of death, the death of that which was and can never be again.

This process of separation and the depressive anxieties that it invokes was described in a 1948 paper, 'On the theory of anxiety and guilt' (Klein, 1952b). It emphasized that depressive anxieties are a part of everyone's normal development, and that the guilt feelings which have developed are understood as part of the imagined harm done to a child's love object.

When this is facilitated it can enable reparation to commence. A child can then show subtle tenderness to those around it and the anxieties and paranoid fears of early infancy can become modified during this period, although these anxieties may be painfully reawakened in the normal mourning processes of later life. Adult depression is known to involve a reactivation of this stage of infantile depression, so Kleinian psychotherapists consider the actual mourning situation a productive period in therapy. When an adult admits to feeling menaced and persecuted, the recriminations and self-reproaches of the depressed patient are interpreted and hopefully understood as a manifestation of the early persecutory impulses which were directed so savagely at the self.

In preceding paragraphs some developmental models have been explained, in particular those of the impulses of destruction, greed and envy, illustrating how the persecutory and sadistic anxieties of early life can disturb the child's emotional balance and inhibit its ability to acquire and maintain good social relationships. Melanie Klein's understanding of what she was later to label 'the depressive position' highlighted the simple truth that human beings feel better when they are labelled as being 'good' than they do when they are made to feel bad. The world in which we now live has taken its toll of childhood. Alongside the obvious signs of materialistic success comes the urgent need to be seen to be a good and successful parent. Whatever the criteria for this measure of success and in order to make sure of being loved, the child has to go along with this fantasy. If they feel unloved, it must be their fault. They are too slow at school, too ugly, naughty, unacademic, lacking in social graces, poor at sport, should have been a boy or should have been a girl. Their self-esteem is low. Their parents have suppressed any recollection of their own innocent and painful childhood experiences. We are terrified of the possibility that hatred can overpower the love we are expected to profess.

Twenty years on from the death of Melanie Klein, Dr Alice Miller wrote:

> Almost everywhere we find the effort, marked by various degrees of intensity and by the use of coercive measures, to rid ourselves as quickly as possible of the child within us i.e. the weak, helpless, dependent creature – in order to become an independent competent adult deserving of respect. When we encounter this creature in our children we persecute it with the same measures once used on ourselves. And this is what we are accustomed to call child rearing ... The methods that can be used to suppress vital spontaneity in the child are: laying traps, lying, duplicity, subterfuge, manipulation, 'scare' tactics, withdrawal of love, isolation, distrust, humiliating and disgracing the child, scorn, ridicule and coercion even to the point of torture. (Miller, 1983: 105)

All human beings, wherever they live, exist only in relationship to other human beings. The physical processes of conception, pregnancy and birth are the same for us all. In the uterus all babies exist in comparative safety; it is only when the baby makes its post-natal appearance, head or feet first or precipitately by Caesarean section, that it learns about the reality of solitary existence.

Acquisition of psychological disturbance

Loss of the parent in any form – breast or hand – gives rise to a primary separation anxiety, which gives way to grief and then to the experience of mourning that which is lost. Aggression is also a major part of the mourning process.

If the normal processes of childhood are disrupted in some way, if fantasy becomes reality and the loved object dies, leaves, neglects, batters, sexually abuses, reacts too possessively, becomes obsessional, it follows that these disruptions of a normal interaction are likely to take a pathological course later in life. This leads not only to an aggressive stance towards society but to self-aggression and abuse. Dr John Bowlby gave the following examples:

> Many of those referred to psychiatrists are anxious, insecure individuals usually described as over-dependent or immature. Under stress they are apt to develop neurotic symptoms, depression or phobia. Research shows them to have been exposed to at least one, and usually more than one, of certain typical patterns of pathogenic parenting, which include:
>
> a) one or both parents being persistently unresponsive to the child's care-eliciting behaviour and/or actively disparaging and rejecting him;
> b) discontinuities of parenting, occurring more or less frequently, including periods in hospital or institution;
> c) persistent threats by parents not to love a child, used as a means of controlling him; threats by parents to abandon the family, used either as a method of disciplining the child or as a way of coercing a spouse;
> d) threats by one parent either to desert or even kill the other or else to commit suicide (each of them more common than might be supposed);
> e) inducing a child to feel guilt by claiming that his behaviour is or will be responsible for the parent's illness or death. (Bowlby, 1979: 136–7)

Cassie Cooper wrote:

> To be a child and especially to be a 'good' child in today's world is not to be a child at all. Instead these children of the twenty-first century, the children of projection, grow up too

quickly to become in their turn mothers, friends, comforters, translators, advisers, support and sometimes lovers of their own parents. In taking care of other siblings, throwing themselves between parents in order to save a marriage, attempting to provide academic kudos, high earnings, sexual titillation and satisfaction, masochistic or sadistic gratification, the child will do anything, anyhow, for parental love and approval. (Cooper, 1988: 12–13)

It is these anxieties which are the cause, if not confronted, of both childhood psychoses and mental illness in adult life.

Perpetuation of psychological disturbance

In Kleinian theory human development is postulated as a series of events: events that have to be endured, experienced and overcome. In particular the theory aims to understand the difficulties experienced in early childhood by both parents and child. It emphasizes that loss of closeness to a parent figure gives rise within the individual to separation anxiety. This feeling of anxiety is internalized by the child and changes as time passes to the experience of bewildered mourning for that which has been lost. Aggression and self-destructiveness become a major part of this mourning process as throughout life the child tries again and again to re-enter that fantasized place of safety to become one with its mother.

We now know (and the dissolution of family life in contemporary society proves the point) that if the normal processes of separation are disrupted in any way, if fantasy becomes reality and the love objects die, leave, reject, batter, disparage, react too possessively or obsessionally, lose face, become depressed, unemployed, redundant, are forced to move home, these disruptions of a normal interaction are likely to take a pathological course later in life.

W.R. Bion postulated that when the infant was accosted by feelings that could not be managed, the fantasy developed that these feelings could be evacuated and then put on to their primary caregiver (i.e. the mother). Obviously if the mother is capable of understanding and accepting the child's anxiety and helplessness without her own balance of mind being disturbed, she can contain these feelings and comfort her child in a way that will make these feelings more acceptable. The child would then feel reassured enough to live with these feelings in a way that is manageable. However, if this process goes wrong – and it can go wrong, particularly if the mother herself is distressed and cannot take the child's projections – the child is forced to internalize these anxieties, repress and bottle them up, empty them out of mind, so that he or she does not have to bear those unpleasant feelings. If this condition persists, the child is well on the way to psychotic behaviour later in life.

There is no such thing as a person who does not have areas of psychological disturbance within their personality; equally, in every person there are areas of their personality which are neurotic and capable of forming good relationships, however ephemeral these relationships may seem to be. In psychoanalytic psychotherapy, provided this healthier part of a patient's ego is in evidence, it is possible to work with this patient with the professed aim of strengthening this healthy part and enabling it to become dominant in relation to the disturbed part of the personality.

In her work with small children, Melanie Klein was of the opinion that infantile neurosis was the structure which defends the child against primitive anxieties of a paranoid and depressive nature. She subsequently maintained that it is this form of psychotic anxiety that in later years blocks off the growth of symbol formation and the development of the ego. It is the resolution of this anxiety that is the aim of therapy, in that this frees the ego to develop and re-establish its symbolic processes.

> It is our contention that psychotic illness is rooted in the pathology of early infancy where the basic matrix of mental function is formed … In psychosis it is all these functions that are disturbed or destroyed. The confusion between the external and the internal, the fragmentation of relationships and the ego, the deterioration of perception, the breakdown of symbolic processes, the disturbance of thinking: all are features of psychosis. Understanding the genesis of the development of the ego and its object relationships and the kind of disturbance that can arise in the course of that development is essential to understanding the mechanisms of the psychotic. (Segal, 1986: 153)

The ability to contain the infant's anxiety by a mother or caregiver capable of understanding is the beginning of stability. If this does not happen, the anxiety is introjected and can grow and develop into the experience of an even greater terror, a nameless fear of excessive destructive omnipotence. In the psychotherapeutic setting these intolerable feelings can be projected on to the therapist, who is capable of tolerating and understanding these terrifying projections – this can be acknowledged and understood by the patient, who feels that the situation becomes more tolerable. With careful interpretation and thought this patient can identify and allow the growth of a part of their personality – the part which is capable of real commitment, caring and understanding.

Change

Kleinian psychotherapy adheres to the common principles which underlie psychoanalytic theory: stressing the unconscious mechanisms which operate within the human psyche and which dominate the process of change for every human being. However, Klein had more to add to this original concept.

Let us take the well-used analogy that, at birth, every human being is a *tabula rasa*, a white tablet, a clean slate: the circumstances of one's life are then written on the white surface. To this end the human being learns to live with their history and the alternating vicissitudes and pleasant episodes of life. What is important here is the emphasis placed by Kleinian therapists on two factors:

1   There is no gain in life without a subsequent loss and the ambivalent feelings that temper any form of progress, i.e. the baby gains approval from its parents when it takes its first mouthful

of solid food – but the breast is then lost to it for ever. The pride a baby will experience when learning to walk diminishes when it acknowledges that the intimacy of helplessness is relinquished.

2 Survival in a dangerous world depends on one's ability to reconcile oneself to the fact that every 'have' is balanced by a 'have not'.

The well-known game played by children, 'I'm the King of the Castle', is a case in point. The consciousness of the self and the feeling of enjoyment in winning are transient. As the child grows up it becomes more aware of the effect of its behaviour on other people and it learns to compromise and to understand the implications of frustration. The process of change can never be viewed as a clear and shining goal; rather it is the development of a growing sense of wise detachment towards life. Developing from this detachment comes the sense of personal identity which enables us to go through life with a tolerant irony and strengthens our resistance to the temptations of fame, wealth and self-aggrandizement and enables us to take what comes. Hinshelwood identifies the change processes within Kleinian theory as:

1 the development of the subject's awareness of psychic reality;
2 balancing the currents of love and hate which run within the self. (Hinshelwood, 1989: 19)

In our therapeutic work we may find that an adult has emerged from this therapeutic process, an adult whose ego can organize and substantiate its own defences against the anxieties that belong to primary separation and loss.

PRACTICE

Goals of therapy

Melanie Klein never altered the technical principles which were the foundation of her early work, *The Psychoanalysis of Children* (1932). This continues to form the basis of the psychodynamic work undertaken by Kleinian psychotherapists and colours their concepts of mental functioning.

It is important to stress here that the theories of Melanie Klein have never been popular. Freudian and post-Freudian doctrines have had more appeal. It was perhaps easier to accept Oedipal conflicts and the 'tidy' process of oral, anal and later libidinal development than to take on board the confrontation with a life and death struggle which lies at the root of Kleinian thinking. To tilt at the precious idealization of the 'loving' mother and to confront instead the infantile struggle for 'survival' are unpleasant and uncomfortable. In Kleinian therapy we have to take a long, hard look at our fantasies of parental love: if these are removed, what bleak prospect of life does the therapist provide?

Patients who undertake this kind of psychotherapy are bound to come to the first session full of hopes and fears, with deep-rooted fantasies and phobias about themselves and their therapist. They present material in the very first session which concerns anxieties that are central to them at that moment. Predominantly they want to feel 'better', to obtain relief from suffering (Colby, 1951), and are seeking, like an infant, immediate gratification of their needs. Wish-fulfilment is not confined to those who seek psychotherapy. Eavesdrop on any everyday conversation and you will conclude that people always hope to get what they feel they need to make them happy and want to obtain it in the shortest possible time and with a minimum of effort: powerful wishes for a magical solution rather than facing up to the realities that underline our complex psychological make-up.

In Kleinian psychotherapy it is maintained that anxiety can act as a spur to development and personal achievement, providing this anxiety is not excessive. At the commencement of therapy it is important to work with the patient's unconscious fantasies about themselves and others, and in particular how such fantasies relate to the reality of the outside world, the way life has been experienced both in the past and in the present.

This may sound simplistic. When studying certain isolated aspects of human behaviour the reductive approach is very appealing. The plain facts are, however, that human beings are complex and that the very process of functioning as a person requires a conceptual level that does justice to what is revealed of these complex forces. Behaviour which is as thoughtless, demanding and extortionate as the infant's relationship with its mother reflects the need to exhaust and exploit the therapist and to experience yet again the feelings of guilt and anxiety which are associated with such behaviour.

A Kleinian therapist would have it that psychotherapy has more in common with an educational experience than a form of medical treatment. Successful psychotherapy should begin a process of learning and personal development which moves along at its own pace. The foundation stone of this process must be the relationship between therapist and patient. If this goal is similarly perceived and worked upon by both parties, the outcome will be the achievement of some mutual satisfaction.

Melanie Klein was quite clear about the efficiency of her method in the treatment of adults. Her primary goal was the reduction of immediate anxiety by encouraging patients to face their inhibitions and to facilitate a more positive relationship with their therapist. This in turn would enable patients to experience themselves as real people in a real world able to maintain a balance between the feelings of love and hate which alternate in every psyche.

At the end of therapy it is hoped that patients will feel able to form full and satisfactory personal relationships, and will have gained insight into their personal situation and feel released from their early fixations and repressions. They will be less inhibited and better able to enjoy the good things of life while remaining sensitive, open and capable when problems arise. They will be able to assess their internal world, possess a quiet reassurance and ego strength which stems from the knowledge that even in times of great stress they will survive and, perhaps even more importantly, that they will want to survive. The means by which true reparation (growth, in the Kleinian sense) takes place are essentially mysterious. It is something which happens when the 'mental atmosphere is conducive to objects repairing one another. The frame of mind of tolerance, of pain, of remorse over one's destructiveness' (Meltzer, 1979: 18–19). These reparative mental conditions follow when there is an understanding of one's infantile dependency upon internal objects – an idealized mother and father at the moment of one's own creation – so that one can in life accept oneself as a product of what was past and is in the future in an atmosphere of tolerance and acceptance. Melanie Klein stated:

> My criterion for termination of analysis is, therefore, as follows: have persecutory and depressive anxieties been sufficiently reduced in the course of analysis, and has the patient's relation to the external world been sufficiently strengthened to enable him to deal satisfactorily with the situation of mourning arising at this point? (Klein, 1950: 78–80)

Selection criteria

Only uncommonly aware and brave people seek to know about themselves and to face up to what psychotherapy can reveal. There are many patterns to therapy and many different approaches to the relief of psychic pain. Patients have a choice in the kind of treatment they would prefer, and can and do move from individual to group therapy, from group therapy to family therapy, if they so wish, and in whatever sequence seems beneficial to them at a particular time.

Initially the referral of a patient for psychotherapy would be made by their psychiatrist or general practitioner. With luck, the would-be patient and their doctor have discussed a preference for one modality or another. There is a need for each patient to accept responsibility for their problem and, in seeking amelioration of their situation, to actively participate in making the decision, choosing to work on a one-to-one basis in individual therapy or deciding that they would gain greater motivation and strength from the support and challenge that can be offered in a therapy group or a family group setting.

In selecting patients for individual therapy there are criteria which the Kleinian psychotherapist would seek to fulfil:

- that the patient has problems which can be clearly defined in psychodynamic terms;
- that the patient appears motivated enough for change and insight into their previous behaviour;
- that the patient has enough internal strength to cope with the demands and tensions that are to be created by the process of interpretation and confrontation;
- that the patient produces evidence that they are able to accept and sustain a long-standing relationship with the therapist and with significant others in their immediate surroundings.

Patients may arrive with little knowledge of how Kleinian therapy differs from other forms of treatment, how the procedure works, and even less knowledge about the outcome of psychotherapy. Initially the psychotherapist will indicate that therapy involves a detailed process of examining and discussing problems. Patients are told that it could be distressing and painful, that there are no guaranteed 'cures', but that they can be enabled to help themselves to identify the origin of their symptoms, the reaction to these symptoms and the ways in which these symptoms constrict their life.

The therapist has the right to decide if he or she is prepared to work with a specific patient. Personal feelings will obviously affect the outcome of an initial diagnostic interview. Conversely, the patient may decide that he or she will be unable to work with the therapist. It is essential to respect the rights of both parties in such a delicate transaction. What is important is that the relationship between therapist and patient can be one in which there is mutual respect, the respect of one human being for another and hope for the potentialities of this other person. This is termed the 'therapeutic alliance'. It is hoped that each patient has the capacity to come out of therapy with the opportunity to love well, to play well and to have some optimism for the future.

A Kleinian psychotherapist finds it most suitable to work with patients whose underlying conflicts are towards the narcissistic side, whose egos have undergone considerable deformation or weakening. Patients may come into therapy expressing inability to love or to be loved by others, with conflicts about dealing with people in a social, sexual or work setting, general intellectual and academic underfunctioning, symptomatic phobias, anxiety states and minor perversions.

With some patients there may be a need to limit the period of treatment. It is useful anyway to indicate that the treatment will not go on indefinitely, that it will end at a certain time. A statement of this kind may not be indicated for all patients, but could be necessary in certain instances. In contrast to psychoanalysis, Kleinian psychotherapy gives a realistic indication that the treatment will terminate some day. The therapist will point out that the therapeutic relationship will come to an end. This is an important and necessary factor in working through the attachment process, a process which is repeated throughout life when some aspect of a 'good object' is given up.

Qualities of effective psychotherapists

Kleinian psychotherapists are always in short supply. As with other modalities, it is an expensive and prolonged training, in most cases a postgraduate training, and in every case a training which involves the student in an extensive commitment both of time and money over many years; they must tailor their lifestyle to personal therapy four or five times a week.

It is a training which centres on the personality of the would-be therapist, and this understanding of the self is tuned to perfect pitch like the finest violin. The therapist is encouraged to become an instrument which can interpret, colour and respond to the musical score, resonate and bend beneath the fingers of the musician, constantly changing and developing their diagnostic sensitivities in interpretation and technique. Kleinian psychotherapists will have experienced this long-term period of personal analysis, three years (minimum) of theoretical input, followed by a shorter period of training analysis at one of the formal institutes, plus ongoing supervision of their work with individual clients. In *The Psychoanalysis of Children*, Melanie Klein wrote:

> The analysis of children at puberty demands a thorough knowledge of the technique of adult analysis. I consider a regular training in the analysis of adults as a necessary foundation ... No one who has not gained experience adequately and done a fair amount of work on adults should enter upon the technically more difficult field of child analysis. In order to be able to preserve the fundamental principles of analytic treatment in the modified form necessitated by the child's (and the adult's) mechanisms at the various stages of development, the therapist must besides being fully versed in the technique of early analysis possess complete mastery of the technique employed in analysing adults. (Klein, 1932: 342)

It is the Kleinian view that an analyst or a psychotherapist who dogmatically believes that they and only they, plus a few other chosen spirits who adhere rationally and rigidly to their particular school and their particular form of dogmatism, will not, in Kleinian terms, have advanced beyond the paranoid-schizoid position to be capable of doubt as to whether they, or anyone else has the key to understanding the complexity of a human being. This is important since the fundamental concepts of the paranoid-schizoid and depressive positions naturally affect the ways in which the Kleinian psychotherapist will view their patients' presentations

In dealing with the early anxieties which arise from the relationship between the baby and the breast, faced by the harsher and more persecutory anxieties which lie in the deepest strata of the mind and the primitive processes that are aroused by this process, it is vital for the Kleinian therapist to remain consistent, namely to refer the anxiety back to its source and resolve it by systemically analysing the transference situation.

The therapist will need to be sensitive to those embryonic features of emotional problems which are present in all human beings and which are clearly reflected in the patient. The therapist will be aware that possible events in one's life, both in reality and in imagination, which did occur and which could have developed, should not be denied and repressed.

The transition from childhood to adulthood requires an understanding of the fact that in every person lies the capacity to have been something and someone else. The therapist should be able to encourage the flowering of this inner self in the patient, while remaining for most of their professional life in a situation where their own self-expression is forbidden.

The steady, accepting but neutral attitude of the Kleinian psychotherapist differs from the more responsive, manipulative and role-playing attitudes advocated by certain other strategies of intervention. Power is acknowledged and interpreted but in Kleinian psychotherapy the therapist allows himself or herself to be used as an object. In this way the psychotherapist actually intrudes but does not obtrude.

Making clear the transference manifestations which develop during this process is regarded as the primary means by which the patient is helped towards better health, and able to maintain continuing psychic functioning. The personality of the therapist – calm, interested, helpful, giving full attention to each minute detail of the patient's behaviour and language – re-creates in the therapeutic alliance an opportunity to correct the infantile distorsted view of object relationships that has constricted the patient's life. It provides incentive and reward in a benign relationship that encourages the patient to achieve the tasks that are imposed by the discipline of therapy and provides each patient with a model of strength and an identification with a reality: the real person of the therapist.

At times the psychotherapist, guided by the ethical goals of treatment and the understanding obtained from their own training and personal psychotherapy, must safeguard against any interference with a professional attitude to the patient based on prior knowledge of their own difficulties and the problems which stem from their own ethical values, attitudes and boundaries. For instance if the therapist is mourning the death of a parent or partner it may be difficult to work with a patient in a similar position.

Therapists are not empty husks; they have prejudices, fears, painful trigger spots. It is better for both therapist and patient to acknowledge and identify these feelings. This may mean that at times the therapist will decide not to take a particular patient into treatment. This is a serious decision for patient and therapist alike and must be handled in such a fashion that making a referral to another agency or individual does not further disturb the patient and cause more pain.

Therapeutic relationship and style

Kleinian technique is psychoanalytic and based – as are others – on classical Freudian analysis. This means that the setting for therapy is formal and the number of sessions will vary (an analysis offers five or six sessions each week), but in psychotherapy this is the exception rather than the rule. However, the session time is the same (50 minutes) and the patient can be offered a choice of either couch or chair.

The therapist uses the techniques of free association and interpretation and in all essentials, other than the frequency of sessions, psychoanalytic principles are strictly adhered to. The therapist is confined to listening and interpreting the material brought by a patient. Criticism, encouragement, reassurance and advice-giving is avoided. However, the atmosphere is relaxed and facilitative.

To understand and appreciate the difference between the Kleinian relationship in therapy with the patient and other methodologies, one must look at the nature of the interpretations given to the patient. Klein changed the emphasis in the analytic process from formal Freudian theories to aspects of material not seen before. She was impressed by the prevalence and power of the mechanisms of projection and introjection and highlighted the fact that these introjections led to the building of the inner complex being, with its projections which colour the world and our perceptions of reality. Once verbalized and 'seen', as it were, these revelations of our primitive levels of experience can be understood and detected in the material provided by our adult patients.

Kleinian therapists are aware that if a patient gains control in psychotherapy their difficulties will be perpetuated in later life. The patient will continue to live a life constricted by the paranoid-schizoid symptoms which caused them to seek therapy in the first place. It follows that however neutral and laid back the therapist may contrive to be, in successful therapy the therapist maintains control of the kind of relationship that will operate.

'In all forms of psychoanalytic psychotherapy, therapist and patient are confronted with a basic problem, the problem of object need. Every patient regards the psychotherapist as real, regards all the manifestations of the treatment situation as real and strives to regard the therapist as a real object. The therapist too wants to regard the patient as real and to respond to the patient as a real object' (Tarachow, 1970: 498–9). The primary urge in this relationship is the temptation to turn back the clock, to regress, to restore the symbiotic parental relationship that initially occurred with the mother: to lose the boundaries and fuse, to re-create the past as it was, and return to the time of ultimate dependency, replete, at one, inside the mother.

In no way should the therapist confuse the therapeutic function with the parental function. The therapist may give over part of their mind to this experience, since they come so close to the patient's life experience, but in essence the therapist must also remain detached from it, holding on to professional anonymity. The therapist will be aware of the seductive danger of imagining him/herself (even for the briefest time) as the ideal parent figure for the patient. The therapist uses these skills of awareness and identification to assess and understand the complexities of the interaction of the patient with the parent parts of the therapist.

We may be deeply affected, feel involved, but paradoxically this affection and involvement are distilled, detached, separated in a way which is impossible in the true relationship between a parent and child.

The Kleinian psychotherapist works assiduously to develop this therapeutic alliance, the intimate, real and close working together of two minds. For this to come about both the therapist and the patient undertake a controlled ego splitting (where either good or bad parts of the self are split off from the ego and projected into love or hatred of external objects: i.e. parental figures or caregivers) in the service of the treatment. The therapist and the patient work together in constructing a barrier against the need for a constricted object relationship. The therapist is not a breast, a hand or a voice, but a human being who is complete in every way. The therapist as well as the patient has to struggle constantly against the array of temptations which lead them to believe that they can allow themselves to become closer to their patient, with consequent dissolution and camouflaging of the existing ego boundaries. These temptations are further compounded because certain aspects of the therapeutic alliance are real. The therapist behaves in a caring, concerned, real and human way to the patient, and the patient is able to glean over a period of time real things about the therapist: that the therapist may be single or married, the family is away on holiday, that the therapist smokes, prefers one colour to another, that there is a secretary, a family pet, small children and that the therapist may share accommodation with other psychotherapists, etc.

These realistic aspects of the treatment relationship must be understood by a psychotherapist. Among other things they lead to identification with the reality aspects of the therapist, who uses them wordlessly to correct transference distortions and to supply the motivation necessary for the therapeutic work of transference interpretation. Close attention to what may be happening in the immediate present has many analogies with what could have been happening in the reconstructed past. What is important is the urgent need that the transference process serves in the here and now and this should not be disregarded in the therapist's search for its meaning in the past.

Every interpretation made by a therapist results in a loss or a deprivation for the patient. It can frustrate, denying the patient an opportunity to gratify their fantasy wishes, often placing them in the position of relinquishing some infantile object: 'It is a paradox that the interpretation – the act of the therapist that deprives the patient of the infantile object – also provides him with an adult object in the form of the sympathetic therapist' (Tarachow, 1970: 498–9).

Despite many changes in current practice and in how unresolved issues are being tackled by therapists, there is a strong continuity in the way in which fundamental principles have endured:

- the process – the overriding importance given to the responses to interpretation;
- the transference – the centrality of interpreting the transference; the emphasis on the patient's early childhood experiences and their level of functioning in this period;
- the belief that love and hate go side by side and that the turmoil caused by the sense of destructiveness is counterbalanced by love.

Major therapeutic strategies and techniques

The role of the psychotherapist is centred entirely on transference and its interpretation. The therapist listens intently to the patient's material, and endeavours not to be involved at all in giving practical advice, encouragement, reassurance or to offer any active participation in the life of the patient or the patient's family.

Transference interpretation

The concept of transference relates not only to an understanding of the 'here and now', the situation which is actually evolving between the psychotherapist and the patient, but to an understanding of the way facts and fantasies which relate to past relationships, especially those of internal figures from the patient's inner world, are transferred on to the therapist. The transference is expanded as a total situation which includes the functioning of the patient as well as the symbolic meanings placed on to the therapist.

This lively process takes in current problems and relationships, which are again related to the transference as it develops. The psychotherapist is aware of the transference at the very beginning of therapy, but in giving interpretations careful attention must be paid to the way they are handled, the timing, the order and the language used, and especially to the amount of interpretation.

Understanding of transference and counter-transference and their effect on therapy are the tools which are used to investigate both positive and negative feelings directed towards the therapist. Counter-transference was first seen as a neurotic disturbance in the therapist which prevented him or her from obtaining a clear and objective view of the patient, but now it is understood to be an important source of information about the patient as well as a major component in understanding the interaction of the therapist and the patient. In other words, we are deeply affected and involved but also paradoxically uninvolved with our patients. These feelings bring with them the pressure to identify with the counter-transference situation and to act it out in ways either unconsciously and subtly or obviously and aggressively.

Interpretation of these feelings should be sparse and succinct, using everyday language, avoiding technical and analytic terms which may give satisfaction to the therapist but are of little value to the patient. If your patient cannot understand you, they may as well go home. The best initial interpretations are simple restatements of the problem as presented by the client but relayed back in dynamic terms.

If it is difficult to teach psychotherapy, it is even more difficult to describe the techniques of psychotherapy. In an earlier paragraph I stressed that the Kleinian psychotherapist will have learned skills through long-term psychoanalytic psychotherapy, a process not unlike the age-old system of apprenticeship to a master or skilled craftsman of some repute and proven worth. The technique of psychotherapy is not static, and psychotherapists regularly attend case discussion groups, supervision sessions, seminars and study groups to meet and compare experiences and to learn from each other in a lively fashion.

Contemporary Kleinian technique emphasizes:

- the immediate here and now situation; all aspects of the setting – i.e. the room where therapy takes place; the importance of understanding the content of the anxiety;
- 'the consequence of interpreting the anxiety rather than the defences only (so called deep interpretation)' (Spillius, 1983: 321–2).

Winnicott humorously remarked, 'of course you can acknowledge that there is a war going on', but political statements or discussion of other issues do not belong in the consulting room. In this way the client is enabled to make contact with an expectation which relates more closely to the emotions that are experienced as a result of therapy, than they do to what is happening at that moment in the external world.

The past is connected to the present gradually. Interpretations are given in a certain sequence: preparatory interventions, interpreting resistances and defences, gauging the patient's readiness to accept the interpretation and wording it carefully. In the Kleinian model, interpretations go from the surface to the depth; from what is known or imagined to occur in the present, to what exists in the past, which is less well known or unknown, the earliest mental processes of childhood, and to the later more specialized types of mental functioning, which are the unconscious infantile archaic wishes and fantasies – those which focus on the therapist as a possible source of gratification.

The change process in therapy

Atholl Hughes, in 'Contributions of Melanie Klein to psycho-analytic technique', gives a particularly clear definition of the change process in Kleinian therapy:

> As the patient is helped to distinguish good experiences they can identify with the analyst as a person who can care for their own insight and well being and the way is open for the patient to do the same. As the patient's envy lessens it becomes possible to appreciate positive qualities in oneself and others, acknowledged along with destructive qualities. Integration of split off parts of oneself is comparable to a process in the development of the normal infant who begins, at about three months of age, to tolerate loving and hating the same object with less splitting and projection.
>
> On the basis of a repeated satisfying experience, the child is able to introject, that is to take into their own personality, ideas and feelings of a good mother with less hostility and idealisation. The child is then in a position to tolerate feelings of concern and responsibility towards the mother in whom the capacity to introject is crippled. (Hughes, 1974: 113–14)

During treatment, the patient comes to understand that feelings of aggression and love can be valuable, and so it is possible to value them. Early responses to interpretation which were felt by the patient to be prohibitive, unkind or unduly harsh, and which tended either to frustrate desire or to punish, permitting, even commanding, the patient to enter in fear and trepidation the forbidden areas of primitive and passionate feelings, these regressive infantile expectations are overcome and are replaced by a rationality that can be accepted and understood. Melanie Klein opened the door to insights which enable us at least to attempt to contend with human behaviour. We are confronted in life with a view of ourselves in a succession of social relationships which are disrupted by hatred, jealousy, rivalry, greed and other destructive feelings. The process of change in therapy enables us at least to establish more constructive relationships. It is said that as Freud discovered the child in the adult, so Klein discovered the infant in the child.

Patients change as they become more open and free to acknowledge their constant struggle between love and hate. Facilitated by their therapy, knowledge of the destructive elements which are present in the psyche can lead to clearer judgement, increased tolerance of themselves and others, with the ability to remain in control and to be less fearful.

Change can be identified as a desire for reconciliation and reparation. The patient can begin to identify with other people in a caring and sensitive way. The patient can let go of the negative aspect of the painful frustrations and suffering of the past and believe once again in their own capacity to love and to expect to be loved in return. In making this reparation for the past the patient makes good the imagined injuries both given and received in infancy and moves on to relinquish their guilt.

Limitations of the approach

There is a proliferation of different methods of psychotherapy, some of which do not emphasize self-awareness, and which question the causation of therapeutic change. They argue that change is not engendered by the growth of self-awareness. Questions are frequently asked about the extent to which the theories and concepts of Kleinian therapy affect the technique of psychoanalysis.

Scientific examination of the causes of therapeutic change must question the examination and description of the variables which, in context, facilitate such change. Experimental methods can then be evolved to test the hypotheses which are formed. Kleinian psychotherapy, as judged by these contemporary standards, is still unable to provide the scientific evidence necessary to meet the basic criteria of disconformability. Moreover it becomes increasingly evident that it is an oversimplification to look at psychopathology as if it can be isolated from the changing attitudes of the nuclear age.

But what of the Kleinian method both as a focus of enquiry and as a therapy? Some Kleinian therapists find it difficult to acknowledge the outside environment that their patients have created and in which they function. In seeking to re-create the patient's internal and fantasized world of childhood, the Kleinian is perhaps too eager to divorce patients from their social and cultural background.

We have, after all, moved on considerably from the early 1900s and have come to realize (I hope) that our patients are a specific group of people who have reacted in a specific way to their problems and who come, specifically, to seek help from Kleinian psychotherapy. A human being cannot develop in a sterilized plastic bubble. A baby is conceived at the coming together of its parents, who contribute to this act of creation the essence of their own personalities at that given moment. The baby is born at a predicted time and season of the year, in a special place and in a particular way and significantly others become involved in its well-being. It depends throughout life on the availability and proximity of other human beings. In the wheatfields of America, a man will sow the wheat that provides bread for this child, and in the sweatshops of India another child will labour to cut its clothes.

In the heat of the moment, focusing mainly on early childhood experiences and/or recollections, the broader social context and subjective processes which brought these two human beings together can sometimes get left out of the consulting room, especially if the focus is on manoeuvrability and tactics. Psychotherapy has held the view that external events are not of primary importance, but we know that these events can exacerbate or alleviate certain aspects of the personality.

Inevitably the decision on what process to use with the patient in effecting change is shaped by one's theoretical approach. However, if the therapist practises therapy all day and every day from only one viewpoint, then there is a real danger of the Kleinian therapist becoming subsumed and consumed by their own stance. The rigorous adherence to basic psychoanalytic methods should not become rigidity. This contrasts sharply with other strategies of intervention where the emphasis has shifted from the processes within an individual to those in the context of his or her relationships with others (i.e. attachment therapy, family therapy and personal construct psychology).

B.J. Farrell (1981) criticizes the limitations imposed by strict adherence to one kind of analytic theory, and makes the point that Kleinian theory was (and still is) innovative. In continuing to extemporize and to employ new forms of psychoanalytic method, the Kleinian therapist will seek to obtain affirmation of any novel input from the patients themselves.

It was a technical invention – the technique of child analysis – which gave Melanie Klein the idea that the free play of young children can be interpreted psychoanalytically, giving access to the more primitive areas of the mind; this still provides the Kleinian therapist with a wealth of new material and has continued to provoke considerable revision of analytic theory. This technique influenced theory.

When the Kleinian therapist continues to report new case material and new findings, how is it possible to decide whether the therapist has, in fact, just misinterpreted basic Kleinian theory? If the therapist is hesitant about challenging results, does this imply that the original theory itself is 'shaky' and in need of amendment?

For every therapist the nagging doubts must persist. The crucial question remains: what effect does the use of Klein's theories have on the behaviour of this therapist? Do interpretations always dictate the therapist's goals for patients? Do Kleinian therapists only seek out what they expect to find? Do therapists, in order to fit their own expectations, distort what information patients provide? The deeper the analytic work, the more primitive the processes mobilized, the more essential it is to adhere to the boundaries of the psychodynamic model.

Therapists tend to forget that because they see their patients in such a strictly controlled analytic setting, they are immolated from a view of their patient in the external world. True, the patients report on their daily life, but these reports are highly selective and often only pertinent to the failures rather than the successes of life outside the consulting room. Anxious behaviour by one patient can be interpreted as a repression of unconscious ideas which are threatening to become conscious. The same anxious behaviour in another could be viewed externally as a way of appealing for a sympathetic approach from the therapist. These two interpretations of behaviour represent astonishingly different theoretical systems. In this way the therapist's viewpoint can be distorted.

The reader of this book will note that various theorists differ considerably on the postulation of central motives or goals for all human beings. Why do they differ so much? Is it not that the task of ferreting out the central motives of all human beings is impossible? Is it not an unattainable goal to poll every patient on their expectations of life and their private responses to the slings and arrows of outrageous fortune?

Would Kleinian psychotherapy suffer if each patient's motives were seen as unique? Psychoanalytical psychotherapy has been defined as a perspective which is essentially pre-theoretical in nature, but perspectives are often constricted by ideological underpinnings whether we are aware of them or not.

It was Huxley who wrote: 'Give me good mothers and I shall make a better world', but it is the converse which is true: 'Make me a good world and I shall give you good mothers.' It is hoped that Kleinian therapy can eventually be more explicit in stating that the amelioration of at least some areas of maternal deprivation and childhood abuse will only be possible when these intrinsic requirements can be met.

In looking forward to the future, R.D. Hinshelwood wrote:

> Increasingly throughout the 20th century human beings have been understood as psychological beings. Their difficulties have therefore been increasingly seen as psychological and less as moral. The impetus for this change has comprised many elements, but psychoanalysis has figured prominently among them. In very large measure, across the whole of our culture, the general apperception of mental illness and disturbance has been moulded by psychoanalysis itself. As psychoanalytic ideas have spread, so the presentation of psychological difficulties has become permeated by a psychoanalytic sophistication. This has created a particular situation for psychoanalysts. They face a moving target. New kinds of patients mean new ideas which in turn mean new ways of working, but they also mean patients with new ways of presenting themselves and thus a new target for the psychoanalytic probe. (Hinshelwood, 1994: 240)

Case example

Kleinian analysts are sometimes accused of not taking sufficient interest in the effect of external environmental influences in the life of their patients. This is not so. Those who use a Kleinian framework in their therapeutic work consider that external events can exacerbate or alleviate certain characteristics in the patient. To this end, I believe the history and circumstances of my patient whom I will call Jessica, and her family, are very relevant to the outcome of our therapeutic relationship.

The client

In 2003 Jessica (now 52) living alone and working as an administrator for an organisation which provided play groups in the community re-entered therapy (having previously worked with two therapists whom she described as 'unsatisfactory'). Initially we agreed to meet once a week for one hour. There were additional twice weekly sessions in 2004 during her mother's illness. Jessica not only gave her permission, but has made a significant contribution to this case presentation. She is a committed patient, hard working, insightful, consistent and punctual. This is her history

Over the last 100 years vast upheavals have taken place in Europe. 35 million people have migrated to seek a new life elsewhere. Fleeing from wars, poverty, famine and persecution, they forsook their homelands, culture and families in search of fabled destinations which appeared to offer refuge, wealth and employment.

They flooded into Britain and the USA until government restraints halted the tide, but many found their adopted countries hostile, unwilling to accept them. Seduced by promises of security and prosperity, it left many facing life with an uncertain future in an unknown land.

The life story of my patient, Jessica, reflects some of these challenging circumstances, and they are factors which led her to seek psychotherapy. Jessica's great grandparents were farmers living in a small Jewish rural community in Rumania. After 1875 when restrictions on the movement of Jews were lifted, twelve members of her family decided to emigrate to the USA. However, tales of Californian gold mines and rich acres of farmland ready for the taking soon proved to be a myth. Undeterred, the family moved again in search of gold and looked instead to the underdeveloped continent of Africa.

Again, dreams of gold mines came to naught but as shopkeepers and traders to the native population, the Rumanian families settled in Zambia and prospered. Large houses and businesses were developed, schools and synagogues were built and the Jewish community was re-established. A third generation soon developed and these children, unlike their parents, were sent to study at the now established Universities in South Africa. After graduation, returning to Zambia to meet and marry within the Community.

Jessica's parents (in their late twenties) married in 1949. It was an arranged marriage and, later, not a happy one. Jessica's father entered his family's prosperous business enabling them to live in style. Jessica's mother was irritated by her placid, good natured and unambitious husband. She longed for 'European' culture, social recognition and status within a society that had become increasingly materialistic and competitive.

Their community, trying to emulate the lost 'delights' of European civilisation, experienced culture shock. They were caught up in a consuming desire for fashion, food and pursuits which were not remotely African. Jessica's mother was affected with the desire to be 'perfect' in manner and form, ambitious to be seen and acknowledged as a member of the higher echelons of Zambian Society.

Two children were born of the marriage, Jessica and her brother Ralph, two years between each birth. They were well looked after, dressed immaculately, sent to the best schools. Three years later (Jessica was then six) Pauline was born. The new baby was born with a rare genetic disorder and kept in intensive care after the birth.

Jessica's maternal Rumanian grandmother was called in to help. A sturdy woman of pioneer stock she had been widowed when her own two children were small. She was a forceful and racially bigoted character, severely critical of her own children and with a violent temper, but with her grandchildren, Jessica and Ralph, she behaved differently. She was gentle, loving and uncritical. Jessica said 'we loved staying with her – always kind and supportive. We could relax and enjoy ourselves'.

Their relationship with their grandmother now became doubly important. The new baby, grossly disabled, hovered between life and death. Her mother's social life was in ruins and the family faced the prospect of a future with a mentally and physically disabled child. Aghast at the turn of events, Jessica's mother disputed the diagnosis. This could and should not happen to someone like her! Jessica and Ralph were hurriedly sent to their grandmother's house and the parents took the baby to Johannesburg for treatment. Later they flew to London for further consultations.

It was four months before the parents returned to Zambia. During this time Jessica was told that the baby (whom she had never seen) might die. 'I didn't really understand what was happening. It was like a heavy weight inside. At bedtime I felt frightened and cried but grandmother was around to comfort me. It was lovely staying with her – I could do no wrong and we got used to staying there. Eventually my parents returned and brought with them a special nurse to look after the baby. This let me off the hook, I wasn't expected to do anything and my parents were free to give us some attention, but the nurse left and everything came out into the open. My mother's anger at the doctor's diagnosis of 'brain damage', arguments going on at home, talk about finding a 'school' for Pauline and my mother's insistence that Pauline could be one of the lucky ones and grow out of "it"'.

Jessica (at 10) became the main target of her mother's frustration and anger, screaming at the servants and accusing her husband of not helping. 'Don't provoke your mom' he warned the children. At night, Jessica was aware of a noise made by her mother vomiting in the bathroom. There were signs of her binge eating, wolfing down the icing on cakes in the kitchen and later making herself sick in the lavatory. Jessica was terrified. She did not know what to do or what to say to her mother and so kept silent.

Dress and appearance were now even more important. Jessica was criticised for being fat and untidy. Large amounts of money were spent on clothes but moments of affection and comfort were rare. In increasing denial, her mother resumed French lessons, studied French culture and fashion and bought French perfume and cosmetics. Still bingeing at night whilst putting Jessica on a strict diet. 'My mother thought her vomiting was a secret but it wasn't. I could never comfort her and thought, resentfully, one rule for her and another for me. I did not speak with her about it ever although I suspected that her later stomach cancer had its origins in the secret vomiting which carried on for years'.

Nothing helped Pauline's disability and instability, which increased with age. Inevitably there were social problems for Jessica at school, and she was now having to share a bedroom with Pauline. Mindful of her mother's temper, Jessica could only sulk. 'I didn't want her to be here. God, I'm stuck with her. I felt no affection for her, no sympathy and still don't, but I could not openly resent her'. The bitter disappointment at what could not be expected of Pauline was projected on to Jessica. Music and dancing lessons, French lessons, dressmakers, scholastic achievement, extra homework, nothing appeased or gratified her mother.

Having done well at school, Jessica was allowed (following fashion) a gap year when family friends in the USA offered hospitality. 'I spent the happiest year of my life with such good people'. Returning to Zambia she knew she had to escape and opted for a British University. Resisting her mother's attempt to place her in a 'Jewish environment' she enrolled at Exeter intending to read French.

Shy, inhibited, petite (4ft 11) convinced of her lack of attraction and sophistication, a Jewish virgin with little sense of self or her own pleasant appearance and sexuality, she was overjoyed to be away from Zambia, her parents and especially Pauline, and was able to find new friends and eventually to enjoy sex and the fun of university life. 'I always found it easier to have friendships with men. Women made me feel awkward, self deprecation would kick in – I never feel as attractive or assertive as other women do. I had several boyfriends but anticipated, sooner or later, they would end the relationships. I accepted this from everyone. There were regular dreaded visits from my parents, always with Pauline, but I disassociated as soon as they left still, dragging her around to doctors searching for hope. They left me alone. She was the main preoccupation and I was able to do what I wanted. I got a mediocre degree still not sure what to do. I wasn't good enough to be a French interpreter and settled for teacher training in London. I felt like an alien. A Zambian trying to teach in a London primary school. It was mayhem. 27 nationalities. Being a 4ft 11 teacher with an inferiority complex did not help. My confidence was nil.

My parents were in London when my father had a minor stroke and was very ill. I used his illness as an excuse to give up teaching. I always felt closer to him. Even when he was ill my mother still put Pauline first. Where we went and what we did still depended on her behaviour at the time. It became obvious that my family would not return to Zambia. As they were still chasing cures all over the place, they decided to buy me a flat in London.

I started a relationship with a Zambian I met at a party. He was married with children. I knew he would never leave his wife for me, why would any man stay with a woman who had no self esteem? I accepted this. I went on to meet Roger who married me. I wasn't in love but admired his intellectual ability. He was an opportunist, attracted to me because I had a home of my own and thought he was on to a good thing. He was writing a book, his primary occupation. I took a part-time job working with children, carrying on with this job during pregnancies when my two sons were born. Roger was unloving, unhelpful, egocentric and critical of my parents who, he said, were coercive, interfering and strict. He was unpleasant to Pauline. She was 'obnoxious'. It's true her behaviour was always giving cause for concern. For a short time I took care of her to give my parents a break. She loved my two little boys and could look after them for brief periods, but I was relieved when my parents returned. I decided to leave Roger. With my parents' help I bought a house and they moved into my small flat. My father relinquished his business ties with Zambia but died shortly afterwards in 1995. Mom stayed on in the flat and we got some minimal help from social services for Pauline'.

The therapy

Based on her history, three themes traversed the process of therapy and in my opinion, prompted Jessica to seek my help.

1. After the death of her father in 1995, London became her mother's permanent home. She was now 78, in poor health and constantly preoccupied with Pauline's well being. In 2004 she was diagnosed with terminal stomach cancer. Jessica was accompanying her mother to hospital for frequent treatments and caring for her on discharge.
2. Brother Ralph, married with 2 children had always been unwell with kidney disease and a diabetic (as was his father). He could only offer limited help to the family.
3. Pauline was provided with sheltered accommodation and social services had become involved but her uncontrollable and bizarre behaviour needed surveillance and support. Jessica organised help for mother and sister whilst continuing to work part-time and care for her two children.
4. Jessica's sons (now in their twenties) were at university and enjoying their studies. They had frequent contact with their mother, returning home for holidays. Contact with their father was rare. He had now remarried.
5. Jessica, unmarried, continued to have male relationships both long and short-term. One, she described as 'entirely inappropriate'. She was currently involved with another married man even though there were good reasons for his unsuitability. He had several women in tow and was clearly unfaithful to her, offering little interest or concern with her family problems. The attraction was, as before, to a sexual relationship which echoed her depressed feelings. She could only aspire to being a 'kind of second best'.

Jessica had approached me as a Kleinian psychotherapist with little anticipation of the process of treatment or its outcome. I was determined to avoid jargon (which is of little use to the patient) and to refrain from remote and authoritative interpretations. I knew that Jessica would respond to a close intelligent wish to acknowledge her individuality, and to provide a reliable holding function, avoiding moral judgments.

My immediate reaction to Jessica's complex story of love and hate was that, as her therapist, I would need to focus on my own and Jessica's uncertainties, to react to the need for further developments without pushing too hard at this early stage in our relationship, and without becoming fanatically dogmatic about Kleinian interpretation or, in contrast, arrogantly dismissive of Jessica's own interpretation of her current situation and needs.

During the opening sessions of therapy I was relatively still, speaking calmly and reassuringly to Jessica who lay on my couch evidently exhausted by this stream of recollections and observations of her past history which I did not interrupt.

Jessica confided that in her previous 'brushes' with therapy, she had felt intimidated and antagonistic to the therapists, both of whom had reminded her of her mother's disapproval. They, too, had initially kept silent, but it had felt hostile rather than helpful. She felt relaxed with me as she preferred to see her therapist's face.

One could see, as well as sense, Jessica's urgent need for approval. When she entered my room, her smallness, the neatness of her petite 4ft 11ins stature, folding her hands and tucking herself so neatly and so quietly and so passively on the couch. Her bodily presentation was deferential and it could be interpreted as her defence. Don't hurt, don't attack me, don't let me down, an unspoken plea, obviously used many times as there were the tears on the brink of her big dark eyes.

I have highlighted, previously in this chapter, that the practice of psychodynamic psychotherapy with its unique methodology based on transference and countertransference, the analytic setting, the intensive individual study of the patient, and the interventions of myself as therapist, is usually based, initially on the formation of a hypothesis even if it is not immediately substantiated by the factual evidence given in a patient's presentation.

The use of hypotheses and the need to verify them is part of an irreducible need in myself. Kleinians have been described as therapists who have a 'psychoanalytic poetic' imagination. Sometimes the truth of psychoanalytic theory consists only in its exaggerations which can encourage and facilitate our patients to speak openly and exactly of what cannot be spoken about.

My hypothesis was that the origins of Jessica's depression and her perceptual dismantling appeared to stem from her experience of her emotionally exhausting mother who, even now, was still in a position to confuse her, alternating as she did between periods of hostility and affection.

Jessica had withdrawn in the face of her mother's furious onslaughts and had retreated to a feeling of terrifying 'isolation' and 'inertia'. Her mother appeared oblivious and insensitive to her feelings, whilst her brother could only try to be supportive.

It was important to understand what Jessica was saying, consciously. She needed to convey many things and so it was important to pay attention to her history, in depth, thus assuring her that her therapist was attentive and giving her the human emotional and intellectual respect she deserved. Respect as Jessica, in her own right, separate from the heavy responsibilities which had beset her. This was, in itself, therapeutic.

I explained to Jessica that it is usual that older siblings of disabled children experience their childhood overshadowed by the family traumas which surround such an event. However, in response Jessica was anxious to establish that, prior to the birth of Pauline, she and Ralph had enjoyed a 'normal' childhood. They had been breast fed and, as other middle class families in Zambia, there were always black nannies and servants to care for their every need.

But Jessica's mother was not 'motherly'. Socially ambitious, she was obsessed by fashion and appearance. Discontented in her marriage she continued to struggle to maintain her 'position' in a competitive society but never quite 'getting there', projecting on to Jessica her failures, criticising her as she had been and still was continually criticised by her own mother (Jessica's grandmother).

When Jessica's mother became pregnant with a third child it presented no problems. It was the norm, something to be welcomed by a Jewish housewife and mother in this stratum of Zambian society. Presumably there would be no difficulty in accessing the nannies, maids and extra help which were readily available and had already been mobilised for the care of Jessica and her brother, Ralph. She did not need to be a 'hands on' mother. No one anticipated that there would be a serious problem in caring for a new baby.

The birth of their mentally handicapped and disfigured baby girl threw the whole family off balance. Chaos ensued. Both parents were unable to cope, and her mother became hysterical. Jessica could feel nothing but ill towards the baby whose arrival exacerbated the distance she already felt from her mother.

At an early stage in her therapy, Jessica gave evidence to the thought that she had contributed to her mother's mental instability. She was not conscious of this idea, but she acknowledged that her mother's behaviour was strange and had bordered, at times, on the bizarre. As her mother evidently showed psychotic features in her personality, although she was never hospitalised, it is understandable that Jessica felt alarm when she had unconscious thoughts, expressed in her depressed foreboding, that she had contributed to her mother's frailty. At a conscious level she knew that her destructive feelings were not in themselves responsible for her mother's mental problems, but she was aware that it was aspects of her own personality that could also have a detrimental effect on others. It was a response to her mother's coldness and lack of involvement with her other children and friends that brought Jessica into therapy in the first place. In her unconscious she showed repeatedly how aware she had always been of her mother's attack on life in all its objects.

This included life in her husband's work, in his creativity and potency and in her children's development and even in her own occupational endeavours. She saw them fostered by others and so belonging to others, be they family friends, parents of other children, teachers, doctors, anyone who tried to help. In Jessica's response to the analytic process, it was possible to illustrate how destructive her own manoeuvres had been to the development of her own sense of self and that this destructiveness had permeated all areas of her life. She was bleak about the future.

Jessica's reactions to her mother's behaviour suggested that, at an unconscious level, she thought that she had made her mother and her breasts impotent and lifeless as she had tried, at times, to make herself. Jessica reasoned aloud that her behaviour could have a pernicious effect on others. If the idea that her beliefs and behaviour could affect others, then she should be able to stop this, if she so desired. Thus she could have restored the mental equilibrium of her mother if she had reacted differently to her mother's distress and been more sympathetic. She had opted for co-operation to avoid confrontation.

Melanie Klein described in many papers the ways in which an infant dealt with feelings of a persecutory nature, accentuated by resentment over frustration and hatred if dependency combined with feelings of envy for the all powerful (and in Jessica's case the withdrawing) mother. Jessica experienced this as a form of abandonment, feeding her envious destructiveness, emphasising her fears of loneliness, isolation, depression and guilt.

In tears, on the couch, Jessica tended to seek to blame herself for matters for which she had no guilt. In therapy, she became self focused and inflicted on herself endless soul searching to find visible proof for her feeling of not being liked by her mother. Her mother's hostility was prompted because she (Jessica) was not handicapped like her sister.

Her mother's penetrating looks (now that Jessica had a therapist) her rejection of any suggestion made to alleviate her obsession with Pauline, even in the face of her illness and encroaching death, completely absorbed Jessica. In the transference I had become her Rumanian grandmother eager to hear about her mother's failings.

Jessica would ruminate on her mother's moods unable to see any way out of her future responsibilities with her sister. Seemingly unsupported at this time with a dead father, a divorced husband, a lack of a male relationship that she could trust, these were thoughts she could share with the one person who had given her a sense of love and belonging – her grandmother. I could take them and contain them non-judgementally.

Desiring her sister's death was unacceptable, unthinkable and dangerous to her own well-being as well as the structure of the family. Perhaps her mother echoed these murderous feelings, but Jessica could never be sure. 'My mother was a loose cannon, unpredictable, unapproachable, one minute loving, the next minute thrashing out to all of us. All I ever wanted was to escape and build a separate life for myself. Now my mother is dying, and, as I dreaded, nothing has been organised for my sister'.

Jessica was now attending therapy twice a week. She was torn by the feelings of anger and hate which now arose to the surface. 'Where is my pity, my sadness?' she would berate herself.

Prior to this period Jessica was producing written material which she wanted me to keep. A letter from Great Ormond Street Hospital explaining the diagnosis of Pauline's abnormalities, a genealogical table of the extended family of both parents with explanatory notes about their past histories. She was preparing herself and me for her mother's imminent death.

Her forebodings proved to be true. (Kleinian therapists consider the actual mourning situation a productive period in therapy). Jessica's mother died of her cancer in 2005. Amazingly, Pauline appeared to cope with the sudden loss of attention. Jessica was left to organise the situation and was also surprisingly calm. She realised that she and her brother now had the power to decide what would be best for themselves. I encouraged Jessica to accept that she was now in control of what happened next. Pauline would continue to receive care from social services. Jessica could release herself from her part-time job and plan to travel as she had always wanted. There was a new note of optimism. Pauline need not be such a concern. Obviously her mother's possessive guilt had exacerbated the problem. She could be contained. Jessica now looked again for reassurance from me. 'I loved being a mother. I never lost my temper with the boys and we are always loving and close. I am so glad I had boys – girls would have caused me to over-compensate. I would have felt insecure and lacked confidence as a role model. I would have felt at a loss. With the boys, I have always been consistent with them and never unfair'.

None of her mother's social friends offered any help or even enquired about Pauline's future. They, too, had found her difficult and even distasteful. Practical matters were taking over our sessions. The estate, the will, the belongings and then, unexpectedly, Pauline became seriously ill with a stomach infection and needed urgent surgery. She was sympathetically treated in hospital and even enjoyed the time she spent recuperating. This gave Jessica the incentive to seek extra care for Pauline and to ask for shared responsibilities from social services without much success.

At this stage I felt it was perfectly in order to abandon interpretation in terms of concrete partial objects, and to focus more on a shared understanding of Jessica's here and now.

It was painful to sort through her mother's possessions. Drawers full of scarves, wardrobes full of clothes and cosmetics, pictures of parties and social events in the past. Friends came to the funeral but most avoided the subject of Pauline. It was sad listening to Jessica's reminiscences, not only of what had been but, more painfully for her, of what could have been. 'Should I have done more but it was so difficult to reach my mother? There were times when I envied her. Her ability to entertain, her taste in dress and manners. She could be charming to others who had no under-standing of how difficult she could be. When she was dying she did say that I had been a good daughter'.

These were difficult times for Jessica. In therapy, reflecting back with me she became angry with her mother and herself, realising that Pauline's behaviour could have been better managed if her mother had allowed herself to let go of her controls. I reinforced her desire to release herself from guilt and self-imposed inhibitions. Jessica made a new relationship. This time she chose well, a gentle man who responded to the possibility of a mutual attraction and commitment. Jessica's despondency was lifting, 'I am happier than I have ever been. I feel I can have a happy normal life like other people. I don't feel outside watching other people live. I am better able to deal with Pauline, not feeling guilty about her. I am changing the work situation, I don't feel trapped. I know this was never about my not loving my mother. I see now that she needed help for herself. She was a sick person, but I don't feel guilty about blaming her – she could have got proper help and support. The damage was done; it was the inevitable result of circum-stances. Some people change, some never change. Pauline was the centre of attention and I lacked confidence. It was upsetting and difficult to have such a "special person" in one's family. Zambia was a stifling society. I would have vis-ited but never returned to live there. The whole dynamic of Pauline made me try hard to run away. I never felt good enough. I came up to scratch academically, but at a huge cost that was never acknowledged. I loved my father; he would have liked to be comfortable, benign, under no pressure, but he was not allowed to feel comfortable either. I now know that I envied my mother. She was always more attractive than me. She made a play for all my friends convincing them that she was more clever and cultured than me. I used to think: if they only knew the truth, but even in her old age, even in ill health, she could put on a wonderful show. She was generous; maybe I haven't mentioned this enough. She would buy lovely presents and give things away to friends. If she came to visit, her idea of flowers was to bring orchids. It was always impressive'.

Jessica was now acknowledging that she envied her mother. It was a revelation. Melanie Klein who wrote at length about envy argued that envy was the earliest direct externalisation of the death instinct. The death instinct can best be understood as a struggle between the forces aiming for growth, order, integration and structure (an upward energy force for life) and forces which lead to contraction, disorder, frag-mentation and chaos (a downward spiral). Envy is both a reactive and inherent force in every individual. It depends on the relative scale of vitality and good fortune between what the envier perceives, and how they experience things in themselves. Envy is not just a curse but a consequence of consciousness.

The most dangerous aspect of her envy was not envy itself but the denial of it. In denial the envious impulse cannot be modified by loving, grateful and reparative wishes, the envier is more likely to disassociate from within themselves their own destructiveness. Jessica envied her mother who, in turn, was full of murderous rage. The more possessions she had the more impoverished she felt, the more angry she got with others and with herself for hating and feeling so empty. This was Jessica's role model, she grew up in the atmosphere of the excessive projection of self-destructiveness demonstrated by her mother. Because the world appeared so dangerous, Jessica's own negative envy induced in her an inability to receive and return love.

Envy depletes others. Triumphs over life are discounted and experienced as painful feelings of inadequacy, inferiority and impotence, the final stages in a long history of unhappiness, but at this time, Jessica seized the opportunity in therapy (without fear of retribution or rejection) to give voice to her ambivalent feelings of love, hate, envy and rage.

Melanie Klein introduced the concept of a paranoid/schizoid position which arose from persecutory anxiety in the individual. Jessica's behaviour, in early childhood and indeed throughout most of her life, illustrated this position. At one level idealizing her mother and at another experiencing her mother's behaviour as horrendous. She knew, early on, that life was a mixture of good and bad, that people we idolize can let us down. As time went on she anticipated only disappointment. The very painfulness of confronting such feelings brought with it feelings of persecution and rage. Her reality was distorted by fear and hostility.

Threatened by the losses she incurred (always exacerbated by the overwhelming needs of Pauline) Jessica was unable to sustain a secure inner world. There was no internalised 'caring' mother to promote her self-esteem. Loss and disappointment combined with her vulnerability could only lead to her subsequent depression. Without an intimate confiding relationship with her mother Jessica had developed a hopelessness in response to life events.

In consideration of why people develop generalised hopelessness following loss and disappointment, such a vulnerability often arises from the relative paucity and inaccessibility of positive memories in childhood. In Jessica's situation one can see how such pessimistic generalisations were formulated. The level of self-esteem is intimately related to the size of such a fund of positive memories. She had very few. With a sense of self-esteem and mastery at low ebb, a young girl was less likely to imagine herself emerging unscathed.

Depression can then be understood as a response to the psychic pain which erupts when the discrepancy between the actual and ideal self becomes unbearable. Helplessness at not being able to restore a wished for state of well-being can only lead to depression. Jessica gave up on herself.

I have asked of myself and Jessica if the Kleinian criteria for a successful outcome for therapy are in place. These criteria will always remain the same. To lift a sense of repression, and to gain the insights which free the patient from early fixations and inhibitions, thus enabling her to form full and satisfactory relationships. Will she be able to maintain these insights in situations of stress when seeking to rebuild her inner world, to allow herself to grieve and to feel some security, harmony and peace? Good things are happening for Jessica which I hope she is able to accept.

The process of psychotherapy seems to show me (as others) that there is something in the process which defies any definitive answer if, at the closing stages of therapy we are simply seeking for criteria of evidence or non-evidence in the worthiness of our discipline.

I put this to Jessica who responded by saying that she understood her progress in therapy as something she had learned 'to live with'. Because it is a part of human nature, reflection is rooted in our very way of being, which psychotherapy seemed to express so well to her in its contradictions and its intuitive ways of thinking.

I acknowledge to the now no longer obsequious but positive woman in front of me that we both can acknowledge that whilst all babies are born flawless, the damage to the psyche occurs after birth but, in the nature of things, no individual can possibly receive an unfalteringly empathetic mothering experience, and to the degree that this fails, we all become affected.

REFERENCES

Bion, W.R. (1952) 'Group dynamics – a review', *International Journal of Psycho-analysis*, 33: 235–47.

Bion, W.R. (1988) 'The differentiation of the psychotic from the non-psychotic personalities' (1957), in E. Bott Spillius (ed.), *Melanie Klein Today*, Vol. I: *Mainly Theory*. London: Routledge. pp. 61–78.

Bowlby, J. (1979) *The Making and Breaking of Affectional Bonds*. London: Tavistock.

Colby, K.M. (1951) *A Primer for Psychotherapists*. New York: Ronald Press.

Cooper, C. (1988) 'The Jewish mother', in H. Cooper (ed.), *Soul Searching*. London: SCM Press.

Farrell, B.J. (1981) *The Standing of Psycho-analysis*. London: Oxford University Press.

Hinshelwood, R.D. (1989) *A Dictionary of Kleinian Thought*. London: Free Association Books.

Hinshelwood, R.D. (1994) *Clinical Klein*. London: Free Association Books.

Hughes, A. (1974) 'Contributions of Melanie Klein to psycho-analytic technique', in Y.J. Varma (ed.), *Psychotherapy Today*. London: Constable.

Klein, M. (1932) *The Psychoanalysis of Children*. London: Hogarth.

Klein, M. (1950) 'On the criteria for the termination of a psycho-analysis', *London International Journal of Psycho-analysis*, 31: 78–80: 204.

Klein, M. (1952a) 'Notes on some schizoid mechanisms', in J. Rivière (ed.), *Developments in Psycho-analysis*. London: Hogarth.

Klein, M. (1952b) 'On the theory of anxiety and guilt', in J. Rivière (ed.), *Developments in Psycho-analysis*. London: Hogarth.

Klein, M. (1957) *Envy and Gratitude*. New York: Basic Books.

Klein, M. (1960) *Our Adult World and its Roots in Infancy*. London: Tavistock.

Meltzer, D. (1979) *The Kleinian Development*. London: The Clunie Press.

Miller, A. (1983) *For Your Own Good*. London: Virago Press.

Piontelli, A. (1992) *From Foetus to Child* (New Library of Psychoanalysis, 15). London: Routledge.

Rivière, J. (1936) Unpublished paper.

Segal, H. (1973) *Introduction to the Work of Melanie Klein*. London: Institute of Psychoanalysis/Karnac Books.

Segal, H. (1986) *Delusion and Artistic Creativity and Other Psycho-analytic Essays*. London: Free Association Books.

Spillius, E.B. (1983) 'Some developments from the work of Melanie Klein', *International Journal of Psycho-analysis*, 64: 321–2.

Tarachow, S. (1970) *Introduction to Psychotherapy*. New York: International University Press.

Waelder, R. (1937) 'The problem of the genesis of psychical conflict in earliest infancy', *International Journal of Psycho-analysis*, 18: 406–73.

SUGGESTED FURTHER READING

Klein, M. (1961) *Narrative of a Child Analysis*. London: Hogarth.
Likierman, M. (2001) *Melanie Klein: Her Work in Context*. London: Continuum.
Piontelli, A. (1992) *From Foetus to Child* (New Library of Psychoanalysis, 15). London: Routledge.
Quinodoz, J.M. (1992) *The Taming of Solitude* (New Library of Psychoanalysis, 20). London: Routledge.
Sayers, J. (2000) *Kleinians: Psychoanalysis Inside Out*. Oxford: Blackwell.

4

Psychodynamic Therapy: The Jungian Approach

Ann Casement

HISTORICAL CONTEXT AND DEVELOPMENT IN BRITAIN

Historical context

Analytical psychology is the term employed by the Swiss psychiatrist, Carl Gustav Jung (1875–1961), to depict his approach to depth psychology and psychotherapy. Though congruent with a psychodynamic perspective, Jung's approach to the human psyche and its drives displays several distinctive features, notably a marked stress on the interrelation of psyche and body.

Jung's childhood was marred by physical illness and emotional uncertainties. His relations with his pastor father and his mother were problematic (Jung, 1963). He happily asserted that his personal library and the cultural influences to which he was subjected were the formative factors in the evolution of his ideas, referring to the personal equation in saying that 'every psychology – my own included – has the character of a subjective confession' (Jung, 1961: 336).

Jung exemplified the anthropologist, Claude Lévi-Strauss's (1908–) term 'bricoleur', an intellectual handyman who finds inspiration everywhere. The quest the two men shared was for universal structures underlying the mind/ psyche, which led to borrowing a metaphorical screw from here, a figurative nut from there and, from elsewhere, an imaginative bolt. This 'bricolage' reflects Jung's view of the diversity and complexity of the psyche.

The first part of this chapter will present some of the main intellectual influences on Jung's work, which stretch as far back as the pre-Socratic thinkers like

Heraclitus and include Plato's ideas. The latter are the forerunners of Jung's theory of archetypes, which concern the inherited patterns in the psychosomatic unconscious. This is Jung's way of linking two sets of opposites: psyche and soma, and instinct and image, the concept of opposites being central to his psychology.

Western philosophy, particularly German Idealism and Romanticism, has had a general impact on analytical psychology. Kant's view of the 'moral order within' is echoed everywhere in Jung's work, while some would say that his 'starry heavens above' are more evident in Jung's ideas than in his own. Kant's theory of knowledge is important, in particular what he termed the noumenal. 'This latter he also called the "thing-in-itself" which come to have great importance for Jung in the development of his theory of archetypes' (Casement, 2001: 42)] Herder, the father of German Expressionism, also influenced Jung's populist and pluralistic approach to the psyche.

Given that Hegel synthesized Kantian reason and morality with Herder's ideas on desire and sensibility, he is a great, though largely unacknowledged influence on Jung. This lack of acknowledgement was perhaps due to Hegel's worldliness and his writings on the state, which were not to Jung's taste. Hegelian dialectics may be compared to the coming together of psychological qualities and elements hitherto seen as opposites. In Jungian therapy, these form into a new third position and the dialectic begins again.

Other strong influences on Jung were Schelling with his view that nature is a visible spirit; Rousseau's 'voice of nature within', and, crucially, the writings of Goethe, particularly *Faust*. Jung claimed to be distantly related to Goethe and therefore felt a strong affinity with him.

The 19th-century German Romantics Schopenhauer and Nietzsche, with their idea of the Will and the Übermensch, also contributed to what we would now call 'Jungian' psychology. The Vitalists such as Bergson and Driesch were the inspiration for ideas of the world as process rather than a static mechanistic view of the world. In such a world view, nature is animated by spirit as opposed to being regarded as inert matter. Monists such as the 3rd-century Neoplatonist, Plotinus, contributed their theory of the oneness of all things. Jung sometimes compared his work to Gnosticism, which became the first heresy in early Christian times. One of its teachings is that initially there was a primordial oneness of all reality and existence and that there is an inherent longing for a return to this unity. The Gnostics also held that wisdom comes through direct experience leading to individual insight rather than through received dogma backed up by authority. Jung's attitude to Freud's intellectual leadership reflected these Gnostic values. Manichaeism, which has its origins in Gnosticism, held that there was an essential dualism to everything. Hence evil was not just an absence of good but a force in its own right, equal in power to good. The 'reality of evil' was a phrase Jung often used in relation to the sadistic and inhumane aspects of psyche and society alike.

Alchemy, another below-the-line phenomenon, was first brought to Jung's attention by the Sinologist, Richard Wilhelm. Knowing of Jung's long-term interest in oriental ideas, Wilhelm sent him a Chinese alchemical text, 'The Secret of the Golden Flower' (Jung, 1967). Following his study of this text, Jung joyfully announced that the alchemists – Eastern and Western – had discovered a way of exploring the path to what Jung later called individuation, meaning the realization or actualization of the potentials inherently existing in the self. The alchemical process by which base matter is transformed into gold may be compared to the corresponding 'stages' in a classical Jungian analysis in which the patient 'individuates', becoming a more or less whole person. Neurosis is transformed into selfhood. These analytical stages will be more fully described below.

At the turn of the century there was a proliferation of spiritualist groups and cultic nature movements, some of which centred around sun worship. Jung's fascination with mysticism and the occult drew him to these – and he often cites the vivid imagery, centred on the sun's phallus, of a psychotic patient of J.J. Honegger, one of his students at the Burgholzi mental hospital. Psychiatry was Jung's first profession and the major influences here were Pierre Janet, Theodore Flournoy and Eugen Bleuler.

The best-known influence of all on Jung was that of Freud, with whom Jung collaborated from 1907 to 1913. Their inherent personality, cultural and conceptual differences led to an irreparable split growing up between them. From today's standpoint, their theoretical views remain highly complementary and Jung's analytical psychology is, in part, a blend of Freud's psychoanalysis and Alfred Adler's individual psychology.

Development in Britain

A Jung club had existed in London since 1922 but the need and wish for increasing professionalization of analytical psychology led a group of analysts under the leadership of Michael Fordham to found the Society of Analytical Psychology (SAP) in 1946. This was the first Jungian training institute in the world and Jung was persuaded to be its first president in spite of the fact that he was always anti-institutional and once said: 'Thank God I am not a Jungian!'

A further development in the UK was Fordham's collaboration with Gerhard Adler, who was also a founder member of the SAP, and Sir Herbert Read to produce the English edition of Jung's *Collected Works*.

Fordham felt strongly that the split between Jung and Freud in 1913 had been a disaster and devoted himself to repairing this split. In the course of his pioneering work with infants and children, he began to bring together Jungian archetypal theory with Kleinian 'phantasies', which are the primary contents of unconscious mental processes. One of Fordham's most radical extensions of classical Jungian theory was to postulate that a 'primary self' is at work in infants from the beginning (Fordham, 1993). Instead of the psyche increasingly working towards synthesis, Fordham concluded from his work with infants and children that this 'primary self' 'de-integrates' from a state of inner wholeness to bring the infant into relation with the environment (ibid.). In this way the infant's expectation of feeding evokes the appropriate response from mother's breast in the external world. Following psychoanalytic object relations theorists, who also postulated the existence of an ego from the start, Fordham filled a gap in both classical psychoanalytic and analytical psychology theory in showing that a primary self exists from the beginning of life.

Classical theory had always seen the self (sometimes the Self) as an underlying unifying principle in the psyche–soma of the human organism which did not become directly important until the second half of life, say from a person's late thirties. 'The self is … as a rule in an unconscious condition to begin with. But it is a definite experience of later life, when the fact becomes conscious' (Jung, 1977: 725).

Fordham also introduced new ideas on the transference–countertransference into Jungian clinical practice. What happened in London, where analytical psychology was being blended with psychoanalytic theory and practice, came to be known as the developmental school of Jungians as it spread to other countries (see Samuels, 1985).

These and other departures from classical Jungian theory have replicated the original Jung/Freud split. Broadly speaking, there are now three groups of Jungian analysts internationally. Andrew Samuels (ibid.) has constructed a tripartite classification of analytical psychology into schools: the developmental school, which incorporates psychoanalytic theory and practice; the classical school, seeking to extend Jung's own ways of thinking and working; and the archetypal school, concentrating on the play of images in the psyche.

Analysts such as Gerhard Adler, the founder of the Association of Jungian Analysts, disagreed with Fordham about the Jung/Freud split being a disaster, regarding the work of the two men as incompatible (Adler, 1979). According to Adler, Jung was essentially a *homo religiosus* for whom the meaning of anyone's life was of paramount importance. This is in direct contrast to Freud's anti-religious stance. If we compare the work of the two men, we see that Freud's system is rational, logical and limited, whereas Jung's is non-rational, religious and aims at a wide but imprecise image of wholeness.

THEORETICAL ASSUMPTIONS

Image of the person

Theory of opposites
The last paragraph of the previous section attempted to give a brief picture of the differences that exist in the Jungian community. Some practitioners would be placed firmly at the archetypal end of a spectrum of concerns, others would be called Kleinian Jungians and there are many who have a syncretistic approach to their work. The present chapter is a pluralistic attempt (Samuels, 1989a) to hold a balance between the diversity of analytical psychology today and the unity it still

possesses as having been inspired by Jung's own work. It is necessary to state Jung's premises here before going on to indicate subsequent developments.

The theory of psychological opposites lies at the basis of Jung's own approach to the psyche. He said, for instance, that opposites are the indispensable preconditions of all psychic life (Jung, 1955–56). To give a simple example, when someone is murderously angry with another person, their desire to destroy the other competes with its opposite – concern for other people backed up by parental and religious teachings. How it works out depends on the individual's ego holding the tension between the opposites of anger and concern – he or she may shout, or bite the bullet, or seek the intercession of another, or engage in self-reflection that undermines the 'justification' felt in relation to the anger. On a cultural level, opposites such as spirituality and sexuality also have to be reconciled in some way. For Jung, on both the individual and cultural levels, neurosis consists of resolution of the tension and interplay of opposites by the neurotic taking up a position aligned with one extreme or another. These days, it is widely accepted that there are usually more than three positions (the two extremes and their resolution) and 'the opposites' are usually presented as a spectrum of possibilities.

Analytical psychology itself is a synthesis of two opposites: a spiritual quest for self-knowledge with a scientific approach to the workings of the psyche. However, the spiritual and religious elements in Jung's work have made it difficult for him to be found acceptable in academic and intellectual circles, and some Jungians eschew this aspect of Jung (see Tacey, 1997). On the other hand, the empirical psychologist is equally a part of him, for instance in his experimental work with the word association test. This discovered the existence of feeling-toned 'complexes', which are relatively autonomous aggregates of emotions and experiences in the psyche clustered around an archetypally patterned core. This method initially attracted Freud's attention as he felt Jung was providing verification of the existence of the unconscious. However, Freud was repelled by the mystical and 'occult' Jung.

To do Jung's work full justice it is essential to maintain a balance between these two opposing forces. He pointed to the 'transcendent function' as the symbolical way of holding a balance between them and of withstanding the pull of one or the other, which would lead eventually to a rigid and rational psychology, or to its opposite: an equally rigid love of the irrational. To try to rationalize Jung by discarding the spiritual elements which speak of concerns for purpose and meaning is to reduce him to the status of a disciple of Freud. But to treat him only as a mystic leaves out the great body of work he contributed to empirical psychology. Readers are referred to the work of Joseph Cambray, George Hogenson, Jean Knox and Margaret Wilkinson.

Transcending that which presents itself to us as opposite is a chief dynamic running through Jung's work and the 'self' is a 'symbol' of this transcendence. In Jung's language, a symbol may be thought of as the intuitive way of knowing the as yet not fully knowable. 'The ... central archetype of "self" ... seems to be the point of reference for the unconscious psyche, just as the ego is the point of reference for consciousness. The symbolism associated with this archetype expresses itself on the one hand in circular, spherical, and quaternary forms, in the "squaring of the circle"; on the other hand in the image of the supraordinate personality' (Jung, 1977: 484).

The influences from the past on Jung's theory of opposites include Heraclitus' 'enantiodromia', which encompasses the idea that sooner or later everything turns into its opposite. An abrupt change from one strongly held position to an extreme other would be an example of this and is a time of great inner conflict for an individual. This is the Jungian equivalent of the object relations theory of 'splitting'. At this point there is a concentration of 'psychic energy', Jung's more neutral term for Freud's 'libido', which Jung saw as sexually loaded, in order to resolve the conflict by seeking for a new position. This method is also directly related to Hegel's dialectical scheme of thesis/antithesis/synthesis.

The object/subject dichotomy is another aspect of opposites exemplified, for instance, in what Jung terms the 'objective psyche'. This points to the 'reality of the psyche' as both a source of objective knowledge with its own autonomous way of functioning and as a container of more than personal or subjective contents. The latter aspect of the objective psyche Jung equated with the 'collective unconscious', the locus of universal motifs shared by all humans throughout time and space. One example is that of the personal mother of an individual, which has aspects in common with the universal image of the objective mother.

'Syzygy' is a term Jung applied to any set of yoked opposites, particularly sexually based ones like male/female, masculine/feminine, and yang/yin which he took from Chinese philosophy. Jung's own terms of 'animus/anima' denote the sexually opposite inner figures of a woman (animus) and a man (anima). This dichotomy has been modified by viewing anima/animus as interchangeable and as functioning equally in men and women to produce what might be seen as creative animation in both (Clark, 1987).

As stated above, the theory of archetypes concerns inherited patterns in the psychosomatic unconscious. It is Jung's way of linking two sets of opposites: psyche and soma and instinct and image. 'Synchronistic' experiences, which Jung claimed were acausal, underwrite this continuum, as the psychic can behave like the non-psychic and vice versa.

Synthesizing opposites is central to Jung's approach. It is also evidence of his personal pathology and points to an inner split that needed healing, which he attempted to do creatively through his work. Winnicott diagnosed Jung as having had a childhood psychosis, when he reviewed Jung's autobiographical work, *Memories, Dreams, Reflections*, and saw Jung's lifelong quest as one in search of healing (Winnicott, 1964). The mercurial and paradoxical tone that runs through so much of Jung's work stems from his fascination with opposites and this is why his writings are often experienced as being elusive (as well as allusive) and difficult to pin down.

Metapsychology

As far as metapsychology is concerned, Jung owes much to Freud's model. For instance, they have in common a dynamic, economic and topographical interaction as their centre. The dynamic and economic attributes in Jung's model are articulated by the investment of 'psychic energy' in varying degrees of equivalence amongst the topographical spheres of 'consciousness', 'personal unconscious' and 'collective unconscious.'

Consciousness has the 'ego' as its centre, this being the agent in the psyche that an individual identifies with as 'I'. 'Persona' lies also in the conscious sphere and is the mask that the individual presents to the world. The 'shadow' lies in the personal unconscious and represents all those aspects that are seen to be undesirable by the ego and which are, therefore, repressed. Interested reader are referred to Casement (forthcoming). 'Anima' and 'animus', like all 'archetypes', originate in the 'collective unconscious' and act unconsciously through projection when activated by an outer object, for example falling in love. The 'self' as the totality of the psyche is immanent throughout and functions both as the beginning and the end of all psychic activity. It mediates the opposites of good/evil, creativity/destruction, divine/human, etc., and offers the possibility of achieving wholeness or 'individuation' through the conjunction of opposites, or 'coniunctio'. Its presence is experienced as 'numinous', i.e. mysteriously powerful, and this is especially prevalent when there is a great deal of archetypal activity at work in an individual as, for instance, when collective unconscious contents are beginning to push through into consciousness.

Typology

Typology, the theory of innate personality differences, is an important, if highly problematic, part of Jung's work. Some time will be spent on its definition according to the Myers-Briggs model, one of the systems used to measure these differences (Myers, 1962).

One reason for Jung's interest in typology was the break with Freud, not only his own but also Alfred Adler's. By examining these and other 'personality clashes' throughout history, Jung sought to clarify his own position by showing how people with inbuilt differences can find it difficult to understand each other. The two basic concepts here are those of orientation of attitude to the world and of ways of 'functioning' in it. Attitude is measured on a scale ranging from extraversion at one end to introversion at the other. Individuals who are extraverted tend to focus on the outer world of people and the external environment. Extraverting in this way means that the individual is energized by what goes on in the outer world and that is where energy tends to be directed. Extraverts usually prefer to communicate more by talking than by writing and need to experience the world in order to understand it and thus tend to like action.

Introverts focus more on their own inner world and while introverting, energy is invested in that direction. Introverts tend to be more interested and comfortable when their work requires a good deal of their activity to take place quietly inside their heads. They like to understand the world before experiencing it, and so often think about what they are doing before acting.

The four functions concern ways of perceiving or acquiring information: sensation, intuition, thinking and feeling. Sensing is a way of perceiving through the senses of sight, hearing, smell, touch and taste. These inform an individual of what is actually happening out there and keep one in touch with the realities of a situation. Sensing types tend to accept and work with what is given in the here-and-now, and have a realistic and practical approach to life. They are adept at working with facts.

Intuiting is the other way of perceiving and is directed to the meanings and possibilities that go beyond information given through the senses. Intuition takes in the whole picture and tries to grasp the essential patterns at work in any situation. Intuitives value imagination and inspiration and are expert at seeing new possibilities.

Once information is acquired through one of the two perceiving functions, it is necessary to make decisions or judgements about it. This is done through the two functions of thinking and feeling.

Thinking predicts the logical consequences of any particular choice or action. Decisions are made objectively on the basis of cause and effect and of analysing and weighing the evidence inherent in any situation. Individuals with a preference for thinking seek an objective standard of truth and are good at analysing what is wrong with something.

Feeling, on the other hand, considers what is important without requiring it to be logical. Values to do with the human domain are at the basis of this way of functioning and the emphasis is upon how much one cares about any situation. Individuals with a preference for feeling like dealing with people and tend to respond in a sympathetic, appreciative and tactful way to others. Feeling as used in Jung's typology is to be differentiated from actual feelings or emotions and is, instead, to do with a capacity for making judgements or decisions based on humane values.

The four functions are heavily modified by the two attitudes and an extraverted sensation type is quite different to an introverted sensation type in being orientated to the outer world. There is usually a primary and secondary way of functioning: for example an individual may have extraverted sensation as their primary function and introverted feeling as their secondary one. The two primary functions will be in the conscious part of the psyche and will be more differentiated. The two functions that are less developed will be unconscious, and when activated will bring forth unconscious material. This is why Jung stated that a great deal can be learned from the least differentiated function. This also applies to the attitudes; for instance, an extravert will have introversion in the unconscious.

The final scale that applies to all this shows how a perceiving type orientates to life in a different way to a judging one. Perceiving through sensing and intuiting will lead to a flexible, spontaneous lifestyle. Individuals with this preference seek to understand life rather than control it. They prefer to stay open to experience, enjoying and trusting in their ability to adapt to the moment.

Individuals who have a judging approach through thinking and feeling tend to live in a planned and orderly way and want to regulate and control life. Decisions are taken which lead to closure and to a passing on to something else. Individuals with a preference for judging tend to be structured and organized in their approach. It is important to differentiate 'judging' used in the above context from judgmental; any of the types may be prone to the latter.

Conceptualization of psychological disturbance and health

The psychologically healthy individual is conceptualized as one who is free to interact with a degree of autonomy, in relation both to the environment and to the inner world of the psyche. The disturbed individual, on the other hand, is conceived as being the inverse of this in finding both inner and outer worlds too persecutory to relate to freely.

In analytical psychology, the unconscious is conceptualized as consisting of two realms: the 'personal unconscious' into which unacceptable contents are repressed, and the 'collective unconscious' which is the container of human-kind's psychic inheritance and potential. Psychological disturbance may be associated with both realms. For instance, too much repression of personal material that is unacceptable to the individual's conscious mind will result in neurotic symptoms. These will also manifest if innate potential is denied existence and not integrated more consciously into the individual's life. To summarize, severe repression in relation to either of these unconscious realms will result in pathological functioning on the individual's part.

The inherent split in Jung between the empirical psychologist and his mythopoeic side are evident in his approach to psychopathology. It has already been stated that he began work as a psychiatrist. In the course of this work he was increasingly interested in schizophrenia and came to conceptualize it as a psychogenic disorder within a psychosomatic framework. This insight pointed to the possibility of using a psychological approach to the treatment of schizophrenia in particular, and psychosis in general. An example of this is given in the section below.

Practice

This was revolutionary at the time in relativizing the view that every psychosis was a purely neurological disorder. Instead, Jung suggested that schizophrenia resulted in part from the invasion of consciousness by contents from the collective unconscious, which, in turn, pointed to the possibility that there was meaning in the utterances and behaviour of schizophrenics.

However, Jung's ambivalent attitude to psychopathology can be seen in the following: 'clinical diagnoses are important, since they give the doctor a certain orientation ... they do not help the patient. The crucial thing is the story' (Jung, 1963: 145). This has led to a concentration in treatment by some Jungian thera-pists on the story or myth of the individual as a way of helping an individual to achieve psychological health. 'The general ambivalence in depth psychology concerning psychopathology is to be found *par excellence* in the Jungian world' (Samuels, 1989b).

As a result, analytical psychology was greatly lacking in clinical teaching and had to borrow heavily from psychoanalysis to fill this gap. In this way, concepts such as ego defences, transference–countertransference and acting-out have been introduced into Jungian practice. This, combined with the mythopoeic stance, can produce effective results in restoring health and potency to individuals.

Acquisition of psychological disturbance

Jung questioned Freud's theory of early traumatic experience as the cause of neu-rosis and eventually rejected it as being too deterministic. The former said that looking for causes in an individual's past kept the person tied for ever to that past.

For Jung, on the other hand, there was an archetypal core at the centre of each neurotic symptom and he concentrated his attention on seeking this out. This is what is called the teleological approach in classical analytical psychology and is based on Aristotle's doctrine of final causes. This point of view looks at psycho-logical phenomena to find out what they are for and where they are leading to, which, in turn, gives symptoms a purpose that results in them being experienced as not only pathological. Jung called his approach 'synthetic' in contrast to what he termed Freud's 'reductive' method. The synthetic approach puts the empha-sis on what emerges from the starting point rather than on the starting point itself.

Depression seen from this viewpoint is both pathological as well as a manifes-tation of psychic energy being drawn from the conscious realm into the uncon-scious. This may arise when change is being signalled, for instance at the time of a major life event for an individual when the status quo has to be abandoned in favour of new life. If this is thwarted, the depression may well become chronic. There are many instances of this but a few will serve to illustrate the point: a young person who is unable to leave the parental home in order to take up the challenge of life; or an unhappily married person failing to deal with marital problems.

Perpetuation of psychological disturbance

A central feature for Jung in perpetuating psychological disturbance is the inabil-ity to separate from the mother, both personal and archetypal. He set out to demonstrate the failure to do so on the part of a young woman patient in his book *Symbols of Transformation* (Jung 1911–12). The patient's case history was sent to him by the psychiatrist, Flournoy, and, although Jung himself never met her, he conducts a long-distance analysis from her notes, which ends with a negative prognosis of schizophrenia. However, a close reading of the book reveals that the real patient is Jung himself simultaneously working through his break with Freud and developing his own ideas through self-analysis.

The main theme of the book is to show that remaining in a state of what Jung thought of as psychological incest is a prime cause for the perpetuation of neurosis and even psychosis. This is in contrast with Freud's Oedipal theory of incest, which is a longing for actual coitus with the mother. Jung, on the other hand, splits the image of mother into a duality – the personal and the archetypal – and states that symbolic re-entry into or union with the mother is necessary in order to be reborn. Thus, the individuated person is 'twice-born', the first time physically from the personal mother and the second time symbolically from the objective mother. The book was an expression of Jung's own rebirth in his late thirties and its contents signalled the split between him and Freud.

Splitting is seen in Kleinian theory as an early defence used in controlling the object by dividing it into a good and bad part-object. In the above, Jung is referring to splitting the image of the mother into personal and archetypal and into good and bad. Another similarity with psychoanalytic pathology is Jung's theory of 'participation mystique' which he took from the anthropologist, Lévy-Bruhl. This entails an identification between subject and object so that the latter is experienced as being a part of the former, e.g. a spirit or a fetish object. Looked at psychologically, this represents a neurotic dependence on another object because it is experienced as being part of the self and in this way has tremendous influence over the individual. This theory of Jung's is the equivalent of projective identification where part of the self is projected into another person and is then experienced as the projected part. For a critique of participation mystique see Shamdasani (2003).

In addition, there is the psychoanalytic concept of ego defences. These act to prevent unwanted personal and archetypal unconscious contents from breaking through into consciousness through the mechanisms of repression, denial and reaction-formation.

Another neurotic defence is that of extreme introversion which manifests in narcissistic feelings of grandiosity that act to keep an individual from being involved in interpersonal relationships. There is a place for healthy introversion as described above under 'Typology', but Western culture is identified with an extraverted thinking/sensation way of functioning so that many people feel forced to comply with this. If this compliance becomes pathological, they need to be helped to achieve a better balance between introversion and extraversion. In this way, it may be said that extreme extraversion can be as neurotic as extreme introversion. Change towards a healthier way of functioning is conceptualized in the Jungian canon as leaving a collective way of being and moving towards a more highly differentiated position as an individual. This is summed up in the Jungian concept of individuating. But as Kenneth Lambert has pointed out, Jung may have overemphasized the beneficial effects of transformation 'so sharply as to suggest that normality equals false conformity' (Lambert, 1981: 33).

Although Jung tended to see individuating as relating to the Jungian path towards selfhood, Samuels states that Klein's view of healthy normality is very similar and may be summed up as 'emotional maturity, strength of character, capacity to deal with conflicting emotions, a reciprocal balance between internal and external worlds, and, finally, a welding of the parts of the personality leading to an integrated self concept' (Samuels, 1985: 132).

Certainly both Klein and Jung would agree with Freud in seeing psychic health as the outcome of the transformation of neurosis as a result of the change that occurs through the successful outcome of therapy. This change may be viewed positively by family and friends if the individual is experienced as being more flexible and spontaneous and less rigid in interacting with the environment. However, the reverse also arises, and the person may be experienced as having become more selfish and less compliant – in other words as having changed for the worse.

PRACTICE

Goals of therapy

Goals of all kinds are of great importance in the classical Jungian approach to therapy, and its major concepts reflect this. These are based on a telelogical or goal-directed view enshrined in a doctrine of final causes. This views the self as functioning essentially to push an individual towards the fulfilment of his or her destiny whether or not the ego concurs with it. This is what Jung means by the reality of the psyche. The classical approach has largely been orientated to therapy for individuals in the second half of life, i.e. in their late thirties and over, and the goal is that of individuation or attaining wholeness by the individual. This telelogical view of the workings of the self points to an essentially religious attitude to life in its awareness of an immanent animated presence in all matter. Gerhard Adler's book, *The Living Symbol*, is an account of the individuating process at work in the analysis of a woman in the second half of life (Adler, 1961).

The first half of life was regarded by Jung as a period of extraversion where an individual is naturally orientated to worldly concerns such as marriage, children and career. It is in the late thirties that an individual's 'myth' challenges him or her to begin to separate from a collective worldly stance and to follow the quest for his or her own separate identity. Because of the heroic nature of this endeavour, Jung conceptualized it as a mythical confrontation with a dragon. This is, of course, a symbolic, inner dragon which is both the personal and the objective mother that seduces the individual into an attitude of inertia *vis-à-vis* life. The treasure which is hard to attain is that of the person's identity.

Both Jung's *Symbols of Transformation*, where the real 'patient' is Jung himself, and Adler's *The Living Symbol* are classical accounts about the goal of individuating in the second half of life. As previously mentioned, Fordham's reworking of the self as primary has resulted in his view that individuation as a goal is not confined to the second half of life. He cites Jung's claim that individuation is to be equated with achieving consciousness through differentiation of subject from object and shows that the child's gradual separation from the mother during its first two years of life is likewise a process of individuation (Fordham, 1976). In his synthesis of object relations theory and analytical psychology, Fordham demonstrated how, after birth, the infant's primary self de-integrates, and, through increasing identification with the mother, begins to move towards early object-relating. Control over bodily functioning is increasingly mastered and the beginnings of a conscience and consciousness are set in train, which includes a synthesizing of opposites such as good/bad and from this there develops a capacity for concern. All these, combined with the start of the process of symbolization, are the prerequisites of the goal of individuation.

In this way, Fordham broadened Jung's goal-centred theory of individuation to include infancy and childhood and by doing so has established that it is a natural part of the goal of maturing rather than a work against nature, as Jung claims. The latter does allow for the fact that individuals individuate unconsciously but claims that this is not comparable with individuating through a long analysis. A further consequence of Fordham's revision of individuation is the modification of the first half/second half of life dichotomy.

Rosemary Gordon talks of a twofold goal in analysis: one is that of curing, which is to do with the expansion of ego through assimilation of contents from the personal and the collective unconscious; the other goal is that of healing, which is involved in the individuating process and the working towards a more complex wholeness of the individual (Gordon, 1979).

The above has largely concentrated on the positive aspects of the individuation process as a goal but there is a great deal of pathology involved in it as well. One danger is that of breakdown when archetypal activity is very strong and the patient may be overwhelmed with contents from the collective unconscious. Another danger is that of identifying with the mana-like power of these contents, which can lead to inflation of the ego. Jung points to Nietzsche's identification with the semi-legendary Persian prophet Zarathustra, which eventually contributed to his madness (Jarrett, 1988). Jung states that if Nietzsche had been more aware that Zarathustra was an archetypal figure calling him – Nietzsche – to explore his own inner world, he would not have seen himself as a prophet and broadcast his message of the Übermensch. This is an example of individuating but with a lack of the conscious integration which would have grounded Nietzsche.

Depression is another consequence of the individuating process: it becomes pathological when an individual elevates the unconscious to a position of moral supremacy over the conscious part of the personality. The latter then feels inferior and worthless and the result is that the individual becomes depressed. According to Jung, Nietzsche, on the other hand, identified with the mana personality and his ego became inflated (Jung, 1953). For a critique of this see Casement, 2001 and Huskinson, 2004.

A further complication of the goal of individuation concerns the behaviour of an individual intent on fulfilling his or her potential in respect to others. An extreme example of this would be a psychopath, but on a more mundane level every individual must to a greater or lesser extent curb potential fulfilment in relation to other people. Jung's awareness of these limitations is expressed in his saying: 'Certainly that consciousness, which would enable us to live the great Yea and Nay of our own free will and purpose, is an altogether superhuman ideal. Still, it is a goal' (Jung, 1953: 59).

To go back to Gordon's model of curing, one of the goals of Jungian therapy would be the enlargement of the ego, in other words an increase in consciousness of both outer and inner worlds. This in turn would lead to a greater balance of the two and a spontaneous flow of energy between them. In short-term therapy, the goal would be to enable an individual to reach a better-adapted relationship to problems posed by the environment through supportive work by the therapist.

Selection criteria

Jungian therapists usually refer to individuals who come into therapy as 'patients' rather than 'clients', which has to do with the concept of suffering inherent in that word, the extension of this being the fact that every therapist has been through his or her own painful therapy. The term also expresses the patience that will be needed in a long therapy. Lastly, 'analysis' and 'therapy' are the terms used in the treatment of 'patients' who are being seen two or more times weekly. This is a simple way of differentiating this type of therapy from 'counselling', which applies to work with 'clients' on a once-weekly basis. However, it must be stressed that these are not hard and fast definitions as a patient seeing a therapist once a week may well be in analysis rather than counselling.

The terms 'analysis' and 'psychotherapy' are difficult to clearly differentiate. One way of doing so is to view analysis as working in greater depth and for longer duration than psychotherapy. In addition, Jungian psychotherapy may be understood as a method that employs some Jungian ideas.

There are no disorders that cannot be alleviated in some way by analysis or psychotherapy, and this will be demonstrated below. But there are a few caveats which it is important to bear in mind. Any persisting physical symptom must be treated by a medical practitioner and not viewed only as psychosomatic hysterical conversion which could justify analytical treatment. Another point to bear in mind is that the analytic process is primarily a relationship between two people and that a genuine rapport is necessary between them for any creative work to be made possible. If there is no 'fit' between analyst and patient from the start, it would be unwise to begin the treatment. It would be preferable to refer the patient to another practitioner.

At this point it would be useful to give an example of how a physical symptom may be treated both organically and analytically. A woman patient started analysis with me 11 years ago and her presenting problem was the messy breakdown of her marriage, combined with an increasingly problematic relationship with her teenage son. It was soon apparent that she was caught in a negative mother complex, which dominated all her relationships in a destructive way. A few months after starting therapy, she was diagnosed as having cancer of the breast and underwent major surgery. She needed many months of supportive therapy throughout this period but when she was ready to work on herself analytically, she began to see that the physical cutting out of 'mother' had been necessary in order to give her a chance to begin to separate herself from her complex and to find her own identity quite apart from that of 'mother'.

Traditionally, Jungian practitioners, in contrast to psychoanalysts, had a tendency to take on highly disturbed patients. Freud held to the view that psychoanalysis was really only suitable as a treatment for the neuroses but he looked to Jung's work with schizophrenic patients, initially as a psychiatrist, then as an analyst, to extend the frontiers of psychoanalysis to the treatment of the psychoses.

Winnicott's claim that Jung's quest for self-healing, rather than resolution through analysis, came from the latter's psychotic illness (Winnicott, 1964), is not borne out by early psychotherapeutic work done by Jung in the treatment of schizophrenia. In a paper he wrote in 1919 (Jung, 1960), Jung explores the possibility of psychotherapy for the psychoses. Initially he summarizes the difficulties of any such endeavour, e.g. that any apparent cure would be seen only as a remission of symptoms, and admits that he is not optimistic in this regard. He stresses the importance of searching out the psychological aetiology and course of psychosis and says that this is more easily done in comparatively simple cases.

He gave the example of a young girl who suddenly became schizophrenic. She was a peasant's daughter, who had trained as a teacher and who until that time had displayed no abnormal symptoms. One night she heard the voice of God, and Jesus also appeared to her. When Jung saw her, she was calm but completely uninterested in her surroundings, and her answers to questions were given without any accompanying affect – as Jung comments, she might as well have been talking of the stove which she was standing next to, rocking gently back and forth all the while.

Jung asked her if she had kept any notes of her conversations with God and, saying yes, she handed him a piece of paper with a cross on it. Eventually, after a long period of questioning her, Jung discovered that the young woman felt herself to be in a state of sin because she had been attracted to a man she saw the day that her symptoms appeared. That night she experienced a religious conversion and God appeared to her.

Jung acknowledged that there must be a predisposition in someone who becomes schizophrenic but held that it is possible to discover the psychogenic causes of the disease and in this way to alleviate the symptoms. In Jung's view, psychosis was the result of a poorly differentiated consciousness and a sparsely stocked personal unconscious so that the subject is at risk of invasion by arche-typal contents from the realm of the collective unconscious. This is why he advo-cated the identification of mythological motifs in the expressions of psychotics. He went on to associate psychosis with anima/animus and the neuroses with the workings of the ego (Jung, 1951).

All Jungian analysts have an internship in psychiatry as part of their training and work psychotherapeutically with psychotic and borderline patients, in cir-cumstances where these patients are contained in a holding environment and are also on medication. Most of the work done with these patients would be psy-chotherapeutic rather than analytic, i.e. supportive and aimed at alleviating symptoms rather than the long and complicated inner journey that a full analy-sis involves. To summarize, as long as the practitioner is not over-optimistic about outcome and as long as the patient is contained in a holding environment, Jungian therapy can be applied effectively to psychosis.

Addiction is another complicated area that some Jungians have worked with therapeutically. The Italian, Luigi Zoja, has worked intensively in therapy with drug addicts and has come to see that the underlying motivation amongst young addicts is a need for the kind of initiation rituals that are so lacking in Western society (Zoja, 1985). He points to the need for treatment that is aimed at helping addicts to give up drugs and to heal damaged organs, also taking into account the underlying psychological needs that are expressed by addiction. He advocates bringing people together in a community which instils a common spirit and goal and in this way creates an atmosphere of being part of a mysti-cal group. This gives meaning both to the addiction and to the process of treatment.

All of this echoes work done by anthropologists and sociologists; for instance the French anthropologist, Arnold van Gennep, in his writing about rites of passage described every ritual as having three distinct phases (van Gennep, 1960). The first is that of separation from the profane world; the second is being contained in the sacred world that exists outside normal social intercourse; the third is reincorporation into the world but with a new identity. The present writer works with the idea that a whole analysis or therapy is a rite of passage, as well as every session, with separation, containment and reincorporation being part of the process in each case.

To elaborate further the need for meaning and containment there is also the need for 'communitas', the term Victor Turner, the anthropologist, applies to a mystical coming together for a joint purpose, in which individual identity is sub-merged in a meaningful way into community feeling as, for example, on a pil-grimage (Turner, 1969). The negative correlate of this is what the sociologist, Erving Goffman, calls the 'stripping process', which is to be seen at work in total institutions, e.g. the Army, prison and hospitals (Goffman, 1961). This involves stripping the person of any individual identity in a brutal fashion by making them wear a uniform, by giving them a number instead of a name, etc. Many hospitals and psychiatric wards exemplify this negative stripping process at work rather than any positive group feeling of *communitas* and asylum. It is this dimension that psychotherapy can bring to bear on psychiatry.

Phobias are also amenable to analytical insight, although the symptoms may persist, e.g. fear of flying. When a patient is able to relate this fear to the anxiety that comes from being out of control – as in the sensation of being out of touch with the earth combined with not being at the controls of the plane – then it may be possible to connect the phobia to its origins in infancy or childhood. One patient was able to recall being terrified every time her father threw her up in the air. Another managed to remember the fact that she had been dropped as an infant. Some behavioural therapy may also be required in working with phobic patients.

In addition, it may seem beneficial for a patient to have family or couples therapy when these sorts of problem begin to dominate the therapeutic work in each session. Another way of locating a major problem at any time is through working with dreams. These tend to throw up a constant stream of images related to a problem when it moves into the acute stage.

Where a patient is in both individual and another form of therapy at the same time, it is vital for the analyst to be aware of any signs of splitting between the two modalities, e.g. all the good being seen as belonging in one and all the bad in the other. An example of this is a patient I have who is also going to Alcoholics Anonymous, who began to split between the good analyst and the bad sponsor. By becoming aware of this in the analytic work, she was enabled to modify her projections on to both. Some analytic patients come from GPs and psychiatry and are on medication such as antidepressants or psychotropic drugs. In these cases, it is important for the therapist not to become involved in the medical treatment, although the therapist may well have to liaise with the medical practitioner involved with the patient. This must be done with the consent of the patient at all times, the only exception being when a patient may be a danger to him/herself or to others, particularly a child. Once again the therapist must be aware of possible splitting between, say, a GP and the therapist and to take steps to counteract this.

It is clear from all the above that therapy not only does not preclude treatment by other modalities but actively welcomes this as long as discrete boundaries are maintained and there is sufficient awareness of splitting and idealization.

Qualities of effective therapists

Therapy is a vocational profession and therapists may experience an inner calling which usually arises from their own deep psychic wounds. If these are left largely unhealed, there is a danger that a therapist will react to patients pathologically from neurotic counter-transference feelings, e.g. retaliating to or overidentifying with patients' disturbed behaviour. Where these wounds have been sufficiently healed, a therapist will be able to empathize with a patient's trauma and be of service. Self-awareness on the therapist's part combined with empathy are the key to effective therapeutic intervention.

Every therapist has an extensive training analysis lasting for several years. This is preceded by pre-training analysis. For the duration of training, a trainee therapist also works under supervision with two senior analysts or therapists with clinical cases. The developmental school has started to require candidates to undertake a two-year infant observation with an attendant discussion group as part of training. However, it is important to pay attention here to Daniel Stern's recent writings on the difference between the psychoanalytic infant and the observed infant (Stern, 1985).

A training candidate does not need to be medically qualified but has to have had some experience of working in a psychiatric unit. Candidates also need to have a background in the helping professions, for example as teachers, social workers or counsellors.

It was Jung who first pointed out in 1911 the necessity of a training analysis for all would-be analysts while he was President of the International Psychoanalytic Association from 1910 to 1914 (Jung, 1961). The therapist's most important tool in therapeutic work is his or her own personality and character, which needs to be married to a capacity for awareness of limitations with regard to the level of disturbance that can be tolerated from patients. This capacity for self-awareness must be combined with what Gerhard Adler called the four 'Hs': honesty, humanity, humility and humour which, in turn, need to be linked to skills acquired during a long training lasting for several years. This includes personal therapy and supervision, theoretical seminars and scientific and clinical meetings which seek to build on an inherent psychological-mindedness in the trainee therapist. Continuous professional development is needed to ensure that a practitioner stays up to date with new theoretical and clinical ideas.

Therapeutic relationship and style

Above all a therapist must to be able to combine spontaneity with an appropriate observance of boundaries. The first session is taken up with information-giving on the part of the patient and setting up of the therapeutic 'contract'. This includes agreeing between the therapist and patient the amount to be paid per session, the number of sessions that will be necessary per week across a spectrum that ranges from one session weekly to five, and whether the patient would benefit from being on the couch or in a chair. This 'contract' or therapeutic alliance is negotiated with what may be thought of as the functioning part of the patient's personality and will be needed throughout the work in relation to the more pragmatic side of analysis, as detailed above.

After establishing the contract, it is necessary to create a holding environment wherein the patient can feel safe to regress and to reflect on experiences that happen in therapy. There is no set plan for each session and this can often feel threatening for a patient, who will need to be able to endure not knowing what may happen. In order for this to take place, the therapist must communicate a feeling of security to the patient that he or she will not be let down. In this holding environment, the therapist must be sensitive to the feeling-tone of a session, for instance, whether silence represents an angry withholding or resistance on the patient's part, or whether it is a creative silence which is allowing the patient to be truly in touch with his or her inner world.

The therapeutic approach is passive/receptive rather than active or directive. It is also somewhat formal and there is no physical contact between the two participants. Added to this, there is virtually no self-disclosure on the part of the majority of therapists apart from the minimum information required by the prospective patient to make an informed choice of therapist. It is always possible, even after years of experience, to be tempted into revealing personal details about oneself. In a recent session, a long-standing patient of mine recounted a dream which portrayed precisely an aspect of my personal life which she could not consciously know. I had to struggle momentarily with responding in a congratulatory manner about her wonderful intuition and with a desire on my part to show off, as it was a positive thing that she had intuited. Humour is a necessary quality for any therapist but so is the awareness that too much of it in a session may represent a manic defence.

In the final stages of a long therapy, a practitioner will begin to be more open in the interaction, perhaps at times admitting to liking something, or vice versa. But, on the whole, boundaries are all-important to this approach so that the analyst's stance will remain largely neutral and formal.

Major therapeutic strategies and techniques

Some Jungian analysts and therapists only use the couch, some only the chair, whereas others, like the writer, use either depending on the patient, or even both at different stages in the analytic work with the same patient. The couch is beneficial for a patient who is strongly resistant to regression, when this is necessary, to a more infantile stage. Resistance involves unconscious ego defences such as repression, denial, reaction-formation and 'acting-out' or 'acting-in' in various ways. The latter can include almost anything, but some examples would be flooding sessions with dream material, being consistently late or bringing an 'agenda' each time. The therapist needs to be sensitive to the timing of when it is safe to dismantle defences. This is most likely to be when the patient has sufficient ego strength to do so. To sum up, it may be said that the couch is appropriate to a more psychoanalytic approach.

The chair, on the other hand, is suited to the classical Jungian strategy which is based on a dialogue between therapist and patient.

Transference/countertransference, as defined by psychoanalysis, are central to a developmental therapist's approach. In Freud's words, transferences are:

> new editions or facsimiles of the impulses and phantasies which are aroused and made
> conscious during the progress of the analysis; but they have this peculiarity, which is
> characteristic for their species, that they replace some earlier person by the person of the
> physician. (Freud, 1912)

Countertransference applies to the therapist's unconscious reactions to the patient, particularly to the latter's transferences. Jung was alert to the utility of these reactions, referring in 1920 to countertransference as 'an important organ of information' (Jung, 1954). Freud tended to depreciate countertransference as residual neurosis on the part of the therapist but Jung's greater flexibility enabled Fordham to develop a detailed theory of there being two kinds of countertransference. The first he calls 'syntonic', which is when an analyst may be so in tune with a patient's inner world that he finds himself feeling or behaving in a way that he comes to realize, on reflection, shows that there are aspects of his patient's inner workings projected into him (Fordham, 1957). This process puts at the disposal of the patient parts of the therapist that are spontaneously responding to the former in a way that is needed.

The other sort of countertransference Fordham hit upon when he made a recording of a session of analysis he conducted with a boy of 11 who had problems with aggressive feelings. Later, on listening to the recording of this session, Fordham discovered that his own aggression had been in evidence, in that a reactivation of a past situation from his own childhood had replaced his relation to the patient. During that time, no analysis of the patient was possible. This phenomenon Fordham termed 'illusory' countertransference.

A therapist working with these concepts of personal transference and countertransference in mind would use interpretation both in and of the transference as a central strategy. All this is directed towards reparation of the patient's damaged inner object world and to an improved interaction with the environment. Working with the above kind of transference/countertransference represented a major change of strategy to Jung's original one, the end-goal of which is individuation.

The change process in therapy

The change process in Jungian therapy has already been signalled. Pathological symptoms are usually what bring an individual into therapy and may be seen as the opener of the way into a deeper awareness on the part of that individual. This chapter has already stated that if there are physical symptoms they need to be diagnosed by a medical practitioner in order to ascertain that medical treatment is not necessary alongside analysis. If the symptoms appear to be largely neurotic, i.e. originating in the psyche, then they can be treated analytically. In fact, symptoms may well persist as the therapy progresses.

The work of therapy, in this regard, is to identify what lies behind the symptom. For instance, repressed emotional disturbances will often manifest somatically if they are not attended to. Above all, therapy is an inner journey and the goal of this quest is the individual's true identity, which may have been hidden for a whole lifetime under a 'false self'. It is, in fact, in the patient's symptom or wound that his or her true identity lies hidden and here we see again the analogy with alchemy of the base metal being transformed into gold. Jung's depiction of an analyst as a 'wounded healer' stems from this 'telelogical' view of pathology.

Alchemy grew more important in Jung's work and he saw what he thought of as the archetypal transference/countertransference reflected in the alchemical text, *Rosarium Philosophorum* (Jung, 1954). For his own purposes he used 10 of the woodcut prints that make up the *Rosarium*. These illustrate the story of an incestuous couple, sometimes depicted as king and queen, sometimes as brother and sister, and at others as sun and moon. The human figures are fully clothed in some of the pictures and naked in others. Jung thought that these 10 pictures contained the overall structure of an in-depth analysis culminating in individuation.

These pictures are for Jung a representation of the criss-crossing of both the conscious and unconscious relationship of analyst and patient. This is multifaceted, i.e. on the personal as well as collective unconscious level, and involves the anima/animus of both individuals. As the analysis deepens beyond the persona and conventional level the couple are shown without clothes in the third picture called 'The naked truth' (Jung, 1954: Figure 3). Figure 4 shows the two still trying to hide their 'shadow' from each other: when it comes into the analysis it can lead to the termination of the work.

If the analysis survives this stage a conjunction takes place between the two protagonists, who are then joined together in working towards greater consciousness. This is depicted in 'The conjunction' (Jung, 1954: Figure 5), which shows the couple having intercourse. However, as the whole of the analytic process is an 'as if' rather than a concrete endeavour, this is a symbolic conjunction and physical gratification between the two has to be forgone. This sacrifice leads to death-like feelings, which are depicted in the next picture. The two have to endure the difficulties that ensue from this stage of the analysis and the analyst needs to withstand the temptation to 'explain' what is happening and to give reassurances to the analysand.

If the analytic container can withstand all the difficult feelings up to this point, there will come a time when the analysand begins to be aware of experiencing the beginnings of 'new life'. This is the coming into being of the capacity for symbolization and is depicted in 'The new birth' (Jung, 1954: Figure 10) as an androgynous figure symbolizing the union of opposites. Eros is central to this kind of Jungian analysis, not just that which is sexually charged but also that which is to do with soul. In both meanings of the word, psyche needs eros.

The *Rosarium*, according to Jung, depicts the structure of a classical Jungian analysis, during the course of which dream analysis takes place through 'amplification' of dream images, which connects them to mythological and cultural motifs. 'Active imagination' may also be part of the work. Jung described this as dreaming with open eyes (Jung, 1921).

The developmental approach would look at change as reparation, through work in the transference, of damaged inner objects and an increased capacity for more real interaction with the environment. Compulsive behaviour will be modified, symptoms will be recognized as having inner meaning, and the capacity for tolerating anxiety and guilt will increase.

The lack of change is usually due to fear of relinquishing old patterns of behaviour even though they cause suffering. A patient may cling to a pathological way of functioning because it maintains fantasies of omnipotence, which are dependent on the pathology being experienced as the only thing the patient has in life. In some instances, the internalized parental voice is so strong that the person cannot go against it as doing so incurs unbearable feelings of guilt about getting better.

Ambivalence is common: patients often present with a compliant conscious wish to change and an unconscious defence against doing so. A male patient brought a dream early on in the analysis which showed him coming to the defence of a weak man who was losing a fencing match against an unknown but stronger opponent. We looked at this as his strong ego defending the vulnerable parts of himself that felt under attack from me in the sessions.

Limitations of the approach

Jung was an empiricist and his metapsychology evolved out of his phenomenological observations. There are Jungian hypotheses which could lend themselves to even more rigorous epidemiological research than has so far been done, e.g. the word association test and psychological types. There is much in the writings which is prospective and has potential for further elaboration.

There is also much that is faulty, as scholars are increasingly discovering. A recent example is Richard Noll's debunking of the solar phallus man alluded to above. In his book, Noll asserts that popular literature detailing myths about sun cults from antiquity was easily available at the time. This undermines Jung's claim that the patient's vision gave credence to his discovery of the 'collective unconscious' (Noll, 1994). For a critique of Noll, readers are referred to Shamdasani, 1998.

Deficiencies in Jungian clinical theory and practice were corrected by Michael Fordham's work in synthesizing analytical psychology and psychoanalysis. Apart from work in transference/countertransference, Jungians have benefited from incorporating into their ethos insights on ego defences and resistance and from using the couch, where patients may be enabled to get in touch with persecutory anxiety and envy.

In recent years there has been an increase in the serious charges levelled at Jung, and, by extension, at analytical psychology. Post-Jungians are becoming more rigorous in their efforts to face honestly Jung's failings in regard to his alleged attitudes of racism, anti-Semitism and sexism.

There are instances of these sentiments on Jung's part, although Geoffrey Cocks offers in his defence that 'Jung conceded more to the Nazis by his words than his actions' (Cocks, 1985: 134). Casement, 2001, contains a number of accounts of this, including a contribution by Jung's secretary, Aniela Jaffé. Several analytical psychologists are represented, amongst whom are James and Thomas Kirsch, Erich Neumann and his son, the psychoanalyst Mishal Neumann, and Andrew Samuels. My own research produced a file from the British Foreign Office dated 1946 in which Jung is accused of being a Nazi collaborator. This was sent to the British War Crimes Executive at Nuremberg by the Legal Advisor at the Foreign Office suggesting the best thing that could be done with it was to put it straight into the waste paper basket.

The concepts of 'self' (supraordinate personality) and 'numinosity' have tremendous potential for healing but, conversely, can be extremely hazardous when they lead to inflation of the ego. This arises when an individual becomes identified with the archetype of the Redeemer and loses touch with his or her common humanity. The danger then is that instead of using these concepts as a psychological tool, analytical psychology can be turned into a religious cult with all that that means in the impulse to convert, proselytize and to become a closed system.

Case example

The client

The case below is a fiction as are all the vignettes included above. In presenting this I will be attempting to illustrate Jungian therapy in relation to working with a patient suffering from obsessive-compulsive disorder (OCD). First, though, I would like to give a brief description of a patient of Jung's who was severely afflicted with this disorder and whom he attended while working as a psychiatrist at the Burghölzli Hospital from 1900–1910. I am drawn to this case for two reasons: one is that the compulsive symptom reminds me of the poignant fictional character of Dr Manette in Dickens' *A Tale of Two Cities*. The other is that it illustrates how even before he met Freud, Jung was thinking psycho-dynamically in seeing severe mental disease as having a psychogenic origin. I will give a brief outline of that patient before presenting a fictional case to demonstrate how Jungian therapy affords some understanding of what may underlie obsessive-compulsive disorder.

The woman described by Jung had been an in-patient at the Burghölzli for 35 years and had neither spoken nor reacted to anything. She lay in bed with her head bowed, her back bent with the knees slightly drawn up all the while making continuous rubbing movements with her hands. As a result 'thick horny patches developed on the palms. She kept the thumb and index finger of her right hand together as if sewing'(Jung, 1960: 172). Prior to becoming bedridden, the patient had been sitting in the same attitude in which she afterwards lay in bed but in earlier days she had made rapid sweeping movements of the arms across her right knee as if she were sewing or polishing shoes. After her death, her 70-year-old brother came to the funeral at which Jung asked if he remembered what had caused the sister's illness. The brother told Jung that it was due to a failed love affair with a shoemaker.

The 'case' I am presenting is of a woman in her mid-fifties whom I will call Catherine. She has attended therapy for twice-weekly sessions over a period of five years but never used the couch although she is aware it is there and could lie on it if she chose. She alludes to it from time to time but says lying down would make her feel too vulnerable. Her presenting problem was that she suffered from severe anxiety diagnosed by her general practitioner on one of her periodic visits to him, who then referred her to me for therapy. I have come to see her as suffering from obsessive-compulsive disorder (OCD) which manifests in ritualized compulsive behaviour that increasingly makes life problematic, for instance, bodily functioning like using the lavatory. She spends at least two hours in the morning in the bathroom trying to urinate and have a bowel movement which has become a ritualized part of her daily routine. She has to use a particular brand of toilet paper which has to be kept folded in a certain way, needs to shower after each visit to the lavatory and can only have a successful evacuation in her own bathroom.

The other tasks she needs to perform are equally ritualized and she spends several hours a day cleaning her small flat. Her work and social life are severely restricted as she can only leave the house for short periods of time and is unable to hold down a regular job of any kind. In the past she did occasionally try to do temporary office work but her obsessive attention to detail makes it impossible for any task to be completed. It also antagonized colleagues at meetings where she would become obsessed, like a dog with a bone, with one item on the agenda. In the last few years she has lived on social security implemented by an allowance from her aging mother.

She is an only child and was both doted on but also used by her parents as a pawn in their marital discord. As this was a strongly religious household, the discord could not be expressed openly but was covert and insidious and she has gradually been able to admit that her childhood often felt insecure with out-of-control feelings between the parents just below the surface calm. The only thing she felt she had control over from an early age was her bodily functioning. As a result, this became the one area that felt safe as she could control it by holding in her urine and faeces for long periods of time. This has now become so much part of her functioning that she cannot 'let go' even when she wants which has led to physical symptoms she often consults her doctor about.

The therapy

The first session is devoted to assessing whether the patient is suitable for Jungian therapy – my own criterion being whether any creative work can be done together. Given the severity of Catherine's presenting problems and her lack of psychological insight, I assessed the goals here needed to be realistic but as the session progressed it seemed possible to aim for an improvement in the paucity of her life at least on an inner level. Once we had agreed to start the therapy, I then dealt with the practical issues involved in setting up the therapeutic contract like frequency of sessions and payment.

From the outset of the therapy, she has never asked to use the bathroom but, instead, constantly evacuates her rage with the world which she experiences as being the cause of her feelings of frustration. The same issues are aired in each session which include her feelings of isolation, her frustration with her own lack of initiative usually followed by making excuses for it, and her complaints about other people, i.e. neighbours or 'friends' – the latter being the few people who inhabit her world at a superficial level. She arrives for each session on the dot and lets me know in advance if she is going to be even five or ten minutes late due to a visit to the doctor. Visits to the doctor are the only outings she has apart from coming to therapy. Her sole companions are the fishes she keeps in an aquarium which she ritually buries in the small garden at the back of her flat when any of them dies.

From time to time she develops a crush on a man she happens to see somewhere and she can spend months fantasizing about developing a friendship with him. It is always thought of in terms of friendship and she avoids any exploration of sex either to do with herself, her parents' married life or any public figure in the news due to a sexual indiscretion. My sense of her is that she is not asexual but that her sexuality is deeply repressed. Any sexual fantasies she may have are never mentioned or brought to the sessions and she avoids attempts on my part to explore them with her.

She has brought dreams to the sessions almost from the start of the therapy but this is more from her conviction that that is what she is supposed to do than out of any real interest in them. The Jungian approach to dreams is that they are complementary to what happens in conscious waking life and this is the case with Catherine. Her dreams are always full of people but until recently none of them, apart from her parents who make frequent appearances, can be distinguished as individuals. I have interpreted that to mean that she cannot relate to others as individuals in their own right as they are only an amorphous mass for her. This has changed in recent months when she has had dreams which show her being attracted to a man even to the point of wanting to marry him. The man usually resembles someone she has known slightly in the past and felt drawn to but in the dreams there is usually a father figure who disapproves of any possible union. I have interpreted this as both her personal father in the outer world and the harsh authoritarian father that inhabits her inner world. The fact that this has now become constellated in her dreams may point to her beginning to become more conscious that it is this inner figure which dominates her life and keeps her imprisoned in her solitary state. That she is now dreaming of uniting with her inner masculine side or animus is a sign that she is slowly reaching towards the wholeness that would enable life to become more fulfilling.

Although at one level, Catherine seems to have no insight into what is wrong with her as she remains stuck in her obsessive and compulsive behaviour, she does at the same time display some awareness about the fact that her repeating actions – the ritualized cleaning of herself, her flat, the aquarium – intrusive and inappropriate as they are may also serve the purpose of neutralizing her anxiety, at least to some extent and then only temporarily. Although she does go to her doctor at frequent intervals and has medication prescribed, including for her anxiety, she never takes any of it. One reason for this is that she was brought up in a strictly religious household where it was considered self-indulgent to try to alleviate suffering but instead it had to be borne without complaint. Another reason, not as yet consciously acknowledged by her, is that this is not the answer and would at best act to suppress her anxiety rather than get to the core of it.

Catherine displays many of the characteristics of OCD set out in the *DSM-IV* such as a preoccupation with details, perfectionism that interferes with task completion, inflexibility about matters of morality, inability to discard anything even when it has no sentimental value, miserliness both towards herself and others, and she displays both rigidity and stubbornness.

Although she does not practice the religion in which she was brought up, much of her behaviour can be seen as ritualistic. In childhood she had to perform many religious acts but as an adult she discarded them as meaningless. However, they continue to live on in the highly ritualized way she performs everyday acts, including coming to therapy. This is where Jungian therapy can offer some insight and Jung himself stated: 'We are still as much possessed by autonomous psychic contents as if they were Olympians. Today they are called phobias, obsessions, and so forth; in a word, neurotic symptoms. The gods have become diseases…' (Jung, 1967: 37).

As Catherine has gained some awareness of the hidden numinous meaning in her symptoms, she has begun to feel less anxious and distressed about them. Although she continues to have the symptoms she is more accepting of them. My role as therapist is not to direct her to the nearest religious centre but to continue working with her on increasing the insight that may enable her eventually to find a more creative way of living the underlying religious meaning in her symptoms.

Epilogue

I would like to end this chapter by returning to Jung and to the intellectual historian, Henri Ellenberger's account of what he calls Jung's 'creative illness' during the period 1913–19 (Ellenberger, 1970). This followed the break with Freud (who had also undergone the experience of a 'creative illness') in 1913 when Jung felt deserted by all his friends and went through an emotional illness akin to a psychotic episode. He continued his work with patients and his relations with his family but spent a great deal of time alone brooding by Lake Zurich and relating to unconscious processes through 'active imagination'. This method of dreaming while still awake involves starting from an image, word or picture and allowing fantasies associated with it to evolve. This can create a new situation which allows unconscious contents to surface (Jung, 1955–56).

Ellenberger goes on to say that a 'creative illness' remits suddenly and is followed by a short period of euphoria and increased activity. The end result is a permanent change in personality evinced by feelings of being freed from the burden of social conventions and a move towards valuing one's own subjective feelings and ideas. This helps to throw light on the ideological battles that have taken place in the analytical world since the beginning of the last century and that continue to take place up to the present time.

REFERENCES

CW refers to The Collected Works of C.G. Jung. London: Routledge & Kegan Paul.
Adler, G. (1961) The Living Symbol. New York: Pantheon Books.
Adler, G. (1979) Dynamics of the Self. London: Conventure.
Casement, A. (2001) Carl Gustav Jung. London: Sage.
Casement, A. (2006) 'The Shadow' in Renos Papadopoulos (ed.), Handbook of Jungian Psychology: Theory, Practice and Application. London: Routledge.
Clark, G. (1987) 'Animation through the analytical relationship: the embodiment of self in the transference and countertransference', Harvest, 13: 104–14.
Cocks, G. (1985) Psychotherapy in the Third Reich: The Goering Institute. London and New York: Oxford University Press.
Ellenberger, H.F. (1970) The Discovery of the Unconscious. New York: Basic Books.
Fordham, M. (1957) New Developments in Analytical Psychology. London: Routledge & Kegan Paul.
Fordham, M. (1993) The Making of an Analyst. London: Free Association Books.
Fordham, M. (1976) The Self and Autism. London: Heinemann.

Freud, S. (1912) Standard Edition Vol XII ed. and trans. J. Strachey. London: Hogarth Press.

Goffman, E. (1961) *Asylums*. New York: Anchor Books.

Gordon, R. (1979) 'Reflections on curing and healing', *Journal of Analytical Psychology*, 24(3).

Huskinson, L. (2004) *Nietzsche and Jung*. Hove and New York: Brunner-Routledge.

Jarrett, L. (ed.) (1988) 'Nietzsche's Zarathustra: notes of the seminar given in 1934–39 by C.G. Jung', *Bolingen Series XCIX*. Princeton, NJ: Princeton University Press.

Jung, C.G. (1911–12) *Symbols of Transformation*, in *CW*, Vol. V.

Jung, C.G. (1921) *Psychological Types*, in *CW*, Vol. VI.

Jung, C.G. (1951) *Aion*, in *CW*, Vol. IX(2).

Jung, C.G. (1953) *Two Essays on Analytical Psychology*, in *CW*, Vol. VII.

Jung, C.G. (1954) *The Practice of Psychotherapy*, in *CW*, Vol. XVI.

Jung, C.G. (1955–56) *Mysterium Coniunctionis*, in *CW*, Vol. XIV.

Jung, C.G. (1960) *The Psychogenesis of Mental Disease*, in *CW*, Vol. III.

Jung, C.G. (1961) *Freud and Psychoanalysis*, in *CW*, Vol. IV.

Jung, C.G. (1963) *Memories, Dreams, Reflections*. London: Collins/Routledge & Kegan Paul.

Jung, C.G. (1967) *Alchemical Studies*, in *CW*, Vol. XIII.

Jung, C.G. (1977) *The Symbolic Life*, in *CW*, Vol. XVIII.

Jung, C.G. (1988) *Nietzsche's Zarathustra*, ed. James L. Jarrett. Princeton, NJ: Princeton University Press.

Lambert, K. (1981) *Analysis, Repair and Individuation*. London: Academic Press.

Myers, L. (1962) *The Myers-Briggs Type Indicator*. Palo Alto, CA: Consulting Psychologists Press.

Noll, R. (1994) *The Jung Cult*. Princeton, NJ: Princeton University Press.

Samuels, A. (1985) *Jung and the Post-Jungians*. London: Routledge & Kegan Paul.

Samuels, A. (1989a) *The Plural Psyche: Personality, Morality and the Father*. London: Routledge.

Samuels, A. (1989b) *Psychopathology*. London: H. Karnac Books.

Shamdasani, S. (1998) *Cult Fictions*. London: Routledge.

Shamdasani, S. (2003) *Jung and the Making of Modern Psychology: The Dream of a Science*. Cambridge: Cambridge University Press.

Stern, D. (1985) *The Internal World of the Infant*. New York: Basic Books.

Tacey, D. (1997) 'Jung in the Academy: devotions and resistances', *Journal of Analytical Psychology*, 42(2).

Turner, V. (1969) *The Ritual Process: Structure and Anti-Structure*. London: Routledge & Kegan Paul.

Van Gennep, A. (1960) *Rites of Passage*. London: Routledge & Kegan Paul.

Winnicott, D.W. (1964) 'Book review: *Memories, Dreams, Reflections*, by C.G. Jung', *International Journal of Psychoanalysis*, 45.

Zoja, L. (1985) *Drugs, Addiction and Initiation: The Modern Search for Ritual*. London: Sigo Press.

SUGGESTED FURTHER READING

Casement, A. and Tacey, D. (eds) (2006) *The Idea of the Numinous: Contemporary Jungian and Psychoanalytic Perspectives*. London and New York: Brunner-Routledge.

Kirsch, T. (2000) *The Jungians: A Comparative and Historical Perspective*. London: Routledge.

Knox, J. (2003) *Archetype, Attachment, Analysis*. Hove and New York: Brunner-Routledge.

Papadopoulos, R. (ed.) (2006) *The Handbook of Jungian Psychology: Theory, Practice and Applications*. London and New York: Routledge.

Shamdasani, S. (2003) *Jung and the Making of Modern Psychology: The Dream of a Science*. Cambridge: Cambridge University Press.

5

Adlerian Therapy

Jenny Warner and Gerhard Baumer

HISTORICAL CONTEXT AND DEVELOPMENT IN BRITAIN

Historical context

Alfred Adler (1870–1937) was a doctor in Vienna who became interested in functional disorders (neuroses) in which physically healthy patients complained of and genuinely suffered from physical symptoms which disrupted their lives. In 1911, he founded a new society which later became the Society for Individual Psychology. From 1902 to 1911 Adler attended the Wednesday evening meetings of the Viennese Psychoanalytical Society at Freud's invitation. Adler was the most active member of this group and Freud held him in high esteem. Adler's book *Study of Organ Inferiority and its Psychical Compensation: A Contribution to Clinical Medicine* (1917), first published in 1907, was well received by Freud and considered by him to complement psychoanalytical theory. In this book Adler described the relative weakness of an organ or a system in the body and the reaction of compensation either by the weak organ, another organ or the nervous system. In 1910 Adler became President, and Stekel Vice-President, of the Vienna Psychoanalytical Society; both men were joint editors, under Freud, of their new journal, *Centralblatt*. By 1911, however, it became obvious that Adler's views differed greatly from Freud's; Adler and Stekel resigned their positions and with a few others left to form a new society.

In 1912 Adler published *The Neurotic Constitution*, outlining his theory of neurosis, and laying down many of the basic tenets of Individual Psychology. Adler was now specializing in treating psychiatric patients, neurotic rather than psychotic. In 1914 the *Journal for Individual Psychology* was founded and Adler's ideas spread to Europe and the USA.

Adler was mobilized into the Austrian-Hungarian army in 1916 and worked as an army physician in a military hospital in Cracow. On returning from the war to a destitute Vienna, Adler directed his energies towards educating people about Individual Psychology. His concept of Gemeinschaftsgefühl or 'social interest' fitted well into the new atmosphere of rebuilding a nation. (There is no direct translation in English of Gemeinschaftsgefühl and Adler was said to prefer the term social interest.) As well as a welfare programme and a housing and health programme, educational reforms were taking place in Vienna. Adler held open sessions with teachers and their problem children so that as many people as possible could learn about his ideas to enable children to grow up mentally healthy. He also lectured to teachers and at the teachers' request he was appointed professor at the Pedagogical Institute of Vienna in 1924.

In 1923 Adler lectured in England for the first time, at the International Congress of Psychology in Oxford, although he spoke very little English. In 1926 he was invited back to England by a few interested medical and psychological societies and by 1927 an Individual Psychology Club was founded in Gower Street, London; this club later became political and Adler dissociated himself from it. In 1927 Adler's book *Understanding Human Nature* was published. Based on a year's lectures given at the People's Institute in Vienna, it gives a complete description of Individual Psychology and its aim is to enable people to understand themselves, and one another, better. From 1926 to 1934 Adler spent the academic term in the USA and June to September in Vienna with his family. He went on lecture tours all over the USA; he was appointed lecturer at Columbia University from 1929 to 1931 and in 1932 a chair of medical psychology was established for him at Long Island Medical College. In 1933 he published *Social Interest: A Challenge to Mankind*, which described the concept of Gemeinschaftsgefühl (social interest) and placed it at the centre of his psychological theory. By 1934 Adler had settled permanently in the USA, where he was eventually joined by his family. A year later he founded the *International Journal of Individual Psychology* in Chicago. The theory of Individual Psychology and its application in medicine and education was now spreading throughout Europe and the USA. In 1937 Adler had planned a lecture tour in Holland, England and Scotland. In Holland, he gave over 40 lectures in three weeks, but suffered severe angina before he left for Britain. He and his daughter, Dr Alexandra Adler, herself a psychiatrist, had public and private lectures as well as university vacation courses booked at Aberdeen, York, Hull, Manchester, London, Edinburgh, Liverpool and Exeter. Sadly Adler died of a heart attack on the fourth day in Aberdeen while taking an early morning walk; he was 67 years old. Alexandra Adler arrived in Britain and fulfilled most of her father's and her own lecture commitments. She and her brother Kurt, also a psychiatrist, formed an Adlerian group in New York, which is still functioning today.

During the 1920s Rudolf Dreikurs, a young doctor, had worked with Adler's followers in their child guidance clinics in Vienna. In 1937 he went to the USA and soon established an open centre for family counselling in Chicago. From 1942 to 1948 he was professor of psychiatry at the Chicago Medical School where he exposed medical students to Adler's theories of personality, behaviour and psychopathology. By 1950, he was teaching a postgraduate course in child guidance at Northwestern University. Manford Sonstegard, who attended this course, afterwards went on to develop child guidance centres and parent education in Iowa and West Virginia and on his retirement as professor in counselling he went to Britain.

Development in Britain

A new Adlerian Society had been formed in London just before Adler's death, with Adler as its president. This stopped meeting during the Second World War but afterwards was reconstituted with Dr Alexandra Adler as its president. It was and still is called the Adlerian Society of Great Britain, and was affiliated to the Individual Psychological Medical Society which had been founded in the 1930s.

Dr Joshua Bierer, who was personally trained by Adler, emigrated to Britain and founded the first self-governed social therapeutic group for acute and chronic inpatients at Runwell Hospital, Wickford, Essex. He also set up a social psychotherapy centre – now a day hospital – and clubs for outpatients and discharged patients. Group therapy and community psychiatry are legitimate offspring of Alfred Adler's thought and work, according to Ellenberger (1970).

In 1958, Rudolf Dreikurs visited England and Scotland and lectured at Edinburgh, Aberdeen, Liverpool and London universities at Dr Joshua Bierer's invitation. Dreikurs found the Adlerian psychologists in England were engaged in private practice but were not training parents, teachers, other psychologists or psychiatrists. Adler, during the last 20 years of his life, had emphasized the need to educate teachers, who have influence over large numbers of children so that the ideas of Individual Psychology could benefit future generations and prevent mental illness. Dreikurs too concentrated his efforts on teaching parents and teachers so that children could be enabled to grow up mentally healthy and psychologically able to participate in a democratic society. In 1976 Sonstegard came to England and trained a group of health professionals in Buckinghamshire. These people joined the Adlerian Society of Great Britain, some of whose members had worked with Adler in Vienna. Sonstegard visited England annually and started to train people to do family counselling, lifestyle assessment, group counselling, self-awareness and psychotherapy. He was particularly interested in training lay counsellors and encouraging parents to form study groups and family education centres.

There are no formal Adlerian psychotherapy training courses in Britain recognized by the Institute for Individual Psychology, which is the training division of the Adlerian Society of Great Britain. In Europe, Adlerian therapists undergo many years of training. British Adlerian therapists have travelled to America, Israel and Europe to continue their training as well as attending the International Committee for Adlerian Summer Schools and Institutes (ICASSI) which takes place annually in different countries.

THEORETICAL ASSUMPTIONS

Image of the person

The holistic socio-teleological approach of Adlerian therapy based on Adler's Individual Psychology, maintains that people should be viewed in their social contexts in order that their goal can be identified. People choose their own goals based on their subjective perceptions of themselves and their world, their bodies, minds and feelings in harmony with their consistent movement towards these goals. Adlerians consider that people are creative, responsible, self-determined and unique. The holistic socio-teleological approach can be defined as having three parts.

Holistic
The term 'individual', of Individual Psychology, was used by Adler to describe the indivisibility of a person: as such it is a holistic approach to psychotherapy. Adler wanted to stress the self-consistent unity of a person as opposed to other theories which described conflicting divisions of the personality.

Social
Human beings are socially embedded and their actions can be understood only when observed within a group.

Teleological
All behaviour has a purpose and consequently it is possible to identify people's short- and long-term goals, which are of a social nature and reveal the total personality. Individual Psychology emphasizes that people are unaware of their goals and the private logic which underpins their movement towards the goals.

People can always choose how to respond to their inherited qualities and to the environment in which they grow up. People's basic concept of themselves and of life provides a guiding line, a fixed pattern; this is called the life style. The ideas and beliefs according to which a person operates are called private logic. They are not common sense but biased apperception. Common sense is shared and understood by all people; private logic is owned and understood by one individual and characterizes his or her own biased perceptions of his or her experiences. A person's private logic is created in childhood and contains generalizations and oversimplifications. Individuals create their own unique life style and are therefore responsible for their own personality and behaviour; they are creative actors rather than passive reactors. The life style concept, the theory of private logic and goal orientation and the idea of repeating early life style patterns are psychodynamic descriptions.

People will have developed their own characteristic life style by the time they are five years old, based on their own creative and unique perceptions of their situation in their family. Parents and their values and the atmosphere they create in the family will set the scene for each child to begin to make some assumptions about themselves, their world and their chosen direction of movement. Siblings and their choices of direction will have a major effect on the individual child.

The Adlerian view is that everyone is born with a desire to belong – to the family, to larger groups, to society and to the whole human race. Everyone is born in an inferior position and strives to overcome this position. If this striving for superiority takes place in the context of social interest, the whole group, all society and the future human race, benefit. The feeling of belonging (or Gemeinschaftsgefühl) is an innate potentiality in every human being. If this potentiality develops in a person he or she feels an equal member of the human race, with a useful part to play, willing to contribute and co-operate; this potentiality can become severely limited or be non-existent when individuals feel inferior to their fellows, unsure of their place and unable to make a useful contribution.

The meaning we attribute to life will determine our behaviour so that we will behave as if our perceptions were true. Life will turn out as we expected and people will respond as we expected; this is a self-fulfilling prophecy.

Conceptualization of psychological disturbance and health

Mental health can be measured by the amount of social interest a person has. Mentally healthy people are assured of their place and contribute to the tasks of the groups to which they belong; they co-operate with their fellow human beings and are part of a community. The human race, when looked at from an evolutionary point of view, is always moving towards an improved position from a minus to a plus. The word courage is used by Adlerians to describe activity plus social interest, and a person who is said to be acting with social interest is encouraged. The encouraged individual has a positive attitude towards him or herself and has self-confidence and self-respect. The goal of mentally healthy people is to belong as social equals in the family, in larger groups and in the whole of humanity, making their unique and useful contribution to these groups. Social equality was a concept that Rudolf Dreikurs developed and wrote about: '[Social equality] implies that each individual is entitled to respect and dignity, to full and equal status, regardless of any personal quality or deficiency' (Dreikurs, 1967: 39).

A person who has social interest will feel equal to other people and will treat others as social equals. The mentally healthy person is moving on a horizontal plane towards others and is task orientated. Their behaviour is useful and is determined solely by the demands of the situation and by common sense. Their feeling of belonging enables them to identify with all human beings and to empathize with them.

Adler considered there were three major life tasks required of each member of the human race: work (or occupation), friendship and love. Dreikurs added two more: getting on with oneself and relationship to the cosmos. In Adler's time the way that people could fulfil the life tasks was seen as getting a job, having a social life and friendships, getting married and having children. Successful completion of these life tasks was seen as essential to the healthy perpetuation of the human race.

More recently, Adlerians have given a broader definition of the three life tasks to take account of unemployment and homosexual relationships. Of the three life tasks the intimate relationship with one partner is considered to be the most testing of a person's social interest and willingness to co-operate.

Psychological disturbance occurs when an individual feels inferior and unworthy of an equal place amongst his or her fellows. Social interest, which is an innate potentiality in every human being, does not grow in the presence of strong feelings of inferiority. The inferiority feelings are substituted by a compensatory striving for personal superiority. People who feel inferior and act superior cannot adequately fulfil the life tasks of occupation, friendship, and marriage because they are concerned with preserving their own prestige rather than responding to the needs of the situation and making their contribution to these tasks. Their movement is on a vertical plane away from the group, withdrawing from some or all of the life tasks. An unrealistic, unattainable goal of personal superiority is set by the individual and in the neurotic individual alibis then have to be found to explain why the goal is never reached. Neurotic symptoms or behaviours serve as such excuses and the mistaken ideas and attitudes that justify the useless behaviour are called private logic. An example of private logic might be 'I am the best at everything I do – unfortunately, I get bad headaches when I am under stress so I am never able to perform at my best.' The goal of being best at everything is unrealistic and unattainable, and the headaches are a neurotic symptom which safeguards the individual from having to admit that he is not as superior as he thinks he is. He likes to think he is superior because he feels inferior; the reality of the situation is that he is socially equal to all human beings. If his feelings of equality and social interest could be developed, he could divert his attention from his own self-esteem, personal security and prestige and concentrate on making his contribution to the tasks of living. His private logic could then be replaced by common sense: Adler's 'ironclad logic of social living' (Terner and Pew, 1978).

Psychotic individuals in the presence of certain predisposing conditions escape totally from the logic of social living and assume a reality of delusions and hallucinations that conforms to their own private logic. Psychopaths openly reject common sense and, like neurotics and psychotics, are motivated only by self interest but, unlike the other two, have no conscience; they do not need the neurotic's excuses and symptoms nor the psychotic's distorted reality.

Acquisition and perpetuation of psychological disturbance

All human problems are essentially social in nature. (Dreikurs, 1967: 104).

We do not develop neurotic symptoms or behaviour as long as we feel we can function adequately. Neurosis will develop as soon as we feel unable to fulfil our obligations in one of the life tasks – at work, in friendships, in an intimate relationship. The symptoms and behaviour will be the excuse for not fulfilling the tasks adequately, not engaging in them at all, or retreating from them. Rather than facing failure and being found to be inadequate the symptom enables the discouraged individual to hesitate or evade and yet not lose face. Neurotics may not appear to have any difficulties until they meet a crisis for which they feel unprepared. For example, a crisis for one individual might be having to find a job when she feels incapable of fulfilling the demands of employment. Facing the demanding task of marriage might become a crisis situation for another individual, so forcing her to break off an engagement. Rather than developing a symptom, an individual may choose safeguarding behaviour such as being totally absorbed in one life task, so leaving no time or energy to engage in the other two life tasks in which they feel inadequate.

Individuals feel unable to find their place due to varying degrees of inferiority feelings. As children they learned to feel inferior. Their parents may have spoiled them and given in to their demands, in which case they would have developed the mistaken idea that they were very special people who should be served by others. They may have learned to use displays of emotion to get this service: temper tantrums, tears or sulks. Adler uses spoiling and pampering synonymously in his writings. Sonstegard makes a distinction between the two: spoiling is giving in to a child's demands whereas pampering is doing for the child those things that the child can do for himself. Pampering is regarded by Sonstegard as the most disabling form of parenting. Pampered children feel unable to accomplish many tasks and constantly seek help from others. They lack self-confidence when they grow into adulthood because they have such limited experience of learning and doing for themselves. Their parents' over-protection stunts their growth, so they doubt their ability to be independent or to make choices or to take risks and face hardships. Spoilt children in adult life will still be expecting others to serve them and let them have their own way. Pampered and spoilt people feel that the world is their enemy because it does not respond in the same way as did their parents. Adler pointed out that children play an active part in enlisting help in the case of pampering, or in demanding service in the case of spoiling. Criticized children grow up afraid of taking risks and making mistakes. Neglect is far less common than pampering and spoiling but was acknowledged by Adler to produce discouraged children. Dreikurs was convinced that the parenting methods and education of our competitive society did not encourage mental health. Mistake-centred education and 'you could do better' parenting discourage children.

People's perception of their position in their family constellation forms the basis of their life style. The parents set family values and create a family atmosphere and the children decide their place in the family. A competitive family will produce discouragement, the children competing against each other and eventually channelling themselves into separate spheres of success. They each choose something they can be best at, even if that is being naughty. As each child strives for superiority this necessitates putting the other siblings down. An eldest child is an only child for a while, possibly the centre of attention until the second child arrives and dethrones the first child. The first child has several options, one of which is to strive to retain her superiority. The second child may want to catch up with the first child and may succeed, in which case the first child will feel discouraged. The second child may give up because the first child is too capable and too far ahead. The youngest child may remain a baby for a long time, the other children acting as pampering parents; they have a vested interest in keeping the youngest a baby, as it enhances their superiority. However, some youngest children can become the most accomplished members of their families; they are never dethroned and strive to overcome all the other children. Individual children make their choice and choose their goals supported by mistaken ideas or private logic, interpreting their position in the family constellation. Neither the child nor the adult is aware of these goals or their private logic.

Even though people may not be co-operating and may not be fulfilling all of the life tasks, as long as their life style is in harmony with their environment, there will be no disturbing behaviour or distressing symptoms. An adult, spoilt as a child, may find partners, relatives, children, friends who are willing to give in to her demands. An adult, pampered as a child, may find sufficient rescuers, helpers and advisers to take over responsibility for his life. If these individuals should lose their slaves or supports a crisis would ensue and disturbing behaviour might emerge in order to attract more applicants for the vacant posts. People may consciously regret their symptoms and seek treatment for them. They may convince themselves and others of their good intentions to get rid of their symptoms or their disturbing behaviour. Their efforts to fight the symptoms merely aggravate and perpetuate them. People's private logic maintains their mistaken and unrealistic life goals. Adler referred to this as a 'yes-but' personality where the individual is aware of their social obligation (yes) – (but) due to their private logic they have to continue with their useless behaviour. The feared situation is still avoided, the task or duty is evaded and the obligations of a relationship are sidestepped. Sometimes the symptom is cured but it recurs or is replaced by another symptom if its safeguarding tendency is still needed.

Change

Any occurrence in people's lives may become an encouraging experience, so causing them to change their perceptions. New behaviours which challenge the old premises of the life style may cause a revision in social interest with a consequent decrease in inferiority feelings. The new behaviour may be embarked upon as a result of encouragement from another person or, less often, due to an independent decision on the part of the individual. Changed circumstances – for example, leaving home, partners or parents, or being left by partners or parents, leaving school, passing exams or failing exams, getting a job or losing a job – can start the changed behaviour. If the new behaviour has encouraging results then the private logic which underpinned the old behaviour is challenged and possibly revised.

As mentioned in the previous section, people may change their overt behaviour without any change in their motivation. Adlerians would consider that a behavioural change is superficial if not accompanied by an alteration of perception and an increase in social interest. People need to gain some insight into their mistaken ideas after changing their behaviour. Substituting acceptable behaviour for unacceptable behaviour is not a change in life style if people still do not feel equal to their fellows. People who feel they must always be the centre of attention, and who change from unacceptable behaviour to acceptable behaviour, are still focused on their own superiority and sense of being special; they are not concentrating on what they can contribute to the task and the needs of the situation.

PRACTICE

Goals of therapy

Adlerian psychotherapy is a learning process where there is re-education of clients' faulty perceptions and social values, and modification of their motivation. It is intended that clients should gain insight into their mistaken ideas and unrealistic goals, both of which are a source of discouragement. After insight there is a stage of reorientation of short- and long-term goals and readjustment of personal concepts and attitudes. The clients' original feelings of inferiority are superseded by a growing social interest. They feel encouraged as they recognize their equality with their fellow human beings. They concentrate on making their contribution and co-operating instead of looking at their personal status within groups.

There are four phases, each with its own goal in the Adlerian psychotherapy process:

1. establishing and maintaining a relationship with the client;
2. uncovering the dynamics of the client;
3. giving insight;
4. encouraging reorientation.

Selection criteria

There are no rigid guidelines for selecting individual therapy rather than couples therapy or group therapy. Individual choice on the part of both the therapist and the client is respected, although clients' rights to choose their kind of therapy are limited by what is available. Some therapists prefer to work with people in a group, acknowledging that each individual's problems are of a social nature, the group acting as an important agent in the psychotherapeutic process. Some therapists are reluctant to work with married individuals unless their partner is aware of the implications of psychotherapy and the changes it may encourage. When working with children, Adlerian therapists work with the whole family – parents and siblings – as they realize that if one child makes changes then the whole family will need to change too. Dreikurs, Mosak and Shulman (1952, 1982) introduced multiple psychotherapy: several therapists working with one client. This provides an ideal training opportunity. The client enjoys the attention of more than one therapist, and since the atmosphere is educational, discussion of interpretation of the client's lifestyle, including disagreements between therapists, is enlightening and encouraging to the client. The client participates as an equal in explaining and understanding his or her private logic. It does happen that clients move from individual to group therapy or from a group to individual therapy and this move is mutually agreed between clients and therapists. Some clients receiving group therapy may have additional individual sessions from the group therapist. If a couple have a relationship problem the therapist may want to work with them as a couple; however, it may emerge that one or both partners need to do some individual work, in which case they would have some individual therapy. Clients who feel ridiculous if they share feelings and personal ideas tend to prefer individual therapy, one therapist being less threatening than a group of people.

Qualities of effective therapists

The effective Adlerian therapist feels truly equal to all human beings, and this includes clients and children. The therapist shows respect to the client, but this does not necessarily mean that the therapist is always nice and kind and accepting of all the client's behaviours. The relationship with the client is one of mutual respect, so that the therapist shows herself respect by not tolerating unacceptable behaviour from the client and by giving honest feedback. The therapist shows respect towards the client by genuinely acting as if he had full responsibility for his decisions and actions. The therapist is warm and accepting of the person as he is and sincerely interested in understanding without judgement his life style, his unique perception of life and his chosen life goals. The Adlerian therapist models social interest and shows herself to be a fallible human being who is making her own contribution, unafraid of making mistakes. The Adlerian approach is based on a clear philosophy of life and the therapist will espouse social values that enable all human beings to live together in harmony as equals now and in the future. The relationship with the therapist may be the first one where the client experiences a democratic, co-operative partnership between equals. The therapist needs to have the skills to win people over as well as the personal maturity to model social interest. Many clients resist entering a partnership between equals because this gives them too much responsibility. The therapist must resist the temptation to dominate, rescue, manipulate or fight with the client; all these therapist behaviours are disrespectful and belong to an authoritarian relationship rather than a democratic one.

There are many varied, creative and adaptable Adlerian therapists who use different modes of gaining insight and encouraging reorientation. Art therapy, psychodrama, non-verbal exercises, group exercises and dream analysis are some of the major approaches that Adlerian therapists use.

Therapeutic relationship and style

There is no prescribed style for Adlerian therapists but the relationship is one of equality. Initially, the therapist will respond sensitively to the client in order to quickly establish an atmosphere of trust and acceptance. The setting is usually relaxed and comfortable with the therapist and client facing each other in chairs of equal height. After the presenting problem has been briefly described by the client, some Adlerian therapists will want to move on to gathering information in order to be able to understand the client's life style. The client may be surprised to be moved away from the problem and although the therapist's style is directive at this point it is respectful, so that an explanation is given as to why the therapist wishes to move on and the client's agreement is sought. Other therapists gather life style information in a more informal way during the course of therapy. Both client and therapist embark upon this educational voyage of discovery actively as partners, the client providing the information and the therapist giving interpretations. The therapist's style will vary according to each client's needs, so that empathy is established. For instance, the therapist might use the client's vocabulary, seeking clarification if she is not sure what the client is saying; the therapist might give time and space for clients to express their feelings or might use humour during the sessions, and some therapists may self-disclose in order to give clients feedback on their behaviour in the session. Gradually the private logic will be uncovered and understood by the therapist. Interpretations need to be put to the client as they are merely hypothesized by guessing on the part of the therapist. The therapist will wish to see whether the client acknowledges if the therapist has made a true interpretation. The whole educational process will not take place unless therapist and client are co-operating and sharing mutually agreed goals. It is in the last phase – reorientation – that it becomes clear whether both therapist and client share the same therapy goals. Clients have the right to gain insight and then decide not to make any changes. If the client does wish to make some changes, the therapist is there to guide him. Task-setting and completing the assignments also require a co-operative relationship. There will be difficult times, there may be strong emotions to work through, disagreements between therapist and client, but their resilient relationship endures these tests. The time-scale for the last phase (reorientation) will vary with each client. Some clients spend useful time with their therapist when they want to make some changes; others may need to be away from the therapist, having decided to stick to old familiar patterns. The door is always open for them to return when they feel ready to work on themselves again. The therapist demonstrates complete faith in the client by giving him total responsibility for his own reorientation.

Major therapeutic strategies and techniques

Adlerian psychotherapy can be described as a co-operative educational enterprise between equals – the therapist and client. The first stage of therapy is to establish a co-operative relationship, one between equals that is recognized by the presence of mutual respect. A co-operative relationship requires mutually agreed goals. An open approach towards stating goals will prevent ineffectual therapy between a therapist and a client who have different goals. If it is not possible to find mutually agreed goals psychotherapy will be ineffectual and may as well be terminated. Mutual respect is established by the therapist showing herself respect by refusing to play any games with the client, by only working towards agreed therapy goals and by openly commenting about behaviour towards herself that she finds unacceptable. If transference takes place the therapist can reveal this to the client as part of the educational experience. The therapist shows respect for clients by listening and accepting and acknowledging clients' rights to make their own decisions and take responsibility for their lives. The client needs to feel that the therapist cares but will not manipulate, dominate nor rescue. Dictatorial prescription and rescuing are equally disrespectful behaviours on the part of the therapist. This democratic relationship becomes part of the client's retraining; it is an action experience.

The second stage of the therapy is to gather information and understand clients' life styles and then to show clients how the presenting problem fits into their overall characteristic pattern of movement. From the first minutes of meeting clients, information will be available to the therapist from non-verbal clues – how clients enter the room, where they choose to sit, their posture, how they speak, etc. Adler was reportedly very clever at picking up information from this non-verbal behaviour. Verbal information is also available in the client's short description of the presenting problem, the subjective situation. The Adlerian therapist will not want to spend too long initially on the presenting problem, as she will need to discover the client's life style before the significance of the problem can be understood. The objective situation of the client is also explored as the therapist finds out how the client is functioning in the three life tasks: work, friendships and intimate relationships. Some therapists may also enquire about relationships to God and moral–ethical beliefs. If clients are complaining of symptoms then they are asked, 'the question', i.e. 'what would be different if you were well/if you did not have this symptom?' Clients' answers will reveal the particular area of difficulty for them and their unrealistic goals.

The therapist will then move on to life style assessment, which consists of understanding the client's family constellation and interpreting his early memories. A child creates his own unique life style in the context of his family and in relation to his siblings. The therapist, therefore, asks the client to describe himself and his siblings as children. Family constellation is not just a reflection of birth order. Adlerians might describe typical eldest, second, youngest, middle and only children but as Adler said, 'Everything can also be different', and children may interpret their positions in the family constellation quite differently. An eldest child chooses how to respond to family values and to the experience of being dethroned by a younger child; all elder children experience being only children for a time. A second child chooses whether to compete with the eldest by overtaking them or by doing something or being something entirely different. A youngest child may decide to remain the baby of the family or to surpass all the siblings in achievement. Family values will determine whether the competition takes place in academic achievements or in being an acceptable person or in some other realm of behaviour important to that family. Many children will decide to rebel against family values, either silently or openly. Most families are competitive; very few are democratic.

The therapist will want additional information, in order to verify the hypothesis that she is beginning to form about the client's life style. Dreikurs said that you needed two points on a line before you could make a hypothesis about a person's life style. The therapist asks the client for some of his early memories. Adler found that people remembered incidents, often innocuous and ordinary, that fitted in with their life style. Clients are asked to think back as far as they can and tell the therapist the first thing they think of, if possible something that happened to them before they were five years old. People select, out of all their life experiences, those memories that depict a certain aspect of their life style. It may be their view of themselves, their view of their world and the people in it, their view of how life should be or how they have to behave. The therapist has to interpret the early memories and align this information with that already gleaned from the description of the family constellation. The therapist wants to find out clients' life goals and their underlying mistaken assumptions, i.e. their private logic. The overall movement of the client needs to be recognized. The presenting problem and future problems will fit into this basic pattern of living.

The third phase of interpretation and giving insight is now entered. The therapist's approach is to find enough points on a line to begin to make a hypothesis. This informed guess is then put to the client, so that it can be verified. The therapist is looking for the client's recognition. Previously, clients were unaware of their goals and private logic, so this phase of the therapy is where the therapist particularly needs to demonstrate her empathy; she needs to be able to describe the client's goals and mistaken ideas in words that the client understands, recognizes and owns. This disclosure does not have to be perfect at the first attempt. The therapist shows her fallibility and encourages the client to help her shape the life style summary, so that it feels right for the client. The summary usually takes the form of 'Life is…'; 'Others are…'; and 'I am…' themes. The therapist explains how clients choose their particular goals, so that there is no mystique in the interpretation of the life style. Private logic once it is verbalized begins to lose its strength. The overgeneralizations, oversimplifications and unrealistic ideas can be challenged. 'Is it reasonable to expect…?'; 'Is this really how people are?'; 'Is it realistic for you to expect to always be…?'.

Dreams may also be analysed. Adler said dreams were the 'factory of the emotions'; they set the mood that fuels people's actions. Remembered dreams that clients produce always fit within a person's life style and never contradict it.

The therapist places the client's concerns and problems in the context of the life style and shows how certain situations, relationships or demands can cause a crisis because they challenge the client's life style. Neurotic symptoms can be understood as alibis which were necessary because the client was pursuing unattainable goals. Making clients aware of the purpose of their neurotic symptoms was described by Adler as 'spitting in the patient's soup'. The patient can persist with the symptoms but they will not give the same satisfaction as before.

The re-orientation phase follows on from gaining insight. The Adlerian therapist will use a mirror technique to show clients familiar patterns of movement towards consistent goals in all their behaviour. Attainable assignments may be set for clients that challenge their private logic. If the assignments are completed successfully then there is a weakening of the client's private logic. Clients will begin to catch themselves pursuing the same goals and making the same justifications for their behaviour. Clients will catch themselves after, during, and then before they engage in the useless behaviour. Each 'aha' experience increases clients' new learning and growing understanding of their own personality. Each individual, once they have some insight, will decide whether or not to change and if to change, over how long a period. The old patterns are well tried and tested, automatic, and to some extent feel comfortable. New patterns are scary. One method that Adler used when a client was fighting against a symptom or behaviour and actually increasing both was to encourage the client to increase the symptom or behaviour; this is known as paradoxical intention.

The change process in therapy

Once people's mistaken goals are revealed to them they can no longer pursue them with such conviction. Once their mistaken ideas are revealed to them they can choose to change. Gaining insight and choosing to change is one choice; gaining insight and choosing not to change is another. Insight will develop as individuals begin to recognize their patterns of behaviour. New behaviours which challenge the old assumptions are then tested out. New behaviours or assignments may be successful – the old private logic is then challenged and weakened and replaced by common sense. New behaviours may have disastrous outcomes, in which case clients may be tempted to retreat to old ways and to feel comfortable with familiar private logic. As their private logic decreases and common sense grows they will display increased social interest in all spheres of their lives and they will take on responsibility for their own life goals, perceptions and behaviours. As soon as they accept full responsibility for their own behaviour they enable themselves to make changes. Their increased sense of belonging and feeling of equal worth will be a source of encouragement to them. Inferiority feelings will diminish; their focus of interest will be on their personal contribution to the task in hand. They will feel content with themselves. Their unattainable goals will be replaced by the courage to be imperfect, an acknowledgement that all active, co-operating human beings make mistakes. The new behaviours and new goals will be followed by new assumptions. This process can be instant in a child, as when one of the Four Mistaken Goals of Misbehaviour (Dreikurs and Soltz, 1995) is revealed to them, very quick in a teenager and increasingly slower in a mature adult. It is harder for adults in established relationships to make changes as these changes will inevitably have an effect on partners in intimate relationships, and on close friends. The therapist, who has always treated the client as an equal, encourages the client to contribute as an equal. Clients may make a partial or complete change of personality, their private logic replaced by common sense, their inferiority feelings replaced by social interest and a feeling of belonging. The correction of one mistaken concept will enable growth and release further courage to tackle new behaviours and additional mistakes. The therapist will respect the client's right to choose when and how much to change. Behaviour change can occur years after initially gaining insight. It is best for the therapist not to fight with the client during times of inactivity; the therapist can be available when the client wants to make some changes but does not know how to. Each person, if they choose to change, will do so in their own unique and creative way.

Limitations of the approach

Adler's theory of personality provides Adlerian therapists with a complete understanding of all human behaviour. The practice of Adlerian therapists is very varied but always based on the foundation of a holistic socio-teleological view of people. Much of Adler's Individual Psychology has permeated other approaches in psychotherapy and counselling; many of his ideas are incorporated into other people's theories without acknowledgement. Adlerian theory appears to have widespread acceptance and relevance to students of human behaviour.

The psychotherapeutic procedures practised by Adler himself and by Rudolf Dreikurs are used today by therapists and any technique which a therapist finds helpful is added to the basic approach. The insight and the skills are only part of Adlerian psychotherapy. Psychotherapists need to have social interest and need to use their skills 'for the purpose of establishing an ideal community' (Dreikurs, 1953: v). The Adlerian approach can give a great deal of insight; to use the insight and understanding of people with social interest is an exacting demand on every therapist. Many people, including therapists, have grown up in families where power was used either openly in the form of control by anger or disguised in the form of manipulation. Therapists have to work on understanding their own skills in the arena of power before they can work with clients in a truly equal cooperative relationship. Many clients will find the idea of being responsible for their own behaviour distasteful and unacceptable.

The client may leave therapy with insight but unwilling to change. If therapy outcomes are looked at over too short a time the long-term effects of the insight may not be recorded. Changes have been seen several years after a life style assessment was done. It is always worthwhile enabling a person to gain insight. It is never worthwhile fighting with them afterwards in order to force or persuade or shame them into change.

There are limitations to using Adlerian psychotherapy only in a one-to-one situation. So much information can be gained by observing clients in groups. So much can be gained by clients when trying out new behaviours in a safe group. So much can be gained by clients experiencing equal membership of a group with a shared goal of mutual growth.

Case example

The client

Pierre (40) came to see me (GB) in London because of his difficulties with his wife (31) whom he had married four months previously. The relationship had always been difficult but after they were married they had even more rows. They had twin girls aged six months. He had been unemployed for quite a while and was not trying very hard to get a new job. He had trained as a social worker, but had never worked as one. He had done unskilled work on building sites, worked in pubs or on fishing boats, had travelled a lot around the world and was always somehow on the move, running away from himself. He met his wife two years previously when he was in hospital with a broken leg. She was a doctor in the hospital. Now she was the breadwinner of the family. He explained that she was attracted by his reserved, cold attitude, curious to find out what might be behind the façade of that tall, good-looking man. It seemed she liked challenges. Pierre told me in his first session that he still went to prostitutes after getting drunk at least once or twice a month, sometimes weekly. He described this behaviour as an addiction that had started when he was 22. He now had terrible guilt feelings afterwards, connected with a lot of self blame. The reply to my question about whether he loved his wife was very honest, 'If there is any love between us it is on her side. I feel numb.' Pierre admitted that his feelings for others easily turned to boredom and disinterest. He said of himself, 'I am a loser, disconnected from others and still very boyish, not willing to take responsibility for myself and for others, but I don't want to end up as a complete failure and I don't want to disappoint my little girls. That is the reason I am coming to you for therapy.'

Next we talked about the possible setting. I offered him a place in an ongoing group but he refused. He mentioned that his wife was already in psychodynamic group therapy and because of that he wanted something different. And he added that he might easily get bored with the other people in the group and drop out. I decided not to get into a power struggle, thereby giving our relationship a chance to be democratic and respectful, and offered him one-to-one sessions.

The therapy

What I describe here is a process that took more than 30 sessions. I had to allow this client to take the lead, as he was very self-centred and unduly sensitive to outside pressure; any imposed structure would have felt like a prison. We started in the usual Adlerian way, doing a life style assessment and began with the family constellation. I asked him to describe his parents when he was a child.

Pierre said his father was born in the French part of Switzerland. He studied medicine, had worked in several underdeveloped countries, came to England, married a posh English middle-class woman and had settled down in a small town in Wales, practising as a GP. Pierre's grandfather was also a doctor who had worked for the World Health Organisation. I suggested to Pierre that his father wanted live up to this ideal and be seen as a very good person and a very good doctor and so he worked long hours to achieve this. Pierre described his father as calm, gentle and quiet – a workaholic. He was a loner, who was not really there for his family apart from holidays when he liked to do a lot of outdoor activities with the children. He had an aura of being special, was idealized by his wife and, Pierre found out in his later life, by other women too. It appears that his father was a womanizer, a very shattering discovery for my client in puberty. I suggested to Pierre that as a child he too had idealized his father, but later he had come to the conclusion that his father did not live up to his expectations; this was a tremendous disappointment to him.

Mother was described as very English and a snob who refused to be part of the Welsh community they lived in. She always said things like, 'We are better than our neighbours'; 'Don't mix with the plebs'; 'You should tell the people in the street that your father is a doctor'; 'They should know we are special'. He agreed with my comment that this resulted in the family being quite isolated and inward looking. This had a tremendous impact on my client's social ability and his view of himself and the world. Mother suffered from long bouts of depression and tried to bolster her self-esteem by being the perfect housewife and mother. When I asked him, Pierre told me he experienced her as 'intruding and nagging'. She and the boys had power struggles from very early on. She felt she did a lot for her family but they did not appreciate this so she picked on the children and started arguing with them, ending in fierce rows which prompted Father to came out of his surgery next door and tell the children off. The family atmosphere was tense with little room for happiness. I asked him to think back to when he was very young and to give me the first thing he could remember. He said that his first early memory was when he was 6 years old. At that time he was very fond of stories about knights; his favourite was King Arthur. In the early memory he was sitting on a swing in the garden dreaming that he was introduced to King Arthur and honoured because he rescued a little girl from a burning house. At the very moment King Arthur said, 'You are very special', Pierre was pushed from the swing by his brother and his friend. My client continued, 'It is still very vivid for me. I decided at that moment not to trust my brother and other ordinary people any more'.

When we had reached that point of the exploration the client was already beginning to gain insight into what had influenced his life style. He accepted he had taken on many of the family values that I had identified, such as it having been very important to be special and unique and it having been important to be successful and the best. I pointed out that this striving for superiority made it hard for him to feel connected to others, feel equal, fit in, get a sense of belonging and find deeper meaning and satisfaction in life. He had to pay the price of loneliness.

We continued with the family constellation by my asking him to tell me about his siblings when they were young. He had a brother one year older, another brother three-and-a-half years younger and a sister five years younger, who was slightly physically handicapped and needed a lot of extra care when she was young. Pierre agreed with my guess that there was a lot of competition between the brothers. There were many fights, especially between Pierre and his elder brother, and a lot of rivalry over who was the clever one, the stronger one and who got the most attention from their parents. Pierre was the youngest child for three-and-a-half years and I suggested to him that he felt dethroned and very put down when his younger brother was born. Pierre remembered that when his mother came home from the hospital he told her to take the baby back immediately as there would not be room at home for him. Mother was hospitalized from time to time with depression when the children were little, and she was not able to give much love nor help him get over losing his place as the youngest. Neither could Father help as he avoided being part of the family. He understood when I commented that, in that family situation, it was very hard for Pierre to cope with the experience of being dethroned by his younger brother. I suggested that his brother had taken the special place he had been given in the family and his parents could not help him regain it so he built up a lot of distrust, felt put down and went into the mode of revenge. Pierre confirmed that he became spiteful after his brother's birth and when I asked him how he felt he said, angry and miserable. Having heard how he related to his brothers when he was a child, I was not surprised that, later on, he felt that boys were a threat. He had many fights with them in the street and was proud of his scars. He shared in one session that he had a lot of problems with men, always getting into power struggles. I pointed out that this was due to the perception which had started in childhood and which had become part of his belief system: beware of other males, they put you down or take your place. His bitter disappointment with his father showed itself in therapy as a very strong transference. Initially he had idealized me, like his father, but later he tested me to see whether I would become as useless and unreliable as his father. This caused a very stormy phase for about six months when he drank more, missed appointments and expressed doubts as to whether I would be good enough to help him. I asked him why he thought that and let him discuss things with me in a non-threatening atmosphere, so that it was possible to work through the transference in therapy. I showed him how it connected to the disappointment with his father and the tremendous rivalry towards his brothers and on to his present attitude and behaviour towards other men. I showed him how he was still striving and failing to be special, like his father, and as a result was restless and unsettled, unable to relate to his wife and children. He accepted that he needed help. One result was that he was now able to join AA, admitting that he had a drinking problem. That was quite a step forward.

Pierre told me in one session that he had built up a good relationship with his little sister. He helped her a lot, looking after her. That gave him some positive attention and acknowledgement from her and a feeling of being useful and, very important from an Adlerian perspective, it helped to build up a basic sense of social interest and feeling of belonging through cooperation. He developed a willingness to help others – at least to a certain degree – which had made him undergo training as a social worker. It was important to encourage this very discouraged client. Helping his sister and working as a social worker helped to maintain his striving for superiority but they were positive behaviours rather than negative ones so I remarked that this was a valuable thing to do.

Pierre had a special relationship with his grandfather who admired him because Pierre looked like him. Grandfather was considered to have second sight and he was convinced that Pierre would develop this gift as well. Pierre produced this as an early memory. It was his fifth birthday when Grandpa told him this 'secret', and it made Pierre feel he was 'being chosen'. Grandpa's prophecy made Pierre very special in the family and strengthened his narcissistic, superior attitude. When we started therapy he was still convinced about the prophecy and was waiting for inspiration. In a way, that made it easier to work with him. There was still some kind of hope, he was at least interested in finding out about himself and what made him special.

Being very unprepared for cooperation and having few social skills, his time as a pupil in boys' school was very difficult. His private logic, made him feel 'as if he were surrounded by 30 brothers'. This caused tremendous emotional stress and alerted all his defence mechanisms to survive this 'dangerous' situation. He became an outsider from the start, got into power struggles, was bullied and, as most of his classmates had more physical strength than him, he had to play the clown more and more in order to survive. Playing the clown was helpful in one way, but it lowered his dignity and he felt very shamed and hurt. He went into revenge-seeking behaviour; he harmed smaller children, animals and sometimes himself. He damaged his own playthings. He clearly viewed himself as 'the bad guy' when he was about eight or nine and withdrew from social contact and group activities. I pointed out to him that this was a pattern in his life that he strove to be superior and failed and then he felt hurt and went into revenge. I put it to him that his view of the world was that it was a very hostile place full of people who wished to hurt him. He agreed and became aware that that was his perception. These mistaken ideas that had been in his private logic, driving his motivation had been verbalized for the first time so he could examine them in the cold light of day. This client accepted and, in the ensuing weeks, began to modify his view.

His uncertainty about himself and his inferiority feelings were compensated for in a fantasy life as we saw in his early recollection – already mentioned – on the swing. He entitled it 'me and my best friend King Arthur'. I interpreted to Pierre that this early memory shows a desire to connect but only with a very special person whom you can trust in all circumstances as he explained in that session. He agreed that this was what he believed. He never found such a person in real life. (We discussed how realistic it would be to expect anyone to be so special.)

After about 30 sessions Pierre was able to change his private logic. We had spent many hours looking at and interpreting his family constellation and his early memories and this had given him a lot to think about. I had needed to be very careful about how I helped him gain insight into how he viewed himself and others and his way of coping in the world. He was a very discouraged individual who was sensitive to criticism so my comments during therapy had to be respectful and non-threatening. Part of the process was to let him see that it was no longer necessary to be special and that indeed he was not special and never would be and that that was a good thing as his striving for that unobtainable goal had caused him much disappointment and loneliness. I suggested that he needed to appreciate himself and the people in his life.

As we moved on to reorientation we discussed his participation in the life tasks. He had described himself as boyish at the beginning of therapy and I now asked him how he could play a more adult role. He answered that he needed to take more responsibility in his marriage, get involved with the family, and get a job. During therapy one important change in his marriage was that he began to respect his wife more and to avoid power struggles. He tried to be more cooperative at home. He accepted a job working with children with behaviour disorders, 'even though it was not a job I had dreamt of and would have gone for a year ago'. In the twenty-third session he said, 'I think it was quite good for me that she insisted on having a relationship with me'. With the help of AA and the therapy he was able to stop his drinking excesses. The enormous inner tension – which had driven him in an almost hyperactive way – reduced so that he became able to experience more closeness and intimacy with his wife and children. When he stopped putting his wife down and provoking her, their sex life started again and became 'bearable', as he phrased it. His critical attitude towards himself and others reduced to mild sarcasm and he started to laugh about himself. He was very proud when he told me, 'I have rejected financial help from my parents, I am no longer the boy who is dependent on his parents'. That was the session when he told me that he felt fine and that he thought he needed no more support. It was the thirty-fourth session when we parted.

REFERENCES

Adler, A. (1912) *The Neurotic Constitution*. London: Kegan Paul, Trench, Trubner & Co.

Adler, A. (1917) *Study of Organ Inferiority and its Psychical Compensation: A Contribution to Clinical Medicine*. New York: Nervous and Mental Diseases Publishing.

Adler, A. (1933) *Social Interest: A Challenge to Mankind*. London: Faber & Faber.

Adler, A. (1992) *Understanding Human Nature*, trans. Colin Brett (1927). Oxford: Oneworld Publications.

Dreikurs, R. (1953) *Fundamentals of Adlerian Psychology*. Chicago, IL: Adler School of Professional Psychology.

Dreikurs, R. (1967) *Psychodynamics, Psychotherapy and Counselling: Collected Papers*. Chicago, IL: Adler School of Professional Psychology.

Dreikurs, R. and Soltz, V. (1995) *Happy Children* (1964). Melbourne: Australian Council for Educational Research.

Dreikurs, R., Mosak, H.H. and Shulman, B.H. (1952) 'Patient–therapist relationship in multiple psychotherapy II: its advantages for the patient', *Psychiatric Quarterly*, 26: 590–6.

Dreikurs, R., Mosak, H.H. and Shulman, B.H. (1982) *Multiple Psychotherapy: Use of Two Therapists with One Patient*. Chicago, IL: Adler School of Professional Psychology.

Ellenberger, H.F. (1970) *The Discovery of the Unconscious*. New York: Basic Books.

Terner, J. and Pew, W.L. (1978) *The Courage to be Imperfect: The Life and Work of Rudolf Dreikurs*. New York: Hawthorn Books.

SUGGESTED FURTHER READING

Adler, A. (1964) *Superiority and Social Interest: A Collection of Later Writings*, ed. H.L. Ansbacher and R.R. Ansbacher. New York: Norton.

Adler, A. (1992) *What Life Could Mean to You*, trans. Colin Brett (1931). Oxford: Oneworld Publications.

Ansbacher, H.L. and Ansbacher, R.R. (eds) (1967) *The Individual Psychology of Alfred Adler*. New York: Harper & Row.

Corsini, R.J. (ed.) (1984) *Current Psychotherapies*. Itasca, IL: Peacock.

Dreikurs, R. (1971) *Social Equality: The Challenge of Today*. Chicago, IL: Henry Regnery.

6

Person-centred Therapy

Brian Thorne

HISTORICAL CONTEXT AND DEVELOPMENT IN BRITAIN

Historical context

Dr Carl Rogers (1902–87), the American psychologist and principal originator of what has now become known as person-centred counselling or psychotherapy, always claimed to be grateful that he never had one particular mentor. He was influenced by many significant figures, often holding widely differing viewpoints, but above all he claimed to be the student of his own experience and of that of his clients and colleagues.

While accepting Rogers's undoubtedly honest claim about his primary sources of learning there is much about his thought and practice which places him within a recognizable tradition. Oatley has described this as

> the distinguished American tradition exemplified by John Dewey: the tradition of no non-sense, of vigorous self-reliance, of exposing oneself thoughtfully to experience, practical innovation, and of careful concern for others. (Oatley, 1981: 192)

In fact in 1925, while still a student at Teachers College, Columbia, New York, Rogers was directly exposed to Dewey's thought and to progressive education through his attendance at a course led by William Heard Kilpatrick, a student of Dewey and himself a teacher of extraordinary magnetism. Not that Dewey and Kilpatrick formed the mainstream of the ideas to which Rogers was introduced during his professional training and early clinical experience. Indeed when he took up his first appointment in 1928 as a member of the Child Study

Department of the Society for the Prevention of Cruelty to Children in Rochester, New York, he joined an institution where the three fields of psychology, psychiatry and social work were combining forces in diagnosing and treating problems. This context appealed to Rogers's essentially pragmatic temperament.

Rogers's biographer, Kirschenbaum (1979), while acknowledging the variety of influences to which Rogers was subjected at the outset of his professional career, suggests nevertheless that when Rogers went to Rochester he saw himself essentially as a diagnostician and as an interpretative therapist whose goal, very much in the analytical tradition, was to help a child or a parent gain insight into their own behaviour and motivation. Diagnosis and interpretation are far removed from the primary concerns of a contemporary person-centred therapist and in an important sense Rogers's progressive disillusionment with both these activities during his time at Rochester marks the beginning of his own unique approach. He tells the story of how, near the end of his time at Rochester, he had been working with a highly intelligent mother whose son was presenting serious behavioural problems. Rogers was convinced that the root of the trouble lay in the mother's early rejection of the boy but no amount of gentle strategy on his part could bring her to this insight. In the end he gave up and they were about to part when she asked if adults were taken for counselling on their own account. When Rogers assured her that they were she immediately requested help for herself and launched into an impassioned outpouring of her own despair, her marital difficulties and her confusion and sense of failure. Real therapy, it seems, began at that moment and was ultimately successful. Rogers commented:

> This incident was one of a number which helped me to experience the fact – only fully realised later – that it is the client who knows what hurts, what direction to go, what problems are crucial, what experiences have been deeply buried. It began to occur to me that unless I had a need to demonstrate my own cleverness and learning, I would do better to rely upon the client for the direction of movement in the process. (cited in Kirschenbaum, 1979: 89)

The essential step from diagnosis and interpretation to listening had been taken and from that point onwards Rogers was launched on his own path.

By 1940 Rogers was a professor of psychology at Ohio State University and his second book, *Counseling and Psychotherapy*, appeared two years later. From 1945 to 1957 he was professor of psychology at Chicago and executive secretary (his own term) of the university counselling centre. This was a period of intense activity, not least in the research field. Rogers's pragmatic nature has led to much research being carried out on person-centred therapy. With the publication of *Client-Centered Therapy* in 1951 Rogers became a major force in the world of psychotherapy and established his position as a practitioner, theorist and researcher who warranted respect. In an address to the American Psychological Association in 1973 Rogers maintained that during this Chicago period he was for the first time giving clear expression to an idea whose time had come. The idea was

> the gradually formed and tested hypothesis that the individual has within himself vast
> resources for self-understanding, for altering his self-concept, his attitudes and his self-
> directed behavior – and that these resources can be tapped if only a definable climate of
> facilitative psychological attitudes can be provided. (Rogers, 1974: 116)

From this 'gradually formed and tested hypothesis' non-directive therapy was born as a protest against the diagnostic, prescriptive point of view prevalent at the time. Emphasis was placed on a relationship between counsellor and client based upon acceptance and clarification. This was a period, too, of excitement generated by the use of recorded interviews for research and training purposes and there was a focus on 'non-directive techniques'. Those coming for help were no longer referred to as patients but as clients, with the inference that they were self-responsible human beings, not objects for treatment. As experience grew and both theory-building and research developed, the term 'client-centred therapy' was adopted which put the emphasis on the internal world of the client and focused attention on the attitudes of therapists towards their clients rather than on particular techniques. The term 'person-centred' won Rogers's approval in the decade before his death, because it could be applied to the many fields outside therapy where his ideas were increasingly becoming accepted and valued and because in the therapy context itself it underlined the person-to-person nature of the interaction where not only the phenomenological world of the client but also the therapist's state of being are of crucial significance. This 'I–Thou' quality of the therapeutic relationship indicates a certain kinship with the existential philosophy of Kierkegaard and Buber and the stress on personal experience recalls the work of the British philosopher/scientist Michael Polanyi (whom Rogers knew and admired). In the years before his death, Rogers also reported his own deepening respect for certain aspects of Zen teaching and became fond of quoting sayings of Lao-Tse, especially those that stress the undesirability of imposing on people instead of allowing them the space in which to find themselves. The interest in Zen was also a significant indication of Rogers's late-flowering interest in the spiritual dimension of experience and its importance in the therapeutic relationship.

Since Rogers's death in 1987 the influence of his work in the United States of America has rapidly declined but in Europe person-centred therapy is strongly represented in many countries (Thorne and Lambers, 1998) and there is continuing interest in the approach in both South America and the Far East. There now exists a World Association for Person-Centered and Experiential Psychotherapy and Counseling whose constitution was formally approved at an international conference in Chicago in 2000. The Association also has its own influential journal *(Person-Centered and Experiential Psychotherapies)* as well as convening bi-annual international conferences.

Development in Britain

In Britain the ideas of Carl Rogers first appeared in the context of the development of the Marriage Guidance Council (now called Relate) during the late 1950s and early 1960s. Client-centred therapy was first introduced into British universities, mainly by visiting Fulbright professors from America, in the late 1960s as part of the curriculum for those training to become counsellors in schools. The enthusiasm for humanistic psychology in general which took London by storm at the end of the 1960s resulted in the emergence of a loosely knit network of persons, mainly working in education and social work, for whom Rogers became a major source of inspiration.

The turning point came, however, in 1974 when Rogers himself had planned to come to Britain in order to attend a workshop initiated by a young psychologist from Scotland, Dave Mearns, who had studied with Rogers in California in 1971–72. In the event, the grave illness of his wife prevented Rogers from coming but the workshop went ahead and a key participant was Dr Charles (Chuck) Devonshire from the College of San Mateo in California, director of the Center for Cross-Cultural Communication and a close associate of Rogers. In the years following, the co-operative efforts of Devonshire, Mearns, Elke Lambers, a Dutch client-centred therapist living in Scotland and myself, led to the founding of the Facilitator Development Institute which provided annual summer residential workshops for members of the helping professions who wished to learn more of person-centred theory and practice especially as it applied to small and large groups. In 1985 the Institute (afterwards renamed Person-Centred Therapy (Britain)) began to offer full-scale training for person-centred therapists. During the same period Devonshire was developing programmes throughout Europe and his Person-Centred Approach Institute International began to offer a British programme in 1987. A splinter group from Devonshire's original staff team subsequently founded the Institute for Person-Centred Learning. All three of these private institutes, which have in recent years been joined by several others (e.g. Metanoia in London and Temenos in Sheffield) have offered professional training at a basic or advanced level during the past twenty years.

Since 1990 person-centred therapy has established a firm foothold in British universities with significant centres for training and research at the Universities of Strathclyde and East Anglia where Mearns and Thorne respectively held the first Chairs in counselling. Another person-centred practitioner, Professor John McLeod, has established a formidable research reputation, initially at the University of Keele and subsequently at Abertay University in Dundee, while at the University of East London Tony Merry provided a powerful person-centred presence in the metropolis until his early death in 2004. This significant power-base – buttressed by a succession of influential publications (Mearns, 1994, 1997, 2002; Mearns and Cooper, 2005; Mearns and Thorne, 1988, 1999, 2000; Thorne, 1992, 1998, 2002, 2003, 2005; McLeod, 1994, 2003; Merry, 1995, 1999) – does much to resource the many courses currently accredited by the British Association for Counselling and Psychotherapy which identify person-centred therapy as their core theoretical model. The strength of the approach is further indicated by the existence of two strong professional associations, the British Association for the Person-Centred Approach (BAPCA) founded in 1989 and its earlier sister organization the Association for Person-Centred Therapy

(Scotland). Recent years, too, have seen the emergence of a new generation of scholar-practitioners who have made substantial contributions to the professional literature (e.g. McMillan (2004), Keys (2003), Purton (2004), Tolan (2003), Embleton Tudor et al. (2004), Wilkins (2003)). The approach is now also admirably served by PCCS Books Limited of Ross-on-Wye who under the inspirational leadership of Pete Sanders and Maggie Taylor-Sanders have become the foremost publisher of person-centred material in the world.

THEORETICAL ASSUMPTIONS

Image of the person

Person-centred therapists start from the assumption that both they and their clients are trustworthy. This trust resides in the belief that every organism – the human being included – has an underlying and instinctive movement towards the constructive accomplishment of its inherent potential. Rogers (1979) often recalled a boyhood memory of his parents' potato bin in which they stored the winter supply of potatoes. This bin was placed in the basement several feet below a small window, yet despite the highly unfavourable conditions the potatoes would begin to send out spindly shoots groping towards the distant light of the window. Rogers compared these pathetic potatoes in their desperate struggle to develop with clients whose lives have been warped by circumstances and experience but who continue against all the odds to strive towards growth, towards becoming. This directional, or actualizing, tendency in the human being can be trusted and the therapist's task is to help create the best possible conditions for its fulfilment. Such a task should not blind the therapist, however, to the social realities of a client's life. Encouraging a client's growth can sometimes lead to foolhardy behaviour which is much to the client's detriment. The therapist needs to be attentive to those signals which indicate 'not for growth' areas and not override them in a mistaken zeal for growth at all costs (see Mearns and Thorne, 2000: 114–16). The actualizing tendency can itself generate resistance from a client's social life space and an interim term for this resistance is the force of 'social mediation' (see Mearns and Thorne, 2000: 182–3).

The elevated view of human nature which person-centred therapists hold is paralleled by their insistence on individual uniqueness. They believe that no two persons are ever alike and that the human personality is so complex that no diagnostic labelling of persons can ever be fully justified. Indeed, person-centred therapists know that they cannot hope to uncover fully the subjective perceptual world of the client and that clients themselves can do this only with great effort. Furthermore clients' perceptual worlds will be determined by the experiences they have rejected or assimilated into the self-concept.

For Rogers the term 'self-concept' was equated with the term 'self'. For him this was a pragmatic decision because it rendered the notion 'self' open to investigation by research. By seeing 'self' as available to the conscious awareness of the person, Rogers placed himself firmly outside the psychoanalytic tradition with its emphasis on the importance of unconscious dimensions. In an extension of the theory my colleague, Dave Mearns, and I have proposed a modification of Rogers's concept of self to include material which is on the edge of awareness. (Rogers used the expression 'subceived' to indicate this 'almost but not quite' conscious material.) By widening the definition of self so that it = self-concept + edge of awareness material we accept the legitimacy of 'focusing' – a method developed by Eugene Gendlin for deepening inner awareness – as a dimension of person-centred therapy and we also make it possible to consider new 'configurations' of self as they emerge during therapy which alter – sometimes radically – the structure of the self-concept (Mearns and Thorne, 2000: 175).

Conceptualization of psychological disturbance and health

The self-concept is of crucial importance in person-centred therapy and needs to be contrasted with the actualizing tendency. It is the actualizing tendency which gives access to the essential resources for living and to the organismic valuing process which enables an individual to make judgements about his or her existence. The human organism can essentially be relied upon to provide trustworthy messages and this is discernible in the physiological processes of the entire body and through the process of growth by which a person's potentialities and capacities are brought to realization. As life proceeds, the actualizing tendency is informed by the promptings of social reality and the need for belonging but it never loses its capacity to provide unerring guidance to the heart of a person's unique and essential personhood. Such an organismic valuing process and its trustworthiness, even if at times it does not easily reveal its wisdom, is to be contrasted with the self-concept which is a person's conceptual construction of him or herself (however poorly articulated) and does not by any means always find itself in harmony with the promptings of the actualizing tendency and its allied organismic valuing process. On the contrary, it is possible, and not at all rare, for a self-concept to become so firmly entrenched that the actualizing tendency becomes almost totally obscured from consciousness.

The self-concept develops over time and is heavily dependent on the attitudes of those who constitute the individual's significant others. It follows that where a person is surrounded by those who are quick to condemn or punish (however subtly) the behaviour which emanates from the promptings of the actualizing tendency, he or she will become rapidly confused. The need for positive regard or approval from others is overwhelming and is present from earliest infancy. If behaviour arising from what is actually experienced by the individual fails to win approval an immediate conflict is established. A baby, for example, may gain considerable satisfaction or relief from howling full-throatedly but may then quickly learn that such behaviour is condemned or punished by the mother. At this point the need to win the mother's approval is in immediate conflict with the promptings of the actualizing tendency which engender howling. In the person-centred tradition disturbance is conceptualized in terms of the degree of success or failure experienced by the individual in resolving such conflicts. The badly disturbed person on this criterion will have lost almost complete contact with the experiencing of his or her organism, for the basic need for self-regard can in the most adverse circumstances lead to behaviour which is totally geared to the desperate search for acceptance and approval. The signals from the organismic valuing system in such cases are silenced and a self-concept is developed which bears little relationship to people's deepest yearnings, from which they are essentially cut off. Not surprisingly, perhaps, such attempts to create a self-concept which runs counter to the actualizing tendency cannot in the long run be successful.

In most cases individuals who come for therapy, whatever face they may present to the world, hold themselves in low esteem and a negative self-concept is usually a further sign of disturbance at some level. In those rarer instances where the self-deception is more extreme the self-concept may at a conscious level appear largely positive but it will be quickly evident to others that such self-affirmation has been won at the cost of a deliberate and sustained refusal to allow adverse judgements into awareness, whether these threaten from within or from outside sources. Disturbed people can seldom trust their own judgement and for the person-centred therapist another sure mark of disturbance is the absence of an internalized locus of evaluation. This somewhat cumbersome term describes the faculty which determines individuals' capacity to trust their own thoughts and feelings when making decisions or choosing courses of action. Disturbed people show little sign of possessing such a faculty: instead they constantly turn to external authorities or find themselves caught in a paralysis of indecision. In summary, then, disturbance may be conceptualized as a greater or lesser degree of alienation from the actualizing tendency and the organismic valuing process prompted by the fundamental need for self-regard. The resulting self-concept, usually negative and always falsely based, is linked to a defective capacity to make decisions, which in turn indicates the absence of an internalized locus of evaluation.

If individuals are unfortunate enough to be brought up amongst a number of significant others who are highly censorious or judgmental, a self-concept can develop which may serve to estrange them almost totally from their organismic experiencing. In such cases the self-concept, often developed after years of denying the promptings of the organism, becomes the fiercest enemy of the individual's true and unique identity and must undergo radical transformation if the actualizing tendency is to reassert itself.

The person-centred therapist is constantly working with clients who have all but lost touch with the actualizing tendency within themselves and who have been surrounded by others who have no confidence in the innate capacity of human beings to move towards the fulfilment of their potential. Psychologically healthy persons on the other hand are men and women who have been lucky enough to live in contexts which have been conducive to the development of self-concepts which allow them to be in touch for at least some of the time with their deepest experiences and feelings without having to censure them or distort them. Such people are well placed to achieve a level of psychological freedom which will enable them to move in the direction of becoming more fully functioning persons. 'Fully functioning' is a term used by Rogers to denote individuals who are using their talents and abilities, realizing their potential and moving towards a more complete knowledge of themselves. They are demonstrating what it means to have attained a high level of psychological health and Rogers has outlined some of the major personality characteristics which they seem to share.

The first and most striking characteristic is *openness to experience*. Individuals who are open to experience are able to listen to themselves and to others and to experience what is happening without feeling threatened. They demonstrate a high level of awareness, especially in the world of the feelings. Second, allied to this characteristic, is the *ability to live fully* in each moment of one's existence. Experience is trusted rather than feared and is the moulding force for the emerging personality rather than being twisted or manipulated to fit some preconceived structure of reality or some rigidly safeguarded self-concept. The third characteristic is the *organismic trusting* which is so clearly lacking in those who have constantly fallen victim to the adverse judgements of others. Such trusting is best displayed in the process of decision-making. Whereas many people defer continually to outside sources of influence when making decisions, fully functioning persons regard their organismic experiences as the most valid sources of information for deciding what to do in any given situation. Rogers put it succinctly when he said 'doing what "feels right" proves to be a … trustworthy guide to behavior' (1961: 190).

Further characteristics of the fully functioning person are concerned with the issues of personal freedom and creativity. For Rogers a mark of psychological health is the sense of responsibility for determining one's own actions and their consequences based on a feeling of freedom and power to choose from the many options that life presents. There is no feeling within the individual of being imprisoned by circumstances, or fate or genetic inheritance, although this is not to suggest that Rogers denies the powerful influences of biological make-up, social forces or past experience. Subjectively, however, people experience themselves as free agents. Finally, the fully functioning person is typically creative in the sense that he or she can adjust to changing conditions and is likely to produce creative ideas or initiate creative projects and actions. Such people are unlikely to be conformists, although they will relate to society in a way which permits them to be fully involved without being imprisoned by convention or tradition.

Acquisition of psychological disturbance

In person-centred terminology the mother's requirement that the baby cease to howl constitutes a *condition of worth*: 'I shall love you if you do not howl.' The concept of conditions of worth bears a striking similarity to the British therapist George Lyward's notion of contractual living. Lyward believed that most of his disturbed adolescent clients had had no chance to contact their real selves because they were too busy attempting – usually in vain – to fulfil contracts, in order to win approval (Burn, 1956; Thorne, 2005). Lyward used to speak of usurped lives and Rogers in similar vein sees many individuals as the victims of countless internalized conditions of worth which have almost totally estranged them from their organismic experiencing. Such people will be preoccupied with a sense of strain at having to come up to the mark or with feelings of worthlessness at having failed to do so. They will be the victims of countless introjected conditions of worth so that they no longer have any sense of their inherent value as unique persons. The proliferation of introjections is an inevitable outcome of the desperate need for positive regard. Introjection is the process whereby the beliefs, judgements, attitudes or values of another person (most often the parent) are taken into the individual and become part of his or her armamentarium for coping with experience, however alien they may have been initially. The child, it seems, will do almost anything to satisfy the need for positive regard even if this means taking on board (introjecting) attitudes and beliefs which run quite counter to its own organismic reaction to experience. Once such attitudes and beliefs have become thoroughly absorbed into the personality they are said to have become internalized. Thus it is that introjection and internalization of conditions of worth imposed by significant others whose approval is desperately desired often constitute the gloomy road to a deeply negative self-concept as individuals discover that they can never come up to the high demands and expectations which such conditions inevitably imply.

Once this negative self-concept has taken root in an individual the likelihood is that the separation from the wisdom of the organism will become increasingly complete. It is as if individuals become cut off from their own inner resources and their own sense of value and are governed by a secondary and treacherous valuing process which is based on the internalization of other people's judgements and evaluations. Once caught in this trap the person is likely to grow more disturbed, for the negative self-concept induces behaviour which reinforces the image of inadequacy and worthlessness. It is a fundamental thesis of the person-centred point of view that behaviour is not only the result of what happens to us from the external world but also a function of how we feel about ourselves on the inside. In other words, we are likely to behave in accordance with our perception of ourselves. What we do is often an accurate reflection of how we evaluate ourselves and if this evaluation is low our behaviour will be correspondingly unacceptable to ourselves and in all probability to others as well. It is likely, too, that we shall be highly conscious of a sense of inadequacy and although we may conceal this from others the awareness that all is not well will usually be with us.

The person-centred therapist recognizes, however, that psychological disturbance is not always available to awareness. It is possible for a person to establish a self-concept which, because of the overriding need to win the approval of others, cannot permit highly significant sensory or visceral (a favourite word with Rogers) experience into consciousness. Such people cannot be open to the full range of their organismic experiencing because to be so would threaten the self-concept which must be maintained in order to win continuing favour. An example of such a person might be the man who has established a picture of himself as honourable, virtuous, responsible and loving. Such a man may be progressively divorced from those feelings which would threaten to undermine such a self-concept. He may arrive at a point where he no longer knows, for example, that he is angry or hostile or sexually hungry, for to admit to such feelings would be to throw his whole picture of himself into question. Disturbed people are by no means always aware of their disturbance, nor will they necessarily be perceived as disturbed by others who may have a vested interest in maintaining what is in effect a tragic but often rigorous act of self-deception.

Perpetuation of psychological disturbance

It follows from the person-centred view of psychological disturbance that it will be perpetuated if an individual continues to be dependent to a high degree on the judgement of others for a sense of self-worth. Such persons will be at pains to preserve and defend at all costs the self-concept which wins approval and esteem and will be thrown into anxiety and confusion whenever incongruity arises between the self-concept and actual experience, an incongruity which may sometimes uncomfortably be 'subceived' below the level of conscious awareness while remaining unacknowledged in accurate symbolization. In the example above the 'virtuous' man would be fully subject to conscious feelings of threat and confusion if he directly experienced his hostility or sexual hunger, although to do so would, of course, be a first step towards the recovery of contact with the organismic valuing process. He will be likely, however, to avoid the threat and confusion by resorting to one or other of two basic mechanisms of defence – perceptual distortion or denial. In this way he avoids or stifles confusion and anxiety and thereby perpetuates his disturbance while mistakenly believing that he is maintaining his integrity.

Perceptual distortion takes place whenever an incongruent experience is allowed into conscious awareness but only in a form that is in harmony with the person's current self-concept. The virtuous man, for instance, might permit himself to experience hostility but would distort this as a justifiable reaction to wickedness in others: for him his hostility would be rationalized into righteous indignation. *Denial* is a less common defence but is in some ways the more impregnable. In this case individuals preserve their self-concept by completely avoiding any conscious recognition of experiences or feelings that threaten them. The virtuous man would therefore be totally unaware of his constantly angry attitudes in a committee meeting and might perceive himself as simply speaking with truth and sincerity. Distortion and denial can have formidable psychological consequences and can sometimes protect a person for a lifetime from the confusion and anxiety which could herald the recovery of proper contact with the actualizing tendency and the organismic valuing process.

Change

For people who are trapped by a negative self-concept and by behaviour which tends to demonstrate and even reinforce the validity of such a self-assessment, there is little hope of positive change unless there is movement in the psychological environment which surrounds them. Most commonly this will be the advent of a new person on the scene or a marked change in attitude of someone who is already closely involved. A child, for example, may be abused and ignored at home but may discover, to her initial bewilderment, that her teachers respect and like her. If she gradually acquires the courage to trust this unexpected acceptance she may be fortunate enough to gain further reassurance through the discovery that her teachers' respect for her is not dependent on her 'being a good girl'. For the young adult a love relationship can often revolutionize the self-concept. A girl who has come to think of herself as both stupid and ugly will find such a self-concept severely challenged by a young man who both enjoys her conversation and finds her physically desirable. There are, of course, dangers in this situation, for if the man's ardour rapidly cools and he abandons her the young woman's negative self-concept may be mightily reinforced by this painful episode. Where love runs deep, however, the beloved may be enabled to rediscover contact with the organismic core of her being and to experience her own essential worth. For clients beginning therapy the most important fact initially is the entry of a new person (the therapist) into their psychological environment. As we shall see, it is the quality of this new person and the nature of the relationship which the therapist offers that will ultimately determine whether or not change will ensue.

PRACTICE

Goals of therapy

The person-centred therapist seeks to establish a relationship with a client in which the latter can gradually dare to face the anxiety and confusion which inevitably arise once the self-concept is challenged by the movement into awareness of experiences which do not fit its current structure. If such a relationship can be achieved the client can then hope to move beyond the confusion and gradually to experience the freedom to choose a way of being which approximates more closely to his or her deepest feelings and values. The therapist will therefore focus not on problems and solutions but on relational depth, or on what has been described as a person-in-person relationship (Boy and Pine, 1982: 129). Person-centred therapists do not hesitate to invest themselves freely and fully in the relationship with their clients. They believe that they will gain entrance into the world of the client through an emotional commitment in which they are willing to involve themselves as people and to reveal themselves, if appropriate, with their own strengths and weaknesses. For the person-centred therapist a primary goal is to see, feel and experience the world as the client sees, feels and experiences it and this is not possible if the therapist stands aloof and maintains a psychological distance in the interests of a quasi-scientific objectivity.

The theoretical end-point of person-centred therapy must be the fully functioning person who is the embodiment of psychological health and whose primary characteristics were outlined above. It would be fairly safe to assert that no client has achieved such an end-point and that no therapist has been in a position to model such perfection. On the other hand there is abundant evidence, not only from the USA but also, for example, from the extensive research activities of Reinhard Tausch and his colleagues at Hamburg University (Tausch, 1975) and of Germain Lietaer at the University of Leuven in Belgium (e.g. Lietaer, 1984), that clients undergoing person-centred therapy frequently demonstrate similar changes. From my own experience I can readily confirm the perception of client movement that Rogers and other person-centred practitioners have repeatedly noted. A listing of these perceptions will show that for many clients the achievement of any one of the developments recorded could well constitute a 'goal' of therapy and might for the time being at least constitute a valid and satisfactory reason for terminating therapy. Clients in person-centred therapy are often perceived to move, then, in the following directions:

1 away from façades and the constant preoccupation with keeping up appearances
2 away from 'oughts' and an internalized sense of duty springing from externally imposed obligations
3 away from living up to the expectations of others
4 towards valuing honesty and 'realness' in oneself and others
5 towards valuing the capacity to direct one's own life
6 towards accepting and valuing one's self and one's feelings whether they are positive or negative
7 towards valuing the experience of the moment and the process of growth rather than continually striving for objectives
8 towards a greater respect and understanding of others
9 towards a cherishing of close relationships and a longing for more intimacy
10 towards a valuing of all forms of experience and a willingness to risk being open to all inner and outer experiences however uncongenial or unexpected. (Frick, 1971: 179)

Selection criteria

Person-centred therapy has proved its effectiveness with clients of many kinds presenting a wide range of difficulties and concerns. Its usefulness even with psychotics was established many years ago when Rogers and his associates participated in an elaborate investigation of the effect of psychotherapy on schizophrenics. More recently the innovative work of Garry Prouty (1995) has extended the application of person-centred theory to what he calls pre-therapy with hospitalized patients many of whom are severely dysfunctional. Rogers himself, however, offered the opinion that psychotherapy of any kind, including person-centred therapy, is probably the greatest help to the people who are closest to a reasonable adjustment to life. It is my own belief that the limitations of person-centred therapy reside not in the approach itself but in the limitations of particular therapists and in their ability or lack of it to offer their clients the necessary conditions for change and development. Having said this I freely admit that in my own experience there are certain kinds of clients who are unlikely to be much helped by the approach. Such people are usually somewhat rigid and authoritarian in their attitude to life. They look for certainties, for secure structures and often for experts to direct them in how they should be and what they should do. Their craving for such direction often makes it difficult for them to relate to the person-centred therapist in such a way that they can begin to get in touch with their own inner resources. Overly intellectual or logically rational people may also find it difficult to engage in the kind of relationship encouraged by person-centred therapy, where often the greatest changes result from a preparedness to face painful and confusing feelings which cannot initially be clearly articulated. Clients falling into these categories often turn out to be poorly motivated in any case and not infrequently they have been referred in desperation by an overworked medical practitioner, priest or social worker. Inarticulacy is in itself no barrier to effective therapeutic work, for inarticulate people are often brimming over with unexpressed feeling which begins to pour out once a relationship of trust has been established.

Clients who perhaps have most to gain from person-centred therapy are those who are strongly motivated to face painful feelings and who are deeply committed to change. They are prepared to take emotional risks and they want to trust even if they are fearful of intimacy. In my own work I often ask myself three questions as I consider working with a prospective client:

• Is the client really desirous of change?
• Is the client prepared to share responsibility for our work together?
• Is the client willing to get in touch with his or her feelings, however difficult that may be?

Reassuring answers to these three questions are usually reliable indicators that person-centred therapy is likely to be beneficial.

The person-centred approach has made significant contributions to small group and large group work and the person-centred therapy group (with two therapists or 'facilitators') is a common modality. Clients who give evidence of at least some degree of self-acceptance and whose self-concept is not entirely negative may well be encouraged (but never obliged) to join a group from the outset. More commonly, however, membership of a counselling group will occur at the point when a client in individual therapy is beginning to experience a measure of self-affirmation and is keen to take further risks in relating. At such a stage membership of a group may replace individual therapy or may be undertaken concurrently. In all cases it is the client who will decide whether to seek group membership and whether or not this should replace or complement individual therapy.

The person-centred therapist will be at pains to ensure that a client whose self-concept is low is not plunged into a group setting prematurely. Such an experience could have the disastrous outcome of reinforcing the client's sense of worthlessness. In such cases individual therapy is almost invariably indicated.

Person-centred therapists can work successfully with couples and with family groups but in these contexts much will depend on the therapist's ability to create the environment in which the couple or the family members can interact with each other without fear. In order for this to be possible it is likely that the therapist will undertake extensive preparatory work with each individual in a one-to-one relationship. Ultimately the principal criterion for embarking on couple or family therapy (apart, of course, from the willingness of all members to participate) is the therapist's confidence in his or her own ability to relate authentically to each member. (For further discussion of this issue see Mearns, 1994: 56–60.) Such confidence is unlikely to be achieved in the absence of in-depth preliminary meetings with each person involved. Indeed, in couple therapy it is common for the therapist to agree to work for a negotiated period with each partner separately before all three come together in order to tackle the relationship directly. With a family the process is clearly more complex and the preparatory work even more time-consuming. Perhaps this is the main reason why person-centred family therapy remains comparatively rare. It may well be, however, that this situation will change in the years immediately ahead not least because a book is now available devoted to person-centred work with couples and families. The author, Charlie O'Leary, provides fascinating evidence of the effectiveness of the person-centred approach in this area of practice and his passionate enthusiasm is sure to inspire others to follow his example (O'Leary, 1999). Certainly the increase in marital and partnership breakdown underlines the need for such work.

Qualities of effective therapists

It has often been suggested that of all the various 'schools' of psychotherapy the person-centred approach makes the heaviest demands upon the therapist. Whether this is so or not I have no way of knowing. What I do know is that unless person-centred therapists can relate in such a way that their clients perceive them as trustworthy and dependable *as people*, therapy cannot take place. Person-centred therapists can have no recourse to diagnostic labelling nor can they find security in a complex and detailed theory of personality which will allow them to foster 'insight' in their clients through interpretation, however gently offered. In brief, they cannot win their clients' confidence by demonstrating their psychological expertise for to do so would be to place yet another obstacle in the way of clients' movement towards trusting their own innate resources. To be a trustworthy person is not something which can be simulated for long and in a very real sense person-centred therapists can only be as trustworthy for another as they are for themselves. Therapists' attitudes to themselves thus become of cardinal importance. If I am to be acceptant of another's feelings and experiences and to be open to the possible expression of material long since blocked off from awareness I must feel a deep level of acceptance for myself. If I cannot trust myself to acknowledge and accept my own feelings without adverse judgement or incapacitating self-recrimination it is unlikely that I shall appear sufficiently trustworthy to a client who may have much deeper cause to feel ashamed or worthless. If, too, I am in constant fear that I shall be overwhelmed by an upsurging of unacceptable data into my own awareness then I am unlikely to convey to my client that I am genuinely open to the full exploration of his or her own doubts and fears.

The ability of the therapist to be congruent, accepting and empathic (fundamental attitudes in person-centred therapy which will be explored more fully later) is not developed overnight. It is unlikely, too, that such an ability will be present in people who are not continually seeking to broaden their own life experience.

Therapists cannot confidently invite their clients to travel further than they have journeyed themselves, but for person-centred therapists the quality, depth and continuity of their own experiencing becomes the very cornerstone of the competence they bring to their professional activity. Unless I have a sense of my own continuing development as a person I shall lose faith in the process of becoming and shall be tempted to relate to my clients in a way which may well reinforce them in a past self-concept. What is more, I shall myself become stuck in a past image of myself and will no longer be in contact with the part of my organism which challenges me to go on growing as a person even if my body is beginning to show every sign of wearing out. It follows, too, that an excessive reliance on particular skills for relating or communicating can present a subtle trap because such skills may lead to a professional behavioural pattern which is itself resistant to change because it becomes set or stylized.

Therapeutic relationship and style

Person-centred therapists differ widely in therapeutic style. They have in common, however, a desire to create a relationship characterized by a climate in which clients begin to get in touch with their own wisdom and their capacity for self-understanding and for altering their self-concept and self-defeating behaviours. Person-centred therapists' ability to establish this climate is crucial to the whole therapeutic enterprise, since if they fail to do so there is no hope of forming the kind of relationship with their clients which will bring about the desired therapeutic movement. It will become apparent, however, that the way in which they attempt to create and convey the necessary climate will depend very much on the nature of their own personality.

The first element in the creation of the climate has to do with what has variously been called the therapist's *congruence*, realness, authenticity or genuineness. In essence this congruence depends on therapists' capacities for being properly in touch with the complexity of feelings, thoughts and attitudes which will be flowing through them as they seek to track their clients' thoughts and feelings. The more they can do this the more they will be perceived by their clients as people of real flesh and blood who are willing to be seen and known and not as clinical professionals intent on concealing themselves behind a metaphorical white coat. The issue of the therapist's congruence is more complex than might initially appear. Although clients need to experience their therapists' essential humanity and to feel their emotional involvement they certainly do not need to have all the therapist's feelings and thoughts thrust down their throats. Therapists must not only attempt to remain firmly in touch with the flow of their own experience but must also have the discrimination to know how and when to communicate what they are experiencing.

It is here that to the objective observer person-centred therapists might well appear to differ widely in style. In my own attempts to be congruent, for example, I find that verbally I often communicate little. I am aware, however, that my bodily posture does convey a deep willingness to be involved with my client and that my eyes are highly expressive of a wide range of feeling – often to the point of tears. It would seem that there is frequently little need for me to communicate my feelings verbally: I am transparent enough already and I know from experience that my clients are sensitive to this transparency. Another therapist might well behave in a manner far removed from mine but with the same concern to be congruent. Therapists are just as much unique human beings as their clients and the way in which they make their humanity available by following the flow of their own experiencing and communicating it when appropriate will be an expression of their own uniqueness. Whatever the precise form of their behaviour, however, person-centred therapists will be exercising their skill in order to communicate to their clients an attitude expressive of their desire to be deeply and fully involved in the relationship without pretence and without the protection of professional impersonality.

For many clients entering therapy, the second attitude of importance in creating a facilitative climate for change – *unconditional positive regard* – may seem to be the most critical. The conditions of worth which have in so many cases warped and undermined the self-concept of the client are the outcome of the judgmental and conditional attitudes of those close to the client, which have often been reinforced by societal or cultural norms. In contrast, the therapist seeks to offer the client an unconditional acceptance, a positive regard or caring, a non-possessive love. This acceptance is not of the person as she might become, a respect for her as yet unfulfilled potential, but a total and unconditional acceptance of the client as she seems to herself *in the present*. Such an attitude on the part of the therapist cannot be simulated and cannot be offered by someone who remains largely frightened or threatened by his or her own feelings. Nor again can such acceptance be offered by someone who is disturbed when confronted by a person who possesses values, attitudes and feelings different from his or her own. Genuine acceptance is totally unaffected by differences of background or belief system between client and therapist, for it is in no way dependent on moral, ethical or social criteria.

As with genuineness, the attitude of acceptance requires great skill on the part of the therapist if it is to be communicated at the depth which will enable clients to feel safe to be whatever they are currently experiencing. After what may well be a lifetime of highly conditional acceptance clients will not recognize unconditionality easily. When they do they will tend to regard it as an unlikely miracle which will demand continual checking out before it can be fully trusted. The way in which a therapist conveys unconditional acceptance characterized by positive regard will again be dependent to a large extent on the nature of his or her personality. For my own part I have found increasingly that the non-verbal aspects of my responsiveness are powerfully effective. A smile can often convey more acceptance and regard than a statement which, however sensitive, may still run the risk of seeming patronizing. I have discovered, too, that the gentle pressing of the hand or the light touch on the knee will enable clients to realize that all is well and that there will be no judgement, however confused or negative they are or however silent and hostile.

The third facilitative attitude is that of *empathic understanding*. Rogers (1975) himself wrote extensively about empathy and suggested that of the three 'core conditions' (as congruence, unconditional positive regard and empathy are often known), empathy is the most trainable. The crucial importance of empathic understanding springs from the person-centred therapist's overriding concern with the client's subjective perceptual world. Only through as full an understanding as possible of the way in which clients view themselves and the world can the therapist hope to encourage the subtle changes in self-concept which make for growth. Such understanding involves on the therapist's part a willingness to enter the private perceptual world of the client and to become thoroughly conversant with it. This demands a high degree of sensitivity to the moment-to-moment experiencing of the client so that the therapist is recognized as a reliable companion even when contradictory feelings follow on each other in rapid succession. In a certain sense therapists must lay themselves aside for the time being with all their prejudices and values if they are to enter into the perceptual world of the other. Such an undertaking would be foolhardy if the therapist feels insecure in the presence of a particular client for there would be the danger of getting lost in a perhaps frightening or confusing world. The task of empathic understanding can be accomplished only by people who are secure enough in their own identity to move into another's world without the fear of being overwhelmed by it. Once there, therapists have to move around with extreme delicacy and with an utter absence of judgement. They will probably sense meanings of which the client is scarcely aware and might even become dimly aware of feelings of which there is no consciousness on the part of the client at all. Such moments call for extreme caution for there is the danger that the therapist could express understanding at too deep a level and frighten the client away from therapy altogether. Rogers, on a recording made for *Psychology Today* in the 1970s, described such a blunder as 'blitz therapy' and contrasted this with an empathic response which is constructive because it conveys an understanding of what is currently going on in the client and of meanings that are just below the level of awareness but does not slip over into unconscious motivations which frighten the client.

If the communication of congruence and unconditional positive regard presents difficulties, the communication of empathic understanding may be even more challenging. Often a client's inner world is complex and confusing as well as a source of pain and guilt. Sometimes clients have little understanding of their own feelings. Therapists often need to marshal the full range of their emotional and cognitive abilities if they are to convey their understanding thoroughly. On the other hand, if they do not succeed there is ample evidence to suggest that their very attempt to do so, however bumbling and incomplete, will be experienced by the client as supportive and validating. What is always essential is the therapist's willingness to check out the accuracy of his or her understanding. I find that my own struggles at communicating empathic understanding are littered with such questions as 'Am I getting it right? Is that what you mean?' When I do get a complex feeling right the effect is often electrifying and the sense of wonder and thankfulness in the client can be one of the most moving experiences in therapy. There can be little doubt that the rarity of empathic understanding of this kind is what endows it with such power and makes it the most reliable force for creative change in the whole of the therapeutic process.

It was Rogers's contention – and he held firm to it for over 40 years – that if the therapist proves able to offer a relationship where congruence, unconditional positive regard and empathy are all present, then therapeutic movement will almost invariably occur. Towards the end of his life, however, he pointed to another quality which he saw not as additional to the core conditions but as sometimes resulting from their consistent application. This he called 'presence' and having first called attention to it in *A Way of Being* (Rogers, 1980: 129) he returned to it in an article published shortly before his death (Rogers, 1986). He talks of 'presence' in terms which seem somewhat at variance with the pragmatic, hard-headed tone of the scientific scholar of earlier years but I have come to see this later statement as capturing the essence of the therapeutic relationship when it is functioning at its most effective level.

Rogers wrote:

> When I am at my best, as a group facilitator or a therapist, I discover another characteristic. I find that when I am closest to my inner, intuitive self, when I am somehow in touch with the unknown in me, when perhaps I am in a slightly altered state of consciousness in the

> relationship, then whatever I do seems to be full of healing. Then simply my *presence* is releasing and helpful. There is nothing I can do to force this experience, but when I can relax and be close to the transcendental core of me, then I may behave in strange and impulsive ways in the relationship, ways which I cannot justify rationally, which have nothing to do with my thought processes. But these strange behaviors turn out to be *right*, in some odd way. At those moments it seems that my inner spirit has reached out and touched the inner spirit of the other. (Rogers, 1986: 199)

It is my own belief that the therapist's ability to be 'present' in this way is dependent on his or her capacity to be fearlessly alongside the client's experience even to the extent of being willing on occasions *not* to understand what is occurring in the client's world (Mearns, 1994: 5–9). Such a capacity is likely to develop in a relationship where counsellor and client have established a deep level of trust and where mutuality is increasingly possible (see following section). It explains, too, why the most fruitful relationships will be characterized by a developing ability on the part of both counsellor and client to move between different levels of experiencing with ease and confidence. As therapy proceeds, seriousness and humour, for example, will alternate and the pattern of interactivity will shift frequently as client and counsellor adopt, by turns, more active or passive roles. Furthermore a therapist's way of being fully present to his or her client is again likely to be indicative of the unique personality of the therapist. I find that when I am able to be totally present in the moment this releases in me a quality which I have defined as 'tenderness' (Thorne, 1985, 2004). This in turn enables me to live with paradoxes and gives me the will to wait in hope when I am feeling powerless. With Rogers, who later in the same article acknowledges that his account 'partakes of the mystical' and goes on to speak of 'this mystical, spiritual dimension', I am persuaded that the relationship in person-centred therapy is at its most liberating and transforming when it 'transcends itself and becomes part of something larger' (Rogers, 1986: 199).

Major therapeutic strategies and techniques

There are no strategies or techniques which are integral to person-centred therapy. The approach is essentially based on the experiencing and communication of attitudes, and these attitudes cannot be packaged up in techniques. At an earlier point in the history of the approach there was an understandable emphasis on the ebb and flow of the therapeutic interview and much was gained from the microscopic study of client–therapist exchanges. To Rogers's horror, however, the tendency to focus on the therapist's responses had the effect of so debasing the approach that it became known as a technique. Even nowadays it is possible to meet people who believe that person-centred therapy is simply the technique of reflecting the client's feelings or, worse still, that it is primarily a matter of repeating the last words spoken by the client. I hope I have shown that nothing could be further from the truth. The attitudes required of the therapist demand the highest level of self-knowledge and self-acceptance and the translation of them into communicable form requires of each therapist the most delicate skill, which for the most part must spring from his or her unique personality and cannot be learned through pale imitations of Carl Rogers or anyone else.

In *Person-Centred Counselling in Action* (Mearns and Thorne, 1988, 1999) attention is drawn to the fact that the most productive outcomes seem to result from therapeutic relationships which move through three distinct phases. The first stage is characterized by the establishing of *trust* on the part of the client. This may happen very rapidly or it can take months. The second stage sees the development of *intimacy*: during this stage the client is enabled to reveal some of the deepest levels of his or her experiencing. The third stage is characterized by an increasing *mutuality* between therapist and client. When such a stage is reached it is likely that therapists will be increasingly self-disclosing and will be challenged to risk more of themselves in the relationship. When it occurs this three-stage process becomes so deeply rewarding for the therapist that a cynical critic might view it as the outcome of an unconscious strategizing on the therapist's part. So insidious is this accusation that I am now deeply concerned to monitor my own behaviour with the utmost vigilance in order to ensure that I am *not* embarked on a manipulatory plot aimed at achieving a spurious mutuality which may be deeply satisfying for me but quite irrelevant to the client's needs.

The realization that person-centred therapy at its best may give access to a quality of relating which embraces the spiritual raises important questions about the counsellor's fitness for such a task and the personal discipline that this implies (Thorne, 1994, 2002; Mearns and Thorne, 2000). In an approach which explicitly turns its back on strategies and techniques as being contrived and potentially abusive of a client's autonomy, it becomes of the utmost importance that the therapist is preserved from self-deception, not only by the challenge of rigorous supervision but also by the willing acceptance of a discipline which has as its aim the most thorough integration of belief and practice. Without such integration the person-centred therapist runs the risk of mouthing and peddling the core conditions as if they were little more than behavioural conditions to be applied mechanically by a psychological technician after a few hours' 'skills training'. Such a travesty of the approach has led in the past to the ill-informed notion that person-centred therapy is 'easy' or that it can be useful *as a technique* in the early stages of therapy before more sophisticated and effective methods are introduced (Mearns and Thorne, 1999: 5).

The change process in therapy

When person-centred therapy goes well clients will move from a position where their self-concept, typically poor at the entry into therapy and finding expression in behaviour which is reinforcing of the negative evaluation of self, will shift to a position where it more closely reflects the person's essential worth. As the self-concept moves towards a more positive view so, too, clients' behaviour begins to mirror the improvement and to enhance their perception of themselves. The therapist's ability to create a relationship in which the three facilitative attitudes are consistently present will to a large extent determine the extent to which clients are able to move towards a more positive contact with the promptings of the actualizing tendency.

If therapy has been successful clients will also have learned how to be their own therapist. It seems that when people experience the genuineness of another and a real attentive caring and valuing by that other person they begin to adopt the same attitude towards themselves. In short, a person who is cared for begins to feel at a deep level that perhaps she is after all *worth* caring for. In a similar way, the experience of being on the receiving end of the concentrated listening and the empathic understanding which characterize the therapist's response tends to develop a listening attitude in the client towards herself. It is as if she gradually becomes less afraid to get in touch with what is going on inside her and dares to listen attentively to her own feelings. With this growing attentive-ness comes increased self-understanding and a tentative grasp of some of her most central personal meanings. Many clients have told me that after person-centred therapy they never lose this ability to treat themselves with respect and to take the risk of listening to what they are experiencing. If they do lose it tem-porarily or find themselves becoming hopelessly confused they will not hesitate to return to therapy to engage once more in a process which is in many ways an education for living.

In Rogers and Dymond (1954) one of Rogers's chapters explores in detail a client's successful process through therapy. The case of Mrs Oak has become a rich source of learning for person-centred therapists ever since, and towards the end of the chapter Rogers attempts a summary of the therapeutic process which Mrs Oak has experienced with such obvious benefits to herself. What is described there seems to me to be so characteristic of the person-centred expe-rience of therapy that I make no apology for providing a further summary of some of Rogers's findings.

The process begins with the therapist providing an atmosphere of warm car-ing and acceptance which over the first few sessions is gradually experienced by the client, Mrs Oak, as genuinely *safe*. With this realization the client finds that she changes the emphasis of her sessions from dealing with reality problems to experiencing herself. The effect of this change of emphasis is that she begins to experience her feelings in the immediate present without inhibition. She can be angry, hurt, childish, joyful, self-deprecating, self-appreciative and as she allows this to occur she discovers many feelings bubbling through into awareness of which she was not previously conscious. With new feelings there come new thoughts and the admission of all this fresh material to awareness leads to a *breakdown of the previously held self-concept*. There then follows a period of disorganization and confusion although there remains a feeling that the path is the right one and that reorganization will ultimately take place. What is being learned during this process is that it pays to recognize an experience for what it is rather than denying it or distorting it. In this way the client becomes more open to experience and begins to realize that it is healthy to accept feelings whether they be positive or negative, for this permits a movement towards greater completeness. At this stage the client gradually comes to realize that *she can begin to define herself and does not have to accept the definition and judgements of others*. There is, too, a more conscious appreciation of the nature of the relationship with the therapist and the value of a love which is not possessive and makes no demands. At about this stage the client finds that she can make relationships outside of therapy which enable others to be self-experiencing and self-directing and she becomes progressively aware that at the core of her being she is not destructive but genuinely desires the well-being of others. Self-responsibility continues to increase to the point where the client feels able to make her own choices – although this is not always pleasant – and to trust herself in a world which, although it may often seem to be disintegrating, yet offers many opportunities for creative activity and relating (Rogers, 1954). I would add that for those clients who repeatedly experience those moments in therapy where 'inner spirit touches inner spirit' there is a strong likelihood that their sense of the numinous will be awakened or rekindled and that the search for meaning will be strengthened. Not infrequently clients towards the end of therapy report a new acknowledgement of spiritual reality which in some cases leads to a re-engagement with previously rejected religious observances or, more often, to the exploration of hitherto uncharted spiritual terrain.

Person-centred therapy is essentially an approach to the human condition based on trust. There is trust in the innate resourcefulness of human beings, given the right conditions, to find their own way through life. There is trust that the direction thus found will be positive and creative. There is trust, too, that the process of relating between counsellor and client will in itself provide the primary context of safety and nurture in which the client can face the pain of alienation from his or her own actualizing tendency and move towards a more integrated way of being. Where blocks occur in therapeutic process they can almost invariably be traced back to a lack or loss of trust on the part of client or counsellor or both in the basic premises of the approach, and more particularly in the essentially healing process of the therapeutic relationship. In many instances where the lack of trust is firmly lodged in the client, the person-centred therapist has the unenviable but clear task of learning to wait, of exercising patience while committing himself or herself to the consistent offering of the core conditions in the face of the client's fear, hostility or increasing pain.

The situation is potentially more grave when the lack of trust resides in the therapist. He or she doubts his or her capacity to offer the core conditions to this particular client and is consumed with a fear of mounting failure. In such a situation, where supervision fails to resolve the stuckness, the therapist has no option but to address the issues with the client, not knowing whether this will herald movement forward or the end of the relationship. An ebbing of trust in the relationship itself can often be guarded against by an agreement at the outset between therapist and client to review their process periodically *as a matter of course*. Such 'stocktaking' facilitates an openness between counsellor and client which ensures that difficulties and doubts are not allowed to fester but can be faced squarely and in this way serve to strengthen rather than undermine the therapeutic relationship. This practice also reinforces the essentially shared nature of the therapeutic work and makes more likely the achievement of the 'relational depth' where the most profound changes can occur (Mearns, 1996). It also offers the client the opportunity, as therapy proceeds, to invite the therapist to respond in new ways. Not infrequently, for example, clients wish to enlist the therapist's support in implementing new behaviours which are more in keeping with their changing self-concept and greater confidence. Progress can be unnecessarily impeded if in such instances clients believe that the therapist is interested solely in their state of being and is not concerned to help initiate action or to involve others in their development. Regular stocktaking will ensure that such misconceptions are rapidly dispelled. Would that such a practice was commonly adopted by married couples and others in close relationships!

Limitations of the approach

After 37 years as a person-centred therapist I am drawn to the conclusion, as I stated earlier, that the limitations of the approach are a reflection of the personal limitations of the therapist. As these will clearly vary from individual to individual and are unlikely to be constant over time I am sceptical about the usefulness of exploring the limitations of the approach in any generalized fashion. None the less I am intrigued by the question with respect to two particular issues. I believe that person-centred therapy has been in danger of selling itself short because of its traditional emphasis on the 'here and now' and because of what is seen as its heavy reliance on verbal interaction. Both these tendencies are likely to be reinforced when the therapist's congruence remains at a relatively superficial level.

In my own practice I have discovered that the more I am able to be fully present to myself in the therapeutic relationship the more likely it is that I shall come to trust the promptings of a deeper and more intuitive level within myself. Cautiously and with constant safeguards against self-deception I have come to value this intuitive part of my being and to discover its efficacy in the therapeutic relationship. What is more, when I have risked articulating a thought or feeling which emanates from this deeper level I have done so in the knowledge that it may appear unconnected to what is currently happening in the relationship or even bizarre to my client. More often than not, however, the client's response has been immediate and sometimes dramatic. It is as if the quality of the relationship which has been established, thanks to the consistent offering of the core conditions, goes a long way towards ensuring that my own intuitive promptings are deeply and immediately significant for the client. Often, too, the significance lies in the triggering of past experience for the client – not in the sense simply of locating memories of past events but in releasing a veritable flow of feeling whose origin lies in past experience which is then vividly relived. Commonly, too, the therapist's intuitive response seems to touch a part of the client's being which cannot find immediate expression in words. I am astonished how often at such moments the client reaches out for physical reassurance or plunges into deep but overflowing silence or into convulsive sobbing in which new movement is mysteriously generated.

There are many in the person-centred tradition whose frustration with the essentially verbal nature of the therapy has led them to supplement the approach with methods culled from other disciplines (e.g. Tausch, 1990). Rogers's own daughter, Natalie, has pioneered an approach she calls person-centred expressive therapy (Rogers, 1993) which incorporates movement, art, music, pottery and creative writing as well as other essentially non-verbal channels of expression. Eugene Gendlin, referred to earlier, has developed the method of focusing for deepening inner experience (Gendlin, 1981). Gendlin's work is particularly impressive, giving access as it does to a level of self-knowledge which is initially just outside the bounds of conscious awareness. Indeed, focusing has developed into what is now known as experiential psychotherapy but its kinship to person-centred therapy is reflected in the title of the new World Association which seeks to embrace both in the same family. In Britain the work of Campbell Purton and Judy Moore at the University of East Anglia has further enhanced the close relationship between the two.

Those who would see a limitation of the approach as being its unwillingness to entertain the notion of working with the unconscious can perhaps find some reassurance in Gendlin's contribution. Focusing works on the premise that there *is* material outside of awareness and that it can profitably be tapped into and integrated into the self-concept. The same is true of the innovative work undertaken in recent times by Dave Mearns on 'configurations' within the self. Person-centred practitioners by their willingness to enter into relational depth with their clients make it safe enough for them to engage with parts or dimensions of their being which they had not previously dared fully to encounter. These 'configurations' – denoting a coherent pattern of feelings, thoughts and behavioural responses – do not constitute material derived from 'working with the unconscious' for the client remains at the centre of the therapeutic endeavour and dictates his or her own path and pace into awareness. The therapist, as always, is the faithful companion who by his or her commitment to authentic relating makes the path less frightening and the pace manageable (Mearns and Thorne, 2000: 101–43). Far from being a limitation, person-centred therapy's refusal to work directly with the unconscious can lead to a mutuality of in-depth relationship where fear can be faced and advances in awareness achieved. These do not depend on elaborated maps of the unconscious but on the therapist's willingness and ability to be fully present to him or herself as well as to the client. Rogers discovered towards the end of his life that simply his presence could be healing for others in ways he had not previously conceptualized. He found, in effect, that to be fully congruent was a constant challenge to his own integrity and trust in life. It is on the continuing response to that challenge that the further development of person-centred therapy must ultimately depend with all the existential and spiritual questionings which that will inevitably entail.

Case example (provided by Caroline Kitcatt)

The client

Melanie was a striking woman in her late thirties, who came for counselling following the break up of her marriage six months before. She was struggling to cope emotionally and had been off work with stress for four weeks. One of her friends had suggested counselling, but she was by no means sure that this was what she wanted to do. She described herself as confident and outgoing but for some reason she was finding herself breaking down in tears frequently, not sleeping, and this was affecting her at work. She said she felt she had 'dealt with' the break up of her marriage, was trying to move on and to this end had joined a gym where she went most days 'to get herself back in shape again' and had met a few men through internet dating. She could not understand why she was not feeling happier.

The therapy

As I listened to Melanie I was aware of feeling confused. She did indeed appear confident and outgoing and to be accepting of the break up of her marriage. She presented me with her situation as if it was a package neatly wrapped and this made it difficult to relate to her in any depth. At the same time I was aware that her tearfulness, insomnia and time off work for stress suggested a vulnerability and a level of distress that she was reluctant to acknowledge.

In my responses to her in the first session I was careful to convey my acceptance of her as a confident and competent person, while at the same time responding to her as someone who was struggling and suffering. This was delicate work, because she was at pains to stress that she was 'dealing with it' and was sure she was really OK. Although I responded to her unhappiness, she did not give much away about her inner feelings. I was aware that the offering of empathy and establishing of trust were not going to be easy.

By our third session I felt that we were still not meeting at any depth. Then I realised that actually it was I who was failing to invest myself fully in the relationship. After she had recounted the events of her week and asked for my support in attempting what she felt was a promising relationship with someone she had met on the internet, I risked expressing something of what I was experiencing. I told her that it felt as if she was trying to convince me that she was doing well, and yet at the same time I sensed a deep despair and I was not quite sure where that was coming from. At this, Melanie immediately burst into tears and began to sob deeply. After five minutes I leant forward and asked gently if she could tell me what she was feeling. To my surprise she then became quite angry, and almost shouted at me that she was perfectly alright. I did not feel unnerved by this anger; on the contrary Melanie's response enabled me to come closer to her for I felt I was being admitted into the rawness of her inner contradictions.

I experienced a huge compassion for this fragile woman, so desperately holding on to her dignity in the face of rejection. I decided to take a further risk and openly expressed my compassionate understanding of her predicament. She looked at me, stopped sobbing, and seemed very confused. It was clear this was not the response she had expected. Met by my acceptance and empathy she came to a sudden reali-sation. She admitted that I had taken her by surprise. She had been waiting to be told to pull herself together and to get on with it. She expected that I was going to tell her where she was 'going wrong' and then she would be able to change and become an OK person who could be loved and not abandoned. She said she knew she didn't look good at the moment, felt she was fat and unattractive, and not really a very nice person at all. She 'ought' to be able to pull herself together, get her weight down and cheer up. She was terrified of being single, feared she would never have a family, was no good at relationships and was only popular if she was the life and soul of her social group. From this catalogue of perceptions and anxieties I con-cluded that she was labouring under many conditions of worth, and that her locus of evaluation was clearly in no way internalized. It was a great relief, however, that she was now trusting me sufficiently to give me access to her inner world.

She arrived the following week with the words 'I want to talk to you about my rela-tionship with my mother'. During the interval since our previous session she had realised how hard she always tried to 'get it right', and how much of a failure she felt. She saw her mother as a slim, elegant, happily married woman with a large social circle. She had realised that she was trying to 'live up to' her mother's expectations and had always felt a failure. Gradually a picture emerged of a lonely childhood, a successful brother who could do no wrong and shone in social situations, whereas she had struggled until she had developed a bubbly outgoing personality who could entertain and amuse. Behind this exterior she hid the shy girl who had no confidence in herself and did not really know who she was. As all this emerged she felt very disloyal to her mother: 'if she was here, she would see it differently, you're only getting one side of it'.

The following week there was a phone call from Melanie to say she was unwell, and the same thing happened the following week too. I was increasingly concerned, took my anxiety to supervision, and concluded as I often do, that I needed to trust my uneasy feelings. Over the years as I have attempted to come to terms with the more painful parts of my own life, I have learned to trust the inner promptings of my own disquiet and to put them at the service of my client.

When, mercifully, Melanie came for her next session, she said she felt much bet-ter, had lost weight, was dating a new man and was convinced everything would now be OK. In the face of her seeming optimism, my feelings of unease became stronger, and I decided to risk sharing what had been happening for me during her absence. Once more she looked surprised, was very quiet, and then in a small voice said that following our previous session her mother had telephoned her. With her new found awareness Melanie had risked telling her she was having counselling, whereupon her mother had been dismissive of the value of counselling, and hoped she was not 'blaming everything on her parents'. Her mother had then told her to pull herself together. She had tried to do this and this was the reason for missing two sessions. A part of her felt she 'ought' to be able 'to pull herself together' but another part, of which she was increasingly aware, knew she needed to face her feelings of low self-esteem, her lack of confidence and her fears about herself. I shuddered to think how I might easily have dismissed my unease and been convinced by her assertions that she was OK. As I shared this with her, our relationship seemed to move to a deeper level of trust.

As therapy progressed, Melanie was able to explore her relationship with her mother, her childhood experiences, her marriage, and most importantly, her relationship with herself, including her body. She realised how severely her mother had undermined her and she began to have vivid dreams in which she was very angry with her mother. She started to write a journal, decided she was not going to date anyone for the time being, and cut down her visits to the gym.

One weekend she discovered a photograph of herself aged around eleven, and was struck by how lovely she had been as a child, not at all fat or ugly. She had bought a frame for the photo and had it by her bed. She brought the photo with her, and I was very moved by both the trust that she felt in showing it to me and by the lovely child I had pictured in my imagination being brought physically into the session and our relationship. I am sure Melanie sensed the lump in my throat as I said how touched I felt by the child with a cheeky smile but such wistful eyes. This was a moment when we both experienced a moment of togetherness that was transformative.

At times we moved between movement and stuckness, but I was always careful to respond to the 'not for growth' parts as well as the 'for growth' parts of her, following my anxiety when she had failed to appear at the earlier stage of therapy. Having explored her relationship with her mother, she made some startling connections to her relationship with her ex-husband, initially blaming herself for the break up of her marriage, but then working through to a clearer place where she felt she had greater understanding and therefore more confidence for the future. Her stress levels fell and she was able to return to work. She became more accepting of herself and, as this happened, she developed a greater acceptance of her mother. Their relationship remained a challenge, but she was able to hear her mother's criticisms without taking them into herself and falling prey to them as had previously happened with such unfortunate results.

REFERENCES

Boy, A.V. and Pine, G.J. (1982) *Client-centered Counselling. A Renewal*. Boston, MA: Allyn & Bacon.

Burn, M. (1956) *Mr Lyward's Answer*. London: Hamish Hamilton.

Embleton Tudor, L., Keemar, K., Tudor, K., Valentine, J. and Worrall, M. (2004) *The Person-Centered Approach: a Contemporary Introduction*. Basingstoke: Palgrave/Macmillan.

Frick, W.B. (1971) *Humanistic Psychology: Interviews with Maslow, Murphy and Rogers*. Columbus, OH: Charles E. Merrill.

Gendlin, E. (1981) *Focusing*. New York: Bantam Books.

Keys, S.(ed.) (2003) *Idiosyncratic Person-Centred Therapy. From the Personal to the Universal*. Ross-on-Wye: PCCS Books.

Kirschenbaum, H. (1979) *On Becoming Carl Rogers*. New York: Delacorte Press.

Lietaer, G. (1984) 'Unconditional positive regard: a controversial basic attitude in client-centered therapy', in R. Levant and J. Shlien (eds), *Client-Centered Therapy and the Person-Centered Approach*. New York: Praeger. pp. 41–58.

McLeod, J. (1994) *Doing Counselling Research*. London: Sage.

McLeod, J. (2003) *Doing counselling Research*, 2nd edn. London: Sage.

McMillan, M. (2004) *The Person-Centred Approach to Therapeutic Change*. London: Sage.

Mearns, D. (1994) *Developing Person-Centred Counselling*. London: Sage.

Mearns, D. (1996) 'Working at relational depth with clients in person-centred therapy', *Counselling*, 7(4): 306–11.

Mearns, D. (1997) *Person-Centred Counselling Training*. London: Sage.

Mearns, D. (2002) *Developing Person-Centred Counselling*, 2nd edn. London: Sage.

Mearns, D. and Cooper, M.(2005) *Working at Relational Depth in Counselling and Psychotherapy*. London: Sage.

Mearns, D. and Thorne, B.J. (1988) *Person-Centred Counselling in Action*. London: Sage.

Mearns, D. and Thorne B.J. (1999) *Person-Centred Counselling in Action*, 2nd edn. London: Sage.

Mearns, D. and Thorne, B.J. (2000) *Person-Centred Therapy Today: New Frontiers in Theory and Practice*. London: Sage.

Merry, T. (1995) *Invitation to Person-Centred Psychology*. London: Whurr.

Merry, T. (1999) *Learning and Being in Person-Centred Counselling*. Ross-on-Wye: PCCS Books.

Oatley, K. (1981) 'The self with others: the person and the interpersonal context in the approaches of C.R. Rogers and R.D. Laing', in F. Fransella (ed.), *Personality*. London: Methuen.

O'Leary, C. (1999) *Couple and Family Counselling: A Person-Centred Approach*. London: Sage.

Prouty, G.F. (1995) *Theoretical Evolutions in Person-centered/Experiential Therapy*. Westport, CT: Praeger.

Purton, C. (2004) *Person-Centred Therapy: The Focusing-Oriented Approach*. Basingstoke: Palgrave/Macmillan.

Rogers, C.R. (1942) *Counseling and Psychotherapy*. Boston, MA: Houghton-Mifflin.

Rogers, C.R. (1951) *Client-Centered Therapy*. Boston, MA: Houghton-Mifflin.

Rogers, C.R. (1954) 'The case of Mrs Oak: a research analysis', in C.R. Rogers and R.F. Dymond (eds), *Psychology and Personality Change*. Chicago: University of Chicago Press.

Rogers, C.R. (1961) *On Becoming a Person*. Boston, MA: Houghton-Mifflin.

Rogers, C.R. (1974) 'In retrospect: forty-six years', *American Psychologist*, 29(2): 115–23.

Rogers, C.R. (1975) 'Empathic: an unappreciated way of being', *The Counseling Psychologist*, 2: 2–10.

Rogers, C.R. (1979) 'The foundations of the person-centered approach', unpublished manuscript. La Jolla, CA.

Rogers, C.R. (1980) *A Way of Being*. Boston, MA: Houghton-Mifflin.

Rogers, C.R. (1986) 'A client-centered/person-centered approach to therapy', in I. Kutash and A. Wolf (eds), *Psychotherapist's Casebook*. San Francisco: Jossey-Bass. pp. 197–208.

Rogers, C.R. and Dymond, R.F. (eds) (1954) *Psychology and Personality Change*. Chicago: University of Chicago Press.

Rogers, N. (1993) *The Creative Connection*. San Francisco: Science and Behavior Books.

Tausch, R. (1975) 'Ergebnisse und Prozesse der klienten-zentrierten Gesprächspsychotherapie bei 500 Klienten und 115 Psychotherapeuten. Eine Zusammenfassung des Hamburger Forschungsprojektes', *Zeitschrift für praktische Psychologie*, 13: 293–307.

Tausch, R. (1990) 'The supplementation of client-centered communication therapy with other validated therapeutic methods: a client centered necessity', in G. Lietaer, J. Rombauts and R. van Balen (eds), *Client-Centered and Experiential Psychotherapy in the Nineties*. Leuven: Leuven University Press. pp. 448–55.

Thorne, B.J. (1985) *The Quality of Tenderness*. Norwich: Norwich Centre Occasional Publications.

Thorne, B.J. (1991) *Person-centred Counselling: Therapeutic and Spiritual Dimensions*. London: Whurr.

Thorne, B.J. (1992) *Carl Rogers*. London: Sage.

Thorne, B.J. (1994) 'Developing a spiritual discipline', in D. Mearns, *Developing Person-centred Counselling*. London: Sage. pp. 44–7.

Thorne, B.J. (1998) *Person-Centred Counselling and Christian Spirituality*. London: Whurr.

Thorne, B.J. (2002) *The Mystical Power of Person-Centred Therapy*. London: Whurr.

Thorne, B.J. (2003) *Carl Rogers*, 2nd edn. London: Sage.

Thorne, B.J. (2004) *The Quality of Tenderness*, revised edn. Norwich: Norwich Centre Occasional
      Publications.
Thorne, B.J. (2005) *Love's Embrace: the Autobiography of a Person-Centred Therapist*. Ross-on-Wye:
      PCCS Books.
Thorne, B.J. and Lambers, E. (eds) (1998) *Person-Centred Therapy: a European Perspective*. London:
      Sage.
Tolan, J. (2003) *Skills in Person-Centred Counselling and Psychotherapy*. London: Sage.

SUGGESTED FURTHER READING

Mearns, D. and Thorne B.J. (2000) *Person-Centred Therapy Today: New Frontiers in Theory and Practice*.
      London: Sage.
Mearns, D. and Thorne. B.J. (2007) *Person-Centred Counselling in Action*, 3rd edn. London: Sage.
Rogers, C.R. (1951) *Client-Centered Therapy*. Boston, MA: Houghton-Mifflin.
Rogers, C.R. (1961) *On Becoming a Person*. Boston, MA: Houghton-Mifflin.
Thorne, B.J. (2003) *Carl Rogers*, 2nd edn. London: Sage.

7

Personal Construct Therapy

Fay Fransella, Peggy Dalton, and
Grant Weselby

HISTORICAL CONTEXT AND DEVELOPMENTS IN BRITAIN

Historical context

George A. Kelly (1905–1967) was not a man of his time. He was a revolutionary thinker who had dreams of what the psychological study of human beings should be like. These dreams were in direct contrast with the current psychological ethos of behaviourism. His ideas expressed in the philosophy of *constructive alternativism* can be traced back to the dim distant past, as can those of his contemporary, Jean Piaget. It was largely the approach of these two men that has triggered off the interest, starting in the 1980s, in the philosophy of 'constructivism' and 'constructivist therapies'.

This approach to the study of human beings is also in direct conflict with the science of the past. No longer are there facts to be found and truths to be gleaned. All we can hope to do is come to a 'best guess' that we know will be superseded by a better 'best guess' in due course. In Kelly's terms, 'there are always alternative ways of looking at any event'. We each live in our own personal world although we may, of course, share with many others our perceptions of events if we come from the same culture or the same family.

In Kelly's theory we act upon our world rather than respond to it as the behaviourists would have us do. We are actors, we create our own lives and can therefore re-create them if we find ourselves not to our own liking. We are also forms of motion. We are alive, and one aspect of living matter is that it is always on the move. What needs explaining is why we behave as we do. Here Kelly turned behaviour, described by the behaviourists as a response *to* something, into a question. That is, we make sense of our world by applying to it the personal constructs we have created in the past. These personal constructs are our mini-theories about how things are. In this way we can predict what may happen as the result of some action. Having made a prediction that, say, this client has normal hearing, we put this prediction to the test *by behaving* 'as if' this client can hear what is being said. Now, that prediction may be correct or incorrect, but the behaviour was asking the question, 'Am I right in thinking this person can hear well enough?'

Kelly received his PhD in psychology – with particular emphasis on physiology – in the early 1930s. He became professor and director of clinical psychology at Ohio State University in 1946. However, in order to gain a fuller insight into the context in which his ideas developed it is important to know something of his earlier studies: in 1926 he obtained a BA degree in physics and mathematics, later a Master's degree in educational sociology, and in 1930 a Bachelor of Education degree at Edinburgh University.

His university courses in physics and mathematics took place around the time when Einstein's ideas were shaking the world of science, as were those of quantum mechanics. With this early training, it comes as no surprise to find that Kelly's model of the person is couched in the language of science, as is his whole theory (see Fransella, 1984 and 2000 for a more detailed discussion of how training in physics and mathematics may have influenced Kelly's psychological theorizing). But Kelly's is a science based on the philosophy of constructive alternativism: a science in which there are no 'facts', only support for current hypotheses. These hypotheses may lead to other hypotheses, which encompass new events, and so on. He argues that there *is* a reality 'out there' and at some infinite moment in time we may learn all there is to know about the universe, but this is unlikely since the universe, like the person, is in a constant state of motion (see Fransella, 1995 for details of George Kelly the man and his psychology).

Development in Britain

George Kelly, an American, found receptive readers first and foremost in Britain. He believed that the attention given to his theory by British psychologists would determine whether his work would stand or fall. Only from the 1980s has there been a quickening of interest in his work in its country of origin. Neimeyer (1985a) has described its development in the context of the sociology of science. He uses Mullins's (1973) model of the sociohistorical development of new theory groups, which focuses on the changing patterns of communication.

The development of personal construct theory goes, according to Neimeyer, something like this. Before and for some time after the publication of Kelly's *magnum opus*, *The Psychology of Personal Constructs* in 1955, he and others worked largely in isolation, However, by 1966 workers in Britain had attained a cluster status; that is, local groups with a minimum of seven people had developed and there had been a publication explosion. The major force behind the development of interest in the theory in Britain was the lecturing and publications of Don Bannister.

Neimeyer finds that by 1972 the major clusters in Britain were beginning to dissolve and that personal construct theory was steadily establishing itself as a mature speciality; by contrast, America and the rest of Europe only started to enter the cluster stage of development in the 1980s.

Up to 1978 there was surprisingly little work published on the application of personal construct psychology (PCP) to psychotherapy – surprising since this is its 'focus of convenience'. But things have changed, and the quantity of publications in the therapy field is now considerable. Interest in Kelly's theory and philosophy is worldwide. Fay Fransella convened the first international congress in Oxford, UK in 1977 and since then these have taken place every two years in different countries around the world. Continental conferences also take place in the intervening years in Australia, the United States, and Europe. In 1981, Fay Fransella founded the first centre devoted solely to the teaching and applications of personal construct psychology in London.

THEORETICAL ASSUMPTIONS

Image of the person

Kelly suggests we might look at the person 'as if' you and I were scientists. By this he means that we could all be seen as doing the same sorts of things that scientists traditionally do. We have theories about why things happen; erect hypotheses derived from these theories; and put these hypotheses to the test to see whether the predictions arising from them are validated or invalidated. We test our predictions by behaving. Viewing all behaviour 'as if' it were an experiment is one of Kelly's unique contributions to our understanding of the person.

We approach the world not as it *is* but as it appears to us to be; we gaze at our world through our construing *goggles*. We make predictions about events constantly and continually – there is no let-up. We are active beings, 'forms of motion'.

He suggests that we might come to understand ourselves and others in psychological terms by studying the personal constructs we have each evolved to discriminate between events and to help us predict other events in the future. Construing is not all going on in the head, though; we construe just as much with our bodies as with our minds. Kelly gives as an example our digestive system. Our stomach anticipates food, secretes gastric juices, behaves towards what it receives in an accepting manner if the food is in line with expectation, or rejects the food if it is not up to expectation and so forth. Kelly considers dualistic thinking a hindrance to our understanding of the person. At any given moment it is just as appropriate to ask what a person is feeling as what he is thinking, for many of our constructs (discriminations between events) were formed either before we had created the words to express them or else those discriminations have never acquired verbal labels. Personal construct theory is thus very much a theory of human experiencing.

For example, a young child may discriminate between types of voice: a harsh, grating voice and a soft, smooth one. The harsh, grating voice is related to feelings of reassurance, a large body to snuggle up to, and is there before the child goes to bed. The soft, smooth one gives conflicting messages: sometimes it is comforting like the harsh, grating one, but at other times – often when it is particularly soft and smooth – there are feelings of unease, of all not being well. Later, as an adult, that person may never be able to put into words exactly why he cannot abide women who have soft, smooth voices and why he himself has developed a harsh, grating one. His pre-verbal construing is being applied in adult life.

Conceptualization of psychological disturbance and health

Kelly argues fiercely against the use of the medical model in the field of psychological disorder. Like many others, he believes that those with psychological problems are not 'ill' and therefore should not be 'treated' by medical doctors. He argues further that the use of the medical model hampers our attempts to understand people and to help them deal with whatever it is that is troubling them. If there is no 'illness' there can be no 'health'. For Kelly, all personal constructs are bipolar.

Instead, he suggests that we might use the concept of functioning (e.g. Kelly, 1980). A person who is functioning fully is one who is able to construe the world in such a way that predictions are, for the most part, validated. When invalidation does occur, the person deals with it by reconstruing. For example, you are at a party and go up to a stranger whom you construe as likely to be friendly. You start a general conversation and, before a few moments have passed, that 'friendly' person is arguing fiercely with you and being quite unpleasant. He is certainly not being 'friendly'. You have been invalidated in your prediction that this was a 'friendly' person. If you are a well-functioning person, you will accept this invalidation and reconstrue the person, perhaps as someone who has a very deceptive façade and that you were stupid not to have seen through the veneer. You leave the incident behind you and put it down to experience.

But someone else, who is incapable of dealing with such invalidation, may not come out so unscathed. She may become more and more embarrassed, flustered and bereft of words. She would then become increasingly anxious since she has been confronted by an event which she now has difficulty in construing at all. Not only is she unable to predict the outcome of this event, but she finds she is increasingly unable to predict herself. The situation is a traumatic one.

Hopefully, either someone will soon come to her rescue, or the stranger will move off. The person who experiences a considerable number of such predictive failures will often consider herself to 'have a problem'.

Another way of dealing with invalidation is to 'make' things work out the way we have predicted. When we do this we are being 'hostile' (we are extorting validational evidence for a social prediction that we have already seen to be a failure). For example, having construed the stranger as friendly, you might behave as if you were going to faint. He then puts his arm under your elbow to support you and guides you towards a chair. Now you can say to yourself: 'There you are! I knew he was really a friendly person!' Such hostility as this is well known in counselling and therapy. Yet there is nothing essentially 'bad' about hostility; it is a way of dealing with events when our construing lets us down.

Nevertheless, the person who functions reasonably well is one who does not use too much hostility to deal with invalidation and does not find himself too often confronted by events he cannot construe (and thus be overwhelmed with anxiety). The well-functioning person has been able to 'update' those potentially troublesome pre-verbal constructs. That is, he has been able to explore, at some level of awareness, those early childhood discriminations. For instance, is it valid, in adult life, to take an instant dislike to people who have soft, smooth voices? Perhaps the construction does not now lead to useful predictions.

Acquisition of psychological disturbance

It makes no theoretical sense to ask how a disturbance in construing is acquired. Personal construct theory takes the position that we act upon the world and construe (predict) events in the world, we cannot 'acquire' something as if we were buying it in a shop or having it imposed upon us, like measles.

A client may construe his incapacitating headaches as a 'bodily symptom' which he 'acquired' as a result of some stressful psychological event. It is the client's construing that the therapist has to understand. However, to the therapist, the headaches are as much to do with construing as is the way the client describes them. *There is no body/mind dichotomy in Kelly's theory*. As the therapist examines the client's construing system (in verbal and non-verbal terms) she may examine the context within which the headaches arose. She will be asking herself such questions as: 'What experiment is my client conducting when he has these headaches?' 'What answers is he seeking from himself or others around him by behaving in that way?'

It is important always to remember that behaviour is the experiment. So we look at the event as if the child's first headache (or the way the client remembers it) was his way of asking a question of his world. It may have gone something like this: 'My mother does not cuddle me as much as I need. But when I have a headache she does. She is ignoring me again now. I feel a headache coming on. Yes, she is coming towards me.' Has he 'acquired a disturbance'? We think not.

He has tried an experiment which, according to the way in which he construes the world, works. He gets his love.

We need to stress that, although we have spelled out a possible process in words, this does not mean that the thought goes consciously through the child's head in this way. A great deal of our experimenting goes on at a non-verbal level.

Perpetuation of psychological disturbance

The headaches are perpetuated because 'they work'. The child's predictions are validated. He may have started the process whereby whenever he feels unloved, he gets stressed and develops headaches.

Invalidation of our important notions of our selves comes most often, of course, from other people in our lives. Our experiments in life succeed or fail in relation to our understanding of others' understandings of us. But it can also come from within. Problems may persist until the person is able to find acceptable alternative ways of dealing with the world. Many long-standing problems, such as stuttering, become enmeshed in the person's core-role construing. The person comes to see himself as 'a stutterer', 'a headache sufferer', 'an unlovable person'.

The reasons for problems persisting must be sought within a person's construing of himself and his world. He behaves in a particular way because that is most meaningful to him; it is in that way he is able to achieve maximal control over events – and over himself. The problem becomes enmeshed in his core-role superordinate construing system. The longer the problem persists, the more difficulty the person is likely to have in changing – to change the construing of one's self is no easy undertaking.

Change

Since part of the model of the person in personal construct psychology is that we are a form of motion, the process of change is built into the theory. Kelly wrote his theory at two levels. There is the structure in the form of postulate, corollaries and other theoretical constructs. There is also the theory of human experiencing in the form of cycles of movement and transitions.

The *fundamental postulate* states that 'a person's processes are psychologically channelized by the ways in which he anticipates events'. Three of the elaborative corollaries are specifically concerned with change.

The *experience corollary* states that 'a person's construction system varies as he successively construes the replication of events'. Merely being in a situation does not, of itself, mean that one has had experience. An agoraphobic woman placed in a situation at some point in her behaviour therapy hierarchy will only have experience of that situation if her construing of the world is in some way different after it from what it was before. Kelly equates experience with learning:

> The burden of our assumption is that learning is not a special class of psychological process; it is synonymous with any and all psychological processes. It is not something that happens to a person on occasion; it is what makes him a person in the first place. (Kelly, 1991, Vol I: 53)

The *choice corollary* states that 'a person chooses for himself that alternative in a dichotomized construct through which he anticipates the greater possibility for extension and definition of his system'. This is a basic motivation construct. As living beings we strive to make our world a more predictable and personally meaningful place. We may not like the world in which we are living, but it is preferable to live in it than to launch ourselves into a vast sea of uncertainty.

In a certain sense, the client is 'choosing' to remain as he is rather than change. The person who has stuttered since early childhood sees no alternative but to continue stuttering in adulthood; that is the way he can make sense of himself interpersonally. If he were to suddenly become a fluent speaker, he would be launched into chaos (Fransella, 1972). In much the same way, smoking becomes personally meaningful for the smoker, obesity for the obese and depression for the depressed.

A personal construct approach involves helping the client construe what he or she is going to become and not simply eliminating the undesired behaviour.

The *modulation corollary* discusses a third aspect of change. It states that any variation within a construing system 'is limited by the permeability of the constructs within whose range of convenience the variants lie'. Construing new events is difficult if many of a person's constructs are not open to receive them; they are pumice stone rather than sponge. Someone who stutters and knows too precisely how people respond to his attempts at communication will find it difficult to employ new constructions of those interactions. He will not 'see' different responses.

While the corollaries of personal construct theory describe the theoretical structure underpinning change, the cycles of movement describe the change process. These are the cycles of experience, creativity and decision-making (CPC cycle).

The cycle of experience is about the process of reconstruing itself. The whole of psychotherapy therefore is seen in terms of human experiencing rather than as treatment. Kelly puts it like this:

> Psychotherapy needs to be understood as an experience, and experience, in turn, understood as a process that reflects human vitality. Thus to define psychotherapy as a form of treatment – something that one person does to another – is misleading. (Kelly, 1980: 21)

In the first place we have to have anticipation. Behaving is our experimentation to test out our anticipations about what confronts us. But we also have to be committed to these anticipations. We have to care about what happens. We have to invest something of ourselves in our experiments. The problem with problems is that we continue to conduct the same old experiments again and again without adding the final, essential component – reconstruing. As reconstruing completes one cycle of experience, so others start.

The *creativity cycle* starts with loosening up our construing of events and then tightening them again, hopefully in a different pattern. We have a problem in life. We go for a long walk and 'mull it over'. We allow ideas to come and go as they please (we are construing loosely). Then we suddenly have a flash of inspiration. Quickly, before it can slip away, we tighten things up again so we can look to see whether or not we have indeed found a solution. This cycle of creativity, like that of experience, repeats itself again and again. Kelly puts it like this:

> The loosening releases facts, long taken as self-evident, from their rigid conceptual moorings. Once so freed, they may be seen in new aspects hitherto unsuspected, and the creativity cycle may get under way. (Kelly, 1991, Vol. II: 301)

The ability to loosen the construing of events is often one of the first lessons the client has to be taught. Problems very often result in our tightening our construing so as to make it more manageable, more predictable. It can therefore be quite threatening to a client to be asked to let go the anchors that hold the construing together – even for a short time. Tightened construing was a problem with Grace (who will be discussed later).

The *decision-making or CPC cycle* is independent of tightening or loosening construing. We have a decision to make. First of all we look at the alternatives available to us (we Circumspect). Eventually we focus on the way that makes the most sense (we Pre-empt the issue). Now we are in a position to make a Choice and so are precipitated into action.

PRACTICE

Goals of therapy

The person with a psychological problem is seen as being 'stuck' – she keeps repeating her behavioural experiments over and over again. Since personal construct psychology views the person (amongst other things) as a form of motion, enabling the person to 'get on the move again' becomes the goal of therapy. As Kelly puts it:

> The task of psychotherapy is to get the human process going again so that life may go on and on from where psychotherapy left off. There is no particular kind of psychotherapeutic relationship – no particular kind of feelings – no particular kind of interaction that is in itself a psychotherapeutic panacea. (Kelly, 1969: 223)

Selection criteria

Since everyone is seen as a construing process, no one person would be deemed unsuitable for personal construct psychotherapy. What usually provides the limiting factor is the context in which the therapy will take place. Not all places can deal with the overactive, the catatonic, the violent. There is also another limiting factor, but one less easy to define – the psychotherapist him or herself. There are very few therapists who would wish to say they are equally successful with any client with any type of problem. The limitations are thus in the physical therapy context and in the therapist, and not in the client.

There are a few criteria which help the therapist decide whether or not the client is likely to benefit from personal construct psychotherapy. But none would automatically lead to a rejection of the client. One is that the client should be willing to go along with the idea that the therapist does not have the answers – the client does. All the therapist has is a theory about how people may go about the business of making sense of themselves and the world around them. If the client is basically looking for psychological 'pills', then they are not likely to take to the idea that psychotherapy means work.

A good prognostic sign is that the client has some existing construct to do with psychological change. Not only that it is possible to change, but that they, themselves, may find it possible to change.

In choosing whether the client is most likely to be able to contemplate change in the one-to-one situation or in the presence of others, a number of factors have to be considered. For instance, a very withdrawn adult would rarely be seen without any contact being made with those caring for that person. The choice is then between only seeing the client in the company of one or two relatives; seeing client and relatives on different occasions; or seeing the client alone for part of the session with the relative(s) joining later. The choice will depend on the problem as seen by all parties. If the problem seems to be very definitely one that focuses on interactions and the withdrawn client not seeming to want to communicate more, then the emphasis would probably be on seeing client and relative(s) together. If the client is clearly withdrawn and experiencing some internal turmoil, most work would be done with the client alone.

However, the die is not cast for ever. As the withdrawn client becomes less so, the relatives may increasingly be brought into the sessions; as they come to understand what their interactions with their client are all about *from the client's point of view*, and vice versa, the client may well increasingly be seen alone.

Clients are referred for group therapy if their problem is clearly related to interpersonal issues: for instance, if they feel poorly understood by others or that others are something of a mystery to them. It is of interest to note that for Kelly group work was the preferred method, certainly within a hospital setting.

It is not uncommon for a client to be seen both individually and in a group. Here it is important that the same therapist is not involved in both. The client needs to be able to separate out the two experiences. There are experiments which the client may wish to conduct with or upon the therapist individually which would not be appropriate in a group. This requires very close collaboration between the therapists, for it is they who must ensure that the client moves along a single path toward reconstruing and does not get mixed messages. For instance, it would be counter-therapeutic for one therapist to be working with the client on the basis that the client needs to be helped to 'tighten' aspects of their construing while the other therapist is focusing on 'loosening'.

Qualities of effective therapists

Establishing the qualities of personal construct therapists more likely to lead to success or failure with clients is proving a very difficult and complex task (for details see Winter, 1992). However, Kelly specifies a number of skills he believes they need to acquire. These are outlined below.

A subsuming system of constructs

Above all, therapists must have a 'subsuming construct system' and be skilled in its use. Every therapist needs a set of professional constructs within which to subsume the client's own personal system of constructs. For the analyst, it is spelt out in psychoanalytic terms; for the cognitive therapist, in cognitive terms; for the personal construct therapist it is spelt out in terms of the theoretical constructs stated in the psychology of personal constructs. Kelly describes it thus:

> Since all clients have their own personal systems my system should be a system of approach by means of which I can quickly come to understand and subsume the widely varying systems which my clients can be expected to present. (Kelly, 1991, Vol. II: 28)

A therapist should be able to specify precisely what constructs are being used whenever a therapeutic decision is made. For example, if he systematically uses the writing of a self-characterization (see pp. 186–7) with clients, he should be able to state precisely what this procedure is designed to do.

In personal construct therapy, the subsuming system is that which defines the theory itself. Those constructs most commonly used in psychotherapy are referred to as 'professional constructs'. One already mentioned is *loose* versus *tight*: is the client using constructs in a way that leads to varying predictions (loosened construing) or to predictions which state that events will definitely be one way or another (unvarying or tight construing)? Bannister (1962) based his theory of the origins and maintenance of schizophrenic thought disorder on this construct.

To be effective the personal construct therapist must be able to 'work within' a client's construing system whether it be overly tight or overly loose. She has to understand these process differences both experientially and theoretically. Therapists who lack an adequate knowledge of the professional constructs or who lack the skill of suspending their own value system in order to subsume that of the client, may fail to help a client change. Once the therapist allows his own construing to intervene between himself and the client, he not only fails to be of use to the client but may also find himself being used by that client and have difficulty extricating himself. Grant Weselby refers to his own difficulty in suspending his own construing in the case example.

Creativity, versatility and aggression

Given the focus on the client and therapist as personal scientists, the therapist needs to be creative, versatile and aggressive. Kelly comments that 'Every case a psychotherapist handles requires him to devise techniques and formulate constructs he has never used before.' Such creativity means the readiness to try out unverbalized hunches, and a willingness to look at things in new ways:

> Creation is therefore an act of daring, an act of daring through which the creator abandons those literal defences behind which he might hide if his act is questioned or its results proven invalid. The psychotherapist who dares not try anything he cannot verbally defend is likely to be sterile in a psychotherapeutic relationship. (Kelly, 1991, Vol. II: 32)

To be creative the therapist must be able to adopt a variety of roles and be aggressive in testing out hypotheses (personal construct aggression being the active elaboration of one's construing). In psychotherapy, both client and therapist must be prepared to be aggressive and to take risks.

It must be borne in mind that an unwritten basic tenet of personal construct psychology is that we have created ourselves and can therefore re-create ourselves if we so wish.

Verbal ability

The therapist must be skilled both verbally and in observation. A therapist must be able to speak the client's language in addition to having a wide-ranging vocabulary. By understanding the meanings that word-symbols have for the client the therapist can minimize the risk of misunderstandings.

Therapeutic relationship and style

The personal construct therapist's relationship and style can best be understood by looking once again at the model of the 'person as scientist'. Client and therapist are partners in the struggle to understand and so find a solution to the same problem. The therapist, like a research supervisor, knows something about designing experiments, has experience of some of the pitfalls involved in any type of research and knows that, ultimately, only the research student can carry out the research.

This supervisor/research student model may sound cold and calculating, but it is not. Anyone who has ever been in one or both of those positions knows only too well how totally involving and challenging is the task. One important aspect of such a relationship is that both client and therapist must have a personal commitment to solving the problem and to the necessary work and experimentation that this involves.

A central feature of the therapeutic relationship is spelled out in the *sociality corollary*. This says that we may be seen as playing a role in relation to another if we try to see the world through the eyes of the other. The personal construct therapist, above all else, is struggling to see things as the client sees them. Only by being successful in this can any meaningful therapeutic strategy be undertaken.

To start with the therapist adopts the *credulous approach*; all personal evaluation is suspended; there are no judgements. Everything the client says is accepted as 'true'. This cannot, of course, go on, but it is essential to the establishment of the initial role relationship. As the therapist gains increasing access to the client's world and begins to formulate hypotheses about the nature of the problem, the therapist begins to put these to the test. However, being active in therapy does not mean that the therapist necessarily adopts a directive role; she may, in fact, be very quiet and give the client absolute freedom to do, say or think whatever he wishes. Nevertheless, the role is decided on by the therapist. Her construing of the client's constructions leads her to consider that this 'quiet' role is something the client can use *at this stage of the therapy.*

This all means that the personal construct therapist will change style according to what is most likely to help the client's reconstruing process. A therapist may be humorous at one time and serious at another; active and then passive, or formal and then informal. Self-disclosure, as with all these other styles, will only be used if the client can make use of the disclosure, otherwise it is self-indulgence on the part of the therapist. The personal construct therapist, therefore, is a *validator or invalidator of the client's construing.*

One implication of construing the therapist as validator of the client's construing, is that she uses the relationship as another valuable 'tool' for helping the client's reconstructions. For instance, 'transference' or 'dependency' is not a general problem to be 'dealt with'. At a particular stage in therapy it may be useful to use the construct of 'dependency', such as when the client attempts to verbalize pre-verbal constructs; at another time or with other clients, dependence on the therapist may prevent the client from conducting useful experiments outside the therapy consulting room.

The therapeutic style is thus dictated by the ways in which the therapist construes the needs of the client, always remembering that client and therapist are both in the experimenting and reconstruing business and work as partners.

Major therapeutic strategies and techniques

The therapist hopes that all interactions with the client will aid the client in reconstruing. The therapist's principal goal is to help the client find alternative ways of looking at himself, life, and the problem. But before the therapist can be reasonably sure about these possible alternative ways, she has to have a moderately clear idea of what it is that is holding the client back from doing this on his own.

Most of the techniques stemming directly from personal construct psychology are concerned with providing the therapist as well as the client with information on how the client views the world at the present time. In that sense the methods can be called 'diagnostic'. Only fixed role therapy is a therapeutic tool in its own right – designed specifically to bring about reconstruing (alternative constructions). However, the diagnostic techniques do themselves bring about reconstruing in many instances, although this is not their prime aim.

Kelly talks about techniques thus:

> Personal construct psychotherapy is a way of getting on with the human enterprise and it may embody and mobilize all of the techniques for doing this that man has yet devised. Certainly there is no one psychotherapeutic technique and certainly no one kind of interpersonal compatibility between psychotherapist and client. The techniques employed are the techniques for living and the task of the skilful psychotherapist is the proper orchestration of all of these varieties of techniques. Hence one may find a personal construct psychotherapist employing a huge variety of procedures – not helter-skelter, but always as part of a plan for helping himself and his client get on with the job of human exploration and checking out the appropriateness of the constructions they have devised for placing upon the world around them. (Kelly, 1969: 221–2)

A few specific methods that have arisen from Kelly's work are outlined below.

Repertory grid technique

This technique has been modified a number of times since Kelly first described it in 1955 (see Fransella et al., 2004). Its uses are many and, although the raw data can give rise to many useful insights, there are a variety of methods of statistical analysis. It is basically a technique which enables the therapist to obtain some degree of quantification of the relationships between constructs and how these relate to individuals who are being construed, as can be seen with Grace in the case study. Many different types of grid have been designed for specific purposes. For instance, Neimeyer describes a 'biographical grid' in which the client construes elements that are important events in his or her life (Neimeyer, 1985b) and Ravenette (1999) a 'self-description grid' for use with children.

Though grids have a place in the psychotherapy setting, they are not essential to it. A grid is only useful if the therapist sees it as such. It can be used to validate therapists' hunches, for monitoring change over time, or in helping clients explore their construing of events more fully. In all cases grids are a part of the therapy as the results are fed back to the client.

Laddering, pyramiding and the ABC model

These are all methods for exploring construct relationships without getting into the complexities of statistical analyses that are often necessary with repertory grids.

Laddering helps the client explore the relationships between constructs at more and more abstract levels (Hinkle, 1965). For instance, if the client uses the construct 'dominant' versus 'submissive', the client would be asked which he would prefer to be. If the answer was submissive, the therapist would ask 'Why do you prefer to be that? What are the advantages of being a submissive rather than a dominant person?' The client might answer that submissive people do not get attacked, whereas dominant people do. The client is again asked why he prefers not to be attacked. The reply might be that he would not know how to respond if he were attacked, he would not know what to do. And so the questioning goes on, until the construing has reached such a superordinate level that it has nowhere else to go (in this example, it might be something to do with self-preservation).

Laddering is not easy to learn. It can go round in circles or produce answers that block all further enquiry. But having learned how to make it work, most people find it an invaluable tool for gaining insight very quickly into the most important values the client holds about himself and others. Not only does it enable the therapist to learn about the client, but frequently it also enables the client to gain considerable insight into his own construing.

Pyramiding (Landfield, 1971) aims at identifying the more concrete levels of the construing system of the client. Instead of asking 'Why?', the client is asked: 'What?' or 'How?': 'What sort of person is a submissive person?' 'How would you know that a person is being submissive?' This method can be very useful when planning behavioural experiments.

The ABC model involves finding out the advantages and disadvantages to the client of each pole of a construct (Tschudi, 1977). This can be used to advantage with constructs connected with 'the problem'. A woman whose 'problem' is being overweight might be asked for an advantage of being the desired weight (perhaps she would be able to wear nice clothes); then for a disadvantage of being overweight (perhaps she gets out of breath when going upstairs). Next, she is asked for a disadvantage of being the normal weight (perhaps she would find there was too much choice around and so get confused), and finally for an advantage of being overweight (perhaps men do not bother her). These answers are regarded not as 'truths' but as guidelines for understanding and further explorations. (For more details of these methods see Fransella, 2005.)

The self-characterization

Kelly says that if he were to be remembered for one thing only, he would like it to be his first principle: 'If you do not know what is wrong with a person, ask him, he may tell you' (Kelly, 1991, Vol. I: 241). A working model for this is the self-characterization he described. The instructions are carefully worded as follows:

> I want you to write a character sketch of (e.g. Harry Brown) just as if he were the principal character in a play. Write it as it might be written by a friend who knew him very intimately and very sympathetically, perhaps better than anyone ever really could know him. Be sure to write it in the third person. For example, start out by saying 'Harry Brown is.' (Kelly, 1991, Vol. I: 242)

There is no formal method of analysis. However, one might look at the first sentence as if it were a statement of where the person is now and at the last as a statement of where the person is going. One might look for themes running through the whole piece. What one tries to do is go beyond the words and glimpse inside where the person lives. These character sketches can be written from a variety of standpoints: 'Harry as he will be in ten years' time', '... as he will be when his problem has disappeared', or any other form which seems to offer the person a way of exploring and communicating his constructions of the world. An example of the use of the self-characterization as the main therapeutic instrument can be found in Fransella (1981). Jackson (1988) has developed ways of using the self-characterization with children and adolescents. It also plays an important part in the case example at the end of this chapter.

Fixed role therapy

This is the only method that is offered by Kelly as a therapeutic tool in its own right. He gave it as an example of the theory in action and based it on the self-characterization. In his description of fixed role therapy, he also gives an implicit account of the way we invent and create ourselves. Kelly acknowledges his indebtedness to Moreno (1964) and his methods of psychodrama here.

The therapist writes a second version of the client's original self-characterization. This is not a replica of the first, since that would only lead back to where the client is now; nor should it be a complete opposite, since no one will readily turn his life on its head. Instead, the client's fixed role sketch is written so as to be 'orthogonal' to the first. For instance, if the client is using the construct 'aggressive' versus 'submissive' in relation to his boss, the sketch might talk of being respectful.

When the sketch has been written, client and therapist pore over it together. They modify it until it describes a person the client feels it would be possible for him to be. The client now lives the life of that person for a few weeks: he eats what his new person eats, dresses as he would dress and relates to others as this person would relate. During this period of fixed role enactment the therapist has to see the client fairly frequently. The sessions focus on what the client sees as going on, which ventures were successful and which were not, what messages he is getting from others and so forth.

The purpose of this fixed role enactment is to get across the idea that we can, indeed, change ourselves; that even the client can change, though he seems so stuck at the moment. He learns about self-inventiveness; he learns what happens when he alters a particular item of behaviour, and whether it is useful to explore this line of enquiry further or whether he should try something else. He discovers how the way we construe others and behave towards them influences how they behave towards us. He learns to read new messages from others. This is particularly important since the person we have invented is, in large part, the result of the way we have construed the reactions of others to us.

Fixed role therapy is certainly not suitable for everyone, but it can be very useful in modified form. For instance, the client and the therapist may choose to work out just one experiment for the former to carry out during the period before the next appointment. This might be to experiment with being respectful to his boss on just one occasion and see what difference it makes to how the boss reacts, and to how the client feels about himself. These 'mini' fixed roles need to be worked out carefully with the client, but can give useful insights into the direction in which both client and therapist think he might profitably travel. This procedure was used with the client discussed at the end of this chapter.

Techniques from other therapies

The choice of technique is always determined by the current formulation of the problem, which is couched in the language of the professional theoretical constructs. Personal construct therapists find the use of dream material, guided fantasy, systematic desensitization and many other techniques of great value for specific purposes, but it must be emphasized that the choice of technique is guided by theory.

The change process in therapy

There are no clear stages in the change process that are applicable to all clients. We have to ask questions derived from the theory. How permeable is the client's construing in the problem area? What is at stake for him if he were to contemplate changing in some radical way? How loosely or tightly knit is his construing in areas relating to anticipated change? And so on. In other words, the change process will be determined by the 'diagnosis' the therapist makes of why the client is unable to move forward on her own.

Diagnosis is the planning stage of treatment for the therapist. This does *not* imply that the therapist is placing the client in some medical pigeonhole such as 'depression', 'schizophrenia' or 'psychopathy'. Personal construct diagnosis does not imply any illness or disturbance on the part of the client. It is couched in the language of the theory to provide guidance for the therapist as to a possible way forward for the client. There is no one way forward for all-comers.

There are some specific factors that may impede the reconstruction process by the client. These factors are often to be found in the constructs to do with transition. The change process can involve anxiety, threat or hostility. All can impede movement if not dealt with sensitively by the therapist.

Any change is accompanied by anxiety as we move into areas we find it difficult or impossible to construe for a while. But this is rarely a problem if the client moves forward in moderate steps. Threat can bring the client up short as she perceives that, if things go on as they are at the moment, she will have to change how she construes some essential aspect of her 'self'. As one client put it after writing a self-characterization:

> Writing the self characterisation focused on something which I suppose has been associated with panic – although not consciously associated with panic – the feeling that I was going to have to change more drastically – in a sense either remain more or less the same or the

change would have to be more drastic than I had thought. Writing the self characterisation focused my attention on not wanting to change. Not wanting to change because I felt that if I was going to have to change as dramatically as I was feeling was necessary, I'd lose 'me'.
(Fransella, 1981: 228)

If a client is able to put the threat into words like that, it is usually possible to move on forward from there. The client had to elaborate precisely what the 'me' was that was in danger of being lost and whether, on close examination, that was necessarily true. But some clients are not able to put the threat into words. Often the client realizes, at some level of awareness, that these radical changes are just too much to be contemplated. She relapses. She has made a positive choice – in her terms – and has signalled that an alternative therapeutic strategy is required. Relapse is not a negative event, but the client's safety-net. This happened briefly with Grace in the case study.

The problem becomes particularly difficult if the client defends her position by becoming hostile: that is, by extorting evidence to prove that she really should be the sort of person she always knew herself to be. She can 'make' the therapy fail. It is really the therapist's fault not the client's. She can produce evidence that there has really been no great change at all by pointing out that the experience indicating psychological movement to the therapist was really 'a chance event – that combination of circumstances will never happen again!'

Hostility is dealt with by discovering, on the one hand, what it is that is so important for the client to retain and on the other hand, exploring areas of construing that will help elaborate the sort of self the client wants to become. Exploration with the client just mentioned revealed that the 'me' he was afraid of losing was 'the child me'. This was to do with a rich fantasy life and a world of deep experiencing. He evolved for himself a way in which he could change to becoming 'an adult' and yet retain areas of living in which he could still experience the valued childlike qualities.

Limitations of the approach

A major undeveloped area for personal construct therapy is group work. Although Kelly advocated its use and devoted a chapter to working with groups of people, little use has been made of it. Its focus has nearly always been on the one-to-one situation. One exception has been Landfield's Interpersonal Transaction (IT) groups (see Neimeyer, 1988).

Apart from this, limitations lie with the therapist rather than with personal construct therapy. The therapist finds it easier if she has the full co-operation of the client – at least implicitly. She finds it easier to work with those who are verbally fluent – but that is not essential. She finds it easier to work with those from a culture similar to her own but, again, this is by no means essential. If all human beings are seen as experiencing, construing beings, then personal construct therapy should be able to be used by all.

Case example

The account covers a period of therapy lasting approximately one year, consequently there are omissions. However I hope to convey some of the flavour of the encounter and the natural ebb and flow of the creative cycles in operation.

The client

Grace is in her late 30s. She is a slight woman, on the dangerously thin side. She spent much of the first interview hunched and rocking in an agitated fashion. I later learnt that the rocking was a self-comforting activity she had developed as a child during asthma attacks. This was her first stay on an acute ward and it followed two incidents in which she had seriously self-harmed by wrist cutting and overdose.

Grace had been married for 20 years and is the mother of two children, aged 9 and 11. She had been brought up as a Catholic. She did not feel that her childhood had been particularly extraordinary. However, she described her Italian father as 'harsh' to the point of being scary at times. She described her mother as being 'quiet and cold', whilst wielding the 'real' power in the family. She had a restricted upbringing, for example she was chaperoned by her elder brother until she was 19 (when she married). Both parents still live locally to her but her brother and sister have now moved away.

Exploring the problems

The present crisis was related to Grace's recent disclosure to her husband of her affair with one of his work colleagues. The affair had ended a couple of months ago. Grace was tormented with guilt while at the same time appeared to be longing for the specialness she had experienced during it. I was struck by the contrast between her rather sober history and her involvement in the affair, and also by the conflicting emotions she was experiencing – guilt (dislodgement from her core role) and longing. An exploration of these features became the focus of our initial meetings.

I shared my observation of this contrast with Grace. She told me with an expression of despair that what she feared most was a return to the 'humdrum non-existence' of her former life as opposed to being special. I began to construe Grace's affair as a kind of radical and aggressive experiment directed towards finding a way out of her despair.

Therapeutic goals

Grace and I agreed to spend some time understanding her core role from which she had transgressed and to hold in mind the possibility that some revision of this role might be useful. In other words rather than to respond to her guilt by retreating to her familiar unsatisfying role we would examine this role and find out whether she might escape her 'humdrum non-existence' in less emotionally painful ways.

I asked Grace to write a Self-Characterization (see page 186-7) for two reasons, first as one way of gathering further information about her existing core role and secondly to help Grace loosen from her constraining focus on the recent affair. To summarize the characterization, Grace described a woman with chameleon-like powers, capable of blending and bending to the needs of others. These powers were reflected in her constructions around being seen to cope, appearing dutiful, capable and being ever helpful. Her primary aim is to be liked. In contrast to these images she painted a second picture, of an angry, brooding person who provokes attack, judges herself and others harshly and who is painfully sensitive to the slightest criticism. She feels taken for granted, 'like a bit of the house furniture, just "there" to accommodate people/things'.

In seeking an understanding of Grace's core role with a view to finding a more feasible way of escaping her 'humdrum non-existence' we decided to explore Grace's 'Chameleon-like' powers, which contrast with her ability to make herself powerfully present by numerous self-destructive acts. We explored this using Tschudi's ABC technique taking the headings 'Not standing out' versus 'Being seen' (see page 186). Grace observed that although whilst hiding she could avoid judgmental criticism, she tended to be taken for granted. This in turn led her to feel resentment. On the other hand, although 'Being seen' left her fearing that she would be open to criticism it might lead to acknowledgment by others. However, since we choose to be the way that is most meaningful to us (Choice Corollary), Grace could not change to someone who 'is seen' until that has been more fully elaborated.

The therapy

The process of exploration and loosening facilitated by the conversational techniques, the self-characterization and Tschudi's ABC technique, had provided us with a possible alternative way of achieving her therapeutic goal. If Grace could find a way to experiment with 'being seen' she might find new ways of living that were less frustratingly humdrum and did not evoke the criticism of others.

Around this time Grace arrived at a session in a distraught and self-berating mood, threatening to end her life. She had attempted to make contact with her ex-lover, failed, but had been 'found out' by her husband. It seemed peculiar that Grace should have resorted to this apparently destructive action at this particular point in our work when it appeared that a constructive alternative might be emerging. I was also concerned and anxious about my capacity to predict and support Grace effectively. I came to construe the event in terms of Grace's response to threat. Our work to this point had begun to seriously raise the prospect of real change. Her behaviour could represent a hostile attempt to extort validatory evidence in support of failing construction. A kind of last-ditch attempt to make old, failing constructions work. This together with work in supervision exploring the way my anxiety was unhelpfully tightening my responsivity to Grace led to two important observations. First, given the level of threat around for Grace it would be crucial to find means of minimising this experience in our future work. Secondly, my own response to the event demanded some personal reflection upon the apparently inevitable experiences of personal and professional invalidation I was experiencing.

We began to discuss and anticipate more directly her experiences of threat, guilt and anxiety and reflected on the need to proceed with caution, for example, working at the 'periphery' of her life before turning to more central aspects.

The period that followed this event was extremely productive for Grace. She seemed to have dilated her construing in a creative and productive manner. For example, she joined an amateur dramatics group who performed plays in Italian. She observed how when performing and speaking in Italian she felt somehow 'different, freer'. In my mind this triggered thoughts about future fixed-role therapy (see page 187) as a possible treatment intervention.

As a way of continuing our work on elaborating 'being seen' and at the same time managing threat we made use of techniques that drew upon Grace's creative and imaginational capacities. To paraphrase Kelly's assertion, the window to change is through the door of make-believe. For example, Grace made powerful use of Miller Mair's 'Community of Self' (1977). She explored herself as if a 'courtroom', with witnesses, prosecutors, a judge and jury, and various 'accused' selves. Perhaps the most telling observation was the absence of a 'defence lawyer' in her community. The exercise raised further ambivalence and discontent with her customary construing and led naturally into an exploration of alternative versions of the court system.

The preceding work had provided a weight of evidence suggesting both Grace's capacity and desire for reconstructive work, along with a wealth of ideas she was keen to test. The fixed-role procedure was introduced following a fairly traditional form with an enactment sketch centred on the idea of 'Being somebody, being seen'. A few days later, when we next met, Grace was dressed subtly differently, was more relaxed and seemed somehow 'lighter'. To my surprise the first thing she did was give me a note. The note was from the 'real' Grace (she had wanted to remain in role in our sessions as we had agreed). The note explained that she had really struggled to stay in role but had solved the problem by imagining her real amateur dramatics director standing permanently at her side 'commanding', in her characteristically robust fashion, 'Stay in role!'.

Over the course of the next two weeks Grace made a number of important discoveries. She accepted invitations, visited the theatre with a friend, 'failed' to make the children's lunch boxes, took time to dress in the morning and experimented with physically being seen by doing her shopping wearing a striking platinum blond wig. She described an emerging ability to find perspective in life. Most significantly, perhaps, she discovered that she could live and enjoy life without being punished or unfairly criticized. As I accompanied her back to the waiting room following her final enactment session Grace remarked, 'It's sad really (to have to finish the enactment)…but then it's up to me if I want to….' (she didn't finish the sentence).

Outcome

The enactment proved to be a disturbing success in that within her new found capacity to be different Grace also found personal responsibility. This realisation together with awareness of missed opportunities provided a further wave of experience upon which she and I continued to work. She is presently separated from her husband and lives with her children. She has continued to courageously experiment with her constructions around 'being somebody' by starting a degree course and seeking a new direction in her career. Her older self-constructions and associated behavioural solutions (e.g. self harm, dietary control) are much reduced but remain potentially viable. Grace has to work hard to ensure that her newer, emerging self and its associated behaviour remain for the most part, prominent.

REFERENCES

Bannister, D. (1962) 'The nature and measurement of schizophrenic thought disorder', *Journal of Mental Science*, 108: 825–42.

Fransella, F. (1972) *Personal Change and Reconstruction: Research on a Treatment of Stuttering.* London: Academic Press.

Fransella, F. (1981) 'Nature babbling to herself: the self characterization as a therapeutic tool', in H. Bonarius, R. Holland and S. Rosenberg (eds), *Personal Construct Psychology: Recent Advances in Theory and Practice.* London: Macmillan.

Fransella, F. (1984) 'What sort of scientist is the person-as-scientist?', in J.R. Adams-Webber and J.C. Mancuso (eds), *Applications of Personal Construct Theory.* Ontario: Academic Press.

Fransella, F. (1995) *George Kelly.* London: Sage.

Fransella, F. (2000) 'George Kelly and mathematics', in J.W. Scheer (ed.), *The Person in Society: Challenges to a Constructivist Theory.* Giessen: Psychosozial-Verlag.

Fransella, F. (2005) 'Some skills and tools for personal construct users', in F. Fransella (ed.), *The Essential Practitioner's Handbook of Personal Construct Psychology.* Chichester: John Wiley & Sons.

Fransella, F., Bell, R. and Bannister, D. (2004) *A Manual for Repertory Grid Technique.*(2nd edn). Chichester, UK: John Wiley & Sons.

Hinkle, D. (1965) 'The change of personal constructs from the viewpoint of a theory of construct implications'. Unpublished PhD thesis, Ohio State University.

Jackson, S. (1988) 'A self-characterization: development and deviance in adolescent construing', in P. Maitland and D. Brennan (eds), *Personal Construct Theory: Deviancy and Social Work.* London: Inner London Probation Service and Centre for Personal Construct Psychology.

Kelly, G.A. (1969) 'The psychotherapeutic relationship', in B. Maher (ed.), *Clinical Psychology and Personality: The Selected Papers of George Kelly.* New York: Krieger.

Kelly, G.A. (1980) 'A psychology of optimal man', in A.W. Landfield and L.M. Leitner (eds), *Personal Construct Psychology: Psychotherapy and Personality.* New York: Wiley.

Kelly, G.A. (1991) *The Psychology of Personal Constructs* (1955), Vols I and II. London: Routledge.

Landfield, A.W. (1971) *Personal Construct Systems in Psychotherapy.* New York: Rand McNally.

Mair, J.M.M. (1977) 'The community of self', in D. Bannister (ed.), *New Perspectives in Personal Construct Theory.* London: Academic Press.

Moreno, J.L. (1964) *Psychodrama* Vol. I. New York: Beacon.

Mullins, N. (1973) *Theories and Theory Groups in Contemporary American Sociology.* New York: Harper & Row.

Neimeyer, R.A. (1985a) *The Development of Personal Construct Psychology.* Lincoln, NE: University of Nebraska Press.

Neimeyer, R.A. (1985b) 'Personal constructs in clinical practice', in P.C. Kendall (ed.), *Advances in Cognitive Behavioral Research and Therapy.* San Diego, CA: Academic Press

Neimeyer, R.A. (1988) 'Clinical Guidelines for conducting interpersonal transaction groups', *International Journal of Personal Construct Psychology*, I, 181–90.

Ravenette, A.T. (1999) 'Personal construct psychology in the practice of an educational psychologist', in *Personal Construct Theory in Educational Psychology: a Practitioner's View.* London: Whurr.

Tschudi, F. (1977) 'Loaded and honest questions', in D. Bannister (ed.), *New Perspectives in Personal Construct Theory*. London: Academic Press.
Winter, D. (1992) *Personal Construct Psychology in Clinical Practice: Theory, Research and Applications*. London: Routledge.

SUGGESTED FURTHER READING

Dalton, P. and Dunnett, G. (2005) *Psychology for Living* (2nd edn.) London: Whurr Publications.
Epting, F., Gemignani, M. and Cross, C.C. (2005) 'An audacious adventure: personal construct counselling and psychotherapy',. in F. Fransella (ed.), *The Essential Practitioner's Handbook of Personal Construct Psychology*. Chichester: John Wiley & Sons.
Fransella, F. and Dalton, P. (2000) *Personal Construct Counselling in Action*. (2nd edn). London: Sage Publications.
Winter, D. (2004) 'The evidence base for personal construct psychotherapy', in F. Fransella (ed.), *International Handbook of Personal Construct Psychology*. Chichester: John Wiley & Sons.
Winter, D. and Viney, L.L. (eds) (2005) *Personal Construct Psychotherapy: Advances in Theory, Practice and Research*. Chichester: John Wiley & Sons.

8

Existential Therapy

Emmy van Deurzen

HISTORICAL CONTEXT AND DEVELOPMENT IN BRITAIN

Historical context

The existential approach is first and foremost philosophical. It is concerned with the understanding of people's position in the world and with the clarification of what it means to them to be alive. It is also committed to exploring these questions with a receptive attitude, rather than with a dogmatic one. The aim is to search for truth with an open mind and an attitude of wonder rather than to fit the client into pre-established frameworks of interpretation.

The historical background to this approach is that of 3,000 years of philosophy. Throughout the history of humankind people have tried to make sense of life in general and of their personal predicaments in particular. Much of the philosophical tradition is relevant and can help us to understand an individual's position in the world. The philosophers who are especially pertinent are those whose work is directly aimed at making sense of human existence. But the philosophical movements that are of most importance and that have been directly responsible for the generation of existential therapy are phenomenology and existential philosophy.

The starting point of existential philosophy (see Warnock, 1970; Macquarrie, 1972; Mace, 1999; Van Deurzen and Kenward, 2005) can be traced back to the 19th century and the work of Kierkegaard and Nietzsche. Both were in conflict with the predominant ideologies of their time and committed to the exploration of reality as it can be experienced in a passionate and personal manner.

Kierkegaard (1813–55) protested vigorously against Christian dogma and the so-called 'objectivity' of science (Kierkegaard, 1941, 1944). He thought that both were ways of avoiding the anxiety inherent in human existence. He had great contempt for the way in which life was being lived by those around him and believed that truth could ultimately only be discovered subjectively by the individual in action. What was most lacking was people's courage to take the leap of faith and live with passion and commitment from the inward depth of existence. This involved a constant struggle between the finite and infinite aspects of our nature as part of the difficult task of creating a self and finding meaning. As Kierkegaard lived by his own word he was lonely and much ridiculed during his lifetime.

Nietzsche (1844–1900) took this philosophy of life a step further. His starting point was the notion that God was dead (Nietzsche, 1961, 1974, 1986) and that it is up to us to re-evaluate existence in light of this. He invited people to shake off the shackles of moral constraint and to discover their free will in order to soar to unknown heights and learn to live with new intensity. He encouraged people not to remain part of the herd, but to dare stand out. The important existential themes of freedom, choice, responsibility and courage are introduced for the first time.

Husserl (1859–1938). While Kierkegaard and Nietzsche drew attention to the human issues that needed to be addressed, Husserl's phenomenology (Husserl, 1960, 1962; Moran, 2000) provided the method to address them in a rigorous manner. He contended that natural sciences are based on the assumption that subject and object are separate and that this kind of dualism can only lead to error. He proposed a whole new mode of investigation and understanding of the world and our experience of it. Prejudice has to be put aside or 'bracketed', in order for us to meet the world afresh and discover what is absolutely fundamental and only directly available to us through intuition. If we want to grasp the essence of things, instead of explaining and analysing them we have to learn to describe and understand them.

Heidegger (1889–1976) applied the phenomenological method to understanding the meaning of being (Heidegger, 1962, 1968). He argued that poetry and deep philosophical thinking can bring greater insight into what it means to be in the world than can be achieved through scientific knowledge. He explored human being in the world in a manner that revolutionizes classical ideas about the self and psychology. He recognized the importance of time, space, death and human relatedness. He also favoured hermeneutics, an old philosophical method of investigation, which is the art of interpretation. Unlike interpretation as practised in psychoanalysis (which consists of referring a person's experience to a pre-established theoretical framework) this kind of interpretation seeks to understand how the person herself subjectively experiences something.

Sartre (1905–80) contributed many other strands of existential exploration, particularly in terms of emotions, imagination, and the person's insertion into a social and political world. He became the father of existentialism, which was a philosophical trend with a limited life span. The philosophy of existence on the contrary is carried by a wide-ranging literature, which includes many other authors than the ones mentioned above. There is much to be learned from existential authors such as Jaspers (1951, 1963), Tillich and Gadamer within the Germanic tradition and Camus, Marcel, Ricoeur, Merleau-Ponty and Levinas within the French tradition (see for instance Spiegelberg, 1972, Kearney, 1986 or van Deurzen-Smith, 1997). Few psychotherapists are aware of this literature, or interested in making use of it. Psychotherapy has traditionally grown within a medical rather than a philosophical milieu and is only just beginning to discover the possibility of a radical philosophical approach.

From the start of the 20th century some psychotherapists were, however, inspired by phenomenology and its possibilities for working with people. Binswanger, in Switzerland, was the first to attempt to bring existential insights to his work with patients, in the Kreuzlingen sanatorium where he was a psychiatrist. Much of his work was translated into English during the 1940s and 1950s and, together with the immigration to the USA of Tillich (Tillich, 1952) and others, this had a considerable impact on the popularization of existential ideas as a basis for therapy (Valle and King, 1978; Cooper, 2003). Rollo May played an important role in this, and his writing (1969, 1983; May et al., 1958) kept the existential influence alive in America, leading eventually to a specific formulation of therapy (Bugental, 1981; May and Yalom, 1985; Yalom, 1980). Humanistic psychology was directly influenced by these ideas, but it invariably diluted and sometimes distorted their original meanings.

In Europe existential ideas were combined with some psychoanalytic principles and a method of existential analysis was developed by Boss (1957a, 1957b, 1979) in close co-operation with Heidegger. In Austria Frankl developed an existential therapy called logotherapy (Frankl, 1964, 1967), which focused particularly on finding meaning. In France the ideas of Sartre (1956, 1962) and Merleau-Ponty (1962) and of a number of practitioners (Minkowski, 1970) were important and influential but no specific therapeutic method was developed from them.

Development in Britain

Britain became a fertile ground for the further development of the existential approach when Laing and Cooper took Sartre's existential ideas as the basis for their work (Laing, 1960, 1961; Cooper, 1967; Laing and Cooper, 1964). Without developing a concrete method of therapy they critically reconsidered the notion of mental illness and its treatment. In the late 1960s they established an experimental therapeutic community at Kingsley Hall in the East End of London, where people could come to live through their madness without the usual medical treatment. They also founded the Philadelphia Association, an organization providing alternative living, therapy and therapeutic training from this perspective. The Philadelphia Association is still in existence today and is now committed to the exploration of the works of philosophers such as Wittgenstein, Derrida,

Levinas and Foucault as well as the work of the French psychoanalyst Lacan. It also runs a number of small therapeutic households along these lines. The Arbours Association is another group that grew out of the Kingsley Hall experiment. Founded by Berke and Schatzman in the 1970s, it now runs a training programme in psychotherapy, a crisis centre and several therapeutic communities. The existential input in the Arbours has gradually been replaced with a more neo-Kleinian emphasis.

The impetus for further development of the existential approach in Britain has largely come from the development of a number of existentially based courses in academic institutions. This started with the programmes created by van Deurzen, initially at Antioch University in London and subsequently at Regent's College, London and since then at the New School of Psychotherapy and Counselling, also in London. The latter is a purely existentially based training institute, which offers postgraduate degrees validated by the University of Sheffield and Middlesex University. In the last decades the existential approach has spread rapidly and has become a welcome alternative to established methods. There are now a number of other, mostly academic, centres in Britain that provide training in existential counselling and psychotherapy and a rapidly growing interest in the approach in the voluntary sector and in the National Health Service.

British publications dealing with existential therapy include contributions by Jenner (de Koning and Jenner, 1982), Heaton (1988, 1994), Cohn (1994, 1997), Spinelli (1997), Cooper (1989, 2003), Eleftheriadou (1994), Lemma-Wright (1994), Du Plock (1997), Strasser and Strasser (1997), van Deurzen-Smith (1997); van Deurzen (1998, 2002); van Deurzen and Arnold-Baker (2005); van Deurzen and Kenward (2005). Other writers such as Lomas (1981) and Smail (1978, 1987, 1993) have published work relevant to the approach although not explicitly 'existential' in orientation. The journal of the British Society for Phenomenology regularly publishes work on existential and phenomenological psychotherapy. An important development was that of the founding of the Society for Existential Analysis in 1988, initiated by van Deurzen. This society brings together psychotherapists, psychologists, psychiatrists, counsellors and philosophers working from an existential perspective. It offers regular fora for discussion and debate as well as major annual conferences. It publishes the *Journal of the Society for Existential Analysis* twice a year. It is also a member of the International Federation for Daseinsanalysis, which stimulates international exchange between representatives of the approach from around the world. An International Society for Existential Psychotherapists also exists.

THEORETICAL ASSUMPTIONS

Image of the person

The existential approach considers human nature to be open-minded, flexible and capable of an enormous range of experience. The person is in a constant process of becoming. I create myself as I exist and have to reinvent myself daily. There is no essential self, as I define my personality and abilities in action and in relation to my environment. This impermanence and uncertainty give rise to a deep sense of anxiety (Angst), in response to the realization of one's insignif- icance, and simultaneous responsibility to have to create something in place of the emptiness we often experience. Everything passes and nothing lasts. We are never able to hold on to the present. We are always no longer or not yet what we would like to be. We find ourselves somewhere in the middle of the passing of time, grappling with the givens of the past and the possibilities of the future, without any sure knowledge of what it all means.

Existential thinkers seek to avoid restrictive models that categorize or label people. Instead they look for the universals that can be observed cross- culturally. There is no existential personality theory which divides humanity into types or reduces people to part components. Instead there is a description of the dif- ferent levels of experience and existence with which people are inevitably confronted.

The way in which a person is in the world at a particular stage can be charted on this general map of human existence (Binswanger, 1963; Yalom, 1980; van Deurzen-Smith, 1984). One can distinguish four basic dimensions of human exis- tence: the physical, the social, the psychological and the spiritual. On each of these dimensions people encounter the world and shape their attitude out of their partic- ular take on their experience. Our orientation towards the world defines our reality. The four dimensions are obviously interwoven and provide a complex four- dimensional force field for our existence. We are stretched between a positive pole of what we aspire to on each dimension and a negative pole of what we fear.

Physical dimension

On the physical dimension (*Umwelt*) we relate to our environment and to the givens of the natural world around us. This includes our attitude to the body we have, to the concrete surroundings we find ourselves in, to the climate and the weather, to objects and material possessions, to the bodies of other people, our own bodily needs, to health and illness and to our own mortality. The struggle on this dimension is, in general terms, between the search for domination over the ele- ments and natural law (as in technology, or in sports) and the need to accept the limitations of natural boundaries (as in ecology or old age). While people gener- ally aim for security on this dimension (through health and wealth), much of life brings a gradual disillusionment and realization that such security can only be temporary. Recognizing limitations can bring great release of tension.

Social dimension

On the social dimension (*Mitwelt*) we relate to others as we interact with the public world around us. This dimension includes our response to the culture we live in, as well as to the class and race we belong to (and also those we do not belong to). Attitudes here range from love to hate and from co-operation to competition. The dynamic contradictions can be understood in terms of acceptance versus rejection or belonging versus isolation. Some people prefer to withdraw from the world of others as much as possible. Others blindly chase public acceptance by going along with the rules and fashions of the moment. Otherwise they try to rise above these by becoming trendsetters themselves. By acquiring fame or other forms of power, we can attain dominance over others temporarily. Sooner or later we are, however, all confronted with both failure and aloneness.

Psychological dimension

On the psychological dimension (*Eigenwelt*) we relate to ourselves and in this way create a personal world. This dimension includes views about our character, our past experience and our future possibilities. Contradictions here are often experienced in terms of personal strengths and weaknesses. People search for a sense of identity, a feeling of being substantial and having a self. But inevitably many events will confront us with evidence to the contrary and plunge us into a state of confusion or disintegration. Activity and passivity are an important polarity here. Self-affirmation and resolution go with the former and surrender and yielding with the latter. Facing the final dissolution of self that comes with personal loss and the facing of death might bring anxiety and confusion to many who have not yet given up their sense of self-importance.

Spiritual dimension

On the spiritual dimension (*Überwelt*) (van Deurzen-Smith, 1984) we relate to the unknown and thus create a sense of an ideal world, an ideology and a philosophical outlook. It is here that we find meaning by putting all the pieces of the puzzle together for ourselves. For some people this is done by adhering to the dogma of a religion or some other prescriptive world view, for others it is about discovering or attributing meaning in a more secular or personal way. The contradictions that have to be faced on this dimension are often related to the tension between purpose and absurdity, hope and despair. People create their values in search of something that matters enough to live or die for, something that may even have ultimate and universal validity. Usually the aim is the conquest of a soul, or something that will substantially surpass mortality (as for instance in having contributed something valuable to humankind). Facing the void and the possibility of nothingness are the indispensable counterparts of this quest for the eternal.

Conceptualization of psychological disturbance and health

Disturbance and health are two sides of the same coin. Living creatively means welcoming both. Well-being coincides with the ability to be transparent and open to what life can bring: both good and bad. In trying to evade the negative side of existence we get stuck as surely as we do when we cannot see the positive side. It is only in facing both positive and negative poles of existence that we generate the necessary power to move ahead. Thus well-being is not the naive enjoyment of a state of total balance given to one by Mother Nature and perfect parents. It can only be negotiated gradually by coming to terms with life, the world and oneself. It doesn't require a clean record of childhood experience, or a total devotion to the cult of body and mind. It simply requires openness to being and to increasing understanding of what the business of living is all about. From an existential perspective psychological well-being is seen to be synonymous with wisdom. This results from being equal to the task of life when it is faced honestly and squarely. Psychological disturbance is seen as a consequence of either avoidance of truth or an inability to cope with it. Discontent is generated for many people through self-deception in a blind following of popular opinions, habits, beliefs, rules and reasons. Others are at a loss to make sense of the paradoxes of life that they are forcefully confronted with and that overwhelm them.

To be authentic is to be true to oneself and one's innermost possibilities and limitations. Finding one's own authority and learning to create an increasingly comfortable space inside and around oneself, no matter what the circumstances, is a considerable challenge. As the self is defined by its vital links to the world around it, being true to oneself has to be understood as being true to life. This is not about setting one's own rules or living without regard for others. It is about recognizing the necessities, givens and limitations of the human condition as much as about affirming freedom and insisting on one's basic rights. Many people avoid authentic living, because it is terrifying to face the reality of the constant challenges, failures, crises and doubts that existence exposes us to. Living authentically begins with the recognition of one's personal vulnerability and mortality and with the acknowledgement of the ultimate uncertainty of all that is known. It is superficially far more rewarding to play at being certain, role-defined and self-important. Even the self-image of sickness or madness can seem more attractive than having to struggle with yourself and face your vulnerability in an uncertain world.

Ultimately it is the essential human longing for truth that redeems. We are reminded of truth by the pangs of conscience, which may expose our evasion of reality. A sense of courage and possibility can be found by stopping the dialogue with the internal voices of other people's laws and expectations. In the quietude of being with myself I can sense where truth lies and where lies have obscured the truth. The call of conscience reaches me through a feeling of guilt, that is, existential guilt, which tells me that something is lacking, something is being owed to life by me: I am in debt to myself.

The call of conscience comes through an attitude of openness to possibilities and limitations. This openness leads to Angst as it exposes me to my responsibilities and possible failure, but when I accept this anxiety it becomes the source of energy that allows me to be ready for whatever the future holds in store. And so, in facing the worst, I prepare myself for the best. I can live resolutely only when I can also surrender and release myself. I can be free only when I know what is necessary. I can be fully alive only when I face up to the possibility of my death.

Acquisition of psychological disturbance

When well-being is defined as the ability to face up to the disturbing facts of life, the notion of disturbance takes on a whole new meaning. Problems and obstacles are not necessarily an impediment to living well, for any potentially distressing situation can be seen as a challenge that can be faced. Problems are first of all problems in living and will occur at any stage in human development. In fact the only thing you can be sure of is that life will inevitably confront you with new situations that are a challenge to your established ways and evasions of the human paradox. When people are shocked out of their ordinary routine into a sudden awareness of their inability to face the realities of living, the clouds start to gather. Even though we may think of ourselves as well-adjusted people who have had a moderately acceptable upbringing, unexpected events, such as the death of a loved one, the loss of a job or another significant sudden exposure of our vulnerability, may still trigger a sense of failure, despair or extreme anxiety. Everything around us suddenly seems absurd or impossible and our own and other people's motives are questioned. The value of what used to be taken for granted becomes uncertain and life loses its appeal. The basic vulnerability of being human has emerged from behind the well-guarded self-deception of social adaptation. Sometimes a similar disenchantment and profound disturbance arise not out of an external catastrophe but out of a sense of the futility of everyday routines. Boredom can be just as important a factor in generating disturbance as losses or other forms of crisis.

No matter how securely a person is established in the world some events will shake the foundations of that security and transform the appearance of existence. For some people, however, such false security is not at first available. They never achieve 'ontological security' (Laing, 1960), which consists of having a firm sense of one's own and other people's reality and identity. Genetic predisposition obviously makes some of us capable of greater sensory awareness and psychological susceptibility than others. People who have such extraordinary sensitivity may easily get caught up in the conflicts that others are trying to avoid. If they are exposed to particularly intense contradictions (as in certain family conflicts) they may fall into a state of extreme confusion and despair and withdraw into the relative security of a world of their own creation. Both the ontologically secure person who is disturbed by a crisis (or boredom) and the ontologically insecure person who is overwhelmed by the less pleasant sides of ordinary human existence are struggling with an absence of the usual protective armour of self-deception. Life is suddenly seen in all its harshness and paradoxical reality. Without the redeeming factor of some of the more positive aspects of life such realism can be distressing.

This does not mean that this kind of crisis or generation of anxiety should be avoided. It can be faced and integrated by making sense of it. The existential view of disturbance is that it is an inevitable and even welcome event that every-one will sooner or later encounter. The question is not how to avoid it but on the contrary how to approach it with determination and curiosity.

Perpetuation of psychological disturbance

Problems start to become more serious when the challenge of disturbance is not faced but evaded. Then a self-perpetuating negative spiralling downward can happen which leads to confusion and chaos. This is most likely to occur if we are not linked to a vital support system. As long as our family or other intimate networks of reference are strong and open enough to absorb the contradictions in which we get caught up, distress can be eased and overcome: the balance can be redressed. But if we find ourselves in isolation, without the understanding and challenge of a relative, a partner or a close friend, it is easy to get lost in our problems. Society's rituals for safeguarding the individual are these days less and less powerful and secure. Few people gain a sense of ultimate meaning or direction from their relationship to God or from other essential beliefs. Many feel at the mercy of temporary, ever-changing but incessant demands, needs and desires. In time of distress there seems all too often to be nowhere to turn. Relatives and friends, who themselves are barely holding their heads above water, may be unavailable. If they are available, they may want to soothe distress instead of tackling it at the root. Spiritual authority has gradually been eroded and has been replaced with scientific authority, which is unable to address moral or spiritual dilemmas. It is hardly surprising that people turn increasingly to psychotherapists or counsellors. Unfortunately, there is little evidence that psychotherapy and coun-selling are able to lessen distress. To some extent a reliance on therapeutic cure may present another perpetuation of disturbance, as long as the basic existential issues are not dealt with and the client is kept in a passive role.

Paradoxically, the institutions in our society often seem to encourage the very opposite of what they are supposed to be about. When the family becomes a place of loneliness and alienation instead of one that fosters togetherness and intimacy, when schools become places of boredom and reluctance instead of inspiring curiosity and learning and when doctors' surgeries become places of dependence and addiction instead of centres of healing and renewal of strength, it is time for essentials to be reconsidered. Much disturbance is not only gener-ated but also maintained by a society that is out of touch with the essential prin-ciples of life. Often it is in the distress of those who face a crisis that the disturbance of society is expressed. It is therefore hardly surprising that we are inclined to want to obliterate this reminder of failings at the heart of our own existence. If we are willing to attend to the message of such distress we give ourselves a chance to be reminded of the ways in which we perpetuate our own misunderstanding and avoidance of life.

Change

Life is one long process of change and transformation. Although people often think they want to change, more often than not their lives reflect their attempts at maintaining the status quo. As a person becomes convinced of the inevitability of change she may also become aware of the many ways in which she has kept such change at bay. Almost every minute of the day people make small choices that together determine the direction of their life. Often that direction is embarked upon passively: people just conform to their own negative or mediocre predictions of the future. But once insight is gained into the possibility of reinterpreting a situation and opting for more constructive predictions a change for the better may come about. This requires the person to learn to live deliberately instead of by default, and it can only be achieved by first becoming aware of how one's daily attitude and frame of mind is set to a form of automatic functioning that keeps one repeating the same mistakes.

It is not easy to break the force of habit, but there are always times when habits are broken by force. Crises are times when old patterns have to be revised and when changes for the better can be initiated. This is why existential therapists talk about a breakdown as a possible breakthrough and why people often note with astonishment that the disaster they tried so hard to avoid was a blessing in disguise. In times of crisis the attention is refocused on where priorities lie so that choices can be made with more understanding than previously.

Whether such an event is self-imposed (as in emigration or marriage) or not (as in natural disasters or bereavement) it has the effect of removing previously taken for granted securities. When this happens it becomes more difficult for us to obscure the aspects of existence that we would rather not think about, and we are compelled to reassess our own attitudes and values. In the ensuing chaos we must make choices about how to proceed and how to bring new order into our lives. If we can tolerate the uncertainty of such situations instead of fleeing towards a new routine, such times can be an opportunity for rectifying life's direction.

Once a crisis has been faced in such a constructive manner it becomes easier to be open to change at other times as well. People can learn to re-evaluate their values and reassess their priorities continually, thus achieving a flexibility and vitality that allows them to make the most of life's naturally transformative character. Many people dread change and hide from it but they have to face it at a time of crisis. Existential therapy can be particularly helpful in those circumstances.

PRACTICE

Goals of therapy

The goals of existential therapy are to enable people to:

- take stock of their situation, their values and beliefs;
- successfully negotiate and come to terms with past, present and future crises;
- become more truthful with themselves;
- widen their perspective on themselves and the world around them;
- find clarity on what their purpose in life is and how they can learn from the past to create something valuable and meaningful to live for;
- understand themselves and others better and find ways of effectively communicating and being with others;
- make sense of the paradoxes; conflicts and dilemmas of their every day existence.

The word 'authenticity' is often used to indicate the goal of becoming true to oneself and therefore more real. This is a much-abused term, which misleadingly suggests that there is a true self; whereas the existential view is that self is relationship and process – not an entity or substance. Authenticity can also become an excuse for people who want to have their cake and eat it. Under the aegis of authenticity anything can be licensed: crude egoism may very well be the consequence. In fact, authenticity can never be fully achieved. It is a gradual process of self-understanding, but of the self as it is created in one's relationships to the world on all levels. Helping people to become authentic therefore means assisting them in gaining a greater understanding of the human condition, so that they can respond to it with a sense of mastery, instead of being at its mercy. To be authentic means to face one's human limitations and possibilities.

The task of the therapist is to have attained sufficient clarity and openness to be able to venture along with any client into murky waters and explore (without getting lost) how this person's experience fits into a wider map of existence. Clients are guided through the disturbances in which they are caught and are helped to examine their assumptions, values and aspirations, so that a new direction can be taken. The therapist is fully available to this exploration and will often be changed in the process. The poignancy of each new adventure over the dangerous ground of life requires the therapist to become aware of previously unrecognized aspects of life. Therapy is a journey that client and therapist embark upon together. Both will be transformed, as they let themselves be touched by life.

Selection criteria

Clients who come specifically for existential therapy usually already have the idea that their problems are about living, and are not a form of pathology. This basic assumption must be acceptable to clients if they are to benefit from the approach. A genuine commitment to an intense and very personal philosophical investigation is therefore a requirement. A critical mind and a desire to think for oneself are an advantage. People who want another's opinion on what ails them and who would prefer symptom relief to a search for meaning might be better referred to other forms of therapy.

The approach is especially suitable for people who feel alienated from the expectations of society or for those seeking to clarify their personal ideology. The approach is relevant to people living in a foreign culture, class or race, as it does not dictate a specific way of looking at reality. It also works well with people confronting adversity in their lives or who are trying to cope with changes of personal circumstances (or want to bring those about). Bereavement, job loss or biological changes (in adolescence, middle age or old age) are a prime time for the reconsideration of the rules and values one has hitherto lived by. Generally speaking the existential approach is more helpful to those who question the state of affairs in the world, than to those who prefer the status quo. This approach seems to be most right for those at the edge of existence: people who are dying or contemplating suicide, people who are just starting on a new phase of life, people in crisis, or people who feel they no longer belong in their surroundings. It is less relevant for people who do not want to examine their assumptions and who would rather not explore the foundation of human existence.

Even though existential work consists in gaining understanding through talking, the client's level of verbal ability is not important. Very young children or people who speak a foreign language will often find that the simpler their way of expressing things, the easier it becomes to grasp the essence of their world view and experience. The approach is not about intellectualizing, but about verbalizing the basic impressions, ideas, intuitions and feelings a person has about life.

The existential approach can be applied in many different settings: individual, couple, family or group. When it involves more than one person at a time, the emphasis will be on clarifying the participants' perceptions of the world and their place in it, in order to encourage communication and mutual understanding. The focus is always on the individual's experiences and relationships. A dimension of existential exploration can easily be added to almost any other approach to psychotherapy, but it will soon be found that this makes a re-evaluation of one's method necessary. Many of the more directive or prescriptive forms of therapy are in flagrant contradiction of existential principles. Interpretative methods such as psychoanalysis or analytical psychology betray the existential rule of openness to the different meanings that emerge for individuals. In the final analysis existential work requires a commitment to a philosophical investigation, which necessitates its own guidelines and parameters.

Qualities of effective therapists

Good existential therapists combine personal qualities with accomplishment in method, but on balance it is more important that they have strength of character as people than that they have a high level of skill. Qualities can be described as falling into four categories: (a) life experience, (b) attitude and personality, (c) theoretical knowledge, (d) professional training.

Life experience
Existential therapists will be psychologically and emotionally mature as human beings. This maturity will manifest itself in an ability to make room in oneself for all sorts of, even contradictory, opinions, attitudes, feelings, thoughts and experiences. They will be open-minded about the many different facets of human living. Rather than clinging to one point of view, existential therapists will be capable of overseeing reality from a wide range of perspectives. They will also be able to tolerate the tension that such awareness of contradictions generates. There are a number of life experiences that appear to be particularly helpful in preparing people for such maturation and broad-mindedness. Cross-cultural experience is an excellent way to stretch the mind and one's views on what it means to be human. People who have permanently had to adjust their whole way of perceiving and dealing with the world (especially when this includes a change of language) have had the all-important experience of questioning previous assumptions and opening up to a new culture and perspective.

Raising a family, or caring for dependants in a close relationship, is another invaluable source of life experience relevant to creating an open attitude. Many women have great practical experience in this area. Their life experience can become one of the building blocks of the kind of maturity needed to become an existential therapist.

The experience of having been immersed in society from several angles, in different jobs, different academic studies, different social classes and so on, is a definite advantage. The existential therapist is likely to be someone who has lived seriously and intensely in a number of ways and not just through the caring professions. People opting for psychotherapy as a second career are often especially suitable. Finally, the *sine qua non* of becoming an existential therapist is to have negotiated a number of significant crossroads in one's personal life. Existential therapists will have had their share of existential crises. Of course they will also have had to develop their ability to deal with these satisfactorily, so that their own lives were enriched rather than impoverished by the experience. Although all this maturity conjures up the image of someone advanced in age, it must be noted that maturity is not always commensurate with years. Some young people may have weathered greater storms than their elders and, what is more, may have lived their relatively shorter lives with greater intensity, maturing into fuller human beings.

Attitude and personality

Existential therapists should be capable of critical consideration of situations, people and ideas. They are serious, but not heavy-handed, downtrodden or cynical. They can be light-hearted, hopeful and humorous about the human condition, whilst intensely aware of the tragic poignancy of much of existence. They should be capable of self-reflection, recognizing the manner in which they themselves represent the paradoxes, ups and downs, strengths and weaknesses that people are capable of. They should have a genuine sense of curiosity and a strong urge to find out what it means to be human. They should be capable of sustaining an attitude of wonder. Existential therapists will now and then abandon psychological theory altogether and reach for poetry, art or religion instead. They will tend to be quite personal in their way of working. Before anything else they must demonstrate their ability to tolerate experiences of anxiety and despair without faltering and without succumbing.

Theoretical knowledge

A basic working knowledge of philosophy, that is of the controversies and perspectives that the human race has produced over the centuries, is more useful to this approach than any other kind of knowledge. Included in this would be a familiarity with the history of psychology and psychoanalysis and a wide study of the many different approaches to psychotherapy that have been developed over the years. This will provide a map of different views on human nature, health and illness, happiness and unhappiness, which again will train and broaden the mind and personal outlook of the therapist. In addition a practical knowledge of human interaction and the dynamics of the therapeutic relationship is essential.

Professional training

The existential therapist needs the kind of training that an eclectic therapist needs: a generic one. But instead of borrowing bits and pieces of technique from each to produce a complex amalgam, essentials are distilled and applied within a consistent philosophical framework. Specific skills of dialectical interaction can then be developed. Training should consist of a significant amount of therapeutic work under supervision and of self-reflection and analysis. Here again it is the quality that will be judged instead of the quantity. Numbers of hours of individual and group therapy are irrelevant. Some people will not reach the necessary perspective and depth with any amount of therapy. Others will be well ahead by having engaged in a discipline of self-reflection for years. The degree of readiness usually becomes obvious in supervision sessions, for one's response to other people's troubles is an excellent test of one's own attitude to life and level of self-knowledge. Existential training will enable therapists to think creatively about complex human dilemmas.

Therapeutic relationship and style

It is important for the existential therapist to have a flexible attitude towards therapeutic style. Not only do different therapists interpret the approach in diverse ways, but clients also have their own individual requirements, which may vary over time. The existential therapist is ready and willing to shift her stance when the situation requires this. In a sense this variability is characteristic of the existential therapeutic style.

There are, of course, common features running through all of this. All existential therapists, for example, strive to recognize and question their preconceptions and prejudices as much as possible in their work. There is also a consistent appreciation of the unique situation of the client. The existential therapist strives to take the dilemmas of the client seriously – eschewing recourse to diagnoses and solutions. This seriousness includes openness and wonder as essential attributes of the existential attitude and does not preclude humour when appropriate.

Existential therapists are fundamentally concerned with what matters most to the client. He or she avoids making normative judgements, and renounces any ambition to, even implicitly, push the client in any particular direction. The attitude is non-directive, but not directionless. The client is assisted in finding his or her own perspective and position in the world in relation to the parameters and limits of human existence. At times the therapist might facilitate the client's investigations through an attitude of relative passivity and silent intervention. At other times active dialogue and debate are required. On such occasions the therapist intervenes to point out contradictions in or implications of the client's avowed point of view. The use of confrontation to offer opinions or moral evaluations of the client is not consistent with the existential attitude.

The existential therapist resists the temptation to try to change the client. The therapy is an opportunity for the client to take stock of her life and ways of being in the world. Nothing is gained from interfering with these. The client is simply given the space, time and understanding to help her come to terms with what is true for her. What she wants to do with this afterwards is up to her. The therapist does not teach or preach about how life should be lived, but lets the client's personal taste in the art of living evolve naturally within the context of existential and social constructions.

The only times when the therapist does follow a didactic line is when she reminds the client of aspects of a problem that have been overlooked. She gently encourages the client to notice a lack of perspective, think through consequences and struggle with contradictions. She puts forward missing links and underlying principles. The therapist never does the work for the client but makes sure that the work gets done. The client's inevitable attempts to shirk and flee from the task in hand are reflected on and used as concrete evidence of the client's attitude to life. The same can be said of the actual encounter between the client and the therapist, which is also reflected on and seen as evidence of the client's usual ways of relating.

Generally speaking the therapeutic style follows a conversational pattern. Issues are considered and explored in dialogue. The rhythm of the sessions will follow that of the client's preoccupations – faster when emotions are expressed and slower when complex ideas are disentangled. Existential therapists need to learn to allow clients to take the amount of space and time in this conversation that they need in order to proceed at their own pace. Existential therapists create sufficient room for the client to feel that it is possible to unfold their troubles.

Existential sessions are usually quite intense, since deep and significant issues often emerge. Moreover, the therapist is personally engaged with the work and is willing to be touched and moved by the client's conflicts and questions. The human dilemmas expressed in the therapeutic encounter have as much relevance to the therapist as to the client. This commonality of experience makes it possible for client and therapist to work together as a team, in a co-operative effort to throw light on human existence. Every new challenge in the client's experience is grist for the mill. The therapeutic relationship itself brings many opportunities to grasp something of the nature of human interaction. The therapist, in principle, is ready to consider any past, present or future matter that is relevant to the client. The therapist is constantly aware of her own bias in approaching the client's difficulties and aims to recognize it sufficiently for it not to interfere with the work on the client's bias.

Major therapeutic strategies and techniques

The existential approach is well known for its anti-technique orientation. It prefers description, understanding and exploration of reality to diagnosis, treatment and prognosis. Existential therapists will not generally use particular techniques, strategies or skills, but they will follow a specific philosophical method of enquiry, which requires a consistent professional attitude. This method and attitude may be interpreted in various ways, but it usually includes some or all of the following ingredients.

Cultivating a naive attitude

By consistently meeting the client with an open mind and in the spirit of exploration and discovery a fresh perspective on the world will emerge. This requires a great deal of intellectual discipline on the part of the therapist, who continuously has to observe and question her own prejudice and bias.

Themes: clear themes will run through the apparently confused discourse of the client. The therapist listens for the unspoken links that are implicit in what is said. When the theme is obvious and has been confirmed several times, the client's attention can be drawn to it. Personal myths and stories are recognized and beliefs and fantasies about the world unveiled. Existential work enables people to create more satisfactory life narratives (Tantam, 2002).

Assumptions: much of what the client says will be based on a number of basic assumptions about the world. Generally people are unaware of these. Clarifying implicit assumptions can be very revealing and may throw new light on a dilemma. Every statement we make reveals our assumptions, and therapists need to make sure these become explicit.

Vicious circles: many people are caught up in self-fulfilling prophecies of doom and destruction without realizing that they set their own low standards and goals. Making such vicious circles explicit can be a crucial step forward. Self-fulfilling prophecies can become positive instead of negative.

Meaning: often people assume that they know what they mean when they talk about something. But the words they use can hide, even from themselves, the significance of what they mean. By questioning the superficial meaning of the client's words and asking her to think again of what she wants to express, a new awareness may be brought about.

Values: people live their lives by standards and principles that establish values which they often take for granted and of which they are only dimly aware. Getting clarity about what makes life worth living and which aspects of life are most important and deserve making sacrifices for is a key step towards finding one's sense of direction and purpose.

Facing limitations

As the existential approach is essentially concerned with the need to face the limitations of the human condition, the therapist will be alert for opportunities to help the client identify these. This means facing up to ultimate concerns, such as death, guilt, freedom, isolation, meaninglessness, etc.

Self-deception: much of the time we pretend that life has determined our situation and character so much that we have no choices left. Crises may provide us with proof to the contrary. The safe crisis of the therapeutic interaction is a suitable place for rediscovering opportunities and challenges that had been forgotten.

Existential anxiety: the anxiety that indicates one's awareness of inevitable limitations and death is also a dizziness in the face of freedom and a summoning of life energy. Existential anxiety is the *sine qua non* of individual awareness and full aliveness. Some people have dulled their sensitivity so as to avoid the basic challenges of life, others are overwhelmed by them and yet others have found ways of disguising them. Optimal use of anxiety is one of the goals of existential work. The therapist will recognize the client's existential anxiety and will assist in finding ways of living with it constructively.

Existential guilt: the sense of being in debt to life and owing it to oneself to accomplish certain tasks before it is too late can give us essential insight into our limitations and priorities. Therapists watch for existential guilt hidden in various disguises (such as anxiety, boredom, depression or even apparent self-confidence).

Consequences: clients are sometimes challenged to think through the consequences of choices, both past and future. In facing the implications of one's actions it becomes necessary to recognize limitations as well as possibilities.

Some choices become easier to make; others become less attractive. Existential therapy does not condone the client's tendency to want only support and accept-ance and wallow in a sense of their own suffering; it encourages clients to confront their own responsibilities in relation to the world, other people and themselves.

Paradoxes: in helping the client to become more authentic the concept of par-adox can be of great help. If people are inclined to evade the basic human dilemma of life and death and contradictions that flow from it, their self-affirmation may look more like egocentricity. Checking that a person is aware of her capacity for both life and death, success and failure, freedom and necessity, certainty and doubts, allows one to remain in touch with a fundamental search for truth.

Exploring personal world view

The existential approach is open to all of life's dimensions, tasks and problems, and the therapist will in principle explore together with the client all information that the latter brings along. It is essential to follow the client's lead and under-stand her particular take on the world.

The fourfold world: using the model of four dimensions of existence dis-cussed earlier it becomes possible to listen to the client's account of herself as revealing her preoccupations with particular levels of her existence. A system-atic analysis of how the client expresses her relationship to the physical, social, psychological and spiritual dimensions of her world can provide much insight into imbalance, priorities and impasses. An impression can be formed of where on the whole territory of human existence the client is struggling for clarity. Intuitions, feelings, thoughts, sensations, dreams and fantasies are all grist for the mill.

Dreams: listening to dreams with this model in mind can be extremely enlightening. The dream is seen as a message of the dreamer to herself. The dream experience reflects the dreamer's attitudes on the various dimensions of existence and the client's dream existence and world relations in it are consid-ered as concrete as those of waking life.

Of course the same applies to the fantasies or stories that the client reports. Each of these is a miniature picture of the way in which she relates to the world and much can be learned from examining them carefully.

Questioning: exploring the client's world view is an ongoing enterprise and it is best done with an observation-orientated attitude. Questions are often asked in order to check whether a certain event or situation is seen in a particular light. Existential therapists will make observations and inferences and elicit further material that will either confirm or disconfirm hypotheses. The therapist draws the client's attention to what seems to be the case. Sometimes an enquiry might be made in order to clarify a perception, along the lines of an exploration: 'What makes this so important to you?', or 'What is this like for you?', or 'What does it mean to you?' The question never suggests a solution or judges right or wrong, but investigates the client's personal opinion and inclination. Initial explanations will almost always be questioned and explored in greater depth.

Enquiring into meaning

All investigations eventually lead to a greater understanding of what makes the world meaningful to the client. The idea is to assist the client in finding purpose and motivation, direction and vitality. In the process a number of irrelevant and misleading motivations may be encountered and eliminated. Quite often new interpretations of past or present events are arrived at, altering the client's orientation to life and the future.

Emotions: feelings are of great help in this process. Understanding the meaning of one's emotions and moods and the message they contain in terms of what one aspires to or is afraid to lose is of crucial help in finding the pattern of purpose currently at work. Each emotion has its own significance (van Deurzen, 2002) and the whole range of the emotional spectrum can be used as a compass in indicating one's direction in life. Emotions like shame, envy and hope are indicators of values that are still missing but implicitly longed for. Love, joy and pride are within the range of emotions that indicate a sense of ownership of what is valued. Whereas jealousy and anger express an active response to the threat that what is valued may be lost, fear and sorrow come with the giving up and eventual loss of what really mattered.

Beliefs: all observations on the client's preoccupations lead to a picture of her opinions, beliefs and values. It is important to extract these respectfully. Nothing can be gained from opposing the client's values with an alternative set of values. It is the client's conscience that has to be uncovered and revitalized. If deeply held values are contested or criticized conformity will be encouraged rather than reliance on an inner sense of purpose. Light is thrown on the ways in which personal beliefs may fail to take into account wider implications for others. This will expand the system of beliefs into something that can encompass the facts of life and a broader frame of reference.

Talents: many talents, abilities and assets will have been hidden by the client's preoccupation with what is wrong with her. The therapist will attend to these and strive to draw attention to the wisdom and strength that are lying fallow. Often it is useful for the therapist to build on the example of the client's abilities as they come to the fore and use them as the point of reference for further understanding.

Recollection: memories will be seen as malleable and open to new interpretation. While clients often set out with fixed views of their past they discover the possibility of reconsidering the same events and experiences in different ways. It is essential to encourage clients to discover how they influence their future with their own version of the past and how it is within their power to re-collect themselves in new ways, thereby opening new vistas. When the client realizes that she is the ultimate source of the meaning of her life, past, present and future, living is experienced as an art rather than a duty.

The change process in therapy

The aim of existential therapy is not to change people but to help them to come to terms with the transformative process of life. The assumption is that when people do face reality they are likely to find a satisfactory way forward. People are often hurried and under the impression that they can speed life up and force great rewards out of it with relatively little effort. One of the aims of existential therapy is to enable people to stop deceiving themselves about both their lack of responsibility for what is happening to them and their excessive demands on life and themselves. Learning to measure one's distress by the standards of the human condition relieves pressure and at the same time provides a clearer ideological basis for making sense of personal preoccupations and aspirations. Clients change through existential therapy by gradually taking more and more of life's ups and downs in their stride. They can become more steadfast in facing death, crises, personal shortcomings, losses and failures if they accept the reality of constant transformation that we are all part of. They can find ways of tuning into these changes, instead of fighting them or trying to speed them up.

In other words they can acquire a measure of wisdom in learning to distinguish between the things they can change and those they cannot change. They can come to terms with the givens and find the courage to tackle the uncertainties. They can find out what matters enough to them to be committed to it, live for it and ultimately perhaps even die for it.

As they are constantly reminded to do their own thinking on these issues, people can learn to monitor their own actions, attitudes and moods. The therapy gives clients an opportunity to rediscover the importance of relating to themselves and taking time for contemplation and recreation. Existential therapy teaches a discipline for living which consists of a frequent process of checking what one's attitude, inclination, mood and frame of mind are, bringing them back in line with reality and personal aspirations.

Change is initiated in the sessions, but not accomplished in them. The process of transformation takes place in between the sessions and after therapy has terminated. The therapeutic hour itself can never be more than a small contribution to a person's renewed engagement with life. It is only a kind of rehearsal for life. The change process is never-ending. As long as there is life there will be change. There is no place for complacency or a self-congratulatory belief in cure.

As existential therapy has no criterion for cure, it could in theory be an endless process. To make sure it does not become this, the criterion for finishing a series of sessions is simply to stop when the client feels ready to manage on her own again. To encourage such self-reliance, relatively short-term therapy is encouraged (three months to two years), though sometimes the process will take a little longer.

Limitations of the approach

The emphasis that the existential approach places on self-reflection and under-standing can lead to certain limitations. The approach often attracts clients who feel disinclined to trust other human beings because they perceive the existential approach as leaving them in total control. This limitation can only be overcome by a therapist who neither fights the need nor leaves it unchallenged, but who assists the client in turning such self-reliance to a positive end.

The approach is also often misconstrued as 'intellectual'. Some existential therapists tend to emphasize the cognitive aspect of their clients' preoccupations and some clients are attracted to the approach with the hope of avoiding senses, feeling and intuition. A good existential therapist would heed all these different levels of experience, as full self-understanding can be achieved only through openness to all different aspects of being. Nevertheless the emphasis on self-reflection remains central and the criticism is therefore a valid one to some degree.

The practical limitations of the approach have already been referred to in the section on selection criteria. As the approach does not stress the illness–health dimension, people who directly want to relieve specific symptoms will generally find the existential approach unsuitable, though they may discover that symptoms tend to disappear when more fundamental life issues are addressed.

The existential therapist neither encourages the client to regress to a deep level of dependency nor seeks to become a significant other in the client's life and nurture the client back to health. The therapist is a consultant who can provide the client with a method for and systematic support in facing the truth, and in this sense is there to allow the client to relate to herself more than to the therapist. This might be considered a limitation of the approach by clients who wish to regress and rely on the therapist as a substitute parental figure. Good existential therapists obviously enable the client to confront that issue just as bravely as any other issue and come through with greater self-understanding.

Perhaps the most absolute limitation is that of the level of maturity, life experience and intensive training that is required of practitioners in this field. It should be clear from the above that existential therapists are required to be wise and capable of profound and wide-ranging understanding of what it means to be human. The criteria of what makes for a good existential therapist are so high that the chances of finding bad existential therapists must be considerable.

One can imagine the danger of therapists pretending to be capable of this kind of wisdom without actual substance or inner authority. Little would be gained by replacing technological or medical models of therapy, which can be concretely learned and applied by practitioners, with a range of would-be existential coaches who are incapable of facing life's problems with dignity and creativity themselves. The only way around this is to create training organizations that select candidates extremely carefully on personal qualities and experience before putting them through a thorough training and a long period of intensively supervised work.

Case example

The client

Jerry R. enters my consulting room with a combination of confidence and coyness. He immediately strikes me as a young man with more than his fair share of gravitas, which he somehow seems to carry as a burden. With great aplomb he pauses to shake my hand and introduce himself. I indicate an armchair by the fire and invite him to take a seat. Before sitting down, he carefully folds his raincoat and places it over another chair, glancing at me sideways, checking for approval. Every gesture is made with precision and attention to detail. He unbuttons his smart black jacket and crosses his legs, exposing perfectly matched blue socks and shirt. He wears pristine black patent leather shoes which he taps gently in rhythm with his words. His appearance is handsome and he carries his rather sultry Mediterranean looks with self-assurance. He brushes a lock of wavy black hair off his forehead with panache and poses both elbows on the armrests of his seat, folding his hands into a neat dome; index fingers pressed firmly together pointing upwards. He retains this posture with great poise and dignity for at least ten minutes. His manner is polite and friendly. He smiles hesitantly with one corner of his mouth when I ask him what brings him to my practice. When he speaks it is to express his hesitance in coming to see me upon his solicitor's recommendation and his voice is sophisticated and melodious. I encourage him to give me some background in spite of his doubts about therapy and without much further prompting he provides me with a full and systematic picture of his life.

Background

He tells me again that his name is Jerry R. (and he puts great emphasis on his last name as if I ought to recognize it). He is a single man of thirty-two. He was born in Paris, but raised in London where his father is an executive director for a large French company. He confirms that both his parents are French though he now has dual nationality himself. When I remark that his name sounds English, he blushes unexpectedly and explains that he is really called Jérôme and that he has adopted a more English sounding name in order to fit in with his peers. I say affirmatively: 'to avoid teasing', whilst looking at him enquiringly. He agrees with one firm nod that makes his hair flop back onto his forehead, but instead of pushing it back with his fingers, this time he tosses it back with an energetic movement of his head. He grins at me disarmingly and I hold his gaze, noticing that his brown eyes are watering, belying his exterior poise. He is still blushing. 'There was a lot of teasing', he says quietly and I can hear a hint of a French accent for the first time.'You went to an English school then?' I speculate. He nods again, vigorously and tells me that he is an only child and has always been very close to his mother. He went to the French school in London for his primary education but for his secondary education his father insisted that he should be sent away to a boarding school somewhere in the Home Counties. There he had to fit in with the English upper middle classes and he had decided it would be wise to change his name. He never felt at ease in his school and used to complain about this bitterly to his parents. His mother tried to convince his father for many years to let him be educated at home instead, but his father was adamant that Jerry should tough it out and stop being a mother's boy.

Jerry thinks he has never forgiven his father for this callousness, but all the same he does take some pride in having managed to comply with his father's expectations, sticking it out till his final exams. He pauses for a minute before admitting (blushing again) that he did have regular illnesses during this period of his life which afforded him time off at home being cosseted by his mother. He tells me, animatedly, that she is a fantastic and elegant woman with a great sense of beauty and fun. His genuine admiration for his mother is refreshing and touching but it also arouses my suspicion, because it is rare in one so young. He informs me with relish that he has always been the apple of her eye. She did not fail to convey to him that she favoured him over his father, who was often absent. He has no siblings, though his mother had a miscarriage soon after the family moved to England when he was about two years old.

After his secondary education he went to University in York, at which point his parents, at his mother's insistence, bought a country house in Yorkshire, where he would usually spend his weekends with mother, while father was in the flat in London or the apartment in Paris. After his degree he lived in the London flat himself for a few years, sometimes sharing with his father. This was a relatively good time in his life, especially when Dad was away in Paris or elsewhere. He had really enjoyed his professional training in photography, making portraiture his speciality. Since then he has been working as a freelance photographer and enjoys his job when it leaves him enough room for creativity. He has occasionally done photography jobs for his father's company at official functions. He has mixed feelings about working with Dad, who is rather controlling.

Jerry has many friends, some very successful in their careers, some unemployed and he spans between these two worlds with ease and relish. He tells me with pride that he has had two girlfriends and that the second one, Jessica, is still part of his life now. From the way in which he describes Jessica in a rather detached and photographic manner, I catch myself wondering whether there have been any boyfriends as well. He seems to expect my reaction and pre-empts a question by volunteering somewhat shyly that before his first girlfriend, he used to 'occasionally indulge in sexual play' with male friends. Here again he blushes and averts his eyes to avoid my gaze. I ask him if he finds men and women equally attractive and he confirms this, saying tentatively: 'I suppose I could be described as bi-sexual'. I weigh these words for a moment, pondering his hesitancy before asking him kindly whether this is indeed how he would describe himself. Now he looks at me rather mischievously and he sounds relieved and rather reckless as he replies: 'That all depends on who I am speaking to. My parents for instance do not know about any of this and Jessica certainly does not have a clue.' His voice trails off. I declare sympathetically: 'Ah, so you lead a double life!' He nods regretfully and tells me of his inner conflicts in relation to his choice of partners and of his mother's insistence that he should behave the same way as his cousins and all of her friends' children, who by his age generally were married. He feels he has tried, for he has lived with Jessica occasionally over the past three years, but they decided to go their separate ways after his accident. I reckon there is a little bit more to it. There is a pause. We look at each other meaningfully. We both know we need to pursue this particular path for a bit. 'Your accident then … ' I state calmly and look at him to invite his account of what has brought him to my consulting room today.

Presenting problem

Jerry reminds me that he is coming to see me for post-traumatic stress. His solicitor has referred him to me to help him overcome the after effects of a motorbike accident. About nine months ago Jerry was coming back from a holiday in France when he got caught sideways by a lorry on the slip road to a petrol station. He was dragged along for thirty yards and remained in a coma for several hours, had multiple fractures, including a skull fracture, and severe concussion. His physical recovery is nearly complete though he is still walking with some difficulty, something I only fully observe when he leaves my office at the end of the session.

Mentally and emotionally he feels a wreck. He says that he has terrible trouble sleeping since the accident. He feels anxious and depressed most of the time. He is incapable of doing work and cannot concentrate. He hates being with people. He has some flashbacks even though he has retrograde amnesia that stops him clearly recollecting the accident. Mostly he just doesn't think the world is a safe place anymore. He figures he has had too much time to lie in bed and worry about things and a lot of his old problems have come back to haunt him. He sounds casually and painfully dismissive of his own plight and I stop him in his tracks by raising my eyebrows questioningly. He takes my cue immediately and informs me that these were his Dad's words. Mum and Dad have had arguments over his illness. Dad has written it off as 'all in the mind'. Mum has been over-protective. He does not know what to think of it himself and he hates having to go through all the legal stuff and psychiatric examinations to get the settlement sorted. He doesn't want to come across as weak and wishes he could just get back to normal. Yet, when he has tried to resume his old life, he has felt incapable of doing so. He has had to bail out of a photographic assignment in London, when he started to panic and feel queasy on the train down for instance. He does not recognize himself anymore. Somehow the accident has changed him and he thinks that nothing can ever be the same again. He thinks he could do with some help in getting his self-assurance back. We agree to work together for as long as it takes to build up his confidence and re-establish his independence again.

Therapy

Initial phase

Formulating the predicament: As Jerry engages with the therapy and reveals more about himself and his shocking lack of self-confidence his previous front of cool composure melts like snow before the sun. His posture shifts markedly as he slumps in the chair, pulling his legs underneath him and hugging himself. He says he has lost the capacity to enjoy himself and feels unable to socialize. Other people just seem to him to talk nonsense, especially Jessica. He has told her he does not want to see her any-more. She doesn't like coming up to Yorkshire anyway and she hates dealing with his illness, so the break-up has suited them both, he says cynically. He is also quite happy to avoid seeing his Dad now that he is not going to London anymore. Dad has been insensitive about the entire accident and just keeps talking about 'getting back into the saddle', he sneers. He makes a face and I invite him to put his grimace into words. I am aware that he is dismissing all the people in his life and I gently keep him exploring his disappointment rather than letting him pretend to not care. At first though he just needs encouragement to speak his frustration with the way he feels treated by others.

Rethinking the predicament: He says his Dad is always in the saddle and has no other way to live. He has no time for anyone but himself or his business. Dad, he says with a pained expression, is a sad and twisted figure. I help Jerry look at this slightly differently by suggesting that he simply cannot take his Dad seriously anymore. He agrees wholeheartedly and adds that he does not understand why he used to feel so overawed by his father. He feels Dad understands nothing about other people at all. When I query what people he means, Jerry recognizes that he feels Dad understands him least of all. But he can also see how Dad is ruining his mother's life by not lov-ing her and by having regular affairs in London and abroad. He is strongly dismissive of his father's conduct. I meekly point out that he speaks as if he feels superior to his Dad and this surprises him. Upon reflection he thinks he is probably beginning to feel strong enough to take his Dad on. He does not understand why his mother accepts his father's odious behaviour. I point out he is now also challenging his mother's behaviour and ask him if he himself has stood up to his Dad about this. He can see now that he used to turn a blind eye to his father's deceitful way of life and that he was too cowardly to confront him. He is tearful again but is annoyed with himself for crying. When I reassuringly suggest that his accident has made him more sensitive to all these experiences and that there may be some good in allowing the process to unfold, he gratefully accepts this idea. He does want to allow himself to experience and understand what was previously out of his ken. This is the first time he acknowl-edges that something positive may come out of what so far has seemed mostly neg-ative. This will become a repeated theme: that the accident has revealed things that were previously hidden and that he wants to be in a new and better position to con-tend with all this. At the moment he sees human tragedy, danger and risk every-where and he feels overwhelmed by it. He is very concerned that he has lost his touch: he perceives and understands more than before but he lacks the strength to deal with it.

He sighs: 'The world has become overpowering. It is all too much … '. He looks down avoiding my gaze and his voice trails off as if he can't cope anymore and is appealing for mercy. But rather than folding and going along with his weakness I now up the stakes: 'Because you are both more vulnerable and more aware now. There is a great challenge to you here. You cannot hide any longer.' He nods thought-fully, but he doesn't look up. I wait before I continue speaking very slowly and whilst carefully observing his reaction: 'and you also just acknowledged that this is freeing you from some old ideas and gives you a new perspective on other people, for instance on your father'. 'Yes', he says softly, hesitantly, as if he is wondering whether or not to pick up the gauntlet thrown at him: 'but it makes me feel as if I am losing it. It feels as if I am reverting to what I used to be in secondary school: I feel different to other people.' As I say nothing, he carries on: 'I just feel so weak'. There is a brief silence between us. I speak tentatively when I reply eventually: 'It is your feeling of weakness that is the real problem then?' 'Hmmm', he mumbles. I want to establish whether we are on the same page and continue: 'if you were able to feel stronger in relation to your new sensitivity and clear observations about others, then this new way of being might actually become a good thing, you think?' He ponders and sways from side to side as he considers my point, literally wavering. Then a frank smile breaks through on his face as if a new idea has just sprung to mind. He hazards an interpretation: 'Well, yes, it would actually. If I could hold on to my understanding of what is happening around me and would not feel so overwhelmed by it all the whole time, then I could really quite enjoy it. It is quite creative in a way.' He glances at me sideways as if to check my response. I smile encouragingly and he carries on: 'You know, it's a bit like artistic inspiration. I am in a new groove.' I nod, smiling too. I say nothing. He beams and looks at me expectantly. I know he needs me to nail it down for him, summarize it somehow. I speak unhurriedly, finding the words little by little by thinking back to what he has discovered and articulated so far. He listens attentively, all ears, as if it is all coming together at last. What I say is nothing new, but somehow it needs saying. He needs to hear his predicament summarized and brought down to manageable size. He needs to be reminded of what he is up against, so that he can get ready to deal with it. 'Something awful and important has happened in your life: a terrifying experience, an accident, out of the blue, shaking everything up, bringing you close to death, making everything seem different, giving you lots of new insights, a new perspective, different ideas about the world'. He approves. I look at him, wondering whether that is enough and whether he can take over and pursue the thought further, or whether he wants me to continue. He looks into my eyes now, openly, kind of confirming that he can stand it after all. He knows now that I don't think him ridiculous or outrageous and that I value his struggle. He can begin to trust me. He can work with me and he does as he steps in to correct me: 'But sometimes it doesn't feel like that though', he hastens to add. 'Sometimes I just feel like I have been smashed to bits.' 'Yes', I say mildly, 'you still need to digest and process all this new experience so that you can integrate it and use it to good effect. You need to build new strength gradually, so as to be equal to your new sensitivity.' He agrees again, enthusiastically. He feels buoyed up by my explanation of his weakness and the implied remedy for it. I see a glint of hope in his eyes as he smiles broadly.

Tackling the predicament: Then he tells me spontaneously how he has actively been avoiding his former group of friends and fears he is becoming a bit of a recluse. As is so often the case my encouragement makes him able to expose his lack of courage. I only need to prompt him a little bit for him to acknowledge that all this avoidance keeps him weak. We immediately agree that he has needed to avoid people for a while just to protect himself. It is alright. He really could not cope with all these people while he was so unwell. My approach is one of approving his past coping strategy whilst exposing its current redundancy. He speaks with gusto of how much he hates being in London nowadays. He cannot tolerate the noise and the traffic and he is scared of buses and trucks. This is a bit of a problem. He knows he will have to tackle it eventually. He feels much better in his mother's country house, away from it all and cannot see himself going back to work. He has been living in Yorkshire with his mother ever since he came out of hospital and hopes to get a big insurance pay-out to allow him to continue living like this for a long time to come. Mother is worried about him, but enjoys fussing over him and she has told him and her friends that the accident has been a blessing in disguise because it has brought her son back to her. I point out that he looks both pleased and worried about this. This brings a wry smile to his lips. He is relieved to be able to speak the unspeakable love/ hate relationship he has with his Mum. We spend a long time debating this. He wants closeness with her and yet feels squashed by her. He agrees it will be best not to stay living at home for too long. This makes it so the more important for him to engage with the therapy.

He is beginning to formulate now what he wants from therapy: processing the distress and help him to get a new understanding of his past and present life, so that he can make something good out of the pieces he seems to have broken into when the lorry hit his head. He would like to sleep properly again and to feel less insecure when he goes out, but he does not want to go back to his old life. That is out of the question. He checks with me about the confidentiality of our conversations and then admits freely that he wants to get as much money out of the insurance company as possible and has no particular motivation to get back to normal. At the same time he does not want to end up as a disabled person, nor as someone who lacks in moral fibre or who is afraid all the time, as he is now. He is worried about his panic attacks and his lack of appetite for life. He cannot carry on this way and will make sure he gets himself sorted out as we work together over the next few months.

We agree then that he will use this time of weakness and incapacity to take stock of his life and make a new start. He can see how having hit rock bottom provides him with an opportunity to rebuild himself from scratch. He does not want to pretend and try to be the popular boy who pleases his mother and father anymore. He wants to rebuild his life on solid ground this time. He now feels therapy is a real chance of getting things right and he becomes a bit of a fan, reading therapy books and self-help books for fun.

Middle phase

Recognizing the vicious circles: By taking things so seriously Jerry quickly gets the hang of therapy and makes the most of it. He brings his concerns openly and does not hide his feelings and fears. Although he tries to play his PTSD symptoms down it becomes clear that the accident has nonetheless left a serious mark on him: the world seems unpredictable and sometimes he feels terrified in the face of things he used to take for granted as part of everyday life. Essentially he cannot face any form of transportation; he hates trains and cars and feels uncomfortable even on an ordinary bike. During the first months of therapy his mother drives him into Sheffield for the sessions and this becomes quite an issue since it brings out the conflicts in his relationship to her. His physical dependency on his Mum feeds the craving for her affection, but it also makes him increasingly impatient with her. I just encourage him to speak about it all and help him become aware of the old vicious circle. I also draw his attention to his frustration and his desire to escape from it.

Facing limitations: I keep telling him to simply observe his relationship to his Mum rather than to try to change it. This frees him to realize he wants to change it for his own sake. He starts noticing that she seems to encourage his reliance on her. Then, with very little prompting, he begins to think about her dependency on him. It strikes him for the first time that she has always needed him as much as he needed her. It occurs to him that his mother has claimed him as the special person who can shield her from the world in the same way in which he needs her to shield him from the world just now. The difference is that he wants to get independent of her, whilst she seems to want him to remain dependent. But then he is not certain about this either. There is much evidence to the contrary too and sometimes he feels confused about it. In many ways it is him who is clinging to her. He wonders: 'Is it wrong for my mother and I to feel comfort in each other's company?' and he returns to this question regularly. It is the central dilemma of his life. Sometimes it is phrased as: 'should I be independent and suffer alone or should I rely on another and learn to be close?' At other times it is formulated as: 'is it possible to tolerate the difficulties of a hazardous world without hiding in a safe place?' By allowing these questions to emerge out of his struggles with the concrete problems of his daily existence he begins to reflect on his life in a way he has not done before. He comes to accept that his mother's love has always been an essential part of his self-confidence and that there is nothing wrong with reclaiming it at this point in his life to help him to find his feet again. Once he feels entitled to making the most of their closeness and stops fighting it, he can begin to see the limits of their mutual dependency as well. It becomes obvious to him that it can stop them both from exploring further afield and can hinder as much as help his recovery. He is starting to see how it is stopping his mother from moving on in her own life as well. She spends time with him, protecting him from his panic attacks instead of finishing her interior decorating course. He notices how she reproaches his father for not spending more time with them in Yorkshire to be with their injured son, rather than confronting the reality of the long standing estrangement in the marriage. Quite quickly simply by being able to talk about his observations and understand what is going on, he becomes able to confront her on her hypocrisy rather than siding with her against Dad as he used to in the past. He can even tell her that he knows how she has always encouraged Dad to live his own life and has pushed him away because she would rather just be with her son anyway. He is surprised to find that his mother is grateful to him for saying these things to her rather than feeling hurt. It proves to him that he is now getting stronger than he has ever been before and he relishes this idea.

Finding new meaning: We generally talk very little of his post-traumatic symptoms, though we spend a little time thinking about suitable strategies in relation to insomnia and fear of public transport. By sticking to the very basic daily struggles he brings to therapy and helping him to clarify and understand his own experience and observations, he begins to recognise his own capacity for solving each of these problems. He comes for some twenty sessions before he realizes that he is dealing with his daily life in a new way. He is getting stronger. He isn't fighting his symptoms and fears anymore but looks forward to facing them because in doing so he can take up the challenge of understanding the underlying dynamics. He recognizes that the trauma of the accident has opened his eyes to the complexities and dangers of living in a way he had never thought possible and he admits one day that he is beginning to enjoy the work of relearning to exist and that he now looks forward to therapy sessions.

His general therapeutic reading is moving towards a focus on existential literature and he becomes an expert at arguing with me about philosophical interpretations of his experience. He enjoys sitting up at night reading books and he stops complaining of insomnia all together. I challenge him to apply his newly found philosophical expertise to the concrete problems that persist in his physical existence and he starts experimenting with ways of overcoming his fear of transportation at this stage. He begins a programme of country walking, working up from two miles a day to seven or eight miles a day. He is aware that walking is safer for him than relying on mechanical means of transport, even though he finds it quite challenging to walk on the side of A-roads where cars and trucks rush past him. As he gets used to the traffic on these roads, he feels his confidence returning and he starts riding his old push bike along small country lanes. He finds the freedom of this experience so exhilarating that he acquires a new cross-country bike and a lot of sophisticated biking equipment and learns new skills in negotiating the hills of the Yorkshire countryside. He has no interest in going back on a motorbike, but without even mentioning it to me, he resumes driving a car to come into town to attend sessions or to pick up new materials for his bike.

End phase

Facing anxiety and guilt: Jerry's fears of traffic are slowly abating as he finds a way to negotiate the world of transportation by relying on his own wits. He is somewhat concerned at his progress, for we are now some 30 weeks into the therapy and his insurance claim for the posttraumatic stress has still not been settled. He worries that his forthcoming psychiatric report will not corroborate his original PTSD diagnosis, since he is now 'nearly cured', and that his insurance claim will be in jeopardy. This is a strange, but not unusual, predicament and we talk about it quite a bit. He agrees that it is not worth pretending to be ill for the sake of a pay-off if the price of this is to stop him getting better. Honesty and facing up to his experience have been the core of his improvement. He cannot undo this now. Would it be so bad if he did not have a huge pay out? Might it even be better to challenge himself and pick up his life by himself rather than being cushioned by the insurance company? We think about how he might cope if he were destitute and alone. He gets great comfort from the idea that he would actually relish the challenge.

Getting real: When the psychiatric assessment does come, he finds, to his relief that the assessment is mainly related to his professional life. The fact that he has not resumed his job and is not likely to fully do so for another few months, makes all the difference to the settlement. We both breathe a sigh of relief when this is sorted, for now there is nothing more to stop his improvement. I had grave doubts about his willingness to get back to work until his compensation claim had been put behind him. Now we can finally discuss his ambivalent attitude towards his job. Eventually he comes to the conclusion that he misses his photography but not the work in London.

   The moment the case is settled he starts to take his camera out on his rides into the hills and gets engrossed in landscape photography, very quickly building up a portfolio of work which leads to some professional contracts. When he finally receives the money from the insurance company for loss of income and in compensation for the physical and emotional trauma he has suffered, he decides to stay in the area rather than moving back to London and he buys a flat in an up and coming area of town, from which he decides to set up a new photography business. His Mum and Dad are both surprised at his regeneration and each in their own way respond with some ambivalence. This leads to some arguments and rows. Jerry needs quite a bit of help in thinking his way through these at times, but it is all his doing that he doesn't give up and keeps sorting things out with them. At first it is his father who begins to treat him in a more mature and respectful way. At this point Jerry decides to revert back to his given name, Jérôme, and feels he is well on the way towards a full recovery, capable of standing up for himself.

Conclusion

After about a year and a half of weekly sessions Jérôme/Jerry starts seeing me fortnightly. We talk mostly about his relationships now, rather than about physical or psychological problems. His relationship to his mother is still problematic and he is still in two minds about how much to condone her desire to be close. This same question arises about his relationship to me. As a mother substitute I have become quite necessary to him as well. He agrees with me that finding a new distance from me will help him in doing the same with his mother. A few months later he switches to coming to see me once a month and continues to see me on this basis for another ten sessions.

I am not surprised when some time during this period he tells me that he has found a new partner, Josh, also a photographer, eight years his senior. Very quickly they build a mutual and committed relationship and when Jérôme comes to see me for the final session, he and Josh have started not only to work but also live together. He brings his partner along to introduce us to each other. Jérôme appears full of confidence and is brimming over with plans and projects in his new life. The two of them seem extremely happy together: as far as I can tell they are relaxed and affectionate with each other. He introduces me as: 'the lady who changed my life' and when I correct him with: 'you mean, the lady who helped you to see how *you* could change your life', I laugh at my own impudence disguised as false modesty. For really, it was neither me nor him who did the work, for all we did was to let life guide him through the complexity of his accident, so that he could thrive on rather than suffer from the far reaching effects it had on his life.

REFERENCES

Binswanger, L. (1963) *Being-in-the-World*, trans. J. Needleman. New York: Basic Books.

Boss, M. (1957a) *Psychoanalysis and Daseinsanalysis*, trans. L.B. Lefebre. New York: Basic Books.

Boss, M. (1957b) *The Analysis of Dreams*. London: Rider.

Boss, M. (1979) *Existential Foundations of Medicine and Psychology*. New York: Jason Aronson.

Bugental, J.F.T. (1981) *The Search for Authenticity: An Existential-Analytic Approach to Psychotherapy*. New York: Irvington.

Cohn, H.W. (1994) 'What is existential psychotherapy?', *British Journal of Psychiatry*, 165(8): 669–701.

Cohn, H.W. (1997) *Existential Thought and Therapeutic Practice*. London: Sage.

Cohn, H.W. (2002) *Heidegger and the Roots of Existential Therapy*. London: Continuum.

Cooper, D. (1967) *Psychiatry and Anti-psychiatry*. New York: Barnes & Noble.

Cooper, R. (ed.) (1989) *Thresholds between Philosophy and Psycho-analysis*. London: Free Association Books.

Cooper, M. (2003) *Existential Therapies*, London: Sage.

De Koning, A.J.J. and Jenner, F.A. (1982) *Phenomenology and Psychiatry*. New York: Academic Press.

Deurzen-Smith, E. van (1984) 'Existential therapy', in W. Dryden (ed.), *Individual Therapy in Britain*. London: Harper & Row.

Deurzen-Smith, E. van (1997) *Everyday Mysteries: Existential Dimensions of Psychotherapy*. London: Routledge.

Deurzen, E. van (1998) *Paradox and Passion in Psychotherapy*. Chichester: Wiley & Sons.
Deurzen, E. van (2002) *Existential Counselling and Psychotherapy in Practice*, 2nd edn. London: Sage.
Deurzen, E. van and Arnold-Baker, C. (2005) *Existential Perspectives on Human Issues: a Handbook for Practice*. London: Palgrave/Macmillan.
Deurzen, E. van and Kenward, R. (2005) *Dictionary of Existential Psychotherapy and Counselling*, London: Sage.
Du Plock, S. (1997) *Case Studies in Existential Psychotherapy*. Chichester: Wiley & Sons.
Eleftheriadou, Z. (1994) *Transcultural Counselling*. London: Central Book Publishing.
Frankl, V.E. (1964) *Man's Search for Meaning*. London: Hodder & Stoughton.
Frankl, V.E. (1967) *Psychotherapy and Existentialism*. Harmondsworth: Penguin.
Heaton, L.M. (1988) *The Provocation of Levinas*. London: Routledge.
Heaton, L.M. (1994) *Wittgenstein for Beginners*. Cambridge: Icon.
Heidegger, M. (1962) *Being and Time*, trans. J. Macquarrie and E.S. Robinson. New York: Harper & Row.
Heidegger, M. (1968) *What is Called Thinking?* New York: Harper & Row.
Husserl, E. (1960) *Cartesian Meditations*. The Hague: Nijhoff.
Husserl, E. (1962) *Ideas*. New York: Collier.
Jaspers, K. (1951) *The Way to Wisdom*, trans. R. Manhneim. New Haven and London: Yale University Press.
Jaspers, K. (1963) *General Psychopathology*. Chicago: University of Chicago Press.
Kearney, R. (1986) *Modern Movements in European Philosophy*. Manchester: Manchester University Press.
Kierkegaard, S. (1941) *Concluding Unscientific Postscript*, trans. D.F. Swenson and W. Lowrie. Princeton, NJ: Princeton University Press.
Kierkegaard, S. (1944) *The Concept of Dread*, trans. W. Lowrie. Princeton, NJ: Princeton University Press.
Laing, R.D. (1960) *The Divided Self*. Harmondsworth: Penguin.
Laing, R.D. (1961) *Self and Others*. Harmondsworth: Penguin.
Laing, R.D. and Cooper, D. (1964) *Reason and Violence*. London: Tavistock.
Lemma-Wright, A. (1994) *Starving to Live. The Paradox of Anorexia Nervosa*. London: Central Book Publishing.
Lomas, P. (1981) *The Case for a Personal Psychotherapy*. Oxford: Oxford University Press.
Mace, C. (ed.) (1999) *Heart and Soul: The Therapeutic Face of Philosophy*. London: Routledge.
Macquarrie, J. (1972) *Existentialism: an Introduction, Guide and Assessment*. Harmondsworth: Penguin.
May, R. (1969) *Love and Will*. New York: Norton.
May, R. (1983) *The Discovery of Being*. New York: Norton.
May, R. and Yalom, L. (1985) 'Existential psychotherapy', in R.S. Corsini (ed.), *Current Psychotherapies*. Itasca, IL: Peacock.
May, R., Angel, E. and Ellenberger, H.F. (1958) *Existence*. New York: Basic Books.
Merleau-Ponty, M. (1962) *Phenomenology of Perception*, trans. C. Smith. London: Routledge & Kegan Paul.
Minkowski, E. (1970) *Lived Time*. Evanston, IL: Northwestern University Press.
Moran, D. (2000) *Introduction to Phenomenology*. London: Routledge.
Nietzsche, F. (1961) *Thus Spoke Zarathustra*, trans. R.J. Hollingdale. Harmondsworth: Penguin.
Nietzsche, F. (1974) *The Gay Science*, trans. W. Kaufmann. New York: Random House.
Nietzsche, F. (1986) *Human, All Too Human: A Book for Free Spirits*, trans. R.J. Hollingdale. Cambridge: Cambridge University Press.
Sartre, J.P. (1956) *Being and Nothingness: An Essay on Phenomenological Ontology*, trans. H. Barnes. New York: New York Philosophical Library.
Sartre, J.P. (1962) *Sketch for a Theory of the Emotions*. London: Methuen.
Smail, D.J. (1978) *Psychotherapy, a Personal Approach*. London: Dent.
Smail, D.J. (1987) *Taking Care*. London: Dent.
Smail, D.J. (1993) *The Origins of Unhappiness: A New Understanding of Personal Distress*. London: HarperCollins.
Spiegelberg, H. (1972) *Phenomenology in Psychology and Psychiatry*. Evanston, IL: Northwestern University Press.
Spinelli, E. (1997) *Tales of Unknowing*. London: Duckworth.

Spinelli, E. (2005) *The Interpreted World: An Introduction to Phenomenological Psychology*, 2nd edn, London: Sage.

Strasser, F. and Strasser, A. (1997) *Existential Time Limited Therapy*. Chichester: Wiley & Sons.

Tantam, D. (2002) *Psychotherapy and Counselling in Practice: a Narrative Approach*, Cambridge: Cambridge University press.

Tillich, P. (1952) *The Courage to Be*. Harmondsworth: Penguin.

Valle, R.S. and King, M. (1978) *Existential Phenomenological Alternatives for Psychology*. New York: Oxford University Press.

Warnock, M. (1970) *Existentialism*. Oxford: Oxford University Press.

Yalom, I. (1980) *Existential Psychotherapy*. New York: Basic Books.

SUGGESTED FURTHER READING

Cohn, H.W. (2002) *Heidegger and the Roots of Existential Therapy*. London: Continuum.

Cooper, M. (2003) *Existential Therapies*. London: Sage.

Deurzen, E. van (2002) *Existential Counselling and Psychotherapy in Practice*, 2nd edn. London: Sage.

Macquarrie, J. (1972) *Existentialism: an Introduction, Guide and Assessment*. Harmondsworth: Penguin.

Yalom, I. (1980) *Existential Psychotherapy*. New York: Basic Books.

9

Gestalt Therapy

Malcolm Parlett and Juliet Denham

HISTORICAL CONTEXT AND DEVELOPMENT IN BRITAIN

Historical context

Gestalt therapy did not appear in a flash. As is usual with any movement, there were preceding ideas forming a fertile substratum, out of which grew this radical revision of psychoanalysis.

The two primary founders of the approach were Frederick (Fritz) Perls (1893–1970) and his wife and collaborator, Laura Perls (1905–92). The pre-history of Gestalt therapy begins in Germany, where they were born and educated and where, throughout the 1920s, they were exposed to the ideas and experimental culture that flowered at that time. Philosophy, education, the arts, politics and psychology were all in creative upheaval. The young couple were of the radical avant-garde.

Fritz Perls, after active service in the First World War, trained and practised as a neuropsychiatrist and had analysis with several orthodox Freudians and then with Wilhelm Reich. Laura Perls was taught by leading members of the then popular Gestalt school of psychology; she also studied with Paul Tillich and Martin Buber. Some of the 'ancestors' of Gestalt therapy can be identified: Freud, with his instinct theories; Reich, with his emphasis on the body; Buber, with his passionate views on the need for human 'meeting'; the Gestalt psychologists (Wertheimer, Kohler, Koffka and Lewin), with their criticism of reductionist psychology and their view of perception and thinking being organized in coherent patterns, or *gestalts*.

Before their analytic trainings, Laura and Fritz had met at the neurological institute directed by Kurt Goldstein, whose views of 'self-actualization' and 'organismic self-regulation' (he coined the terms) also fed into the eventual synthesis. This was their first experience of holistic thinking. The Perls were also exposed to the radical philosophy of existentialism and to phenomenology, both of which became major foundations of the Gestalt approach. Fritz was involved in theatre with the director Max Reinhardt – his love of dramatization was later reflected in his training workshops; Laura, an accomplished musician, was involved in dance, movement, and Eastern philosophy.

This extraordinary cultural epoch did not, of course, survive. By 1933, Fritz and Laura Perls were on the Nazi blacklist as left-wing radicals. They fled to Holland, and then to South Africa, where they remained working as psychoanalysts till 1946. They continued to lap up other ideas and influences, for example holism, as first written about by Smuts, the South African philosopher and prime minister. Perls's first major statement, *Ego, Hunger and Aggression* (Perls, 1969a but first published in 1942) criticized psychoanalysis and suggested a new approach to therapy. After the war they emigrated to the USA.

Post-war New York was another place and time marked by great cultural ferment. The Perls became a focus for a group of writers, political activists and therapists, including the poet, educator and social critic Paul Goodman, who was to write a major part of the 'founding book': *Gestalt Therapy* (Perls et al., 1994/ 1951). The first Institute of Gestalt Therapy was set up in New York in 1952 and Laura Perls continued to be a key figure until her death in 1992. In contrast, Fritz Perls began moving restlessly between different locations. He was not successful until he turned up at the famed Esalen Institute in California. Then, at the height of the 1960s counterculture, he became widely known. At this time Gestalt therapy became linked to the human potential movement, encounter, and the development of humanistic psychology generally.

Numerous stereotypes and misconceptions about Gestalt stem from this period. Many would-be Gestalt practitioners imitated Perls and his personal style of work, taking the techniques he was experimenting with to be the essence of the whole approach. For many, Gestalt became equated with what Fritz Perls did, and the full depth and substance of the Gestalt philosophy and practice were not communicated. The history of Gestalt therapy since that time has included returning to European philosophical roots, and building on other founding influences and teachers. The depth and effectiveness of the approach have been reaffirmed, and many of the original ideas have been developed greatly (Woldt and Toman, 2005).

For a time, misinformation persisted, with Gestalt regarded as confrontational or as lacking a theory, or that it was confined to one or two techniques, or only carried out in groups. Such misperceptions have been displaced by growing acknowledgement of Gestalt therapy's professionalism and influential place among therapies. In particular, its extensive skills base grounded in a dialogic relationship (Joyce and Sills, 2001), its attention to body experience (Kennedy, 2005), its sensitivity to the situation (Wollants, 2005), and its emphasis on present-centred awareness (Spagnuolo-Lobb and Amendt-Lyon, 2003) are all now endorsed by therapists of many persuasions. Gestalt therapy is flexibly applied – including for brief therapy (Houston, 2003) and in NHS settings (Denham-Vaughan, 2005) as well as in long-term therapy (Jacobs, 2000).

Development in Britain

There were some early developments in the 1970s – mainly visitors or émigrés from America offering short training experiences – but it was not until the 1980s that Gestalt therapy began to be taught in an organized way. The Gestalt Psychotherapy and Training Institute and the Gestalt Centre, London, became founder member organizations in the UK Council for Psychotherapy. Training programmes were established in major cities (such as Manchester, Bristol and Edinburgh) and prominently within psychotherapy training institutes (such as Metanoia in London and Sherwood in Nottingham).

In the 1990s the trend was for trainings to become linked with universities, so that Masters level courses could be undertaken. There was an inevitable shift towards more emphasis on the underlying theory and philosophy of Gestalt therapy and on writing and thinking. This academic development has prompted some questioning: Gestalt began as a radical and innovative approach, with an anti-establishment ethos. Some believe the pendulum has swung too far – that the sparkle of Gestalt has been dulled by respectability. Overall, though, the emphasis on higher training standards (including the requirement for extensive personal therapy) and on rigorous ethical and professional practice have strengthened Gestalt therapy. Its roots in holism, relationship, present-centered experiencing and experiment remain axiomatic.

With Gestalt therapy newly arriving in many other countries, British Gestalt therapists have become more cosmopolitan in outlook. The *British Gestalt Journal,* an acclaimed international journal, began publishing in 1991. British writers, such as Mackewn (1997), Philippson (2001), Joyce and Sills (2001) and Houston (2003), have contributed to the rapid expansion in books about the approach. A strong web presence and international network, with a host of international meetings, are signs of increased influence and long-term confidence. However, in Britain as elsewhere, challenges face the Gestalt community – its values and vision of health are more expansive than those in political favour and so far Gestalt therapists have not risen to the research challenges posed by evidence-based practice to demonstrate to others the effectiveness of the approach.

THEORETICAL ASSUMPTIONS

Image of the person

Gestalt therapy has a central idea that human beings are in constant development. The person is regarded as an exploring, adapting, self-reflecting being, in a process of continuous change. We are constantly making and remaking ourselves. Gestalt therapy focuses on the process of experiencing this unfolding life.

Such change comes about inevitably through our constantly interacting with others and dealing with life's challenges, possibilities and problems. This leads to another assumption, namely that human beings should not be theorized about as if they have some isolated, independent existence (and psychology). The individual is seen as always being 'in relation' – as one pole within a constantly changing 'field' (Parlett, 2005) encompassing both the individual and her/his milieu. 'Inner' and 'outer' realms of existence cannot be separated. Thus, family, colleagues, work, organizational, communal and national life, as well as being 'other', are also so much part of the actual experience of life and living that they are, in effect, 'part of oneself'.

The lack of a hard and fast cut-off point between the person and the physical and social world is evident at every level. Breathing and the presence of air are so interlinked that to separate them is an academic abstraction. In a similar way, lovers require a beloved, a person is not an 'employer' without others who are employed, people can only be 'therapy clients' because therapy and therapists exist. Neither pole exists without its accompaniment. The whole of life involves such interdependent relationship. Thus, human beings are communal animals, each 'carrying' the language and values of their cultural heritage and embodying attitudes and behaviours derived from family and society, work, home and the media. Given this outlook, confronting sexism, racism, homophobia and other cultural and societal prejudices is an essential therapeutic priority for the Gestalt therapist. Anti-oppressive practice is seen as having direct clinical relevance.

The Gestalt perspective on the image of the person is therefore holistic and inclusive. Likewise, the individual is viewed as a complex biological organism. Just as a child without a 'growing up context' is inconceivable, so is a mind or soul without a body. Human beings have inbuilt psychological patterns of reacting (for instance to shock), physical needs which dictate a lot of daily life, with muscular involvement and constant bio-chemical changes accompanied by a phenomenological 'felt sense' that is part of every thought and action taken. All experience is embodied and the process of living involves immersion in the physical realities of feeling states, the emotions, and in the life of our bodies – e.g. our state of health, fluctuations of energy, ageing, sensual satisfactions, pain and the quality of sleep.

Gestalt therapists believe that enquiring into the *actually lived experience* of the person leads inevitably to a holistic, rather than reductionistic, perspective. Human life and experience cannot be divided into parts. Our lived existence is grounded both in the social and familial realities of our present world – its technologies, its economics, its pressures – *and* in the 'experience of our body [which is] experience of our self, just as our thinking, imagery, and ideas are part of our self' (Kepner, 1987: 10).

Creative adjustment

The Gestalt approach emphasizes that each person is actively 'self-organizing'. At every level we are managing the conditions and possibilities of life, minimizing discomfort, seeking to meet our needs (with or without awareness), dealing with the demands and obligations of the systems that are part of our field or life space. Much of life relates to preserving ourselves in equilibrium. Thus, we 'self-regulate' ourselves at an organismic level – e.g. sleeping when tired, crying when in grief, eating when hungry. Biologically, these capabilities allow the person to live in a state of health. At the same time, obviously, we also choose sometimes intentionally to disturb our equilibrium – extending ourselves in order to meet some broader need for, say, stimulation at a party or to serve others through self-sacrifice. So the ways we self-organize are many and complex.

Existence as a whole calls for continuous 'creative adjustment' (Perls et al., 1994/1951). Adjustment is not only reactive but also proactive – a process of 'approaching, laying hold of, and altering old structures' (ibid.: 9) within the field. Thus, the person both adapts to, and seeks to modify, obstacles, habits, traditions and systems within the field in ways that meet needs, improve conditions, or sustain life through assimilation and learning. These modifications might take the form of destroying part of 'what is other' (as in eating or throwing away old papers), or 'aggressing upon it' (as in editing someone's writing, or questioning authority), or 'deconstructing' it (such as altering the shape of a garden or the nature of a relationship). Again, the idea that we are changers and makers of our life and reality as well as adapting to it underlines the participatory or 'co-created' nature of our lived existence.

Altogether, then, the person is viewed in a more fluid, continuously interactive way than is perhaps common in psychology and in conventional ways of thinking about the person. The self is not regarded as a 'thing-like mental entity', but as 'the process of experiencing' (Wolfert, 2000). As a process, 'selfing' is an activity, 'a dynamic relation which is ever-moving, ever-changing – an organisation shaped by and shaping experiences in the play of the forces in the field' (ibid.: 77). The theory which goes with this view is radical: the self is variable, and at times of maximum intensity and involvement there is greater 'self' than at times when energy is low and the person feels directionless or unfocused.

The view of the self espoused in the Gestalt approach fits with many present-day notions of what it means to be human. In a postmodernist time, and with the new discoveries of physics and the changing cosmology of our time, we have become used to abandoning fixed structures, categories and mechanisms – the static framework for thinking about human being – in favour of a more dynamic, relativistic, fluid picture of what it means to be human. Gestalt therapy and theory are in tune with these developments. They emphasize processes – continuous development, ever-changing responses to evolving conditions, and shifting perspectives – rather than mechanisms, causes and effects, fixed diagnostic categories and treatment plans.

The bias towards acknowledging fluidity and change does not mean that the opposites are ignored; 'stuckness', fixity and resistance to change are also part of what Gestalt therapists attend to. There are patterned sequences and continuities, habits of thought and body structures, as well as social, family, economic, cultural and organizational structures that provide the necessary counterpoint influences of stability in a person's lived existence. In other words, although life is continuously forming and re-forming, and the self and field are always in flux, there are also consistent patterns to self-organizing. It is to these habitual responses and patterns of responding that we turn next.

Conceptualization of psychological disturbance and health

Given what has been said so far, it is not surprising that Gestalt therapists are wary of language and assumptions that seem to 'fix' a person or pattern of experience as 'disturbed'. They argue that we are all 'disturbed' at times. The incidence of mental ill health, of depression and anxiety in particular, in present-day society suggests that we are talking of wide-scale phenomena that, in certain cases and at certain times, become acute and debilitating. Given adverse enough circumstances, any human being may come to operate in a way that can be seen as disturbed. The overwhelming sense of how human beings operate, however, is that they organize themselves and their lives as well as they can, even if their life skills and human abilities are not always well developed (Parlett, 2000).

Disturbance is therefore not conceived as some kind of personal dysfunction that is attributable to an individual's psychological history or character. Rather it is seen in a wider, 'whole field' way which takes into account the family, work, and societal pressures that are acting in the person's life space – pressures that many have to cope with, and which 'reach breaking point' in certain individual lives at certain times.

A definition of health

Many approaches avoid defining health, by referring to it as 'absence of disturbance or illness'. In Gestalt therapy we suggest that health is a living expression of a person's present field relationships: whether their lives feel integrated (or 'together'); the extent to which they are creatively adjusting to present challenges and opportunities; and whether they feel 'in balance' physically and energetically.

The notion of health derives from regarding human experience as being most rewarding when we feel most alive and are well supported. As energized, embodied, focused centres of consciousness, human beings are able to engage fully with whatever life situation they are presently encountering. At such moments (or periods of time), they are able to apply their life knowledge freely – that is, without self-consciousness, loss of focus, inhibitions or intellectualizations.

Existence calls for versatility, a capacity to learn from experience and self-orienting principles by which to live and to exercise choice and self-responsibility. Obviously for most people in a broad range of circumstances the same impulse is there: to improve one's life or to evolve. Even in unfavourable conditions (e.g. as hostages or in situations of grinding poverty) people can often retain a capacity to operate creatively. They make choices and are not overwhelmed, whereas for others there is insufficient support in the field at that time for them to adjust creatively in the face of obstacles. Such individuals, at least at that time, require more benign and supportive circumstances before they can act with dignity or elegance, or 'with good form' (Zinker, 1994). The Gestalt approach rests on the belief that anyone can, if they want to and have sufficient support (incentives, back-up, urgency of need), learn how to function in life with greater skill and satisfaction.

Disturbance

To be disturbed at times, then, is to be expected. The individual is responding to the whole field, and the field may be in chaos or crisis, which impacts those within it. However, there are sometimes individual patterns of repeated confusion and distress. Human beings are creatures of habit. In situations where we are not comfortable and are not managing, we are likely to fall back on repertoires and responses that were once adequate solutions (or creative adjustments) but that do not 'work' in present circumstances. In 'healthy' modes we are capable of the necessary involvement with what is actually in front of us; in 'disturbed' modes we can seem fixated in inappropriate habitual patterns of thinking, feeling and reacting in ways that interfere with functioning in the circumstances being encountered in the present. Life calls for us continuously to extend our abilities to maintain ourselves in changing conditions, rather than perpetuating obsolete responses, or 'fixed gestalts', which are self-limiting. In times of personal or collective chaos, graceful and creative qualities are often among the first casualties.

The exact ways in which individuals act stereotypically, do not 'flow', and experience themselves as adrift become the foci for Gestalt investigation (as do their creative opposites).

The management of 'gestalts'

Gestalt therapists are interested in how people organize their experience. Human beings are preoccupied with differing things at different times, and with various degrees of intensity. For example, if I meet an old friend in the street, how exactly I relate to him will be a function of the field conditions as a whole. Thus, I may be pleased to see him but I may also have a critically important appointment in a few minutes' time. Alternatively, I may have a longing for human contact and bumping into him is particularly welcome. The total situation or field includes constraints (e.g. the lack of privacy or time available); needs (e.g. to quell a sense of loneliness, or not to be late); and ongoing structures (e.g. assumptions about the social 'etiquette' of meeting old friends and the physical arrangement of the street).

Life is full of these processes – these temporary configurations of a person's experience, the patterns or *gestalts* of a life, which form and, when completed, dissolve. When a person becomes more interested in something (whatever it happens to be), attention becomes more focused, and the field is reorganized. The matter in hand becomes more *figural*, giving competing interests and concerns lower priority. What is not attended to becomes correspondingly dimmer, vaguer or more distant-seeming (becomes part of the *ground*).

As we continue to focus on a particular figure, coming more and more in contact with this 'other' (e.g. a mathematical problem, a lover, a conversation), we eventually reach a point where the sense of difference between the problem (or lover, etc.) and 'me' lessens. The 'contact boundary', at the point of fullest contact between self and other, dissolves altogether, and the field of one's experience is momentarily full and unified. Such a state alters again, as we lose interest following completion of the task (the problem is solved, or the lovemaking complete), and 'we come back to ourselves' with a renewed sense of 'self' and 'other'.

This model of involvement (Perls et al., 1994/1951) highlights that our attention and interest vary, along with our sense of energetic engagement or contact, and also our sense of self. Our conscious experience is forever changing. We may be acutely interested in the whereabouts and relative qualities of restaurants before lunch, but do not notice them after lunch. Another matter of persistent interest arises in its stead – for example, the meeting we are going to.

When adjusting in a creative and effective way to circumstances arising in life, the configurations of existence (that we call gestalts) tend to be well formed, graceful and fulfilling, and when complete or finished they disappear into the background. However, when gestalts are left *unfinished* (e.g. a conversation is interrupted) they tend to continue to occupy some of our attention intermittently. Some gestalts are *not well-formed* in the first place (e.g. the meeting starts off 'on the wrong foot'), or are short of energy (e.g. the participants in a project are half-hearted in their enthusiasm), and these do not satisfy us. The Gestalt therapist attends to the quality of a person's experiences: disturbance is manifested in the very processes of gestalt formation and destruction.

Of course, it is not just small life-episodes that interest us. While some gestalts are short-lived, many are of long duration. Many different gestalts operate in someone's life at any one time. Our creative adjustment involves seeking overall balance within our experiential field or life space. Some *interrupted* gestalts have a huge effect on the course of a person's life (as for instance when a young person's studying stops through having to take over the family business); and some *fixed* gestalts dominate everyday life (such as addiction to alcohol).

Often, gestalts have a life-cycle. Whether it is with a street encounter, or having a baby, or taking an exam or completing a major life project, there are discernible phases in how the cycle unfolds; and they relate to both energy and time. Typically, there is a build-up of interest and vital energy as we become more focused and more involved – say, in preparing for an exam. There is usually a discernible high point in the cycle, when 'something happens' which is significant (in this case, writing the exam paper), and thereafter the energy slowly or rapidly dissipates: the examinee becomes less involved and more easily distracted by other priorities (new needs emerging). The arising and receding of different gestalts is a continuous process. If interrupted, a gestalt may not complete its life-cycle. (If the exam were cancelled, the examinee might be 'left hanging'.) A state of feeling unfulfilled results from such interruptions, many of which are self-induced and repetitive. For some, the satisfaction of completing gestalts and moving on is rarely achievable.

Some interruptions to the natural flow of experience are environmental (e.g. someone arrives as I am about to say goodnight to my child). Other interruptions are consciously chosen, and wisely so – if I have an urge to assault a traffic warden, interrupting that particular gestalt is a wise and mature choice. More often, however, interruptions are self-constructed (e.g. 'people are not interested in what I have to say'); and involve lack of awareness, (e.g. I do not register my dissatisfaction with a conversation till it is over).

Present-centred awareness

Such abilities of self-organizing are enhanced by having an awareness of present, ongoing experience. Being unable to 'tune in' to what is actually arising in one's experience, or to notice what one is doing in the moment, is a major impediment in coping with the world as it is encountered. Awareness includes noticing, recognizing, being in touch with … Its opposites include being distracted, oblivious, desensitized or out of touch. Part of being aware relates to the five senses and the capacity to take in information from our surroundings. It also involves recognizing feeling states and bodily sensations.

Awareness of self and of the world involves direct experience, not merely talked-about or conceptualized versions of it. We all engage in self-talk – e.g. planning, remembering, futurizing and arguing with oneself – and these are essential for human living; but they can displace our capacity to hear, see, smell, and to tune into bodily reactions and emotional feelings. The person with a rich, sensation-filled somatic and emotional life feels generally more alive than someone who identifies him/herself only with what is going on 'in the mind'.

The issues are philosophically difficult, but there is, in Gestalt therapy, a conviction that despite the importance of thinking and rationality, a person is limited if s/he is out of touch with his or her primary experience. Knowing what one feels 'in one's bones', or recognizing one's 'heart's desire', is essential for the refining of values. To know that something does not 'feel right' is a human sensibility that collectively and individually needs cultivating if we are to assume full personal responsibility. In Gestalt therapy the body is regarded as a source of wisdom, a provider of organismic truth; and client perception as a more reliable guide than applying a concept or principle (Kennedy, 2005).

Contact styles

Gestalt therapists also attend to the 'contact boundary', the relationship between person and situation, noticing the exact patterns of how people connect (or fail to connect) to their surroundings and circumstances. Particular attention has been given in Gestalt therapy to four kinds of transaction at the contact boundary (Mackewn, 1997).

The first relates to the way in which the contact boundary is subjected to overload or potential invasion from the outside. For instance, suppose an employee receives a repeated message from his boss (e.g. that he is 'careless'). The man may take on the message without question, as an automatic given, so that it becomes a part of his outlook. He has *introjected* it. Alternatively, the man may incline to the opposite response and reject utterly any message from 'authority'.

If he is adjusting creatively – i.e. responding flexibly to current field conditions – there will be times when he introjects to good effect (introjecting instructions in an emergency might be life-saving); and other times when he sensibly rejects, say a gratuitous insult, out of hand. The contact boundary here operates like a membrane with different degrees of permeability – sometimes letting information in, sometimes keeping it out. The more situations that evoke out of date reactions, the less likely he/she is to operate flexibly: a fixed pattern of managing contact at the boundary results. For example, always (or never) rejecting what is said to one would represent a self-defeating contact style. In most circumstances, operating 'semi-permeably' allows us to be influenced to a degree by what impinges on us, neither 'swallowing it whole' nor 'spitting it out', but instead 'chewing it over' before assimilating and digesting it.

A second kind of contact boundary transaction relates to containment or expression of feelings, responses or energy. Again a failure of adaptability is evident if, say, a man has grown into adulthood rarely able to contain his angry feelings, so he flies into uncontrollable rages when frustrated. Another may have the opposite tendency, repeatedly to hold in or hold back – or *retroflect* – all his angry feelings, so that he becomes held in muscularly, in his voice, and with some possible accompanying somatic problems. A profoundly unbalanced life could follow from either habitual submergence of angry energy or from its repeated expression.

Again, most situations call for some combination of expression and control, with the contact boundary operating flexibly. We recognize that in some contexts release and full-bodied expression of feelings, or of our opinions, is appropriate and safe, whilst in other settings the consequences of expressing them might be serious. If, however, we are 'stuck' in either habitually retroflecting or alternatively expressing ourselves without attention to the circumstances, we are likely to suffer unpleasant consequences of one kind or another.

A third contact boundary disturbance of particular interest in Gestalt therapy is where 'what belongs to self' is located as 'belonging to the environment'. Thus, a woman who is not owning her intelligence may be delighted by how intelligent her colleague seems. She *projects* her own qualities on to the other. When she learns to acknowledge that she herself is intelligent, the fascination with the other person's qualities may be less.

Projection is present universally, and is by no means always dysfunctional. Indeed, empathy and identifying with others' experience depend upon it, and in certain situations the complete absence of an ability to project would suggest a profoundly insensitive or even psychopathic response. Much projection, however, is limiting and the basis for much intractable human conflict in relationships and communities (e.g. two sides of a conflict regarding each other as aggressive and unreasonable).

A fourth focus of particular interest in contact styles relates to the extent to which the contact boundary separates 'self' from 'other'. If a boy joins a gang and his identity is altogether submerged, his separateness is temporarily put aside: he has become *confluent* with his environment. If, by contrast, he cannot fit in, feels altogether different and regards the situation as completely alien, he leans in the opposite direction of extreme differentiation or isolation.

If the contact boundary is operating flexibly, we can experience times both of 'losing ourselves in' and 'of not going along with' something in our environment. Both can be functional. If, however, we habitually and without awareness lean towards one or the other pole, regardless of circumstances, then there are bound to be occasions when the result interrupts creative living.

There are a number of other contact transactions which form part of what Gestalt therapists notice, e.g. relating to how attention is sustained or deflected; and the degree to which individuals 'watch themselves' as they engage in an activity or, alternatively, 'surrender' to the experience (Clarkson, 1989). Since the Gestalt therapist is focusing on the ongoing act of living, the focus on contact styles is inevitably central. (Fuller descriptions are available elsewhere, e.g. Mackewn, 1997).

Acquisition of psychological disturbance

Gestalt therapists are more inclined to approach human distress with an 'injury' model in mind rather than one implying 'illness'. They think of traumas and setbacks – such as disappointments, humiliations, being terrorized, rejections – as times when a person's field or life space is disrupted, perhaps massively or repeatedly. They endorse the widespread view that such emotional injuries are likely to be more disruptive the earlier in life that they occur. Research into post-traumatic stress reactions (Wilson et al., 2004) reveals that experiences of terror, pain or other acute distress often have long-term effects for those who have experienced them. These include dissociation and desensitization (both interruptions of present awareness), relational problems (including extreme contact styles of the kind described above), and damage to the sense of self.

When a person experiences herself, say, as deeply misunderstood by a teacher, there is a 'rupture in the relational field' (Wheeler, 1995). She may feel awkward or embarrassed (which are varieties of the experience of shame) and – not feeling supported or 'met' by the environment – she adapts as resourcefully as she can. This may mean retroflecting or holding back her tears, recognizing that she may be

further shamed if she cries; and/or she may decide to conform exactly to the teacher's wishes. Her spontaneous response is thereby partly or wholly replaced with a newly learned deliberate response. The episode, while over, has not as a gestalt been satisfactorily resolved. Her learning has taken a certain path, away from being a 'natural' or organismic reaction involving all of her. At the moment of trauma – when feeling secure is suddenly lost – certain feeling states, body positions, thoughts, sensory experiences and biochemical secretions arise and occur together, and the situation is seen as dangerous or distressing. These holistic reactions form a specific gestalt which, if appropriate support were promptly reinstated, and the relational field rebalanced, might well 'run its course'. Thus, were a traumatized child physically held by someone she trusted, the trauma might be short-lived and recovery swift. When, however, the loss of support is perpetuated, this gestalt remains unresolved as a *fixed gestalt*, frozen in time, and the adaptive responses may become a fixed part of the repertoire of responses available to the child (Gerhardt, 2004).

What happens is that this painful, perhaps consciously forgotten, traumatic time can be easily restimulated, with a concurrent re-emergence of the field conditions (including feelings or thoughts) which constituted aspects of the frozen or unresolved gestalt. When this occurs, the immediate response is to avoid further re-entry to this state of being. The learned adaptive response (e.g. the conformity to the powerful other) often appears as the known way to avoid its being reawakened, and is replayed.

Altogether, what happens as a result of an early emotional injury is that deliberate, stylised or self-protective responses are often substituted for fully spontaneous reactions to situations. In many circumstances, the individual is less free to be 'fully him/herself', and other ways become a norm. There may be suppression of feeling states, muscular armouring, loss of self-esteem, shame, anxiety, and so on, all of which in turn limit the person's capacity to live freely and creatively in certain kinds of situation. He or she needs certain conditions in order to be able to resume the task of completing whatever gestalt was left unfinished, or meeting the need that was never met.

There are obviously many degrees of emotional injury. Life invariably has setbacks and problems, even for the most privileged. For some, who have been persistently abused or traumatized at an early age, their whole way of self-organizing and adjusting to life may have become dislocated, such that most contact with others and their ability to self-manage in a complex society has become affected. Such inability may be perceptual, in not taking in information but relying on fantasy (or in being hyper-vigilant, or both); or physically, in that the person may have little sensitivity (or alternatively may be 'allergic' to the slightest touch). Sometimes the person may be thought-disordered (or take refuge in logical intellectualizing). In some cases people begin to operate and relate in ways that strike others as bizarre or 'sick'. Tracing the origins, however, reveals that usually there is some particular set of field circumstances which were themselves strange or horrifying, and that the individual 'adjusted' to these conditions by adopting a particular style of being.

Perpetuation of psychological disturbance

It is central to Gestalt thinking that even though a person's pattern of disturbed functioning may have originated in the past, the manifestation of the disturbance is played out and witnessed in the present, and can only be undone (deconstructed) in the present. Individuals' fixed patterns (of adapting, getting by, manipulating, etc.) are often so habitual and taken for granted that they are not easily accessible to the person's present awareness. Indeed, he or she may not realize at all how much he/she is 'operating on automatic', and that alternative choices might be possible that would be more life-enhancing or creative.

As we have seen, these automatic patterns of thinking, moving and feeling arise as a result of some form of re-enactment of a previously unresolved, frozen or fixed gestalt. Suppose, for instance, that someone has to confront an angry person in a work setting. This evokes or triggers the memory (in or out of awareness) of an earlier traumatic situation (like being shouted at by an angry teacher). Then the old reactions, feeling state and sense of powerlessness are likely to be at least partially reawakened. An up-to-date, more mature or 'healthy' response may be possible, provided that the individual has enough self-support (a feeling of inner strength) and environmental support (in the form, say, of an assertive colleague being present when she confronts the angry person). However, if the present total situation is no more supportive than at the time of the original trauma, then the old response is likely to be experienced similarly to how it was in the past.

The undoing or deconstructing of a fixed gestalt requires experimenting with a different solution, usually experienced as a dangerous enterprise. Feeling unable to deal 'healthily' with the present situation may well lead to anxiety, a sense of confusion, and experiences of shame – which include 'feeling awkward', embarrassed or shy. To change, and to update oneself, requires existentially entering the unknown. Catastrophizing is common – e.g. 'If I allow myself to feel sad, I'll fall apart altogether', or 'If I say "no" to him, he will walk out.' Only by changing the balance of forces, as it were, so there is sufficient backing and encouragement, will the person be able to take the risk of doing something new. The provision of adequate support is therefore crucial.

Given that it is so unsettling to deconstruct a fixed way of being – even if the person recognizes that the pattern is self-damaging or self-limiting – it is not surprising that disturbed patterns of behaviour and feeling are very difficult to shift. Moreover, in cases of more severe disturbance there often has to be extensive initial work of becoming more aware and finding ways to access available support in the field, before these experiments can be countenanced. So the familiar, if unwelcome, patterns are unlikely to alter for some time, even after therapy is under way.

Two further factors help to keep the fixed gestalt intact. The version of the self, which forms a part of that gestalt (e.g. my 'frightened self'), is only one of many versions. Another may be the 'self-critical self' (Polster, 1995). What often happens is that when one version appears the other soon follows, and an internal debate is set up between them. The individual recognizes that 'part of me wants to do X, but another part of me knows that it will be hopeless if I try'. This is a very frequent kind of confusion. So part of how 'disturbance' is maintained is by the endless circulating through these contradictory versions of self, without integration or their 'working together'.

Secondly, the person, existing in a relational world, does not create a version of himself in isolation, but always with a 'self–other' referent. If he creates himself as 'a failure' he is probably creating others in his field as 'condemning of his failure' or as 'successful', and then he acts towards these imagined versions of the other as if these fantasies were true. Such expectations are well known to be often self-fulfilling. For instance, a man who was abused by a woman as a child, may believe that 'no women are trustworthy'. He therefore breaks eye contact, disregards evidence (that others may see) that the woman in front of him is kindly looking and 'safe', and seizes on the slightest evidence to confirm his view that she is unsafe. Finding confirmation of belief systems leads often to unaware manipulation of other people or of groups, and is a major way in which disturbed approaches to living are maintained.

Change

Gestalt therapy can be thought of as a potent means for speeding up the evolution of a person, yet development occurs anyway. People 'grow up', 'take on a new lease of life', 'come to their senses', or 'are forced to come to terms with things', as a result of changes in their life situation – like promotion at work, meeting a new partner, coping with illness, becoming a grandparent, or redundancy.

A person fixed in their relating to human situations has a reduced capacity for dealing with novel or stressful situations. Yet Gestalt therapists operate with the belief that the human being has an inbuilt urge to complete situations and to find an inner sense of balance and good form. They see themselves as assisting a natural life process of human creativity, potential resourcefulness and a desire to grow. A man, say, has a pattern of retreating from social contacts; it does not mean he will retain this as a fixed personal characteristic throughout life. He may find himself in a new work group where he is stimulated and encouraged to break his habit of withdrawal, and then finds that he 'is taken out of himself'. The next time he may be a little less reluctant to take part. Such growth experiences occur for all of us, throughout life, and many people change, mature and mellow as a result of unlearning patterns of avoidance and stereotyped reactions they acquired earlier in life. Some make these changes through therapy, others through life experience or a combination of both.

Gestalt therapy is based on a model of the change process that builds on these normal ways in which people develop and mature, and extends them. In offering a supportive relationship and context, Gestalt therapists provide opportunities for personal exploration of how the client flourishes in the world and how he/she concurrently limits and distorts life experience in certain ways. The process of therapy becomes itself one of life's new situations: it offers an opportunity to experience life differently and to extend the range of ways in which a person can operate in the world with greater satisfaction.

Incremental change through assimilating new life (or therapy-generated) experiences is quite different from intentional self-reform or 'improvement' according to rules (as in diets or some religious teachings). This difference is reflected in Gestalt therapy in what is called the 'paradoxical theory of change' (Beisser, 1970). This says that change occurs when a person 'becomes what he is, not when he tries to become what he is not'. In other words, deliberate attempts to change by conscious control or acts of will are usually doomed: they set up an unconscious conflict between the will of the person and the unconscious 'saboteur' or 'underdog'. Instead, for individuals to 'move on' in life they need to begin with accepting what they are already doing. They may realize how they have left gestalts incomplete (e.g. by not mourning a loss or expressing a resentment) and risk trying a new adaptation or response. Ordinary life situations call for these personal innovations, which are usually accompanied by fear reactions (from 'stage fright' to intense anxiety) but which, once achieved and practised, become part of the person's natural repertoire.

PRACTICE

Goals of therapy

The task of the therapist is to create a situation rich in possibilities for human meeting, emotional healing, increased awareness of self process and experimentation in a supportive setting.

Current research in neuroscience supports the centrality in Gestalt of a genuine dialogue between client and therapist in effective therapy. For example, Schore (2003) shows evidence that such a dialogue can literally alter the neocortical networks of both client and therapist.

The work of Stern (2004) provides evidence that supports Gestalt's emphasis on the present-centred, co-created nature of the therapeutic relationship. The stress in Gestalt on the therapist's use of herself alongside her ability to enter the phenomenological world of her clients enables the therapist to gain the non-verbal 'implicit' relational knowledge (Stern, 2004) that current research suggests is at the 'core of therapeutic change' (Schore, 2003: 53).

Intrinsic to creating a learning-rich therapeutic milieu, the client is encouraged to recognize his own expert status, with the first priority being to build a therapeutic alliance where he is encouraged to empower himself. The emphasis is on people finding their own goals and discovering their potential to meet these goals.

Gestalt therapy values individuals finding unique solutions to unique situations, recognizing the special nature of each person's history, circumstances, values, needs and preferences. Gestalt therapy has never been an 'adjustment' therapy (Perls et al., 1994/1951), and given that there are many ways that our culture fails to support human well-being, the client may develop ways of living which run counter to normative expectations.

Selection criteria

The Gestalt therapy approach orientates the work of its practitioners, but each therapist applies Gestalt principles in individual ways and uses different methods according to her/his training, professional background and personal style.

It follows from this that each therapist–client pairing is also individual and that to argue that certain persons are 'suitable' for Gestalt therapy as such, while others are unsuitable, does not make sense. A clinical psychologist working, say, in a hospital setting and from a Gestalt therapy base, may work therapeutically with severely fragmented and disoriented individuals, applying Gestalt principles appropriately and effectively. A school counsellor, on the other hand, though trained in Gestalt, would almost certainly not work with such individuals, although she might be well qualified to apply Gestalt thinking and practice to working with the children referred to her.

The most likely course of action for a practitioner, faced with an enquirer, will be to have an introductory meeting in order to assess what the individual might benefit from most – perhaps once- or twice-weekly individual sessions, joining an ongoing therapy group, or participating in a weekend workshop.

Practitioners of Gestalt therapy give emphasis to the unique nature of each person's therapeutic needs. Suppose, for instance, that the extent of disturbance is such that a client has little stability, and has been labelled 'psychotic' or 'borderline'. A high degree of environmental support and time, commitment and attention on the part of the therapist may be called for. This could entail residential care, with the therapist seeing the client every day for a specified period of time. Such conditions, even in hospital settings, are often not available, and it would be irresponsible to engage such a client in intensive exploration without sufficient environmental support.

Obviously, then, initial meetings and contacts are very significant. The person's presenting problem may indicate one form of intervention rather than another – a relationship problem might best be explored with the partner in couples therapy; someone cut off and lonely might benefit from a group. But the stress is on the special nature of each enquiry, not on any rule.

In weighing up what the person might benefit from most, the Gestalt therapist does not ignore the usual psychiatric diagnostic categories. However, she will want most to observe how aware the person is of his own process – i.e. of the current direction of his interest, bodily state, physical and social needs, feeling sense, and how capable he is of articulating his inner experience as it unfolds, i.e. in the 'here and now'. She will also note how he communicates with her (the client's contact style or functions), how he interrupts or blocks the flow of his experiencing himself, and how aware he is of doing so. The therapist may also think in terms of polarities, and be influenced by what strikes her as 'missing' with this person: e.g. he may manifest no assertiveness or, though married, fail to mention his wife or children. All of this may suggest to the therapist the appropriateness of a specific course of action. At this stage, one-to-one therapy might be suggested for someone who was unaware of, or unable to externalize, his inner experience. Joining a group might be thought desirable at a later stage, when the person has become more familiar with the Gestalt method – i.e. has acquired facility with its self-investigative procedures (which constitute both a demand for, as well as a means to, greater awareness).

Qualities of effective therapists

Basic to all training of Gestalt psychotherapists is that all trainees have prolonged individual and group therapy themselves. Gestalt therapy is an approach which is based on developing a full sensory awareness of self and others, and has to be learned by active participation. It decidedly cannot be learned solely from books and lectures. The approach has to be known from the inside, experienced as a powerful means of self-enquiry and progressively incorporated into one's own personal life and work as a therapist. It has to be embodied (Parlett, 2001).

Effective Gestalt therapists, aside from having an adequate level of integration themselves, vary greatly in their personal and professional qualities. However, they are expected to manifest authenticity and openness about their feelings and reactions; as well as (hopefully) being skilful in handling a broad spectrum of interpersonal transactions (including intimacy, conflict, appropriate physical contact, emotional expression, separation and endings, and maintaining clear boundaries). In addition, they need to have acquired the ability to recognize their own preoccupations and problems and to deal with them in such a way as to be fully present and available for the client. On occasions when they are unable to do this they need to acknowledge that they are not competent to practise for the time being. They need to have a strong ethical base in other ways as well, and to be non-exploitative, having a fundamental respect for the integrity of the therapy process.

Therapeutic relationship and style

Although there are wide differences between Gestalt therapists, most would conceptualize what they do along the following (or similar) lines.

They aim to provide a relationship and setting which supports and provokes the person's exploring her 'here and now' experience – that is, what she is aware of in the actual, present context of being in the therapy room, relating to the therapist (or, in a group, with the other members). A further aim is to explore how the patterns that emerge in the therapy room or relationship may relate to the patterns that occur in the rest of the client's life – and especially the patterns that have brought him to therapy.

The emphasis given to exploring present reality in Gestalt therapy can easily be misunderstood: it does not mean that references to past and future are banned – that would be absurd. But when dwelling on past or future events, what the person is currently and actually doing is *remembering* or *anticipating*, both of which involve constructing an imagined reality in the present. Exactly *how* the person reconstructs her past, or formulates a vision of the future, is part of what she is doing at the moment. It is an essential part of the investigation of what the person actually does in the present, which is often more significant than what she says or reports about another time or place.

The emphasis on working with present experience as it arises in the consciousness of the client, moment by moment, places Gestalt broadly in the tradition of phenomenology (Spinelli, 1989). The Gestalt therapist is interested in first, rather than second thoughts; in the immediacy of images, however fleeting, and in passing ideas about himself rather than lengthy self-descriptions. The therapist may interrupt long discourses, inviting the client instead to notice what is happening now, in their immediate experience.

For the kind of exploratory work favoured by Gestalt therapists, a strong and supportive therapeutic relationship is necessary. The therapist's personal presence, interest in the client's life, and her commitment to the client's well-being, are taken for granted as being necessary foundations. A strong and loving connection supports the work of open-ended enquiry, the focus on the immediacy of exploring live experience in the therapy room, and on experimental action rather than on merely gaining insight. These can flourish only within a relationship where each party meets the other as a person, not as a role. The two parties engage in dialogue, not in one-way communication (Yontef, 1993; Jacobs, 2000). Gestalt therapists let themselves be themselves and encourage those they work with to do the same. Sometimes they may communicate (selectively) some of their own life experience, or express their own feelings. Obviously, this needs to be done with respect and a sense of timing, honouring the validity of the other's reality and not imposing their own views and values. Relating dialogically also calls for the therapist to 'show his caring by his honesty more than by his constant softness' (Yontef, 1984: 47). The major emphasis on the 'dialogic relationship' in present-day Gestalt therapy was inspired by the work of Martin Buber (1970), with his views of the healing power of meeting another person in an authentic way.

In addition to offering the possibility of a person-to-person relationship, and the focus on present experience and its direct investigation, Gestalt therapists also emphasize experimentation ('try it rather than talk about it': Zinker, 1977). 'All therapy is play,' said Fritz Perls, and the effective Gestalt therapist is skilled in creating experimental situations and methods to provide learning experiences which extend a person's repertoire. Experimenting enables the therapist and client, working together, to create (or re-create) conditions of the person's life space or field that can provide 'rehearsal space' for the development of new strategies, behaviour, or non-habitual modes of relating, moving, sensing, etc.

When it comes to the therapist's individual style it is difficult to generalize. The competent Gestalt therapist employs different styles according to person, situation and stage of therapy. His choices are based on skills and experience; his response to a particular instance depends on his creativeness (e.g. in finding ways to heighten the person's awareness of their surroundings). The therapist may at times be challenging, pointing out how he feels manipulated by a certain response of the client; at another time he may extend a hand, literally, to establish a channel of support when the client momentarily falters before taking a risk. He may listen intently and sympathetically to an emotionally laden account of an early trauma now being recounted for the first time. In contrast, with another person at another time, he may report his sense of losing interest by the repeated recital of well-known facts. He is, after all, attending to individuals' unfolding realities, to their unique experiences; and this demands authentic, spontaneous and creative responses – not rehearsed reactions and 'therapy techniques', which demean the relationship.

Each Gestalt therapist is enjoined to find his or her own way of integrating and applying the philosophy and methodology of Gestalt therapy in a creative, intelligent, sensitive and ethical fashion that does justice to their talents, personality and background (Parlett, 2001). Each is encouraged to continue to develop their own ways of working skilfully.

Major therapeutic strategies and techniques

The exact way in which a Gestalt therapist will work varies from person to person and occasion to occasion. However, Resnick (1995) has suggested that (1) *attention to phenomenology*, (2) *dialogue in the relationship,* and (3) *holding a field perspective* all need to be present, for the therapy to be designated as Gestalt therapy. The three are closely related. For instance, in building a therapy relationship based on dialogue and trust, the co-created field of 'therapist and client' and how the therapy fits within the person's wider life, are central and significant; and the exploration proceeds via investigating the 'live experience' of both the client and the therapist – i.e. their phenomenological realities. Within these broad parameters, there are also areas of concentration.

Support

The establishment of a sufficiently supportive context for therapy is perhaps the most important single feature of the approach in practical terms. Successful Gestalt therapy is indicated by a 'subject–subject' relationship between therapist and client, rather than one that is 'subject–object' (Wheeler, 1995). We exist, and grow, in relationship. Establishing the relationship as a real one based on a level of respectfulness equivalent to love is healing in itself (Latner, 1995). Inauthenticity or lack of being fully present can be deleterious to establishing a degree of openness and sense of security, which are necessary for risky life changes to be attempted.

Providing the right kind and level of support is a crucial skill. Sometimes challenging self-destructive behaviour is the most supportive thing a therapist can do (Perls, 1992). What is supportive – i.e. assists the process of enquiry and the client's 'flow' – has to be discovered in each case. Automatically handing a weeping client a box of tissues may be highly supportive for some, but for others who, when young, had parents who forbade their crying, the box of tissues arriving could be seen as a covert demand that they come out of the experience. (Of course, if the therapist makes a 'mistake' about such matters, it can be itself informative; if the therapist goes on to apologize for the 'rupture', it can sometimes be a therapeutic turning point: Jacobs, 2000.)

Almost intrinsic to therapy are shame reactions of various kinds. The client may be bringing issues that are intimate, difficult to talk about, and embarrassing. Some feel huge degrees of shame about aspects of their life, or about being in therapy at all. The therapist needs to be acutely aware of the possibility of heightening feelings of exposure, embarrassment or shame, often inadvertently or without recognizing that he or she is doing so. For some clients, even asking questions or making statements that are felt as 'personal' can be shaming. Taking 'a professional stance', including the making of interpretations by the therapist, can be subtly diminishing of the client from being 'subject' to 'object', and can be shaming.

Some degree of experienced shame is usually inevitable, given the nature of the therapeutic process and the broad intention of experimenting with novel behaviour. It is important that the experience of feeling ashamed is seen as a normal reaction to the feeling of being unsupported by others (Lee and Wheeler, 1996) and that clients discover they do not need to feel 'ashamed of their shame'. Ultimately, learning to tolerate the experience of shame is more useful to the client than trying to avoid it completely. Working with shame issues requires a particularly supportive setting: developing a therapy relationship where shame reactions can be safely addressed is of the first importance.

Increasing Awareness

An important priority in Gestalt therapy is the focus on awareness. The approach offers an equivalent (some say) to Zen training or other forms of meditation. Awareness is the key to personal experiment and change. If a man has suppressed his feelings, say, of love for his father, the process of becoming aware of *how* and *what* he suppresses is the first and necessary stage. He may simply wake up to what he is doing, or practise allowing the feelings to be expressed and even communicated to his father in person.

Awareness work involves practising attending to the bodily 'felt sense'. Through education in heightened awareness, individuals are effectively acquiring a 'biofeedback'system. By more accurately attuning themselves to their actual physical and emotional experience, moment by moment, they can recognize more accurately when they are tensing up, withdrawing, suppressing a feeling and, with this additional information, can choose to relax, breathe differently, speak out or withdraw, or whatever they need to do in order to feel more balanced or satisfied. The greater awareness of her process a person has, the more she can influence her life choices and destiny.

Working with polarities

The Gestalt therapist not only reacts to what is presented – the client's behaviour and experience in the session itself – but is also interested in 'what is missing'. It is a central tenet of Gestalt therapy that all of us have within us the potential for acting and experiencing differently from how we usually do. Each time someone identifies strongly with a particular 'quality' the more likely he is to have 'alienated' (Perls et al., 1994/1951) or rejected its polar opposite. Thus, if a man is always tidy and organized, he may be losing out on the experience of letting a little disorder and unpredictability into his life. He may represent the latter to himself as 'chaos and catastrophe'.

Gestalt therapy involves attending to such polarities, often renaming them in less pejorative language, exploring the associated feeling reactions to them, and uncovering gently the potentialities latent in the hitherto rejected behaviours and experiences.

Recognizing interruptions and avoidances

Human beings stop the flow of their naturally unfolding experience in numerous different ways. We may attempt to avoid painful or unpleasant memories, or certain emotions, or uncomfortable realizations. We interrupt awareness or restrict feelings by holding the breath, at the same time as tensing the musculature in certain parts of the body. Inhibition (wholesale avoidance of certain impulses), intellectualizing (often in the form of 'explaining away'), and displacement (e.g. instead of dealing with his wife he takes it out on his employee), are among other common patterns of avoidance.

By 'tracking' – or following closely what is happening for a person who is attending to and reporting his moment-by-moment thoughts, percepts, and feelings – the therapist is able to spot points of 'interruption of flow' in the ongoing process: e.g. shifts in vitality, changes in eye contact, movements in body position, a sentence left unfinished. All may indicate something withheld, glossed over, blotted out or diverged from. The therapist may sometimes draw attention frequently to such interruptions. At other times she may not intervene for long periods, perhaps letting the person tell his story (Polster, 1987) or leaving him to struggle to articulate some hitherto undefinable feeling. All depends on the total situation and the moment. Becoming aware of interrupted gestalts and avoidances in contact with others is the first step to relearning.

Working with the theme

Identifying a theme of a specific session, usually based on identifying something which energizes the client in the moment (not necessarily what they have planned to bring to therapy to discuss) permits the session to have a form – a gestalt in itself. Often it helps to clarify the theme, including a statement of something the individual *needs* (wants, craves, is determined to have) and pointing out how the person is *resisting* getting what she wants (holding back through fear of retribution, an imagined rejection, etc.). The therapist signals that she has no investment in a particular outcome, but is interested in the client exploring equally both the desire and the reluctance, the need and resistance.

It is easy to fall into imagining that if a client refuses a suggestion the therapist makes, he is 'resistant'. Yet resistance (rather like the French Resistance) can be celebrated as fighting spirit or sensible reluctance. In the field in which, say, 'holding back' was learned as a pattern, the choice then made (to hold back) was the best creative adjustment of which the client-as-child was then capable. In exploring the theme in the present, a realignment becomes possible, provided there is enough support in the present 'field of forces', which includes the presence and sensitivity of the therapist.

Working with transference

Transference reactions inevitably arise in the therapeutic relationship. However, in building the relationship, Gestalt therapists are continuously seeking a real rather than a transferential relationship. The therapist respectfully invites clients to use their eyes and ears to see and listen to the actual person behind their projections. The process of dissolving the transference is probably never fully completed but the whole tenor of the work is to acknowledge, investigate, and then move on from the imaginings a client may have, not to allow them to continue uninvestigated. Being able to maintain an 'adult to adult' relationship in parallel with episodes and periods of regression is a necessary part of integrating the therapy experience into the wider field of a person's present life. Important as is visiting the 'past-that-arises-in-the-present', Gestalt therapy is primarily about living present life, which includes in therapy a real relationship with a real human being.

Experimentation and techniques

Gestalt therapy provides experiential learning and the experiment is central: 'It transforms talking about doing into doing, stale reminiscing and theorizing into being fully here with all one's imagination, energy and excitement' (Zinker, 1977). It is the pursuit of greater awareness through active behavioural expression, entailing senses, skeletal muscles and full bodily and emotional involvement.

Experiments grow out of themes emerging during the tracking of ongoing awareness and are ways of 'thinking out loud (concretizing) one's imagination' (Zinker, 1977). There are no set structures or techniques, though necessary preconditions for a successful experiment include ensuring that the person is 'grounded' and has sufficient self-support; that the experiment is pitched at the right level of risk for the individual at the time; and that he understands what he is doing and has agreed to it. It also needs to incorporate the person's own language and images. The therapist's creativity in expanding on these ideas is also important.

More usually, experiments are simply minor additions to 'tracking' – i.e. following the awareness reporting of the client. Thus, a man reporting that he is 'fed up with working' may be hunching his shoulders as he says it. The therapist might invite him to exaggerate the posture of his body, or to stay in the hunched position to explore what it may represent. Alternatively the experiment might be exploring an 'opposite' body position. All of these would be designed to fill out the experience – always more than a verbal description.

Other experiments may involve deliberately rearranging the field to provide for a risky-seeming 'first try' at a new behaviour which the client wishes to explore – perhaps asking fellow members of a group for feedback about her appearance. The task of the therapist is to help design and focus the experiment, checking that there is sufficient support in the field (e.g. enough encouragement, time, freedom from interruptions) to enable the person to try out what she wants. The conditions should not be so safe that the client finds the experiment 'too easy' with no extending of her experience.

Experimentation can employ any of a whole variety of media, from dramatizations, dance or other physical movement, to dialogues between parts of the self, sculpting, artwork, working with dreams, fantasy trips, trying out specific language or behavioural changes. Often the therapist will encourage metaphorical and intuitive thinking, which in the majority of people is less developed than their capacity to be verbal and explanatory.

Some experiments have become classics – for instance the 'empty chair', in which a person speaks to someone with whom she has unfinished business, or to another part of herself, a polar opposite (her 'weak' side may speak to her 'strong' side). She may then move to the other chair and react from that position – either being the other person or the other aspect of self.

'Two-chair work' has been widely copied and used by therapists from other schools, so we shall say more about it. As a means of exploring communication between different aspects of self (or between 'self' and 'other'), physical shifts – such as moving from seat to seat – can assist in symbolizing profound changes in field conditions, i.e. how a life scene is seen from one position or from another. However, many Gestalt therapists use other ways of differentiating the field, perhaps by inviting the client to take two particular body positions or turning the lights down or up, and do not rely on chairs. If they do set up this particular experiment they are likely to adapt it according to circumstances – which can never be anticipated. What is important is to attend to what is needed at the time: perhaps turning the experiment into moving between three places, or the therapist taking one of the parts herself, or upturning or reversing or elevating one chair to make a point. The precise 'technique' is irrelevant, because the focus is actually upon, say, heightening differentiation and exploring possible integration of different versions of the self, and there are any number of ways in which this can be done, once the principle has been understood.

Gestalt therapy experimentation needs to be perpetually innovative to accord with exactly what is required in a unique situation. Although Gestalt techniques have been widely copied, their use in isolation from the rest of the Gestalt therapy system is highly questionable. They are not recipes. As Yontef has remarked: 'There is no Gestalt therapy cookbook ... therapy is an art [requiring] all of the therapist's creativity and love' (1988: 32).

The change process in therapy

Work with awareness lies at the heart of Gestalt therapy: attending to present experience, noticing what the person is doing, and recognizing her processes of contact and avoidance. Yontef (1988) has suggested a developmental sequence within therapy in which initially the client may talk about her problem but may have little awareness of what she is actually doing. In the course of therapy she recognizes how unaware she was previously; she begins to notice her characteristic style of avoidance. In time, she learns to recognize the ways she has been interrupting the natural process of gestalt formation and completion. She becomes aware of being aware and (paradoxically) of being unaware. The next stage is when the person 'becomes aware of [her] overall character structure', her general patterns and the conditions which give rise to her being less aware. Finally, the high level of awareness reached in therapy 'permeates the person's ordinary life' (Yontef, 1988).

Another way that Gestalt therapists think of change is in terms of figure formation and completion of gestalts. Movement in therapy is signalled by the person being more skilful in completing unfinished situations from the past and also with new gestalts arising in the present. He learns to avoid his avoidance; he interrupts more of his interruptions as they happen. In the process he acquires greater facility in forming and completing gestalts, and experiences more fulfilment and less dissatisfaction.

Limitations of the approach

The major limitation of Gestalt therapy is the reverse side of one of its strengths. Because it requires a high level of therapeutic participation and creativity, and an ability to work in numerous different ways, there are real difficulties in teaching the approach, in communicating its essence to those who have not directly experienced it, and in codifying its methods and concepts in ways that are helpful to practitioners and trainees while not oversimplifying it.

Another result of its distinctiveness is that, having given specialist meanings to such terms as 'contact', 'process' and 'support', all of them in common usage, there is scope for misunderstanding. As a result, Gestalt specialists can incline to insularity and disengagement from other forms of psychotherapy. Gestalt therapists, too, rarely engage in evidence-based quantitative research; the inquiry methods are deemed unsuitable. Again, this is self-defeating and isolating instead of boldly challenging conventional thinking.

More generally, certain criticisms of therapy (see, for instance, Hillman and Ventura, 1992) strike home hard for Gestalt therapists. Acknowledging the environment or situation as a major co-determinant of the person's mental health means there is an obvious responsibility for linking therapy with activity directed at social, community-orientated or political change (Parlett, 2000). Yet by and large Gestalt therapists have done little in this regard, working with individuals and couple systems without attending to the wider field of society and the times we live in. They are not alone in this among therapists, but the model of Gestalt therapy offers no comfortable justification for avoiding such involvement.

Case example

The client

Dave came to see me for individual therapy for two years after spending some months in a group led by me (JD). He requested individual therapy as he did not want to discuss some aspects of his childhood in a group: partly due to his sense of shame, and partly as he felt this would not be 'honouring' his parents. The individual work opened up a new phase of the work we did together, though several of the issues had been pre-figured in the work he had done in group.

With his initial interview, I had some first impressions of Dave. He was tall and slight and wore jogging pants and trainers. His voice was shaky and hesitant and he seemed younger than his forty years. I noticed I felt protective towards him. He seemed to devalue himself and looked to me for what to do and to give him answers.

He came in part because he felt inhibited in speaking up in a group. That is why, at first, I recommended a therapy group. Later, important unfinished situations emerged, moving the work in new directions – the focus for the individual therapy.

Overall, I came to understand that his behaviour, 'lying low' and self-devaluing, was a creative adjustment – necessary and supportive in his past but now a fixed way of being. At one point I asked him who devalued him in the past: he had felt undermined and underestimated by his parents and his elder sister; he still repeated to himself disparaging words they had said to him. I was shocked by his lack of life in telling his story. I told him sadness and anger were evoked in me as he spoke of feeling belittled, controlled, unseen, and unsupported for being himself. It was difficult for young Dave to own his feelings when his parents 'only valued thinking'.

The therapy

As the therapy proceeded, Dave and I became increasingly aware of his deflecting intimate contact via humour or changing the topic. Every time I said anything positive about him, I had the impression he countered it by asking me to tell him something he 'could do better'. It seemed he could not believe anyone would value him. He related this to his father, who continued to criticize the way Dave chose to live his life.

I invited Dave to imagine his father was present in the room and to tell him how he felt. He looked excited and keen to try the experiment. Dave told his father how angry he was that he had dominated him as a child, never listened to him, spent lots of time with other children (his father was a head teacher), and had no time for him. He had longed for his father to talk with him and to play football together.

Following this, Dave seemed more grounded and in contact with himself and with me. His voice deepened; he sounded more adult. He spoke of years of responding to others in the same way as to his father – making other people bigger and better than him. He was animated in telling me his parents' 'stiff upper lip' values were not his own and that he was keen to explore his own values without making his parents 'bad'. To his surprise, Dave was able to talk to me about his beliefs in a clear, assertive way. He seemed very different from the diffident man of only a few months earlier.

One session, Dave arrived looking shaky and anxious as he sat down. He cried as he told me he had been sexually molested as a child by a family friend. I was moved by his deep distress, and shocked when he told me that a previous counsellor had 'brushed it aside' as unimportant. I told him 'it sounds very important'. He felt relieved I had heard him; unlike his parents (who prevented further abuse, but refused to discuss it).

We had several sessions with Dave sobbing as he grieved the abuse. He spoke of six year old Dave feeling in a 'dark hopeless forest, darker than you can imagine'. I said 'you seem very sad and small and very alone. I want to reach you, but don't know how to'. Would he let me be there with him? He said he wanted to let me in, yet was scared; I might reject him as his mother had, or even abuse him. I said 'I can see how hard it is for you to trust me now when you were let down so often in the past'. I sat quietly with Dave as he cried some more for all the times he had felt alone and rejected; occasionally I would say a word or two, to reassure him I was still there.

Dave spoke of wanting to 'get rid of' or even 'kill' the small, anxious part of him ('little Dave') whose continuing grief was 'getting in the way of me leading my life'. I asked him what 'little Dave' needed. He replied: to 'be listened to and comforted, allowed to talk about what had happened and told that it was not my fault.'

The following week, Dave initiated a piece of two chair work, speaking to his 'little' polarity; he was able to comfort and reassure himself. Step-by-step – it often felt like slow work – Dave began to trust me more and his recognition that the abuse was not his fault deepened. He expressed shock no one in his family had been willing to talk to him about it. His parents' message was 'pretend it didn't happen'. As Dave continued to grieve and express his outrage at the paedophile he reported feeling 'bigger and stronger, like I've got more space inside me'.

Further work

We reviewed our work together after six months and celebrated the changes Dave had made. He requested further sessions to explore relating to his parents in a healthier way. He recognised he could easily blame all his problems on the sexual abuse, avoiding what happened in his family. He did not want to do this.

Part of this work involved breaking his confluence with his mother who he felt 'suffocated' him and kept him 'under her wing'. He realised that he transferred these feelings onto me, and was anxious about disagreeing with me as I would 'chuck him out of therapy'. I challenged him to experiment with telling me ways in which he disagreed with me. He told me he believed that 'only men should be church leaders' and that 'sex is only okay if it is heterosexual and in the context of marriage'. He asked me for a response to his views. I told him the truth – I found his views sexist and homophobic – but that I still liked him and was happy to continue working with him. Dave felt relieved and delighted we could disagree and still have a relationship. His contact with his mother improved; he reported feeling 'separate and not entangled' as he experimented with airing disagreements with her over political and religious issues.

Dave also wanted to do some two chair work with his mother. I was concerned about over-using this particular method of work, yet it suited him. He told her he was angry that she never saw or valued him: 'I no longer want to keep your rules; I need to do it my way; I will not let you control me any more'. The following weekend, visiting his parents, he was able briefly to leave the table during a meal – despite a family rule of 'you must never leave the table'. He seemed elated as he reported his success.

Dave spent several sessions working with the shame and betrayal he felt when publicly jilted by his girlfriend as an adolescent. This betrayal, the childhood abuse, the confluence with his mother, and his father's absence had left him 'diminished as a man'. As well as grieving what was lost, I helped Dave support his symbolic entry into the world of men by imagining four strong male friends standing behind him offering him support and accepting him as a man. He began to meet other men socially, joined a men's group, and told me: 'I am coming out of my father's shadow into my power'.

Having done a fairly menial job below his capability, Dave applied for and got a senior position with more money and responsibility. Occasionally, he would come to therapy feeling wobbly and small again. I suggested he used these sessions to practice reaching out and getting support from his place of grief. As he did this, Dave noticed that his negative introjects of the type 'be strong, show a stiff upper lip', lost much of their power over him. I helped him develop skills of self-soothing and self support, including breathing and grounding. Several times Dave came to therapy excited about how he had supported himself during the week. He was discovering ways to stay with working through his feelings of grief or rage as they emerged during the week, rather than waiting for our session and expecting me to 'fix' him, as he had earlier in our relationship.

We discussed the approaching end of our work. Before then Dave wanted to tell his parents about his experiences of childhood. He told me 'It's only because I've grown so much that I can do this'. We discussed how he would feel if they refused to listen, or denied his reality. Sounding strong and clear, he replied 'I know that might happen, but I need to tell them. I know that whatever happens, this will help me move on'. The meeting with his parents went well. He reported being clear, honest and non-defensive with them. And he had felt heard and accepted: they expressed sadness at how hurt he had felt and apologised for their part in it. Dave told me he was 'up-beat' about his future, and was ready to leave therapy.

During the final sessions, as he continued to try out new things, Dave moved between being excited and anxious. He gave his first party in several years and was very distressed when a woman he 'fancied' did not attend. This triggered childhood memories and feelings of 'I'm not good enough'. As he explored this introject he smiled and said, 'I'm actually doing really well, aren't I?' We investigated ways Dave could support himself when triggered into old patterns of distress. He was better at returning to up-to-date self-organisation. Ways he found helpful, aside from deeper, slower breathing and physically grounding himself, included remembering that most people feel anxious when trying out new things. Dave found it useful having this 'toolbox' of skills he could continue to practise on leaving therapy.

Watching him leave the room at the end of our last session I felt moved at how different he was to the anxious, fearful man who had first come to see me. Dave had re-connected with himself and was ready to move on.

ACKNOWLEDGEMENTS

The authors acknowledge with gratitude the contribution of Judith Hemming – co-author of this chapter in the previous edition.

REFERENCES

Beisser, A. (1970) 'The paradoxical theory of change', in J. Fagan and I. Shepherd (eds), *Gestalt Therapy Now*. New York: Harper & Row.

Buber, M. (1970) *I and Thou*. New York: Scribner's.

Clarkson, P. (1989) *Gestalt Counselling in Action*, 2nd edn. London: Sage.

Denham-Vaughan, S. (2005) 'Brief Gestalt therapy (BGT) for clients with bulimia', *British Gestalt Journal*, 14(2): 128–34.

Gerhardt, S. (2004) *Why Love Matters: How Affection Shapes a Baby's Brain*. Hove: Brunner-Routledge.

Hillman, L. and Ventura, M. (1992) *We've Had a Hundred Years of Psychotherapy and the World's Getting Worse*. New York: Harper.

Houston, G. (2003) *Brief Gestalt Therapy*. London: Sage.

Jacobs, L. (2000) Interview 'Respectful dialogues' with J. Mackewn, *British Gestalt Journal*, 9 (2): 105–16.

Joyce, P. and Sills, C. (2001) *Skills in Gestalt Counselling and Psychotherapy*. London: Sage.

Kennedy, D.J. (2005) 'The lived body', *British Gestalt Journal*, 14(2): 109–17.

Kepner, J. (1987) *Body Process. A Gestalt Approach to Working with the Body in Psychotherapy*. New York: Gardner Press (Gestalt Institute of Cleveland Press).

Latner, L. (1995) Letter to the Editor, *British Gestalt Journal*, 4(1): 49–50.

Lee, R. and Wheeler, G. (eds). (1996) *The Voice of Shame*. Cleveland: GIC Press.

Mackewn, J. (1997) *Developing Gestalt Counselling*. London: Sage.

Parlett, M. (2000) 'Creative adjustment and the global field', *British Gestalt Journal*, 9(1): 15–27.

Parlett, M. (2001) 'Being present at one's own life', in *Embodied Theory*. London: Continuum.

Parlett, M. (2005) 'Contemporary Gestalt therapy: field theory', in A.L. Woldt and S.M. Toman (eds), *Gestalt Therapy: History, Theory and Practice*. Thousand Oaks, CA: Sage.

Perls, F.S. (1969a) *Ego, Hunger and Aggression: The Beginning of Gestalt Therapy* (1942). New York: Vintage Books.

Perls, L. (1992) *Living at the Boundary*. Highland, NY: The Gestalt Journal Press.

Perls, F.S., Hefferline, R.F. and Goodman, P. (1994) *Gestalt Therapy: Excitement and Growth in Human Personality* (1951). Highland, NY: Gestalt Journal Press.

Philippson, P. (2001) *Self in Relation*. Highland, NY: Gestalt Journal Press.

Polster, E. (1987) *Every Person's Life is Worth a Novel*. New York: Norton.

Polster, E. (1995) *A Population of Selves*. San Francisco: Jossey-Bass.

Resnick, R. (1995) Interview 'Gestalt therapy: principles, prisms and perspectives' with M. Parlett, *British Gestalt Journal*, 4(1): 3–13.

Schore, A. (2003) *Affect Regulation and the Repair of the Self*. New York: Norton.

Spagnuolo-Lobb, M. and Amendt-Lyon, N. (2003) *Creative License: The Art of Gestalt Therapy*. Wien/New York: Springer-Verlag.

Spinelli, E. (1989) *The Interpreted World*. London: Sage.

Stern, D.N. (2004) *The Present Moment in Psychotherapy and Everyday Life*. New York: Norton.

Wheeler, G. (1991) *Gestalt Reconsidered: A New Approach to Contact and Resistance*. New York: Gardner Press.

Wheeler, G. (1995) 'Shame in two paradigms of therapy', *British Gestalt Journal*, 4(2).

Wilson, J.P., Friendman, M.J. and Lindy, J.D. (2004) *Treating Psychological Trauma and PTSD*. New York: Guilford.

Woldt, A.L. and Toman, S.M. (2005) *Gestalt Therapy: History, Theory and Practice*. Thousand Oaks, CA: Sage.

Wolfert, R. (2000) 'Self in experience, Gestalt therapy, science and Buddhism', *British Gestalt Journal*, 9(2): 77–86.

Wollants, G. (2005) Interview 'Therapy of the situation' with M. Parlett, *British Gestalt Journal*, 14(2): 91–102.

Yontef, G.L. (1984) 'Modes of thinking in Gestalt therapy', *The Gestalt Journal*, 7(1): 33–74.
Yontef, G.L. (1988) 'Assimilating diagnostic and psychoanalytical perspectives into Gestalt therapy', *The Gestalt Journal,* 11(1): 5–32.
Yontef, G.L. (1993) *Awareness, Dialogue and Process*. New York: The Gestalt Journal Press.
Zinker, J. (1977) *Creative Process in Gestalt Therapy*. New York: Brunner Mazel.
Zinker, J. (1994) *In Search of Good Form*. San Francisco: Jossey-Bass.

SUGGESTED FURTHER READING

Clarkson, P. and Mackewn, J. (1993) *Fritz Perls*. London: Sage.
Joyce, P. and Sills, C. (2001) *Skills in Gestalt Counselling and Psychotherapy*. London: Sage.
Mackewn, J. (1997) *Developing Gestalt Counselling*. London: Sage.
Woldt, A.L. and Toman, S.M. (2005) *Gestalt Therapy: History, Theory and Practice*. Thousand Oaks, CA: Sage.
Yontef, G.L. (1993) *Awareness, Dialogue and Process*. New York: The Gestalt Journal Press.

10

Transactional Analysis

Keith Tudor and Robin Hobbes

HISTORICAL CONTEXT AND DEVELOPMENT IN BRITAIN

Historical context

Transactional analysis (TA) was founded by Eric Berne (1910–1970), a Canadian psychiatrist who originally trained as a psychoanalyst. Its theories of personality, child development and psychopathology offer a comprehensive theory of therapy, whilst its theory of communication, applied to social (*inter*-personal, *extra*–psychic) as well as psychological (*intra*-personal, *intra*-psychic) systems, offers a framework for understanding and analysing groups and organisations (see Berne, 1963, 1966). Historically, its philosophical and intellectual roots lie in empiricism, phenomenology, existentialism and humanism, roots nourished by the context of the political radicalism of aspects of American and, specifically, Californian culture in the 1960s and 1970s.

The history of TA is well-documented – see, for instance, James (1977), as well as previous editions of this handbook (Collinson, 1984; Clarkson and Gilbert, 1990; Clarkson et al. 1996; Tudor and Hobbes, 2002). Here we identify the historical context and development of TA in terms of the influences on Berne, both personally and philosophically.

Two major influences on Berne were Paul Federn (1870–1950) and Eric Erikson (1902–1994) with both of whom he was in analysis and from whom he derived and developed key ideas in TA:

- an interest in ego psychology (Federn, 1952) which was seminal in Berne's later development of the ego state model of personality (see below, pp. 263–6).

- a concern in working with severely disturbed patients in the context of psychiatric hospitals (again from Federn), which informed Berne's development of TA as a model for understanding and working with disordered thinking (contamination) and regressiveness (exclusion) (see below, p. 265–6).
- the structured and sequential view of human development (Erikson, 1951), which has informed TA's theory of 'life script' (although more recent studies in child development have questioned this linear view, a critique which has been taken up within TA, see Cornell, 1988).
- the view that personality can only be understood in a psycho-*social* context (Erikson, 1951, 1968), a perspective which is echoed in Berne's (1975a/1961) view of TA as a 'social psychiatry' and, fundamentally, a *group* psychotherapy.

As we have indicated, four major philosophical influences may be discerned in the history and development of TA.

Empiricism

Whilst Berne was clearly influenced by psychoanalysis, he was critical of its over-theorising and of its elitism. This led him to construct a theory, which, whilst psychodynamic in concept, could be checked out directly against observations. For Berne (visual) observation 'is the basis of all good clinical work, (1966: 65–6) and, ideally, the therapist should use all five senses in diagnosis, assessment and treatment planning. This emphasis has led to a strong cognitive-behavioural strand to TA (see, for instance, Mothersole, 2002). The requirements for a valid therapeutic contract in TA – that it is behavioural, observable and finishable (as well as bilateral) – clearly reflects empiricism. Stewart suggests that observability is important in Berne's theory for three reasons:

1   It means that TA is effective as a social psychology …
2   It makes TA practice relatively easy to replicate, and therefore relatively straightforward to teach.
3   It renders the theory of TA testable (1992:18).

Phenomenology

The view that we can best understand the world by direct personal experience finds its expression in TA in one of the (four) requirements for ego state diagnosis which is only validated 'if the individual can finally re-experience in full intensity, with little weathering, the moment or epoch when he assimilated [in this case] the parental ego state' (Berne, 1961/1975a: 76). Indeed, with its structural analysis of ego states, Berne viewed TA as a 'systemic phenomenology' which (then) filled a gap in psychological theory.

Existentialism

There are many different views of existentialism and differences of emphasis, especially between American and European traditions. Berne (1971b: 8), who was a dedicated poker player, used this to describe what he meant by existentialism:

poker is one of the few really existential situations left in the world … everybody's on their own. Nobody's going to feel sorry for you. You're fully responsible for everything you do. Once you've put the money in the pot, you've put it in the pot. You can't blame anybody else. You have to take the consequences of that.

TA's three basic philosophical tenets – that people are OK, that everyone has the capacity to think, and that people decide their own destiny (and that these decisions can be changed) – are generally viewed as reflecting existential thinking, attributable to the influence on Berne of Virginia Satir who coined the phrase 'I count. You count. Context counts'. C. Sills (personal communication, May 2001), however, suggests that the true existential position is 'I am, You are' and that the attributed value of OKness is a humanistic influence. Nevertheless, Berne's 'I'm OK, You're OK' (I+ U+) life position was a significant addition to the previous Kleinian 'positions': paranoid (I+ U–), depressive (I– U+) and schizoid (I– U–). In his last work, *What Do You Say After You Say Hello?* (1975b/1972), Berne extended these four two–handed positions to include third parties thus: I+ U+ They+ – a significant development, the importance of which for human conduct is, in our view, underestimated both within and outside TA (see Tudor, 1999b).

Humanism

A number of TA's theoretical strands and principles derive from humanism and, historically, both drew on the (then) emerging 'third force' humanistic psychology and contributed to its development:

- TA's therapeutic slogans (Berne, 1966): Above all do no harm, (a belief in) the curative power of nature, and the notion that 'I treat, Gods cures'.
- TA's therapeutic attitudes (Berne, 1966), including the importance of the therapist's authenticity. This is also echoed in the importance of mutuality in TA, as represented, for example, in the bilaterality of the therapeutic method and, specifically, therapeutic contracts.
- Open communication and accessibility. Berne once said that 'anything that can't be said in front of the patient isn't worth saying' and he was one of the first psychiatrists to develop staff-patient case conferences (see Berne, 1968b). Berne's insistence on accessibility extended to theory. The translation of complex ideas – Freud's 'repetition compulsion' becomes 'psychological games' – has been one of the great contributions of TA to psychology and psychotherapy in general, and, at the same time, has laid it open to accusations of 'pop psychology', charges not helped by the misrepresentation of TA theory from both outside and, at times, within TA.

TA's humanistic roots, identity and location are the subject of some debate amongst both generic writers and within TA: Stewart (1992), for instance, places TA within the psychodynamic stream and Moiso and Novellino argue vociferously for TA as 'the most promising form of neo-psychoanalytic psychotherapy' (2000: 186). Whilst clearly drawing on elements from the other two 'forces' in psychology – indeed, humanistic psychology itself is, as Maslow acknowledged, an *epi*-psychology (epi = 'building upon') – we consider TA to be essentially (i.e. ontologically), epistemologically and methodologically a humanistic psychotherapy (see Tudor, 1996) and as consistent with core beliefs of humanistic psychology theory and practice (see Association of Humanistic Psychology Practitioners, 1998).

Now, 50 years on from Berne's early writings, TA has developed both theoretically and organisationally, for details of which see the *International*

Transactional Analysis Association (ITAA) website www.itaa-net.org; and Stewart and Joines (1987). This development is supported by a number of publications – the international quarterly *Transactional Analysis Journal (TAJ)* and monthly newsletter *The Script*, both produced by the ITAA; and, in Britain, the journal *Transactions*, produced by the Institute of Transactional Analysis (ITA). The developing theory and practice of TA psychotherapy is also well represented in publications over the last five years: Hargaden and Sills (2002); Joines and Stewart (2002); Kouwenhoven et al. (2002); Lister-Ford (2002); Martorell (2002); Schneider (2002); Tudor (2002); Cassoni (2003); Filippi (2003); Moursund and Erskine (2003); Munari Poda (2003); Schmid (2003); Sills and Hargaden (2003); Ligabue (2004); Mazzetti (2004); Novellino (2004); Cornell and Hargaden (2005); Ligabue (2005); Sills (2006); Tudor (2007, in press). In addition to the clinical field, which encompasses psychotherapy and counselling, TA has recognised applications in the educational field (see Pierre, 2002; Barrow and Newton, 2004); and the organisational field (see Le Guernic, 2004; Mountain, 2004; Risto, 2004; Vogelauer, 2005a, 2005b). A recent book by Jabandzic (2005) on the war in Bosnia transcends these 'fields of application' and reflects the continuity of TA as a social psychology. In TA, reflecting the diversity of thinking and practice within the field of psychotherapy in general, there are a number of distinct 'schools' or traditions (see next section p. 261–3).

Development in Britain

The beginnings of TA in Britain have been recorded by Allaway (1983) and Collinson (1983) and summarised in previous editions. Collinson describes three broad and overlapping stages to the development of TA in Britain, beginning in 1962 with the first TA classes run by John Allaway and Joe Richards at the University of Leicester. The second stage was marked in April 1972 by the establishment of a TA discussion group in London initiated by Lawrence Collinson and David Porter, and in November 1972 by the first official '101' introductory course in Sheffield, organised by Alan Byron and run by Warren Cheney, a psychotherapist and Teaching Member of the ITAA. The third stage began in 1973 with the establishment of TA groups and workshops with the authorisation of the ITAA. In the previous edition, in the spirit of the narrative turn of psychotherapy, we invited Michael Reddy, one of the people most associated with the development of TA in Britain in its early days, and the first British Teaching Member of the ITAA, to take up its story.

> 1973 was a watershed year for TA in the UK. I was back in London after 6 years abroad mostly in the USA. A diffident young man called David Porter tracked me down via ITAA and introduced me to a TA Study Group which met somewhere in Hampstead or Highgate. David later became the first Editor of ITA's tiny Bulletin. Margaret Turpin was a member of that group. She and I were the only professionals involved (from medicine and psychology, respectively) and it was not long before we found four others keenly interested in TA: two doctors, David Connell from London and Alan Byron from Sheffield, Emeritus Professor John Allaway from Nottingham, and Paul Brown a London–based psychologist. We six formed a

Steering Group which I chaired, most of our meetings taking place at 39 Fitzjohns Avenue, Hampstead. We produced a Constitution and became the Founders of the Institute of Transactional Analysis, doing all the things a professional body does: running approved courses, setting training standards, mounting conferences and seminars, and producing a house journal. We would have called it The British Association for Transaction Analysis but the use of 'British' had (then) been recently banned so we chose 'Institute' as best expressing the professional standing for which we were aiming.

By now TA in the UK was growing rapidly. ITA conferences were well attended, membership grew, and standards were being developed, 'though I have to admit my own Clinical Member (CM) exam would scarcely have passed muster today! The core of the exam was Jack Dusay, a psychiatrist and President of the ITAA, role-playing a florid paranoid schizophrenic in a café on the Boulevard St Germain in Paris. My strongest recollection is of the place emptying rather quickly!

Alan Byron remained active for quite some time and to some extent David Connell, but it is Margaret Turpin who has devoted half a lifetime to TA. I went on to chair the Steering Group for the European Association for Transactional Analysis (EATA), following an inspired initiative in 1974 by Bob Goulding when an amazing number of people turned up for the first European Congress at Villars in Switzerland. Most of the prominent Americans were there but what surprised us was the large number of practitioners from every corner of Europe. Konstanz Robertson–Rose (Switzerland), Arnold Van Westering (Netherlands) and I put our heads together, held an inaugural meeting on the spot and EATA was born. I stayed with EATA as Chair and then first President.

THEORETICAL ASSUMPTIONS

As we indicated, there are a number of different 'schools' or traditions within TA, which represent differences of theory and practice within TA, and which draw on a broad range of influences from outside TA (see Table 10.1). A little while after Berne's death in 1970, three 'schools' of TA were recognised: the Classical School, the Redecision School and the Cathexis School (see Barnes, 1977) and, until 2001, it was a requirement for qualification and accreditation that all TA practitioners were familiar with the theory and practice of these three schools. In 1978 Woollams and Brown expanded the original division by recognising other 'schools'; more recently Lee (2001) has identified ten different approaches within TA, and Campos (2003) five 'branches' of the tree of TA. As part of his contribution to the previous chapter, one of the authors (KT) formulated the present categorisation of seven traditions as most coherently representing the current strands of thinking and practice within TA (see Table 10.1). In the present schema, the original 'Classical School' is divided into two, representing both psychoanalytic and cognitive–behavioural influences on Berne and his work. The lost tradition of radical psychiatry is reclaimed although, arguably, it could be widened to include more recent social/political writings and analysis. The integrative tradition is retained as TA practitioners refer to it, although it is unclear that the three works on 'integrative' TA (Erskine and Moursund, 1988; Clarkson, 1992; Erskine and Trautmann, 1996) represent a school or tradition, or any meta-theoretical view by which such integration is effective or, indeed, defined (see Tudor, 1996). Interestingly, none of the authors cited on integration actually claim their work as 'integrative *TA*'. As a revision to the previous edition, here 'constructivist TA' replaces 'narrative TA'. This is a clarification as constructivism is a philosophical tradition, founded on the premise that, by reflecting on our experiences, we construct our own understanding of the world, whilst narrative therapy is a particular form of therapy which draws largely but not exclusively on constructivist ideas (see Allen and Allen, 1995). In this sense a therapist may tell – and encourage the client to see and reflect on – a 'narrative' which encompasses all the theoretical traditions of TA; and, indeed, it may be argued that TA, with its emphasis on script, is one of the original narrative therapies. J. Allen (personal communication, 21 January 2006) identifies three types of constructivist TA:

1   The construction of meaning and narrative – which fits for scripts, and for the idea of a constructivist overarching framework for all our traditions in TA.
2   The ongoing construction and deconstruction of relationships, including transactions and games.
3   The neurodevelopmental – or the neuroconstructive – which encompasses and involves environment-dependent gene expression, the development of new synapses, actual changes in neural networks and also brain structure as a result of experience, and especially interpersonal experience.

In Table 10.1 the focus, key theories and methods and theorists of each tradition are summarised, and some influences on each tradition external to TA are identified.

In the past five years, and reflective of debates in the wider psychotherapeutic world, as well as the impact of research in neuroscience on psychotherapy there has been more explicit recognition of TA as a relational psychotherapy. In many ways this goes back to the roots of TA in the analysis of transactions between client and therapist. However, more than this, beginning with the publication of *Transactional Analysis: A Relational Perspective* (Hargaden and Sills, 2002), and continuing with a recent, edited collection comprising articles previously published in the *TAJ* (Cornell and Hargaden, 2005), transactional analysts are tracing, reclaiming and developing a more intersubjective and relational paradigm in TA. Rather than viewing 'relational TA' as a tradition, we consider it as a lens through which to observe, understand and practice TA in different ways. This acknowledges relational TA as comprising a number of different perspectives (faces of the lens), informed by different theories, and that it thus, like narrative, offers a meta-perspective on TA.

Of course, each tradition, drawing on and emphasising different theory and models, carries different and, at times, differing underlying theoretical assumptions. In this section (and, indeed, in the chapter as a whole) we aim both to represent TA whilst acknowledging and, in part, to reflect the complexity and diversity of contemporary TA theory and practice. In each of the following sub-sections we summarise the key elements of TA theory, introduce relevant concepts with examples and offer our own view of more recent and critical developments in TA theory.

Table 10.1   Seven traditions in TA

Tradition	Focus	Key theories and methods	TA theorists	Influences external to TA
'Classical School' (Psycho-dynamic)	On re-enactment of original protocol (early script) and palimpsest (later script).	Structural ego state analysis; analysis of games (repetition compulsion) and transactions, including transferential and countertransferential transactions.	Eric Berne (early work); Carlo Moiso (1983, 1985), Michele Novellino (1984, 1990) (see Novellino and Moiso, 1990); Diana Shmuckler (1991).	Psychodynamic theory (Freud, Kernberg, Racker, Bollas); ego psychology (Weiss, Federn); object relations (Klein, Winnicott, Fairbairn; Guntrip); self-psychology (Kohut).
'Classical School' (Cognitive-behavioural)	On script, social control and symptomatic relief	Functional ego states; strokes (Steiner); permission (Crossman); drama triangle (Karpman); options (Karpman); egogram (Dusay); contracts.	Eric Berne; Claude Steiner. See Mothersole (2002).	Cognitive-behavioural therapies; cybernetics (Korzybski, Weiner); neuro-linguistic programming (see Stewart, 1996).
'Redecision School'	On original relationship experience; early decisions	Games; rackets; injunctions (the Gouldings); impasses (Mellor); Parent interview (McNeel); redecision.	Bob and Mary Goulding (1979); John McNeel (1977); Barbara and James Allen (1995); J. Allen, (1998). See McClendon and Kadis (1983).	Gestalt therapy (Perls); family systems therapy (Satir, Minuchin).
'Cathexis School'	On unhealthy symbiosis; passivity; grandiosity; thinking disorders	Frames of reference; confronting symbiosis, passivity, discounting and redefining; reparenting and regression.	Jacqui Schiff (Schiff et al., 1975). See Childs-Gowell (1979), and Kouwenhoven, et al. (2002).	Social work and psychiatric approaches to work with severely disturbed and psychotic patients, especially those with schizophrenia (Rose).
Radical psychiatry	On alienation; oppression; institu-tionalisation; and power	Script types (Steiner); stroke economy (Steiner); contracts; permission, protection and potency (Crossman, Steiner, the Allens).	Claude Steiner; Hogie Wyckoff (1976). See Agel (1971), and Steiner (2000). More recently, Pearl Drego (1983); Alan Jacobs (1987).	Social movements and radical politics of the 1960s and 1970s; 'anti-psychiatry' and critical psychology (including Fanon, Basaglia, Laing, Berke, Jones).
Integrative	On disowned, unaware, and unresolved aspects of the self; defence mechanisms.	Integration; enquiry, attune-ment, and involvement; relational needs; contact-in-relationship (Erskine).	William Holloway (1977); Richard Erskine, Janet Moursund and Rebecca Trautmann (Erskine and Moursund, 1988; Erskine and Trautmann, 1996); Petrūska Clarkson (1992).	Gestalt conceptualisations of the ego; self-psychology (Kohut); integrative psychology (Stolorow, Brandchaft and Atwood).

Table 10.1   (Continued)

Tradition	Focus	Key theories and methods	TA theorists	Influences external to TA
Constructivist	On discourse, meaning, and evolving constructions of 'reality'.	Construction; intersubjectivity; dialogue; co-creativity (Summers and Tudor); Integrating Adult (Tudor).	Barbara and James Allen (1991, 1997, 2000); Bruce Loria (1991; Loria & J. Allen, 1997); Graeme Summers and Keith Tudor (2000).	Field theory (Lewin); social constructivism (White, Hoyt); intersubjectivity, and dialogic psychotherapy (Friedman).

Image of the person

TA is based on three basic philosophical propositions, all of which centre on the innate capacities of the person, namely:

1 That people are OK, having intrinsic worth, the capacity to relate and to resolve problems.
2 That people can think.
3 That people make decisions and decide their own destiny – and that these decisions can be changed (and hence 'redecisions').

Berne (1971a: 98) also talked about the force of Nature or *physis* 'which eternally strives to make things grow and to make growing things more perfect' and whose existence made it easier to understand the human being, which he described as:

> a colourful energy system, full of dynamic strivings ... continually trying to reach a state of tranquillity ... whose tensions give rise to wishes which it is his task to gratify without getting into trouble with himself, with other people, or with the world around him'. (1971a; 65–6).

This describes the aspirational and transformative quality of human beings or persons – *and* reflects Berne's own conservatism and conformity: a dynamic and tension which we see manifested in the theory, practice and organisation of TA in a number of ways.

The central concept in TA regarding the image of person is that of ego states. Drawing on research on memory and the brain (notably, Penfield, 1952), Berne (1961/1975a) described an ego state as follows: 'phenomenologically as a coherent set of feelings related to a given subject, and operationally as a set of coherent behavior patterns; or pragmatically, as a system of feelings which motivated a related set of behavior patterns'. From Weiss (1950) and Federn (1952), Berne drew on the notion of an ego state:

1 As actually experienced reality.
2 As retained in potential existence within the personality.
3 Which, under special conditions may be 're-cathected' or re-energised (Berne originally cited hypnosis, dreams and psychosis as such conditions).

Berne (1961/1975a) identified three systems or organisations of the ego which he referred to as psychic organs: an elaborative system connected to the

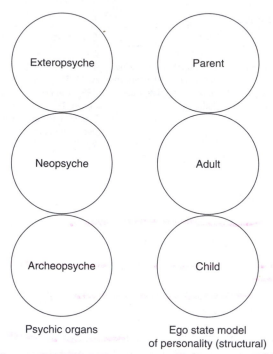

Figure 10.1   **Psychic organs and corresponding ego states (Berne, 1961/1975a)**

mental/emotional analysis of the here-and-now (*neopsyche*); a system aimed at organising introjected psychic material (*exteropsyche*); and a system linked to the organisation of instinctual drives, basic needs and primary emotional experiences (*archeopsyche*) which he termed, respectively: Adult, Parent and Child (see Figure 10.1).

Following Lapworth et al. (1993) we prefer a further clarification of: Introjected Parent, Integrated (or *Integrating*) Adult and Archaic Child. Whilst Berne implied correspondence between psychic organs and three ego states, he himself and other TA writers and clinicians since have proposed a number of ego states especially as conceived within the Parent and Child. It is thus more accurate and consistent to think in terms of three psychic organs but many ego states (see Jacobs, 2000; Tudor, 2003).

In the 40 years since Berne's original formulation, ego state theory has been the subject of much debate within TA (for summaries of which, see Friedlander, 1988; Clarkson, 1992; Midgley, 1999; Sills and Hargaden, 2003). Our own view is a constructivist one which is, broadly, that ego states are ways of describing intrapsychic and interpersonal *processes* with regard to personality. They are constructed, deconstructed and reconstructed in an ongoing, interpersonal process, based on dialogue, i.e. transactions: 'this perspective shifts the therapeutic emphasis away from the treatment of ego-state structures and toward an exploration of how relational possibilities are cocreated on a moment-to-moment basis' (Summers and Tudor, 2000: 36).

Conceptualisation of psychological health and disturbance

TA's conceptualisation of health and disturbance is reflected in its four theoretical foundations: ego states, transactions, scripts and games. Like many other approaches to psychotherapy, TA has, in our view, overemphasised disturbance and pathology at the expense of health. As Cornell observes: 'like many clinicians, Berne became possessed by the effort to understand pathology. He lost track of health' (1988: 32). With some others, we believe that, alongside its detailed theory of psychopathology, TA also offers a psychology of health, albeit one which needs further development. Thus, psychological health may be conceived, in terms of *ego states*, as being a state of flexibility and one which emphasises the here-and-now, present-centred Integrating Adult. Similarly, *transactions*, which in themselves are also neutral, may be viewed as representing and supporting healthy interactions comprising stimuli and responses. Berne's classification of *scripts* includes a 'winning' script, defining a 'winner' as 'someone who accomplishes his declared purpose', to which Bob Goulding added 'and makes the world a better place as a result' (cited in Stewart and Joines, 1987). Berne's definition of a *game* as 'an ongoing series of complementary ulterior transactions progressing to a well-defined, predictable outcome' (1964/1968a: 44) offers a non-pathologising view of a 'game' as a confirmation of a transactional or relational pattern. Acknowledging TA as a health psychology and following Summers and Tudor (2000), we consider transactions as co-creative relationships, ego states as co-creative personalities in process, script as co-creative identity, and games as co-creative 'confirmations'.

This said, we turn our attention to the conceptualisation of disturbance in terms of ego states, scripts and games. Whilst a number of transactions contribute towards the acquisition and maintenance of psychopathology, we do not think of transactions themselves in terms of 'disturbance' (see next section pp. 267).

Ego states
In terms of ego states psychological health is conceived as being a state of flexibility, and disturbance, one of inflexibility. There is a debate within TA about the nature of ego states (see Sills and Hargaden, 2003) which partly focuses on the nature of the Adult ego state as representing a state – or process – of flexibility and fluidity (see Tudor, 2003). There is no dispute about the three primary inflexible states which are:

1   *Excluding ego states* in which one ego state excludes awareness of the other two. Paranoid states can be understood as states where a Parent ego state excludes awareness of Child and Adult material, whilst hallucinatory states can be conceived as excluding Child ego states in which the Child excludes awareness of Parent and Adult functioning.
2   *Contaminating ego states* refers to disturbance that is specifically related to discrete experiences such as prejudice (Parent contaminating Adult) or phobias (Child contaminating Adult).

In contrast to exclusions, contaminations are much less pervasive and tend to result in inflexibility only in specific situations such as a perceived threat or the presence of spiders.

3   *Symbiotic ego states* refers to a type of relational dependency in which two people rely very heavily on each other, leading to the development of dependant personalities: they sense that they can only exist relationally if they only have three ego states between them. This is often perceived and presented as when one person in the relationship cathects Parent and Adult ego states whilst the other occupies the Child position.

Scripts

Transactional analysts conceive of script as an ongoing psychological process in which meaning is given to life experiences. As Stewart (1992) points out, similar concepts may be found in the work of Otto Rank, Carl Jung, Eric Erikson and, particularly, Alfred Adler and his concept of 'life goal', on whose work Berne drew. In TA, life script is essentially thought of as a decisional process which takes place from the cradle to the grave and is an essential component of the life process that influences the course of action somebody will take throughout their life. Whilst a healthy script is conceived as a 'winning script', there are two types of unhealthy scripts:

*   *losing or harmartic script* in which the meanings and actions arising from those meanings are such that the person turns away from life, either ending up dead or in an institution unable to care for themselves.
*   *a non-winning or banal script* in which the meanings and actions arising from those meanings are such that the person never fully engages in life and fails to reach their full potential.

Again, over the years, the concept of script has developed. Berne himself refined his definition over 15 years (Berne, 1958, 1972/1975b) and others such as Steiner (1966, 1974) have also developed the concept and analysis of script (for a summary of which see Müller and Tudor, 2001).

Games and rackets

Games and rackets refer to relational and emotional patterns that people create to maintain the script decisions they have taken. Here, transactional analysts identify relational disturbance. This disturbance is found to lie in the relational patterns people develop to maintain the sense of identity they have established through their script. Essentially these patterns are another way to understand transference phenomena in which the projections that people make onto each other are acted out with each other, and these 'dramas' are often repeated. Karpman (1968) famously applied role theory to the drama in a game. He identified three roles: Rescuer, Persecutor and Victim and suggested that in a game each person adopts one of these roles and then (like all good drama) switches roles, say, from Persecutor to Rescuer. A 'racket' refers to emotional patterns people develop that, again, result in an emotional inflexibility. English (1971) considered the main feature of a racket was that it was a substitute feeling; thus, a depressed person may substitute depressive feelings for angry feelings.

Table 10.2   Simon's script system (based on Erskine and Moursund, 1988)

Script Beliefs	Script Displays	Reinforcing Experiences
About self: There's something wrong with me	Observable behaviours Hesitant style of voice Not finishing sentences	Current events Unsatisfactory relationships Little interest in work
About others: They are not interested in me	Smiling and biting lower lip Reported internal experiences	Old emotional memories
About the quality of life: Be cautious	Fluttery sensations in tummy 'tightening up'	Father leaving home Mother enjoying having son around
Intrapsychic processes	Fantasies	Memories of the fantasies as real
Repressed needs and feelings:	No one will really know me – that keeps me safe	Father making promises and not keeping them Mother being there when needed
To be protected by a stable other		
Anger and grief		

Acquisition of psychological disturbance

Much of the discussion in the previous section explains both the conceptualisation TA has of psychological disturbance as well as its acquisition. Nevertheless, there are a number of ways in which TA conceptualises the acquisition of disturbance, one of which is the script system (Erskine and Moursund, 1988). Based on some original work by Erskine and Zalcman (1979), the script system is one in which the various components of script are categorised. The script system is described by Erskine and Moursund (1988) as a collection of beliefs, current behaviours, memories and fantasies that 'serve as a defense against awareness of childhood experiences, needs, and related emotions while simultaneously being a repetition of the past' (p. 29-40). Table 10.2 shows the script system of 'Simon', the client whose work is discussed below (pp. 278–81).

Of course, it is the daily transactions – stimuli and responses – which maintain and confirm or question and challenge the script. Unsurprisingly, TA – the analysis of transactions – has developed a sophisticated language for describing various types of transactions e.g. complementary, crossed and ulterior (for explanations of which see Stewart and Joines, 1987) which Berne (1961/1975a) linked to three rules of communication. Other types of transaction include redefining transactions which discount either the stimulus, the response or both.

Perpetuation of psychological disturbance

Building on the notion that it is the transactions people engage in (or do not) that stimulate the acquisition of psychological disturbance, it is primarily the psychological games people play in order to reinforce their script which perpetuates their distress or disturbance. In this statement, of course, is embedded the humanistic slogan that 'defences are for protection': so-called 'games' may perpetuate something which both therapist and client may regard as unhealthy; however, playing a game may also help a person to protect him or herself against greater disturbance and to survive. One way of understanding a psychological game is as an example of transference phenomena in which early relationships are replayed, for example, a woman who had a distant and remote father is drawn to distant and remote men. When playing a game – and in his book *Games People Play* Berne (1964/1968a) identified many variations – we also embody a desire that this time things will turn out differently. E. Ruppert (personal communication, 1982) goes further, suggesting that Berne failed to realise the full implications of his own theory, as games can be understood as only being resolved by a movement into intimacy, and thus are an attempt to enter into relating intimately rather than avoiding this. One positive aspect of game analysis is its emphasis on the relational: it takes two to tango and two (at least) to play a game. TA therapists may take this as a modern day Zen koan through which to study humility, or as a challenge to be mindful of 'Ah–ha' moments and certainties, and as a way of avoiding such consulting room games as identified by Berne (1964/1968a) such as 'I'm only trying to help you' or 'Psychiatry'.

Change

There are two views of change in transactional analysis psychotherapy. One emphasises the notion of cure, the other that the process of change is given. The first, somewhat medical model view of cure, derives from Berne (1972/1975b) who identifies four goals and stages of cure whereby clients achieve: *social control* over their symptoms or dysfunctional behaviours; *symptomatic relief* from the subjective discomfort of the dysfunction; *transference cure* (defined as staying out of script but only by substituting the therapist); and *script cure*. Traditionally, this is effected through identifiable and observable (usually behavioural) changes, through contractual psychotherapy. The other stream emphasises the existential truism that, as organisms, human beings and persons, we are in a constant process of change and development, a drive or 'force for Nature' which Berne (1963, 1971a, 1972/1975b), drawing on ancient writings, referred to as '*physis*'. In response to this, the psychotherapist's role is to help the client to harness this developmental drive.

Whilst the focus of the first two stages of cure is on behavioural change, in both views of change the therapeutic relationship is the medium for change. This is borne out by psychotherapy research and is increasingly emphasised in TA, despite the differences between 'schools' and practitioners regarding the use of transference (see Tudor, 1999b). From a constructivist and co-creative perspective, therapist and client share the responsibility to create, explore and learn from the process of establishing, contracting about, working through and ending the therapeutic relationship. In this sense, just as there has been a movement from cure to change, there may be a further movement in emphasis from change to *learning* as defining the process and focus of TA psychotherapy (G. Summers, personal communication, May 2001).

PRACTICE

Goals of therapy

Transactional analysis psychotherapy has as its primary goal the creation and development of a meaningful relationship within which transformation and development can occur. The therapist will pay a lot of attention to the development of a working alliance in which goals are mutually arrived at and agreed. Therapists differ as to their attention to therapeutic goals, this difference being reflected in the multiplicity of orientations TA therapists take. On one end of the continuum TA practitioners will take a cognitive/behavioural approach devising behavioural goals the attainment of which is the focus of their therapy; at the other end of the continuum practitioners will take an approach which sees the developing relationship as primary and in which a multiplicity of developments will occur as a healing relationship is established. In this, the therapist refrains from emphasising behavioural goals so as to minimise overadaptation.

Generally the goal of TA therapy is autonomy. The TA therapist understands autonomy to consist of three dimensions: awareness, spontaneity and intimacy (Berne, 1964/1968a). Awareness is where the client knows both experientially and cognitively those parts of their experience that are regressive (i.e. that reside in the Child ego state), those parts that are introjected (Parent ego state), and those parts of experience that are directly related to the here-and-now (Adult ego state). Therefore awareness is knowing the self. Spontaneity, the second component of autonomy refers to the client recovering freedom to express this growing awareness without censorship. The third component of autonomy is intimacy, which is the capacity to be aware and spontaneous with someone else in a way that accounts for both people. An example of this process is a client who, in the course of his therapy, develops from a depression into some sense of inner and outer contentment. This is achieved in many dimensions but includes the development of the awareness of angry feelings. The awareness may be that his father expressed uncontrolled anger in a violent way (internalised in his Introjected Parent) and that they adapted to that experience by deciding to inhibit their experiencing of that feeling in case they themselves became violent (Archaic Child). As the therapy develops, spontaneity of expression of angry feelings evolves while at the same time the capacity to express those feelings with others (intimacy) is frequently explored. This involves questions like: 'Who can I be angry with?', 'How can I express my anger?', 'When can I express my anger?' This movement through awareness, spontaneity and intimacy occurs multidimensionally in TA therapy resulting in the attainment of autonomy.

Selection criteria

Berne was very concerned to avoid selection criteria for suitability for therapy that was based on a diagnostic category. He thought these selection processes were arbitrary and would result in ineffectual, elitist therapy: 'the real issue … is not the one commonly debated, "What are the criteria for the selection of patients?", but the underlying, usually unstated assumption "Criteria for selection are good"' (Berne, 1966: 5). There is also another assumption embedded in the concept of selection that 'People are usefully categorised in terms of "client groups"'. As we have already said, TA was devised as a method of psychotherapy that could be applied to those 'groups' who previously were debarred from psychotherapeutic (and psychiatric) interventions because they were deemed 'too disturbed' to be able to tolerate the experience of therapy. This is topical as regards current debates about the 'treatability' of people diagnosed as having personality disorders. The TA practitioner working with individual clients then does not select clients based on diagnostic categories or 'client population groups', believing that everyone has the potential to benefit from TA therapy.

Nevertheless, a TA therapist will be *selective*, according to the criteria for making a contract, originally identified by Steiner (1971a) and based on the requirements for legal contracts, i.e. *mutual consent, valid consideration, competency* and *lawful object*. Informed *mutual consent* means that the client and therapist freely chose to be in therapy together. The therapist will expect the client to be intelligently involved in his or her own therapy. As TA takes the approach that theory used by the therapist is put on the table between therapist and client, the client is involved in his or her own treatment planning and there are no case conference secrets. If a client has been sent to therapy or has not chosen to work with the particular therapist or is not willing to be involved in his or her own assessment and the planning of therapy, then they are unlikely to be selected. TA therapists expect some *valid consideration* or exchange to occur between therapist and client, believing that an exchange of services equalises the relationship and encourages the realisation of autonomy. This can range from being paid for the therapy to the client demonstrating an equality of involvement in the psychotherapeutic process. A high proportion of TA therapists are in private practice and this may be because of this basic belief.

To decide *competency* the therapist needs to find out if they have the resources and expertise to help this particular client with the particular development that this client wants to make. This often involves the therapist in making a time-specific agreement to work with a client to assess her or his own competency. The therapist will question their own competency for a number of reasons: if the therapist considers themself insufficiently experienced to work with the client or if the therapist does not have the resources that the client needs for effective psychotherapy to take place, such as being unable to meet a twice-weekly appointment commitment. If the therapist considers that they cannot develop sufficient flexibility to effectively engage the client because of, say, boundary issues;

for example, the client is in a training group that the therapist was once in, then the therapist is unlikely to agree to work with the client. Finally the TA practitioner will want to be clear that the request for psychotherapeutic involvement and the desired outcome of the therapy is *lawful*. The practitioner is unlikely to agree to help someone develop inner security in their chosen career of bank robbery! These requirements have informed the ITAA's (1989) statement of ethics and the EATA's (1998) ethics guidelines as well as the clinical, organisational and educational applications of TA. Updating Steiner's requirements in terms of British contract law, three elements create a legal, written contract: valid consideration, dates and signatures.

Having ascertained if a client's request for therapy meets these criteria the therapist is likely to offer different modes of therapy. One mode will be individual therapy, usually weekly or fortnightly. (The other mode will be weekly group therapy. TA was originally a group psychotherapy and this tradition is still very strong in the TA community. Trainee transactional analysts are required to have group work experience and demonstrate it to an exam board before they can be accredited.) There is a variety of criteria applied to whether individual or group psychotherapy is recommended. The establishment of a therapeutic alliance is usually seen as a precursor to group work, although Tudor (1999a) questions the assumption that individual therapy is the default setting for the therapy of choice. Nevertheless, the therapeutic goals of the client influence the decision for groupwork. If the client wishes to focus on developing relationship skills then often a group, with its variety of potential relationships, is chosen. As ever, in terms of the emphasis on mutuality, the mode of psychotherapy needs to be the choice of the client as well as the psychotherapist – and this is still, most often, individual therapy.

Qualities of effective therapists

From TA's basic philosophy (see above) and Berne's (1966) therapeutic attitudes and slogans, it is clear that the qualities of an effective TA therapist must include: respect for self and others; a belief in self-responsibility and autonomy; a factual humility; and authenticity as a therapist (see Tudor, 1999b). In discussing the requirements of the (group) therapist, Berne cites an ability 'to use all five senses in making a diagnosis, assessing the situation, and planning the treatment' (1966: 65) – and, indeed, some of the practical qualities and skills of well trained and effective TA therapists are: fine observation skills, phenomenological awareness and an ability to analyse transactions. Other qualities which are required for certification as a certified transactional analyst include:

- ability to describe their own ideological beliefs and to relate them to the philosophical assumptions of TA, including the implications of cultural, racial and social identities and their significance.
- capacity to conceptualise psychotherapy in terms of TA.

- ability to integrate theory into practice.
- ability to demonstrate creativity and effectiveness, including discussing interventions within the context of the relationship.
- capacity for self-reflection (see EATA, 1999/2001/2005).

Finally, in our view, two further qualities define effective therapists (derived, respectively, from psychoanalysis and the person-centred approach): that of therapeutic neutrality and independence, and non-defensiveness.

Therapeutic relationship and style

Whilst there is increasing emphasis on and understanding of the therapeutic relationship in TA (for discussions of which see Clarkson, 1992; Clarkson et al., 1996; Tudor, 1999a; Hargaden and Sills, 2002), there is great richness and diversity of styles embodied by transactional analysts. Underpinning therapeutic 'style' is the requirement for the therapist to be authentic. Working with the philosophical principle of mutual OKness ('I'm OK, You're OK'), the TA therapist takes as their starting point that all psychological problems are potentially solvable, given sufficient resources and enough expertise. The practice of psychotherapy is thus essentially a collaborative one, in which both client and therapist are actively and intelligently involved. The requirement for authenticity, together with the requirement to be therapeutic and relational, and to promote the client's innate and/or desired development, results in the TA therapist using a wide variety of styles of communication: interruptive, directive, requestive, nurturative and emotive – styles which Kahler (1979) defines as the five communication channels (in order, in terms of the increasing intensity of stroking).

This range of styles used can be illustrated by examining the various approaches a transactional analyst might use to understand and work with ego states. To assess or diagnose ego states the therapist will both observe the client and pay close attention to their own experiences which are emerging as the therapeutic relationship develops. The therapist will draw tentative hypotheses as to the ego state structure of the client, based both on the observations they are making (behavioural diagnosis) and on the internal responses they are experiencing in being with the client (social diagnosis). Thus we could say that self-experiencing, or the phenomenology of the psychotherapist, has a strong influence on the style the psychotherapist uses. To confirm their provisional diagnosis, the therapist may enquire about the client's experience (historical and phenomenological diagnoses). In order to do this, the therapist may adopt an empathic approach, attuning to the perceived inner experience of the client, or they may become more purposefully active, involving themselves through sharing their own experience of being with the client. In order to help the client in recognising and distinguishing between ego states, the practitioner remains receptive to preconscious and unconscious processes, again both through the observation of transactions and through self–observation. The therapist's awareness is then available to the client. This process becomes a kind of relational dance between psychotherapist and client in which these three primary styles of enquiry, attunement and involvement weave a complex matrix of relational development.

As ego states are recognised, the psychotherapist has a variety of stylistic responses available to her or him. An interruptive response in which the therapist adopts a commanding and directional manner such as 'Breathe, look at me, notice what you can smell and hear' tends to be used to direct clients to a body-based awareness when the client needs to integrate thinking and feeling with bodily responses. 'Tell me what you are thinking' utilises a directive channel in which the therapist encourages the client to strengthen ego states' boundaries through cognitive work. Straightforward, non-directive cognitive transactions such as 'What do you want to focus on today?' are requestive. Empathic transactions in which the therapist shares her or his here-and-now experience such as 'I feel sad as you talk' are predominantly emotive. Finally, a practitioner may seek to contain or hold the client within the relationship by establishing and maintaining contact, by noticing relational needs as they emerge and responding to them by using a nurturative channel of communication. As an example, Simon starts his therapy session in an agitated state. The therapist interrupts the agitation by saying 'Simon, calm down, look at me, breathe and notice your breath' (interrruptive channel). The therapist goes on to say 'When you get excited like that, what are you thinking?' (directive). The therapist then says 'What do you want to work on?' (requestive). Simon then focuses on how he finds fear hard to contain. The therapist responds in a caring and non-directive manner: 'Maybe you need to know I am here when you feel frightened' (nurturative) and 'I feel sad when you say you were left all alone to look after yourself' (emotive channel).

Major therapeutic strategies and techniques

Traditionally, from Berne onwards, transactional analysts have adopted a strategic view of the progress of psychotherapy. Stewart suggests that there is always 'a three-way interplay between ... choice of interventions, the treatment contract ... and diagnosis of the client' (1989: 9) – a perspective which has led to the concept of the *treatment triangle* (in which these three elements are represented as diagnosis, contract and treatment planning (or treatment direction) (see Stewart, 1996). For us, this model, based in the medical tradition, overemphasises diagnosis and the external authority of the psychotherapist/diagnostician. It is mediated, however, by TA's emphasis on the contractual method and the more recent emphasis within TA on *process* (e.g. Kahler, 1979; Lee, 1997) which contributes to our understanding of all three elements of the treatment triangle, and on the *therapeutic relationship* (e.g. Hargaden and Sills, 2002). Traditionally, TA has been viewed (from both within and without) as a 'technical' therapy and, indeed, it has developed a number of techniques to facilitate therapeutic change. Berne (1966) himself defined eight, sequential 'therapeutic operations': interrogation, specification, confrontation, explanation, illustration, confirmation, interpretation and crystallisation which he defines precisely and TA psychotherapists are trained in their use and application – for further elaboration and discussion of which see Müller and Tudor (2001), and Hargaden and Sills (2002). Nevertheless, as Berne himself put it: 'observation is the basis of all good clinical work, *and takes precedent even over technique*' (1966: 65–6, our emphasis). Indeed, detailed observation and (literally) the analysis of transactions, may be viewed as the most desirable and effective quality of the transactional analyst as well as their most effective 'technique'. Other key therapeutic strategies and techniques include:

- the *decontamination* and strengthening of the Adult ego state (from the intrusion of archaic material), often effected by means of Berne's therapeutic operations and an intersubjective therapeutic relationship (see Hargaden and Sills, 2002).
- the *deconfusion* of the Child ego state whereby unmet archaic needs and feelings are identified and expressed. This may be through catharsis or by means of parenting and reparenting techniques (see James, 1974, 1981; Osnes, 1974; Schiff et al., 1975), or through the client internalising the therapist's empathic transactions (see Hargaden and Sills, 2002).
- the resolution of different degrees of *impasse* based on early script decisions, often through use of two-chair work – a theory and practice particularly developed in redecision therapy (see Goulding and Goulding, 1979; Mellor, 1980; Allen and Allen, 1995).
- much of the above also applies to *therapeutic work with the Parent ego state* which, as this comprises introjected or incorporated parental figures, may take the form of therapeutic 'interviews' with a psychic entity whose origins lie in a historical figure, personal to the client (see Dashiell, 1978; Mellor and Andrewartha, 1980).
- the therapist's use of herself or himself within the therapeutic relationship, whether informed by psychoanalytic perspectives (see Novellino, 1984; Moiso, 1985; Hargaden and Sills, 2002) or narrative, gestalt and person-centred perspectives (see Allen and Allen, 1995; Summers and Tudor, 2000) (see Table 10.1).

For further details of these techniques see Stewart and Joines (1987); Stewart (1989, 1996); Clarkson et al. (1996); and Hargaden and Sills (2002).

Whether actionistic and directive (in its traditional form) or more reflective and relational, TA is an interactive psychotherapy in which strategies and techniques are continually evolving within the psychotherapeutic space which both client and therapist are uniquely co-creating. Some contemporary views of TA eschew defined, prescribed procedures in favour of more focus on the process, co-creation and narrative of the therapeutic relationship.

Change process in therapy

Traditionally, the process of change in TA psychotherapy has focused on and emphasised *cure* (see pp. 268–9), the journey to which may be more or less structured, depending on the client, the nature of the issue or problem and on the person of the therapist. Berne's (1975b/1972) original 'treatment planning' sequence i.e. establishing a working alliance, decontamination, deconfusion, and relearning has (in our view) suffered from over-elaboration (see Woollams and Brown, 1978; Clarkson, 1992; and summarised in Clarkson et al., 1996). For us, change or learning takes place in and informs the complex interactional and relational processes between client and therapist, through which the client makes sense of and integrates past experiences into an expanded and expanding Adult ego state (see Tudor, 2003). In this sense, and with the support of evidence from neuroscientific research, we can talk about effecting both psychological and neurological change. This process of integration allows for the development of a flexible, fluid, autonomous person who can be freely active and engaged in her or his world. Having largely eschewed technique, strategy and sequence, the change process in TA psychotherapy may be viewed as comprising three overlapping processes: *building the working alliance*, *restructuring* and *reorganisation* (Clark, 1991).

Building the working alliance

As much research in the field has now shown, the single most important factor in determining the effectiveness of psychotherapy is the impact of the therapeutic relationship: the relationship *is* the therapy. Thus, as with many of their colleagues of different therapeutic orientations, the TA psychotherapist (of whatever tradition) focuses on the establishment, maintenance, development and ending of the therapeutic relationship. Although there is some debate about the relation between the therapeutic relationship and the working alliance (see, for instance, Barrett–Lennard, 1985), we view both as important and as ongoing. As Bordin (1975) conceptualises it, the working alliance comprises: the establishment of *an emotional bond*, and *an agreement* – or, in TA terms, a *contract* – about the goals and tasks of therapy. The TA practitioner seeks to establish contact with the client and often uses an initial period to make an assessment and provisional diagnosis, and to agree a contract which, in turn, traditionally informs their treatment planning and direction. Such 'treatment' is, nevertheless, subject to the contractual method and, therefore, agreed, bilateral, specific – and changeable.

In the early days of working with a client, many TA therapists also want to ensure that the client has closed their self-harming 'escape hatches' (see Holloway, 1973). An escape hatch is a term for destructive behaviours: self-harm or suicide, hurting others or going crazy. Transactional analysts have tended to view serious failure of self-care, suicide, homicide and madness as ways in which clients flee from problem-solving and the promotion of their own development. It is considered a way clients enter into *not* solving their problems, and the self-limiting behaviours that reinforce the script decisions they have taken. The procedure for 'closing escape hatches' is one of asking clients to make a commitment to themselves to stay alive, to stay sane, to take care of themselves, and to respect the lives of others, *no matter what experiences they have*. Formerly this technique was used rather ritualistically with the resulting consequences that existential issues such as questioning the meaning and purpose of life were shelved by clients who, consciously or unconsciously, perceived the therapist as communicating a 'no go area' for these issues. Over the past five years, this practice has been questioned (see, for instance, Mothersole, 1996, 1997) and a much more flexible approach has emerged in the practice of TA by which the technique of escape hatch closure is applied appropriately and sensitively only to those clients who are seriously at risk of a lack of self-care, of ending their own lives, of killing someone or ending up in a psychiatric hospital.

Restructuring

The restructuring of the personality occurs as the client develops awareness. Awareness relates to clients being able to understand their own experiences and responses to others in terms of ego states, that is, that they become aware which experiences and responses are borrowed from significant others (Parent), which are old, regressive patterns of thinking, feeling and behaving (Child), and which are a direct response to the here-and-now (Adult). Whether adopting a traditional cognitive behavioural or a more relational TA approach at this stage, the strategy is to promote awareness so that the client develops symptom or social control and symptomatic relief – the first two of Berne's (1972/1975b) four stages of cure (see pp. 268). As the client develops insight into the courses of action they have chosen for their unfolding life, so they can exercise greater control over their lives.

The approaches used by the TA psychotherapist relate to ego state awareness and the awareness of how the client uses ego states with others (i.e. transactions). Hence the transactional analyst might teach the client key concepts from TA so that the client becomes intelligently involved in their own decontamination. The client will develop awareness of her or his own games, rackets and scripts. The TA practitioner may use actionistic techniques borrowed from gestalt therapy (such as two-chair work) to encourage awareness of internal ego state dialogues. S/he will also use inquiry to facilitate the decontamination process. This process as a whole is referred to as restructuring and is often understood and encapsulated by such expressions as 'I now know why I do/ think or feel that ... '

Reorganisation

Reorganisation refers to the more emotionally intense, regressive processes that occur in psychotherapy in which clients develop and change their internal responses to stressful situations. Essentially they reorganise themselves and develop autonomy. The strategy of this stage of psychotherapy is to facilitate this reorganisation, especially through deconfusion. The reorganisation occurs through the client integrating Parent and Child ego state material into their Adult ego state. The integration occurs through the client fully identifying with and expressing the ego state.

Transactional analysts generally take one of two approaches at this stage in therapy. They may decide to take an actionistic approach to the Child and Parent ego state material that emerges. This can include setting up early scenes in which the client replays key early experiences in their past in which they externalise their inner ego state dialogues, or the psychotherapist may directly address either the Child or Parent ego states. Addressing the Child, the client identifies a parenting response that was missing and devises with the therapist a way for that parenting to be provided now. In therapy, the therapist 'parents' the client's Child ego state Addressing the Parent, the client cathects their relevant Parent ego state and the TA psychotherapist in effect conducts a therapy session with the client's 'mother', 'father' or significant parental figure.

The second approach the transactional analyst may use is to focus on the developing relationship to provide a space for holding and containing the intensity that emerges in the deconfusion stage. The TA practitioner attunes and involves themself with their client's process, perhaps paying particular attention to the presence of relational needs. The transactional analyst will notice the transactions taking place between herself and her client and through inquiry, attunement and involvement facilitate an integrative process (Erskine and Trautmann, 1996). As the therapeutic relationship develops the practitioner may notice the presence of relational needs, for example the need for recognition by a stable significant other. She may notice how the client has defended against the experience of the failure of this need as a child, and may encourage the client to dissolve those defences and to find more satisfying ways to relate to people when the client experiences that need. The 'techniques' emphasised in this approach are less actionistic and require more rhythmic, receptive and empathic responses (see Hargaden and Sills, 2002). As we have noted, in recent years there has been more interest in relational approaches to TA.

Limitations of the approach

As we value the contribution TA as a social psychiatry makes in encouraging both practitioners and clients to be interested in the social dimension of their own and each other's psychology, so we are concerned about any theory, practice and organisation in TA which limits open communication, autonomy, mutuality and co-creativity. Here we refer to three possible limitations.

Motivation

In TA motivation is often explained and understood in terms of social reward or punishment, often described as the client establishing a system for recognition in their early life in which they seek positive or negative strokes and establish a pattern for human contact. This pattern is considered to be the primary motivation for human interaction. This is too limiting an explanation for why people do things and why they relate to others in specific ways. In this, no account is given of either biological or spiritual drives that influence human interaction. This means that the practitioner has to broaden her or his outlook to accommodate these wider understandings into her or his work as a therapist. It may mean, for example, that practitioners miss the important dimension of the need and yearning for spiritual fulfilment and mistake it for the effect of a social experience such as an unavailable mother. With few, rare exceptions, the lack of a coherent spiritual dimension to the main body of TA theory and method means that this is a fertile field for development (see, for example, Midgley, 1999).

Pathology

As we have noted, TA, along with most other psychotherapies, overly emphasises the psychopathology of the client at the expense of acknowledging her or his health, and erroneously places that pathology in the nuclear family. In this case an entire course of therapeutic exchanges may take place which are more the result of practitioners following expectations arising from their theory, rather than the result of careful observation and mutual consideration with the client. Despite this medical background, which, in large part, derives from Berne himself, there is also a strong strand of positive psychology in TA (see, for instance, Cornell, 1988; Summers and Tudor, 2000).

Conservatism

Despite its radical roots and its contribution to the development of radical psychiatry (as noted above pp. 260–2), TA today appears very traditional. The influence of the medical model, especially on notions of 'cure' and (ironically) adaptation to social norms; the predominance of the nuclear family as the basic social and theoretical unit; the largely uncritical acceptance (with the exception of Steiner, 1971b) of diagnosis and diagnostic formulations; and the hierarchical and hegemonic nature of its organisation – all give TA a flavour of being part of the social and psychotherapeutic establishment. This is also offered as a criticism by both Yalom (1970) and Kovel (1976) – and whilst these criticisms are largely rebutted by Stewart (1992), this is no basis for complacency in TA which, in our view, needs to revisit and continue to learn from its radical roots and continue to develop its application to wider social issues (see, for example, Tudor and Hargaden, 2002; and Jabandzic, 2005).

Case example (RH)[1]

The client

One day I received a telephone call from a rather hesitant sounding young man called Simon requesting psychotherapy. I agreed to see him to discuss this. He arrived at my office as planned, and presented as a tall, somewhat scruffily dressed, curly-haired man with an attractive smile. He was 29 years old and working as a child care social worker. He was in a permanent heterosexual relationship. He said he wanted 'to find out more about himself'. He didn't think he had any 'problems' but wanted to make sense of his life.

I later found out that he was the middle child of three boys. He had moved a lot as a young child, estimating that he had lived in five different towns in his first nine years. His father had walked out of the family home when Simon was 9 years old and Simon had had no contact with him since that time. He said this had upset him at the time but he had 'managed fine without him'. He was close to his mother who, he said, had cared well for him and his two brothers. He talked briefly of a step-father from whom he was distant. When Simon was 11 he was sent to a boarding school, a move which he described in terms of great loss, but did not communicate the 'felt' loss of this experience to me. He described his educational experiences as being 'difficult' and described himself as succeeding in getting a university place 'in spite of the teachers'.

Simon had had a number of relationships, none of which had lasted, and he talked of being rejected a number of times. He was currently in a relationship of about six months standing. He spoke highly of his current partner and hoped to establish a long-term relationship.

The therapy

In writing this case study, for ease of reading, I describe a linear process. In fact, the three strands of my TA psychotherapy practice – building the working alliance, restructuring and reorganisation – follow a much less linear or ordered path. In an earlier section (see pp. 275–7 above) we described these strands as 'overlapping'. In the actuality of psychotherapy, the client and I often move from alliance to restructuring to reorganisation and then sometimes back to restructuring and alliance-building again as the relationship develops and more issues emerge.

Establishing and building the therapeutic/working alliance

Simon greeted me nervously, with a distinct shakiness to his voice, and, at the same time, smiled engagingly. I felt engaged with him very quickly and felt rather flattered by his apparent appreciation and respect for me. He treated me as an expert to whom he would defer. There was also a slightly menacing feel to this as if I must be as he expected – rewarding, pleasant and interested in him. I immediately thought about ego states and made tentative guesses as to where he was placing his ego state energy. None of these guesses seemed right to me so I disregarded them, and concentrated on the content of what he was saying.

As I inquired about his life, I was drawn to the narrative Simon told me, and was intrigued by his place in this narrative. He talked about himself a lot but primarily as a man of action. I had no idea as to the inner life of this young man. He talked of 'winning and losing' people, but the 'winning and losing' seemed to have little or no impact on him. A key script narrative he introduced early on centred on his relationship with his father. Again, within his narrative, there seemed to be no place for someone emotionally impacted by his life experiences. I started to imagine that I was talking to Simon's Parent ego state that was protecting his Child ego state from sharing expression with me.

Mindful of our task to establish a working alliance, I began to conceive of one being established around this principal narrative theme of a boy/man who has no father and few means to express his emotional reality. Simon was drawn to establishing more confidence in his life, particularly when he had to exercise authority either at work or in his relationships. As he told me about his long-term wishes for a more satisfying job, and the development of a meaningful relationship, I was able to suggest psychotherapy as way to help him achieve this. I think of psychotherapy as one avenue to develop a greater sense of aliveness. Simon was drawn to psychotherapy as a means for finding this aliveness and I was confident that I could make a contribution to this. Simon quickly demonstrated the establishment of an emotional bond through his interest in me as a therapist. I also felt engaged with him and keen to involve myself in his development. This coupled with his explicit goals around work and love meant that we had established a therapeutic contract leading to an establishment of a working alliance.

Restructuring

Simon then started to embark on the therapeutic task of developing awareness. This enabled him to strengthen his Adult ego state boundary. I have a range of therapeutic actions open to me to encourage Simon in this work.

At the beginning of his therapy Simon focused a lot on me. He would often ask me how my week had gone, and what I had been up to. I would inquire about the nature of my importance to him but to little effect. He would accuse me of 'trying to be like a therapist' and say things like 'Can't I just ask an ordinary question sometimes?' It seemed to me that focusing on the content of his transactions was not succeeding in facilitating the development of his awareness.

I started to notice a transactional pattern emerging whereby Simon did not complete transactions associated with his emotional life. At the same time I was aware of a number of ulterior transactions where he communicated strong anxiety, especially when he sensed that I might not be in agreement with what he was saying, at which moments he chewed his lower lip and squeezed his hands. I began to notice a game emerging between us whereby, in response to these ulterior transactions, I found myself being overly pleasing towards him in case he might get irritated or angry with me. As I inquired about these processes it became apparent to us both that an old drama was unfolding between us in which he anxiously sought out a 'good' father in me – a good father being one who is only pleasing and wholly responsive towards his wishes and needs. At this point in the therapy, Simon decided to attempt to trace his missing father, a decision which indicated to me a strengthened Adult ego state with greater internal resources to deal with the felt experience of his 'father loss'.

Simon started to reflect on his experiences of being with me. He talked about his ambivalent feelings towards me: 'I really want you to like me but also you seem distant, not really interested in me.' He told me how similar his experience of me was to that which he experienced with men in authority at work. He told me how he sought out older men for companionship while, at the same time, being highly self-conscious and cautious about expressing himself. I recognised that he was developing the ability to observe himself: to notice his own experience and to comment upon it with me.

Reorganisation

Simon was now able to engage in the next therapeutic task, that of working through early experiences so that Child and Parent ego state material becomes integrated into the Adult ego state. This involved him living his experiences with me and, specifically, finding a way that he could express and release regressive experiences and feelings so that their potency diminished. He did this in two ways. First his decision to find his missing father provided a whole variety of intense experiences, including recovering past memories that were highly emotionally charged. Secondly, the transactional dramas that emerged between us provided an intensity of experience that enabled him radically to change his way of being with men, and this included him reassessing what being a man meant to him.

At this point in the therapy Simon actually found his missing father. Simon had hoped that, once found, his father would express a new found interest in him. However, this was not to be. Indeed, his father repeated his earlier gross lack of interest in his son, a rejection which resulted in Simon both reliving the past experience and experiencing a 'here-and-now' loss.

While all of this was going on, the game process between us also reached its apotheosis. I was aware of being over–accommodating towards Simon, changing appointment times to fit in with his schedule at times when it was seriously inconvenient for me. I became aware that I was also feeling and limiting the expression of my wishes in relation to Simon. I would rationalise this in terms of 'meeting the client's needs'. Eventually I said 'No' to a request he made for me to change an appointment time. His reaction was surprising and intense. He angrily attacked me for being overly self-interested and not considering his needs. I stood my ground and did not change the appointment time. My willingness to hear his enraged response, and not caving in to it, meant that he was able to start working through the rageful and murderous feelings towards his father that he had kept hidden. For example, in one session, he explored a fantasy of murdering me: holding my dead body in his arms and then feeling the great loss and regret that such an action would cause him.

Simon was now integrating Child ego state experiences into his Adult ego state. He was doing this both through engaging with me in the therapeutic relationship and, specifically, through revealing the difficult and painful fantasies he had about me; and, outside therapy, by taking steps in his life that stimulated new experiences. As the therapy progressed he made a number of highly significant life changes – he changed career to a more satisfying job and he embarked on a new long-term relationship. He seemed to develop the inner confidence in his own masculinity that he lacked when I first met him. We had worked together for a couple of years. The experience had been satisfying and challenging for both of us. At this point I fully supported his decision to leave, having experienced and witnessed him having achieved his contractual goals.

NOTE

1 The personal details of this case example have been written in such a way that the client is not identifiable.

REFERENCES

Agel, J. (ed.) (1971) *The Radical Therapist.* New York: Ballantine.

Allaway, J. (1983) 'Transactional analysis in Britain: [t]he beginnings', *Transactions: Journal of the Institute of Transactional Analysis*, 1: 5–10.

Allen, J. (1998) 'Redecision therapy: through a narrative lens', in M. Hoyt (ed.), *The Handbook of Constructive Therapies.* San Francisco, CA: Jossey-Bass.

Allen, J.R. and Allen, B.A. (1991) 'Towards a constructivist TA', in B. Loria (ed.), *The Stamford Papers: Selections from the 29th Annual ITAA Conference,* pp. 1–22. Madison, WI: Omnipress.

Allen, J.R. and Allen, B.A. (1995) 'Narrative theory, redecision therapy, and postmodernism', *Transactional Analysis Journal,* 25 (4): 327–34.

Allen, J.R. and Allen, B.A. (1997) 'A new type of transactional analysis and one version of script work with a constructivist sensibility', *Transactional Analysis Journal,* 27 (2): 89–98.

Allen, J.R. and Allen, B.A. (2000) 'Every revolution should have dancing: biology, community, organization, constructivism, and joy', *Transactional Analysis Journal,* 30 (3): 188–91.

Association of Humanistic Psychology Practitioners (1998) 'The AHPP statement of core beliefs', *Self & Society,* 26 (3): 3–6.

Barnes, G. (ed.) (1977) *Transactional Analysis After Eric Berne.* New York: Harper's College Press.

Barrett-Lennard, G. (1985) 'The helping relationship: crisis and advance in theory and research', *The Counseling Psychologist,* 13 (2); 279–94.

Barrow, G. and Newton, T. (eds) (2004) *Walking the Talk: How TA is Improving Behaviour and Raising Self-Esteem.* London: David Fulton.

Berne, E. (1958) 'Transactional analysis: a new and effective method of group therapy', *American Journal of Psychotherapy,* 11: 293–309.

Berne, E. (1963) *The Structure and Dynamics of Organizations and Groups.* New York: Grove Press.

Berne, E. (1966) *Principles of Group Treatment.* New York: Grove Press.

Berne, E. (1968a) *Games People Play.* Harmondsworth: Penguin. (Original work published 1964.)

Berne, E. (1968b) 'Staff–patient staff conferences', *American Journal of Psychiatry,* 123 (3): 286–93.

Berne, E. (1971a) *A Layman's Guide to Psychiatry and Psychoanalysis.* Harmondsworth: Penguin.

Berne, E. (1971b) 'Away from a theory of the impact of interpersonal interaction on non–verbal participation', *Transactional Analysis Journal,* 1 (1): 6–13.

Berne, E. (1975a) *Transactional Analysis in Psychotherapy.* London: Souvenir Press. (Original work Published 1961.)

Berne, E. (1975b) *What Do You Say After You Say Hello?* London: Corgi. (Original work Published 1972.)

Bordin, E.S. (1975) 'The generalizability of the psychoanalytic concept of the working alliance', *Psychotherapy: Theory, Research and Practice,* 16: 252–60.

Campos, L.P. (2003) 'Care and maintenance of the tree of transactional analysis', *Transactional Analysis Journal,* 33 (2): 115–25.

Cassoni, E. (ed.) (2003) *Trame ed Esistenze* [The Warp and Weft of Life]. Milano: La Vita Felice.

Childs–Gowell, E. (1979) *Reparenting Schizophrenics: The Cathexis Experience.* North Quincey, MA: The Christopher Publishing House.

Clark, B.D. (1991) 'Empathic transactions in the deconfusion of ego states', *Transactional Analysis Journal,* 22 (2): 92–98.

Clarkson, P. (1992) *Transactional Analysis Psychotherapy: An Integrated Approach.* London: Routledge.

Clarkson, P., and Gilbert, M. (1990) 'Transactional analysis', In W. Dryden (ed.), *Individual Therapy: A Handbook.* Buckingham: Open University. pp.199–225.

Clarkson, P., Gilbert, M. and Tudor, K. (1996) 'Transactional analysis', in W. Dryden (ed.) *Handbook of Individual Therapy.* London: Sage. pp. 219–53.

Collinson, L. (1983) 'Autonomy soon?: A brief history of transactional analysis in Britain', *Transactions: Journal of the Institute of Transactional Analysis,* 1: 11–12.

Collinson, L. (1984) 'Transactional analysis', In W. Dryden (ed.) *Individual Therapy: A Handbook,.* London: Harper Row Press. pp. 205–34.

Cornell, B. and Hargaden, H. (eds) (2005) *From Transactions to Relations: the Emergence of a Relational Tradition in Transactional Analysis.* Chadlington: Haddon Press.

Cornell, W.F. (1988) 'Life script theory: a critical review from a developmental perspective', *Transactional Analysis Journal,* 18 (4): 270–82.

Dashiell, S.R. (1978) 'The Parent resolution process: reprogramming psychic incorporations in the Parent', *Transactional Analysis Journal*, 8 (4): 289–95.

Drego, P. (1983) 'The cultural Parent', *Transactional Analysis Journal*, 13 (4): 224–7.

English, F. (1971) 'The substitution factor, rackets and real feelings', *Transactional Analysis Journal*, 1(4): 225–30.

Erikson, E. (1951) *Childhood and Society*. New York: W.W. Norton.

Erikson, E. (1968) *Identity, Youth and Crisis*. New York: W.W. Norton.

Erskine, R. and Moursund, J. (1988) *Integrative Psychotherapy in Action*. Newbury Park, CA: Sage.

Erskine, R. and Trautmann, R. (1996) 'Methods of an integrative psychotherapy', *Transactional Analysis Journal*, 26 (4): 316–28.

Erskine, R. and Zalcman, M.J. (1979) 'The racket system: a model for racket analysis', *Transactional Analysis Journal*, 9 (1): 51–9.

European Association for Transactional Analysis. (EATA) (1998) 'Ethics guidelines', in *Training and Examination Handbook*. Nottingham: EATA.

European Association for Transactional Analysis (EATA) Professional Standards and Training Committee. (2001) *PTSC Telegram No.15*. Aix-en-Provence: EATA.

European Association for Transactional Analysis (EATA) Professional Standards and Training Committee. (2005) *Core Competencies – Psychotherapy*. Aix-en-Provence: EATA. Available online at: http://www.eatanews.org/content/view/8/69/. (Original work published 1999.)

Federn, P. (1952) *Ego Psychology and the Psychoses*. New York: Basic Books.

Filippi, S. (ed.) (2003) *Incipit: I Modi del Primo Colloquio* [Incipit: The Characteristics of the Initial Meeting]. Milano: La Vita Felice.

Friedlander, M.G. (ed.) (1988) Ego states [Special issue]. *Transactional Analysis Journal*, *18*(1).

Goulding, M. and Goulding, R. (1979) *Changing Lives Through Redecision Therapy*. New York: Brunner-Mazel.

Hargaden, H. and Sills, C. (2002) *Transactional Analysis: A Relational Perspective*. London: Routledge.

Holloway, W.H. (1973) 'Shut the escape hatch', Monograph IV in *The Monograph Series I–X*. Medina, OH: Midwest Institute of Human Understanding. pp. 15–18.

Holloway, W.H. (1977) 'Transactional analysis: an integrative view', in G. Barnes (ed.) *Transactional Analysis After Eric Berne*. New York: Harper's College Press. pp.169–221.

International Transactional Analysis Association. (ITAA) (1989) *Statement of Ethics*. Available from the ITAA, 2186 Rheem Drive #B–1, Pleasanton, California, CA 94588.

Jabandzic, N. (2005) *Wenn der Krieg patriotisch ist, ist der Frieden matriotisch? Zur Krise der bosnischen Identität* [If War is Patriotic, is Peace Matriotic? The Crises of Bosnian Identity]. Klagenfurt: Wieser.

Jacobs, A. (1987) 'Autocratic power', *Transactional Analysis Journal*, 17 (3): 59–71.

Jacobs, A. (2000) 'Psychic organs, ego states, and visual metaphors: speculation on Berne's integration of ego states', *Transactional Analysis Journal*, 30 (1): 10–22.

James, M. (1974) 'Self–reparenting: Theory and process', *Transactional Analysis Journal*, 4 (3): 32–9.

James, M. (1977) 'Eric Berne, the development of TA and the ITAA', in M. James (ed.), *Techniques in Transactional Analysis for Psychotherapists and Counsellors*. Reading, MA: Addison-Wesley.

James, M. (1981) *Breaking Free: Self–Reparenting for a New Life*. Reading, MA: Addison-Wesley.

Joines, V. and Stewart, I. (2002). *Personality Adaptations: A New Guide to Human Understanding in Psychotherapy & Counselling*. Nottingham: Lifespace Publishing.

Kahler, T. (1979) *Process Therapy in Brief*. Little Rock, AR: Human Development Publications.

Karpman, S. (1968) 'Fairy tales and script drama analysis', *Transactional Analysis Bulletin*, 7 (26): 39–43.

Kouwenhoven, M., Kiltz, R.R. and Elbing, U. (2002) *Schwere Persönlichkeitsstörungen: Transaktionsanalytische Behandlung nach dem Cathexis–Ansatz* [Severe Personality Disorders: TA Treatment Following the Principles of Cathexis]. Vienna: Springer.

Kovel, J. (1976) *A Complete Guide to Therapy*. Harmondsworth: Penguin.

Lapworth, P., Sills, C. and Fish, S. (1993) *Transactional Analysis Counselling*. Bicester: Winslow.

Lee, A. (1997) 'Process contracts', in C. Sills (ed.), *Contracts in Counselling*. London: Sage. pp. 94–112.

Lee, A. (2001). *The Schools of Change.* Workshop presentation, The Berne Institute, Kegworth, June.

Le Guernic, A. (2004) *États du Moi, Transactions et Communication: Savoir enfin que Dire après Avoir dit Bonjour!* [Egostates, Transactions and Communication: Knowing What to Say After You Say Hello!]. Paris: InterEditions.

Ligabue, S. (ed.) (2004) *Linguaggi in Connessione* [Connecting Languages]. Milano: La Vita Felice.

Ligabue, S. (ed.) (2005) *Dedicato ai Sogni* [Dedicated to Dreams]. Milano: La Vita Felice.

Lister-Ford, C. (2002) *Skills in Transactional Analysis Counselling and Psychotherapy.* London: Sage.

Loria, B. (ed.) (1991) *The Stamford Papers: Selections from the 29th Annual ITAA Conference.* Madison, WI: Omnipress.

Loria, B. and Allen, J. (eds) (1997) 'TA and Constructivism' [special issue], *Transactional Analysis Journal,* 27(2).

Martorell, J.L. (2002) *El Analisis de Juego Transactionales: Un Estudio Empirico* [The Concept of Transactional Games: An Empirical Study. Madrid: Uned.

Mazzetti, M. (ed.) (2004) *La Supervisione: Scambi di Saperi* [Supervision: Exchanging Knowledge]. Milano: La Vita Felice.

Mclendon, R. and Kadis, L.B. (1983) *Chocolate Pudding and Other Approaches to Intensive Multiple–Family Therapy.* Palo Alto, CA: Science & Behavior Books.

McNeel, J.R. (1977) 'The seven components of redecision therapy', in G. Barnes (ed.), *Transactional Analysis After Eric Berne* New York: Harper's College Press. pp. 425–41.

Mellor, K. (1980) 'Impasses: a developmental and structural understanding', *Transactional Analysis Journal,* 10 (3): 213–20.

Mellor, K. and Andrewartha, G. (1980) 'Reparenting the parent in support of redecisions', *Transactional Analysis Journal,* 10 (3): 197–203.

Midgley, D. (1999) *New Directions in Transactional Analysis Counselling: An Explorer's Handbook.* London: Free Association Books.

Moiso, C. (1983) L'analisi strutturale delle relazioni transferali. [Structural analysis of transferential relations]. *Neopsiche,* 1(1): 16–19.

Moiso, C. (1985) 'Ego states and transference', *Transactional Analysis Journal,* 15 (3): 194–201.

Moiso, C. and Novellino, M. (2000) 'An overview of the psychodynamic school of transactional analysis', *Transactional Analysis Journal,* 30 (3): 182–87.

Mothersole, G. (1996) 'Existential realities and no–suicide contracts', *Transactional Analysis Journal,* 26 (2): 151–60.

Mothersole, G. (1997) 'Contracts and harmful behaviour', in C. Sills (ed.), *Contracts in Counselling* London: Sage. pp.113–24.

Mothersole, G. (2002) 'TA as short–term cognitive therapy', in K. Tudor (ed.), *Transactional Analysis Approaches to Brief Therapy.* London: Sage. pp. 64–82.

Mountain, A. (2004) *The Space Between: Bridging the Gap between Workers and Young People.* Lyme Regis: Russell House.

Moursund, J. and Erskine, R. (2003) *Integrative Psychotherapy: The Art and Science of Relationship.* Belmont, CA: Wadsworth Publishing.

Müller, U. and Tudor, K. (2001) 'Transactional analysis as brief therapy', in K. Tudor (ed.), *Transactional Analysis Approaches to Brief Therapy.* London: Sage. pp. 19–44.

Munari Poda, D. (2003) *L'adolescenza Accade* [Adolescence Happens]. Milano: La Vita Felice.

Novellino, M. (1984) 'Self-analysis of countertransference in integrative transactional analysis,' *Transactional Analysis Journal,* 14 (1): 63–67.

Novellino, M. (1990) 'Unconscious communication and interpretation in transactional analysis', *Transactional Analysis Journal,* 20 (3): 168–73.

Novellino, M. (2004) *Psicoanalisi Transazionale; Manuale di Psicodinamica Relazionale per Psicoterapeuti e Counsellor* [Transactional Psychoanalysis: A Manual of Psychodynamic Relations for Psychotherapists and Counsellors]. Milano: Franco Angeli.

Novellino, M. and Moiso, C. (1990) 'The psychodynamic approach to transactional analysis', *Transactional Analysis Journal,* 20 (3): 87–92.

Osnes, R.E. (1974) 'Spot reparenting', *Transactional Analysis Journal,* (3): 40–6.

Penfield, W. (1952) 'Memory mechanisms', *Archives of Neurology and Psychiatry,* 67: 178–98.

Pierre, N. (2002) *Pratique de l'Analyse Transactionnelle dans la classe* [Applying Transactional Analysis in the Classroom]. Issy–les–Moulineaux: ESF.

Risto, K.H. (2004) *Konflikte lösen mit System* [Solving Conflict in Systems]. Paderborn: Junfermann.

Schiff, J.L., Schiff, A.W., Mellor, K., Schiff, E., Schiff, S., Richman, D., Fishman, J., Wolz, L., Fishman, C. and Momb, D. (1975) *Cathexis Reader: Transactional Analysis Treatment of Psychosis.* New York: Harper & Row.

Schmid, B. (2003) *Systemische Professionalität und Transaktionsanalyse* [Systemic Professionalism and Transactional Analysis]. Köln: Edition Humanistische Psychologie.

Schmuckler, D. (1991) 'Transference and transactions: perspectives from developmental theory, objects relations, and transformational processes', *Transactional Analysis Journal,* 21 (3): 127–35.

Schneider, J. (2002) *Auf dem Weg zum Ziel* [Achieving your Goal]. Paderborn: Junfermann.

Sills, C. (ed.) (2006) *Contracts in Counselling',* 2nd edn. London: Sage.

Sills, C. and Hargaden, H. (eds) (2003) *Ego States.* London: Worth Reading.

Steiner, C. (1966) 'Script and counterscript', *Transactional Analysis Bulletin,* 5 (18): 133–5.

Steiner, C. (1971a) *Games Alcoholics Play.* New York: Grove Press.

Steiner, C. (1971b) 'Radical psychiatry: Principles', In J. Agel (ed.), *The Radical Therapist.* New York: Ballantine. pp. 3–7.

Steiner, C. (1974) *Scripts People Live.* New York: Bantam.

Steiner, C. (2000) 'Radical psychiatry', in R.J. Corsini (ed.), *Handbook of Innovative Therapy,* Chichester: Wiley. pp. 578–86.

Stewart, I. (1989) *Transactional Analysis Counselling in Action.* London: Sage.

Stewart, I. (1992) *Eric Berne.* London: Sage.

Stewart, I. (1996) *Developing Transactional Analysis Counselling.* London: Sage.

Stewart, I. and Joines, V. (1987) *TA Today.* Nottingham: Lifespace Publishing.

Summers, G. and Tudor, K. (2000) 'Cocreative transactional analysis', *Transactional Analysis Journal,* 30 (1): 23–40.

Tudor, K. (1996) 'Transactional analysis *intra*gration: a metatheoretical analysis for practice', *Transactional Analysis Journal,* 26: 329–40.

Tudor, K. (1999a) *Group Counselling.* London: Sage.

Tudor, K. (1999b) '"I'm OK, You're OK – and They're OK": therapeutic relationships in transactional Analysis', In C. Feltham (Ed.), *Understanding the Counselling Relationship.* London: Sage. pp. 90–119.

Tudor, K. (ed.) (2002) *Transactional Approaches to Brief Therapy or What Do You Say Between Saying Hello and Goodbye?* London: Sage.

Tudor, K. (2003) 'The neopsyche: the integrating Adult ego state', in C. Sills and H. Hargaden (eds), *Ego States.* London: Worth Reading. pp. 201–31.

Tudor, K. (2007, in press) *The Adult is Parent to the Child: Using Transactional Analysis Working with Children and Young People.* Lyme Regis: Russell House Press.

Tudor, K. and Hargaden, H. (2002) 'The couch and the ballot box: the contribution and potential of psychotherapy in enhancing citizenship', in C. Feltham (ed.), *What's the Good of Counselling and Psychotherapy?: The Benefits Explained.* London: Sage. pp. 156–78.

Tudor, K. and Hobbes, R. (2002) 'Transactional analysis', in W. Dryden (ed.), *Handbook of Individual Therapy,* 4th edn. London: Sage. pp. 239–65

Vogelauer, W. (2005a) *Coaching Praxis.* München: Luchterhand.

Vogelauer, W. (2005b) *Methoden ABC im Training* [Using ABC Methods in Training]. München: Luchterhand.

Weiss, E. (1950) *Principles of Psychodynamics.* New York: Grune & Strutton.

Woollams, S. and Brown, M. (1979) *Transactional Analysis*. Dexter, MI: Huron Valley Institute.
Wyckoff, H. (ed.) (1976) *Love, Therapy and Politics: Issues in Radical Therapy – The First Year*. New York: Grove Press.
Yalom, I.D. (1970) *The Theory and Practice of Group Psychotherapy*. New York: Basic Books.

SUGGESTED FURTHER READING

Berne, E. (1975a) *Transactional Analysis in Psychotherapy*. London: Souvenir Press. (Original work Published 1961.)
Cornell, B. and Hargaden, H. (eds) (2005) *From Transactions to Relations: the Emergence of a Relational Tradition in Transactional Analysis*. Chadlington: Haddon Press.
Erskine, R. and Trautmann, R. (1999) *Beyond Empathy: A Therapy of Contact–in–Relationship*. New York: Brunner/Mazel.
Stewart, I. (1992) *Eric Berne*. London: Sage.
Tudor, K. (ed.) (2002) *Transactional Approaches to Brief Therapy or What do You Say Between Saying Hello and Goodbye?* London: Sage.

11

Cognitive Analytic Therapy

Mark Dunn

HISTORICAL CONTEXT AND DEVELOPMENT IN BRITAIN

Historical context

Cognitive Analytic Theory (CAT) was developed by Dr Anthony Ryle, Consultant Psychotherapist, over a period of 25 years commencing around 1975. It was his intention to develop an integrative therapy which would make use of the theoretical insights of cognitive-behavioural therapy and the object relations theorists of the British School, hence the therapy's name. The urge towards integration came partly from frustration with the divided nature of psychotherapy practice in the UK, partly from intellectual frustration with the philosophical positions adopted by some mainstream theorists and partly from the urge to give access to psychotherapeutic help to those most often excluded by reason of poor health service provision or through a perception of their insufficient intellectual development. In a nutshell he is against the 'balkanization' of psychotherapy and its resulting tower of psycho-babel, and in favour of pragmatics and public usability.

The integrative theory of CAT was developed to provide an accessible model of mental functioning and a time-limited and focused practice for both the staff and patients of the NHS. It is essentially a constructivist model of how the mind works and how it interacts with other minds; it is based in the language of cognitive psychology which is seen as the most accessible language for describing mental processes; it seeks to build bridges to all theories from a notional starting point, acknowledging that the truth of how the mind works is unlikely ever to be fully known and even less likely to be encompassed by any one theory; it proposes that the more theoretical and practical tools there can be integrated in the psychotherapist's tool box the better.

CAT's historical roots lie in both the European tradition of psychoanalytic thinking and the North American tradition of cognitive psychology. In CAT these ideas are seen as being like flour and yeast in the making of bread and not, as is sometimes suggested, the oil and vinegar in salad dressing which may be shaken together but in reality do not mix. CAT holds that, while the unleavened bread of CBT has nutritional value and the yeast of psychoanalysis has flavour (perhaps an acquired taste like Marmite), needed [sic] together in CAT they are more palatable and satisfying. However, not everything can be translated – CAT tends to see the dynamic unconscious as an unnecessary construction and the information-processing models of cognitive theory to be inhuman. The water in the bread would be the semiotic understanding of the social construction of the mind in the inter-subjective field and how this is expressed in voice, language and the body – gesture.

Development in Britain

Ryle started his career after the Second World War as a GP and became interested in counselling patients with common psychiatric and neurotic problems. He moved to Sussex University health service to provide psychoanalytic type individual and group therapy to students. He developed research into neurosis based on Kelly's (1955) essentially cognitive repertory grid technique attempting to describe psychoanalytic formulations in cognitive behavioural language (Ryle, 1975). He found that 'descriptions of patients' problems based on repertory grid testing produced more precise, acceptable and useful descriptions of the patients' difficulties than did those based on hypotheses based on psychoanalytic theory' (Ryle, 1990: 2). These researches led to an interest in the possibilities for integrating psychotherapy theories by way of a common language, using cognitive language to translate psychoanalytic theory (Ryle, 1978) and naming three common types of neurotic problem understood in this way, as Dilemmas, Traps and Snags (Ryle, 1979).

In 1982 Ryle was appointed to the post of Consultant Psychotherapist at St Thomas's and Guy's Hospitals in London and commenced to develop CAT as a brief, focused, integrative, individual psychotherapy treatment for NHS patients. He published many papers and two main books developing the core integrative theory of the Procedural Sequence Object Relations Model (PSORM) (Ryle, 1982, 1985, 1990). During this period Ryle was also experimenting with practical innovations that would facilitate brief treatment by focusing on target problems including the use of questionnaires such as the CAT Psychotherapy File, prose reformulation letters to the patient summarizing understandings, the use of flow chart style diagrams as well as techniques from CBT such as diary keeping and rating sheets. In keeping with the integrative ethos Ryle would exclude nothing that might support and motivate both the client and the therapist and empower them to make changes.

In the 1990s Ryle continued to pursue the integration of theory and the establishment of CAT in his writings (Ryle, 1994a, 1994b, 1995a; Ryle et al., 1992). He extended the theory and practice to understand personality disorders, particularly Borderlines (Ryle, 1995b, 1997a, 1997b; Ryle and Beard, 1993; Ryle and Marlowe, 1995; Ryle and Golynkina, 1999) and conducted debate with Kleinian and other psychoanalytic writers (Ryle, 1992, 1993, 1995c, 1996, 1998; Ryle and Fonagy, 1995). In collaboration with Finnish psychologist Mikael Leiman he extended CAT theory to integrate the activity theory of Russian psychologist Vygotsky and the semiotic theory of Bakhtin (Ryle, 1991; Leiman, 1992, 1994, 1995, 1997). Psychotherapists who have trained in CAT have published research and practical papers describing the application of CAT in different the settings – eating disorders (Treasure et al., 1995, 1997; Bell, 1996), deliberate self-harm (Cowmeadow, 1994; Sheard et al., 2000), survivors of sexual abuse (Clarke and Llewelyn, 1994), non-compliant diabetics (Fosbury et al., 1997), forensic offenders (Pollock, 1996, 1997; Pollock and Kear-Colwell, 1994), group CAT treatment (Mitzman and Duignan, 1993, 1994), organisational environments and systems (Walsh, 1996; Kerr, 1999), and the treatment of alcoholics (Leighton, 1995, 1997). Three recent books bring CAT up to date: Ryle and Kerr (2002); Pollock (2001); and Hepple and Sutton (2004).

Ryle retired from the NHS in 1995 but continues to write, research and teach part time as Emeritus Consultant Psychotherapist at Guy's Hospital. His special interest is in researching the treatment of Borderline and other personality disorders. His early students formed the Association for Cognitive Analytic Therapy (ACAT) in 1990 to promote research and training and to represent and develop the membership. CAT has been taken up mainly within the NHS (for which it was designed) and there are training courses throughout the UK.

Case example

The client

Anne, a 30-year old white married woman, was referred for psychotherapy due to feeling overwhelmed by obsessive and jealous thoughts about her husband. She had had a difficult and unstable childhood having been brought up mostly by her maternal grandmother and a great-aunt as a result of her virtual abandonment by her widowed mother. She had a history of a generally chaotic and promiscuous life style as a teenager with excessive consumption of alcohol and illicit drugs. She had received a diagnosis of Borderline Personality Disorder (BPD). She had two children, a daughter aged eight, from a previous relationship and a son aged eight months from her current marriage. It became apparent in the early stages of therapy that Anne was pregnant with her third child, although this was not disclosed at the time of her assessment.

The therapy

From the outset Anne appeared to engage well with the therapy, wanting to make the most of the process. At assessment she had welcomed the diagnostic label of 'personality disorder' – she felt that this more appropriately recognised her sense of suffering than being labelled as 'just' depressed. She gave a clear presentation of erratic and fragmented relationships and unpredictable behaviour with an unstable sense of self. Her diagnosis was borne out by the Structured Clinical Interview for DSM-IV Axis II Personality Disorders test (SCID-II).

Anne identified two principal issues that she wanted to focus on:

- The first was her difficulty in managing her jealousy in relation to her husband. She would construct elaborate fantasies about what he might do with other women and she would imagine that he would watch pornographic films on the television after she had gone to bed.
- The second was her wish to deal with the 'lost years' of her early life. This concerned both the disturbed years during her teenage and early twenties as well as her earlier childhood, the neglect by her mother and the strictness of the Catholic upbringing that she had experienced from her grandmother and her great-aunt.

A contract for 20 sessions was made taking account of her pregnancy. She engaged well with the early stages of therapy and with the 'homework' tasks, keeping a 'mood' diary and producing a useful timeline. In her psychotherapy file, as might be expected with someone with a diagnosis of BPD, there were 14 items checked in the section concerned with different self-states.

At the sixth session Anne was given the following reformulation:

Now that we have seen each other for five sessions, the time has come for us to take stock and to summarise some of the main issues that have emerged in your therapy so far. This will help us to prepare for the work that we do together during the next 14 sessions.

You decided to seek help with trying to deal with the 'lost years' of your youth and the way that your behaviour and general life style during that time might have given rise to the difficulties that you currently face. In this connection we have talked about your intense feelings of jealousy and the obsessive thoughts that tend to pre-occupy your mind. We have also discussed your frequent and marked mood swings. You have said that both your obsessive thoughts and your mood swings were moderated by antidepressant medication; however, you have stopped taking this because you are now pregnant.

You have told me something of your childhood and early adult life. This seemed to be dominated by your sense of being abandoned. First by your mother, your father having been stabbed to death in a pub brawl when you were very little, and then later by others whom you relied upon. You were, however, looked after by – in fact more or less brought up by – your maternal grandmother and her sister, your great-aunt.

This abandonment, in conjunction with the very strict regime that your grandmother and great-aunt imposed upon you, led to a sense of rebellion and you running wild as a teenager. You abused alcohol and drugs and became sexually promiscuous from about the age of 13. It was as if you were both seeking to escape from, and perhaps also trying to 'keep up with', the harshness of much of what surrounded you. You became involved in a stormy and mutually abusive relationship with Bill, who is the father of your daughter Mary. This relationship came to an end in your early twenties.

These turbulent times began to diminish when you became involved with Alcoholics Anonymous and then met Tom with whom you have had your son, 'little' Tom. You have not now had any alcohol for seven years and you recognise that your relationship with Tom is fundamentally strong, despite the intense feelings of jealousy, which you often have.

You have told me that you often feel as if there are different parts of you that do not feel as if they belong to each other (you have often described them as 'heaven' and 'hell'). There is that part of you which is confident and content and then there is another part that is consumed with self-doubt and difficult, destructive feelings. You can switch between these two parts of your self, or self-states, very quickly with seemingly the smallest event or feeling triggering the change. It has also become clear that you are inclined to deny or shut off your emotions, in particular those that you have difficulty in dealing with. You seem to be good at describing and analysing yourself at an intellectual level whilst having difficulty in experiencing the emotion that belongs with the description and analysis.

It might be helpful at this point to spend a moment considering a bit of the theory that underlies the therapy model that we are working with. In doing so I don't want you to be daunted or overwhelmed but I do feel that you will be able to get more out of the therapy with this understanding.

It is often the case that what is learnt or experienced by someone as a child informs their thinking and behaviour as an adult. It is as though there is an internal relationship, or dialogue, between the child and the adult. This leads to what we know as reciprocal roles (i.e. the way the adult part, or role, reciprocates the child role and vice versa – this can be in the way someone relates either with themselves or with another person). Sometimes the relationships within and between these roles can create tensions and problems and an understanding of these relationships can be the key to resolving difficulties.

We will want to explore all of this, as it relates to you, as the therapy progresses so that we can try to understand the relevant links with the past that contribute to your feelings and behaviour now. As you will appreciate this is to do with both the way that you relate to yourself as well as the way that you relate to others (including me). It seems to me that there are a number of reciprocal roles that emerge from what you have told me, these include: abandoning–abandoned; abusing-abused; controlling–submissive or rebellious; cut off–withdrawn; perfectly caring–perfectly cared for; forgiving–forgiven. We will discuss these roles more during our sessions together, the ones you take and the ones others take towards you.

We will construct a diagram that will help to recognise and make sense of the origin of your self-states and the way that they are connected to each other in relation to your reciprocal roles. In this way we will hope to be able to devise the means of being able to find better ways of coping. We will thus be able to address the problem you have that can be described as 'I don't know how to maintain a coherent sense of myself'.

I look forward to continuing to work with you Anne. I think that we both know that the journey through therapy may not be easy but I believe that with your determination and commitment it will be one worth making. We must be careful that we

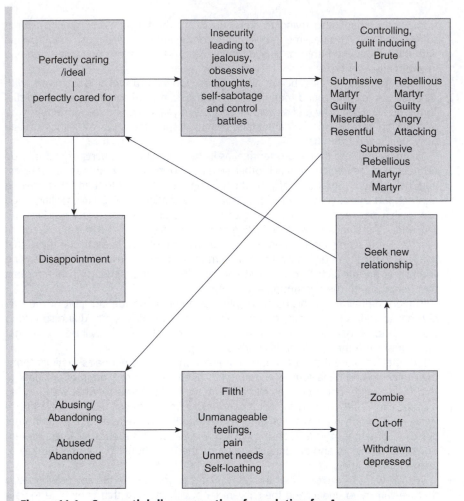

Figure 11.1   Sequential diagrammatic reformulation for Anne

do not become over pressurised or rushed during the therapy by the impending birth of your baby.

An SDR was developed (see Figure 11.1).

As the therapy progressed it was possible to agree a principal target problem: "I know how to maintain a coherent sense of myself". This was underpinned by a number of subsidiary target problems, including:

- jealous and inappropriate rage with her husband.
- uncontrollable mood swings.
- a difficult relationship with her mother due to feeling that, as a child, she never had the mothering that she deserved.
- a need to understand her 'lost years' as a younger person.

The principal procedures that were identified from the large number highlighted in the CAT Psychotherapy File were:

- Social isolation trap
- Depressed thinking trap
- Internal self-sabotage snag
- Brute or martyr self to other dilemma

There were two chief self-states that seemed to describe the difficulties that Anne experienced:

- The first she called the '**filth**' which was the state that was filled with self-loathing and took her back to the times when she had been out of control with the abuse of alcohol and drugs and her promiscuous behaviour.
- The second she referred to as her '**zombie**' state when she felt cut off and disconnected from her feelings; she would retreat to this state to escape from intolerable emotional pain.

Once the reformulation was completed it was possible to begin to concentrate on the task of facilitating the recognition and revision processes. To begin with this was difficult for Anne; she would fill the sessions with superficial rambling so as to avoid having to go beneath the surface where she feared she would not be able to 'breathe'. In due course Anne was able to come closer to the previously unattainable feelings. She said that her emotions were becoming more fluid and flexible than previously. She described having a knot inside her that was full of unexpressed emotion that she experienced as physical pain. One device that seemed to be helpful in trying to access these feelings was for Anne to write a letter to the pain in which she expressed her deep sense of shame and anger.

Anne went on to explore her relationship with her late grandmother ('Nan'). She did this with 'empty-chair' technique to address her grandmother in the room. The relationship with her grandmother became increasingly important in the therapy and provided the exit from the maladaptive procedures and the means to move towards the integration of her dissociated self-states.

As the therapy drew to a close the issue of the ending took on a sharp focus; in Anne's case this was all the more relevant due to the impending birth of her child. In her 'goodbye' letter Anne noted '... I realise the great freedom I have been given from the chains of my past, I no longer feel shackled to it ...' She went on to say '...I had a lot of preconceptions before I came to therapy, like I wanted a woman [therapist], we would deal with this and that, I'd be taught how not to be jealous and obsessive and go away fixed. But it wasn't like that, for a start you turned out to be a man (a very safe man), you were always warm and clear. I didn't feel any badness from you which is rare, almost like God was working through you sometimes ...'. It is clear from this that there was a danger that Anne idealised the therapy and the therapist; however the therapy did appear to have beneficial effect (as borne out by the pre- and post-therapy test scores for the various psychometrics used), notwithstanding this idealisation.

REFERENCES

Bell, L. (1996) 'CAT: its value in the treatment of people with eating disorders', *Clinical Psychology Forum*, 92: 5–10.

Clarke, S. and Llewelyn, S. (1994) 'Personal constructs of survivors of childhood sexual abuse receiving cognitive analytic therapy', *British Journal of Medical Psychology*, 67: 273–89.

Cowmeadow, P. (1994) 'Deliberate self-harm and cognitive analytic therapy', *International Journal of Short-term Psychotherapy* 9, 2/3, 135–50.

Fosbury, J.A., Bosley, C.M., Ryle, A., Sonksen, P.H. and Judd, S.L. (1997) 'A trial of cognitive analytic therapy in poorly controlled Type I patients', *Diabetes Care*, 20 (6): 959–64.

Hepple, J. and Sutton, L. (eds) (2004) *CAT and Later Life, a New Perspective on Old Age*. Hove/New York: Brunner Routledge.

Kelly, G. (1955) *The Psychology of Personal Constructs*. New York: Norton.

Kerr, I. (1999) 'Cognitive analytic therapy for borderline personality disorder in the context of a community mental health team', *British Journal of Psychotherapy*, 15: 425–38.

Leighton, T. (1995) 'A cognitive analytic understanding of "Twelve Step" treatment', *New Directions in the Study of Alcohol Groups*, 20 (November).

Leighton, T. (1997) 'Borderline personality disorder and substance abuse problems', in A. Ryle (ed.), *Cognitive Analytic Therapy and Borderline Personality Disorder: the Model and the Method*. Chichester, Wiley.

Leiman, M. (1992) 'The concept of sign in the work of Vygotsky, Winnicott and Bakhtin: further integration of object relations theory and activity theory', *British Journal of Medical Psychology*, 65: 209–21.

Leiman, M. (1994) 'Projective identification as early joint action sequences; a Vygotskian addendum to the Procedural Sequence Object Relations Model', *British Journal of Medical Psychology*, 67: 97–106.

Leiman, M. (1995) 'Early development', in A. Ryle (ed.), *Cognitive Analytic Therapy: Developments in Theory and Practice*. Chichester: John Wiley.

Leiman, M. (1997) 'Procedures as dialogical sequences: a revised version of the fundamental concept in CAT', *British Journal of Medical Psychology*, 70 (2): 193–207.

Mitzman, S. and Duignan, I. (1993) 'One man's group: brief CAT group therapy and the use of SDR', *Counselling Psychology Quarterly*, 6 (3): 183–92.

Mitzman, S. and Duignan, I. (1994) 'Change in patients receiving time limited cognitive analytic group therapy', *International Journal of Short-Term Psychotherapy*, 9 (2/3): 151–60.

Pollock, P.H. (1996) 'Clinical issues in the CAT of sexually abused women who commit violent offences against their partners', *British Journal of Medical Psychology*, 69, 117–27.

Pollock, P.H. (1997) 'CAT of an offender with borderline personality', in A. Ryle (ed.), *Cognitive Analytic Therapy and Borderline Personality Disorder: the Model and the Method*. Chichester: Wiley.

Pollock, P.H. (2001) *CAT for Adult Survivors of Childhood Abuse*. Chichester: Wiley.

Pollock, P.H. and Kear-Colwell, J.J. (1994) 'Women who stab: a personal construct analysis of sexual victimization and offending behaviour', *British Journal of Medical Psychology*, 67: 13–22.

Ryle, A. (1975) *Frames and Cages*. London: Chatto and Windus.

Ryle, A. (1978) 'A common language for the psychotherapies', *British Journal of Psychiatry*, 132: 585–94.

Ryle, A. (1979) 'The focus in brief interpretive psychotherapy: dilemmas, traps and snags as target problems', *British Journal of Psychiatry*, 134: 46–54.

Ryle, A. (1982) *Psychotherapy: A Cognitive Integration of Theory and Practice*. London: Academic Press.

Ryle, A. (1985) 'Cognitive theory, object relations and the self', *British Journal of Medical Psychology*, 58: 1–7.

Ryle, A. (1990) *Cognitive Analytic Therapy: Active Participation in Change*. Chichester & New York: John Wiley.

Ryle, A. (1991) 'Object relations theory and activity theory: a proposed link by way of the procedural sequence model', *British Journal of Medical Psychology*, 64: 307–16.

Ryle, A. (1992) 'Critique of a Kleinian case presentation', *British Journal of Medical Psychology*, 65: 309–17.

Ryle, A. (1993) 'Addiction to the death instinct? A critical review of Joseph's paper "Addiction to near death"', *British Journal of Psychotherapy*, 10: 88–92.

Ryle, A. (1994a) 'Projective identification: a particular form of reciprocal role procedure', *British Journal of Medical Psychology*, 67: 107–14.

Ryle, A. (1994b) 'Consciousness and psychotherapy', *British Journal of Medical Psychology*, 67: 115–23.

Ryle, A. (1995a) *Cognitive Analytic Therapy: Developments in Theory and Practice*. Chichester: Wiley.

Ryle, A. (1995b) 'Transference and counter-transference variations in the course of cognitive analytic therapy of two borderline patients: the relation to the diagrammatic reformulation of self-states', *British Journal of Medical Psychology*, 68: 109–24.

Ryle, A. (1995c) 'Defensive organizations or collusive interpretations? A further critique of Kleinian theory and practice', *British Journal of Psychotherapy*, 12 (1): 60–6.

Ryle, A. (1996) 'Ogden's autistic-contiguous position and the role of interpretation in psychoanalytic theory building', *British Journal of Medical Psychology*, 69: 129–38.

Ryle, A. (1997a) 'The structure and development of borderline personality disorder: a proposed model', *British Journal of Psychiatry*, 170: 82–7.

Ryle, A. (1997b) *Cognitive Analytic Therapy and Borderline Personality Disorder: The Model and the Method*. Chichester: Wiley.

Ryle, A. (1998) 'Tranceferences and countertransferences: the cognitive analytic therapy perspective', *British Journal of Psychotherapy*, 14 (3): 303–9.

Ryle, A. and Beard, H. (1993) 'The integrative effect of reformulation: cognitive analytic therapy in a patient with borderline personality disorder', *British Journal of Medical Psychology*, 66: 249–58.

Ryle, A. and Fonagy, P. (1995) '*British Journal of Psychotherapy* Annual Lecture 1994: psychoanalysis, cognitive analytic therapy, mind and self', *British Journal of Psychotherapy*, 11 (4): 567–74.

Ryle, A. and Golynkina, K. (1999) 'Time-limited cognitive analytic therapy of borderline personality disorder: factors associated with outcome', *British Journal of Medical Psychology*, 72 (4): 429–46.

Ryle, A. and Kerr, I. (2002) *Introducing CAT: Principles and Practice*. Chichester: Wiley.

Ryle, A. and Marlowe, M. (1995) 'Cognitive analytic therapy of borderline personality disorder: theory and practice and the clinical and research uses of the self states sequential diagram', *International Journal of Short-Term Psychotherapy*, 10: 21–34.

Ryle, A., Spencer, J. and Yawetz, C. (1992) 'When less is more or at least enough', *British Journal of Psychotherapy*, 8: 401–12.

Sheard, T., Evans, J. and Cash, D. (2000) 'A CAT-derived one to three session intervention for repeated deliberate self-harm: a description of the model and initial experience of trainee psychiatrists in using it', *British Journal of Medical Psychology*, 73 (2): 179–96.

Treasure, J., Todd, G., Brolly, M., Tiller, J., Nehmad, A. and Denman, F. (1995) 'A pilot study of a randomised trial of cognitive analytic therapy vs educational behaviour therapy for adult anorexia nervosa', *Behaviour Research and Therapy*, 33 (4): 363–7.

Treasure, J. and Ward, A. (1997) 'Cognitive analytic therapy in the treatment of anorexia nervosa', *Clinical Psychology and Psychotherapy*, 4: 62–71.

Walsh, S. (1996) 'Adapting cognitive analytic therapy to make sense of psychologically harmful work environments', *British Journal of Medical Psychology*, 69: 3–20

SUGGESTED FURTHER READING

Hepple, J. and Sutton, L. (eds) (2004) *CAT and Later Life, a New Perspective on Old Age*. Hove/ New York: Brunner Routledge.

Pollock, P.H. (2001) *CAT for Adult Survivors of Childhood Abuse*. Chichester: Wiley.

Ryle, A. (1995) *Cognitive Analytic Therapy: Developments in Theory and Practice*. Chichester: Wiley.

Ryle, A. (1997) *Cognitive Analytic Therapy and Borderline Personality Disorder: The Model and the Method*. Chichester: Wiley.

Ryle, A. and Kerr, I. (2002) *Introducing CAT: Principles and Practice*. Chichester: Wiley.

12

Cognitive Therapy

Stirling Moorey

HISTORICAL CONTEXT AND DEVELOPMENT IN BRITAIN

Historical context

During the middle years of the 20th century psychology was dominated by the twin edifices of behaviourism and psychoanalysis. For one the individual's internal world was unimportant and his or her actions were determined by environmental events. For the other the internal world was all important, but its workings were unconscious and accessible only with the help of a trained guide. The thoughts which most people regarded as central to their experience of everyday life were seen by both schools as peripheral. There were, however, some lone voices which defended the individual as a conscious agent. Kelly (1955) emphasized the way in which the person seeks to give meaning to the world, and suggested that each of us constructs our own view of reality through a process of experimentation. Ellis (1962) drew attention to the role of irrational beliefs in neurotic disorders, and developed rational-emotive therapy (RET) to change these beliefs systematically. The study of the mental processes which intervene between stimulus and response is termed 'cognitive psychology'. This includes a wide range of activities such as thinking, remembering and perceiving. It was not until the 1970s that psychology began to undergo a 'cognitive revolution' (Mahoney and Arnkoff, 1978) which led to a greater interest in the relevance of cognitive processes to therapy. This revolution came in part from within behaviourism. Starting from a learning theory perspective, some behavioural psychologists began to investigate how cognitions could be treated as behaviours in their own right, and so might be conditioned or deconditioned (Cautela, 1973). Others considered the person's contribution to the management of his or her own behaviour (Kanfer and Karoly, 1972); this led to a theory of self-regulation known as self-control theory. Cognitive theory started to break away from Skinnerian and Pavlovian learning theory with the work of Bandura. He showed that it was possible to understand the phenomenon of modelling from a cognitive rather than strictly behaviourist perspective (Bandura, 1977; Rosenthal and Bandura, 1978). An even more radical step was taken when Mahoney drew attention to the significance of cognitive processes such as expectation and attribution in conditioning (Mahoney and Arnkoff, 1978). This increasing interest in cognition led to the development of various cognitive-behavioural therapies. Although they all have slightly different theoretical perspectives they share common assumptions and it is often difficult to distinguish them in terms of the techniques used in clinical practice. Of these the most influential have been Ellis's rational-emotive therapy (now known as rational emotive behaviour therapy – see Chapter 14), Meichenbaum's cognitive-behaviour modification and Beck's cognitive therapy. Ellis aims through therapy to make the client aware of his or her irrational beliefs and the way in which they lead to maladaptive emotional states. His emphasis is on cognitive processes that are evaluative rather than inferential If, for example, a client reported that she felt depressed when a friend ignored her in the street, rather than asking her if there were any alternative explanation (e.g. her friend was preoccupied and did not notice her) Ellis would home in immediately on the evaluative belief underlying her reaction 'I must be liked by people'. Meichenbaum differs from Ellis in the emphasis he places on the role of cognitive processes in coping. Meichenbaum (1985) studied the use of self-instructions as a means of coping with stressful situations and this led to the development of 'Stress Inoculation Training'. This model has had considerable influence on cognitive-behaviour therapy in general and on stress management in particular, but few therapists in Britain would use Meichenbaum's approach exclusively. There are, however, a larger number of clinicians in Britain who would say that they practice Beck's cognitive therapy. This is certainly the form of cognitive-behaviour therapy which has been most intensively researched (Salkovskis, 1996; Clark & Fairburn, 1997). Beck, like Ellis, was originally an analyst who became disillusioned with the orthodox Freudian tradition of the 1950s. His research into depression led him to believe that this condition was associated with a form of 'thought disorder' (Beck, 1963, 1964), in which the depressed person distorted incoming information in a negative way. The therapy that arose from Beck's cognitive model focused on teaching patients to learn to identify and modify their dysfunctional thought processes. Underlying these negative thoughts are beliefs or assumptions which need to be restructured to prevent further depression. In 1977 Beck's group published the first outcome study comparing cognitive therapy with pharmacotherapy in depressed patients (Rush et al., 1977). This generated great interest, first, because previous studies had shown psychotherapy to be less effective than drug treatment with this group of patients, and second, because psychologists were already becoming interested in cognitive approaches. From its origins in the USA cognitive therapy has become increasingly popular in Europe, especially in Britain and Scandinavia. The approaches of Beck and Ellis could be described as 'rationalist' since they assume that psychological disturbance results from irrational or biased ways of seeing the world. Constructivist cognitive therapies (Guidano and Liotti, 1983; Mahoney, 1995) on the other hand stress the person's active role in constructing reality, and are in a sense 'relativist': we each construct our own world. Therapy then becomes a journey that therapist and client embark on together, neither sure of where they will finally disembark. This form of cognitive therapy, which emphasises developmental issues more strongly than Beck or Ellis, has become influential in Italy and other parts of Europe.

Development in Britain

Cognitive therapy first came to the attention of British psychologists and psychiatrists through the pioneering work of British researchers who sought to evaluate the efficacy of Beck's treatment for depression. Dr Ivy Blackburn carried out an outcome study in Edinburgh (Blackburn et al.,1981), while Dr John Teasdale and Dr Melanie Fennell carried out similar work in Oxford (Teasdale et al., 1984). These studies showed cognitive therapy to be as effective as antidepressants with depressed patients, and also proved that the treatment could be applied outside American private practice in a National Health Service setting. In keeping with the empirical nature of the therapy British cognitive therapists have always been committed to research. Many theoretical and clinical contributions have come from the United Kingdom, particularly in the areas of anxiety disorders and psychosis. Starting in the mid 1980's David Clark and his colleagues at Oxford (and more recently at the Institute of Psychiatry) have identified specific cognitive models for panic disorder (Clark, 1986), obsessive compulsive disorder (Salkovskis, 1985), hypochondriasis (Salkovskis and Warwick, 1986), social phobia (Clark & Wells, 1995) and post traumatic stress disorder (Ehlers & Clark, 2000). Using these conceptualisations as a framework they have developed and tested focused therapies which target the core cognitive and behavioural elements of each disorder. In the past, psychotic patients were thought to be beyond the reach of psychotherapy, but Britain has been in the forefront of the development of cognitive behavioural therapies for psychosis (Chadwick and Lowe, 1991; Birchwood & Tarrier, 1992; Kingdon & Turkington, 1994; Fowler et al., 1995) and for bipolar affective disorder (Lam et al., 2003). An exciting new approach to relapse prevention of depression *(Mindfulness Based Cognitive Therapy)* has come from John Teasdale and Mark Williams in collaboration with their American colleague, Zindel Segal (Teasdale et al., 2000). Cognitive behaviour therapy (CBT) is now widely practised in the National Health Service, particularly by clinical psychologists. The guidelines of the National Institute for Clinical Excellence (www.nice.org.uk) for the treatment of depression, anxiety and schizophrenia all recommend CBT as one of the core components of management of these conditions.

THEORETICAL ASSUMPTIONS

Image of the person

This chapter will concern itself with Beck's cognitive therapy, but many of the theoretical and clinical points described are shared with other forms of cognitive behaviour therapy. Cognitive therapy makes a number of assumptions about the nature of the human individual:

1   The person is an active agent who interacts with his or her world.
2   This interaction takes place through the interpretations and evaluations the person makes about his or her environment.
3   The results of the 'cognitive' processes are thought to be accessible to consciousness in the form of thoughts and images, and so the person has the potential to change them.

Emotions and behaviour are mediated by cognitive processes. This distinguishes cognitive therapy from the extreme forms of behaviour therapy which see the organism as a black box: what goes on inside the box is of little consequence. It also distinguishes it from psychoanalysis, which gives prime importance to unconscious rather than conscious meanings. According to Beck:

> The specific content of the interpretation of an event leads to a specific emotional response … depending on the kind of interpretation a person makes, he will feel glad, sad, scared, or angry – or he may have no particular emotional reaction at all. (Beck, 1976: 51–2)

The behavioural response will also depend upon the interpretation made: if a situation is perceived as threatening the person may try to escape, if it is perceived as an insult the person may take aggressive action, if it is perceived as a loss he may give up. An important concept in Beck's view of normal and abnormal behaviour is the idea of the 'personal domain'. The personal domain is the conglomeration of real and abstract things which are important to us: our family, possessions, health, status, values and goals. Each of us has a different set of items in our personal domain; the more an event impinges on our domain the stronger our emotional reaction is likely to be. The meaning we give to a situation will be determined by the mental set we bring to it. Life is too short to work out what each event means to us afresh. We need rules or guidelines to allow us to make educated guesses about what is likely to happen next. If we did not have an internalized rule that we should stop at red traffic lights, our insurance bills would be considerably higher. Some of these assumptions about the world are shared, but others are intensely personal and idiosyncratic. Cognitive theorists call the hypothetical cognitive structures which guide and direct our thought processes 'schemata'. A schema is like a template which allows us to filter out unwanted information, attend to important aspects of the environment and relate new information to previous knowledge and memories (Kovacs and Beck, 1978). In areas we know well we have well-developed schemata (e.g. schemata for driving a car, or how to behave at a social gathering), whereas in new situations schemata will be less well developed.

Conceptualization of psychological disturbance and health

In psychological health our schemata are sufficiently consistent to allow us to predict likely occurrences, but also flexible enough to allow changes on the basis of new information. Most of the time we are capable of processing information in an accurate or even a slightly positively biased fashion (as evidenced by studies demonstrating that non-depressed subjects make internal attributions for success but external attributions for failure: Alloy and Ahrens, 1987; Bradley, 1978). In emotional disturbance information-processing is biased, usually in a negative distorted way. Beck suggests that we are all capable of functioning as rational problem-solvers at least some of the time. Psychological health requires us to be able to use the skills of reality-testing to solve personal problems as they occur. For instance, an adaptive way of dealing with a failure experience such as being turned down for a job would involve thinking about the interview, assessing one's performance, taking responsibility for any faults or weaknesses that might have contributed to the failure and looking for ways to prevent it happening in the future. In psychological disturbance people revert to more primitive thinking which prevents them functioning as effective problem-solvers (Beck et al., 1979: 15). This thinking tends to be global, absolute and judgmental. So a depressed person who is not successful at a job interview would label herself as a total failure, would conclude that it was entirely her own fault that she did not get the job, and would ruminate about the interview, focusing on all the things that went wrong without thinking about any of the positive factors.

Faulty and adaptive information-processing

When this primitive thinking is in operation information-processing is biased or distorted. Beck (1976) identifies 'logical errors' which characterize the thinking in psychological disorders. Table 12.1 summarizes some of the common logical errors. The tendency to distort information repeatedly in a maladaptive way is one of the factors which distinguishes psychologically healthy from psychologically disturbed individuals. Psychological health is seen as a state where the individual is able to make relatively accurate interpretations and evaluations of events, but this does not imply that psychologically healthy people will always think and act rationally.

Taylor and Brown (1988) argued persuasively from research evidence that a degree of self deception may be necessary for mental health. Beck's original cognitive model was developed to explain emotional disorder and as such did not have a systematic framework for understanding normal functioning and development. In fact, one strand that runs through much cognitive therapy is the assumption that the patient has much more in common with healthy individuals than he thinks. The cognitive therapist is usually able to see how the person's behaviour is not abnormal when the basic premises of his or her belief system become clear. Thus, for someone with obsessive compulsive disorder (OCD), it is not the experience of intrusive thoughts that is the problem (obsessional thoughts are not uncommon in the general population and are indistinguishable

Table 12.1   Cognitive distortions

1   *Arbitrary inference* refers to the process of drawing a specific conclusion in the absence of evidence to support the conclusion or when the evidence is contrary to the conclusion.

2   *Selective abstraction* consists of focusing on a detail taken out of context, ignoring other more salient features of the situation and conceptualizing the whole experience on the basis of this fragment.

3   *Overgeneralization* refers to the pattern of drawing a general rule or conclusion on the basis of one or more isolated incidents and applying the concept across the board to related and unrelated situations.

4   *Magnification and minimization* are reflected in errors in evaluating the significance or magnitude of an event that are so gross as to constitute a distortion.

5   *Personalization* refers to the patient's proclivity to relate external events to himself when there is no basis for making such a connection.

6   *Absolutistic, dichotomous thinking* is manifested in the tendency to place all experiences in one of two opposite categories; i.e. flawless or defective, immaculate or filthy, saint or sinner. In describing himself, the patient selects the extreme negative categorization.

Source: Beck et al., 1979

from those experienced by people with OCD; Rachman and de Silva, 1978; Salkovskis and Harrison, 1984) but the interpretations made about them (Salkovskis, 1985). Instead of accepting that an urge to blaspheme in church is an odd but harmless intrusion, the person with OCD will believe it indicates some deep, dark impulsiveness in their nature which must be controlled at all costs. It is the consequent attempts to supress and neutralise these normal intrusions that give rise to rituals and compulsive behaviours. As cognitive therapists have been confronted by the needs of people with personality disorders, a more systematic model of personality and its development has begun to be constructed (e.g. Beck et al., 1990). Beck has always stressed the importance of having a good theory to describe the condition you are studying or treating. Starting with his pioneering work on depression, cognitive therapists have been mapping the cognitive abnormalities seen in the various psychiatric disorders. Beck (1976) suggests that in depression there is a negative view of the self, the world and the future. In anxiety the cognitive distortions involve an overestimation of major physical or social threat together with an underestimation of the individual's ability to cope with the threat. There is evidence that anxious patients selectively attend to cues which represent threat. Clark and Steer (1997) describe some of the tests of cognitive models of emotional disorders. More specific models of certain types of anxiety disorder have been proposed. Clark (1986) presented a cognitive model of panic, which emphasizes the way in which catastrophic misinterpretations of bodily symptoms create a vicious circle of anxiety leading to more bodily sensations and more panic. Salkovskis and Warwick (1986) adapted this model for hypochondriasis: the hypochondriac misinterprets innocuous bodily sensations such as headache, twinges, etc. as signs of chronic life-threatening illness. Each of these diagnostic groups therefore filters information in a slightly different way. In panic and health anxiety the focus of attention is usually on bodily symptoms, but in generalised anxiety disorder it is worry which is the cause of distress. According to Wells (1997), any negative events can set off worry (e.g. unpleasant news material, intrusive thoughts). Worry is then chosen as a coping strategy (often because of beliefs that it helps problem solving or prevents bad things happening), but once this happens negative beliefs about worry (e.g. that worry can cause stress or that the person will lose control of their thinking) set in and a vicious cycle is set up, perpetuating the anxiety. Clark (for a summary see Clark, 1996) has carried out a number of compelling experiments specifically designed to test his model of panic. More limited evidence is available so far for the other anxiety models (Wells, 1997).

Negative automatic thoughts

People with psychological disorders differ from the non-distressed in the content as well as the form of their thinking. They are prone to frequent, disruptive thoughts known as 'negative automatic thoughts'. These are spontaneous thoughts or images which are plausible when the patient experiences them, but are in fact unrealistic. For instance, an anxious person may repeatedly think 'I can't cope. There's nothing I can do about my problems. Something terrible is going to happen. What if I'm going mad?' and may have images of collapsing, or going berserk. A depressed person may ruminate about his failures, thinking 'I'm useless, I never do anything right, I'm just a fraud.' We all experience these thoughts at times, but they are much more frequent and distressing in people with emotional disorders.

Maintaining behaviours

Cognitive therapists assume that the person's behaviour will be consistent with these thought processes. So in depression, the person who believes he will always fail, doesn't try anything, and the result is a confirmation of the negative belief. In panic disorder, a belief that you are about to die from a heart attack might make you sit down to take the strain off your heart. The role of these behaviours in the maintenance of psychological disturbance is decribed below.

Cognitive schemata

We have already seen how cognitive schemata are necessary for effective functioning in the world. Healthy schemata are reasonably flexible whereas unhealthy ones tend to be more rigid, absolute and overgeneralized. For instance, a belief that 'I must always be nice to everyone' is inflexible and irrationally universal. A more healthy rule might be 'It is generally better to be pleasant to people, but in certain circumstances it is OK to be unpleasant.' The person with the more rigid rule will tend to criticize themselves heavily if they fall short of their excessively high standard. Schemata may vary in the extent to which they are active at a given time. When they are latent they are not involved in information-processing, but when activated they channel all stages of processing (Beck et al., 1990). In a psychological disorder like depression, the negative schemata tend to become more active. Beliefs such as 'If you are not successful you are worthless' seem more plausible if you are depressed and unconditional beliefs like 'I am stupid and unlovable' may generate negative self-referent thoughts.

Some cognitive therapists distinguish between core beliefs and conditional beliefs (Beck, 1995). A core belief is an unconditional, axiomatic assumption about the self, the world or other people. In anxiety and depression these core beliefs may be inactive until a critical incident brings them to life. In personality disorders schemata may be active more pervasively. Someone with a dependent personality disorder may believe they are helpless and unable to survive alone even when they are not depressed. The core belief 'I am helpless' is associated with various conditional beliefs like 'If I find someone to rely on I can survive', and behavioural strategies consistent with the schema (i.e. finding and cultivating relationships where a strong person will look after you). Just as cognitive therapy has identified cognitive disturbances for emotional disorders, the different personality disorders have their own cognitive styles. The paranoid person believes that anyone is a potential enemy and so acts with suspicion and wariness; the narcissistic person believes that he is very special and so acts in a grandiose fashion (Beck et al., 1990). These schemata are more difficult to shift than in disorders such as depression because they are so pervasive and deeply embedded in the individual's belief system.

Acquisition of psychological disturbance

Beck considers that there are many factors which predispose an individual to emotional disturbance. He has considered these factors in relation to various conditions, including depression (Beck, 1987), anxiety (Beck and Emery, 1985) and personality disorders (Beck et al., 1990). He attempts to integrate cognitive factors with other factors to develop a multifactorial theory of psychological disorder. Table 12.2 shows some of the long-term (predisposing) and short-term (precipitating) factors which may be associated with anxiety or depression in adult life.

This suggests a much more complex aetiology for emotional disorders than the simplistic notion that cognitions cause emotions. Beck very clearly asserts that:

> the primary pathology or dysfunction during a depression or an anxiety disorder is in the cognitive apparatus. However, it is quite different from the notion that cognition causes these syndromes – a notion that is just as illogical as an assertion that hallucinations cause schizophrenia. (Beck and Emery, 1985: 85)

The aetiological factors described above can all be seen as operating on the 'cognitive apparatus' in one way or another.

Schemata as vulnerability factors

We have already begun to consider the vital role that schemata play in psychological health and disturbance. Early learning experiences, traumas and chronic stresses can all lead to idiosyncratic beliefs and attitudes which make a person vulnerable to psychological disturbance. For instance, someone who endures long periods of illness as a child and is overprotected by his parents may develop a core

Table 12.2   Long–term and short–term vulnerability factors

Predisposing factors

1   Genetic predisposition.
2   Physical disease (e.g. hypothyroidism and depression, hypothyroidism and anxiety).
3   Developmental traumas which lead to specific vulnerabilities (e.g. loss of a parent in childhood may be associated with depression in adult life).
4   Personal experiences too inadequate to provide adequate coping mechanisms (e.g. parents who provide poor models of how to cope with rejection).
5   Counterproductive cognitive patterns, unrealistic goals, unreasonable values and assumptions learned from significant others.

Precipitating factors

1   Physical disease
2   Severe external stress (e.g. exposure to physical danger may precipitate anxiety, loss of a partner may induce depression).
3   Chronic insidious external stress (e.g. continuous subtle disapproval from significant others).
4   Specific external stress (which acts on a psychological vulnerability).

Source: Adapted form Beck and Emery, 1985: 83

belief that he is frail and vulnerable and needs to be supported by others in order to survive. Someone who is continually criticized for making even small mistakes may elaborate the belief that she must get everything she does completely right. Continuing our view of the person as an active construing agent, we can conceptualize these beliefs as a way the person makes sense of the world by developing ideas about how the world does, or should, operate. The more rigid, judgmental and absolute these beliefs become, the more likely they are to cause problems. Examples of beliefs which predispose to anxiety include the following:

'Any strange situation should be regarded as dangerous.'
'My safety depends on always being prepared for possible danger.'
'I have to be in control of myself at all times.'

Examples of beliefs which predispose to depression include the following:

'I can only be happy if I am totally successful.'
'I need to be loved in order to be happy.'
'I must never make a mistake.'

One of the features of cognitive therapy in recent years has been an interest in developmental factors. Young (1990, 1994) has mapped out various ways in which family experiences can create maladaptive schemata. These assumptions may remain relatively quiescent until an event occurs which is of particular relevance to them. This causes them to be activated and to become the primary mode for construing situations. For instance, because of early childhood experiences a woman may believe that she needs to be loved in order to survive. While she is in a relationship this belief will not be salient, unless she thinks that she might lose the love of the person concerned. But if she is rejected by her lover it is likely to be activated. It acts as a premiss to a syllogism:

'I need to be loved in order to survive.' 'X has left me.' 'Therefore I cannot survive.'

These underlying assumptions become less obvious again when the person recovers from the depression. But they remain dormant as a potential source of vulnerability. Cognitive therapy aims not only to correct faulty information-processing but also to modify assumptions and so reduce vulnerability to further psychological disturbance.

Perpetuation of psychological disturbance

The concept of biased information-processing readily explains how information which is contrary to the client's cognitive schema is filtered out or manipulated in such a way that it is made consistent with her belief system. This is commonly seen in depression, where positive information (e.g. past achievement) is repeatedly disqualified. The depressed person will say that past successes do not count because they were due to luck, or to people helping. As Beck remarks,

> even though the depressive may be reasonably accurate in a cognitive appraisal (for example, 'They seem to like me'), the overall meaning is still a negative one: 'If they knew how worthless I was, they would not like me'. (Beck, 1987: 12)

Behaving in a manner that is consistent with dysfunctional beliefs can also help to maintain negative emotions. A simple example of this can be seen in a phobia, like a dog phobia, where *avoidance* of a feared stimulus (dogs) prevents the person from acquiring information that contradicts the negative belief (that dogs are dangerous). A more subtle form of avoidance is seen in panic disorder. A patient who fears she will collapse while having a panic attack because she feels dizzy, may hold on to chairs or railings to keep herself from falling. This *safety behaviour* prevents the patient from discovering that she will not collapse.

In personality disorders _schema maintenance_ (Young et al., 2003) takes place when cognitive distortions or behavioural strategies lead the individual to think or act in ways that perpetuate the problem. Someone with an abandonment schema believes that she is doomed to be rejected in any close relationship (often as the result of key experiences of rejection, loss or separation in childhood). If her partner is late for a meeting or rings up to cancel, her automatic thought is 'It's happening again. He's just like all the rest. He'll leave me soon.' She may try to prevent rejection by constantly looking for reassurance from her partner and this clinging behaviour may actually have the effect of alienating him and bringing about the very abandonment she fears. An alternative strategy which many people who fear abandonment employ is to keep away from relationships altogether and so escape the pain of rejection. This strategy has been termed 'schema avoidance' (Young et al., 2003).

External factors can also help to perpetuate psychological disturbance. Real-life problems such as unemployment or bereavement make it difficult for depressed people to believe that there is a future, or to believe that they are of value.

Similarly, chronic stress or social rejection can contribute to the continuation of anxiety states. The influence of close personal relationships can be very important in this respect. Hooley et al. (1986) have shown that a relationship in which the partner makes frequent negative comments predicts relapse in depression, The more negative the external environment the more difficult it is to challenge negative thinking.

Change

The cognitive model assumes that emotional and behavioural change is mediated by changes in beliefs and interpretations. In therapy this is achieved through systematic testing of these thoughts and beliefs, but the same process occurs naturally when we are exposed to situations which do not fit our assumptions about the world. If information is not consistent with our schema then we either find ways to incorporate the new information into our existing belief system, or we have to change our belief. Positive life events can therefore lift people out of depression. If your negative thoughts revolve around the idea that you are unloveable, then making a new friend can make you reconsider this. If you think you are a failure, passing an exam you expected to fail can improve your sense of competence. It is often a combination of various external events that leads to natural schema change, but it is by no means clear what allows some people to reconstrue their world in a more positive way while others interpret the new events as evidence that still supports their old beliefs – it is still possible for people to decide that their new friend is just a misfit like them, or that passing the exam was a fluke. Because many of our beliefs are tacit rules, these natural changes often occur gradually and may not be noticed. For instance, someone who has been abused in childhood may not trust anyone, but over time repeated experience of certain people being reliable and honest may lead to revision of this mistrust. Although it does not happen as a conscious re-evaluation, there is a radical change in beliefs about other people. Change in therapy probably occurs through a mixture of learning new coping strategies and modification of schemas.

PRACTICE

Goals of therapy

Cognitive therapy has three main goals:

1   to relieve symptoms and to resolve problems;
2   to help the client to acquire coping strategies;
3   to help the client to modify underlying cognitive structures in order to prevent relapse.

Unlike other forms of psychotherapy which sometimes lose sight of the patient's presenting complaint, cognitive therapy is problem oriented. Whether the complaints are symptoms of psychiatric illness like anxiety and depression, behavioural problems like addiction or bulimia, or interpersonal ones like social anxiety, the primary goal is always to help clients solve the problems which they have targeted for change. In the first session the therapist helps to clarify the problems as the patient sees them and to establish priorities. The therapist tries to target symptoms or problems which are both important to the client and amenable to therapeutic intervention.

The whole course of cognitive therapy can be seen as a learning exercise in which the client acquires and practises coping skills. The aim is to teach skills which can be used to deal with the current episode of distress, but can also be employed if problems recur. Many clients find that the methods of cognitive therapy can be generalized to other situations beyond the initial focus of therapy. This goal of therapy is 'to help patients uncover their dysfunctional and irrational thinking, reality test their thinking and behaviour, and build more adaptive and functional techniques for responding both inter- and intra-personally' (Freeman, 1983: 2). While cognitive therapy seeks to relieve distress it does not set out to change the personality completely. Learning how to navigate the squalls of life in our own battered vessel is often a more realistic objective than trying to rebuild it to someone else's specification as an ocean liner.

The final goal of therapy is the modification of maladaptive schemata. The intention is not to restructure all of a person's irrational beliefs, but only those which are causing problems. Beliefs that are rigid, global and selfreferent (e.g. I can be happy only if I'm successful at everything I do; I need a close relationship to survive) predispose the individual to future emotional disturbance. If these beliefs can be made more flexible, specific vulnerability to psychological disturbance will be reduced.

Selection criteria

Which patients?

Psychotherapy research has shown that a variety of therapies are effective with people in emotional distress but it is still not clear which clients respond best to which type of treatment. It has been suggested that all therapies work through non-specific factors such as establishing a therapeutic alliance and instilling hope, but DeRubeis presents a considered case for how CBT produces its effect through theory based, specific methods (DeRubeis et al., 2005). As with other therapies (including drug treatment) severity and chronicity are associated with poor outcome in the treatment of depression. A recent meta-analysis (Haby et al., 2006) found that more severely ill patients did less well in trials of CBT for depression, panic and generalized anxiety disorder. The quality of therapeutic alliance has also been associated with outcome in CBT for depression, but there is some evidence that the alliance builds as a result of the client making some initial improvements as a result of intervention, rather than the alliance acting as the sole vehicle for change. This is supported by evidence, for instance, that early improvement is associated with better post therapy outcome in CBT for bulimia nervosa (Agras et al., 2000). Another factor which seems to affect outcome is the extent to which the client understands and accepts the cognitive model. Fennell and Teasdale (1987) found that those who accept the rationale for therapy and find their first homework assignment a success are more likely to do well. For depression particularly, it may be the case that people who can easily engage in problem solving might benefit more form CBT (Moorey et al., 2003). The implications are that if the clients do not respond to the idea that their thoughts might have some relevance to the problem during the initial sessions then cognitive therapy may not be the right approach. There are some people who are just not 'psychologically minded', and who find it extremely difficult to introspect even to the extent that cognitive therapy requires.

These factors are usually taken into account when considering patients for cognitive therapy, and a clinician will often test clients' suitability by assessing their acceptance of the cognitive model and their response to cognitive restructuring. Safran and Segal's Suitability for Short Term Cognitive Therapy Scale gives a more systematic method for assessing suitability for short term CBT (Safran et al., 1993). Scores on this predict the outcome of short-term cognitive therapy on multiple dependent measures. As might be predicted clients with personality disorders tend to score lower on alliance potential, security operations, chronicity, personal responsibility for change, and compatibility with the cognitive therapy rationale when this scale is applied (Vallis et al., 2000), which may indicate longer term therapy for these clients.

Individual or group therapy? Although most cognitive therapists would say that group therapy is less effective than individual therapy, results from controlled trials are contradictory. For depression Rush & Watkins (1981) found group therapy to be as effective as individual, but the effects were not as strong; but Scott and Stradling (1990) and Zettle et al. (1992) found the two modalities were equally effective. The advantages of group cognitive therapy in a busy health service are obvious and it can be a very cost effective approach. Gould et al. (1995) carried out a meta–analysis of treatment outcomes for panic disorder and found that group CBT was half the cost of individual CBT.

Some services offer group cognitive therapy as the first intervention for all clients, and only those who do not make significant gains are then given individual therapy. In other circumstances clients may be offered a group because there are specific advantages over individual therapy. There are two main reasons for this decision:

1. If the client's problems are predominantly interpersonal e.g. social anxiety.
2. If there will be major advantages to the client being able to see and learn from others with similar problems e.g. group CBT for people with cancer.

Some patients may initially require individual therapy when they are most distressed but can then go on to a group as their mood improves. This can be especially helpful if interpersonal factors (e.g. lack of assertiveness or fear of disapproval) are considered to be relevant to future relapse. Young (1990) describes a combination of group and individual therapy in the treatment of patients with personality disorders. The group provides a 'laboratory' where the client can test out maladaptive beliefs in relative safety.

Qualities of effective therapists

First and foremost, cognitive therapists need to have good general interpersonal skills. Although the therapy sometimes appears to place a strong emphasis on cognitive and behavioural techniques these are deemed to be effective only if they are used within the context of a good therapeutic relationship. In CBT for depression, both the quality of the therapeutic alliance and the therapist's competence in using the cognitive behavioural approach contribute to a good outcome (Trepka et al., 2004). Warmth, genuineness and empathy are vital components of this relationship:

> We believe that these characteristics in themselves are necessary but not sufficient to produce an optimum therapeutic effect. However, to the degree that the therapist is able to demonstrate these qualities, he is helping to develop a milieu in which the specific cognitive change techniques can be applied most efficiently. (Beck et al., 1979: 45–6)

Cognitive therapists need to have good listening skills, to be able to reflect accurately the cognitive and emotional components of the client's communication, and to demonstrate an active and warm interest in the client. If this is not done there is a real danger that attempts to challenge distorted thinking will be perceived by the client as insensitive or even persecutory. Good therapists seem to be able to get inside the client's cognitive world and empathize while at the same time retaining objectivity.

Many would see the qualities described above as essential to any form of psychotherapy. It is more difficult to specify qualities which make someone a good cognitive therapist rather than a good psychotherapist in general. Perhaps one of the most important factors is the extent to which the therapist can accept the cognitive model. The therapist has to be prepared to work in a problem-oriented way without continually looking for unconscious motives in the patient's self-defeating thinking and behaviour. He or she must be able to blend the interpersonal skills described in the last paragraph with a directive approach which involves a great deal of structure and focus. While specific cognitive therapy skills can be learned the therapist still needs to accept the basic rationale for doing therapy in this way.

No published data exist on factors which predict how well someone will function as a cognitive therapist, although it has been shown that competency in the therapy improves with training (Shaw, 1984). The impression from my own experience of training cognitive therapists is that people with more clinical experience do better than those without, people with a background in behaviour therapy do better than those with a psychodynamic background, and people who take to the model enthusiastically do better than those who are less committed.

Therapeutic relationship and style

The aim of cognitive therapy is to teach the client to monitor thought processes and to reality-test them. Rather than assume that the client's view of the situation is distorted or correct, the cognitive therapist treats every statement about the problem as a hypothesis. Therapy is empirical in the sense that it is continually setting up and testing out hypotheses. Client and therapist collaborate like scientists testing a theory. For instance, a depressed person may believe that there is no point in doing anything because there is no pleasure in life any more.

Hypothesis

If I visit my friend tomorrow I will get no pleasure from it.

Experiment

Arrange to visit from 3 p.m. to 4 p.m., and immediately afterwards rate the amount of pleasure I get on a 0–10 scale.

Most depressed people find they get at least some enjoyment out of activities they used to find pleasurable.

Experiments like this can gradually erode the belief that it is not worth doing anything by providing evidence that there is still pleasure open to them and so increase the person's motivation.

Teaching the client to be a 'personal scientist' is done through collaboration rather than prescription. Wherever possible the therapist will encourage the client to choose problems, set priorities and think of experiments. This collaboration is the hallmark of cognitive therapy and there are a number of reasons for including the client in the problem-solving process as much as possible.

- Collaboration gives the client a say in the therapy process and so reduces conflict
- Collaboration fosters a sense of self-efficacy by giving the client an active role. Collaboration encourages the learning of self-help techniques which can be continued when therapy is ended.
- Collaboration allows an active input from the person who knows most about the problem.

Collaboration also serves to reduce the sorts of misinterpretation that can sometimes affect the therapeutic relationship. In non-directive therapies, the impassive stance of the therapist means that the patient has to construct an image of the therapist based on her own predictions and rules about people. The resulting misinterpretation (transference) can be used therapeutically. Cognitive therapy wants to reduce this and does not use the relationship as the focus of therapy. It sees the therapist and client as partners in the process of problem-solving. This does not prevent the therapist being very active and directive at times, but it always gives space for the client to contribute and give feedback on what the therapist is doing. With more severely depressed clients there is often a need for a lot of direction at first, but as the mood improves and the client learns the principles of cognitive therapy the relationship becomes more collaborative. Ideally by the end of therapy the client is doing most of the work and thinking up his or her own strategies for change. When the therapist is most directive at the beginning of treatment he or she must also be most empathic in order to establish rapport.

In this type of therapeutic relationship the client and therapist are co-investigators trying to uncover the interpretations and evaluations that might be contributing to the client's problems. This is an inductive process of guided discovery. Wherever possible the therapist asks questions to elicit the idiosyncratic meanings which give rise to the client's distress and to look for the evidence supporting or refuting the client's beliefs. This use of questioning to reveal the self-defeating nature of the client's automatic thoughts has been termed *Socratic questioning*.

Another characteristic feature of cognitive therapy is the way in which the session is structured. At the beginning of each session an agenda is set, with both client and therapist contributing to this. Usually the agenda will include a brief review of the last session, developments in the last week and the results of homework assignments. The work then goes on to the major topic for the session. Anyone listening to a cognitive therapy session will also be struck by two further features: the use of summaries and feedback. Two or three times during a session the client or therapist will summarize what has been going on so far. This helps to keep the client on track, which is particularly important if anxiety or depression impairs concentration. Asking the client to summarize also reveals whether or not the therapist has got a point across clearly. The therapist regularly asks for feedback about his or her behaviour, the effects of cognitive interventions, and so on.

Major therapeutic strategies and techniques

Emery (in Beck and Emery, 1985) describes a four-step process of problem-solving in cognitive therapy:

1   Conceptualize the patient's problems.
2   Choose a strategy.
3   Choose a tactic or technique.
4   Assess the effectiveness of the technique.

1.Conceptualization

Cognitive therapy is based on a coherent theory of emotional disturbance, and this theory can be used to conceptualize the patient's problems. The clearer the conceptualization, the easier it becomes to develop strategies (i.e. general methods for solving the patient's problems) and techniques (specific interventions). For instance, a woman presented with complaints of fatigue and memory problems, but did not have any physical cause for these symptoms. The initial formulation was that the symptoms were stress related, and over the course of two assessment interviews the therapist was able to construct a clearer picture of the problem using the cognitive model. The client had a very poor self-image and was in a difficult marriage where her husband was very critical. She described a constant stream of thoughts criticizing herself which occurred whenever she needed to make decisions. She was also able to identify negative thoughts about the marriage ('It's hopeless, I'm trapped'). The cognitive formulation explained her memory problems as a natural result of only partly attending to anything: she was distracted by the running commentary she gave on her actions. Her fatigue probably resulted from the frequent negative thoughts she was having about herself and her marriage.

Because she had a belief that there was nothing she could do about her marital problems she tended to put these thoughts to the back of her mind using 'cognitive avoidance', and selectively focused on the physical symptoms. This in turn led to a further set of negative thoughts – 'Is there something wrong with my brain? Am I going senile?' This formulation allowed the therapist to develop a comprehensive treatment strategy.

2. Therapeutic strategies

Strategies are the general plans the therapist makes to help the client meet their goals in therapy. These will change across the course of treatment. Early on strategies are aimed at helping to socialise the patient into the cognitive model by identifying how thoughts and feelings are linked, to provide coping strategies for immediate crises and to help the client get some distance from the constant flow of maladaptive thinking. In the next phase of therapy the aim is to help the client identify cognitions and behaviours that might be maintaining their problems and to begin to test the validity and helpfulness of these thoughts and actions. The last phase of therapy involves identifying and challenging underlying maladaptive beliefs and developing a relapse prevention plan.

3. Cognitive and behavioural techniques

Identifying negative automatic thoughts Early in therapy the therapist teaches the client to observe and record negative automatic thoughts. Initially the concept of an automatic thought is explained: it is a thought or image that comes to mind automatically and seems plausible, but on inspection is often distorted or unrealistic. Thoughts the client has during the session can be used to illustrate this, e.g. in the first session a depressed client may be thinking 'I don't know why I've come, there's nothing anyone can do for me.' Written material such as the leaflet Coping with Depression (Beck and Greenberg, 1974) is also used to explain the basic features of therapy. The client is then given the homework task of collecting and recording negative automatic thoughts. The exact format of this will depend on the problem. A depressed client will be asked to monitor depressed mood, recording the situation which triggered a worsening of depression, and the thoughts associated with it. Someone with an alcohol problem would monitor cravings for drink, and again record the situations in which they occurred and the thoughts that precipitated them. This phase of identifying thoughts helps clients to start making the link:

Event: negative automatic thought disturbed emotion or behaviour. Identifying thoughts may also be therapeutic in its own right, since just recording negative thoughts sometimes reduces their frequency. Clients should try to record their thoughts as soon after the stressful event as possible, when it is fresh in their mind.

Testing negative automatic thoughts: When the client has learned to identify the maladaptive thinking the next step is to learn how to challenge the negative thoughts. Through Socratic questioning the therapist shows the client how to change his or her thinking. This cognitive restructuring by the therapist usually brings relief in the session, but it takes longer for the client to practise challenging thoughts outside the therapy session, which becomes a situation where the therapist models the process of cognitive restructuring and gives the client feedback on his or her success at the task. Clients are encouraged to use a form to record and challenge their automatic thoughts to help them internalize the process of identifying and modifying negative automatic thoughts.

There are a number of methods the therapist can use to help a client modify negative thinking:

Reality testing: This is probably the most common method of cognitive restructuring. The client is taught to question the evidence for the automatic thoughts. For example, you hear that your five-year-old son has hit another child at school. You immediately think 'He's a bully. I'm a useless parent', and feel depressed. What is the evidence that your son is a bully? Has he done this sort of thing before? Is this unusual behaviour for a five-year-old child? Bullying implies an unprovoked attack. Could he have been provoked? What is the evidence that you are a useless parent? Have you been told by anyone in your family that you are doing a bad job? Is a single instance of bad behaviour in a five-year-old child proof that you are a bad parent?

Looking for alternatives: People who are in emotional crisis, especially if they are depressed, find it difficult to examine the options that are open to them. They get into a blinkered view of their situation. Looking for alternatives is a way of helping them out of this mental set. The therapist gently asks for alternative explanations or solutions and continues until as many as possible are generated. At first these will probably all be negative but after a while the client will start to come up with more constructive alternatives.

Reattribution: A more specialized form of the search for alternatives involves reattributing the cause of, or responsibility for, an event. A client who experiences panic attacks may believe that the physical sensations of dizziness and a pounding heart are signs of an impending heart attack. The therapist, through education, questioning and experimentation, helps the client to reattribute the cause of these experiences to the natural bodily sensations of extreme anxiety. For example, the client who attributes her son's behaviour to her failure as a mother can be taught to change the focus of responsibility; many factors contribute to a child's behaviour, and a parent does not have control of all of them.

Decatastrophizing: This has been termed the 'What if' technique (Freeman, 1987). The client is taught to ask what would be the worst thing that could happen. In many cases when the fear is confronted it becomes clear that it is not so terrible after all. For example, you are preparing to visit a friend for the weekend and do not have much time to pack. You think, 'I can't decide what to pack. I mustn't forget anything.' You get into more and more of a panic trying to remember everything in time. Why would it be so awful if you did forget something? Would it be the end of the world if you turned up without a toothbrush?

Advantages and disadvantages: This is a very helpful technique to enable clients to get things into perspective. If a difficult decision has to be made or if it seems difficult to give up a habitual maladaptive behaviour, the client can list the advantages and disadvantages of a certain course of action.

Behavioural techniques Freeman (1987) considered the behavioural techniques in cognitive therapy to serve two purposes: they work to change behaviour through a broad range of methods; and they serve as short-term interventions in the service of longer-term cognitive change. This second goal differentiates the behavioural tasks used in cognitive therapy from those used in more conventional behaviour therapy. These tasks are set within a cognitive conceptualization of the problem and are used to produce cognitive change. Seen in its simplest form, behavioural work changes cognitions by distracting clients from automatic thoughts early in the process of therapy; and challenging maladaptive beliefs through experimentation. Behavioural methods are often used at the beginning of therapy when the client is most distressed and so less able to use cognitive techniques.

Activity scheduling This is a technique which is particularly useful with depressed clients but can be applied with other problems too. The rationale for scheduling time centres on the proposition that when they are depressed, clients reduce their level of activity and spend more time ruminating on negative thoughts. The schedule is an hour-by-hour plan of what the client will do. As with all the procedures in cognitive therapy, this needs to be explained in some detail and a clear rationale given. It is often set up as an experiment to see if certain activities will improve mood. The therapist stresses that few people accomplish everything they plan, and the aim is not to get all the items done but to find out if planning and structuring time can be helpful. Initially the aim may just be to monitor tasks together with the thoughts and feelings that accompany them. The emphasis is usually on engaging in specific behaviours during a certain period rather than the amount achieved. For instance, a client would be encouraged to decide to do some decorating between 10 a.m. and 11 a.m. on a certain day, rather than plan to decorate a whole room over a weekend. These tasks are set up as homework assignments and the results discussed at the beginning of the next session.

Mastery and pleasure ratings   This technique can be used in conjunction with activity scheduling. Clients rate how much mastery (feelings of success, achievement or control) or pleasure they get out of a task (on a 0–10 scale). Since depressed clients often avoid engaging in pleasant activities, this method allows the therapist to establish which activities might be enjoyable for clients and to encourage them to engage in them with greater frequency. It also challenges all-or-nothing thinking, by showing that there is a continuum of pleasure and mastery rather than experiences which (1) are totally enjoyable or unenjoyable and (2) yield complete success or failure.

Graded task assignments   All-or-nothing thinking can also be challenged using graded task assignments. Many clients think, 'I have to be able to do everything I set myself, or I have failed.' The therapist begins by setting small homework tasks which gradually build up in complexity and difficulty The client is encouraged to set goals that can realistically be achieved, so that he or she completes a series of successful assignments.

Behavioural experiments

We have already seen how behavioural experiments are an important component of cognitive therapy. Hypotheses are continually generated and put to the test. This usually involves a negative prediction of some form. For instance, an anxious client may state that he is too anxious even to read. An experiment can be set up in the therapy session where the client reads a short paragraph from a newspaper, thus disproving the absolutism of this statement. The client can then go on to read articles of increasing length over the following week. Experiments are often set as homework. For instance, a depressed client who firmly believes that she is unable to go shopping could be asked to go shopping with her husband. Even if the client is not able to carry out the assignment the experiment is not a failure because it provides valuable information about what might be the blocks to the activity.

Other behavioural techniques   Cognitive therapy employs a variety of other behavioural techniques where appropriate. Cognitive and behavioural rehearsal is frequently used during the session in preparation for a difficult homework assignment. Role-play can be a very effective cognitive change technique. When clients have practical problems that need to be solved, behavioural techniques based on a skills training model are especially useful. This will usually involve forms of assertiveness training or social skills training for people who have deficits in interpersonal skills.

Schema change methods   All the techniques described so far can be applied to help elicit and change underlying beliefs. In addition some techniques may be specifically applied to change deeply held core beliefs or schemas. *The Historical Review of Schemas* involves testing the evidence for and against the belief across the individual's lifespan. While many clients will find evidence for their belief that they are inadequate or doomed to being abandoned from their recent experience, it is more difficult for them to bias information from early childhood in the same way. *The Continuum Technique* is a method where-all-or nothing thinking is challenged by plotting it on a continuum and the *Positive Data Log* involves collecting daily instances which discount the client's core beliefs. For information on how these techniques are applied the reader is directed to Beck (1995), Padesky (1994), Persons et al. (2001) and Young et al. (2003).

Treating patients with personality disorders   There is not room in this chapter to describe the treatment of personality disorders in detail (see Beck et al., 1990; Young et al., 2003; Linehan, 1993 for useful guidelines). The schema change techniques just mentioned play an important role in working with this client group. Because it can be difficult to establish a therapeutic alliance, and because of the strength with which the dysfunctional beliefs are held, treatment is usually longer than with emotional disorders. Clients often find it difficult to identify automatic thoughts and so much of the work has to be done at the schematic level. Repeated recognition of core beliefs and the behavioural strategies stemming from them is often necessary before change can occur, and sometimes a much more confrontational style is needed to overcome schema avoidance (Young et al., 2003). This can include the use of emotive techniques to activate schemas. For instance, a schema may be activated by reconstructing a traumatic scene from childhood in role play. This is often associated with powerful feelings of fear, hurt and anger. Initially the client is unable to think rationally and is overwhelmed by the feelings, but a skilful therapist can help the client get some distance from the affect without getting caught up in it. Cognitive restructuring can then be used to challenge guilt or blame the person feels for the trauma or abuse, and to challenge beliefs that the past must always poison the present. More active techniques like imagery rescripting can help to change the sense of powerlessness which is often part of the memory. The conceptualization is even more important in this work than in standard cognitive therapy. To guide the interventions the therapist needs a clear picture of how core beliefs were developed as a result of childhood experiences, how compensatory beliefs and coping strategies emerged, and how these schemata operate in the client's present to maintain the maladaptive interpersonal patterns. Sharing this conceptualization with the client can help give meaning to a seemingly chaotic and meaningless present.

The change process in therapy

It is difficult to summarize a typical course of cognitive therapy since strategy and technique depend on the individual client and the problems being treated. There is, however, generally a progression through therapy. At the beginning of therapy the emphasis is on conceptualizing the client's problems, teaching the cognitive model and producing early symptom relief. Techniques aimed at symptom relief in the early stages of therapy tend to be more behavioural. As therapy progresses the client learns to monitor and challenge automatic thoughts and this forms the major focus in therapy. As the client's problems reach some resolution the emphasis shifts to identifying and challenging underlying assumptions, and to work on relapse prevention. There is still debate about which components of cognitive therapy are most important in bringing about change. Is it the learning of new ways of dealing with negative thoughts, or the modification of underlying schemata? The process of change is not always smooth. The client may come with very different expectations of treatment than the therapist. For instance, a client with a hypochondriacal preoccupation will believe that there is a physical cause for his or her problems and will be reluctant to accept the cognitive model. In the early sessions with this type of client the therapist tries to engage the client in the therapy, perhaps examining the evidence for the client's explanation of the symptoms, and getting his or her agreement to try the new approach on an experimental basis. For people who find it difficult to understand the concept of negative automatic thoughts it may take longer to explain and demonstrate their nature. Others are frightened to record such thoughts because they make them feel worse.

This may require that more time be spent in examining possible gains from exposing themselves to short-term distress in order to achieve long-term benefit. With clients who have personality problems, maladaptive patterns of relating to others will be brought into the session and these need to be addressed as part of therapy: for example dependent clients may fail to carry out homework assignments because they hope that the therapist will support and help them without the difficult learning of self-reliance. These patterns often act as blocks to therapy and must be openly discussed with the client.

Limitations of the approach

Many of the limitations of cognitive therapy are the same as those that apply to any form of psychotherapy. People with very severe mental disturbances are not readily treated with talking treatments. This applies particularly to those who suffer from delusions and hallucinations, although experimental cognitive approaches may have something to offer even these clients (Birchwood and Tarrier, 1992; Kingdon and Turkington, 1994). Motivation to change is an important construct that is not always assessable until therapy is under way. The emphasis placed on homework and self-help can be a limitation for some clients. One study of cognitive therapy for depression found that people who endorsed ideas about self-control did well with cognitive therapy, whereas those who did not responded better to drugs (Simons et al., 1986). Subsequent studies have not all supported this finding. As we have seen, the question of acceptance of the theoretical model, and the ability and willingness to carry out self-help assignments, must be taken into account when considering clients for therapy. The more clearly difficulties can be defined as problems the easier it is to do cognitive therapy. With vague characterological flaws which manifest themselves as problems in interpersonal relationships it is sometimes very hard to find a focus. With such clients the form of therapy described here may not be adequate. One major advantage that cognitive therapy has over some forms of therapy is its commitment to the scientific method. It is being applied to a widening field of disorders, and as long as its practitioners continue to evaluate its efficacy the next 10 years should provide answers to the question: what are the areas of application and the limits of this approach?

Case example

The client

Cindy was a 33 year old artist who had been troubled by low mood on and off since her teens. Even when not suffering from depression she had a very poor opinion of herself and doubted her ability to make anything of her life. She berated herself for not having a partner or children, criticised herself for not making more of her career, and considered herself a failure all round. Cindy had problems settling down to mundane tasks or planning her week because she found it hard to concentrate and stick with humdrum chores. It felt like there was one side of her that wanted to live a conventional life, but another side that saw this as boring and ordinary. At weekends she would start drinking with friends in the early evening and then go out clubbing till the early morning. She often found it hard to remember what had happened the night before and feared that she had behaved outrageously. Her inability to restrict her drinking and the effects of her binges further added to her sense of shame and failure.

Cindy described an unhappy childhood. She had never really felt loved and valued and worried that her brother who was two years older was both more able and more appreciated. Her father was a moderately successful artist, but had an erratic, unpredictable character, exacerbated by his heavy drinking. He had left when Cindy was 11 and her contact with him since then had been fitful. She felt they were similar personalities, so they either got on really well or were at each other's throats. Since she had grown up she believed he saw her artistic efforts as competition: he always wanted to talk about his own work and never seemed to praise her for her work. Her mother was somewhat morose; she was very hard on herself but also hard on her daughter, particularly about her heavy drinking. Cindy's brother was working abroad as an IT consultant. Their relationship had improved now they were adults, but she still couldn't help making comparisons: he seemed to have a successful career and was planning to return to England to live with his partner.

Cindy had found school difficult. She wondered if she had been dyslexic because she had always done better at non-verbal subjects. She did not like the rules and regulations of school, but generally complied and did not get into trouble. She was popular with others but was never considered cool. After school she went to Art College and then did various part-time jobs while continuing her art work.

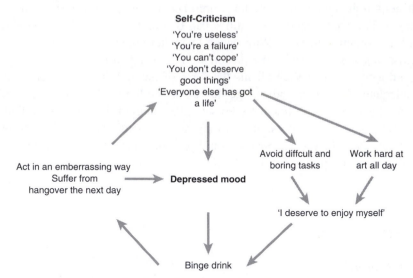

Figure 12.1   Conceptualization of factors maintaining Cindy's problems

Cindy had had a number of relationships, none lasting more than a year. She tended to go out with men she had met while clubbing. Although they seemed exciting initially, she later ususally found them shallow.

The therapy

The two main aims of therapy were to help Cindy control her binge drinking and to improve her self-esteem.

The therapist began by helping her to understand the factors that might be maintaining her low mood and low self-esteem. Cindy's self-criticism seemed to pervade much of her life. She attacked herself for what she didn't do and for what she did do. There was a vicious circle in which her low self-esteem, low confidence and belief that she would never be organised and successful led her to avoid difficult or onerous tasks, but this avoidance simply confirmed her negative beliefs about herself. There was also a vicious circle involving her excessive drinking. Through the week she would either spend her time in a disorganized state escaping from negative thoughts and feelings, or she would throw herself into her art, sometimes working 12 hours a day. By the end of the week she began to feel tense and tired and gave herself permission to relax and unwind: 'You'll feel better if you have a drink. You've worked hard, you deserve to enjoy yourself.' Her binge drinking made her feel unwell for a couple of days, so she was then unable to get her work done and she criticised herself even more. Because she lost her inhibitions when very drunk she often behaved in ways she later regretted, and this further added to her self-disgust. This conceptualization is shown in Figure 12.1.

A cost-benefit analysis of drinking showed that although she enjoyed it, felt relaxed and felt more socially confident, the alcohol tended to make her more depressed and less productive overall. Cindy agreed it might be worth cutting down on her alcohol intake. She kept a record of her drinking and a diary of what she did

Table 12.3   Dysfunctional thought Record

Situation	Automatic thoughts	Emotion(s)	Adaptive response	Outcome
Mother criticising me because I have a hangover.	She's right. I'm a waste of space. I'm never going to get control of my life. I'm never going to change. **Hot Thought: I'm never going to get control of my life. (90%)**	Tired. Depressed. Hopeless. Dejected. (80%)	Beating myself up isn't going to help anything. It will only make me feel worse. This is the first time I've been like this for 3 weeks. I am beginning to get control of my life. I'm drinking less overall, I'm looking after myself better and I'm more balanced and centred more of the time.	Depressed (30%) Belief in auto-matic thought (30%) Belief in adaptive response (60%) **Action Plan: Look after myself till I feel better and then start to plan some healthy activities for next week**

during the week; she rated the activities for pleasure and mastery. The activity schedule was used to help her get a balance in her daily routine, between avoidance and overwork. The therapist helped her to explore what she would like to achieve and how she might get there, as well as encouraging her to find activities which could combat her depressed mood. She felt that avoiding alcohol during the week, exercising and doing her art were all nurturing activities. The therapist also helped her to rehearse in imagination how she could leave a club at a reasonable time instead of staying all night. This involved identifying and challenging some of the permission giving thoughts that encouraged her to drink more and more. She had variable success with this over the first few weeks of therapy. She began to recognise some of the risk factors and decided that she would be better off meeting friends who only drank small amounts and went home early rather than staying with her old circle. She found that in weeks during which she looked after herself she felt much better and was much more productive. Her difficulty in doing this every week was a good source of automatic thoughts. The habit of berating herself up for failures was very strong and she would easily think: 'I've done it again. I'm never going to change. I've got no self-control.' She learned to identify these thoughts in the session and outside the session using the Dysfunctional Thought Record (see Table 12.3). Recording and test-ing these self-critical thoughts became the main component of the middle phase of therapy. She found that she had negative thoughts about many things that hap-pened on a day to day basis as well as things that had happened in the past. She noticed that these seemed to be worse when she was with her mother who was overtly critical of her. Repeatedly using the thought record helped her to feel stronger and not to fall into believing her mother's criticism. Cindy had in the past been quite interested in Buddhism and meditation; the therapist encouraged her to return to meditating as a means of both nurturing herself and helping to break the vicious cycle of depressive thoughts. She began to recognise her self-critical thoughts as sim-ply thoughts and worked on accepting herself as she was rather than demanding she be different.

By this time Cindy was bingeing less frequently and had more weeks during which she achieved the things she wanted to do. Therapy moved on to exploring the

Table 12.4   Cindy's relapse prevention plan

What I have learned from therapy:

I'm not a failure. I have achieved significant things and am appreciated as an artist.
It's more important to me to enjoy and find fulfilment in the act of creating than in outward success.

Techniques which have been most helpful:

1 Activity Schedules – filling my time with things that nurture me.
2 Being compassionate to myself.
3 Reading: Overcoming low self-esteem.

What I have to look out for:

1 Slipping into avoiding things and not doing things I know are good for me.
2 Drinking too much in one night.
3 Beating myself up if I slip.

Relapse prevention:

1 Plan my week so I have some healthy things to look forward to.
2 Meditate regularly.
3 If I have a week where I don't look after myself or drink too much, don't attack myself.
4 Pick myself up and start again if I slip.

underlying beliefs that made her vulnerable to thinking and feeling so badly about herself. She readily understood that the origins of this had been in her childhood. She had seen her brother apparently succeeding effortlessly while everything seemed difficult for her. Her mother modelled a pessimistic, fatalistic view of the world and criticised her directly, while her father modelled some of the out of control behaviour she later fell into herself. She therefore developed the core belief that she was a **useless failure**. This pervaded all she did and thought, and a number of conditional beliefs arose from this 'bottom line'. These included:

'If I don't have a successful career, a long term relationship and children, I'm a failure.'
'If I try to do something I will fail.'
'If people know the real me they'll reject me.'
'If I try to organise my life I'm bound to fail because I'm incompetent.'
Many of the behaviours we had been working on in therapy seemed to arise as compensatory strategies out of these beliefs:
Work really hard non-stop, or give up.
Avoid difficult situations.
Use alcohol to relax and escape from negative feelings.
Use alcohol to increase confidence and feel part of the crowd.
Criticise self in order to do better.

She saw that much of her self-criticism was like an internal bully she had inherited from her mother, who punished herself as well as Cindy in an effort to do better. The therapist helped her to test some of these beliefs for their accuracy and usefulness, replacing them with alternative more helpful beliefs. She found the self-help book *Overcoming Low Self-Esteem* very useful at this stage and was able to create a new 'bottom line' – I'm good enough. I can get fulfilment from my work and life for its own sake.

As therapy came to an end Cindy wrote a blueprint outlining what she needed to do to maintain the gains she had made (see Table 12.4). Cindy attended for 12 weekly sessions and then had two follow-up sessions. At her final follow-up she was still having occasional drinking spells but these were much less frequent and she was far less critical of herself if they happened. She felt she was more productive in her work and more constructive in her life in general. She felt that overall she was beginning to believe her new bottom line.

Finding a Therapist

Cognitive Therapy is available on the National Health Service, but waiting lists are often long. Most therapy is carried out by clinical psychologists, or nurse therapists. Your General Practitioner should know what is available locally and be able to make a referral to the appropriate service. Private therapy is not as much part of the culture of cognitive therapy as it is for other therapies. The organisation to which most CBT therapists (working privately and in the NHS) belong in Britain is the British Association for Behavioural and Cognitive Psychotherapies. A Directory of Members is posted on their website (www.babcp.com).

Training as a Cognitive Therapist

Most cognitive therapists have a basic training as a mental health professional (Clinical Psychology, Nursing, Psychiatry or Counselling) and for this reason most of the courses are postgraduate courses which assume this professional background. A small number of courses will take trainees who do not have a previous mental health training. A list of courses can be found at the BABCP website (www.babcp.com).

REFERENCES

Agras, W. Stewart, Crow, Scott J., Halmi, Katherine A., Mitchell, James E., Wilson, G. Terence., Kraemer, Helena C. (2000) Outcome predictors for the cognitive behavior treatment of bulimia nervosa: Data from a multisite study. *American Journal of Psychiatry*. 157: 1302–1308.

Alloy, L.B. and Ahrens, A.H. (1987) Depression and pessimism for the future: biased use of statistically relevant information in predictions for self versus others, *Journal of Personality and Social Psychology*, 53: 366–78.

Bandura, A. (1977) *Social Learning Theory*. Englewood Cliffs, NJ: Prentice-Hall.

Beck, A.T. (1963) Thinking and depression: 1. Idiosyncratic content and cognitive distortions, *Archives of General Psychiatry*, 9: 324–33.

Beck, A.T. (1964) Thinking and depression: 2. Theory and therapy, *Archives of General Psychiatry*, 10: 561–71.

Beck, A.T. (1976) *Cognitive Therapy and the Emotional Disorders*. New York. International Universities Press.

Beck, A.T. (1987) Cognitive models of depression, *Journal of Cognitive Psychotherapy: An International Quarterly*, 1: 5–39.

Beck, A.T. (1989) *Love is Never Enough*. London: Penguin.

Beck, A.T. and Emery, G. with Greenberg, R.L. (1985) *Anxiety Disorders and Phobias: A Cognitive Perspective*. New York: Basic Books.

Beck, A.T. and Greenberg, R.L. (1974) *Coping with Depression*. New York: Institute for Rational Living.

Beck, A.T., Rush, J.L., Shaw, B.E. and Emery, G. (1979) *The Cognitive Therapy of Depression*. New York: Guilford Press.

Beck, A.T., Freeman, A. and Associates (1990) *Cognitive Therapy of Personality Disorders*. New York: Guilford Press.

Beck, J.S. (1995) *Cognitive Therapy. Basics and Beyond*. New York: Guilford Press.

Birchwood, M. and Tarrier, N. (1992) *Innovations in the Psychological Management of Schizophrenia*. Chichester: John Wiley.

Blackburn, I.M. (1984) *Coping with Depression*. London: Chambers.

Blackburn, I.M., Bishop, S., Glen, A.I.M., Whalley, L.J. and Christie, L.E. (1981) The efficacy of cognitive therapy in depression: a treatment trial using cognitive therapy and pharmacotherapy, each alone and in combination, *British Journal of Psychiatry*, 139: 181–9.

Bradley, G.W. (1978) Self-serving biases in the attribution process: a re-examination of the fact or fiction question, *Journal of Personality and Social Psychology*, 36: 56–71.

Bums, D.D. (1980) *Feeling Good*. New York: William Morrow & Co. Inc.

Cautela, L.R. (1973) Covert processes and behaviour modification, *Journal of Nervous and Mental Diseases*, 157: 27–36.

Chadwick, P.D.J. and Lowe, C.F. (1991) Measurement and modification of delusional beliefs, *Journal of Consulting and Clinical Psychology*, 58: 225–32.

Clark, D.A. and Steer, R.A. (1996) Empirical status of the cognitive model of anxiety and depression. In Salkovskis, P.M. (ed.), *Frontiers of Cognitive Therapy*. New York: Guilford Press,

Clark, D.M. (1986) A cognitive approach to panic, *Behaviour Research and Therapy*, 24: 461–70.

Clark, D.M. (1996) Panic disorder: from theory to therapy. In Salkovskis, P.M. (ed.), *Frontiers of Cognitive Therapy*. New York: Guilford Press.

Clark, D.M. & Fairburn, C.G., (1997) *Science and Practice of Cognitive Behaviour Therapy*. Oxford: Oxford University Press.

Clark D.M., & Wells, A. (1995) A cognitive model of social phobia. In: R.Heimberg, M.Liebowitz, D.A. Hope & F.R. Schneier (eds), *Social Phobia: Diagnosis, Assessment and Treatment*. New York: Guilford Press.

DeRubeis, R.J., Brotman, M.A., Gibbons, C.J. (2005) A Conceptual and Methodological Analysis of the Nonspecifics Argument, *Clinical Psychology: Science & Practice*, 12: 174–83.

Ehlers, A. & Clark, D.M. (2000) A cognitive model of posttraumatic stress disorder. *Behaviour Research & Therapy*, 38: 319–345.

Ellis, A. (1962) *Reason and Emotion in Psychotherapy*. Secaucus, NJ: Lyle Stuart.

Fennell, M.J.V. and Teasdale, L.D. (1987) Cognitive therapy for depression: individual differences and the process of change. *Cognitive Therapy and Research*, 11: 253–71.

Fennell, M.J.V. (1999) *Overcoming Low Self Esteem*. London: Robinson.

Fowler, D., Garety, P. & Kuipers, E. (1995) *Cognitive Behaviour Therapy for Psychosis: Theory and Practice*. Chichester: Wiley.

Freeman, A. (1983) Cognitive therapy: an overview, in A. Freeman (ed.), *Cognitive Therapy with Couples and Groups*. New York: Plenum Press.

Freeman, A. (1987) Cognitive therapy: an overview, in A. Freeman and V. Greenwood (eds), *Cognitive Therapy: Application in Psychiatric and Medical Settings*. New York: Human Sciences Press.

Gould, R.A., Otto, M.W. & Pollack, M.H. (1995) A meta-analysis of treatment outcome for panic disorder. *Clinical Psychology Review*, 15: 819–844.

Guidano, V.F. and Liotti, G. (1983) *Cognitive Processes and Emotional Disorders. A Structural Approach to Psychotherapy*. New York: Guilford.

Haby, M.M., Donnelly, M.C.J and Vos, T. (2006) Cognitive behavioural therapy for depression, panic disorder and generalized anxiety disorder: a meta-regression of factors that may predict outcome,. *Australian & New Zealand Journal of Psychiatry*, 40: 9–19.

Hooley, L.M., Orley, L. and Teasdale, J.D. (1986) Levels of expressed emotion and relapse in depressed patient?, *British Journal of Psychiatry*, 148: 642–7.

Kanfer, F.H. and Karoly, P. (1972) Self-control: a behaviouristic excursion into the lion's den, *Behaviour Therapy*, 3: 378–416.

Kelly, G. (1955) *The Psychology of Personal Constructs*, Vols I and II. New York: Norton.

Kingdon, D.G. and Turkington, D. (1994) *Cognitive Behaviour Therapy of Schizophrenia*. Hove: Lawrence Erlbaum Associates.

Kovacs, M. and Beck, A.T. (1978) Maladaptive cognitive structures in depressions, *American Journal of Psychiatry*, 135: 525–7.

Lam, D.H., Watkins, E.R., Hayward, P., Bright, J., Wright, K., Kerr ,N., Parr-Davis, G. and Sham,P. (2003) A randomized controlled study of cognitive therapy for relapse prevention for bipolar affective disorder: outcome of the first year. *Archives of General Psychiatry*, 60: 145–152.

Linehan, M.M. (1993) *Cognitive-behavioural Treatment of Borderline Personality Disorder*. London: The Guilford Press.

Mahoney, M.J. (ed.) (1995) *Cognitive and Constructive Psychotherapies*. New York: Springer.

Mahoney, M.J. and Arnkoff, D.B. (1978) Cognitive and self-control therapies, in S.L. Garfield and A.E. Bergin (eds), *Handbook of Psychotherapy and Behavior Change*, 2nd edition. New York: Wiley.

Meichenbaum, D. (1985) *Stress Inoculation Training*. New York: Pergamon Press.

Moorey, S., Holting, C., Hughes, P., Knynenberg, P. and Michael, A. (2003) Does problem solving ability predict therapy outcome in a clinical setting? *Behavioural & Cognitive Psychotherapy, 29: 485–95.* .

Padesky, C.A. (1994) Schema change processes in cognitive therapy, *Clinical Psychology and Psychotherapy*, 1: 267–278.

Persons, J.B., Davidson, J. and Tompkins, M.A. (2001) *Essential Components of Cognitive-Behavior Therapy for Depression*. Washington, D.C.: American Psychological Association.

Rachman S.J. and deSilva, P. (1978) Abnormal and normal obsessions. *Behaviour Research and Therapy*, 16, 233–238.

Rosenthal, T.L. and Bandura, A. (1978) Psychological modelling: theory and practice, in S.L. Garfield and A.E. Bergin (eds), *Handbook of Psychotherapy and Behavior Change*, 2nd edition. New York: Wiley.

Rush, A.J. and Watkins, L.T. (1981) Group versus individual cognitive therapy: a pilot study, *Cognitive Therapy and Research*, 5: 95–103.

Rush, A.J., Beck, A.T., Kovacs, M. and Hollon, S. (1977) Comparative efficacy of cognitive therapy and imipramine in the treatment of depressed outpatients, *Cognitive Therapy and Research*, 1: 17–37.

Safran, Jeremy D., Segal, Zindel V., Vallis, T. Michael, Shaw, Brian F., et al. (1993) Assessing patient suitability for short-term cognitive therapy with an interpersonal focus. *Cognitive Therapy and Research*. 17: 23–38.

Salkovskis, P.M. (1985) Obsessive-compulsive problems: a cognitive-behavioural analysis. *Behaviour Research and Therapy*, 23: 571–583.

Salkovskis, P.M. (Ed.) (1996) *Frontiers of Cognitive Therapy*. New York: Guilford Press.

Salkovskis, P.M. and Harrison, J. (1984) Abnormal and normal obsessions: A replication. *Behaviour research and Therapy*, 22: 549–552.

Salkovskis, P.M. and Warwick, N.M.C. (1986) Morbid preoccupations, health anxiety and reassurance: a cognitive-behavioural approach to hypochondriasis, *Behaviour Research and Therapy*, 24: 597–602.

Scott, M.J. and Stradling, S.C. (1990) Group cognitive therapy for depression produces clinically significant reliable change in community-based settings. *Behavioural Psychotherapy*, 18: 1–19.

Shaw, B.F. (1984) Specification of the training and evaluation of cognitive therapists for outcome studies, in L. Williams and R.L. Spitzer (eds), *Psychotherapy Research: Where Are We and Where Should We Go?* New York: Guilford Press.

Simons, A.D., Murphy, G.E., Levine, L.L. and Wetzel, R.D. (1986) Cognitive therapy and pharmacotherapy for depression, *Archives of General Psychiatry*, 43: 43–8.

Taylor, S.E. and Brown, I.D. (1988) Illusion and well-being: a social psychological perspective on mental health, *Psychological Bulletin*, 103: 193–210.

Teasdale, L.D., Fennell, M.J.V., Hibbert, G.A. and Amies, P.L. (1984) Cognitive therapy for major depressive disorder in primary care, *British Journal of Psychiatry*, 144: 400–6.

Teasdale, J.D., Segal, Z.V., Williams, J.M.G., Ridgeway, V., Soulsby, J. & Lau, M. (2000) Prevention of relapse/recurrence in major depression by mindfulness-based cognitive therapy, *Journal of Consulting and Clinical Psychology,* 68: 615–23.

Trepka, C., Rees, A., Shapiro, D.A., Hardy, G.E. & Barkham, M. (2004) Therapist competence and outcome of cognitive therapy for depression, *Cognitive Therapy and Research,* 28: 143–57.

Vallis, T. Michael, Howes, Janice L., Standage, Kevin (2000) Is cognitive therapy suitable for treating individuals with personality dysfunction? *Cognitive Therapy and Research.* 24: 595–606.

Wells, A. (1997). *Cognitive Therapy of Anxiety Disorders.* Chichester: Wiley.

Young, J.E., Klosko, J.S. & Weishaar, M.E. (2003) *Schema Therapy: A Practitioner's Guide.* New York: Guilford Press.

Young, L.E. and Klosko, L.S. (1994) *Reinventing Your Life.* New York: Plume Books.

Zettle, R.D., Haflich, J.L. & Reynolds, R.A. (1992) Responsivity to cognitive therapy as a function of treatment format and client personality dimensions. *Journal of Consulting and Clinical Psychology,* 48: 787–797.

SUGGESTED FURTHER READING

Beck, A.T. (1976) *Cognitive Therapy and the Emotional Disorders.* New York: International Universities Press.

Beck, J.S. (1995) *Cognitive Therapy. Basics and Beyond.* New York: Guilford Press.

Clark, D.M. and Fairburn, C.G. (1997) *Science and Practice of Cognitive Behaviour Therapy.* Oxford: Oxford University Press.

Hawton, K., Salkovskis, P.M., Kirk, L. and Clarke, D.M. (eds) (1989*) Cognitive Behaviour Therapy for Psychiatric Problems.* Oxford: Oxford Medical Publications.

Young, L.E. and Klosko, L.S. (1994) *Reinventing Your Life.* New York: Plume Books.

13

Behaviour Therapy

David Richards

HISTORICAL CONTEXT AND DEVELOPMENT IN BRITAIN

Historical context

The traditional view of behaviour therapy is that it is the practical and clinical manifestation of laboratory-based research work, which itself developed from theories of human behaviour dating from the early part of the 20th century. Central to these theories is 'learning theory', the science of understanding how living beings learn. In particular, classical and operant conditioning models were developed and tested, which went some way to explaining human behaviour.

During the latter part of the century, however, behaviour therapy as a term came to be used more loosely to describe a range of techniques that often relied less on learning theory and more on data from empirical research trials which have demonstrated clinical efficacy. What was more important to many practitioners was that, in contrast to other psychotherapies developed solely from *theoretical* models that stressed past developmental conflicts as the source of psychological distress, a new range of *evidence-based* therapeutic techniques was becoming available. Such techniques attracted the name 'behavioural psychotherapy', the preferred term to describe the clinical techniques described in the rest of this chapter. Behavioural psychotherapy has thus developed via a potent mix of evidence from both basic science and clinical trials. It cannot be stressed too much at the beginning of this chapter that, for many clinicians, the theories of learning most often associated with behavioural psychotherapy matter far less than evidence-based technical eclecticism – i.e. what works for patients.

There have been many historical references to techniques that we would now refer to as behavioural. There is an oft-quoted 17th-century reference whereby the principles of graded exposure were outlined for those who had a fearful child:

> if your child shrieks and runs away at the sight of a frog, let another catch it and lay it down at a good distance from him; at first accustom him to look upon it; when he can do that to come nearer to it and see it leap without emotion; then to touch it lightly, when it is held fast in another's hand; and so on until he can come to handle it as confidently as a butterfly or sparrow. (Locke, 1693)

Buddhist writings, reviewed in detail by Padmal de Silva (1984) refer much to behavioural approaches, particularly relaxation, imaginal and real life exposure. Even Freud noted the efficacy of behavioural approaches when he wrote:

> One can hardly master a phobia if one waits until the patient lets the analysis influence him to give it up … One succeeds only when one can induce them by the influence of the analysis to go and to struggle with the anxiety while they make the attempts. (Freud, 1919)

At this point it is usual to describe the development of those two planks of behavioural thinking – classical and operant conditioning. Unfortunately, the term 'conditioning' is actually a mistranslation from Russian (since Pavlov and others were working in relative isolation from the West it took some time before their ideas were passed on) and it also implies something that one imposes on another. 'Learning' is a better term. Another problem with traditional explanations is that they appear highly mechanistic (as indeed they are) and have produced much disapproval from those that value a sense of choice and self-determination in human behaviour. Although classical and operant learning, as described below, are distinct processes they are laboratory derived and even here require a huge amount of ingenuity to produce a situation where only one is operating at a time. In real life, a complex mixture of reinforcements is acting on an organism and any attempt to explain emotional responding using only one process will be unsatisfactory. Although these terms will be elaborated below, it is important to recognize that their description does not imply adherence to principles of Social Darwinism. Classical and operant learning take place in a sophisticated and complex manner in the real world.

Learning theory got off to a systematic start with the work of Pavlov (1927) on classical learning and others such as Thorndike (1911), Jones (1924) and Skinner (1953) for operant learning. It was shown that reliable and reproducible effects could be demonstrated from the pairing of unconditioned stimuli (i.e. environmental cues which produce an innate physiological or behavioural response in all cases; for example, the blink of an eye in response to a puff of air or salivation in response to food) with previously innocuous cues (for example, a coloured light or a bell). After a number of pairings, living beings come to associate the new, previously innocuous cue with the effects of the unconditioned stimuli and, if presented with the new cue on its own, behave as if it were the unconditioned stimuli. Thus, a coloured light might invoke an involuntary blink, whilst a bell might induce salivation. Such reactions are termed conditioned responses, the new cues are known as conditioned stimuli and the process by which conditioned responses are acquired is called classical learning.

The second plank – operant learning – is basically the assertion that the probability of a behaviour being repeated is determined by its consequences. If the consequences are beneficial the behaviour is more likely to be repeated. If they are harmful the behaviour will be reduced. Consequences which are beneficial are called reinforcers, come in two types (positive and negative reinforcement) and always increase the probability of a behaviour occurring. A positive reinforcement is something that increases the behaviour because it is a pleasant experience, for example a child receiving a chocolate as praise for clearing their toys away. Negative reinforcement also increases behaviour, although in this case it is by the removal of something aversive. For example, if a person feels highly anxious in the presence of a dog and by running away feels a reduction in their anxiety, they will be more likely to repeat the exercise next time they see a dog. Two other types of consequence will reduce rather than increase the probability of behaviours occurring. Behaviours which are punished – associated with aversive events – will reduce, as will behaviours in situations where an expected reward is omitted, a situation called frustrative non-reward.

Few behavioural psychotherapists in current practice spend much of their day reflecting on such definitions. This can be clearly illustrated by the fate of the first theoretically driven behavioural treatment – systematic desensitization. Developed by Wolpe, systematic desensitization was based on classical learning principles. By pairing a pleasant stimulus with a conditioned aversive one, Wolpe was able to demonstrate a change in fear and arousal levels in the face of the aversive stimulus, which gradually lost its power to disturb. Of clear utility for treating phobias, relaxation was used by Wolpe as the inhibitory stimulus; he called his procedure 'psychotherapy by reciprocal inhibition' (Wolpe, 1958). Although it was effective for up to 80 per cent of people with phobias, Wolpe required patients to develop a highly complex hierarchy, work up it very gradually, keeping levels of anxiety always at an absolute minimum, and conducted the treatment using visual imagery techniques. The next decade saw empirical trials which demonstrated that none of these elements was required. Complex imaginal hierarchies and competing relaxation techniques were all proved to be redundant as the singularly most effective psychotherapeutic technique of modern times was developed: graded exposure *in vivo*. Therefore, whereas Wolpe (1976) favoured a strong theory base others (e.g. Marks, 1982a) argued for empirical pragmatism.

This work was accompanied by a general dissatisfaction with traditional psychoanalytical techniques. Eysenck (1952, 1985) was instrumental in drawing attention to the many flaws and irrelevancies in such work. Key was the discovery that improvements attributed to psychoanalysis could be easily explained by spontaneous remission rates. At this time a massive research effort began to take shape in order to develop effective psychotherapy for all.

In amongst this effort arose one element of laboratory theory which many therapists regard as crucial to their understanding of emotion: Lang's three systems theory of emotion (Lang, 1979). In this theory, emotional responses can be conveniently defined as physiological (autonomic responses), behavioural (responses controlled by the individual) and cognitive (internal events such as thoughts and images). The three systems are linked together but often change at different rates during therapy. This analysis of emotion has had an enormous influence on the way behavioural psychotherapists organize their assessment and treatment techniques.

The development of cognitive therapy has added to the early work on behavioural psychotherapy. With the understanding of emotion that came from Lang's 'three systems' model, behavioural psychotherapy and cognitive therapy came together as 'cognitive behavioural therapy' (CBT). Behavioural psychotherapy, CBT and cognitive therapy now lie on both a theoretical and a practical continuum, where the two schools of thought borrow from each other's theoretical, empirical and clinical knowledge bases. Behavioural and cognitive therapists generally adopt a position somewhere along this continuum, which they then use to describe their theoretical rationale and clinical practice. However, there tends to be more debate and difference around theory than one can observe reflected in clinical practice. Furthermore, the empirical evidence base does not support the primacy of behavioural, cognitive or cognitive-behavioural techniques. Studies, reviewed by Lovell and Richards (2000), repeatedly demonstrate that behavioural, cognitive or mixed approaches achieve the same level of satisfactory outcomes for equivalent numbers of patients. More complex, multi-strand combined cognitive and behavioural approaches do not appear to deliver improved outcomes for the majority of clients.

Development in Britain

Britain developed a unique approach to behavioural psychotherapy which can be traced to its publicly funded system of 'socialized medicine', the National Health Service (NHS). One of the characteristics of behavioural psychotherapy in Britain is its multiprofessional practitioner base, a situation rare elsewhere. Psychologists, doctors and nurses are all major professional groups practising behavioural psychotherapy and increasingly it is becoming possible for other health workers such as counsellors to become trained as behavioural or cognitive-behavioural therapists. This healthy multiprofessionalism is due to three reasons.

First, the presence of a group of doctors and psychologists working at the Institute of Psychiatry, Maudsley Hospital, London during the 1960s and 1970s led to a huge surge in collaborative research work. It was during this time that some of the empirical foundations were laid for key techniques such as exposure and response prevention.

Secondly, part of the reason for the vibrant mix of therapists can be ascribed to the establishment in 1972 of the British Association for Behavioural

Psychotherapy (BABP), now the British Association for Behavioural and Cognitive Psychotherapy (BABCP). Set up as an interest group, based around the Maudsley group and a few other British collaborators, the BABCP reflected the pioneering spirit of the times and did not restrict its membership to specific professions. Because the BABCP was not a professional body and did not embark on its practitioner registration scheme until much more recently, it was open to anyone with an interest in behavioural psychotherapy. As such, as well as psychiatrists and psychologists, nurses, social workers, teachers, general practitioners and many more joined.

The third reason for the vibrant mix of professions was the pioneering work of the psychiatrist Isaac Marks, a renowned empirical scientist and part of the Maudsley group. In the mid-1970s Marks was so concerned to spread the availability of the newly developed behavioural psychotherapy, that he conducted a government-funded trial of nurse-delivered behavioural psychotherapy. This first trial of specialist nurse practitioners in mental health proved that they could deliver behavioural psychotherapy as effectively as medical practitioners and others and was so successful that it led to the development of an 18-month post-registration course in behavioural psychotherapy. This course has trained over 250 nurse behavioural psychotherapists who themselves have gone on to disseminate behavioural psychotherapy via local innovative training programmes.

From this secure professional and empirical evidence base, nurses in the UK are now firmly accepted as part of the multiprofessional body of workers who can deliver and develop behavioural psychotherapy. In Britain, unlike some other countries, there have been no sterile debates about who 'owns' behavioural psychotherapy. Behavioural psychotherapy is now owned quite properly by those who have the skills to deliver it effectively.

THEORETICAL ASSUMPTIONS

Image of the person

Behaviourists view a person as a physiological being who under the influence of the environment and genetic predispositions will behave in a particular manner. Behaviourists reject the mind–body dualism prevalent in Western thought and regard concepts such as mind and ego as unscientific and unhelpful since they are explanatory fictions. Because one cannot observe such concepts directly – only infer them by observing behaviour – they do not help explain the human condition. Such non-explanations are termed examples of mentalism. Rejection of mentalism does not exclude consideration of thinking and sensory experiences since these phenomena can be seen as private behaviours (i.e. experienced by one person only) which share all the properties of public behaviours (i.e. experienced by many people). Behaviourists strongly believe that any natural event arises only from other natural events, not from mysterious notions of personality or ego, for example. These are merely explanatory constructions which ultimately impede scientific enquiry. If we are tempted to describe a person as having a depressive personality it is because we are observing certain depressed behaviours such as withdrawal, sleeplessness or tearfulness. We are not able to observe the personality directly.

Behaviourists view a person's past history as extremely important because of the wealth of learning or conditioning events within it. Analogous to evolutionary explanations of species behaviour, an individual's past experiences will have an effect on their current behaviour, even if that experience is some considerable time in the past. In some ways, the concept of natural selection for a species is an identical idea to the learning history of an individual, as both provide explanations for behaviours in the present. They are also similar in that both ideas are more appropriate explanations than a retreat into beliefs about enigmatic internal or external forces directing either behaviour or evolution.

Conceptualization of psychological disturbance and health

Psychological disturbance is considered to be expressed as behaviours which cause the individual problems in their interactions with the environment. Societal norms allow individuals to operate within an envelope of acceptable behaviours. A 'healthy' individual is one who is able to interact with others and the environment in such a way as to derive high rates of positive reinforcement. Mastery and control are usually cited as positive elements of an individual's relationship with the environment. However, all individuals are genetically 'set' at a specific autonomic level – one only has to parent two or more children to appreciate this particular truth. As a consequence the impact of social and other environmental stimuli on two children will vary enormously. As a result, words such as stoicism and nervousness are used to describe individuals at different ends of a genetically determined arousal spectrum. The complex interplay of genetic predispositions and environmental stimuli produces our own uniqueness.

A range of thinkers have coined terms to describe the results of this interplay. Particularly dominant have been the theories of self-efficacy (Bandura, 1977) and learned helplessness (Seligman, 1975). These related ideas concern the ability of an individual to cope with whatever the world throws at them. Coping is often divided into practical, emotional and avoidant categories. Individuals use these strategies to different degrees depending on the situations they face and on their individual abilities and range of personal skills. Women are traditionally seen as more competent in emotional coping – listening, empathizing, etc. – whereas men use more practical coping strategies – doing things to alter the situation – although there is, of course, huge individual variation. Avoidant coping is generally seen as maladaptive given that it may lead to a perpetuation of unhelpful learned helplessness. However, where environmental stimuli are potentially overwhelming, avoidant coping may be extremely effective, at least in the short term.

Acquisition of psychological disturbance

The earlier observations on classical and operant learning are pertinent here. It has been reliably demonstrated that fears can be learned through a process of pairing real aversive stimuli with initially innocuous stimuli and that these stimuli, once established, are extremely difficult to eradicate. A famous example of this is the well-known experience of the poor unfortunate 'Little Albert' who at the tender age of 11 months was conditioned to be afraid of white rats by their pairing with a loud noise (Watson and Rayner, 1920). This effect even extended to other similarly looking stimuli such as the scientist's white hair. However, this simple phenomenon does not explain why humans are apparently more prone to some types of fear than others. Although not unheard of, it is extremely rare for someone to complain of fearing tweed trousers (rather than appropriately merely abhorring them) whereas fears of spiders, snakes, heights and the sight of blood are extremely common. This selectivity in fear acquisition is a central pillar of the argument for genetic evolutionary preparedness in the acquisition of psychological disturbance. However, the term 'innateness' is now used since preparedness assumes that the predisposition must be paired with an aversive experience for it to become activated. For example, preparedness does not explain why in many countries large numbers of people are afraid of snakes despite the fact that the chances of coming across one are infinitesimally small and it is unlikely that anybody will have experienced a conditioning event involving snakes.

The types of innate feared stimuli are many. Isaac Marks (1987) sums this up by reference to the evolutionary merit in the selection of individuals whose make-up is innately programmed to avoid certain stimuli which herald objective danger. Fear is generally brought on by 'stimuli which are abrupt, intense, irregular, and rapidly increasing' (Marks, 1987: 52). Heights, too much or too little space around us, newness, loudness, being looked at, the sight of one of our fellows being injured – all provoke fear even where we have no previous direct experience of an aversive consequence associated with the specific stimulus.

Clearly, not all psychological disorders can be explained by this innateness. Social experience also has a role to play. As discussed earlier, variation across individuals is enormous. There is also variation across gender. For example, the prevalence of agoraphobia is between a 1:2 and 1:3 male to female ratio. Many explanations have been advanced, including the greater ability of women in Western cultures to express their fears or the feminist view that women are sex-stereotyped in a patriarchal society into promoting the display of fear. Potentially, men are enabled to overcome their innate fears by social pressures to go forth into the world and prosper – a process not unlike the clinical procedure of graded exposure *in vivo*.

The impact of environmental experience is most clearly seen in traumatically induced disorders such as post-traumatic stress disorder (PTSD). Commonly, people with PTSD describe no previous experience of pathological psychological disturbance. As a consequence of an encounter with some incident such as an accident or an assault, a severe anxiety disorder can result which the individual experiences as a series of severe autonomic, behavioural and cognitive symptoms. Here, the inducting stimuli may not be of the innate variety and the fearful reaction of people with PTSD to ordinarily innocuous stimuli is a particular feature. This leads us on to the next section – the perpetuation of psychological disturbance.

Perpetuation of psychological disturbance

Most people would be extremely sympathetic towards someone who had just experienced an assault or an accident which involved a real or potential threat to life, even if they had merely witnessed such an event. We would expect them to be in a state of 'shock' – experiencing a range of autonomic symptoms and possessed of a strong desire to talk repeatedly about their experience. However, despite our initial sympathy we would also expect them to recover. Indeed, given time, this is what happens to most of us who are unfortunate to endure a traumatic event. For some, however, recovery does not occur. The mechanisms behind this maintenance of fearful reactions are central to behavioural understandings of both psychological disturbance and, more importantly, their treatment.

In order to advance some understanding of the concept of fear maintenance it is necessary to return to the principles of operant learning. Mowrer (1950) described the deficiencies of psychopathological models based on classical learning alone and integrated them with operant paradigms. Essentially, if a fearful organism engages in behaviours which reduce their anxiety, such as escape or avoidance, the resultant negative reinforcement strengthens the probability of the escape and avoidance still further. This 'two process' theory has been extremely influential. Much behavioural psychotherapy is directed towards assisting clients to modify the operant reinforcers or 'maintenance factors' for their problematic behaviours. This approach has yielded much greater therapeutic fruit than the unproductive attempts at uncovering and modifying postulated early experiences engaged in by many other schools of psychotherapy. Breaking the cycle of fear and avoidance is a central goal of much behavioural psychotherapy.

One important concept in fear maintenance is the failure of a person's fear to 'habituate' in the face of noxious stimuli. Ordinarily, if a person is repeatedly presented with a feared stimulus, provided it is not contiguous with real pain or permanent discomfort, the arousal experienced in the face of this stimulus reduces over time. The person becomes more confident and can face the previously feared situation. This most often happens when faced with novel situations. Initially timid, the person eventually habituates and grows more confident. Someone with agoraphobia, however, has not experienced this natural arousal reduction and continues to be distressed and consequently avoidant in the face of crowds, enclosed spaces, etc.

Explanations involving the psycho-biological processes involved are necessary to shed light on the above phenomenon. When faced with a stimulus which is innately fear inducing, all organisms, from the highest to the lowest, find that their ordinary behaviours are inhibited, selective attention is paid to the new stimulus and they become highly aroused. This 'behavioural inhibition' allows organisms to appraise the potential threat and prepare for subsequent action – fight or flight – without distraction from other competing stimuli. If the organism decides to run, it gives itself no opportunity to ascertain the true threat involved. This is essentially what happens with the maintenance of fear. The person with agoraphobia does not stay with the anxiety-provoking stimulus for a sufficiently long time or frequently enough to lead to this behavioural inhibition system becoming habituated. The phenomenon of habituation can be observed in ordinary life many times, for example in the case of someone living with a loudly ticking clock. Over time they will cease to notice it, although an occasional visitor will find the noise intrusive, at least for a time. Repetition and duration are key principles in effective treatments for fear reduction.

One final principle needs to be explained: that of sensitization. Sensitization refers to the increasing levels of arousal experienced by people when confronted by short, intense exposures to fear-provoking stimuli. Erratic and involuntary contact with previously feared or innately fearful stimuli is most likely to lead to increasing sensitization. Therefore, not only does running away or escape from a feared situation prevent habituation, it may also lead to a net increase in fear via sensitization.

Change

Mental health waxes and wanes in all individuals in response to the complex interplay of biological arousability and environmental pressure. The behavioural view of change is that organisms will be motivated by responding to reinforcers. Rewards, whether in the form of negative or positive reinforcement, will lead to increases in behaviour. Punishment or frustrative non-reward will lead to behavioural reductions. The propensity of individuals to respond to these environmental stimuli varies according to their genetic set. As behavioural changes occur, the autonomic and cognitive systems also move – not always at the same pace – until the three systems of physical arousal, behaviour and cognitions achieve equilibrium again. Further, as individuals learn new and more complex skills, for example by watching others, they may learn how to become more assertive and can exert more choice in their behavioural repertoires. This enables them to employ more diverse responses to the problems and stresses of everyday life.

PRACTICE

Goals of therapy

In all instances, the goals of behavioural psychotherapy are arrived at in a collaborative process of negotiation between therapist and client. Different clients will have different objectives. In general, the goal of most programmes of behavioural psychotherapy will be to assist a client reduce the intensity of their problems such that their difficulties impact less upon their activities of daily living. For some clients an appropriate goal will be the complete eradication of all symptoms, most commonly achieved in specific phobias and PTSD. In other cases clients will seek a reduction in the impact of their difficulties sufficient to allow them to engage in normal activities again – an end-point which sufferers of obsessive-compulsive disorder strive for. Whilst empowerment and personal growth are often a product of behavioural psychotherapy's fundamental principle that clients should be enabled to address their problems using their own resources, therapy is not framed as a search for personal enlightenment.

Therapists seek to use behavioural activities as a way of entering and modifying the three emotional response systems (autonomic, behavioural and cognitive). When the client is assisted to change one of these systems (behaviour) directly, the autonomic and cognitive systems also change, although there is often a lag or de-synchrony between systems. The behaviours targeted for change are those that are implicated in the antecedent/behaviour/consequence sequence of triggers and reinforcement.

Importantly, behaviour therapists do not believe that they are missing some mysterious unacknowledged personal conflict from either the past or present when they target current behavioural symptoms for change. This is because as well as the theoretical rejection of mentalist thought, a key principle is that techniques must be based on the best empirical research evidence available. Research does not support a search for mentalist solutions. Quite the reverse: previous theoretical assumptions of other schools of psychological therapy have proved to be unfounded. Arguments such as 'symptom substitution' have floundered on empirical demonstrations of success in behavioural psychotherapy whilst the maintenance of behavioural treatment gains has been demonstrated with very long follow-up studies. It is a key element of the BABCP's code of practice that therapists should only utilize techniques with such a sound evidence base. The goal of behavioural psychotherapy is, therefore, to deliver the best evidence-based therapy, focusing on the 'here and now', which is action orientated, collaborative and aimed at relieving current distress and disability caused by acute or chronic psychological disturbance.

Selection criteria

The principle of an evidence base is applied right at the start of definitions of suitability for behavioural psychotherapy. Where there is clear evidence that behavioural methods can improve a client's condition the client must be initially considered as suitable for therapy. Such evidence is most believable if it comes from a systematic review, at least one randomized controlled trial or, if these are not available, from other empirical evidence from less robust study designs. As more clinical problems are being researched the list of suitable conditions is growing; it currently comprises all the anxiety disorders including obsessive-compulsive disorder and PTSD, depression, some somatizing disorders such as chronic fatigue, sexual difficulties, habit disorders, eating problems particularly bulimia, nightmares and morbid grief. Recently, in combination with some cognitive techniques, behavioural methods have been shown to be effective with psychosis (Slade and Haddock, 1996).

However, all clients are individuals and each individual will present with a unique constellation of symptoms. Once it has been established that a client has a general type of problem for which there is evidence that behavioural psychotherapy can help, there are several criteria which should be applied (Richards and McDonald, 1990). First, the client's problem should be expressed as observable behaviour. Behavioural psychotherapy is most likely to be useful if a person is complaining of a handicapping excess or deficit of behaviour, such as avoidance or excessive cleaning or waking in the night after frequent nightmares. This does not exclude symptoms such as intrusive images or obsessive ruminations. These are regarded as private behaviours and have been shown to be just as amenable to change as public behaviours.

Secondly, the client's difficulties must be current and predictable. Behavioural psychotherapy techniques usually require the client to address their difficulties regularly and repeatedly. Clients should be able to predict a reasonably consistent degree of handicap in particular situations. This is not to say that their problems cannot vary in intensity or severity from time to time, but the problem should manifest itself by and large in a predictable fashion. It is perfectly possible that a problem's origins may lie in the past – morbid grief would be an example here – however, it should be manifesting itself as a current difficulty to render it suitable for treatment using behavioural psychotherapy.

A third suitability principle is that client and therapist should be able to define and agree on specific goals for therapy. Purposeful and participatory, behavioural psychotherapy cannot work unless client and therapist work together towards achieving clearly defined end-points and intermediary goals, usually expressed as behavioural targets. Fourthly, and in line with the third principle, clients should understand and agree to the type of treatment being offered. Once again, the participatory criterion is being invoked here. Behavioural techniques do not 'do things to people'; rather, people 'do things with behavioural techniques'.

The final criterion should be that there are no contra-indications for behavioural treatment. There are many and varied reasons why a client may present with an apparent psychological problem when in reality there is an underlying physical cause for their distress, for example hyperthyroidism and anxiety or diabetes and impotence. Other contra-indications are very severe depression which might pose a risk to the individual through suicide, self-harm or self-neglect; excessive use of anxiolytic medications such as benzodiazepines; or severe problem illegal drug and alcohol use. These conditions must be treated separately. In the case of depression, antidepressants do not interfere with the psychological processes harnessed in behavioural psychotherapy so treatment can be concurrent.

Qualities of effective therapists

Behavioural psychotherapists display a set of behaviours with their clients which are the outward manifestation of assumptions they make about people who seek help for psychological problems. Chief amongst these are:

- This person is responsive.
- This person is honest.
- This person is trying to cope.

Behavioural psychotherapists believe that these assumptions will drive client responses. If a therapist approaches a clinical situation with negative attitudes it will quickly become apparent to the client, the client will behave in response to these negative assumptions and very little effective work will be undertaken. The reverse, the set of assumptions listed above, will be more likely to elicit a positive response from the client. Belief in client *responsivity* is a prerequisite for collaborative working. The second assumption, *honesty*, reflects the principle of behavioural psychotherapists' valuing the client as a true partner in therapy. Change can only be achieved if clients and therapists know what the client is experiencing. Generally, this must be ascertained through client self-report. A positive assumption must be that the client will report these experiences honestly for progress to be validly monitored. Finally, the principle of *coping* is essential. However different from the norm is the behaviour that is causing the client their life problems, it has to be understood in terms of an attempt to cope with emotional arousal. Avoidances, rituals, excesses and deficits in behaviour are all seen as attempts to cope rather than as discrete pathological processes.

In addition to these essential positive assumptions, behavioural psychotherapists must be able to interview effectively. Patient-centred interviewing is the essential method of information-gathering, treatment planning, review and evaluation. At all times the therapist is interested in the 'here and now', not the client's past history except where it has a direct and crucial bearing on the present. To this end, therapists use an interview process which is free-flowing, has a progressive focus and elicits client-centred information. Typically, therapists start with a general open question then, guided by the client's responses, move to specific open questions and finally ask closed questions to arrive at a mutually agreed accurate problem definition (Richards and McDonald, 1990). Within this structure information on triggers, the three systems of emotion, consequences, frequency, duration and intensity of symptoms is all gathered. The same patient-centred interview process is utilized in subsequent therapy sessions where the therapist will use information from the client to review progress. Many authors regard this whole process and way of working as an essential ethical dimension to behavioural psychotherapy (Fox and Conroy, 2000; Newell, 1994; Newell and Gournay, 2000).

Other qualities of effective behavioural psychotherapists are the ability to tolerate and handle expressed emotion, to be able to plan coherent treatment programmes, to be able to use clinical measures accurately, to be comfortable with 'selling' clinical strategies and to display behaviours consistent with the 'scientist practitioner'. Behavioural psychotherapists must use information from the scientific evidence base, plan personal experiments with clients to test individual hypotheses and report their results in the wider public domain.

Therapeutic relationship and style

The therapeutic style of a behavioural psychotherapist is best described as purposeful and participatory. The aim of the therapist is to assist the client to address their problems and move towards a position of greater health and reduced handicap. The therapist enables the client to make this change through the provision of information and participatory shaping of therapeutic activities. The relationship between client and therapist is not, therefore, developed for its own sake. Indeed, there is much evidence that behavioural psychotherapy can be delivered very effectively without the presence of a human therapist (e.g. Greist et al., 1998). The therapeutic relationship is merely one of a range of potential delivery systems including books, computers, interactive telephone systems for behavioural psychotherapy.

Where face-to-face individual therapy is selected as the delivery mode, the quality of the therapeutic relationship is vital since the therapist may have to assist the client to engage in some therapeutic behavioural activities which might at first appear aversive. The therapeutic relationship is enhanced in the following manner. Attention and continuity are demonstrated by nods, facial expression, eye contact and the setting of the environment to avoid interruptions. Non-intrusive note-taking is also utilized to aid the flow of therapy sessions. Rapport and partnership are established through the totality of the client-centred interviewing process including mutual comments on the progress of the session. Where the therapist has to assist the client to manage emotion, empathy rather than sympathy is used, as is very limited self-disclosure (usually restricted to factually accurate statements to establish a therapist's relevant expertise). Reassurance is also limited to truthful, preferably conservative, predictions about events which are under the therapist's control. In behavioural psychotherapy, therapists do not use interpretation, excessive reassurance, inappropriate probing or evaluative statements.

The techniques described in the previous paragraph are not unique to behavioural psychotherapy. They are used in many individual therapies to develop warm and trusting relationships between helper and the person seeking help. In behavioural psychotherapy, however, the relationship is not an end in itself. Both each session and the treatment programme itself are prefaced by a clear agreement between client and therapist on session time limits and goals. The quality of the relationship should assist both partners in utilizing evidence-based interventions in order to meet these goals. Therapy is a partnership, initially and mutually unequal in that the therapist has more knowledge and professional expertise whereas the client has more personal understanding of their particular circumstances and problems. By the end of therapy the relationship should have become more equal.

Major therapeutic strategies and techniques

Given that they target the behavioural emotional response system, behavioural techniques appear deceptively simple. However, they are extremely subtle and sophisticated in application. The use of a behavioural treatment such as exposure, with its explicit goal of promoting habituation to feared stimuli, requires an understanding of psychobiological mechanisms and the nature of the environmental and personal characteristics necessary to make the most effective use of the techniques. The deceptive simplicity of behavioural techniques can lead unwary therapists into designing poorly understood and ultimately ineffective programmes.

The current view, supported by a considerable evidence base, is that in the application of almost all behavioural techniques it is what the client does between sessions that is the crucial determinant of therapeutic success or failure. In the past, therapists spent a great deal of time 'walking the streets' accompanying clients with agoraphobia. We know now that this is both unnecessary and potentially harmful in that it may lead to client dependence on the therapist. Inter-session 'homework' is the most important part of any programme. The nature of this homework will be determined by the client's problems and the selection of the appropriate evidence-based intervention. The most robust and common of these is prolonged exposure.

Exposure

This is defined as the therapeutic confrontation with a feared stimulus until the physical, behavioural and cognitive responses to that stimulus have habituated (become reduced). In order to facilitate this psychobiological process, key principles have to be observed. First, exposure must be prolonged. Fear does not habituate unless one confronts it for a sufficient length of time. Figure 13.1 details this effect by comparing a typical fear/avoidance response to a feared stimulus, contrasted with a response to the same stimulus in an exposure paradigm. If the person remains in contact with the feared stimulus (exposure 1) prolonged exposure will lead to a gradual reduction in fear over time. This contrasts with the fear/avoidance response where the person escapes from the stimulus as soon as it reaches its peak, experiencing temporary reduction in fear but no long-term improvement. Each subsequent contact with the feared stimulus produces exactly the same fear and avoidance response. In the same time frame, where the

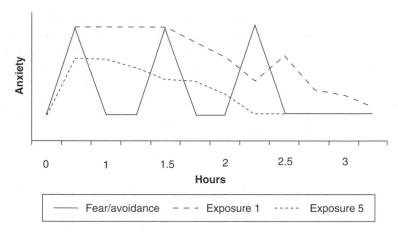

Figure 13.1   Fear and avoidance (the solid line) versus exposure (the broken lines): the effect on anxiety over time

exposure paradigm produces a reduction in anxiety over time, the approach/ avoidance paradigm leads to a continuation of the same level of fear.

The figure also illustrates the second principle of exposure: exposure must be repeated. Subsequent confrontation with the feared stimuli leads both to less initial fear and to a more rapid reduction (habituation) of the fear response. This is shown clearly by the line 'Exposure 5', a hypothetical fifth exposure session for someone undergoing an exposure treatment programme. The number of repeated exposure sessions depends on the individual's response and is ultimately determined by the levels of intra- and inter-session habituation.

A third principle of exposure is that it should be graded. People who fear situations or objects can usually place their fears in a hierarchy. They can then work up this hierarchy, from least to worst feared, moving up as they habituate to lower items via prolonged and repeated exposures.

Most of this happens between sessions as homework. In order for client and therapist to decide together on suitable exposure targets and the speed of progress, the client monitors their levels of anxiety using a simple scale (e.g. 0–8; 0–100). Behavioural psychotherapists use special self-monitoring diary sheets where the client rates their anxiety before, during (every 15 minutes) and after each exposure exercise, particularly those done as homework. Review of these diaries forms a key part of each therapy session.

The stimuli used in exposure exercises are those that the client has selected as most appropriate and are usually those which cause them most anxiety. In general, real-life situations and objects are chosen and are regarded as the most effective. Occasionally it may not be possible to have access to real-life examples of feared stimuli and in these circumstances imaginal exposure may be used (e.g. Richards, 1988). Imaginal exposure is particularly useful in the treatment of PTSD. Here individuals fear memories of their trauma and spend considerable energy avoiding thinking about it. As well as the many theoretical and ethical objections to real-life exposure to situations associated with the trauma, in many cases it is impossible to re-create the trauma situation. Imaginal exposure not only gives access to the evoking stimuli but also enables the feared stimuli to be reproduced so as to resemble as closely as possible the real event, maximizing the effectiveness of exposure. Imaginal exposure is also used with obsessive-compulsive disorder (OCD). OCD often involves covert ritualizing so imaginal exposure to anxiety-provoking cognitive ruminations can be used to promote habituation.

One further type of stimulus useful for exposure is interoceptive cue exposure. People who are hypersensitive to changes in their body often get labelled as 'hypochondriacs'. Exposure to these cues either in imagination or in real life can lead to habituation and reduced sensitivity. An example of interoceptive cue exposure would be the client with an inappropriate fear of having a heart attack brought on whenever s/he experienced a faster pulse rate. In this case, exposure would take the form of a graded exercise regime to produce sustained periods of faster heart rate.

Response prevention
This is an adjunctive technique used with exposure for people who are suffering problems with OCD. As well as fearing and avoiding stimuli which provoke anxiety (for example various 'contaminants') people with OCD also engage in excessive behaviours such as cleaning and checking. These serve to reduce or neutralize the anxiety provoked by confrontation with their feared stimuli, and are rather like the avoidance behaviour undertaken by our hypothetical client in Figure 13.1. Clearly, if exposure is to be effective in OCD, clients also have to desist from their neutralizing behaviours while in contact with the fear-producing situation or object. Response prevention refers to the voluntary cessation of these behaviours during prolonged exposure. The principle of response prevention is also applied to requests from clients with OCD for 'reassurance' which can become extremely excessive and once again are concerned with escape from anxiety (for example, repeated requests from a client with OCD to a partner to confirm that the client has locked the front door on leaving the house). Involving partners and family members in rehearing consensual response prevention statements such as, 'Your therapist has informed me that I cannot answer that question' may be necessary to facilitate prolonged exposure without neutralizing. Again, for imaginal exposure to obsessive ruminations to be successful, it must also be accompanied by response prevention of the neutralizing thoughts and covert rituals.

Other techniques
Generally subsumed under the pragmatic envelope of behavioural psychotherapy are techniques to reduce appetitive behaviours and to learn new behavioural skills.

Appetitive reduction techniques are often used when clients have difficulty controlling behaviours which they regard as excessive. Self-monitoring (like the diary-keeping in exposure) is a highly effective technique in its own right but is more often used to chart the effectiveness of some other technique. These include stimulus control procedures, most often used in disorders where control is poor such as bulimia and alcohol misuse. Identification of individual 'danger' signals and pre-control of stimuli to reduce the incidence of these signals assist clients to control situations: confining eating to certain times and places, only having certain foods in the house, etc. Although behavioural techniques such as meal scheduling are extremely useful in disorders such as bulimia they are usually accompanied by cognitive strategies to assist the client to address the core assumptions which are driving their behaviour (Schmidt and Treasure, 1994).

Less often used are techniques regarded as aversive in that they utilize punishment or frustrative non-reward. Currently, covert sensitization is the only technique in widespread use and is an imaginal procedure for reducing the potency of unacceptable sexual fantasies. The behavioural literature does contain many references to other procedures such as 'response cost' but these are now rarely employed.

Certain training and learning procedures are used, however, to assist clients develop new skills – assertiveness or job skills for example. Social skills training is often conducted in groups so that socially isolated and unskilled individuals can practise in a safe environment. Micro skills such as maintaining eye contact can be practised via role-play, modelling and ultimately real-life practice.

Behavioural activation

Behavioural activation is used to treat people who are depressed. Theoretically, it rests on the contextualist premise that depression is a result of the two-way interaction between an individual and their environment and that this interaction is the most appropriate place to intervene in depression. Behavioural activation, in the form of activity scheduling, is usually erroneously considered to be part of cognitive therapy, delivered in the early stages of this treatment. However, behavioural activation has a strong and distinct theoretical rationale which explicitly rejects the need to intervene directly in patients' cognitions. Originally, behavioural activation was developed by Lewinsohn (1974) and colleagues to increase depressed patients' pleasant activities. However, a more sophisticated analysis of behavioural theory in depression by authors such as Jacobson et al. (2001) and Hopko et al. (2003b) broadened this thinking to include a two process analysis of depression. It is now recognised that when people are depressed their ability to feel pleasure reduces (the anhedonia or absence of pleasure characteristic of depression) and this causes people to withdraw from previously enjoyed activities as these become less positively reinforcing. At the same time, people avoid activities which might be even slightly aversive – social contact for example. This process of negative reinforcement increases their likelihood of further avoidance and reduces their opportunities for positive experiences still further.

This dual process of negative reinforcement and reduction in positive reinforcement leads to greatly reduced activity and a spiralling of low mood, physiological disturbance and depressive cognitions, the three systems of affect identified by Lang (1979). Behavioural activation targets the behavioural disturbance on the understanding that reducing avoidance will lead to improvements in behavioural, physiological and cognitive aspects of depression. Many clients find it easier to 'act themselves out of depression' than 'think themselves out' (Martell et al., 2001). Clients are assisted to schedule a gradually increasing series of activities into their lives in order to reduce the feelings of aversion (similar to exposure for anxiety disorders) and simultaneously increase the possibilities of positive reinforcement. The difference between older models and new ideas about behavioural activation is that the modern therapist focuses on avoidance rather than only attempting to schedule activities which give clients pleasure.

Although behavioural activation in its current form is a relatively new development, there have been a number of trials demonstrating its efficacy (Hopko et al., 2003a; Jacobson et al., 1996). Behavioural activation has now been shown to be as effective as antidepressant medication or cognitive therapy in moderately depressed adults and more effective than cognitive therapy for people with more severe depression. As such, behavioural activation is likely to become more commonly used since it offers a greater degree of simplicity in training and application than the relatively complex skills required of cognitive therapy. It may also be more acceptable to clients than antidepressants.

The clinical method of behavioural activation requires clients to identify lists of routine, pleasurable and necessary activities which they are doing less of during their depression. These lists are then assembled into a hierarchy, similar to an exposure hierarchy in anxiety, but in depression the hierarchy reflects both the desirability and difficulty of the different activities. A diary is then used to help the client plan activities from the hierarchy, starting near the bottom but also paying attention to activities which might be critical – paying bills for example. The therapist supports the client through this process, giving important feedback on the client's progress through review of the diaries and helping the client select new activities from the hierarchy. The case example in this chapter describes this process in more detail.

Self-help techniques

These are not strictly separate from those listed above but have come to increased prominence since the early 1990s. With the definition and isolation of the effective elements of behavioural psychotherapy has come a movement to make such techniques more widely available. There will never be sufficient therapists to meet the massive mental health needs of the population. Further, the emphasis within behavioural psychotherapy on patient empowerment leads one naturally to the ultimate self-reliance strategy – self-care. Given sufficient instruction and explanation there is no reason why many people could not utilize these techniques successfully without a therapist. A recent systematic review of such approaches in primary care (Bower et al., 2001) revealed a considerable evidence base with some indication that self-help applications of behavioural techniques (usually via bibliotherapy) were at least as effective as standard care and might even be more effective. Computer (Ghosh and Marks, 1987) and interactive touch-tone phone systems (Greist et al., 1998) delivering self-care have already been shown to be effective for a number of anxiety disorders and are likely to be increasingly employed.

These studies also show that equivalent outcomes can be achieved with no loss of client satisfaction; in fact there is some indication that clients find it easier to disclose personal information to a computer than to a therapist (Greist et al., 1998). A final route of access for self-care is through service user groups such as Triumph over Phobia (TOP) who run self-care groups for people with anxiety disorders using behavioural techniques. As described by Lovell and Richards (2000), these routes to behavioural psychotherapy are likely to assume greater importance as demand for effective psychotherapy increases.

The change process in therapy

The change process in behavioural psychotherapy goes through several stages. Initially, client and therapist must come to some mutual understanding of the client's problems and agree both a problem formulation and a series of goals to be worked towards during therapy. The client must fully understand what is being suggested by the therapist and agree to implement the therapeutic techniques advised. If the problem is one of anxiety the next stage will be to identify the first exposure exercise in the client's hierarchy and embark on a programme of prolonged and repeated therapeutic exposure, coupled with response prevention if this is necessary. Habituation is measured via the client's self-report of discomfort in the face of their feared stimuli and progress will be monitored by sessional review of their homework diary sheets and anxiety ratings. Habituation is observed through reductions in both peak anxiety levels and duration of symptoms in the face of anxiety-provoking stimuli. Successful habituation will occur most rapidly with specific phobias and least quickly with OCD (Marks, 1987). In general, however, within-session habituation should begin in the first hour of exposure and progress rapidly during the second hour. Changes are most likely to be observed first in the behavioural system (i.e. an increase in approach behaviours rather than the avoidance or escape seen pre-treatment), followed by the autonomic system (i.e. reduction in physical anxiety symptoms) and finally the cognitive system (replacement of fearful thoughts with less fearful ones).

Traditionally, behavioural psychotherapy treatment programmes are scheduled to last for between eight and ten weeks. In practice, this is often much less. Certainly, if progress is not being achieved after three active therapy sessions the therapist should search for potential problems such as distraction during exposure which would render exposure ineffective. If there are no problems, over time, client and therapist should observe a reduction in fear which should begin to generalize to other situations. Successful clients are able to apply the principles of behavioural psychotherapy to new situations and will make rapid progress. Where this does not occur, therapists may occasionally need to accompany clients and observe where things may be going wrong. In OCD in particular, therapists may need to search carefully for micro examples of clients' feared consequences and ensure that exposure addresses these effectively.

Finally, on discharge clients should have a maintenance plan so that gains they have made in therapy do not decay over time. Relapse prevention plans similar in principle to those developed for clients with alcohol and problem drug use (Marlatt and Gordon, 1985) ensure that clients can recognize the triggers which indicate their problems may be relapsing. They then have a series of exercises that can be used immediately to prevent any recurrence of their problems. Such plans are very effective in appetitive disorders associated with eating and drug/alcohol use. In particular, the concept of 'lapse' rather than 'relapse' allows clients to suffer a temporary recurrence of their symptoms without a complete collapse in treatment gains.

Other disorders amenable to behavioural psychotherapy described earlier usually progress along similar lines. Whether it is the learning of new skills or starting to take pleasure in previously enjoyed activities, therapy initially addresses very specific, targeted behaviours with the expectation that improvement will spread out to other situations. As this happens, changes in autonomic and cognitive responses occur, albeit at different rates for different disorders and clients. Maintenance of gains is through planned strategies to identify and nip in the bud any signs of relapse.

Limitations of the approach

Twenty years ago behavioural psychotherapy was limited to approximately 25 per cent of clients with 'neurotic' disorders and 10 per cent of the adult population (Marks, 1982b). However, with behavioural treatments increasingly being used within a cognitive-behavioural therapy (CBT) paradigm, these proportions are increasing all the time. In particular, the development of CBT for psychosis is broadening the population of clients for whom behavioural psychotherapy is now considered useful and for which there is evidence of effectiveness.

Behavioural psychotherapy requires the active participation of the client and as such is limited to those clients that are prepared to engage in purposeful activity. Therapy is not suited to individuals who are embarking on a quest for understanding of personal existential conflicts. As in other therapies, even drug therapies such as antidepressants, approximately 25 per cent of clients either refuse or drop out of therapy in the early stages. This is a phenomenon common to all psychotherapies and only partly accounted for by exposure being an initially discomforting experience. Clients do need to remain anxious until the effects of habituation reduce arousal and this can lead to some clients dropping out of therapy. With these clients, therapists will find mere knowledge of technique insufficient. The engagement and rationale-giving techniques referred to earlier are essential to enable some clients to proceed with therapy.

In very few disorders can one talk about complete cure. An exception might be PTSD, where complete resolution of all symptoms is frequently possible. In most other anxiety disorders no more than a minority of clients are wholly rid of their symptoms. It is much more common for clients to have greatly reduced symptoms but some residual anxiety, hence the discussion of relapse prevention strategies above. This is of little consequence for many clients in that therapy can progress to a sufficient extent to allow them to live a normal life, free from the crippling handicaps and disabilities they previously laboured under. Therapy cannot change the biological set of the individual, merely the impact of the combination of this set, their behaviours and their cognitions on their lives.

Behavioural psychotherapy is not a panacea for all ills. Some clients do not respond to treatment despite client and therapist exploring the details of their problems, searching for specific environmental cues and devising ingenious therapy programmes. Such clients are often resistant to other approaches too and these people have frequently been identified as an urgent priority for research (e.g. Foa and Emmelkamp, 1983). More effort needs to be made to understand the reasons for non-responding and to develop programmes for these clients.

Case example

The client

Samina, 44, has been living with her partner for 20 years. They have three teenage children. Over the last six months Samina had been feeling increasingly low in mood. She found herself unable to get to sleep at her usual time and then when she did get to sleep she had subsequent periods of frequent wakening. She had lost her appetite, was often tearful for no apparent reason and was consumed with an overwhelming feeling of sadness. She found it difficult to concentrate on activities such as reading and she was finding it more and more difficult to motivate herself to do ordinary activities. She had lost pleasure and interest in previously enjoyed activities such as reading, family life and going out with friends. Given her difficulties with motivating herself to do things, she was spending much of her day sitting and doing very little. Previously houseproud, she had stopped cleaning and looking after the house. She was also irritable and tired, with thoughts that she was a failure and life was getting on top of her. She was experiencing occasional thoughts that life was not worth living. However, these were only fleeting thoughts and she had no plans to kill herself, feeling instead that there had to be a way out of this and that her family were worth fighting for. Samia was working as a cleaner at a local school but had been off sick for the last eight weeks.

The problem was clearly impacting on her work, social and private lives. Although the onset was six months ago, it was gradual and she could not determine any specific stressor or life event which caused her to feel down. She had one previous episode of depression in her early twenties for which she received no treatment, which was 22 years ago during a messy divorce.

Samina's GP had prescribed her Fluoxetine 20mg daily. She had decided not to take the tablets as she was very ambivalent about medication. She also thought that she should be able to 'pull herself together' like she did the last time she was feeling this way.

The therapy

Samina met the therapist at her local general practice. After taking the history Samina and the therapist came to a shared decision on a short problem statement defining her difficulties. This was: Low mood, tearfulness, poor appetite, irritability and sleep problems with avoidance of routine and previously enjoyed activities and thoughts that I am a failure, with the consequence that I have stopped looking after the house and am off sick from work. They also agreed some goals together, things that Samina wanted to achieve from her therapy. These included returning to work, getting back on top of her housework and doing more things for herself.

The therapist then outlined the principles of behavioural activation. She described the interlinking of physical, behavioural and cognitive symptoms and how a vicious circle of maintenance was contributing to the persistence of Samina's low mood. The therapist paid particular attention to avoidance – the things that Samina had stopped doing – and how the more that her activities became restricted, the more difficulty she felt in getting back to 'normal'. Due to her concentration difficulties Samina welcomed the idea of a treatment that focused on activity rather than intellectual effort. She was of the view that she should be able to 'pull herself together' like she did last time she was depressed, and really liked the idea of a behavioural activation programme. The therapist then described the three categories of activity which Samina should work on in her therapy – routine, pleasurable and necessary. Together Samina and the therapist thought up two or three examples of each type of activity as examples and began to fill in a worksheet list. Samina agreed to complete the worksheet and keep a dairy of her usual routine activities during the next week.

The next week, Samina and the therapist met again at the general practice. She had completed most of her lists although found it difficult to think of many things she considered necessary. Mostly, her lists were full of routine activities – such as washing up, cleaning the house, cooking meals, washing clothes, ironing and food shopping – and some ideas of pleasurable activities – such as having a meal out with her partner, going to a jewellery party with work colleagues, talking to a friend on the telephone, watching favourite TV programmes like history programmes, going to the cinema. She agreed that the previously identified necessary activities of filling in her local council tax form, paying bills and returning to work were the main items in this category that she was avoiding.

Samina was very unhappy with her diary. She had filled it in carefully and it made her realise just how little she was doing other than the basic activities necessary to keep her family and herself fed. She was getting up late each day, rarely went out and could not identify times when she was doing things for herself. The therapist empathised with Samina and supported her in recognising that this baseline represented a product of her low mood, was not the real 'her' and that she had made a positive move in seeking help. The therapist was careful to work hard in steering a fine balance between offering support to Samina whilst being careful not to make her feel more negative and disempowered through recognition of her lack of activity.

Together, Samina and her therapist placed her identified activities into a hierarchal list, putting easier activities at the bottom and the really difficult ones at the top. They then selected some easier activities and timetabled them into a blank diary. Samina chose to get up one hour earlier each day and decided that she wanted to do some ironing and some tidying up. The therapist helped Samina to break larger activities into smaller sections and they agreed that Samina should do no more than 20 minutes of ironing every two days and that she should decide to tidy only one room per day. The therapist also asked Samina to think about some previously enjoyed activity that she would like to do and to select at least one. Samina decided that she would telephone a friend from work, whom she had not spoken to for the last three weeks. She also decided to ask her partner to go for a drive in their car one afternoon at the weekend.

The next appointment was by telephone. Samina had done very well with her activities and had maintained her goal of getting up earlier every day. She had found the activities a little tiring but had persevered. She had gone out with her partner in the car and the telephone call to her friend had gone well, in fact her friend had invited her to go round and see her. Together, Samina and the therapist decided on the next set of activities, getting up by 9.00a.m. every day apart from the weekends and a range of household tasks. She also decided to telephone her friend again and arrange to visit her.

At the next telephone call, Samina was much less positive. Three days after speaking to the therapist, encouraged by the previous week's activity, she had decided to exercise with an aerobics video-tape she had used previously. However, she found it much harder than she had expected and gave up half way through. She became despondent and went back to bed. Her sleep for the rest of the week was very poor and she missed about half of her planned activities, including telephoning her friend. This setback proved a very useful, albeit challenging, opportunity for the therapist to work with Samina to problem solve what had gone wrong. Paradoxically, it provided the therapist with a chance to help Samina see just how powerful behavioural activation is as a method of overcoming low mood. After exploring the reasons for Samina failing at her exercise viedo – trying to do too much after six months lay off – they used the example of the next few days when Samina did nothing and her mood and depression symptoms got worse to illustrate how mood and activity are closely related.

After this initial setback Samina was more careful in choosing activities and in setting herself expectations. She gradually increased the frequency, duration and variety of activities. After another five weeks of planning her behavioural activation and keeping her diary she was getting up at a time which she found normal for her, her sleep had improved and she was in regular contact with friends. She had been to a jewellery party hosted by a work colleague and although she had anticipated it would be frightening for her, had actually enjoyed it once she had overcome her initial apprehension. She was getting much more satisfaction from her domestic activities and she and her partner had continued to find times to be together on drives at the weekend. She felt able to manage the rest of her behavioural activation programme with reduced support from the therapist, who decreased the frequency of telephone contacts to fortnightly.

Another two months later and Samina had returned to work. Although the first two weeks had been difficult she had been able to negotiate a gradual return to work and had eased herself into her previous routine. She had found her workmates more sympathetic than she had imagined, including one person who confided that she too had had similar symptoms of depression.

The therapist had a last face to face session with Samina to discuss ways of monitoring her mood, looking out for signs of relapse and recommencing her behavioural activation programme if necessary. She agreed to maintain brief telephone contact with Samina monthly for the next six months. Samina remained well during this time and felt confident enough in her ability to manage her own mood that contact with the therapist was concluded at this point.

REFERENCES

Bandura, A. (1977) 'Self-efficacy: toward a unifying theory of behavioural change', *Psychological Review*, 84: 191–215.

Bower, P., Richards, D.A. and Lovell, K. (2001). 'The clinical and cost-effectiveness of self-help treatments for anxiety and depressive disorders in primary care: a systematic review', *British Journal of General Practice*, 51: 838–45.

De Silva, P. (1984) 'Buddhism and behaviour modification', *Behaviour Research and Therapy*, 22: 661–78.

Eysenck, H.J. (1952) 'The effects of psychotherapy: an evaluation', *Journal of Consulting Psychology*, 16: 319–24.

Eysenck, H.J. (1985) *Decline and Fall of the Freudian Empire*. London: Penguin.

Foa, E.B. and Emmelkamp, P.M.G. (1983) *Failures in Behavior Therapy*. New York: Wiley.

Fox, J. and Conroy, P. (2000) 'Assessing clients' needs: the semi-structured interview', in C. Gamble and G. Brennan (eds), *Working with Serious Mental Illness: A Manual for Clinical Practice*. London: Ballière Tindall.

Freud, S. (1919) 'Turning in the ways of psychoanalytic therapy', in *Collected Papers*, Vol. II. London: Hogarth Press/Institute of Psycho-analysis.

Ghosh, A. and Marks, I. (1987) 'Self-treatment of agoraphobia by exposure', *Behaviour Therapy*, 18: 3–16.

Greist, J.H., Marks, I.M., Baer, L., Parkin, J.R., Manzo, P.A., Mantle, J.M., Wenzel, K.W., Spierings, C.J., Kobak, K.A., Dottl, S.L., Bailey, T.M. and Forman, L. (1998) 'Self-treatment for obsessive compulsive disorder using a manual and a computerized telephone interview: a US–UK study', *M.D. Computing*, 15(3): 149–57.

Hopko, D.R., Lejuez, C.W., LePage, J.P., Hopko, S.D., McNeil, D.W. (2003a) 'A brief behavioral activation treatment for depression: a randomized trial within an inpatient psychiatric hospital; *Behavior Modification*, 27: 58–69.

Hopko, D.R., Lejuez, C.W., Ruggiero, K.J., Eifert, G.H. (2003b) 'Contemporary behavioral activation treatments for depression: procedures, principles and progress', *Clinical Psychology Review*, 23: 699–717.

Jacobson, N.S., Dobson, K.S., Traux, P.A., Addis, M.E., Koerner, K., Gollan, J.K., Gortner, E. and Prince, S.E. (1996) 'A component analysis of cognitive-behavioural treatment of depression', *Journal of Consulting and Clinical Psychology*, 64: 295–304.

Jacobson, N.S., Martell, C.R. and Dimidjian, S. (2001) 'Behavioral activation treatment for depression: returning to contextual roots', *American Psychological Association*, D12: 225–70.

Jones, M.C. (1924) 'A laboratory study of fear', *Pedagogical Seminary*, 31: 308–315.

Lang, P. (1979). 'A bioinformational theory of emotional imagery', *Psychophysiology*, 16: 495–512.

Lewinsohn, P.M. (1974) 'A behavioral approach to depression', in R.M. Friedman and M.M. Katz (eds), *Psychology of Depression: Contemporary Theory and Research*. New York: Wiley.

Locke, J. (1693) *Some Thoughts Concerning Education*. London: Ward Lock.

Lovell, K. and Richards, D.A. (2000) 'Multiple access points and levels of entry (MAPLE): ensuring choice, accessibility and equity for CBT services', *Behavioural and Cognitive Psychotherapy*, 28: 379–91.

Marks, I.M. (1982a) 'Is conditioning relevant to behavior therapy?' in J. Boulougouris (ed.), *Learning Theory Approaches to Psychiatry*, New York: Wiley.

Marks, I.M. (1982b) *Cure and Care of Neuroses: Theory and Practice of Behavioral Psychotherapy*. New York: Wiley.

Marks, I.M. (1987) *Fears, Phobias and Rituals*. Oxford: Oxford University Press.

Marlatt, G.A. and Gordon, J.R. (1985) *Relapse Prevention: Maintenance Strategies in Addictive Behavior Change*. New York: Guilford.

Martell, C.R., Addis, M.E and Jacobson, N.S. (2001) *Depression in Context: Strategies for Guided Action*. Norton: New York.

Mowrer, O.H. (1950) *Learning Theory and Personality Dynamics*. New York: Arnold.

Newell, R. (1994) *Interviewing Skills for Nurses: A Structured Approach*. London: Routledge.

Newell, R. and Gournay, K. (2000) *Mental Health Nursing: An Evidence Based Approach*. London: Churchill Livingstone.

Pavlov, I.P. (1927) *Conditional Reflexes*. London: Oxford University Press.

Richards, D.A. (1988) 'The treatment of a snake phobia by imaginal exposure', *Behavioural Psychotherapy*, 16: 207–16.

Richards, D. and McDonald, B. (1990) *Behavioural Psychotherapy: A Handbook for Nurses*. Oxford: Heinemann.

Schmidt, U. and Treasure, J. (1994) *Getting Better Bit(e) by Bit(e): A Survival Kit for Sufferers of Bulimia Nervosa and Binge Eating Disorders*. Hove: Lawrence Erlbaum Associates.

Seligman, M.E.P. (1975) *Helplessness*. San Francisco: Freeman.

Skinner, B.F. (1953) *Science and Human Behavior*. New York: Macmillan.

Slade, P.D. and Haddock, G. (1996) *Cognitive-behavioural Interventions for Psychotic Disorders*. London: Routledge.

Thorndike, E.L. (1911) *Animal Intelligence*. New York: Macmillan.

Watson, J.B. and Rayner, R. (1920) 'Conditioned emotional reactions', *Journal of Experimental Psychology*, 3: 1–14.

Wolpe, J. (1958) *Psychotherapy by Reciprocal Inhibition*. Stanford, CA: Stanford University Press.

Wolpe, J. (1976) 'Behavior therapy and its malcontents', *Journal of Behavior Therapy and Experimental Psychiatry*, 7: 109–16.

SUGGESTED FURTHER READING

Baum, W.M. (1994) *Understanding Behaviourism: Science, Behaviour and Culture*. London: HarperCollins.

Gamble, C. and Brennan, G. (eds) (2000) *Working with Serious Mental Illness: A Manual for Clinical Practice*. London: Ballière Tindall.

Hawton, K., Salkovskis, P.M., Kirk, J. and Clark, D.M. (2000) *Cognitive Behaviour Therapy For Psychiatric Problems*, 2nd edn. Oxford: Oxford Medical Publications.

Marks, I.M. (1987) *Fears, Phobias and Rituals*. Oxford: Oxford University Press.

Parry, G. and Watts, F.N. (eds) (1996) *Behavioural and Mental Health Research: A Handbook of Skills and Methods*, 2nd edn. Hove: Erlbaum.

14

Rational Emotive Behaviour Therapy

Windy Dryden

HISTORICAL CONTEXT AND DEVELOPMENT IN BRITAIN

Historical context

Rational emotive behaviour therapy (REBT) was established in 1955 by Albert Ellis, a clinical psychologist in New York, who originally called the approach rational therapy. Ellis received his original training in psychotherapy in the 1940s in the field of marriage, family and sex counselling. In the course of his practice he realized that this kind of counselling was limited because 'disturbed marriages (or premarital relationships) were a product of disturbed spouses; and that if people were truly to be helped to live happily with each other they would first have to be shown how they could live peacefully with themselves' (Ellis, 1962: 3). He thus embarked on a course of intensive psychoanalytic training and received his training analysis from a training analyst of the Karen Homey group whose technique was primarily Freudian. In 1949 Ellis began to practise ortho-dox psychoanalysis with his patients, but was disappointed with the results he obtained. His patients appeared to improve, claimed to feel better, but Ellis could see that their improvement was not necessarily sustained. He then began to experiment with various forms of face to face, psychoanalytically-oriented psychotherapy. Although he claimed that these methods brought better results and within a shorter period of time than orthodox psychoanalysis, he was still dissatisfied with the outcome of the treatment. In 1953 he began to research a monograph and a long article on new techniques in psychotherapy (Ellis, 1955a,

1955b) which influenced him to practise a unique brand of psychoanalytic-eclectic therapy; still, Ellis remained dissatisfied.

Throughout his career as a psychoanalytically inspired therapist from the late 1940s and 1950s, Ellis had become increasingly disenchanted with psychoanalytic theory, claiming that it tended to be unscientific, devout and dogmatic. He had always maintained his early interest in philosophy and enjoyed thinking about how this field could be applied to the realm of psychotherapy. He used his knowledge of philosophy to help him answer his most puzzling question: 'Why do highly intelligent human beings, including those with considerable psychological insight, desperately hold on to their irrational ideas about themselves and others?' (Ellis, 1962: 14). The writings of Greek and Roman Stoic philosophers (especially Epictetus and Marcus Aurelius) were particularly influential in this respect. These philosophers stressed that people are disturbed not by things but by their view of things. Ellis began to realize that he had made the error of stressing a psychodynamic causation of psychological problems (namely that we are disturbed as a result of what happens to us in our early childhood); instead, he started to emphasize the philosophic causation of psychological problems (namely that we remain disturbed because we actively and in the present re-indoctrinate ourselves with our disturbance-creating philosophies).

From this point he began to stress the importance that thoughts and philosophies (cognition) have in creating and maintaining psychological disturbance. In his early presentations and writings on what has become known as rational emotive behaviour therapy, Ellis (1958) tended to overemphasize the role that cognitive factors play in human disturbance and consequently de-emphasized the place of emotive and behavioural factors. This was reflected in the original name that he gave to his approach: rational psychotherapy. In 1962 Ellis published his pioneering volume, *Reason and Emotion in Psychotherapy*. In this he stressed two important points – that cognitions, emotions and behaviours are interactive and often overlapping processes; and that 'human thinking and emotions are, in some of their essences, the same thing, and that by changing the former one does change the latter' (Ellis, 1962: 122). He concluded that the label rational-emotive therapy (RET) more accurately described his therapeutic approach. In 1993, Ellis decided to change the name of the therapy once more to rational emotive behaviour therapy (REBT). This was in response to critics who claimed, wrongly, that RET neglected behaviour and was purely cognitive and emotive in nature.

As noted above, the theory of rational emotive behaviour therapy has from its inception stressed the importance of the interaction of cognitive, emotive and behavioural factors both in human functioning and dysfunctioning and in the practice of psychotherapy. Ellis has acknowledged, in particular, his debts to theorists and practitioners who have advocated the role of action in helping clients to overcome their problems (Herzberg, 1945; Salter, 1949; Wolpe, 1958). Indeed, Ellis employed a number of *in vivo* behavioural methods to overcome his own fears of speaking in public and approaching women (Ellis, 1973).

Initially, rational emotive behaviour therapy received unfavourable and even hostile responses from the field of American psychotherapy. Despite this, Ellis persisted in his efforts to make his ideas more widely known; and as a result REBT is now flourishing. Its popularity in the United States increased markedly in the 1970s, when behaviour therapists became interested in cognitive factors, and the present impact of cognitive behaviour therapy has helped REBT to become more widely known there. Currently, REBT is practised by literally thousands of mental health professionals in North America and it is taught and practised throughout the world.

Development in Britain

Until the early 1990s, training in REBT was available on an *ad hoc* basis from myself or Dr Al Raitt (now deceased). Since training opportunities in REBT were limited, there were few therapists properly trained in REBT. Then, under the auspices of the Centre for Stress Management in Blackheath, London, I began a programme of certificate, diploma and advanced diploma courses in REBT. These courses, which are now run under the auspices of the Centre for Rational Emotive Behaviour Therapy, attracted and continue to attract people from a range of helping professions, and the number of REBT therapists has increased to the extent that an Association for Rational Emotive Behaviour Therapy (AREBT) was formed in 1993. The association, which publishes twice a year a journal entitled the *Rational Emotive Behaviour Therapist*, is a member of the Behavioural and Cognitive Section of the United Kingdom Council for Psychotherapy (UKCP).

In September 1995, I established an MSc in Rational Emotive Behaviour Therapy at Goldsmiths College, University of London. This course was the first Masters course in REBT to be established in Europe and is now the only one in the world. In 2006, the name of this course was changed to MSc in Rational-Emotive and Cognitive Behaviour Therapy to forge closer links between REBT and CBT.

In 2003, the United Kingdom Institute for Rational Emotive Behaviour Therapy was established in association with the Albert Ellis Institute and the University of Birmingham primarily to run training courses in REBT.

THEORETICAL ASSUMPTIONS

Image of the person

Rational emotive behaviour therapy holds that humans are essentially hedonistic (Ellis, 1976): their major goals are to stay alive and to pursue happiness efficiently, that is, in a non-compulsive but self-interested manner enlightened by the fact that they live in a social world. It is stressed that people differ enormously in terms of what will bring them happiness, so rational emotive behaviour therapists show clients not what will lead to their happiness but how they prevent themselves from pursuing it and how they can overcome these obstacles. Other basic concepts implicit in REBT's image of the person include those listed below.

Rationality

In REBT, 'rational' means primarily that which helps people to achieve their basic goals and purposes; 'irrational' means primarily that which prevents them from achieving these goals and purposes. However, 'rational' also means that which is flexible, non-extreme, logical and consistent with reality, whereas 'irrational' also means that which is rigid, extreme, illogical and inconsistent with reality.

Human fallibility

Humans are deemed to be by nature fallible and not perfectible. They naturally make errors and defeat themselves in the pursuit of their basic goals and purposes.

Human complexity and fluidity

Humans are seen as enormously complex organisms constantly in flux, and are encouraged to view themselves as such.

Biological emphasis

Ellis (1976) argues that humans have two basic biological tendencies. First, they have a tendency towards irrationality; they naturally tend to make themselves disturbed. Ellis (1976) makes a number of points in support of his 'biological hypothesis'. These include the following:

(a) Virtually all humans show evidence of major human irrationalities.
(b) Many human irrationalities actually go counter to the teachings of parents, peers and the mass media (for example, people are rarely taught that it is good to procrastinate, yet countless do so).
(c) Humans often adopt other irrationalities after giving up former ones.
(d) Humans often go back to irrational activity even though they may have worked hard to overcome it. (Ellis, 1976)

Secondly, and more optimistically, humans are considered to have great potential to work to change their biologically-based irrationalities.

Human activity

Humans can best achieve their basic goals by pursuing them actively. They are less likely to be successful if they are passive or half-hearted in their endeavours.

Cognitive emphasis

Although emotions overlap with other psychological processes such as cognitions, sensations and behaviours, cognitions are given special emphasis in REBT theory. The most efficient way of effecting lasting emotional and behaviour change is for humans to change their philosophies. Two types of cognition are distinguished in Ellis' (1962) ABC model of the emotional/behavioural episode. The first type refers to the person's inferences about events and includes such cognitive activities as making forecasts, guessing the intentions of others and assessing the implications of one's behaviour for self and others. Inferences are hunches about reality and need to be tested out. As such they may be accurate or inaccurate. They are placed under 'A' of the ABC of REBT[1] since they do not fully account for the person's emotions and/or behaviours at 'C'. The second type of cognition – beliefs – is attitudinal in nature; such cognitions, which are placed under 'B' of the ABC of REBT, do account for the person's emotions and/or behaviours at 'C'.

Constructivistic focus

Ellis (1994) has argued that REBT is best seen as one of the constructivistic cognitive therapies. In REBT, the constructivistic focus is seen in the emphasis that REBT places on the active role that humans play in constructing their irrational beliefs and the distorted inferences which they frequently bring to emotional episodes.

Concepts of psychological disturbance and health

Irrational and rational beliefs

Early on, Ellis (1962) distinguished between two types of beliefs: irrational and rational. According to REBT theory, irrational beliefs are rigid, extreme, illogical, inconsistent with reality and self-and other-defeating. By contrast, rational beliefs are non-absolute and non-extreme in nature, logical, consistent with reaity and self- and other-enhancing. Table 14.1 provides a summary of irrational beliefs and their rational alternatives.

Psychological disturbance

According to Ellis, irrational beliefs underpin psychologically disturbed responses to life's actual or perceived adversities. The most common of these disturbed responses that appear in the clinic are: anxiety, depression, guilt, shame, hurt, unhealthy anger, unhealthy jealousy and unhealthy envy. These emotions are known in REBT theory as unhealthy negative emotions in that they are negative in feeling tone and discourage people from changing adversities that can be changed and from adjusting constructively to adversities that cannot be changed.

Ellis (1982) also argues that irrational beliefs underpin dysfunctional behaviours such as withdrawal, procrastination, alcoholism, substance abuse and so on.

Of the four irrational beliefs listed to the left of Table 14.1, Ellis (1983a) holds that rigid demands are at the very core of human disturbance and the other three irrational beliefs are derived from these demands.

According to REBT theory there are two types of psychological disturbance: ego disturbance and discomfort disturbance.

Ego disturbance

Ego disturbance takes the form of self-depreciation. This occurs when I make demands on myself and I fail to meet these demands. It involves: (a) the process of giving my 'self' a global negative rating; and (b) 'devil-ifying' myself as being

Table 14.1 Irrational and rational beliefs in REBT theory

Irrational Belief	Rational Belief
Demand	*Non-dogmatic preference*
X must (or must not happen)	I would like X to happen (or not happen), but it does not have to be the way I want it to be
Awfulising belief	*Anti-awfulising belief*
It would be terrible if X happens (or does not happen)	It would be bad, but not terrible if X happens (or does not happen)
LFT belief	*HFT belief*
I could not bear it if X happens (or does not happen)	It would be difficult to bear if X happens (or does not happen), but I could bear it and it would be worth it to me to do so
Depreciation belief	*Acceptance belief*
If X happens (or does not happen) I am no good/you are no good/ life is no good	If X happens (or does not happen), it does not prove that I am no good/, you are no good/life is no good. Rather, I am a FHB/you are a FHB, life is a complex/mixture of good bad and neutral

FHB = Fallible human being
LFT = Low frustration tolerance
HFT = High frustration tolerance

bad or less worthy. This second process rests on a theological concept, and implies either that I am undeserving of pleasure on earth or that I should rot in hell as a subhuman (devil).

Ego disturbance is also found in demands on others (e.g. 'You must treat me well or I am no good') and in demands against life conditions (e.g. 'I must be promoted and if I am not I am useless').

Discomfort disturbance
This form of disturbance stems from the irrational belief: 'I must feel comfortable and have comfortable life conditions'. Conclusions that stem from this premiss are (a) 'It's awful when these life conditions do not exist' and (b) 'I can't stand the discomfort when these life conditions do not exist'. Discomfort disturbance occurs in different forms and is central to a full understanding of a number of emotional and behavioural disturbances such as unhealthy anger, agoraphobia, depression, procrastination and alcoholism. Discomfort disturbance usually gets in the way of people working persistently hard to effect productive psychological change and is thus a major form of 'resistance' to change in psychotherapy.

It is useful to note that according to REBT theory demands made on other people either involve ego disturbance (for example 'You must approve of me and if you don't it proves that I am less worthy') or discomfort disturbance ('You must approve of me and give me what I must have and if you don't I can't bear it'), and thus do not represent a fundamental human disturbance, since they include one or other of the two fundamental disturbances.

Psychological health

According to Ellis, rational beliefs underpin psychologically healthy responses to life's actual or perceived adversities. Healthy alternatives to the eight unhealthy negative emotions listed above are: concern, sadness, remorse, disappointment, sorrow, healthy anger, healthy jealousy and healthy envy. These emotions are known in REBT theory as healthy negative emotions in that they are negative in feeling tone, but encourage people to change adversities that can be changed and to adjust constructively to adversities that cannot be changed.

Ellis (1982) also argues that rational beliefs underpin functional behaviours such as confronting life's adversities, self-disciplined action and sensible use of alcohol.

Of the four rational beliefs listed to the right of Table 14.1, Ellis (1983a) holds that non-dogmatic preferences are at the very core of psychological health and the other three rational beliefs are derived from these non-dogmatic preferences.

According to REBT theory there are two types of psychological health: ego health and discomfort tolerance.

Ego health

The most common form of ego health is unconditional self-acceptance. This occurs when I hold preferences about myself, but do not demand that I must achieve these preferences. When you accept yourself you acknowledge that you are a fallible human being who is constantly in flux and too complex to be given a single legitimate rating. REBT theory advocates that it is legitimate, and often helpful, to rate one's traits, behaviours, etc., but that it is not legitimate to rate one's self at all, even in a global positive manner, since positive self-rating tends to be conditional on doing good things, being loved and approved, and so on.

Ego health is also found in non-dogmatic preferences about others (e.g. 'I want you to treat me treat me well, but you do not have to do so. If you don't, I am the same fallible human being as I would be if you did treat me well') and in non-dogmatic preferences about life conditions (e.g. 'I want to be promoted, but it isn't essential that I am. If I am not, I am not useless. I am acceptable as a human being with good, bad and neutral points').

Discomfort tolerance

Discomfort tolerance stems from the rational belief, 'I want to feel comfortable and have comfortable life conditions, but I don't need to have such comfort in my life.' Conclusions that stem from this premiss are (a) 'It's bad, but not awful when these life conditions do not exist' and (b) 'I can stand the discomfort when these life conditions do not exist.' Discomfort tolerance is central to dealing with a range of psychological problems and is a hallmark of what is known as psychological resilience (Reivich and Shatte, 2002) in that it encourages people to face up to life's adverse conditions and cope with them head on, with difficulty to be sure, particularly in the short term, but ultimately to good effect in the longer term. Discomfort tolerance also encourages people to work hard and to be persistent in effecting productive psychological change and its presence augurs well for change in psychotherapy. Finally, discomfort tolerance forms the basis of a philosophy of long-range hedonism: the pursuit of meaningful long-term goals while tolerating the deprivation of attractive short-term goals which are self-defeating in the longer term.

According to REBT theory, non-dogmatic preferences about people either involve ego health (for example 'I would like you to approve of me but you don't have to do so and if you don't I can still accept myself') or discomfort tolerance ('I want you to approve of me and give me what I must have, but you don't have to do so. If you don't, I can bear it'), and thus do not represent a distinct form of psychological health since they include one or other of the two fundamental types of psychological health.

Criteria of positive mental health

For Ellis (1983a) non-absolutism is at the core of the REBT view of psychological health, as can be seen in the following list of criteria of positive mental health outlined by Ellis (1994): self-interest; social interest; self-direction; tolerance; acceptance of ambiguity and uncertainty; flexibility; and scientific thinking (employing the rules of logic and scientific analysis in solving emotional and behavioural problems). In this respect, psychologically healthy people are not cold and detached, as those with a scientific approach to life are commonly but erroneously assumed to be; indeed, they experience the full range of healthy emotions, positive and negative. Other criteria of psychological health emphasized in REBT include commitment, calculated risk-taking, and as we have seen self- and other-acceptance, acceptance of reality and discomfort tolerance.

Acquisition of psychological disturbance

Rational emotive behaviour therapy does not posit an elaborate theory concerning how psychological disturbance is acquired. This follows logically from Ellis' (1976) hypothesis that humans have a strong biological tendency to think and act irrationally. While Ellis is clear that humans' tendency to make absolute demands on themselves, others and the world is biologically rooted, he does acknowledge that environmental factors contribute to emotional disturbance and thus encourage humans to make their biologically-based demands (Ellis, 1994). He argues that because humans are particularly open to influence as young children they tend to let themselves be over-influenced by societal teachings such as those offered by parents, peers, teachers and the mass media (Ellis, 1994). One major reason why environmental control continues to wield a powerful influence over most people most of the time is because they tend not to be critical of the socialization messages they receive. Individual differences also play a part here. Humans vary in their suggestibility: while some humans emerge relatively unscathed emotionally from harsh and severe childhood regimes, others emerge emotionally damaged from more benign regimes (Werner and Smith, 1982). Ellis strongly believes that we, as humans, are not disturbed simply by our experiences; rather, we bring our ability to disturb ourselves to our experiences.

In doing this we can be said to play a large role in constructing our disturbances (as noted on p. 356). We construct our demands out of our strong preferences and from these demands we construct our overly distorted negative inferences about reality. Having constructed such inferences we then focus on them and construct a further set of demands: that these inferred adversities absolutely should not be as bad as they are, for example. As a result we deepen the intensity of our already constructed disturbance. As will be seen, this is a far cry from models of psychotherapy which place negative life events at the centre of an explanation of how psychological disturbance is acquired.

Perpetuation of psychological disturbance

While REBT does not put forward elaborate theories to explain the acquisition of psychological disturbance, it does deal more extensively with how such disturbance is perpetuated.

First, most people perpetuate their psychological disturbance precisely because of their own theories concerning the 'cause' of their problems. They do not have what Ellis (1994) calls 'REBT Insight 1': that psychological disturbance is largely determined by the irrational beliefs that people hold about the negative events in their lives. They tend to attribute the 'cause' of their problems to situations, rather than to their beliefs about these situations. Lacking 'Insight 1', people are ignorant of the major determinants of their disturbance; consequently they do not know what to change in order to overcome their difficulties.

Secondly, even when individuals see clearly that their beliefs determine their disturbance, they may lack 'REBT Insight 2': that they remain upset by re-indoctrinating themselves in the present with these beliefs. People who do see that their irrational beliefs largely determine their disturbance tend to perpetuate such disturbance by devoting their energy to attempting to find out why and how they first adopted such beliefs instead of using such energy to change the currently held irrational beliefs.

Thirdly, some people who have both insights still perpetuate their disturbance because they lack 'REBT Insight 3': only if we consistently work and practise in the present as well as in the future to think, feel and act against these irrational beliefs are we likely to surrender them and make ourselves significantly less disturbed (Ellis, 1994). People who have all three insights see clearly that just acknowledging that a belief is irrational is insufficient for change to take place.

Ellis (1994) stresses that the major reason why people fail to change is due to their philosophy of 'low frustration tolerance' (LFT). By believing that they must be comfortable, people will tend to avoid the discomfort that working to effect psychological change very often involves, even though facing and enduring such short-term discomfort will probably result in long-term benefit. As Wessler (1978) has noted, such people are operating hedonistically from within their own frames of reference. They evaluate the tasks associated with change as 'too uncomfortable to bear' – certainly more painful than the psychological disturbance to which they have achieved a fair measure of habituation. They prefer to opt for the comfortable but disturbance-perpetuating discomfort of their problems rather than face the 'change-related' discomfort which they rate as 'dire'. Clearly, therapists have to intervene in this closed system of beliefs if psychological change is to be effected. This philosophy of low frustration tolerance which impedes change can take many different forms. One prevalent form of LFT is 'anxiety about anxiety'. Here, individuals may not expose themselves to anxiety-provoking situations because they are afraid that they might become anxious if they did so: a prospect which they would rate as 'terrible' because they believe 'I must not be anxious'.

'Anxiety about anxiety' is an example of a phenomenon that explains further why people perpetuate their psychological disturbances. Ellis (1994) has noted that people often make themselves disturbed about their disturbances; thus they block themselves from working to overcome their original psychological disturbance because they upset themselves about having the original disturbance. Humans are often inventive in this respect – they can make themselves anxious about their anxiety, depressed about being depressed, guilty concerning their anger, and so on. Consequently, people often have to overcome their meta-emotional problems (as these secondary disturbances are now called – Dryden, 2002) before embarking on effecting change in their original problems.

Ellis (1979) has observed that people sometimes experience some kind of perceived pay-off for their psychological disturbance other than the gaining of immediate obvious ease. Here such disturbance may be perpetuated until the perceived pay-off is dealt with, in order to minimize its impact. For example, a woman who claims to want to lose weight may not take the necessary steps because she fears that losing weight would make her more attractive to men: a situation which she would view as 'awful'. Remaining fat protects her (in her mind) from a 'terrible' state of affairs. It is to be emphasized that the REBT therapists stress the phenomenological nature of these pay-offs: in other words, it is the person's view of the pay-off that is important in determining its impact, not the events delineated in the person's description.

Another important way in which people perpetuate their disturbance is that their behaviour and thinking do not support their developing rational beliefs. Thus, I may believe that I do not have to have your approval, but if I behave toward you as if I do and if I think that very bad things will happen if you do not approve of me then this behaviour and thinking will tend to nullify my developing rational belief and reinforce my well established irrational belief (i.e. 'I must have your approval').

A final major way that people tend to perpetuate their psychological disturbance is explained by the 'self-fulfilling prophecy' phenomenon (Jones, 1977; Wachtel, 1977): by acting according to their predictions, people often elicit from themselves or from others reactions which they then interpret in such a way as to confirm their initial self-defeating forecasts. In conclusion, Ellis (1994) believes that humans tend naturally to perpetuate their problems and have a strong innate tendency to cling to self-defeating, habitual patterns, thereby resisting basic change.

Change

REBT theory argues that humans can and do change without psychotherapy. First people can change their disturbance-creating philosophies by reading rational self-help material or talking to people who teach them sound rational principles. I personally derived much benefit in the 1970s from reading and acting on the principles described in Ellis and Harper's (1975) *A New Guide to Rational Living* and helped myself to overcome feelings of inferiority which I experienced from my early teens. Well before that time, I heard Michael Bentine talk on the radio about how he overcame his fear of talking in public due in large part to his stammer. He said that he helped himself by telling himself: 'If I stammer, I stammer. Too bad!' I thought this was excellent advice and because I was scared in my teens to speak in public since I had a stammer, I undertook a similar programme of speaking in public (behavioural exposure) while telling myself, 'If I stammer, I stammer. Fuck it!' (cognitive restructuring with a strong emotive component). The conjoint use of behavioural and cognitive techniques is frequently the hallmark of change when people (whether they are in therapy or not) alter their disturbance-creating philosophies.

People can help themselves overcome or gain relief from their problems in a number of ways other than changing the philosophies that underpin their psychological problems. They may succeed at changing their distorted inferences about negative events at 'A' or they may put their situation into a more positive frame. They may help themselves by learning new skills like assertion or study skills and thereby improve their relationships with people and their performance at college. They may leave a situation in which they experience their psychological problems and find a new, much more favourable situation. Similarly, they may find a job or a relationship which may help them to transform their problems into strengths. Thus, a very obsessive person may flourish in a job environment that values his obsessiveness.

Finally, people may help themselves by telling themselves obvious irrationalities. I might help myself enormously if I tell myself and believe that I have a fairy godmother who will protect me from trouble and strife or if I think that I am a wonderful person because I write books and articles on rational emotive behaviour therapy!

As this chapter shows, the most enduring psychological changes are deemed to occur when someone changes their irrational beliefs to rational beliefs. All the other changes mentioned tend to be more transient and dependent on the existence of favourable life conditions.

PRACTICE

Goals of therapy

In trying to help clients overcome their emotional difficulties and achieve their self-enhancing goals, rational emotive behaviour therapists have clear and well-defined aims. In this discussion it is important to distinguish between outcome goals and process goals. Outcome goals are those benefits which clients hope to derive from the therapeutic process. Ideally, rational emotive behaviour therapists try to assist clients to make profound philosophic changes. These would involve clients (a) giving up their demands on themselves, others and the world, while sticking with their non-dogmatic preferences; (b) refusing to rate themselves, a process which would help them to accept themselves unconditionally; (c) refusing to give others and life conditions a global negative evaluation; (d) refusing to rate anything as 'awful'; and (e) increasing their tolerance of frustration while striving to achieve their basic goals and purposes.

If therapists are successful in this basic objective, clients will be minimally prone to future ego disturbance or discomfort disturbance. They will still experience healthy negative emotions in the face of life's adversities such as sadness, healthy anger, concern and disappointment, since they would clearly retain their desires, wishes and wants; however, they will rarely experience unhealthy negative emotions such as depression, unhealthy anger, anxiety and guilt since they would have largely surrendered the absolutistic 'musts', 'shoulds' and 'oughts' which underlie such dysfunctional emotional experiences. In achieving such profound philosophic changes, clients would clearly score highly on the criteria of positive mental health mentioned earlier (see p. 359). If such ideal client goals are not possible, rational emotive behaviour therapists settle for less pervasive changes in their clients. Here clients may well achieve considerable symptomatic relief and overcome the psychological disturbance that brought them to therapy, but they will not have achieved such profound philosophic changes as to prevent the development of future psychological disturbance. In this case, clients benefit from therapy either (a) by making productive behavioural changes which lead to improved environmental circumstances at 'A' in Ellis' ABC model; or (b) by correcting distorted inferences at 'A'. In reality most clients achieve some measure of philosophic change, while only a few achieve a profound philosophic change.

Process goals involve therapists engaging clients effectively in the process of therapy so that they can be helped to achieve their outcome goals. Here Bordin's (1979) concept of the therapeutic alliance is helpful. There are three major components of the therapeutic alliance: bonds, goals and tasks.

Effective bonds

These refer to the quality of the relationship between therapist and client that is necessary to help clients achieve their outcome goals. Rational emotive behaviour therapists consider that there is no one way of developing effective bonds with clients: flexibility is the key concept here.

Agreement on goals

Effective REBT is usually characterized by therapists and clients working together towards clients' realistic and self-enhancing outcome goals. The role of therapists in this process is to help clients distinguish between (a) realistic and unrealistic goals; and (b) self-enhancing and self-defeating goals. Moreover, REBT therapists help clients see that they can usually achieve their ultimate outcome goals only by means of reaching a series of mediating goals. In addition, some REBT therapists like to set goals for each therapy session, although Ellis (1989) is against this practice because, he argues, it forces clients to identify goals that they do not really have. Client goals can be negotiated at three levels: ultimate outcome goals, mediating goals and session goals. Effective REBT therapists help their clients explicitly to see the links between these different goals and thus help to demystify the process of therapy.

Agreement on tasks

REBT is most effective when therapist and client clearly acknowledge that each has tasks to carry out in the process of therapy, clearly understand the nature of these tasks and agree to execute their own tasks. The major tasks of rational emotive behaviour therapy are: (a) to help clients see that their emotional and behavioural problems have cognitive antecedents; (b) to train clients to identify and change their irrational beliefs and distorted inferences; and (c) to teach clients that such change is best effected by the persistent application of cognitive, imagery, emotive and behavioural methods. The major tasks of clients are: (a) to observe their emotional and behavioural disturbances; (b) to relate these to their cognitive determinants; and (c) to work continually at changing their irrational beliefs and distorted inferences by employing cognitive, imagery, emotive and behavioural methods.

Selection criteria

In response to a question that I once asked Albert Ellis concerning selection criteria, he said the following:

> In regard to your question about placing people in individual, marital, family or group therapy, I usually let them select the form of therapy they personally want to begin with. If one tries to push clients into a form of therapy they do not want or are afraid of, this frequently will not work out. So I generally start them where they want to start. If they begin in individual therapy and they are the kind of individuals who I think would benefit from group, I recommend this either quickly after we begin or sometime later. People who benefit most from group are generally those who are shy, retiring and afraid to take risks. And if I can induce them to go into a group, they will likely benefit more from that than the less risky

situation of individual therapy. On the other hand, a few people who want to start with group but seem to be too disorganized or too disruptive, are recommended for individual sessions until they become sufficiently organized to benefit from a group.

Most people who come for marital or family therapy actually come alone and I frequently have a few sessions with them and then strongly recommend their mates also be included. On the other hand, some people who come together are not able to benefit from joint sessions, since they mainly argue during these sessions and we get nowhere. Therefore sometimes I recommend that they have individual sessions in addition to or instead of the conjoint sessions. There are many factors, some of them unique, which would induce me to recommend that people have individual rather than joint sessions. For example, one of the partners in a marriage may seem to be having an affair on the side and will not be able to talk about this in conjoint sessions and therefore I would try and see this partner individually. Or one of the partners may very much want to continue with the marriage while the other very much wants to stop it. Again, I would then recommend they be seen individually. I usually try to see the people I see in conjoint sessions at least for one or a few individual sessions to discover if there are things they will say during the individual sessions that they would refuse to bring out during the conjoint sessions.

On the whole, however, I am usually able to go along with the basic desire of any clients who want individual, marital, family or group psychotherapy. It is only in relatively few cases that I talk them into taking a form of therapy they are at first loath to try. (Ellis in Dryden, 1984: 14–15)

While I cannot say whether or not other REBT therapists would agree with Ellis on these points, his views do indicate the importance that REBT theory places on individual choice. Within individual therapy, it is important to distinguish between those who may benefit from brief REBT and those who may require a longer period of therapy. In 1995, I published an 11-session protocol for the practice of brief REBT (Dryden, 1995). In it I outline the following seven indications that a person seeking help might benefit from brief REBT:

1   The person is able and willing to present her problems in a specific form and set goals that are concrete and achievable.
2   The person's problems are of the type that can be dealt with in 11 sessions.
3   The person is able and willing to target two problems that she wants to work on during therapy.
4   The person has understood the ABCDEs[2] of REBT and has indicated that this way of conceptualizing and dealing with her problems makes sense and is potentially helpful to her.
5   The person has understood the therapist's tasks and her own tasks in brief REBT, has indicated that REBT seems potentially useful to her and is willing to carry out her tasks.
6   The person's level of functioning in her everyday life is sufficiently high to enable her to carry out her tasks both inside and outside therapy sessions.
7   There is early evidence that a good working bond can be developed between the therapist and the person seeking help.

The more a person meets such inclusive criteria, the more suitable she is for brief REBT. On the other hand if one or more of the following six contra-indications for brief REBT are present, it should not be offered as a treatment modality.

1   The person is antagonistic to the REBT view of psychological disturbance and its remediation.
2   The person disagrees with the therapeutic tasks that REBT outlines for both therapist and client. [These two points are contra-indications for REBT (whether brief or longer-term) as a treatment modality and the person should be referred to a different therapeutic approach that matches her views on these two issues.]

3   The person is unable to carry out the tasks of a client in brief REBT.
4   The person is at present seriously disturbed and has a long history of such disturbance.
     (The above two points do not mean that the person is not a good candidate for longer-term REBT.)
5   The person seeking help and the therapist are clearly a poor therapeutic match. (In this case
     referral to a different REBT therapist is in order. Brief REBT cannot yet be ruled out.)
6   The person's problems are vague and cannot be specified even with therapist's help.
     (While in this case the person is clearly not suitable for brief REBT, she may be suitable for
     longer-term REBT if she can be helped to be more concrete. If she cannot, then REBT may not
     be helpful for her.)

It should be stressed that Ellis' and my views on selection criteria are only suggestions and need to be tested empirically before firm guidelines can be issued on
selection criteria for REBT in general and as an approach to individual therapy in
particular.

Qualities of effective therapists

Unfortunately, no research studies have been carried out to determine the personal qualities of effective rational emotive behaviour therapists. REBT theory
does, however, put forward a number of hypotheses on this topic (Ellis, 1978),
but it is important to regard these as both tentative and awaiting empirical study.

Since REBT is a fairly structured form of therapy, its effective practitioners
are usually comfortable with structure, but flexible enough to work in a less
structured manner when the situation arises.

REBT practitioners tend to be intellectually, cognitively or philosophically
inclined and are attracted to REBT because the approach provides them with
opportunities to fully express this tendency.

Ellis argues that REBT should often be conducted in a strong active-directive
manner; thus, effective REBT practitioners are usually comfortable operating in this
mode. Nevertheless, they have the flexibility to modify their interpersonal style
with clients so that they provide the optimum conditions to facilitate client change.

REBT emphasizes that it is important for clients to put their therapy-derived
insights into practice in their everyday lives. As a result, effective practitioners
of REBT are usually comfortable with behavioural instruction and teaching and
with providing the active prompting that clients often require if they are to follow through on homework assignments.

Effective rational emotive behaviour therapists tend to have little fear of failure
themselves. Their personal worth is not invested in their clients' improvement.
They do not need their clients' love and/or approval and are so not afraid of taking
calculated risks if therapeutic impasses occur. They tend to accept both themselves
and their clients as fallible human beings and are tolerant of their own mistakes
and the irresponsible acts of their clients. They tend to have, or persistently work
towards acquiring, a philosophy of high frustration tolerance, and do not get discouraged when clients improve at a slower rate than they desire. Effective practitioners tend to score highly on most of the criteria of positive mental health
outlined earlier in this chapter and serve as healthy role models for their clients.

REBT strives to be scientific, empirical, anti-absolutistic and undevout in its approach to people's selecting and achieving their own goals (Ellis, 1978). Effective practitioners of REBT tend to show similar traits and are definitely not mystical, anti-intellectual and magical in their beliefs.

REBT advocates the use of techniques in a number of different modalities (cognitive, imagery, emotive, behavioural and interpersonal). Its effective practitioners are comfortable with a multi-modal approach to treatment and tend not to be people who like to stick rigidly to any one modality.

Finally, Ellis (1978) notes that some rational emotive behaviour therapists often modify the preferred practice of REBT according to their own natural personality characteristics. For example, some practise REBT in a slow-moving passive manner, do little disputing and focus therapy on the relationship between them and their clients. Whether such modification of the preferred practice of REBT is effective is a question awaiting empirical enquiry.

Therapeutic relationship and style

Taking their lead from Ellis (1994), most rational emotive behaviour therapists tend to adopt an active-directive style in therapy. They are active in directing their clients' attention to the cognitive determinants of their emotional and behavioural problems. While they often adopt a collaborative style of interaction with clients who are relatively non-disturbed and non-resistant to the therapeutic process, Ellis (2002) advocates that they be forceful and persuasive with more disturbed and highly resistant clients. Whichever style they adopt, they strive to show that they unconditionally accept their clients as fallible human beings and to be empathic and genuine in the therapeutic encounter.

They strive to establish the same 'core conditions' as their person-centred colleagues, albeit in a different style (see Chapter 6, by Thorne and Kitcatt). They, however, do not regard such 'core conditions' as necessary and sufficient for therapeutic change to occur. Rather, they regard them as often desirable for the presence of such change. While research in the more relationship-oriented aspects of REBT is sparse, DiGiuseppe et al. (1993) did find in one study that REBT therapists were rated highly on the core conditions by their clients.

Ellis (in Dryden, 1985) has argued that it is important for REBT therapists not to be unduly warm towards their clients, since he believes that this is counterproductive from a long-term perspective, in that it may inappropriately reinforce clients' approval and dependency needs. However, other REBT therapists do try to develop a warm relationship with their clients. Consistent with this, DiGiuseppe et al. (1993) found that Ellis was rated as being less warm than other REBT therapists in their study.

While an active-directive style of interaction is often preferred, this is not absolutely favoured (Eschenroeder, 1979). What is important is for therapists to convey to clients that they are trustworthy and knowledgeable individuals who are prepared to commit themselves fully to the task of helping clients reach their goals. Therapists must develop the kind of relationship with clients that the latter will, according to their idiosyncratic positions, find helpful. This might mean that, with some clients, therapists emphasize their expertise and portray themselves as well-qualified individuals whose knowledge and expertise form the basis of what social psychologists call communicator credibility. Such credibility is important to the extent that certain clients will be more likely to listen to therapists if they stress these characteristics. Other clients, however, will be more likely to listen to therapists who portray themselves as likeable individuals. In such cases, therapists might de-emphasize their expertise but emphasize their humanity by being prepared to disclose certain aspects of their lives which are both relevant to clients' problems and which stress liking as a powerful source of communicator credibility.

Many years ago, I saw two clients on the same day with whom I emphasized different aspects of communicator credibility. I decided to interact with Jim, a 30-year-old bricklayer, in a casual, 'laid-back' style. I encouraged him to use my first name and was prepared to disclose some personal details because I believed, from what he had told me in an assessment interview, that he strongly disliked 'stuffy mind doctors who treat me as another case rather than as a human being'. However, in the next hour with Jane, a 42-year-old unmarried fashion editor, I portrayed myself as 'Dr Dryden' and stressed my long training and qualifications because she had indicated, again in an assessment interview, that she strongly disliked therapists who were too warm and friendly towards her; she wanted a therapist who 'knew what he was doing'. REBT therapists should ideally be flexible with regard to changing their style of interaction with different clients. They should preferably come to a therapeutic decision about which style of interaction is going to be helpful in both the short and long term with a particular client. Furthermore, they need to recognize that the style of interaction that they adopt may in fact be counterproductive (Beutler, 1979); for instance, they should be wary of adopting an overly friendly style of interaction with 'histrionic' clients, or an overly directive style with clients whose sense of autonomy is easily threatened. No matter which style of interaction REBT therapists may adopt with individual clients, they should be concerned, genuine and empathic in the therapeutic encounter.

Major therapeutic strategies and techniques

The primary purpose of the major therapeutic strategies and techniques of REBT is to help clients give up their absolute philosophies and adhere to more relative ones. However, before change procedures can be used, REBT therapists need to make an adequate assessment of clients' problems.

Assessment of client problems

Clients often begin to talk in therapy about the troublesome events in their lives ('A') or their dysfunctional emotional and/or behavioural reactions ('C') to these events. Rational emotive behaviour therapists use concrete examples of 'A' and 'C' to help clients identify their irrational beliefs at 'B' in the ABC model. In the assessment stage, therapists particularly look to assess whether clients are making themselves disturbed about their original disturbances as described earlier in this chapter.

Cognitive change techniques

Here both verbal and imagery methods are used to dispute clients' irrational beliefs. Verbal disputing involves three sub-categories. First, therapists can help clients to *discriminate* clearly between their rational and irrational beliefs. Then, while *debating*, therapists can ask clients a number of Socratic-type questions about their irrational beliefs: for example, 'Is there evidence that you must ... ?' Finally, *defining* helps clients to make increasingly accurate definitions in their private and public language. These verbal disputing methods can also be used to help correct their faulty inferences (Beck et al., 1979).

To reinforce the rational philosophy clients can be given books to read (bibliotherapy); self-help books often used in conjunction with REBT include *A Guide to Rational Living* by Ellis and Harper (1997) and *Ten Steps to Positive Living* (Dryden, 1994). They can also employ written rational self-statements, which they can refer to at various times, and they can use REBT with others – a technique which gives clients practice at thinking through arguments in favour of rational beliefs.

Written homework, in forms such as those presented in Dryden (2001), is another major cognitive technique used in REBT as is rational-emotive imagery (REI). REI is the major imagery technique used in REBT. Here clients get practice at changing their unhealthy negative emotions to healthy ones ('C') while keenly imagining the negative event at 'A'; what they are in fact doing is getting practice at changing their underlying philosophy at 'B'. Some cognitive techniques (like REI) are particularly designed to help clients move from 'intellectual' insight (i.e. a weak conviction that their irrational beliefs are irrational and their rational beliefs are rational) to 'emotional' insight (a strong conviction in those same points) (Ellis, 1963). Others included in this category are a range of rational-irrational dialogue techniques described in Dryden (1995).

Emotive-evocative change techniques

Such techniques are quite vivid and evocative in nature, but are still designed to dispute clients' irrational beliefs. Rational emotive behaviour therapists unconditionally accept their clients as fallible human beings even when they act poorly or obnoxiously: they thus act as a good role model for clients. In this they judiciously employ self-disclosure, openly admitting that they make errors, act badly, etc., but that they can nevertheless accept themselves. Therapists employ humour at times in the therapeutic process, believing that clients can be helped by not taking themselves and their problems too seriously; such humour is directed at aspects of clients' behaviour, never at clients themselves.

Clients are sometimes encouraged to do shame-attacking exercises in which they practise their new philosophies of discomfort tolerance and self-acceptance while doing something 'shameful' but not harmful to themselves or others: examples might include asking for chocolate in a hardware shop, and wearing odd shoes for a day. Repeating rational self-statements in a passionate manner is often employed in conjunction with shame-attacking exercises and also at other times.

Behaviour change techniques

Rational emotive behaviour therapists can employ the whole range of currently used behavioural techniques (see Chapter 13); however, they prefer *in vivo* (in the situation) rather than imaginal desensitization. Ellis (1994) favours the use of *in vivo* desensitization in its 'full exposure' rather than its gradual form, because it offers clients greater opportunities to change profoundly their ego and discomfort disturbance-creating philosophies. This highlights the fact that behavioural methods are used primarily to effect cognitive changes. Careful negotiation concerning homework assignments, where clients aim to put into practice what they have learned in therapy, is advocated, and it should be realized that clients will not always opt for full-exposure, *in vivo* homework. Other behavioural methods often used in REBT include: (a) 'stay-in-there' activities (Grieger and Boyd, 1980) which help clients to remain in an uncomfortable situation for a period while tolerating feelings of chronic discomfort; (b) anti-procrastination exercises which are designed to help clients start tasks earlier rather than later, thus behaviourally disputing their dire need for comfort; (c) skill-training methods, which equip clients with certain key skills in which they are lacking (social skills and assertiveness training are often employed, but usually after important cognitive changes have been effected); (d) self-reward and self-penalization (but not, of course, self-depreciation!) which can also be used to encourage clients to use behaviour change methods.

These are the major treatment techniques, but rational emotive behaviour therapists are flexible and creative in the methods they employ, tailoring therapy to meet the client's idiosyncratic position. A fuller description of these and other REBT treatment techniques is to be found in Dryden and Neenan (1995).

The change process in therapy

Rational emotive behaviour therapists are quite ambitious in setting as their major therapeutic goal helping clients to effect what Ellis often calls a 'profound philosophic change'. This primarily involves clients surrendering their 'demanding' philosophy and replacing it with a 'desiring' philosophy. In striving to achieve these changes in philosophy, such clients are helped in therapy to:

(a)   adhere to the idea that they manufacture and continue to manufacture their own psychological disturbance;
(b)   acknowledge fully that they have the ability to change such disturbance to a significant degree;
(c)   understand that their psychological disturbance is determined mainly by irrational beliefs;
(d)   identify such irrational beliefs when they disturb themselves and distinguish these from rational beliefs;

(e) dispute such beliefs using the logico-empirical methods of science and replace these with their rational alternatives (more specifically, such clients work towards unconditional self-acceptance and raising their frustration tolerance);

(f) reinforce such cognitive learning by persistently working hard in employing emotive and behavioural methods. Such clients choose to tolerate the discomfort that this may well involve because they recognize that without acting on newly acquired insights, change will probably not be maintained;

(g) acknowledge that as humans they will probably have difficulty in effecting a profound philosophic change and will tend to backslide. Taking such factors into account, such clients re-employ and continually practise REBT's multimodal methods for the rest of their lives. In doing so, they learn to experiment and find the methods that work especially well for them. They specifically recognize that forceful and dramatic methods are powerful ways of facilitating philosophic change and readily implement these, particularly at times when they experience difficulty in changing. (Ellis, 1994)

In helping clients achieve such profound change, effective REBT therapists are unswerving in their unconditional acceptance of their clients. They realize that the achievement of profound philosophic change is an extraordinarily difficult task, and one which frequently involves many setbacks. Consequently, while tolerating their own feelings of discomfort they dedicate themselves to becoming a persistent and effective change agent. They (a) identify and work to overcome their clients' resistances (Ellis, 2002); (b) interpret and challenge the many defences that their clients erect against such change; (c) continually encourage, persuade and cajole their clients to keep persisting at the hard work of changing themselves; and (d) generally experiment with a wide variety of methods and styles to determine which work best for individual clients.

Rational emotive behaviour therapists acknowledge that not all clients can achieve such far-reaching philosophic change. This knowledge is usually gained from clients' responses to the therapeutic process. When deciding to settle for less ambitious outcome goals, REBT practitioners limit themselves to help clients effect situationally based philosophic change; correct distorted inferences (Beck et al., 1979); and effect behavioural changes so that they can improve negatively perceived life events. Profound philosophic change would, of course, incorporate these three modes of change.

Limitations of the approach

I have been practising REBT now for almost 30 years in a variety of settings and I have seen a wide range of moderately to severely disturbed individuals who were deemed to be able to benefit from weekly counselling or psychotherapy. While I do not have any hard data to substantiate the point, I have found rational emotive behaviour therapy to be a highly effective method of individual psychotherapy with a wide range of client problems.

However, I have of course had my therapeutic failures, and I would like to outline some of the factors that in my opinion have accounted for these. I will use Bordin's (1979) useful concept of the therapeutic working alliance as a framework.

Goals

I have generally been unsuccessful with clients who have devoutly clung to goals where changes in other people were desired. (I have also failed to involve these others in therapy.) I have not been able to show or to persuade these clients that they make themselves emotionally disturbed and that they are advised to work to change themselves before attempting to negotiate changes in their relationships with others. It is the devoutness of their beliefs which seems to me to be the problem here.

Bonds

Unlike the majority of therapists of my acquaintance, I do not regard the relationship between therapist and client to be the *sine qua non* of effective therapy. I strive to accept my clients as fallible human beings and am prepared to work concertedly to help them overcome their problems, but do not endeavour to form very close, warm relationships with them. In the main, my clients do not appear to want such a relationship with me (preferring to become close and intimate with their significant others). However, occasionally I get clients who do wish to become (non-sexually) intimate with me. Some of these clients (who devoutly believe they need my love) leave therapy disappointed after I have failed either to get them to give up their dire need for love or to give them what they think they need.

Tasks

As Bordin (1979) has noted, every therapeutic method requires clients to fulfil various tasks if therapy is to be successful. I outlined what these tasks are with respect to REBT earlier in this chapter. In my experience, clients who are diligent in performing these tasks generally have a positive therapeutic outcome with REBT, while those who steadfastly refuse to help themselves outside therapy generally do less well or are therapeutic failures.

It may of course be that I am practising REBT ineptly and that these failures are due to my poor skills rather than any other factor. Ellis (1983b), however, has published some interesting data which tend to corroborate my own therapeutic experiences. He chose 50 of his clients who were seen in individual and/or group REBT and were rated by him, and where appropriate by his associate group therapist, as 'failures'. In some ways, this group consisted of fairly ideal REBT clients in that they were individuals of:

> [1] above average or of superior intelligence (in my judgement and that of their other group therapist); (2) who seemed really to understand RET and who were often effective (especially in group therapy) in helping others to learn and use it; (3) who in some ways made therapeutic progress and felt that they benefited by having RET but who still retained one or more serious presenting symptoms, such as severe depression, acute anxiety, overwhelming hostility, or extreme lack of self-discipline; and (4) who had at least one year of individual and/or group RET sessions, and sometimes considerably more. (Ellis, 1983b: 160)

This group was compared to clients who were selected on the same four criteria but who seemed to benefit greatly from REBT. While a complete account of this study – which, of course, has its methodological flaws – can be found in Ellis (1983b), the following results are most pertinent:

1. In its cognitive aspects, RET ... emphasizes the persistent use of reason, logic, and the scientific method to uproot clients' irrational beliefs. Consequently, it ideally requires intelligence, concentration, and high-level, consistent cognitive self-disputation and self-persuasion. These therapeutic behaviours would tend to be disrupted or blocked by extreme disturbance, by lack of organization, by grandiosity, by organic disruption, and by refusal to do RET-type disputing of irrational ideas. All these characteristics proved to be present in significantly more failures than in those clients who responded favourably to RET.
2. RET also, to be quite successful, involves clients forcefully and emotively changing their beliefs and actions, and their being stubbornly determined to accept responsibility for their own inappropriate feelings and to vigorously work at changing these feelings (Ellis and Abrahms, 1978). But the failure clients in this study were significantly more angry than those who responded well to RET; more of them were severely depressed and inactive, they were more often grandiose, and they were more frequently stubbornly resistant and rebellious. All these characteristics would presumably tend to interfere with the kind of emotive processes and changes that RET espouses.
3. RET strongly advocates that clients, in order to improve, do *in vivo* activity homework assignments, deliberately force themselves to engage in many painful activities until they become familiar and unpainful, and notably work and practice its multimodal techniques. But the group of clients who signally failed in this study showed abysmally low frustration tolerance, had serious behavioral addictions, led disorganized lives, refrained from doing their activity homework assignments, were more frequently psychotic and generally refused to work at therapy. All these characteristics, which were found significantly more frequently than were found in the clients who responded quite well to RET, would tend to interfere with the behavioural methods of RET. (Ellis, 1983b: 165)

It appears from the above analysis that the old adage of psychotherapy applies to REBT: that clients who could most use therapy are precisely those individuals whose disturbance interferes with their benefiting from it. At present, it is not known whether clients who 'fail' with REBT are likely to benefit more from other therapies. Finally, as discussed by other contributors to this book, the practice of REBT is limited by the poor skills of the REBT practitioner.

As I have often said: 'REBT is easy to practise poorly.' There is no substitute, then, for proper training and supervision in the approach.

Case example

The client

Malcolm is a 42-year-old married man who works in IT. He was referred to me by his GP whom he had repeatedly consulted over recent years about various physical symptoms which turned out to be benign but which Malcolm thought pointed to serious illness. In short, Malcolm suffered from health anxiety (which used to be called hypochondria). He had a four year history of consulting doctors both NHS and private and was currently seeing a number of complementary medicine practitioners every week to 'improve my immune system'.

Malcolm is one of three children of two 'overprotective' Jewish parents who are both alive. Both parents are in their 80s and are in poor health. Malcolm routinely accompanied both his mother and father on their frequent hospital visits.

Malcolm grew up in an environment where the focus was very much on illness and the importance of, but impossibility of, avoiding it. When he was growing up, Malcolm generally resented his parents' focus on illness and had always enjoyed good health until he was 38 when he was hospitalised for pneumonia. This triggered a very different attitude in Malcolm and he came to see himself as physically vulnerable. At this point he began to consult doctors and became preoccupied with his health. His GP had for the past three years suggested that Malcolm seek therapy for health anxiety which Malcolm resisted since he claimed he was ill not anxious.

The therapy

In my experience of working with clients with health anxiety, the beginning of therapy is crucial since such clients believe that they are physically ill rather than anxious. As such, at the beginning of my work with Malcolm, I did the following:

1   I gave Malcolm an extended opportunity to talk about why he had come to see me and why he thought his GP had suggested that he consult me. Malcolm said that he thought that his GP was fed up with him and wanted to 'get shot of me, so he has dumped me on you'. He claimed that his GP thought he was neurotic not ill, while he thought that he was ill, not neurotic.
2   I told Malcolm that I did not know whether or not he was ill, but that I did not regard him as neurotic. I did say that he seemed to be quite anxious about his health and that I could help with this if he would like me to. Malcolm was ambivalent about this. I then suggested an experiment. Would Malcolm be willing for a month to proceed as if he was anxious rather than ill to see what happens? If not, this would be fine and I would refer him back to his GP. If he agreed then I would expect Malcolm to give the experiment a proper chance to work and to proceed according to an agreed psychological conceptualization of his problems. Malcolm gave his consent to this.
3   Having elicited this agreement, I gave Malcolm a brief outline of REBT, what he could expect from me and what I expected from him. In this regard I made clear that as in other cognitive-behaviour therapies, clients get the most from REBT when they commit themselves to a regular and extended period of self-help between sessions.
4   I then helped Malcolm to specify his target problem and asked him to set a healthy goal for this problem as follows:

Problem: When I have a physical symptom that I am concerned about and I don't know that it is not serious, I become very anxious, think it is serious, seek reassurance from doctors and others and keep checking the symptom.

Goal: When I have a physical symptom that I am concerned about and I don't know that it is not serious, I want to be healthily concerned about it rather than anxious, refrain from seeking reassurance and stop checking the symptom.

As I discussed above, Malcolm agreed for a month to follow an agreed set of guidelines based on the following conceptualization.

Conceptualization of Malcolm's problems

Here is the conceptualization of Malcolm's problems that I negotiated with him.

Situation: Unexplained symptom

> 'A' = Don't know that it is not serious
> Irrational Belief = I must know now that it isn't serious. I can't stand this uncertainty
> 'C' (emotional) = Anxiety
>   (behavioural) = Reassurance-seeking; checking the symptom
>   (thinking) = 'If I don't know that the symptom is not serious then it is serious'

Goals of therapy

My initial therapeutic goal was to help Malcolm test out his basic idea that he was ill rather than anxious about his health by following a number of principles based on the above conceptualization.

1 To challenge his irrational belief and to act on his alternative rational belief.
2 To refrain from seeking reassurance and checking his unexplained symptoms.
3 To go along with the probability that the unexplained symptom was not serious.

This is shown below:

> Situation: Unexplained symptom
> 'A' = Don't know that it is not serious
> Irrational Belief = I would like to know now that it isn't serious, but I don't have to know this. I can stand this uncertainty and it is worth standing.
> 'C' (emotional) = Concern
>   (behavioural) = Refraining from reassurance-seeking and from checking the symptom
>   (thinking) = 'If I don't know that the symptom is not serious then it is probably not serious'

Therapeutic relationship and style

As I discussed on pp. 367–8, REBT therapists strive to accept their clients as fallible human beings while focusing on the latters' problems in an active-directive manner. This characterized my therapeutic style with Malcolm. Furthermore, my early interactions with him led me to conclude that he would respond better to a formal therapeutic style than to an informal one. Our relationship could be described as friendly, but formal where humour and counsellor self-disclosure were kept to a minimum. As it transpired, we had no reason to focus on our relationship as a microcosm of Malcolm's problems and, indeed, our relationship was never a subject for direct therapeutic exploration.

Major therapeutic strategies and techniques

Before I began to challenge Malcolm's irrational belief, he agreed to do the following:

• He agreed to consult his doctor about any unexplained symptom a week after first discovering it, as long as he refrained from reassurance-seeking and checking (see below). This was done in agreement with his doctor.

- He agreed not to consult any complementary therapists for a month.
- He explained to relevant family and friends that they should refrain from talking with him about his symptoms for a month.

Once Malcolm agreed to do the above, during the early part of therapy I helped him to challenge his irrational belief about uncertainty with respect to whichever unexplained symptom he experienced. After he had challenged his irrational belief:

- I encouraged Malcolm to notice any residual urges he had to seek reassurance (e.g. by consulting his doctor, by talking about his symptoms with friends and family and by looking up symptoms on the internet), but not to act on these urges. Instead, he agreed to pursue one of his hobbies that he claimed he had little time for because of his preoccupation with his health.
- I also encouraged Malcolm to notice any residual urges to check his symptom but to refrain from doing so. Instead, he was again to involve himself in his hobbies.
- Finally, I encouraged him to think that his symptom was probably benign, but that there was a slim chance that it was serious. Thereafter, he should focus his attention elsewhere.

At other times when Malcolm noticed an urge to seek reassurance or to check his symptom or when he thought that his symptom was serious and he hadn't challenged his irrational belief, he agreed to use these as cues to challenge this irrational belief and then to notice, but not act on any residual urges or thoughts that the symptom was serious as before.

    With respect to the above interventions, I explained to Malcolm that he could easily use these strategies in the service of distraction or superstition. Thus, he could use the recognition of an urge to distract himself from his irrational belief rather than as a cue to challenge it and he could use the thought that his symptom was probably benign as a superstitious form of self-reassurance that it was definitely benign. I monitored carefully his inappropriate use of these strategies during the therapy process and intervened accordingly.

The change process

The most important part of therapy with Malcolm was eliciting the agreement at the beginning that he would test out the hypothesis that he was anxious about his health rather than ill. Without this agreement, therapy would have stalled at a very early phase.

    With one or two exceptions which we discussed and analysed in therapy, Malcolm succeeded in challenging his irrational belief about uncertainty and most importantly he refrained from seeking reassurance and from checking as detailed above. The outcome of this early work was startling. At the end of the month, Malcolm was far less anxious about his health and he was convinced now that he had been anxious about his health rather than ill. He considered himself less vulnerable physically.

    We decided to have another 6 sessions initially at fortnightly intervals and then monthly to deal with a number of matters related to health and other matters. First I helped Malcolm to see that feelings of health anxiety were signs that he needed to challenge his irrational beliefs and were unlikely to be premonitions of serious illness as he had previously, but erroneously thought before. Secondly, I encouraged him to involve his siblings in sharing the responsibility of making hospital visits with their parents. This proved to be difficult since it suited his brother and sister for Malcolm to do it all. So I had to help Malcolm to overcome his feelings of guilt about refusing on occasion to accompany his parents to the hospital and I had to teach him to assert himself with his siblings without unhealthy anger. As a result and after much argument, a rota was agreed with all concerned. As a result, his relationship with his sister did become less close. The overall effect of this change in family responsibilities was to help Malcolm to become less focused on matters to do with ill health.

Finally, I helped Malcolm deal with his anxiety about his financial investments, the dynamics of which were very similar to his health anxiety ('I must be sure that there is no risk to my investments' → overestimating financial loss in the face of uncertainty → frequent checking on his investments and calling his broker for reassurance). Having pointed out the similarities between the two problems, I encouraged Malcolm to transfer his learning and skills from one problem to another. When he did that, Malcolm became far less anxious in the financial domain as well as in the health domain.

I had 10 sessions with Malcolm in total and on 6 month follow-up he had maintained his gains. His relationship with his sister was improving although she still felt resentful towards Malcolm for failing to help their parents as much as he once did.

REFERENCES

Beck, A.T., Rush, A.J., Shaw, B.F. and Emery, G. (1979) *Cognitive Therapy of Depression*. New York: Guilford Press.

Beutler, L.E. (1979) 'Towards specific psychological therapies for specific conditions', *Journal of Consulting and Clinical Psychology*, 47: 882–97.

Bordin, E.S. (1979) 'The generalizability of the psychoanalytic concept of the working alliance', *Psychotherapy Theory, Research and Practice*, 16: 252–60.

DiGiuseppe, R., Leaf, R. and Lipscott, L. (1993) 'The therapeutic relationship in rational-emotive therapy: some preliminary data', *Journal of Rational-Emotive and Cognitive-Behavior Therapy*, 11(4): 223–33.

Dryden, W. (ed.) (1984) *Individual Therapy in Britain*. London. Harper & Row.

Dryden, W. (1985) *Therapists' Dilemmas*. London: Harper & Row.

Dryden, W. (1994) *Ten Steps to Positive Living*. London: Sheldon.

Dryden, W. (1995) *Brief Rational Emotive Behaviour Therapy*. Chichester: John Wiley.

Dryden, W. (2001) *Reason to Change: A Rational Emotive Behaviour Therapy (REBT) Workbook*. London: Brunner-Routledge.

Dryden, W. (2002) *Fundamentals of Rational Emotive Behaviour Therapy: A Training Handbook*. London: Whurr.

Dryden, W. and Neenan, M. (1995) *Dictionary of Rational Emotive Behaviour Therapy*. London: Whurr.

Ellis, A. (1955a) 'New approaches to psychotherapy techniques', *Journal of Clinical Psychology* (Brandon, Vermont).

Ellis, A. (1955b) 'Psychotherapy techniques for use with psychotics', *American Journal of Psychotherapy*, 9: 425–76.

Ellis, A. (1958) 'Rational psychotherapy', *Journal of General Psychology*, 59: 35–49.

Ellis, A. (1962) *Reason and Emotion in Psychotherapy*. Secaucus, NJ: Lyle Stuart.

Ellis, A. (1963) 'Toward a more precise definition of "emotional" and "intellectual" insight', *Psychological Reports*, 13: 125–6.

Ellis, A. (1973) 'Psychotherapy without tears', in A. Burton and associates, *Twelve Therapists: How They Live and Actualize Themselves*. San Francisco: Jossey-Bass.

Ellis, A. (1976) 'The biological basis of human irrationality', *Journal of Individual Psychology*, 32: 145–68.

Ellis, A. (1978) 'Personality characteristics of rational-emotive therapists and other kinds of therapists', *Psychotherapy Theory, Research and Practice*, 15: 329–32.

Ellis, A. (1979) 'The theory of rational-emotive therapy', in A. Ellis and J.M. Whiteley (eds), *Theoretical and Empirical Foundations of Rational-Emotive Therapy*. Monterey, CA: Brooks/Cole.

Ellis, A (1982) 'The treatment of alcohol and drug abuse: a rational-emotive approach', *Rational Living*, 17(2): 15–24.

Ellis, A. (1983a) *The Case against Religiosity*. New York: Albert Ellis Institute.

Ellis, A. (1983b) 'Failures in rational-emotive therapy', in E.B. Foa and P.M.G. Emmelkamp (eds), *Failures in Behavior Therapy*. New York: Wiley.

Ellis, A. (1989) 'Ineffective consumerism in the cognitive-behavioural therapies and in general psychotherapy', in W. Dryden and P. Trower (eds), *Cognitive Psychotherapy: Stasis and Change*. London: Cassell.

Ellis, A. (1994) *Reason and Emotion in Psychotherapy*, revised and updated edition. New York: Birch Lane Press.

Ellis, A. (2002). *Overcoming Resistance: A Rational Emotive Behavior Therapy Integrative Approach*, 2nd edn. New York: Springer.

Ellis, A. and Abrahms, E. (1978) *Brief Psychotherapy in Medical and Health Practice*. New York: Springer.

Ellis, A. and Harper, R.A. (1975) *A New Guide to Rational Living*, 2nd edn. North Hollywood, CA: Wilshire.

Ellis, A. and Harper, R.A. (1997) *A Guide to Rational Living*, 3rd edn. North Hollywood, CA: Wilshire.

Eschenroeder, C. (1979) 'Different therapeutic styles in rational-emotive therapy', *Rational Living*, 14(1): 3–7.

Grieger, R. and Boyd, J. (1980) *Rational-Emotive Therapy. A Skills-Based Approach*. New York: Van Nostrand Reinhold.

Herzberg, A. (1945) *Active Psychotherapy*. New York: Grune & Stratton.

Jones, R.A. (1977) *Self-Fulfilling Prophecies: Social, Psychological and Physiological Effects of Expectancies*. Hillsdale, NJ: Lawrence Erlbaum.

Reivich, K. and Shatte, A. (2002) *The Resilience Factor: 7 Keys to Finding Your Inner Strength and Overcoming Life's Hurdles*. New York: Broadway Books.

Salter, A. (1949) *Conditioned Reflex Therapy*. New York: Creative Age.

Wachtel, P.L. (1977) *Psychoanalysis and Behavior Therapy: Toward an Integration*. New York: Basic Books.

Werner, E.E. and Smith, R.S. (1982) *Vulnerable but Invincible: A Study of Resilient Children*. New York: McGraw-Hill.

Wessler, R.A. (1978) 'The neurotic paradox: a rational-emotive view', *Rational Living*, 13(1): 9–12.

Wolpe, J. (1958) *Psychotherapy by Reciprocal Inhibition*. Stanford, CA: Stanford University Press.

SUGGESTED FURTHER READING

Dryden, W. (2002) *Fundamentals of Rational Emotive Behaviour Therapy: A Training Handbook*. London: Whurr.

Dryden, W. and Neenan, M. (1995) *Dictionary of Rational Emotive Behaviour Therapy*. London: Whurr.

Ellis, A. (1994) *Reason and Emotion in Psychotherapy*, revised and updated edition. New York: Birch Lane Press.

Neenan, M. and Dryden, W. (2006) *Rational Emotive Behaviour Therapy in a Nutshell*. London: Sage.

Yankura, J. and Dryden, W. (1994) *Albert Ellis*. London: Sage.

NOTES

1 Where 'A' stands for Activating event, 'B' for Belief and 'C' for the emotional/behavioural/thinking Consequences of holding that belief.

2 Where 'A' stands for Activating event, 'B' for Belief and 'C' for the emotional/behavioural/thinking Consequences of holding that belief, 'D' for Disputing irrational beliefs and 'E' for the Effects of disputing.

15

Solution-Focused Therapy

Bill O'Connell

HISTORICAL CONTEXT AND DEVELOPMENT IN BRITIAN

Historical context

Solution-focused therapy (SFT) is an outcome-oriented, competence-based approach. Solution-focused therapists help clients to achieve their preferred outcomes by facilitating the evocation of solutions. A team of family therapists who worked at the Brief Therapy Center in Milwaukee, USA, founded solution-focused therapy in the 1980s. The team leaders were a married couple, Steve De Shazer and Insoo Kim Berg. According to De Shazer, Berg's contribution was her skilled and innovative work with clients, while his was to articulate the theory behind it. De Shazer's writing and master classes were immensely influential. He died in 2005. Berg continues to teach, write and work with clients.

Families came to the Center in Milwaukee with multiple, chronic and complex problems. Family members often argued about the nature of the problem and who was to blame. Parents and children became defensive in this conflict arena and were unwilling to consider their need to change. After a time the team began to stop asking families about their problems and asked instead about what 'their solutions' would look like. They asked each family member how they would know the situation had improved – what would they notice that was different? Taking this as a starting point, the team found that families spent less time arguing over their problems. The therapists discovered that the more they encouraged family members to notice times when things went better, the more the family seemed to change. When families focused more on their 'solutions', they talked less about their problems.

Since the 1980s solution-focused therapy has built an international following of professionals across the disciplines. It has moved beyond the boundaries of therapy to apply its techniques in a wide variety of fields such as:

- Business – coaching, project management, appraisal, team building
- Education – tutoring, pastoral care, mentoring and teaching
- Mediation, advice and guidance
- Psychology
- Social work, including child protection
- Health – physical and mental settings
- Substance misuse.

SFT is used extensively with groups/teams/couples/families/young people and children. Some practitioners use the approach in a purist form, while others integrate it with other models.

In 1993 the European Brief Therapy Association, with its largely solution-focused membership, began to organise annual conferences which attracted practitioners from all over Europe and beyond. These conferences continue to be run annually in different European cities.

Development in Britain

Three social workers and family therapists – Harvey Ratner, Evan George and Chris Iveson were the pioneers of solution-focused therapy in the UK. In 1987, when they were working and teaching together in London they discovered a mutual interest in brief therapy. They first explored the Mental Research Institute model of brief therapy but were soon persudaded by the work of Steve de Shazer and began to experiment with his solution-focused model. Their success in using the model attracted the interest of other professionals who, in turn, sought training in the approach. To meet this need the team established the Brief Therapy Practice, later to be renamed as BRIEF.

Many of the leading figures in the field – Bill O'Hanlon, Steve de Shazer, Insoo Kim Berg, Yvonne Dolan, Michael Hoyt, Scott Miller, Linda Metcalf and Ben Furman, Michael Durrant and others, began to visit the UK and lead seminars and workshops.

In 2000 Birmingham University became the first academic institution to offer a Masters degree in Solution-Focused Therapy, designed and led by the author. Until then training had taken place mainly through short courses, delivered by practitioner-trainers, or private organisations.

In 2002 a small group of practitioners met in Birmingham to explore the need for a National Association. They agreed that the purpose of such an association would be to:

- Enable practitioners to share good practice.
- Raise the national profile of solution-focused practice.

- Provide to the general public information about the approach and facilitate their access to solution-focused practitioners.
- Explore professional issues such as Accreditation.

In 2003 this founding group established the United Kingdom Association for Solution Focused Practice (UKASFP). It very quickly recruited a membership of almost 200 practitioners. It publishes an online newsletter, has established a successful annual conference now in its third year, stimulated regional groups and launched a website (http://www.ukasfp.co.uk/). The energy, enthusiasm and commitment behind the Association reflects the dynamism which drives the solution-focused movement in the UK.

In the early days, the solution-focused literature was almost entirely American. De Shazer was a prolific writer who contributed a stream of articles and published several books. He was, to a large extent, the intellectual figure head of SFT, although he always credited his partner Insoo Kim Berg for being the innovative practitioner behind the development of the therapy. His books were seminal texts – *Keys to Solutions in Brief Therapy (1985), Clues-Investigating Solutions in Brief Therapy* (1988), *Putting Difference to Work (1991), Words were Originally Magic* (1994).

The first UK authored solution-focused book was *Problems to Solutions* (1990) by Evan George, Harvey Ratner and Chris Iveson. Jane Lethem's work *Moved to Tears, Moved to Action* (1994) was followed by Hawkes, Marsh and Wilgosh's book (1998) describing how the approach could be used in a mental health setting. O'Connell's book in 1998 located the approach within the field of counselling and psychotherapy.

The history of solution-focused therapy in the UK is one of rapid growth and increasing maturity. It has progressed from a small number of pioneers into a major player in the therapeutic field. Its ideas have fired the imagination of many. It has won academic credibility and front line popularity. To some extent it fitted the zeitgeist of the time. SFT offered a time-limited, goal-oriented way of working which suited the needs of a busy society. It clearly focused on finding solutions rather than introspection or history. It appealed to clients as more practical than traditional therapies. Within a relatively short period of time it has made its mark and joined its relatives in the therapy family tree.

THEORETICAL ASSUMPTIONS

Image of the Person

The solution-focused image of the Person is that of a resilient, skilled, imaginative, idiosyncratic problem-solver. Human beings are creative and flexible solvers of the problems presented by their social environment. The human brain is an amazing treasure house of bright ideas and a repository of a lifetime's solution-memories. In response to focused questioning people can become more aware of their signature solutions (they may also recall their patterns of failed solutions!)

Solution-focused therapists communicate to their clients that, 'there's nothing wrong with you that what's right with you can't fix.' Rather than attempt to fix what may be 'wrong', the emphasis is on finding out 'what works' for the client and how they could find ways of doing more of it.

There is in SFT a strong commitment to the empowerment of clients, coupled with a humanistic belief in the inherent goodness of people. Trusting the client means that the therapist takes a pragmatic position that clients are 'doing their best most of the time'. Instead of regarding client 'resistance' as something to work on, the therapist reads it as a message to 'do something different' in order to engage the client on his or her own terms.

Respecting the clients' autonomy is also a warning against rescuing or problem solving on their behalf. The therapist does not find solutions for the client from within her own repertoire, but together they work to find solutions which 'fit' the client. Instead of searching for a 'quick fix,' the emphasis is on finding small steps forward – micro-solutions – in the belief that small changes can lead to big changes.

Some critics dismiss SFT as a version of 'Positive Thinking'. This is a caricature. Pressurising people to see the positives in every life situation minimises or denies the complexity and 'shadow side' of the human condition. Sanctifying positivity creates additional problems for the trauma survivor who feels they have failed to live up to this cultural ideal. SFT acknowledges the negativity, the loss, the pain and the confusion in our lives. Therapists who push people 'to move on' are not working within the SFT framework.

The philosophy behind solution-focused therapy is social constructionism. This epistemology also underpins Kelly's *The Psychology of Personal Constructs* (1955), Neuro-Linguistic Programming (Bandler and Grinder, 1979), the Brief Problem-Solving model developed at the Mental Research Institute (MRI) in Palo Alto in California by Watzlawick, Weakland and Fisch (1974) and the Narrative approach as described by White and Epston (1990). The MRI and the SFT model owe much to the seminal thinking of Gregory Bateson (1972) and Milton Erickson (1980).

Constructionism argues that meaning is created through social interaction and negotiation. It proposes that we have no direct access to objective truth independent of our linguistically constructed versions. It argues that theories are not objective versions of external reality, but a socially constructed framework of ideas that emerge within a cultural, political and social context.

The constructionist position challenges our belief that reality exists independently of us, the observers. The knower actively participates in constructing what is observed. Constructionism sabotages our hopes that reality is discoverable, predictable and certain.

In therapy the client and the therapist explore a range of meanings for the client's experiences and work towards negotiating a 'provisional understanding'. This does not mean that any explanation for a 'problem' will suffice, but it underlines the subjectivity and cultural relativity of the language we use to describe our realities. Therapy becomes a dialogue in which both partners construct what is meant by 'the problem' and 'the solution'. The 'problem' does not carry an objective, fixed meaning. Instead, clients tell and retell their story using language which reshapes the social reality by which they live. In Watzlawick's phrase (1984), 'reality is invented, not discovered'.

For the solution-focused therapist this constructionist foundation means that:

- The client's perceptions and experiences (provided they are legal and ethical) are privileged above those of the professional.
- There is flexibility in negotiating a 'possibility' narrative which will 'open windows' rather than 'close doors'.
- The task is to 'join with' the client in order to co-create a new and empowering narrative.
- The client is viewed as an 'expert' in his or her own life.
- The therapist's expertise lies in guiding the process and keeping the dialogue within a solution-focused frame.
- The therapist pays careful attention to the client's context.
- The therapist builds upon the client's competence and strengths.
- The therapist needs to be aware of her own values, 'blind spots' and biases.

The solution-focused approach claims to be minimalist both in theory and in practice. It has adopted Occam's principle that 'it is vain to do with more what can be achieved with fewer'. Being minimalist means that the therapist works pragmatically with 'what is already there' in the client's life. This principle of utilisation has its roots in the work of Milton Erickson (1980). Utilisation covers not only the positive, solution-oriented aspects of the client's life, but also those elements which might be viewed as neutral or even problematic.

In SFT it is not considered necessary to search for the origins or causes of people's problems. The work is more in the present and about the future, than it is about the past. If a client has a theory about the causes of his problem, the therapist will accept it on certain conditions, namely that it is legal and ethical and increases the chances of the problem being solved, both in the short and the long term.

By containing the amount of problem talk about the possible causes of the problem, the client is able to think 'past' the problem and become more aware of his resources and solutions. Instead of analysing the problem, the therapy focuses on the client's observation of changes and how they came about. This attention shift aims to help the client learn how to maintain or expand the desired changes. When the client is primed to look out for and pay attention to evidence of progressive change, he is more likely to see it.

The therapist elicits the client's pattern of problem-solving strategies by enquiring how the client has dealt with similar problems in the past. Having discovered what works, the therapist encourages the client to keep doing it.

SFT assumes that clients:

- Can construct solutions with minimal, if any, analysis of their problems.
- Have many resources and competences, many of which they, and others, are unaware of. Most people do not use a fraction of their potential.
- Are more likely to be open to possibilities for change if they are connected to experiences of 'success', rather than failure.
- Have many ideas about their preferred futures.
- Are already engaging in constructive and helpful actions (otherwise their situation would be worse!)
- Have memory banks of solutions.

SF therapists accept that some clients believe they must 'get to the roots' of their problems. But for the SF therapist this is not essential, and in some cases it becomes part of the problem. The search for explanations can become a 'blamestorm', as people look for anyone or anything to blame. Looking for causes can become a diversion from finding real and lasting solutions. Added to that, there are often divisive opinions about problem-definition and ownership. Some clients may get 'stuck' because they constantly revisit memories of past events which disempower them and make them fatalistic about the future.

We store our experiences of major life events in our long-term memory and are particularly able to access those with strong emotional resonance. Johnson describes the brain as, 'an associative network in which thoughts are represented by groups of neurons distributed throughout our brains that fire in sync with each other. Certain thoughts have more neurons in common than others. Neurons that fire together, wire together' (2004: 200). When we revisit our memories we trigger off other associated memories. From a SF standpoint the consequences of this are that:

1   The therapist discourages the client from revisiting those 'problem' neural connections which the client has maintained by dwelling upon their problems. By neglecting the problem pathways the neural connections will become weakened.
2   Conversely the therapist encourages the client to build new pathways to solutions. This fires off other neurons associated with memories of solutions in their memory bank. These connections will become stronger the more the client thinks and talks about how to make the changes they want.

When clients live on Problem Island they become experts about the terrain. They know every nook and cranny. They give therapists a guided tour of this island so that they can learn what life is like for them. Some clients will have no idea how to escape Problem Island and emigrate to Solution Island. They may resign themselves to life on Problem Island, with all its limitations and difficulties. For some people, it is too frightening to consider a move. They will need a lot of encouragement and support to go even on a short visit. Some may be willing to risk a brief visit to sample Solution Island life, before they could commit themselves to living there.

By engaging in 'solution-talk' the therapist gives clients the opportunity to 'visit' Solution Island on their own terms, without feeling they cannot return to Problem Island if they wish. Those who had a good visit to Solution Island and who want to return and live there permanently, may wish to develop a new set of strategies. Remembering what they liked about it will motivate them to take the next big step.

Solution-focused therapy breaks the connection between the problem and the solution. Its practitioners have found that they can help clients find solutions without reference to the content of the problem. They reject the view that understanding the problem must necessarily precede a lasting and genuine solution. They challenge the idea that we need to gather detailed information and the history of the problem in order to find solutions that fit. SF therapists work on the basis that the solutions do not need to look like the problem. The fact that the problem has been around for a long time and is complex need not mean that it will take a long time to solve, or that the solution should be equally complex. Since the approach is not dependent upon the content of the problem, a SF therapist will use the same type of interventions with all clients, irrespective of the nature of the problem.

However, although the SF therapist does not need to hear about the problem in detail, the client may want or need to talk about it (Edwards, 2006). Solution-focused practitioners recognise and accept this. Problem talk is important when it clearly meets the needs of the client. It becomes an important spar on the bridge to Solution Island.

Conceptualization of psychological disturbance and health

It may be clear from the above that these medical terms do not sit easy with SFT. Since SFT does not seek to explain problems it does not have a conceptual framework for psychological disturbance.

SFT does not take a position in relation to the interaction between thinking, feeling and behaving. It is however firmly opposed to intra-psychic explanations for problems and prefers a more inter-actional frame which pays attention to the specific context of the client's life.

Acquisition of psychological disturbance

Given what has been written already, it will come as no surprise to say that if you were to ask a solution-focused therapist how she explains psychological disturbance you would be likely to get the response, 'I wouldn't start from here'. SFT does not have a theory to explain how people become 'psychologically disturbed'. It does not believe that understanding pathology is necessary for the client to collaborate with the therapist in the search for solutions. It is sceptical of the power position occupied by the therapist who holds a map or a theory which suggests how people became, and continue to be, 'psychologically disturbed'. Since the starting point for therapy is 'where the client would like to get to, there is minimal attention to history, formulations or speculations about where the client has been. If the client chooses to share with the therapist an account of how they think their problems began, the therapist, of course, listens and empathises. But he or she would not be pro-active in seeking out this information, unless the agency for whom she worked required it (and of course many of them do). Collecting a case history may be useful for research, risk assessment and 'therapist-as-expert' therapies, but it is of secondary importance to a client-centred, future-oriented approach.

Perpetuation of psychological disturbance

When people spend excessive time analysing their problems they strengthen the neural networks attached to the problem memory. Recalling all the details around the problem experience, invites the brain to search for associated memories of other problems. This generates the original feelings of sadness, anxiety, fear or whatever. This re-enactment imprints a fresh memory of the problem experience. When these pathways have developed over a long period of time and been regularly re-visited, it becomes difficult to break the connections. Similarly, when a person reflects upon previous successes, transferable skills and resources, the brain automatically seeks evidence of a similar kind. When positive feelings such as joy, satisfaction and pride accompany the memory, the brain logs this rewarding and empowering experience and reinforces the pathways to solutions. This 'high' brings chemical rewards which in turn motivate the client to repeat the 'solution experience'.

SFT argues that by dwelling upon disturbance, deficits and problems the individual is likely to attract more of the same. People can become experts about their problems, believing that they know *why* they have them, but have no idea how to overcome them. They can become attached to, yet trapped by, professional-inspired labels. The problem-label may become justification for a fatalistic resignation to the status quo. Some drug abusers, for example, use the label of 'junkie' or ' smack head' as a short-hand way to communicate their belief that they are bound for ever to their problem identity.

Change

SFT does not propose a particular sequence or pattern of change applicable to all. Instead, based upon clinical experience, its premise is that people change more quickly when they focus on what they want to happen next, rather than what has happened already. They make further changes as they become aware of changes already happening in their lives. When they realise that their problem is not fixed, rigid or static, but in a constant state of evolution, they become more hopeful that they can influence its course. Change becomes more attractive and attainable when people face it from a position of self-valuing, believing that they have the capacity to rise to the challenge. SFT supports this position by giving clients affirming, honest and life-enhancing feedback, free of blame, criticism and judgement. Most people are far more likely to risk change when given time and space to reflect upon their own unique set of resources, solutions and strategies. People change when:

- they know what to change, when to change and how to change.
- they believe that there is something better than their present circumstances and that they have the ability to make and sustain change.
- they tap into what is best about themselves.
- they find reasons to be hopeful, optimistic and dynamic.

PRACTICE

Goals of Therapy

The goals of therapy are those proposed by the client. These are carefully negotiated in clear, specific and measurable terms at the onset of the work. To be solution-focused is to be client-centred in the sense of staying close to the client's agenda, context and capacity. Solution-focused is a future-oriented way of working which aims to harness the client's resources in a directive process shaped by the client's goals.

Selection criteria

The agency context in which the therapy is taking place may have specific selection criteria in operation but the model itself does not impose set criteria as to who might benefit from the therapy. If it is possible to identify achievable and appropriate therapeutic goals then SFT could be offered as an option. It is currently used with a wide range of challenging clients including offenders, substance misusers, survivors of sexual, physical and emotional abuse, people with learning difficulties and mental or physical health problems.

Macdonald's research (1994) suggests that it offers equal benefits across socio-economic classes but is less helpful for clients with long standing problems. Anecdotal evidence suggests that many clients who did not engage with problem-focused therapy find the solution-focused process more accessible.

While there are many practitioners who see themselves as exclusively solution-focused and are purist in their practice, there are many others who take an integrated position. They use the core interventions and subscribe to the beliefs and values of SFT, but where appropriate they also use interventions from other therapies. This is consistent with the SFT principle, 'if it doesn't work, do something different'. It also embraces the maxim that the model fits the client, not the client the model. Some clients undoubtedly benefit from a fusion of SFT and other approaches.

Qualities of effective therapists

In many respects who you *are* with the client is more crucial than technique. Some 'presences' are more therapeutic than others! As well as having the personal qualities of compassion, warmth and empathy, solution-focused therapists require the ability to:

- Listen attentively and be able to feedback to the client those aspects of the client's narrative which SFT privileges e.g. evidence of the client's resources. A key skill for the therapist is to reflect back the positive aspects of what the client has said and to add a phrase or question which orients the client in the direction of solutions and resources. These 'solution connectors' may, for example, be the conversion of problem statements into goal statements. Throughout the interview the therapist gives undivided attention to the client and matches his language in order to demonstrate that she is on the client's wavelength. This active listening, which includes non-verbal as well as verbal communications, ensures the therapist stays close to the client.
- Time the move from 'problem-talk' to 'solution-talk' and be able to re-think should the client prove unprepared for the shift. Many practitioners new to SFT intervene too early and direct clients down the solution route without first acknowledging and validating the client's concerns and feelings. Forcing the pace often results in the client being less willing to engage.
- Be disciplined in staying on 'solution track' – not being diverted by the search for explanations, e.g. by exploring possible causes of the problem or by trying to delve deeper than the presenting problem.
- Pace the number and frequency of questions. Since the therapist asks a lot of questions she needs to pay attention to the client's body language to ensure that the interview does not feel like an interrogation. The therapist's tone of voice and facial expressions are also important factors in securing the collaboration of the client.
- Be sensitive to the use of language. This is a key skill as careful choice of language can open up or close down possibilities. For example, solution-focused therapists use qualifying phrases such as ' so far' or 'as yet' to suggest that sometime in the future the problem will be resolved.
- Roll with 'resistance'. In SFT the worker views 'resistance' as a signal to change the style or pace or focus of the session. The therapist checks out with the client, 'Is this helpful? Is this what you want to talk about today? Do we need to do anything different?'
- Celebrate diversity. Working with her clients' unique beliefs, values and strategies, requires the therapist to have a mindset that goes beyond mere acceptance of difference, to one that is fascinated and excited by the range of attitudes and life styles her clients choose.
- Keep out of the client's way. In practice, this means trusting the client to know what works best in his life and not short-circuiting his own problem-solving mechanisms by introducing therapist-initiated solutions.

Therapeutic relationship and style

A solution-focused relationship is a respectful collaboration. It is a partnership in which the client's expertise is given equal weight to that of the therapist. The latter's expertise lies in creating a therapeutic environment and setting the direction of the conversation to be consistent with solution-focused principles. The expertise of the clients lies in reflecting upon their experience and coming to a realisation of what 'works' for them. They are also responsible for the agenda – the goals for the work. The therapist's role is not to offer solutions or give advice, but to facilitate client solutions by supportive questions and reflections.

The emphasis is on enabling clients to tap into their own resources – their reservoir of skills, strengths and strategies – which will help them to overcome their problems.

Listening attentively, keeping the client on solution-track, reflecting back the client's competence, promoting the client's use of the imagination, summarising the client's unique set of strategies – these are the key contributions of the solution-focused therapist. Technique does not make a therapist solution-focused. It is the quality of the relationship underpinned by solution-focused values which makes someone genuinely solution-focused.

Having observed many of the major figures in SFT using the approach, I have concluded that there is no one authentic solution-focused style. On the one hand there is a dynamic, high-energy style, exemplified by the charismatic Bill O'Hanlon. On the other, there is the gentle, warm and quiet style, characterised by Insoo Kim Berg. Steve de Shazer himself had a laconic, laid back style that gave the impression he wasn't listening, when in fact he heard and picked up on everything! Generally speaking SFT encourages a relaxed, informal, warm, conversational style. Practitioners tend to disclose more about themselves and their work than perhaps other therapists (obviously there are a lot of qualifications to that). One noticeable feature of solution-focused interviewing is that there is often humour in it. Perhaps the emphasis on the clients' strengths, skills and successes makes it easier for them to see humour in their situation.

Steve de Shazer once said that his only worry about the future of SFT was that someone would try to impose one way of being solution-focused!

Major therapeutic strategies and techniques

Pre-Session Change

From the initial contact the therapist focuses on the theme of change. She uses pre-suppositional language to convey to the client that change is inevitable – that it is already taking place and that it will continue. For example, she will talk about *when* change takes place, not *if* it does. One of the aims of the work is to help clients experience change in their lives as early on in the therapy as possible. As they experience the immediate benefits of change, this will empower them to make further changes. When the client first requests a therapy session he is recruited as an active agent in the process. Either by letter, phone or e-mail, the therapist asks him to notice any changes that take place prior to the first appointment. When he comes for the first session the therapist expresses curiosity about what might have changed. If the client can report beneficial change the therapist will ask, ' How did you do that?' Research (Weiner-Davis et al., 1987; Lawson, 1994) suggests that between 62 per cent and 66 per cent of clients will report positive pre-session change if asked by the therapist in a tone that expects a positive answer. When the client is able to report positive pre-session change it indicates that he has already raised his awareness of 'what works' and has identified specific exceptions to the problem. The discovery of pre-session change gives momentum to the session, as well as a clear message to the client that his observations are key to finding solutions. It underlines the fact that the client has the power and the resources to shape his own future. This is a powerful message for clients who may have felt stigmatised or de-skilled in having to seek or be sent to have therapy. For many clients with a long history of blame, punishment, criticism and failure, this awareness of their strengths and achievements comes as a revelation. It challenges their expectations that the therapist will expose their weaknesses, blind spots and deficits.

Problem-Free Talk

Unless the client is distressed or launches into an urgent account of their difficulties, the therapist takes some time at the beginning of the first session to engage in conversation about the client's interests or leisure pursuits. These conversations are more than icebreakers or rapport builders, they often provide clues about:

- metaphors or illustrations which will resonate with the client
- the client's strengths, qualities and values
- strategies which may work for the client.

Problem-free talk also underlines the fact that there is a lot more to the client than any difficulties s/he may be experiencing. There is a saying in solution-focused circles, 'There's nothing wrong with you that what's right with you can't fix'.

Being Brief

Many solution-focused therapists emphasise the brevity associated with the approach. Although used with long-term clients, it is used most often in time-limited settings. In order to be brief the therapist will:

- Treat every session as if it could be the last, especially the first one.
- Project confidence and hope that much can be achieved in limited time.
- Stay close to the client's view of the problem.
- Trust and consult the client.
- Believe that more does not mean better.
- Be curious only about solutions and sometimes not even about them.
- Intervene as minimally as possible.
- Avoid if possible a focus on the problem itself.
- Match the client's language.
- Deconstruct problems into goals.
- Use what the client brings.
- Negotiate attainable goals.

Competence seeking

Without minimising their problems, solution-focused therapists draw particular attention to examples of their clients' competence. The skilled therapist senses when to reflect back these strengths and qualities. When doing this they invite clients to own them and apply them in the current situation. This feedback should be realistic or the client will reject the picture as being overly positive.

Building on exceptions

Instead of asking questions about the occasions when clients experienced their problems, SF therapists direct their attention toward times when they managed the problems better. These episodes are called 'exceptions' or micro-solutions. There are always exceptions to any problem experience because everyone has highs and lows, ups and downs, good and bad times. Exceptions are evidence of clients' constructive strategies. Highlighting and exploring these exceptions enables clients to become aware of how they made them happen. They can begin to think about how they could repeat and expand these helpful strategies. Freedman and Combs describe the seeking of exceptions as ' ways in which people recover experiences at odds with their dominant story. By highlighting different events, they are opening space for the authoring of new stories,' (1993: 296).

The therapist supportively explores with the client the circumstances in which the exception took place. He or she may use questions such as:

- How did you do that?
- What was the first thing you did?
- How did you know that was going to be useful?
- What needs to happen for you to do that again?

Having unearthed evidence of embryonic solutions the therapist encourages the client to 'keep doing what works.' It is important not to overdo a curiosity about solutions, it could be counterproductive, resulting in a loss of spontaneity on the client's part (Debnam, 2006).

The Miracle Question

The Miracle Question (MQ), devised by Steve de Shazer (1988) is an intervention used by solution-focused therapists in first and subsequent sessions. It is designed to help clients by-pass 'problem talk'. The miracle question is an intervention which encourages the client to leave Problem Island and visit Solution Island. Answers to the MQ become the focus of the work. It can be a powerful intervention, accessing material not easily unearthed by conventional questioning. The MQ can be particularly useful when the client believes that prolonged discussion of his problems will get him nowhere. Paradoxically, the MQ can sometimes clarify, reveal and on occasions 'dissolve' problems. Over the course of a number of sessions the answers to the question are likely to change.

The question is an invitation to the client to use his imagination to describe how his day-to-day life would look when his problems disappeared. Its standard form is:

Imagine one night when you are asleep, a miracle happens and the problems we've been discussing disappear. Since you are asleep, you do not know that a miracle has happened. When you wake up what will be the first signs for you that a miracle has happened?

In asking the MQ the therapist assumes that some of the 'miracle' is in fact already happening and that what the client needs to do is locate these changes and amplify them. The therapist follows up the first answer by further questions, closely linked to the client's answers. 'So after you've managed to …, what will be the next thing the miracle has enabled you to do?' Each answer contributes to the overall shape of the client's preferred scenario and helps to clarify available strategies. The therapist may ask, 'What did the miracle change so that you were able to do that?' As therapists develop clients' miracle answers, they listen for exceptions – times when even a small part of the miracle has happened. They also listen for evidence of strengths, qualities and competence. They use circular questions to scan the client's system or network – 'Who else will notice that the miracle has happened? What will they see that is different? How will they respond? If they respond like that, what do you think you will do?'

The miracle question requires focused concentration by the therapist. Keeping on the solution-track demands a disciplined perseverance which motivates the client to discover more solutions. The therapist asks repeatedly, ' What else will you notice?'

During this intervention the therapist will write down or remember the client's answers as they will be central to the feedback given at the end of the session. A helpful way of drawing the MQ to a close is to ask scaling questions in relation to some of the answers.

Scaling
Although scaling is not exclusive to SFT, the questions used to explore the scale are. Therapists use a scale of zero to ten to help clients:

- measure progress
- build confidence and motivation
- set small identifiable goals
- develop strategies.

Ten on the scale represents 'the best it could be' and zero the worst. Therapists invite clients to think about their position on the scale by asking such questions as:

- Where were you a day or two ago?
- What was happening when you were higher on the scale?
- Where do you hope to be in the next few weeks?
- What needs to happen for that to happen?

Clients are invited to think where other significant people would put them on the scale. Solution-focused therapists encourage clients to consider small steps they can take which will move them one point up the scale. This is consistent with the solution-focused principle that 'small changes can lead to big changes'. It is often the case that when clients commit to making small changes they build momentum which takes them much further than they had originally planned. On the other hand when circumstances are difficult it may be a considerable achievement for the client to hold on to their point on the scale. Scaling is a simple, practical technique which clients can use between sessions to measure their progress and to plan their next steps.

Between session tasks

By the end of the interview the therapist will have elicited many ideas from the client as to what he could do to make things better. In the feedback the therapist will pull these together, usually following the principles of:

a) If it works keep doing it.
b) If it doesn't work stop doing it.
c) Small steps can lead to big changes.
d) Do something different.

In addition to these the therapist may invite the client to carry out:

- A Notice Task. This is an observational task most commonly given to clients who have struggled to answer questions about their experience and who lack the motivation to take action. The therapist asks the client to notice times when the problem is not so bad or times when someone else does something they value or when they do something they feel good about.
- A Pretend Task. This is when the client is asked to behave for a short time as if the miracle has happened and to notice anything that is different in that time.

Feedback

At the end of each session the therapist takes a short break to compose a succinct and positive message for the client. Some therapists will actually leave the client and go elsewhere to do this, returning within five minutes. Others simply remind the client about the break and remain in the room as they quickly scan their notes and compose the feedback. During the feedback the client is not invited to join in as this is part of concluding the session. The feedback follows a clear and simple sequence:

Positive feedback

↓

Summarise client achievements

↓

Link to goals

↓

Negotiate task

Positive feedback   The therapist gives positive feedback about the client's participation in the session. This may include comments such as:

- 'I'd like to thank you …. for coming here today.'
- 'I was really impressed by the way you …'
- 'I appreciated the fact that you …'
- 'I thought it was a great help the way that you …'

These comments should be genuine and grounded in specific examples.

Summarise client achievements   The therapist chooses two or three specific examples of what the client is doing in between sessions to sort out the problem.

- 'It was good to hear that on Monday when you normally would have done …, you managed to do ….instead'.
- 'Another important thing you did this week was to …. and I know that wasn't easy for you to do'.

The purpose of this summary is to reinforce and encourage the client to 'keep doing what works'.

Link to goals   The therapist links this evidence of progress with the client's stated goals.

- 'It sounds as if what you managed to do on Tuesday when you…is just the kind of thing you're working on'.

Negotiate tasks   The two parties agree the next stage of the plan – what the client is going to do before the next meeting – the between-session task.

The change process in therapy

The entire solution-focused process is about eliciting and expanding positive change in the client's life. It is based upon the assumption that change is inevitable but that awareness of the direction in which change is going is vital in order for the client to achieve his goals. Making this awareness explicit is a goal of the work. That is the rationale for targeting exceptions, resources and goals. Right from the start of the work the therapist helps the client to imagine the ending, 'When will you know you don't have to come here anymore?, What will your manager/partner/probation officer have to see before they realise what you have achieved?'

One starting point for the change process can be agreement about what the client does *not* want to change. If it is possible to ringfence this, it frees the client to explore what he *does* want to change. Faced with a complex and chronic set of problems it is possible for client and therapist to be overwhelmed by the task ahead. This is less likely to happen in SFT because the therapist will not get bogged down in the details of the problems and will not believe that they require complex solutions. Whatever the client brings she will focus on increasing his awareness of how change has already been achieved and what he has the resources to tackle next.

However, the solution-focused therapist recognises that not all clients are equally motivated towards change and that it is not helpful to imagine that they are. It characterises the relationship between therapist and client as either:

- Visitor – one in which the client is sent, does not own a problem and does not believe they need to change anything. Trying to persuade the client of the case for change is usually unproductive. It is often better to join with his ambivalence and to explore his current situation in a non-judgemental way. Fisch et al. (1982:39) describe this type of client as a window shopper who slips into a shop in a heavy shower with no intention of buying anything. Sometimes it happens that they end up buying something, but often they don't. It could be argued that SFT has an advantage over problem-focused therapies with this type of client, as there is no need for him to admit he has a problem. He could explore what he would like to keep the same or be different in his life without going down the problem exploration route.
- Complainant – one in which the client owns the problem, but is not ready to change or sees the solution lying elsewhere, often in someone else changing their behaviour. The therapist listens empathically, matches his language and frame of reference and where appropriate, gives positive feedback. She asks coping questions which draw out what he is already doing to 'stop it getting worse' and in some instances this can lead on to how he could make his life better, even if the other person or situation did not change.
- Customer – a relationship in which the client recognises that there is a problem over which he has some control and is ready to do something about it.

Limitations

Although in my experience, SFT is helpful to many clients, there are times when it is not effective. Studies have consistently shown that in general terms it has the same effectiveness rate as other therapies, while using fewer sessions than most other therapies. Gingerich and Eisengart (2000) summarise the state of SFBT research (also available on Gingerich's website www.gingerich.net). Based on anecdotal evidence I suggest that SFT is ineffective when:

- The therapist has a limited understanding of the rationale behind the approach and is simply a technician.
- The therapist combines solution-focused with problem-focused techniques and confuses themself and the clients.
- Clients in crisis cannot access their resources.
- Clients want a 'quick fix' and are unwilling or unable to explore their solutions repertoire.
- Clients who hold themselves in such low esteem they are unable to accept that they have any personal strengths or qualities.
- Clients who are convinced that they cannot find solutions until they have 'got to the bottom' of the problem.
- Clients who think that SFT is too simple and that their problem requires a more complex solution.
- Clients who want the therapist to supply the solutions.

There are many research projects currently underway on SFT in Europe and in the USA. Hopefully these will provide a stronger evidence base and clarify the reason for SFT's success.

Case example

The client

My client Judith was a 37 year old woman, married with one small child, who had recently been promoted at work to a middle-management team leader role. Judith was an intelligent, conscientious and hard working person. Her partner, Michael, was more laid back and although successful enough in his own eyes, to Judith he was failing to fulfil his potential. They rowed frequently over Michael's perception of Judith as 'driven' and her view of Michael as 'lazy and sloppy.' The atmosphere at home was often tense and unhappy.

Due to a recent restructuring at Judith's company, there was a lot of uncertainty about the future. Her new colleagues, fearing for their jobs, were unwilling to take risks or step out of line. Judith found it difficult to manage a team who seemed to her unwilling to raise their game and meet the challenges the situation demanded. Her team failed to meet their targets and Judith was heavily criticised for this. She became acutely anxious and had a number of panic attacks in meetings. Her manager, who was usually unsupportive, recommended that she seek counselling for her problems. She contacted the counselling service which was part of the company's Employee Assistance Programme (EAP).

Judith also found Michael unsupportive. At home her partner was not supportive. He felt that, to a large extent, her problems were of her own making. He said that she shouldn't have allowed herself to be promoted 'beyond her competence.' He also resented the fact that he had to do so much at home to 'cover for her'. Michael also blamed the company for wanting 'more and more for less and less'.

The therapy

It is my practice to explain to clients the model I use and to gain their understanding and consent to it. It is also standard practice with this model to negotiate with the client at the end of each session whether she wants additional sessions, rather than make a contract at the beginning for a specific number. This allows for the possibility that a client may only want, or need, a single session. In this particular case, the Employment Assistance Programme set a limit of six sessions, although it was possible to request further sessions, if a case could be made for them.

After the usual preliminaries (explanation of the model and confidentiality), the interview began with a standard set of questions laid down by the EAP. These focused mainly on the history of the problem while scanning for any possible risk issues.

The first solution-focused intervention was the pre-session change question.

- What has been different in the interval between you making the appointment and coming here today?

Judith's response was that she was feeling slightly better as she had reduced her intake of alcohol over the past week. She felt that her drinking had only been making her more depressed. Michael had promised to be more supportive over the next month as he could see she was making efforts to improve matters.

In the early stages we aim to establish as far as possible the client's goals. I used a combination of the following questions:

- How will you know that coming here is proving useful to you?
- What will you begin to notice that will tell you that you are making progress?
- What are your best hopes for counselling?

Judith answered that:

1 She would be able to manage her anxiety better and reduce or eliminate the panic attacks.
2 She would engage better with members of her team.
3 She would be getting on better with Michael, her partner.

Solution-focused therapists encourage clients to be as specific as possible about their goals. So I asked her:

- What will be the *first* sign for you that you are engaging better with your colleagues?
- What will you/he be doing that will let you know that you are beginning to get on better with Michael?

As the client talked, I listened attentively to her concerns and acknowledged her feelings. SF therapists listen to their clients' problems for as long as the clients find it helpful. While doing so, I also enquired about her resources: 'It sounds as if things have been really difficult for you. How do you cope, how do you manage?' I also asked her how she managed to stop things getting worse. Judith had a number of strategies she was already using to control her anxiety – thinking about something else, reminding herself that these were only feelings and that they would pass and at home, putting on some music and moving around.

Sometimes clients are unprepared for positive questions. Judith was surprised to be asked:

- What do you know about yourself that is going to help you get through this difficult time in your life?
- What got you through other bad patches in your life?
- What do other people see as strengths in you?

I encouraged the client to be aware, not only of her personal qualities and values, but also of her transferable skills and solutions. Judith was able to recall a time in her life when she was anxious when her daughter was very ill. She remembered that it helped to go for walks in nice places and to slow down everything. She felt that she could benefit from doing the latter at the moment as she was making a lot of mistakes at work by trying to work fast. Although she felt weak and something of a failure at the moment she knew that she could be a strong, determined and achieving person too.

In the first session I also listened for evidence of exceptions to the problem.

- Have there been any times recently when you managed to control your anxiety/got on better with Michael/engaged with your colleagues?

Judith was able to recall a team meeting when she felt that her colleagues were more enthusiastic. I asked her 'How did you do that? What was the difference that made the difference?' She was able to describe how she had prepared the meeting, had taken more of a back seat and been positive in her comments to colleagues. At home she thought that the atmosphere had improved since Michael's offer of support and she had also tried to do more at home.

At the end of the first session I fed back to Judith that:

> I know that in many ways you didn't want to be here today and that talking about your situation wasn't easy. I appreciated how honest you were in telling me about what was happening. Although life is difficult at the moment, you really want to improve the situation at home and at work. You have taken a number of constructive steps already. You have also remembered that going for walks and slowing everything down helped you on another occasion when you were anxious. This week perhaps you could notice any times you manage to control your anxiety, any times when things go a little better with Michael and any time when any of your colleagues begin to engage.

The next session began in standard fashion with the question:

- What has been different since we met last time?

Judith's response was that things were still bad at work, but there had been some progress on the home front. She had noticed that Michael did a lot of helpful things of which she had previously been unaware. She had told him how much she appreciated him. He, in turn, had listened to her more and had given her some good advice about work. She had started to practice relaxation exercises to help with the anxiety and had gone for a walk in the local country park at the weekend with Michael and her daughter. She said that she was beginning to feel that she had more control over the situation than she had thought previously.

During this session I used the Miracle Question.

> Imagine that one night soon when you are fast asleep a miracle happens. The miracle is that your anxiety disappears and that you are getting on better at home and at work. Since you were asleep you didn't know that this miracle had happened, so when you wake up what will be the first signs for you that the miracle had happened?

Judith was able to describe step-by-step an anxiety-free day. During this day she would be more optimistic, more confident, more assertive. She would value her own achievements without needing the praise of others. Instead of being so critical of her colleagues, she would be more appreciative of their efforts. When exploring this miracle

I asked, ' What would need to happen for that to happen?' Judith began to identify small steps she could take that accumulatively would add up to a big move forward. She recognised that she did not have to wait for a miracle.

Over the next four sessions I continued to highlight and reinforce Judith's resources and successful small steps. A frequently used intervention was the scaling question. I invited Judith to rate her progress and then asked her questions around her scale: 'On a scale of zero to ten with ten being that you feel you have achieved your goals, where would you say you were this week?' Wherever Judith placed herself on the scale I explored with her the strategies she had used to get or stay there. I asked whether she was thinking of moving up the scale and if so, what would she do to move up just one step?

Judith did not always report progress. In the week of session four she had suffered a major panic attack at work that had been witnessed by several colleagues. She was frightened that this could have consequences for her future with the company.

The six sessions were spread out over a period of ten weeks. In the final session we reviewed progress and discussed strategies she could implement if her anxiety level began to rise again.

Judith returned for two sessions of therapy six months later when there were redundancies in her team. She had begun to feel acutely anxious again and wanted to explore whether she should stay in her job or seek another post elsewhere.

REFERENCES

Bandler, R. and Grinder, J. (1979) *Frogs into Princes*. Moab, UT: Real People Press.

Bateson, G. (1972) *Steps to an Ecology of Mind*. New York: Ballantine.

Debnam, L. (2006) Personal communication.

de Shazer, S. (1985) *Keys to Solutions in Brief Therapy*. New York: W. W. Norton.

de Shazer, S. (1988) *Clues–Investigating Solutions in Brief Therapy*. New York: W. W. Norton.

de Shazer, S. (1991) *Putting Difference to Work*. New York: W. W. Norton.

de Shazer, S. (1994) *Words were Originally Magic*. New York: W. W. Norton.

Edwards, M. F. (2006) Personal communication.

Erickson, M.H. (1980) *Collected Papers. Vols 1–4* (E. Rossi, ed.). New York: Irvington.

Fisch, R., Weakland, J.H. and Segal, L. (1982) *The Tactics of Change – Doing Therapy Briefly*. San Francisco: Jossey-Bass.

Freedman, J. and Combs, G. (1993) 'Invitations to new stories: using questions to explore alternative possibilities', in S. Gilligan and R. Price (eds), *Therapeutic Conversations*. New York: W.W. Norton. pp. 291–303.

George, E., Iveson C. and Ratner, H. (1990) *Problems to Solutions*. London: BT Press.

Gingerich, W. J., and Eisengart, S. (2000) 'Solution-focused brief therapy: a review of the outcome research', *Family Process*, 39: 477–98.

Hawkes, D., Marsh, T. I. and Wilgosh, R. (1998) *Solution Focused Therapy – A Handbook for Health Care Professionals*. Oxford: Butterworth Heinemann.

Johnson, S. (2004) *Mind Wide Open*. New York: Penguin.

Kelly, G.A. (1955) *The Psychology of Personal Constructs*. New York: W.W. Norton.

Lawson, D. (1994) 'Identifying pre-treatment change', *Journal of Counselling and Development*, 72: 244–8.

Lethem, J. (1994) *Moved to Tears, Moved to Action*. London: BT Press.

Macdonald, A.J. (1994) 'Brief therapy in adult psychiatry', *Journal of Family Therapy*, 16: 415–26.

Macdonald, A.J. (2003) 'Research in solution-focused brief therapy', in B. O'Connell and S. Palmer (eds), *The Handbook of Solution Focused Therapy*. London: Sage.

O'Connell, B. (1998/2005) *Solution Focused Therapy*. London. Sage.

Watzlawick, P., Weakland, J. and Fisch, R. (1974) *Change: Principles of Problem Formation and Problem Resolution*. New York: W.W. Norton.

Watzlawick, P. (1984) *The Invented Reality*. New York: W.W. Norton.

Weiner-Davis, M., de Shazer, S. and Gingerich, W. (1987) 'Building on pretreatment change to construct the therapeutic solution: an exploratory study', *Journal of Marital and Family Therapy*, 13 (4): 359–63.

White, M. and Epston, D. (1990) *Narrative Means to Therapeutic Ends*. New York: W.W. Norton.

SUGGESTED FURTHER READING

Jackson, P. Z. and McKergow, M. (2002) *The Solutions Focus*. London: Nicholas Brealey

Nelson, T. S. (2005) *Education and Training in Solution-Focused Brief Therapy*. New York: The Howarth Press.

O'Connell, B. (1998/ 2005) *Solution Focused Therapy*. London: Sage.

O'Connell, B. and Palmer, S. (2003) *The Handbook of Solution-Focused Therapy*. London: Sage.

O'Hanlon, B. and Beadle, S. (1994) *A Field Guide to Possibility Land*. Omaha, NE: Possibility Press.

16

Narrative Therapy

Martin Payne

Practitioners of narrative therapy share certain philosophical positions, and use many similar techniques, but like all therapies it is a developing way of working. I hope the reader will understand that this chapter is one practitioner's attempt to present a consensus; inevitably there are omissions and simplifications. Michael White's practice of referring to people who come to counselling as 'persons' rather than 'clients' is followed throughout.

HISTORICAL CONTEXT AND DEVELOPMENT IN BRITAIN

Historical context

Narrative therapy, as defined here, is a specific strand of family therapy, counselling, social work and community work which originated in Australia and New Zealand in the early 1980s. It is informed by European theoretical positions of post-modernism, and in particular post-structuralism, which have come to permeate much of Western intellectual life since the Second World War. Broadly speaking, the post-structuralist tradition perceives assumed knowledge as deriving from socially constructed linguistic meanings; questions the possibility of achieving objective knowledge in human affairs; defines much assumed 'expert' knowledge as the means by which social institutions perpetuate their power; and sees people as principally influenced in their identity and behaviour by cultural and social norms rather than by inner psychological processes. Michel Foucault, the French historian of ideas, is a major influence on this therapy's theoretical base. Narrative therapy also draws on the 'cognitive turn' intellectual tradition in

America, which puts people's conscious understandings of life at the centre; sociologist Erving Goffman, psychologist Jerome Bruner, anthropologists Gregory Bateson, Glifford Geerz and Barbara Myerhoff, and social psychologist Kenneth Gergen have been influential.

Narrative therapy is appropriate for working with communities, families, couples and individuals, but its use in individual therapy is, of course, the theme of this chapter.

Narrative therapy's originators are Michael White, Co-Director of the Dulwich Centre (for family therapy and community work) in Adelaide, South Australia, and David Epston, an anthropologist and family therapist who is Co-Director of the Family Centre, Auckland, New Zealand. White is the more influential of the two, and in family therapy circles is recognized as a leading figure, certainly one of the most important of our time. He began his career in the 1960s as a social worker and family therapist. He has described how he questioned the taken-for-granted assumptions of social work/therapy training and practice at that period. These cultural assumptions were that people choose careers working with distressed people out of suspect and unacknowledged psychological motives; that 'clients' are under the influence of hidden factors in their past lives producing defects or shortcomings of personality and of skills in living; and that social and political factors impinging on people's lives are of no direct concern to the therapist, whose role is to concentrate on helping them to overcome inner defects by means of specialist expertise. White's reaction against these assumptions led him to develop ways of assisting troubled people which are in striking contrast to such pathologizing and 'expert-based' positions (White, 2000: 117–22, 151–2).

Initially White's therapeutic work took place within the Australian public health system, but he found greater freedom for his practice by becoming Co-Director of the independent Dulwich Centre, where he is still based. In 1981 he met David Epston at a conference. They recognized that they shared common values and purposes, and had independently developed similar approaches to community work, counselling and family therapy. The Dulwich Centre started a publishing venture, the Dulwich Centre Press, publishing a Newsletter and collections of papers by White and Epston as well as books by other therapists who were finding the White/Epston way of working congenial and exciting. In 1989 Epston and White took up a whole issue of the Newsletter with a book-length paper 'Literate Means to Therapeutic Ends', a jointly written account of the theoretical basis of their work and its practical application to therapy. In 1990 a very slightly modified version, significantly with 'Narrative' replacing 'Literate' in the title, was published by Norton. This brought their work to the attention of a wider audience and is still regarded by many as the key text.

Articles by White, Epston and other narrative therapists have proliferated in family therapy journals in many countries, including Britain; over the years the Dulwich Centre Press has published several books in which White gives accounts of his developing thought and practice; and books on narrative therapy have increasingly been brought out not only by the Dulwich Centre Press but by established international publishers such as Norton, Guilford, Jossey-Bass and Sage. From its modest beginnings the *Dulwich Centre Newsletter* has evolved into the *International Journal of Narrative Therapy and Community Work*. Centres offering narrative therapy and/or training in narrative therapy are now established in many countries, including New Zealand, the USA, Canada, Scandinavia, Ireland and the UK, and well attended annual international Narrative Therapy conferences have been held in Australia, America, England, Mexico and Hong Kong. The Dulwich Centre now offers a qualifying Diploma as well as many workshops and Intensives.

Development in Britain

Until the late 1990s family therapy rather than counselling was the context for the development of narrative therapy in Britain, with frequent articles about White and Epston's work appearing in the Association for Family Therapy and Systemic Practice's *Journal* and its magazine *Context*. Family therapists, who have always worked with individuals as well as with couples or whole families, began to experiment with narrative ideas and methods. Qualifying courses in family therapy, such as the Kensington Consultation Centre's Diploma in Systemic Therapy, gave narrative ideas serious attention. White's annual presentations and workshops in Britain were, and still are, organized by family therapists, including the Centre for Narrative Practice in Manchester, Brief Therapy Practice in London, and Mark Hayward, a clinical psychologist and family therapist in Devon who is the Dulwich Centre Press' British representative. As word has spread, counsellors who work one-to-one have attended narrative therapy conferences and courses. Parker et al.'s groundbreaking text (1995) includes much on White's ideas, and Angus and McLeod refer at length to White/Epston narrative therapy when describing narrative in psychotherapy as a whole (McLeod, 1997; Angus and McLeod, 2004). I have written about narrative therapy specifically from a counselling perspective (1993/1996, 2000/2006). Jane Speedy has established an MA in Counselling at Bristol University with narrative therapy modules and her thoughtful articles have reached the counselling world through the BACP Journal. The commissioning of this present chapter is perhaps an indication that in Britain narrative therapy with individuals is now poised to take off in counselling contexts wider than family therapy.

THEORETICAL ASSUMPTIONS

Image of the person

Narrative therapists conceive people as socially and individually complex; never fully knowable or explicable to themselves or others. People's frequent accounts of their experience, repeatedly told to themselves and others and drawn from selective memory, are believed to be the most important factors influencing their sense of themselves and how they view their lives and relationships. This is how the term 'narrative' is used in this therapy; it refers to *self-stories*, the multiply-stranded and often inconsistent images, thoughts and conceptualizations of their past, present and future, and of the world within which experience takes place, which people continually reinforce, expand, revise and explore. Events selected from memory can be combined to make up accounts of life in innumerable ways – 'I find it helpful to conceive of life as multi-storied' (White, 2004b: 60). Since life is perceived as a movement from past to present to imagined future, a sense of temporal sequence underpins and gives an overall structure to selective memories even if these are often recalled and told in a non-sequential or kaleidoscopic fashion.

Personal narratives, 'self-stories', are not merely inert, neutral, passive images. They have emotional resonance. The continual process of self-storying actively feeds back into, and affects, people's attitudes, actions, relationships and sense of identity.

Narrative therapists recognize that people are born with inherited mental potentials, such as a predisposition for understanding and developing language (Bruner, 1990: 69–80). However narrative therapists do not call on ideas of psychological dynamics to define what makes people tick, what produces distress and confusion, and what is needed to improve life. Such 'professional' interpretations are seen as outside the experience of the person herself, an example of control by the therapist, no matter how respectfully applied. People's *own* perspectives as revealed through their told narratives are the focus of this therapy. McLeod has accurately called narrative therapy *'post-psychological'* (in Payne, 2000: viii).

Sociocultural influences, including family of origin, social class, significant relationships, and wider sub-groups inform people's sense of what constitutes normality and how life should be lived. Correspondingly, self-stories embody socially and culturally derived assumptions, values and beliefs, which form lenses through which people perceive and give meaning to their lives. The provisional nature of these norms is frequently unrecognized because they have unthinkingly been absorbed as assumed 'truths'. They form a framework of 'canonical life styles' – stereotypical templates of living, current in the immediate and wider social circles to which people belong. Failure to correspond to these stereotypes can produce self-devaluation and stress. To give examples: one canonical life style in the contemporary Western world, particularly applied to middle class men, is of moving up through status-level stages of a career so as to gain a high income with which to provide for a family originating in a romantic heterosexual attachment. In certain strata of Indian society an otherwise similar canonical story includes the norm of parents advertising for suitable marriage partners for their adult children. A Western middle class man who chose to follow a low-paid vocation while living with a male partner, or an Indian woman in a traditional community who chose her own husband independently of her parents, would be stepping outside the canonical stories by which others in their social context expect them to live. They might however gain validation in these choices through allegiance to non-conforming sub-groups.

Self-stories also incorporate and are expressed through culturally formed, value-laden, unrecognized, and unexamined *linguistic* meanings, such as when a woman identifies herself as insufficiently 'feminine', a young man drawn into criminality says he wants to keep the 'respect' of his peers, or a person conversant with pop-psychology identifies his problem as 'lack of self-esteem'. Such terms not only *reflect* the cultural attitudes and meanings they embody; their use *embeds* those attitudes and meanings.

Narrative theory therefore proposes that since people's identities, values and beliefs are culturally and linguistically derived, and provisional, there is no bedrock of innate, essential or universal self; no psychology common to all people at all times; and no extra-cultural and unchanging human nature. Identity and beliefs are 'negotiated' between people, in a huge variety of social and historical contexts. There is no universal common meaning to superficially similar institutions, actions and belief systems. However, narrative therapists' view of the person is *not* relativist or determinist. People may largely live according to the culturally influenced meanings they give to their experience, but narrative therapists believe that people are fully capable of examining their assumptions, making conscious choices, and basing their lives on those choices. They can to a significant degree *escape* sociocultural and interpersonal influences; they are not inescapably moulded by them. They can evaluate their self-stories and revise them (metaphorically, 're-write' them) and in so doing loosen the grip of previously fixed ways of conceptualizing their lives, opening up possibilities for moving into new 'territories of life' (White, 2004b: 60) which differ from their past in significant ways but which also embody *continuity* with it.

White suggests that if therapists abandon the generalized idea of assisting people to 'become more truly who [they] really are' this opens up the possibility for paying a more specifically focused attention to the concrete details of people's lives; a 'fascination with ... how people's management of the predicaments, dilemmas and contradictions of their lives contribute to possibilities for them to think outside of what they otherwise thought' (2000: 106–7).

Conceptualization of psychological disturbance and health

Narrative therapists do not define human distress in terms of deficit, so 'psychological disturbance' and 'psychological health' are not concepts of this therapy. The unsubtle binary opposition 'psychological disturbance' versus 'psychological health' would not be defined by narrative therapists as actual elements possessed by or internal to troubled people; rather, they would be seen as linguistic constructs of the therapy culture reflecting certain attitudes which narrative therapy does not share. 'In our work we do not construct problems in terms of disease and we do not imagine that we do anything that relates to "a cure"' (White and Epston, 1990: 14). The use of professional-psychological language for reactions to distress and confusion is an example of a medicalized discourse implying that the therapist has access to specialized knowledge in people's lives and relationships which is *superior* to their own, and a correspondingly superior expertise in addressing their problems. People's distresses and dilemmas have, in much of Western professional practice, come to be expressed in the language of physical illness, with metaphors such as healthy, unhealthy, symptoms, dysfunction and so forth being perceived as psychological realities. Narrative therapists working with people whose reactions have been medically defined ask them whether or not they find these terms helpful, with direct questions such as 'Is it helpful to call your problem *obsessive-compulsive behaviour,* like in your doctor's referral, or would you prefer us to use something like *a habit of relying on comforting daily rituals?*'

Locating the source of distress in factors beyond the 'bounded individual' certainly does not deny the reality of anguish, disorientation and confusion which bring people to counselling. Nor does it deny that people feel, think, behave and relate in ways which may be counter-productive, dissatisfying, chaotic or reinforcing of their problems. And narrative therapists acknowledge a physiological aspect to distress and that in some instances medication can play a useful part in alleviation (White, 1995:116). Nevertheless narrative therapy is allied to a movement of re-evaluation and re-definition of psychological or psychiatric concepts (Parker et al., 1995: 70, 108–9, 126; also Parker (ed.), 1999). An example is White's work with people diagnosed as schizophrenic (White, 1989: 47–58; White, 1995: 112–54; Brigitte et al., 1997: 25–36). Narrative therapists have been highly critical of the *DSM* (for example Law, 1998: 119–24). Psychological and psychiatric definitions are questioned on three grounds: first because they give an authoritative stamp of expert and proven knowledge to a range of human distress which has wide, multiple and never fully knowable aspects; secondly because such definitions (for example, the previous *DSM* definition of homosexuality as an illness) are unacknowledged reflections of the thinking and values of a particular society, and a particular, powerful grouping within that society, at a particular historical time; and thirdly because they internalize and pathologize persons' reactions to distress without taking into account multiple factors outside the assumed bounded individual, including family and peer interaction and the effects of social and political power on individual lives and relationships.

Acquisition of psychological disturbance

Narrative therapists see confusion, sadness and despair as reactions to be expected when circumstances are distressing, rather than as indications of something awry in the person seeking assistance.

Narrative therapists pay close and detailed attention to the social, political and cultural origins of much distress, and the ways in which institutional and professional discourse can feed into and exacerbate it. Where such factors are involved, this is the emphasis of therapy. If a man is affected by depression because his boss is setting him impossible tasks *that* is the reason for his distress, not an inability to work hard enough, a failure to be assertive, or the depression produced by the situation. He would be invited to consider the culture of over-work linked with the emergence of hard management in the workplace in the 1980s. He would be invited to consider how that culture arose and whose interests it serves. The therapist would elicit the precise nature of his boss's expectations and pressures, their effects on his life and the lives of people he cares about, and the extent to which the situation is outside his power to control – and in this light, would encourage him to examine his options for staying in the job or leaving. If a woman is confused and unhappy because her male partner keeps telling her she should welcome intercourse every night, *that* is the reason for her confusion and unhappiness, not a lack of libido, or a weakness in failing to resist her partner's demands. A narrative therapist would encourage her to consider (perhaps through recommended reading) the known wide variations of sexual behaviour and of fre-quency of intercourse. She would be invited to think about how men are encour-aged by peers and the media to glorify and normalize frequent intercourse, and how they take on the belief that they have both a need for its frequency and the right to demand this. The power-based techniques used by the man to make the woman feel it is 'her' problem, rather than an issue needing respectful discussion between partners with differing wishes, would also be raised.

Perpetuation of psychological disturbance

Should there be no clearly identified, continuing, external factors perpetuating the person's distress as in the examples above, a narrative therapist would hypothesize that the main perpetuating factor is likely to be embedded self-stories which have come to represent the person's experience to her and which restrain her from seeing beyond those stories. Many of society's institutions and commercial enterprises, ranging from the cosmetics industry to pop-psychology urging continual self-monitoring towards personal growth, have an interest in promoting a sense of failure: 'Never before has the sense of being a failure to be an adequate person been so freely available to people ... ' (White, 2002: 35). Persons' self-stories frequently incorporate self-condemnation, guilt and inade-quacy, reinforced and perpetuated by their sense of not meeting the norms and standards of significant others and/or wider society. Such accounts are 'problem-saturated,' so drenched with negativity and hopelessness that there appears no room for anything else (White, 1989: 37; White and Epston, 1990: 39). But any history of life is selective and partial. The perpetuation of the problem has been encouraged through the person's inability to escape from the problem-saturated perspective. She has been unable to recognize that her story omits more hopeful or encouraging, but un-noticed or forgotten, elements which are not consistent with her pessimistic, dominant story.

Change

White and Epston's ideas about change derive from Gregory Bateson, an anthropologist who developed theories about mental processes which became influential in family therapy in the 1970s and 1980s. Bateson proposed that notions of linear causality in human life are always over-simplistic, since the multiplicity of contributing factors is too complex for the human mind to know. People fit new events or ideas into preconceived frameworks, creating their own versions in harmony with received ideas. This means that the grasp of the unfamiliar depends on how persons 'interpret' events or ideas (make sense of them) out of their existing stock of perceptions and assumptions. If events, including proposals for change, are too differentiated from persons' preconceptions they lack meaning. Too swift or too great a difference is blanked out, or is incomprehensible (Bateson, 1978, 1979; White, 1989: 65–76, 85–100; White and Epston, 1990: 2).

Since perceptual change must mesh with preconceptions, 'new information' has to be absorbed at a pace which allows reconfiguration. A past/present/future framework is inherent to and facilitates this. In other words, *storying;* gradually extending the pre-existing framework of time-structured memories into versions which incorporate different images and possibilities out of the person's past, present and future. Such storying occurs in everyday life, as people scan and explore their experience through internal monologue and in discussion with others such as concerned friends, and it is central to narrative therapy. The as yet untold stories of persons' lives, by their potential richness and variety, have the potential to allow movement towards change without disconnection from the past and without minimizing or dismissing the initial, painful account.

In moving towards a narrative understanding of change White and Epston have found recent literary theory helpful in its considerations of story structures and how storied representations of life impact on the teller and the reader or listener (Iser, 1974, 1978; Bruner, 1986, 1990; White and Epston, 1990: 9–13). From this has come an emphasis on the importance of an *audience* as a vital contribution to the person's creation of new self-stories. The active response of an audience facilitates the stories becoming enriched, confirmed and remembered. In narrative therapy the therapist himself is not seen as the most important audience, and one of his tasks is to discuss with the person whom else, in her private life, she might like to hear the 'new story'. In addition, where acceptable, the therapist may organize an *in-session* audience of one or more people significant to the person, or colleagues of the therapist, or both.

Re-storying in everyday life, and in a more focused way in therapy, is not just a process of talking about problems or distress more hopefully, although this *may* occur. It is a means of *conceptual reorientation* or *re-positioning* in relation both to the problem and to the person's wider life and relationships. It is the embedding of this re-positioning that enables possibilities for change to emerge.

PRACTICE

Goals of therapy

All therapists aim to assist persons to move from distress and confusion to feeling better and moving forward in their lives, and these are the aims of narrative therapy. But narrative therapists do not set preconceived goals for their work, since these would constitute external impositions on the person rather than allowing a sensitive response to the unique story the person brings to therapy. Nor do narrative therapists encourage persons to take part in goal-setting. As therapy begins, people are likely to be dominated by preconceived positions around their lives, identities and relationships, so if they were to set specific goals at that point they would be locked into the conceptualizations they have brought to therapy rather than open to processes of perceptual change through re-storying. For example: a man who defines his marital problems as 'poor communication' and 'constant nagging by his wife' might set goals of their talking together more, and of his wife keeping her temper, which would then act as constraints on considering the implicit verbal and non-verbal signals the couple may in fact be clearly exchanging, what these might mean, and whether 'nagging' might be a word invented by men to describe women's desperate attempts to get through to them. As therapy progresses the discoveries and perceptions achieved by the person are tentative, provisional and subject to further extension, the dominant story only partly revised, the unrecognized sub-plots only partly told. Goal-setting at these later points would constitute a constraint on further and as yet unimagined and unimaginable possibilities (White, 2004c).

A wholly future perspective would also disallow the exploration of personal history, and the discovery and elaboration of helpful elements from that history (White, 1995: 25–6). However narrative therapists do invite persons to envisage a 'preferred future' where the problems they brought to therapy will be absent. But unlike for example in solution-focused work, where the therapist would ask what small steps might now be taken towards this future, a narrative therapist would tend to leave the images to settle and to create their own momentum and meaning for the person as part of their revised past/present/possible future story. If the future images have resonance the person will *discover* their meaning for her and will *discover,* rather than anticipate, what actions she might take to move towards her preferred future. At this later point, conscious decision-making will be undertaken without the therapist's prompting.

Selection criteria

Since narrative therapists are uneasy about taking up 'expert positions' they do not have criteria as to whether any particular individual, couple or family might benefit from this way of working, or whether any specific issues brought to therapy might be inappropriate for narrative work. Judgements about appropriateness are based both on the therapist's *self*-assessment of competence and on choices made by the person seeking assistance. Is the therapist experienced and skilled enough to take on this particular person and the issues she has brought to therapy or would it be best to refer on? Has the person been offered a choice of therapist of her/his own gender? Would she prefer someone of her own sexuality, ethnic group, culture or religious affiliation? Does she know about other sources of assistance which might be more useful than counselling, either now or later? During counselling these questions would be borne in mind, with the therapist checking out whether the person is finding counselling useful, whether it is addressing the concerns she wishes to explore, and whether counselling might end soon or continue. If a person is already attending counselling or group work where different approaches are used the narrative therapist would explain these differences and ask how she felt about attending both – would this give her a wider perspective or would it be confusing? These considerations would be kept under review throughout therapy.

When it becomes clear that the problems and dilemmas brought to counselling by individuals derive from, or are intertwined with, the actions or inactions of others, a narrative therapist may float the possibility of joint or family work rather than, or in addition to, one-to-one counselling. A man who is distressed because he cannot recover from the effects of his wife's sexual affair despite her regrets and apologies may benefit from a combination of joint and individual sessions; a mother who is being driven to despair by her teenage sons' loutish and disrespectful behaviour, while her husband stands back from the problem, may in addition to one-to-one counselling benefit from some sessions with her husband and sons if they will attend, and from some sessions held with these family members when she is not present. Narrative therapists do not consider individual, couple and family therapy to be distinct – indeed the traditional counselling focus on the bounded individual is seen as often masking wider social and political aspects of persons' lives (including the power-politics of interaction with others) and as imposing the whole weight of responsibility for change on one person's already bowed shoulders.

Qualities of effective therapists

The narrative therapy literature contains little explicit definition of 'qualities' necessary to be an effective therapist, although it contains much implicit ethical positioning; for example its moral base and resultant practices imply respect for cultural diversity, and for the beliefs of others where these beliefs are not harmful. Examples of narrative work in books, articles and teaching videos show narrative therapists demonstrating empathy and respect for the persons consulting them, and a genuine interest in their lives. In these respects narrative therapy matches most other therapies. However the overall ethical position of narrative therapy is not to pathologize but always to separate the problem from the identity of the person. Narrative therapy does not work unless the therapist consistently maintains this post-structuralist position (White, 1997: Chapter 11). This means the effective narrative therapist needs to hold to a genuine belief that distressed persons are not intrinsically deficient. They are struggling, always with unrecognized elements of success, to cope with the issues they bring to therapy, while defining themselves negatively (or acting harmfully) under the influence of powerful sociocultural influences woven into their self-stories. Since post-structuralist thinkers question the concept of 'essential', fixed 'qualities' for anyone, including therapists, the nature of the therapist's speech, actions and revealed attitudes in his interactions with persons are the relevant considerations. Despite its specific techniques, narrative therapy is more an ethical position, or attitude towards human life, than an 'approach' (White, 1995: 37–8) so the most important characteristic of a counsellor who wished to explore narrative practices would be openness to post-structuralist concepts. This might mean some degree of reconsideration around his assumptions about the origins and nature of human distress, the nature of self and identity, and the nature and aims of therapy.

Therapeutic relationship and style

Observation of White and other leading practitioners in training sessions, workshop demonstrations or on video-tape reveals some of the values and attitudes implicit in good narrative practice. The atmosphere is purposeful but relaxed. People are treated with respect and acceptance, taken seriously, and consulted on whether the session is proving fruitful for them. Strong feelings are often present, both in the person and in the therapist. Sometimes, even if the matter under discussion is very serious, a spontaneously light-hearted moment or sequence may occur, creating a less constricting atmosphere around the problem when discussion continues. The person's statements are checked out for understanding but there are few or no summaries in the therapist's words – the person's own words are used. Within these generalities there are many different personal styles. Epston tends to be more immediately challenging in his mode of speech than White, and White's manner is exceptionally informal compared, for example, with Jill Freedman and Gene Combs.

The nature of the relationship between the therapist and the person has a rather different emphasis in narrative therapy than in many other therapies. It is taken for granted that the therapist will be respectful, engaged and open, but this way of relating is not defined as promoting some kind of special relationship which is *itself* the key to the therapy's success. The 'relationship' is *not* seen as the means by which change is effected. White emphasises a quite different idea – the deliberate aim of *de-centring* the therapist, of maintaining a persistent orientation toward putting the person's own skills and knowledge of living at the centre of the therapy with the therapist following a little behind, together with acknowledgement and enhancement of the part played in the person's life by his own significant relationships in the present and in the past (White, 1997: Chapter 10). It is the person's relationship with these people, not with the counsellor, which is considered therapeutic.

Therapist de-centring is an ethical position at the core of narrative therapy. It is promoted by specific techniques, including 'taking-back practices' when the therapist acknowledges the resonances from and effects on her own life coming out of conversations with the person, and 'transparency and accountability' when the therapist invites the person to bear in mind the counsellor's limits and constraints of understanding. Therapist de-centring makes it clear to the person that therapy is a *two-way* process, thus counteracting therapist mystique and any assumptions that the therapist wishes to, or can, stand aside from the continuity between herself in the therapy room and herself in her personal life. Despite their importance, de-centring practices take up little time in the session. They are quite distinct in purpose and nature from therapist self-disclosure as a role-model for promoting the 'client's' 'personal growth' (Jourard, 1971: Chapter 18), which finds no place in narrative therapy.

Major therapeutic strategies and techniques

The number of sessions, and the intervals between them, vary according to the nature of the issues brought to therapy. Narrative counsellors tend to hold standard 50 to 60 minute sessions but certain narrative practices such as definitional ceremony (see below) may best be undertaken in sessions of around 90 minutes or more, if conditions allow. Sometimes one session is enough, and sometimes many more may be appropriate, although narrative work tends to be completed in significantly fewer sessions than some traditional therapies assume to be necessary.

'Maps' of therapy

Narrative therapy does not follow a rigid formula, but the overall pattern is always of starting with the person's description of the problem; identifying clues in the story which suggest the possibility of more helpful elements; and asking questions around these elements so that they come to form sub-plots which modify the original story and open up possibilities for change.

White has proposed some 'maps' for this process, consisting of mini-sequences of types of questions to give purposeful structure to the session or to parts of it. When asking questions the therapist attempts to establish a genuinely egalitarian and conversational ambiance. Taking the therapeutic conversation forward by structured sequences of questions and following up the answers with further questions could be called the 'strategies' of narrative therapy. The maps are drawn upon creatively, according to how the conversation develops, and in sensitive response to the person's emerging story. They need to be understood, learned, and practised again and again, so that as with any other skill involving response to the unpredictable they can then be emphasised, underplayed, extended, shortened or modified. The maps are generalized, so within their overall pattern there is the possibility for a range of specific narrative practices geared to certain kinds of problems, issues and concerns. These specific practices could be called the 'techniques' of narrative therapy.

For the sake of clarity the following, simplified descriptions of practice follow a sequential pattern, but actual narrative conversations are less tidy; earlier themes may be returned to, sometimes more than once, and the progress of therapy tends at times to be somewhat 'one-step-back-two-steps-forward' as the therapist and the person move through unfamiliar territory together.

The *Statement of Position* map is used at the start of therapy. There are two stages:

Stage 1: Encouraging a full description of the problem and a telling of the dominant story

1   The therapist encourages the person to describe what has brought her to therapy. Once a natural pause has been reached, a definition of the problem is discussed and agreed. The definition is usually couched in what White and Epston call 'externalizing' language; phrasing which implies a distinction between the problem on the one hand, and the identity of the person on the other (1990: 38–76). Using this definition will help the person to stand back from the problem and to avoid assuming it is inherent and therefore difficult to dislodge. 'My depression' might become 'the depression affecting me'; 'my low self-esteem' might become 'a temptation to think badly of myself'; 'my temper outbursts' might become 'temper's ability to goad me'.

2   Once the definition has been agreed the therapist asks the person to describe the effect the problem is having on his life and relationships, followed by questions designed to assist as full a description as possible. The therapist is alert to any elements of contradiction or ambiguity in the problem-story which suggest that it might be possible for the person, with encouragement, to tell a more helpful or encouraging sub-plot in addition to the dominant story.

3   The therapist asks questions around whether the person finds the present state of affairs acceptable or whether he wishes things to be different. This apparently redundant question encourages a commitment to change through a statement of intent. He has now begun to position himself differently in relation to the problem.

4   Since the person is not usually happy to let things stay as they are, the therapist is now able to explore in detail, through further questions, what in his history has contributed to his ability to make this commitment to change. Throughout narrative therapy memories of the painful past are taken seriously as formative elements of a person's dominant self-story, but the past is principally used as a resource for the discovery and elaboration of hopeful elements. It is never perceived as a source of deficit or pathology.

Stage 2: Encouraging the telling of alternative sub-plots or counter-plots

1   The therapist expresses interest in elements of the person's story which seem to indicate certain unrecognized or undervalued evidence that at times he may, to an extent, have escaped from the problem's influence. Sometimes these clues to alternative sub-plots arise from quickly passed-over elements in the told story, and sometimes a little prompting is needed to reveal them – 'You say that the temptation to think badly of yourself is always with you. So I'm intrigued that you managed to go for that interview. How did you manage that? Are there any other occasions when you were able to push away doubts about yourself?' Entry points to alternative sub-plots of the person's life are usually called 'unique outcomes' (after Erving Goffman, 1961) although some practitioners prefer less obscure terminology such as 'exceptions', 'sparkling moments' or 'initiatives'. Once the unique outcome has been identified a definition is discussed and agreed – the above example might be named as 'moments of confidence'.

2   The therapist draws from the person, by asking questions, a *very detailed* description of this unique outcome and the part it played in his life. The aim is not to contradict or deny the original, problem-based story, but to assist him to widen the story so it more accurately reflects the complex mix of positive and negative of his actual lived experience.

3   The person is asked whether he thinks the effects of the unique outcome were negative, positive, mixed or lacking in significance. The therapist does not just assume that the new story-element is resonant for the person; this is merely a hypothesis until confirmed. Usually the person sees the emerging story-theme as positive, but not always. If the therapist has misjudged, another unique outcome is identified, named and evaluated; if the person answers in the positive the therapist moves to 4.

4   The therapist invites the person to explain why he sees the unique outcome as positive. By continuing to question him around circumstances when the unique outcome has occurred, in the past as well as more recently, the therapist assists him to locate it in his history.

As therapy continues, Stage 2 of the map is repeated and Stage 1 is left behind (unless the person returns to it – a fairly common occurrence since at this early point in therapy the dominant problem-story is more powerful than emerging sub-plots). More unique outcomes are identified and named, and the therapist pursues their meaning and significance for the person in considerable detail: 'What does it tell me about you that you went for the interview? What does it tell you about your ability to face difficult situations? You say that when you weren't offered the job you felt bad for a while, then looked through the paper for other job adverts. How was it you didn't just give up? Can you describe any other times when you've had disappointments then got on with your life despite them? How did you manage to keep hope alive? What techniques did you use then, which you still find helpful?' and so forth. A chain of linked examples creates a sense of continuity. As told unique outcomes begin to form a sub-plot they have a greater chance of being remembered than if the events were seen as unconnected, and this enables their significance to become established in the person's self-perception.

Some of White's maps consist of suggestions for procedures at various specific points of therapy. The *Re-authoring Conversations Map* (1991/1992; 1995: 32–3) offers a structure for the identification and exploration of unique outcomes. It incorporates questions around unique outcomes in the person's present, past and possible future, weaving back and forth between questions about actions and events, and about thoughts and feelings. The aim is to assist the person to revise the negative conclusions he has reached about himself – conclusions derived from others' views which have become embedded in his self-story. This map is particularly appropriate for the effects of trauma arising from abuse and violence, when the focus of therapy is upon recovery of a sense of identity (White, 2004b: 61–3).

As therapy progresses the therapist veers the conversation into other sequences of questions according to the issues and problems which emerge. The overall framework of the Statement of Position Map is maintained, but with certain elements enlarged or more focused upon. An example is the Failure Conversations Map, which assists persons to escape from culturally formed ideas of failure and success and to evaluate previously unacknowledged ways in which they have put their own values into practice in their lives and relationships (White, 2004a: 149–232). By the therapist linguistically externalizing the concept 'failure' and asking questions around the person's acts and thoughts in relation to it, this map assists the person to move from a sense of 'I'm a failure', implying a permanent personal deficit, to a sense of 'I believe in and have done *these* things', implying achievement. White emphasizes that the map may not be suitable for *all* experiences of failure, and needs some adaptation if, for example, trauma is a significant element. Questions invite the person to identify the norms and standards by which she has been judging herself, to consider when these come from others and society, then to define her own values and standards and their origins in her personal history. Finally she is asked how her newly recognized values might sustain her in the future.

Therapeutic documents

Since the spoken word is easily forgotten, narrative therapists use permanent records of counselling to confirm and record persons' thoughts, discoveries and achievements (White and Epston, 1990: 77–187; White, 1995: 199–213; Freedman and Combs, 1996: 207–36; Payne, 2000/2006, Chapter 6; Behan, 2003; Fox, 2003; Speedy, 2004). Unlike much 'secret file' documentation of officialdom, these documents are always fully in the open, shared with the person, and embody the person's own thoughts and discoveries rather than the therapist's ideas. They may be in written form, including letters from the therapist reminding the person of salient points of discovery; copies of the therapist's notes sent for verification and comment next time; and reminders of unique outcomes, written as brief notes by the therapist in the person's own words, and given to her at the session's end. Sometimes documents have a light-hearted tone, especially when the person is feeling rather better – examples include end-of-counselling certificates, produced to look like formal official documents and presented ceremonially. The written word is not the only medium used. Sessions may be tape-recorded (with permission) and the recordings given to the person to take home and listen to, possibly sharing them with a relative or friend who can comment on and discuss them.

The therapist sometimes encourages the person to create her own therapeutic documents, to show to the therapist or to record experiences and thoughts privately, including her ideas about what is coming out of counselling. Narrative therapists are unlikely to encourage the uncontrolled outpouring of feelings as a means of assumed catharsis, but an expression of feeling in the person's writing may assist her to understand herself and her situation better, and poetry as well as prose may be appropriate if she is comfortable with this. Sometimes persons whose experiences have been embarrassing find it easier to describe them to the counsellor through writing rather than in speech. Diaries of progress are particularly useful, with the person noting instances when the problem is more under control, or absent. These unique outcomes can then be discussed in subsequent sessions.

Calling on the assistance of others

Narrative therapists bear in mind that people do not exist as bounded and closed systems. We may be born with certain in-built potentials and characteristics, but the form these take is constructed via social interaction. Our lives can be made miserable by criticism, condemnation and marginalization, and our lives can be made happy and satisfying by support, understanding and acceptance. In addition we live in a wider culture where socialization has led us to accept certain beliefs, norms and behaviours as 'given' and we can feel failure or inadequacy if we do not match up to society's expectations. When people come to counselling they often feel rather isolated. They have often to an extent lost access to sources of assistance – friends and relatives may have tried to help but without much success, and the person may feel she is a nuisance to them. Sometimes the source of pain is the very people who might otherwise be expected to be helpful – an unfaithful or abusive partner, a bullying boss, cold and uninterested parents. Sometimes people close to the person have died, resulting both in grief, and in the loss of the dead person's support role.

Narrative therapy has developed various means of calling on a wider range of people than the therapist to play a part in assisting the person. This is another aspect of therapist de-centring.

Re-membering practices   White's early paper 'Saying hullo again: the incorporation of the lost relationship in the resolution of grief' (1989: 5–28) proposes that rather than assisting the grieving person to say a final goodbye, to accept the finality of loss and to get on with life without the dead person, the therapist would do better to acknowledge and promote the lost person's continuing to play a part in the grieving person's life. By the person's saying 'Hullo again' in imagination rather than 'Goodbye', and through discussing what the dead person would appreciate about him at this point of life, the person tells a story-line of the relationship continuing rather than ending. The grieving person can take lost persons with him rather than leave them behind. White stresses that this is not to deny the pain or reality of loss but rather to assist the person to position himself differently in relation to it.

Hedtke and Winslade (2004) have extended and refined White's ideas about grief therapy, and in wider contexts than grief the concept of calling on the imagined 'voices' of others to contribute to the person's developing self-story has proved fruitful, becoming known as 're-membering.' This pun implies both the activation of memory around a lost other, and that other's re-joining the person as a member of her 'club of life' (White, 1997: 22–4). Persons who have received little or no useful help from others immediately available to them are asked who in their past might have had something helpful to say about the situation, and what this advice might have been. Sometimes this imagined person might have died and sometimes the person might simply have lost touch with them, for example wise and supportive grandparents or a helpful teacher. Where a lack of belief in his own worth is affecting the person, the therapist may ask him to name someone in his past who thought well of him, followed by questions such as, 'What was it about you that she appreciated? What would she say about how you contributed to her life and happiness? What qualities in you did she recognise that others including yourself might not see? How did these qualities show themselves in action? What would she see you doing or not doing today that would tell her you are the same person with the same qualities she valued?'

Bringing 'outsider witnesses' into the therapy room   White and Epston have always stressed the importance of an actual recipient or 'audience' for the person's developing story, in the belief that unless it is told to people in addition to the therapist, and commented upon by them, it may fade in the memory. Questions such as 'Who might you like to tell about the discoveries you have made?' and 'Can you think of anyone who would appreciate hearing about how you are feeling now compared to a couple of months ago?' were and still are asked in later sessions. Narrative therapists now sometimes go to considerable lengths (with the agreement of the person) to make contact with named people to invite them to attend one or more sessions. Similar questions to those quoted in the previous section may be asked, but White has also developed a map for a more systematic sequence of questioning, known as 'definitional ceremony' from the work of anthropologist Barbara Myerhoff (White, 1995: 172–9; 1997: 3–116; 2000: Chapter 4; 2004a Chapter 5). In definitional ceremony sessions outsider witnesses may be friends or relatives of the person, or they may, with the person's consent, be therapists and/or trainees.

Definitional ceremony   Definitional ceremony consists of a sequence of 'tellings and re-tellings'. The therapist encourages the person to tell her story, prompting her with questions where necessary, while the outsider witnesses listen. The outsider witnesses then comment on the story in response to questions by the therapist. The person responds to the outsider witnesses' comments, and then everyone including the therapist discusses the experience and what it has meant for them. As the person tells her story, hears the responses of the outsider witnesses, and then responds to their responses, her story takes on further dimensions of meaning and significance. Not only will she remember it more fully and completely but interwoven with the story she will carry its meaning and significance for others. The role of outsider witnesses is *not* to take an expert position by hypothesizing, advising, analysing motives or sources of action and feelings, or congratulating. The focus is on a response to the 'more neglected aspects' of the person's life (White, 1995: 180) – those aspects which have, through the therapist's exploration of unique outcomes, become woven into the initial self-story but which may still be rather fragile. The therapist also includes questions around aspects of the person's story which may have resonance in the lives of the outsider witnesses themselves, so as to create a sense of commonality between the lives of the person, the outsider witnesses and the therapist.

White suggests that since therapists have an ethical responsibility for what happens in the session, the responses of outsider witnesses cannot usually be left to chance, but must be in response to specific and purposeful questions from the therapist. He focuses on the words, phrases and images used by the person, and what these convey about her beliefs, values, purposes and commitments. The outsider witnesses are asked about resonances in their own lives evoked by the person's words, what images and feelings these resonances produced for them, and what difference hearing the person's account of her history will make to their own lives, perceptions and understandings. The therapist asks the person a similar sequence of questions around what the outsider witnesses have said, continuing to focus on verbal expressions which carry significance.

Counsellors working in constrained circumstances which make it difficult or impossible to organize definitional ceremony sessions with a team of outsider witnesses adapt the practice to fit their situation; for example by inviting a colleague to take an outsider witness role, and returning the favour in the colleague's sessions. Sometimes the person is invited to bring a trusted friend to the session. The definitional ceremony sequence is then followed; asking the colleague or friend definitional ceremony questions, inviting the person to respond, asking the colleague or friend to respond to the person's response, then discussing the session with both (Payne, 2000/2006: Chapter 7).

The change process in therapy

Narrative therapy does not aim to produce change in the person, if by this is meant cure, improvement, fixing of problems, personal growth or alteration to identity. Broadly speaking it is a resource-based rather than a deficit-based therapy. The resource it assists the person to discover is the previously veiled richness of his actual experience in all its diversity and contradiction, including its pain and confusion but also its elements of coping, hope, skills of living, resilience, values and the lost relationships which have the potential to play a renewed part in actuality or in imagination. The telling of richer accounts of life together with hearing others' responses to the emerging story enables the person to gain a more 'experience-near' perspective on his life and problems than the previously restricted perspective embodied in and expressed by his original, problem-saturated or despairing story. The apprehension of this new position, not just as a cognitive restructuring but also as a wholly felt, emotional and releasing experience, frees him to make conscious choices and commitments which were previously blocked by the fogged, enveloping and constraining self-story which had come to represent his life to him. Those aspects of narrative therapy which encourage the person to look beyond the concept of himself as a bounded individual and to recognize the negative power of certain sociocultural norms and expectations have a major role in this opening up of viewpoints and re-positioning.

Limitations of the approach

Narrative therapy is edging into the wider counselling culture from the world of family therapy with the disadvantage that it invites reconsideration of many of the counselling culture's most cherished beliefs and assumptions. Bateson's ideas on the difficulty of a mind-set being able to understand, yet alone accept 'new information,' are particularly relevant here. Much of White's writing is entertaining, sympathetic and clear but when outlining new or developing ideas his prose is sometimes daunting in its complexity of style and references even for experienced narrative therapists, let alone counsellors whose training and practice are based on different assumptions. Family therapists have written books aiming to summarize and clarify White's and Epston's thinking and practice (Parry and Doan, 1994; Freedman and Combs, 1996; Zimmerman and Dickerson, 1996; Monk et al., 1997; Morgan, 2000) but although they include examples of individual therapy their main focus is on family and couple work. My own book attempts to address this imbalance, with many examples of work with individuals (Payne, 2000/2006).

An additional barrier is that at a time when providers are under pressure to demonstrate counselling's effectiveness through objective research, all therapies which cannot be reduced to simplistic, repeatable protocols of practice for comparison with each other are at a disadvantage. The 'medical' research model of randomized controlled trials for the physical treatment of illness is the expected methodology for providing proof of counselling effectiveness. However as Garske and Anderson (2003) point out, if researchers reduce counselling practices to standard protocols, the flexibility and creative moment-by-moment response essential to all good counselling is lost, so the approach is not really being assessed; but if the research is based on observation of actual counselling being performed in all its subtlety, sensitivity, variety and complexity then no precise comparisons between approaches are possible. Narrative therapists have generally taken rather a critical attitude towards research evidence, defining discoveries by the therapist and the person of what is helpful and successful as 'primary' research, with traditional, comparative research methods being called 'secondary' and by implication inferior (Gaddis, 2004: Epston, 2004; Redstone, 2004; Speedy, 2004). Unless narrative therapists become actively involved in, and promote the value of, qualitative research methods such as discourse analysis, and *also* co-operate in random controlled trial methodology and promote its findings as indicatively useful although limited, they together with many other therapists may find their opportunities for employment (and thus assisting troubled persons) severely restricted compared with counsellors using models such as cognitive-behavioural where proponents have more astutely grasped the research nettle.

Case example

The client

Sally was a hairdresser working in a residential home for the elderly, who also spent much time looking after her grandchildren. She was approaching age 60 with physical symptoms which she believed to be stress-related, since blood tests showed nothing untoward. She felt extremely guilty at planning to cut back her work and family commitments, and she hoped counselling would help her to resolve this dilemma.

The therapy

Sally had attended a course in counselling skills, so I tried to explain narrative therapy, which was very different from her course model. After a while I realized to my dismay that my attempt at transparency sounded suspiciously like trying to put her right, but Sally showed considerable tolerance as I tried to haul back from being the 'lecturing expert'.

She loved her part in helping the elderly people to feel valued, she said, by making them look nice and by listening when they reminisced. She confirmed how guilty she was about considering leaving, and about the prospect of spending less time looking after her grandchildren. After discussion we agreed to name her feeling as 'regret' rather than guilt, because alongside her sense of letting people down Sally did recognize that she must consider her own health.

Over the next few sessions, during which time Sally left her job and reduced her babysitting, we explored her personal history in the light of the unique outcome of deciding to prioritize her health. Her parents had been highly critical, which she thought had given her a habit of putting herself second to gain others' approval. This tendency had been reinforced in young womanhood by her being humiliatingly and publicly dismissed from the fundamentalist church to which the family belonged, because of her love of pretty clothes. Ever since, she had missed the belonging and acceptance she had felt when a member of the church community, although she was firm in her conviction that the church had treated her with bigoted cruelty. I asked questions around her refusal to follow the demands of a rigid and punitive culture out of step with her own values of fairness and tolerance, and we related this to her present ability to question the dictates of an over-zealous conscience.

I asked about principled defiance in Sally's history, and what influences might have contributed to it. Sally identified her parents' next-door neighbours as a positive influence in her childhood. Her parents had often left her alone in the house until late at night, and the neighbours made their opinions about this known in no uncertain terms. Despite their resentment at this 'interference' her parents stopped the practice. The neighbours' house was always open to Sally for talk, laughter, and tea and biscuits, and she often defied her parents by secretly going there. In responding to re-membering questions she said that if the neighbours had still been alive they would have advised her to cut down. She could vividly imagine them saying this, and by bringing them into the present in her imagination she felt reassurance and validation.

By the fifth session Sally was reasonably at ease with her decision and I assumed that counselling would be ended after our final session, which was arranged for one week after a check-up at the hospital. However she wrote to tell me she might have to miss the appointment as a large and aggressive breast cancer had been discovered and she had been put on intensive chemotherapy.

When we next met she spoke at length about her experience of physical examination, diagnosis and chemotherapy; about terror, which was preventing sleep and haunting her in the day; and about a distressing return of memories concerning her parents' deaths. In this session there was no question of my doing anything but listening to this unexpected story-line of her life which was dominating her thoughts and feelings, while avoiding any facile reassurance or comfort. It was a time to acknowledge and honour a problem-saturated account rooted in the actuality of events.

Over the next eighteen months we held sessions at varying intervals according to Sally's capacity to attend, totalling around twenty. At an early stage of this new phase of counselling we discussed a metaphorical 'support team' for Sally – people in her present and past who would provide therapeutic sustenance. There were her husband, her daughters, close friends and the imagined presence of her past neighbours. Some available members of the 'team' were invited to sessions. When her husband came Sally paid tribute to his optimism – he never gave up hope for her, and this gave her hope for herself, though at times, she told him, she preferred a cuddle to reassurance. He had not fully understood this before. Her eldest daughter Jane attended several sessions and said how she felt Sally was holding back in talking about the cancer, out of a concern not to worry her, but that Jane wanted Sally to be wholly frank. Sally agreed to this, beginning by talking in the session about her fears, as Jane listened.

Sally continued to tell me about her terror as well as describing how she was sometimes keeping it at bay, and coping with her restricted life. We talked of the social narrative around cancer where people are usually portrayed as 'fighting' and 'courageous', making it difficult for them to acknowledge fear and despair. Sally agreed that at least in the counselling room she was able to resist that stereotyping, but that in her everyday life she did think it important to maintain a balance between honesty with others about her fears, and not distressing them by talking about the fears too much or too often. As well as teaching me about despair she was teaching me about stoicism.

Once when Sally described some particularly bad experiences of feeling ill and frightened I became affected by sorrow for her, and by a more general sense of the inevitability of death, and I lost professional objectivity. Sally saw my distress and immediately reversed roles, inviting me to talk about my response to what she had been saying. I described the resonances for me, in Sally's account, of how my mother had retained cheerfulness and consideration for others as she approached death. Only afterwards was I able to reflect that by not shying away from Sally's fulfilling this counselling/listening role for me I was stepping momentarily into an outsider witness role, and also reinforcing Sally's professional identity at a time when continuity of identity was important for her.

In our early sessions I externalized Sally's illness with phrases like 'the cancer invading your body and thoughts' rather than 'your cancer.' This implied a distinction between Sally's identity, and her loss of that identity when bouts of uncontrolled terror occurred and she did not recognize herself. These bouts were so powerful that she once got near to overdosing on her painkillers. However to my amusement Sally started to call the cancer 'Stanley' – explaining that this mocking externalization referred to Stan Laurel, who was always getting Oliver Hardy 'into another fine mess'.

As the tumour gradually diminished, and as she began to allow the possibility of planning for the future, we tape-recorded our sessions. Sally played the cassettes at night and in the early hours when terror returned and she was most affected by depression and a return of despair. She said that the recordings documenting these therapeutic conversations, with their detailed exploration of 'future unique outcomes', were a useful antidote to the fears.

From childhood Sally had looked forward to witnessing the beginning of the third millennium. As treatment was working well, especially a new and powerful drug only recently available, she believed that this ambition might be fulfilled – as indeed it was. She was realistic about possible relapse and we often discussed this, so I also felt able to encourage her to identify hopes and ambitions now that fears were retreating; her dominant story gradually became cautious optimism, enjoyment of small but significant present pleasures, and a sense that 'I've got a bit of a future.' She thought she might work again, possibly completing counselling training to Certificate level.

Counselling ended when Sally was pronounced clear of cancer.

A few months later I contacted her for permission to use an account of our counselling for a radio programme. She readily agreed, writing characteristically generous comments about how narrative therapy had helped her, to be read on air by an actor. She also told me she had developed secondary tumours, and had only a short while to live. She died a few days after the broadcast.

I was left with both immense sadness, and unease. I wondered whether my encouraging a telling of thoughts and hopes for the future might have seemed bitterly ironical to her, given the final outcome. Writing this account several years later has re-membered her in my life; it has become a therapeutic document for me. I hear her voice reassuring me that I did what I could, in the light of what I thought I knew at the time.

REFERENCES

Angus, Lynne E. and McLeod, John (eds) (2004) *The Handbook of Narrative and Psychotherapy*. London: Sage.

Bateson, Gregory (1972) *Steps to an Ecology of Mind*. New York: Ballantine.

Bateson, Gregory (1979) *Mind and Nature: a Necessary Unity*. London: Fontana.

Behan, Christopher (2003) 'Rescued speech poems: co-authoring poetry in narrative therapy' in Dean Lobovits, David Epston, Jennifer Freeman, (eds), www.narrativeapproaches.com/narrative papers/behan.

Brigitte, Sue, Mem and Veronika (1997) 'Power to our journeys' in *Dulwich Centre Newsletter,* 1.

Bruner, Jerome (1986) *Actual Minds, Possible Worlds*. Cambridge, MA: Harvard University Press.

Bruner, Jerome (1990) *Acts of Meaning*. Cambridge, MA: Harvard University Press.

Epston, David (2004) 'From empathy to ethnography: the origin of therapeutic co-research', *International Journal of Narrative Therapy and Community Work*, 2004 (2): 29–35.

Fox, Hugh (2003) 'Using therapeutic documents: a review', *International Journal of Narrative Therapy and Community Work*, 2003 (4): 26–36.

Freedman, Jill and Combs, Gene (1996) *Narrative Therapy: the Social Construction of Preferred Realities*. New York: Norton.

Gaddis, Stephen (2004) 'Repositioning traditional research: centring clients' accounts in the construction of professional therapy knowledges', *International Journal of Narrative Therapy and Community Work*, 2004 (2): 47–8.

Garske, John P. and Anderson, Timothy (2003) 'Towards a science of psychotherapy research: present status and evaluation' in Scott, D. Lilienfield, Steven J. Lynn and Jeffrey M. Lohr (eds), *Science and Pseudoscience in Clinical Psychology*. New York: Guilford Press.

Goffman, Erving (1961) *Asylums*. London: Penguin.

Hedtke, Lorraine and Winslade, John (2004) *Re-membering Lives: Conversations with the Dying and Bereaved*. New York: Baywood.

Iser, Wolfgang (1974) *The Implied Reader*. Baltimore: Johns Hopkins University Press.

Iser, Wolfgang (1978) *The Act of Reading*. Baltimore: Johns Hopkins University Press.

Jourard, Sidney, M. (1971) *The Transparent Self*. New York:Van Nostrand Reinhold.

Law, Ian (1998) 'Attention deficit disorders: therapy with a shoddily built construct', in Stephen Madigan and Ian Law (eds), *Praxis*. Vancouver: Yaletown Family Therapy.

McLeod, John (1997) *Narrative and Psychotherapy*. London: Sage.

Monk, G., Winslade, J., Crocket, K. and Epston, D. (eds) (1997) *Narrative Therapy in Practice: The Archaealogy of Hope*. San Francisco: Jossey-Bass.

Morgan, Alice (2000) *What is Narrative Therapy?* Adelaide: Dulwich Centre Publications.

Parker, Ian, Georgaca, Eugenie, Harper, David, McLaughlin, Terence and Stowell-Smith, Mark (1995) *Deconstructing Psychopathology*. London: Sage.

Parker, Ian (ed.) (1999) *Deconstructing Psychotherapy*. London: Sage.

Parry, Alan and Doan, Robert, E. (1994) *Story Re-visions: Narrative Therapy in the Postmodern World*. New York: Guilford Press.

Payne, Martin (1993) 'Down-under innovation: a bridge between person-centred and systemic models?', *The Journal of the British Association for Counselling* 4/2. Reprinted in Stephen Palmer, Sheila Dainow and Pat Milner (eds) (1996): *The BAC Counselling Reader*. London: Sage.

Payne, Martin (2000/2006) *Narrative Therapy: an Introduction for Counsellors*. London: Sage.

Redstone, Amanda (2004) 'Researching people's experience of narrative therapy: acknowledging the contribution of the 'client' to what works in counselling conversations', *International Journal of Narrative Therapy and Community Work*, 2004 (2).

Speedy, Jane (2004) 'Using poetic documents in narrative therapy', in Jean Lobovits, David Epston, and Jennifer Freeman (eds) www.narrativeapproaches.com/narrativepapers.

White, Michael (1989) *Selected Papers*. Adelaide: Dulwich Centre Publications.

White, Michael (1991) 'Deconstruction and Therapy' *Dulwich Centre Newsletter*, 3 Reprinted in David Epston and Michael White (1992) *Experience, Contradiction, Narrative & Imagination*. Adelaide: Dulwich Centre Publications.

White, Michael (1995) *Re-authoring Lives*. Adelaide: Dulwich Centre Publications.

White, Michael (1997) *Narratives of Therapists' Lives*. Adelaide: Dulwich Centre Publications.

White, Michael (2000) *Reflections on Narrative Practice*. Adelaide: Dulwich Centre Publications.

White, Michael (2002) 'Addressing personal failure', *International Journal of Narrative Therapy and Community Work*, 2002 (3): 33–76.

White, Michael (2004a) *Narrative Practice and Exotic Lives*. Adelaide: Dulwich Centre Publications.

White, Michael (2004b) 'Working with people who are suffering from the effects of trauma', *International Journal of Narrative Therapy and Community Work*, 2004 (1).

White, Michael (2004c) Personal communication.

White, Michael and Epston, David (1990) *Narrative Means to Therapeutic Ends*. New York: Norton.

Zimmerman, Jeffrey L. and Dickerson, Victoria C. (1996) *If Problems Talked*. New York: Guilford Press.

SUGGESTED FURTHER READING

Freedman, Jill and Combs, Gene (1996) *Narrative Therapy*. New York: Norton.

Morgan, Alice (2000) *What is Narrative Therapy? An Easy-to-read Introduction*. Adelaide: Dulwich Centre Publications.

Payne, Martin (2006) *Narrative Therapy: an Introduction for Counsellors* (2nd edn). London: Sage.

White, Michael (1995) *Re-Authoring Lives*. Adelaide: Dulwich Centre Publications.

White, Michael and Epston, David (1990) *Narrative Means to Therapeutic Ends*. New York: Norton.

17

Integrative and Eclectic Approaches

Henry Hollanders

The title of this chapter clearly places it in a different position from those dealing with specific approaches to therapy – approaches that are sometimes called Purist. For this reason, I have been given liberty by the Editor to digress from the structure provided for the other chapters. Nevertheless, it is my intention to follow that structure as closely as I am able, and, in the process, to point out just where and why it poses problems for someone who is an integrationist in the sense in which I am going to be suggesting. In some respects, the structured outline represents in itself a philosophy of therapy that is likely to be subverted by the integrationist who considers that such concepts as Person (Self?), Human Nature, Psychological Disturbance and Health, and the processes of Change, cannot be encapsulated in any single approach. Thus, it is my intention in this chapter to tentatively explore a philosophy of therapy that is quite different from the kind that is implicit in structures that are most appropriate for purist approaches. It is the need for such a philosophy that the movement towards integration, at least in some of its manifestations, highlights and attempts to address. First, however, I must try to define some terms.

Some definitions of terms

The following represents an attempt to provide tentative definitions of some terms that are used in the literature, sometimes without explanation or clarification. Each term is given a somewhat expanded definition in the hope that this section will serve as a useful introduction to the whole theme of this chapter.

Purism

The purist practitioner identifies herself with only one particular therapeutic approach. She will profess to be true to this approach and will refuse to be seduced by techniques and procedures from elsewhere. The thorough-going purist believes, implicitly if not explicitly, that all that is necessary and sufficient for therapy can be found within the approach she has adopted. That does not mean, however, that she will necessarily be closed to processes of development and change as time passes. Nevertheless, any development that does take place must be built on the foundations once laid, and must be within the confines prescribed by the approach as defined by those considered, formally or informally, to be its custodians. Purism is sometimes (though not necessarily) associated with schoolism, in which advocates of one approach defend passionately the 'truth' of their own school and attack with vigour the 'errors' of rival schools.

Pluralism

The philosopher A. J. Ayer (1982) describes pluralism as 'denying that there is a single world, which is waiting there to be captured, with a greater or lesser degree of truth, by our narratives, our scientific theories or even our artistic representations'. According to this perspective 'there are as many worlds as we are able to construct by the use of different systems of concepts, different standards of measurement, different forms of expression and exemplification' (1982: 13). Samuels considers pluralism to demonstrate 'an attitude to conflict that tries to reconcile differences without imposing a false resolution on them or losing sight of the unique value of each position' (1989: 1). Here, pluralism is an attempt to hold unity and diversity in balance by recognising that it is possible to have a multitude of 'world views' operating within a field of interest that can be described as unified at some level, if only by virtue of the fact that somehow the occupants find themselves rubbing shoulders with each other in spite of having arrived in this 'field' along very different routes (Samuels, 1993)! In therapeutic practice, although a practitioner with a pluralistic 'bent' may work within a single approach as her preference, she will not hold it as *the exclusive truth*. Rather, she will recognise that other approaches also have genuine, and even equal, value. Ideally, a pluralistic practitioner will work closely with colleagues from a number of different orientations to whom she can refer when she considers that a particular client will gain more benefit from an approach other than her own. Moreover, such a referral will not be considered to be a failure on the part of the practitioner for not being good enough at working with her model, or a failure of the client for not being able to make use of the therapist's superior system of therapy!

Eclecticism

Our word eclectic comes from the Greek word 'eklegein', meaning 'to pick out' or 'to choose'. Thus, eclectic practitioners are prepared to select out and make use of a range of techniques and procedures from a number of different approaches.

Integration

Whereas eclecticism places the emphasis on selecting out, integration places the emphasis on putting together. Although in some of the earlier literature the term 'integration' was often used in a way that made it almost interchangeable with 'eclecticism' (Hollanders and McLeod, 1999), today it is mostly used to refer to *theoretical* integration (i.e. the integration of theories as distinct from the eclectic emphasis on the integration of techniques (see below)).

'Integration' is also used in the literature to describe the process of bringing together a number of different modalities or arenas, such as Group, Individual, Couples and Family therapy (Friedman et al., 2005), Psychotherapy and Psychopharmacology (Winston et al., 2005) and Western psychotherapy and healing traditions from other cultures (Moodley and West, 2005; Van Dyke and Nefali, 2005)

In spite of the distinction drawn in much of the recent literature between Eclecticism and Integration, there is some evidence among practitioners at grass-roots level that the integrative 'label' tends to be used simply to indicate an unwillingness to be rigidly confined to one approach. In this respect the finer distinctions between 'eclecticism' and 'integration' seem to carry little practical significance. Generally, therapists who might have called themselves eclectic a decade or so ago are now just as likely to refer to themselves as integrative (Hollanders and McLeod, 1999). This does not indicate a change of practice, just a preference for what might be considered to be the more therapeutically friendly term!

HISTORICAL CONTEXT AND DEVELOPMENT IN BRITAIN

In this section I will give a very brief outline of the way in which integration in counselling and psychotherapy has developed since the first half of the last century. I will attempt to identify some of the key texts, though these are multiplying now so rapidly that I suspect I am bound to miss out some that will be considered essential reading by other integrative practitioners! For those who would like a fuller historical account of developments I will suggest where this may be found.

A Brief History of Integration

The concept of integration in psychotherapy is by no means new or novel. While the early history of counselling and psychotherapy is dominated by the development of different competing, even warring, schools, it is possible to trace another strand of development within that early adversarial climate. As long ago as 1932, French drew the attention of the American Psychiatric Association to what he considered to be the commonalities between Freudian psychoanalysis and Pavlovian conditioning (French, 1933). This received a mixed, but mainly critical, reception and in the years that followed eclecticism/integration failed to flourish openly. There is some evidence, however, for the existence of what has been called a 'therapeutic underground' (Goldfried and Davison, 1976; Wachtel, 1977). This consisted of those practitioners who continued to identify themselves publicly with a single orientation but who, in the privacy of their own studies and consulting rooms, were prepared to open themselves to influences from other approaches. Some lone voices were raised intermittently in favour of a more eclectic/integrative therapeutic stance in the 1930s, 40s and 50s (e.g. Rosenzweig, 1936; Watson, 1940; Dollard and Miller, 1950), but it was only in the 1960s that a discernible movement towards eclecticism/integration began to emerge and gather momentum (e.g. Alexander, 1963; Marmor, 1964; Marks and Gelder,1966; Paul, 1966; Weitzman, 1967; Bergin, 1968; Kraft, 1969). It was in this decade that Jerome Frank (1961) published his important work *Persuasion and Healing*, in which he sought to distil the prime factors that produce change in the lives of individuals. This volume has been described by Arkowitz as 'one of the most influential early writings on common factors' (1992:277). In 1967, Arnold Lazarus, working along different lines from those of Frank, first introduced the concept of making use of techniques from a variety of approaches without being bound by the philosophy that gave rise to them. Lazarus termed this 'technical eclecticism' (Lazarus, 1967).

By the mid-1970s practitioners were beginning to openly identify themselves as eclectic in growing numbers. Surveys of American practitioners conducted by Garfield and Kurtz (1975, n = 855) and Jayaratne (1978, n = 489) both indicated that 55 per cent of those surveyed were prepared to adopt the label 'eclectic' to describe their therapeutic orientation.

In 1975 Gerard Egan published the first edition of *The Skilled Helper*, setting out an eclectic framework for a 'problem management approach' to the counselling process. Egan began from an essentially humanistic position but in subsequent revisions of his work (2004 being the latest, 7th, edition) he shifted progressively towards a more action-oriented form of helping. The counselling process was presented as going through three main stages: Exploration, Understanding and Action (later to be re-titled: Present Scenario, Preferred Scenario and Getting There), with each stage having an appropriate set of skills associated with it. Egan's approach has exerted a major influence on training programmes for counsellors in the UK.

An important contribution to the debate on integration in the 1970s was made by Paul Wachtel (1977) with the publication of *Psychoanalysis and Behavior Therapy: Toward an Integration*. Wachtel retained the psychoanalytic concepts of the unconscious, dynamic conflict, and the influence of the 'inner world' on interactions with the 'outer world'. At the same time, however, he paid attention to a number of behavioural principles, including the importance of the present environmental context in which problematic behaviour takes place; the real influence of present as well as past interpersonal relationships, and the need for active interventions by the therapist in working with clients/patients towards identified goals. In the 1980s Wachtel developed his approach more fully, using the term 'cyclical dynamics' to describe it (Wachtel, 1987).

During the 1980s and 1990s a number of surveys of practitioners indicated that the broad trend among counsellors, psychologists and psychotherapists towards eclecticism/integration was continuing (Hollanders, 2000). However, many of these surveys were conducted in America amongst clinical psychologists. From the few surveys that were conducted in the UK there were some indications that clinical psychologists here were less likely to identify themselves as eclectic than their American counterparts (O'Sullivan and Dryden, 1990; Norcross et al., 1992). In contrast to this, however, a UK multi-level survey of 309 therapists from a broad range of traditions indicated that at each level an eclectic/integrative approach was preferred, and at the level of the use of techniques virtually 95 per cent of respondents revealed a tendency towards eclecticism/integrationism (Hollanders and McLeod, 1999).

The formation of the Society for the Exploration of Psychotherapy Integration (SEPI) was a hugely significant event in the development of a professional identity for integrative practitioners. The society's first newsletter appeared in 1983, and by 1991 there was sufficient growth in the membership to warrant the publication of the first issue of its official journal, the *Journal of Integrative and Eclectic Psychotherapy* (later to become the *Journal of Psychotherapy Integration*). In 1989 SEPI's membership was listed as 394, with 348 in the USA and 46 in the rest of the world spread over 17 countries. At that time the UK had 10 members. By 2005 the overall membership had grown to 687, with 427 in the USA, 260 in the rest of the world spread over 32 countries, with 23 in the UK.

Publications on eclecticism and integration increased dramatically in the 1980s and 1990s, and have continued to appear regularly in the early years of this century. A few of the significant publications that have appeared during these years are listed under suggested further reading at the end of this chapter.

Those readers who are interested in a more detailed history of the eclectic/integrative movement are referred to Hollanders (2000).

THEORETICAL ASSUMPTIONS

In practice, by its very nature, 'integration' covers a wide range of theories, attitudes and perspectives, and for this reason it is not possible to present a unified set of theoretical assumptions in a way that may be possible for other approaches. Nevertheless, we can engage in what I hope will be a useful exercise by taking a step back to examine the main philosophical strands that underpin the integration movement.

Philosophical strands

Two broad, and very different, philosophical strands can be identified.

Modernist/positivist philosophical strand

For some integrationists, working on the basis that over the past decades of therapeutic activity no approach has managed to distinguish itself overall as better than any other, integration is the quest for an approach that will make use of the most effective elements from all the various approaches by combining them into a single therapeutic system. The hope is that such an approach will come out of, and be based upon, the growing body of research in our field. This single system, once discovered, will serve to give definition to the whole field of psychotherapy and enable us, or our professional representatives, to demonstrate a kind of orthodox consistency in our efforts to present to the world at large what psychotherapy is all about. Such a system is likely to incorporate into it a unified understanding of what it means to be a person, what goes wrong and how it can be put right, and, therefore, is likely to be able to conform to the structure supplied for the chapters in a book of this kind (except that one obvious consequence of the discovery of such an approach would be that only the one chapter would be needed!). Because, from this perspective, integration represents a search for the 'truth' about what constitutes health, pathology and therapy – a kind of quest to find a therapeutic 'whole' that will have greater correspondence to 'reality' than any single approach that currently exists – we might think of this as the *modernist* or *positivist* philosophical strand in the movement towards integration.

Post-modern/constructionist philosophical strand

For other integrationists, however, the pathway runs in a very different, almost opposite, direction. These integrationists also recognise that no single approach has proved itself to be more effective (and, therefore, closer to 'the truth') than any of the others, but they draw very different conclusions from this fact. They believe that this realisation should lead us not to search more intensely for *the* single approach, but rather to give up the search altogether. They believe that the world in general, and the world of therapy in particular, can be (and needs to be) constructed in many different ways. There is no objective and absolute 'truth' about anything, least of all about what it means to be a fully-functioning human being – there are only perceptions, ways of seeing, constructions. Moreover, every construction is made under philosophical, social, cultural, economic and political influences. Even what some might like to think of as 'objective scientific truths' are subject to the same non-scientific influences and, therefore, should also be considered to be a particular set of constructions (Kuhn, 1970; Gergen, 1997; Rorty, 1999). From this perspective, in as much as the quest for a single 'grand' system of therapy represents a search for 'the truth' about psychotherapy, it is a mistaken, and even a nonsensical, endeavour. For those who think in this way, integration is about welcoming the rich diversity that is in our field. They want to be able to engage with a multiplicity of concepts of the self, health, pathology and therapy, and to find imaginative ways of using as many different constructions as possible, without succumbing to the illusion that any of them constitutes 'the truth'! Particular constructions will depend largely on:

1   *client variables* – who the client is, her experience, the way she presents her data and where she positions herself, explicitly or implicitly, philosophically, culturally, socially, economically and spiritually.
2   *therapist variables* – who the therapist is, her experience, where she positions herself theoretically and practically, and, crucially from an integrative perspective, her openness to a variety of perspectives.
3   *relationship variables* – how the relationship develops between the client and the therapist, and how they construct its meaning individually and together.

This philosophical strand might be thought of as the *post-modern* or *constructionist* version of integration.

Operational strands

As well as the two broad philosophical strands indicated above, we can identify at least four operational modes within the broad integration movement. By operational modes, I mean ways of going about integration. As we shall see, each of these operational modes can run alongside either of the philosophical strands.

Technical eclecticism
'Technical eclecticism' is a major route towards integration today. As we noted earlier, the term 'eclectic' refers to one who is prepared to 'select out' from a range of approaches and disciplines whatever seems to be useful for the purpose in hand (in our case, therapy). 'Technical' here refers to techniques, skills and strategies, as distinct from theories. To be able to use a technique well it is not necessary to subscribe to the particular theory or approach in which it was first developed, since, by and large, techniques can be lifted out of any particular theory base and be utilised in a variety of ways depending on the imagination and creativity of the one using them. For example, the empty chair (or two chair) technique may be used by a Gestaltist (within whose approach it was first developed), as a way of facilitating an intra-personal dialogue between polarities within the self. Equally it may be used by a Behaviourist to rehearse in the therapy room an inter-personal procedure that is to be practised outside.

In considering technical eclecticism as a route towards integration we need to make a clear distinction between what has been called 'haphazard eclecticism' on the one hand (Dryden, 1984; Lazarus, 1990), and 'systematic eclecticism' (Dryden, 1991; Norcross and Newman, 1992; Lazarus, 1992), on the other. In the former, techniques are grabbed at and used willy-nilly without any comprehensible rationale, whereas, in the latter, practitioners utilise a procedure of some kind for making systematic and coherent interventions that will enable them to work consistently over time. Some eclectic practitioners have adopted a 'mainstream' orientation, to which they add whatever seems to be useful from other approaches for particular clients (see below). Others have chosen a more recognisably eclectic/integrative framework that enables them to make systematic use of a variety of skills and techniques by matching them with different stages in the therapeutic process (e.g. Egan, 2004; Palmer, 2000; Lazarus, 1981; Jenkins, 2000), or with different aspects of the unfolding relationship between the client and the therapist (Clarkson, 2003).

Theoretical Integration

A second major pathway towards integration is what is now generally referred to as 'theoretical integration'. Those travelling towards integration along this route focus their attention primarily on theories rather than techniques, since they are not content simply to make use of techniques regardless of their theoretical underpinnings. In particular, they are seeking to discover the points at which different therapeutic theories converge, with the ultimate intention of melding them into a single theoretical orientation that will be more meaningfully comprehensive than the various parts of which it is made up. Theoretical integrationists believe that if the theoretical foundations are 'right', consistent and well-grounded techniques can be safely built on them, thus creating an integrated 'whole' system of therapy. This is no mean task, since, on the surface at least, and in some cases a good way below the surface, many therapeutic theories seem to be in direct conflict with each other. If the process of integration is to be achieved at this level it is likely to involve a considerable reframing of each of the theories/part theories that are being utilised, together with the development of a therapeutic vocabulary or language that is not tied too closely to any of the pre-existing theories. Two examples of approaches that have come out of this kind of integration are Hobson's Conversational Therapy (Hobson, 1985; Martin and Margison, 2000), now renamed as Psychodynamic Interpersonal Therapy (Margison, 2002), and Cognitive Analytic Therapy developed by Anthony Ryle (Ryle, 1990; Crossley and Stowell-Smith, 2000).

Common factors

The third main route towards integration is usually referred to as the 'common factors approach'. Integrationists on this route are attempting to identify the factors that are effective across each of the therapies, and, if possible, to combine them into a new approach that will have the best of all worlds. In this respect their aspirations are the same as those of both the technical eclectics and the theoretical integrationists. Those integrationists on the common factors route, however, do have a particular contribution to make to the debate. They point out that since, broadly and overall, there would seem to be an 'equivalence of outcomes' across the various orientations (i.e. no approach has shown itself to have more successful outcomes overall than any of the others), it is highly likely that the effective therapeutic factors will be found, not in the distinctive characteristics that mark out the divisions between the orientations, but rather in those less obvious things that they have in common. These are usually called the 'non-specific variables'. 'Non-specific' here means 'not related to any specific theory or technique'. Of course, many non-specifics operate entirely outside the therapy session, and even though some therapists may seem to be reluctant to do so, we have to acknowledge the obvious fact that clients have lives that are not entirely bound up with either the therapist or the therapy hour! Deeply significant events (e.g. a relationship breakdown, a bereavement, a loss of employment, a new relationship, a promotion, etc.) can occur in our clients' lives outside of therapy that have a profound effect both on them and the course that the therapy takes. Of course, such events can be related to the therapeutic process as a whole and be used positively within it. Nevertheless, it is obviously not within the power of the therapist to reproduce them as part of a therapeutic approach. However, there are non-specific factors likely to be operating within the therapy session that are common to all the 'talking' therapies, and it these that are of particular interest to those integrationists following the common factors route. If these factors can be identified and made explicit, it may be possible to develop them into a new approach, or at least to utilise them more effectively within existing approaches. One major area of interest that has come to the fore in recent years is the therapeutic relationship (Clarkson, 2003; Feltham, 1999; Gold, 1996; Kahn, 1997; Lapworth et al., 2001; Mearns and Cooper, 2005; Saffron and Muran, 2000; Stern, 2004; Wosket, 1999). Since all therapies involve some kind of relationship between a therapist and a client, the elements of this that can be identified as having therapeutic significance must be of great interest to us as a focal point for integration. In a recent research study of psychotherapists' development conducted by Orlinsky and Rønnestad (2005), those psychotherapists who experienced themselves predominantly as being able to enter into a 'healing involvement' with their clients were 'personally committed and affirming in relating to patients', able to engage 'at a high level of basic empathic and communication skills', were 'conscious of Flow-type feelings during sessions', had 'a sense of efficacy in general', and were able to deal 'constructively with difficulties encountered if problems in treatment arose'. (2005: 162). In contrast to this, those therapists who experienced themselves as predominantly engaged in a 'stressful involvement' with their clients reported frequent relational difficulties in practice, 'unconstructive efforts to deal with those difficulties by avoiding therapeutic engagement, and feelings of boredom and anxiety during sessions' (2005: 162). On a more anecdotal level, some years ago I was present at a seminar where a prominent psychoanalyst reported an incident during a course of analysis in which a patient tripped and fell to the floor as she entered the room. Leaving both her chair and her therapeutic frame, the analyst gently took hold of the patient and helped her to her feet, exclaiming 'Oh my dear, I'm so sorry!' Later, on completion of the analysis, the client reported this moment of spontaneous human contact to be one of the most significant elements in the therapy, enabling her to see both the therapist and the therapy in a new light.

Assimilative and accommodative integration: a home of your own
A fourth route to integration might be described as having and working from a
'home of your own'. There is some evidence to suggest that a large proportion
of integrative therapists in the UK place themselves under a mainstream orientation label (Humanistic, Psychodynamic, Cognitive-Behavioural etc.) whilst at
the same time practising integratively (Hollanders and McLeod, 1999). The
orientation is a place to work from, providing a kind of theoretically secure base
without excluding the possibility of building into it whatever seems to be appropriately useful for each client. In this way the therapist can enjoy some of the
benefits of identifying with a particular therapeutic community whose language
she both speaks and understands, whilst at the same time being ready to follow
the recommendation of Yalom to 'create a new therapy for each patient!' (2001:
33ff). This process of building integratively into an orientational base may be
assimilative or *accommodative* – or both (Messer, 2001). *Assimilative integration* places the emphasis on adapting and adjusting whatever you are seeking to
incorporate into your approach, in order to make it fit more readily into the home
base. *Accommodative integration* leaves open the possibility of making changes
in the home base itself in order to accommodate some insight or intervention in
its almost 'pristine' form, recognising that it has something important to add to
our current therapeutic perspective. It is likely that, in practice, most integrationists will both assimilate and accommodate as they go on developing their
approach to therapy.

Philosophical strands and operational modes
Each of the operational modes outlined above can be engaged with from within
either of the philosophical strands referred to earlier. Those integrationists who
are working within what I referred to as the *modernist/positivist* strand will be
likely to see each of the operational modes as being en route to the destination
of a grand system of psychotherapy. These operational modes, in one form or
another, are the best that can be managed at present, but the time will surely
come when our objective and essential understanding of the workings of the
human brain, of the self, of what constitutes human development, health, pathology
and therapy, will have advanced to such an extent that a single system of 'orthodox' therapy will be possible. At present, however, although some very interesting developments have taken place along the lines of each of the operational
routes, these integrationists readily acknowledge that they are not yet in a position to discover what might be thought of as 'The Approach at the End of the
Highway'.

Those who practise integration within the *post-modern/constructionist* philosophical strand are likely to consider the operational modes to be simply currently
useful means of developing ways of helping people. They highlight the possibility
of using existing theories and techniques from across the therapeutic board and of
developing new ideas and techniques on a pragmatic basis. However, the operational modes will not be considered to be some kind of developmental stage on the

way to some ultimate, objective point in the future at which we will eventually arrive if only we can discover well enough the pathways that have been laid down for us to follow. This perspective on integration is based broadly on the notion that there is no absolute or essential 'reality' at which to arrive. Everything is open to being constructed from different positions at different times using the touchstone of current usefulness (Rorty, 1989, 1999). At certain moments in the changing movements of cultures, societies, politics, economics etc., we are faced with the challenge to revisit, deconstruct and reconstruct our theories (Karasu, 1996; Caputo, 1997; Parker, 1999). Failure to respond to this challenge will leave us stranded with approaches that are no longer relevant to the world in which we live. This process, however, is not to be seen as a linear advancement towards the goal of a grand theory of everything therapeutic. Rather it is an attempt to ensure that as the world goes around, our theories and our practices will go around with it, so that at any given point in time, we are able to speak with a voice that really does resonate with men and women where they actually are.

PRACTICE

Goals of therapy

As in the previous section of this chapter (Theoretical assumptions), it is not possible to identify a single, overall set of goals that integrative therapy directs itself towards. That does not mean, of course, that individual integrative therapists are without any sense of goal or direction – it simply means that we cannot generalise within the confines of this chapter. Nevertheless, we can say that *the broad and most basic goal of integrative therapy is for the therapist and the client together to construct a therapy in which both will be able to engage progressively in a fully collaborative process.* The way in which such a therapy will be constructed will depend to some extent on whether the therapist considers the locus of integration to be predominantly external (i.e. in a specific approach), predominantly internal (i.e. within the therapist herself), or predominantly 'between' (i.e. within the relationship between therapist and client). If the locus of integration is considered to reside predominantly in a particular approach, then the therapy will be constructed in a way that is predominantly consistent with, and bounded by, the philosophy of that approach. If the locus of integration is considered to reside predominantly in the therapist herself, then the therapy will be constructed in a way that is predominantly consistent with the therapist's own sense of congruency, and if the locus of integration is considered to reside predominantly in 'the between', then the therapy will be constructed in a way that is predominantly determined by the emerging relationship between therapist and client. Of course, in reality, for any effective integration to take place all three loci will be exerting an influence on the way in which therapy is constructed, but a careful examination of the main thrust of the integrative process in which individual practitioners engage is likely to reveal that one or other holds a central position.

Selection criteria

Here again we cannot identify a single set of selection criteria that will be used by all integrative practitioners. The decision on whether or not this therapist, in this setting, can usefully work with this client, who has this problem, will be determined by a complex combination of influences. If the therapist is working integratively by building into a preferred mainstream approach (see section above titled Assimilative and Accommodative Integration: A Home of Your Own) the criteria applicable to that approach will be a dominant influence. Similarly, if an identifiable integrative approach is used (see sections above titled Technical Eclecticism and Theoretical Integration) the criteria relating to that approach will be a major influence. However, where a therapist's integrative approach is largely 'process oriented' rather than 'model oriented' (i.e. focusing on, and working with, the emerging process within the developing therapeutic relationship), it is likely that the broad selection criteria will be related to *this* therapist's sense of competency; the perceived potential and willingness of *this* client to be open to the therapy; and the ability of *both* this therapist and this client to engage in a relationship in *this* setting. Ideally, the decision to proceed with therapy will be made in supervision following assessment. Having said that, however, we must recognise that, in practice, these things can only be estimated over a period of time and often only emerge within the process of therapy itself, which makes the notion of 'selection criteria' somewhat problematic. Moreover, in the reality of today's world, many therapists work in far from ideal institutional settings in which genuine assessment and selection are often little more than theoretical possibilities to which lip service is paid. In such situations there is very considerable pressure to agree to seek to be of some help, in whatever way possible, to those who are allocated to them.

Qualities of effective therapists

Identifying the qualities of effective therapists is as important for integrationists as it is for practitioners from any mainstream orientation. First, I want to make a distinction between integration as a therapeutic activity ('doing integration') and integration as a way of being ('being integrative'). While I do not wish to create a false dichotomy between the two, I do want to suggest that our ability to '*do* integration' effectively will be very closely related to '*being* integrative'. Indeed, I consider that 'doing' will flow naturally out of 'being'. In other words, the more naturally we can *be* integrative in our whole approach to life, the more those with whom we share a relationship, both therapeutically and in other ways, will experience us as being able to embrace possibilities and make use of opportunities. If we can truly *be* integrative through and through, the whole process of our practice will be freer, less anxiously restrictive and more open to new, and, perhaps, surprising insights.

What, then, does it mean to be integrative?

Being integrative goes hand in hand with a philosophy of life and work that is truly pluralistic in its vision. This means having a spontaneous approach to life that is very different from that characterised by what is sometimes referred to as thinking in 'binary oppositions'. Those who engage in binary thinking tend to see the world in clear cut categories – *'good'* over against *'bad'*; *'right'* over against *'wrong'*; *'truth'* over against *'error'*; *'for us'* or *'against us'* etc. It is this kind of thinking that was characteristic of the schoolistic attitudes that so bedevilled psychotherapy in earlier decades, and is still evident in some circles today. One who is truly integrative has moved a long way away from such a limited view of the world. In contrast, she has adopted the kind of vision that Zohar and Marshal describe as being characteristic of what they call a Quantum Society:

> 'It (the Quantum society) must be plural. The old vision of one truth, one expression of real-ity, one best way of doing things, the either/or of absolute, unambiguous choice, must give way to a more pluralistic vision that can accommodate the multiplicities and diversities of our new experience. Learning to live with many points of view, many different ways of expe-riencing reality, is perhaps the greatest challenge of the new, complex society in which we find ourselves. Either/or must give way to both/and. 'My way' must give way to a shared way that respects many possibilities as valid …' (1993: 9).

This is the kind of 'world view' that the integrative counsellor/psychotherapist is most likely to have adopted. She may have adopted it deliberately, by design, or because it has crept up on her somehow, bit by bit, during long hours of work with a great diversity of clients. Perhaps, for most integrationists, it has been a bit of both.

Being integrative means being committed to the whole project of therapy, rather than to a particular approach. Some time ago, before eclecticism in counselling had become as firmly established as it is today, Thomas Szasz deliv-ered a scathing criticism of eclectic practitioners, focusing in particular on what he considered to be the eclectic's non-identity and lack of commitment to any particular form of therapy (Szasz, 1974: 41). In contrast to this view, however, Prochaska (1984) presented a very different perspective on the meaning of com-mitment. Applying Perry's (1970) model of intellectual and ethical development to the development of psychotherapists, Prochaska suggested that the process of maturing psychotherapeutic development runs through four primary stages: 'Dualistic' ('I'm right you're wrong!'); 'Multiplistic' ('We all have some of the truth, but I have more of it than you!'); 'Relativistic' ('We all hold different aspects of the truth equally'), and, finally, 'Committed' ('There is no absolute truth, and since none of us really know very much at all, let us commit ourselves with humility to going on finding out together'). Clearly, in this view the committed practitioner is one who is *not* holding tenaciously to a single approach with an 'I'm right and you're wrong' attitude, but is rather one who accepts with a genuine humility the validity of different systems. Thus mature commitment is not to a narrow school but to *the whole project* of therapy. In line with this attitude, Prochaska suggests that the questions with which the committed practitioner is centrally concerned are:

> ... what is the best way to be in therapy; what is the most valuable model we can provide for our clients, our colleagues, and our students, and how we can help our clients attain a better life. (Prochaska, 1984: 367).

There is a sense in which purist practitioners answer these questions in advance, since they are committed to a particular set of theories and to a broadly predetermined way of working. The integrationist, however, considers that such questions must always remain truly open, and be asked again and again, genuinely, for each client, in every session, without anticipating the answers and without resorting to stereotypical, theory dominated, responses. In this sense, the integrative practitioner has a genuine commitment, not to a particular theoretical approach, but rather to helping her clients by utilising whatever therapeutic process can be usefully employed.

Being integrative means having an expansive vision of life and work. As well as having an implied pluralistic philosophy and a commitment to the whole project of therapy, the integrative practitioner will have an expansive vision. She will look beyond the confines of counselling and psychotherapy theory and seek to gain insights into what it means to be a human being wherever they may be found. This means that there will be no territory that she is forbidden to enter – the world of the sciences and of the arts, of philosophy and philology, of literature and linguistics, of mathematics and mythology, of anthropology and theology – all the 'worlds' in all the world will be legitimate spheres of interest for the integrationist! To be sure, she will not expect to be able to explore all these worlds in a single life-time, but she will take to herself the liberty of choice to venture where she will, refusing to be prohibited from any area of potential interest because it does not accord with a particular theoretical stance. Moreover, and most importantly for the process of integration, she will be prepared to make use of whatever insight she has gained from any field of interest if it can be of help to her client.

Being integrative means being open to experience in both breadth and depth. Vision must lead to venture, and fundamental to both, if they are to be truly useful, is a deep-seated desire to be open to experience. While this must surely be true of therapists from every orientation for the purpose of their own *personal development*, integrative therapists will allow themselves to make creative use of their experience in the *development of their practice* in a way that will not be determined or limited by one particular theoretical approach. Hobson (1985) applied what the poet Rilke had to say about the place of experience in the creation of poetry, to the experience of the psychotherapist in 'creating' what Hobson described as 'an understanding intervention':

> verses ... are experiences. In order to write a single verse, one must see many cities, and men and things; one must get to know animals and the flight of birds, and the gestures that the little flowers make when they open out to the morning. One must be able to return in thought to roads in unknown regions, to unexpected encounters, and to partings that had long been foreseen; to days of childhood that are still indistinct, and to parents whom one had to hurt when they sought to give some pleasure which one did not understand .... There must be memories of many nights of love, each one unlike the others, of the screams of women in labour, and of women in childbed, light and blanched and sleeping, shutting themselves in. But one must also have been beside the dying, must have sat beside the dead in a room with open windows and fitful noises. And still it is not yet enough to have mem- ories. One must be able to forget them when they are many and one must have the immense patience to wait until they come again. For the memories themselves are not yet experiences. Only when they have turned to blood within us, to glance and gesture, name- less and no longer to be distinguished from ourselves – only then can it happen that in a most rare hour the first word of a poem arises in their midst and goes forth from them. (Rilke, in Hobson, 1985: 36).

This is itself a piece of poetic writing, but it conveys well the central place of real experience in the development of the therapist as well as the poet. This kind of experience, to be true to itself, will find expression in many forms and will not fit easily into the confines of a single and narrowly defined approach. There is a world of difference between the response that is a kind of formulaic pro- nouncement determined by a particular model or theory, and that which comes from the kind of experience that has 'turned to blood within us'.

Being integrative means not avoiding anxiety about the unknown by remain- ing defensively within the security of the supposedly known. This is so both of life and of work. From a therapeutic perspective this has been well expressed by both Yalom and Saffron and Muran:

> ' ... the capacity to tolerate uncertainty is a prerequisite of the profession. Though the pub- lic may believe that therapists guide patients systematically and sure-handedly through pre- dictable stages of therapy to a foreknown goal, such is rarely the case: instead ... therapists frequently wobble, improvise, and grope for direction. The powerful temptation to achieve certainty through embracing an ideological school and a tight therapeutic system is treach- erous: such belief may block the uncertain and spontaneous encounter necessary for effec- tive therapy.' (Yalom, 1991:13)
> 'Therapy is an ongoing flow of moments that are woven together through a process of construction ... It is important to remember that new information and new possibilities are constantly emerging in every moment of interaction with the patient. The therapist who is able to let go of his or her current understanding of what is happening in order to see what is emerging in the moment will have more flexibility and adaptability to the situation than the therapist who cannot do so ... it can be very anxiety-provoking to do psychotherapy without the solid ground provided by the concepts one normally uses to impose order on

what is going on … As therapists, we must constantly struggle with the temptation to hold on to fixed conceptions of what is taking place between us and our patients. We must constantly struggle with the temptation to deal with the anxiety and discomfort of ambiguous situations and to establish some sense of security in the midst of the experience of groundlessness, through reification (Saffron and Muran, 2000: 37)

Doubtless, *being* integrative means much more than there is space to explore in this chapter, but two further aspects need brief mention here: *engagement with the process of inner integration on a personal level*, and *some concept of the transcendent dimension of human experience*. The former may come through a multiplicity of channels, including experiencing a variety of different therapies as a client. The latter may lead us into the controversial realm of the place of religion and spirituality in counselling and psychotherapy. All I want to say here is that so much human experience in every age has been expressed in terms related to transcendence and immanence (a sense of that which is 'beyond' and 'within' at the same time), that a failure to explore it in our own experience might be to truncate our own humanness, and to limit our usefulness when working with clients for whom such constructs are an important and pervasive aspect of their lives (Schreurs, 2002; West, 2000, 2004).

Therapeutic relationship and style

As already indicated, the therapeutic relationship has become an important focus for therapists from a number of different schools (Bateman, 2002). For many integrationists, however, it is the very hub around which all else revolves. Clarkson (2003) suggests that the process of psychotherapy involves a multiplicity of relationships, including the working alliance, the transference/counter-transference relationship the developmentally needed relationship, the person-to-person real relationship, and the transpersonal relationship. As therapy proceeds, at any given point, one or other of these will take precedence. Taking it from a slightly different perspective, Kahn (1997) seeks to bring together insights on the therapeutic relationship from Humanistic, Psychodynamic (Object Relations), and Self-Psychology sources. Whereas Clarkson sees a multiplicity of relationships, Kahn sees the therapeutic relationship as singular, all of one piece, though having different facets to it. He invites us to imagine ourselves as therapists who have successfully integrated the work of Freud, Rogers, Gill and Kohut, and then seeks to draw out from these different approaches those elements of the relationship that make for effective therapy. From this we can see that, for Kahn, the therapeutic relationship is one in which the therapist is truly present, active and involved with the client. The 'core conditions' of genuineness, empathy (with a Kohutian flavour) and unconditional acceptance are central:

We will aspire to genuineness: we will strive to be transparent, not wearing our therapist mask and not pretending to be someone we're not. (Kahn, 1997: 166)

We will allow ourselves a good deal of spontaneity. (ibid. 167)
'We will be non-defensive. (ibid. 166)
'Kohut teaches that it is hard to change and grow until someone has really *seen* where we are now. Our empathy is our major therapeutic contribution to our clients. (ibid. 167)

However, such a genuine and empathic relationship does not preclude the development of transference and counter-transference, which emerge anyway within all relationships and are a valuable source of information about the client's developmental pathways. These are to be worked with and interpreted as seems appropriate throughout the therapy:

'We will remind ourselves that when clients give us a bad time, they may be showing us the kind of bad time someone gave them long ago, and we will do well to stay open to that information. (Kahn, 1997:166)
    It is essential that, whatever feelings clients express about us, our response will be interested, encouraging, and without judgement. It is likely that clients have previously gotten very different responses from significant people, and this difference is an important ingredient of the therapy. (ibid. 167)
    We will give our clients a good deal of encouragement to reveal their feelings about us, since in some way they are likely to be connected to the thoughts, feelings and impulses that were originally connected to the situations that bred their current troubles – and we will respond to those revelations with interest, objectivity and *acceptance*. (ibid. 169)
    We will try to understand how clients see us and what they want from us. This effort will … alert us to the deficits in the development of the client's self. We will attempt not to fill the need but rather to acknowledge the importance of it and the pain caused by its lack of fulfilment. (ibid.173)

For Kahn, the relationship between therapist and client is both the main focus of the therapy and the medium through which the therapy works:

The quality of our 'presence' will be as important as our theory. (Kahn, 1997: 177) Helping the client learn about the power of the past is usually not the first order of business. With most clients the therapist will spend much of the earlier phases of the therapy just trying to understand their experience and letting them know it has been understood. And the therapist will continually work to increase each client's awareness of the relationship with the therapist. Then, after a time, having begun to gain some understanding of a client and of the themes of that client's life, the therapist will begin to help the client see that the reactions to the therapist are inevitably determined *in part* by the attitudes and expectations the client carries everywhere. (ibid. 173ff)

Although both Clarkson and Kahn are seeking to provide an integrative perspective on the therapeutic relationship, it is clear that they are primarily interested in combining the humanistic/existential and the psychodynamic/psychoanalytic, without any reference to the kind of relationship likely to be fostered in the technique oriented cognitive behavioural approaches. This third element of the therapeutic relationship is addressed by Gold (1996) and Power (2002).

Therapeutic strategies and techniques

I think it would be true to say that there are no strategies or techniques that are intrinsically closed to the integrationist. That is to say, nothing is forbidden of itself. However, in common with all therapeutic approaches, there are certain principles that the practitioner must be guided by in her choice of interventions.

1. Since it is obvious that you cannot use what you do not know, it is important for the integrative practitioner to be in touch with what is going on across a wide range of therapies and disciplines. No doubt research should have a place in all therapy approaches, but since integrationists claim that they are centrally concerned to use whatever is of use to the clients they work with, research should be of particular interest to them.
2. Since it is also obvious that knowledge about something is not the same as competency in something, the integrative therapist must be wary of taking up what she is not competent to use. Of course, working within our competencies is important for all practitioners regardless of therapeutic orientation, but since integrative practitioners do not accept what might be thought to be the more secure confines of a single approach, the less experienced therapist may be more open to the temptation to use something too quickly, without due consideration of competence. Supervison and continuing professional development are, therefore, of particular importance.
3. Since the therapeutic relationship is recognised by most integrative practitioners to be central to the process of integration, every intervention used by the practitioner must be sensitively 'translated' into the relationship as it develops. This will mean that whatever the source that gives rise to the intervention in the head of the therapist (e.g. formulating a psychodynamic understanding, or experiencing a moment of existential encounter, or identifying negative automatic thoughts and irrational beliefs, etc.), it will be presented to the client in a way that fits the language, concepts and spirit of the relationship that exists between them.
4. In common with all other practitioners, the strategies and techniques used by integrative therapists will be bounded by an ethical framework. However, this is, perhaps, a more complex area for the integrationist than it is for those who work within a single orientation. Apart from the clear boundaries that would be agreed by virtually all approaches, there are areas of difference. What is considered to be bad practice in one approach may be allowed in another (e.g. the boundary of touch is placed differently in different approaches). Those who work within a single orientation will have guidelines to help them decide on what is good and what is bad within their espoused approach. For the integrationist, however, apart from broad ethical frameworks of the kind developed by BACP (2002), it is less clear-cut. Thus it is important to develop an ethical sensitivity in relation to each client, and to be able to give a clear ethical rationale for what is done or left undone. Clearly, supervision takes on an even more important perspective in the light of this responsibility.

Limitations of the approach

Although integration is much more established in the therapeutic world than it was some decades ago, it is still open to the criticism that integrative practitioners do not have sufficient depth in any approach to be of significant use to those who seek help from them. While this kind of criticism does not take into account the fact that many of those who are now prominent integrationists were first grounded in a particular approach, it is, nevertheless, a valid area for concern. It is possible that, for some, integration is a convenient label that covers a failure to be disciplined and well focused in their therapeutic work. Integration does not, and should not, mean that integrative practitioners do not have any real sense of coherence in their work with clients. It has to be acknowledged, however, that it is particularly open to that abuse.

It is peculiarly difficult to provide a good training in integration within the confines of the kind of training structures that are common in the UK. There are now many counselling courses that claim to be integrative in the training they offer. All too often, however, the criticism of Hinshelwood applies to the way it is presented:

> Many trainings advertise themselves as eclectic, offering a non-partisan approach … But what it means … is that students are taught by staff selected from different orientations, leaving the students to try to integrate the systems of thinking that on the whole the teachers have found themselves incapable of doing (1985: 13).

One of the greatest and most urgent needs is for serious and experienced integrationists to focus their attention on how a substantial training in integration can be provided within the time limits and structures available to us in this country. This is a creative task, and, of all people, integrationists should be able to be creative!

Case example

The case example that follows presents briefly the work of one integrative therapist working with one case. It cannot be generalised to a way of working with all clients by all integrative therapists. Nevertheless, it is hoped that it will provide some indication of what integration was about in this particular case, and, perhaps, provide some pointers to the way integration, in a broad sense, can work elsewhere

The client

Max was referred to me by his GP. He was a young man holding down a good job, within which he was making progress, while at the same time studying to advance his career. He was amiable and motivated to make life better for himself and his partner, Alicia, whom he intended to marry in the near future. He attended the first (assessment) session with Alicia, and, as the session unfolded, they described how their life together had been progressively limited by Max's obsessive-compulsive tendencies. He had left one job because of the difficulties caused by his compulsive behaviours, and the manner of his leaving had been somewhat traumatic for him. Now, in his new job he had managed to develop some strategies that enabled him to delay 'cleansing' himself until he reached home, but once inside the house, both he and his partner were bound to observe numerous cleansing rituals. These involved

Max in repeatedly washing himself with bleach-based cleaning agents and then spraying the environment a number of times to ensure that any possible contamination was eliminated. The rituals took a considerable period of time each evening and created a huge amount of tension. If they were not carried out to his complete satisfaction the whole evening would be a disaster. In the past they had made use of a number of different therapies, but though Max considered that he had made some progress, Alicia was clearly becoming more and more distressed by what she saw as the erosion of their life. Since the problem was one in which both Alicia and Max were deeply involved, and since, on the basis of the first session, it was evident that both needed to be involved in the therapy, we agreed to meet as a threesome once a week for a session of one hour.

The therapy

It is, of course, impossible to encapsulate a year of intensive therapy into the few words allowed in the confines of a chapter such as this. However, since the subject of this chapter is integration I will focus on those points that I believe demonstrate the elements of integration in this particular case.

Goals of therapy

The goal of therapy was clearly identified by the end of the first session, namely to work with Max to reduce, and, if possible, eliminate the obsessive-compulsive behaviours that were ruining the quality of his life and threatening his relationships. Within that overall goal, we agreed that it would be useful to gain some insight into what is driving the behaviours, to identify and, where needed, re-structure the thinking and beliefs that maintain and reinforce the behaviours, and to use both insight and new ways of thinking to create strategies for change. It became evident as the therapy progressed that a further goal for Max was to develop a sense of self-identity – a sense of himself as a man who could both maintain his own boundaries and actively take hold of life without having to have recourse to the protective rituals developed at an earlier period. It was in relation to this that the therapeutic relationship proved to be the most effective aspect of the work.

Therapeutic relationship and style

We quickly formed a good working relationship, and, beyond this, during the whole course of the therapy we developed what I felt was a mutual bond of genuine affection. As a therapist I seek to be genuinely present in the sessions. For me this rarely, if ever, means overt disclosure of aspects of my own story, but I do consider myself to be at liberty to share immediate in-session experience, where and when it seems appropriate – though this is usually only after a number of 'inner prompts' to do so! In any event, I regard myself – my own inner state and processes – as an inextricable part of the whole, that, in one way or another, will be picked up and interpreted by the client, and this will need to be worked with at different times in the therapy. In the light of this it will be evident that I do not believe that genuine presence excludes the development of transference and projections of various kinds, the use of which are, for me, an important part of the therapeutic process. Whilst this was individual therapy, with the focus on Max, Alicia was very much part of the therapeutic relationship. She attended each of the sessions and often took part by supporting and, sometimes, challenging Max by letting him know, at times verbally and at other times simply through a quiet show of emotion, what his obsessive-compulsive patterns were doing to her – somewhat after the fashion of 'tough-love'.

Overall process of therapy

The therapy with Max and Alicia involved making use of humanistic/existential, psychodynamic, cognitive, behavioural and systemic concepts within the context of the relationship that evolved between us. Although Max fully endorsed the goals of therapy as set out above, in the early stages we had to struggle together to get an in-depth commitment from him to be on the side of life and liberty, which involved facing what he experienced at times as overwhelming anxiety. We worked together to explore current life situations and to uncover the influence of past experience both on his present self-concept and on current beliefs about how to manage and control life events; we agreed together, eventually, to refuse to follow Max into the maze of convoluted thought processes; we discovered together the ways in which the system that both Max and Alicia had created was working in favour of the 'enemy within' and undermining the process of liberation, and we developed together some 'tough' strategies for progressively reclaiming life. Whilst in general terms each of the above processes received 'optimal' attention more or less in the order presented, it would be misleading to suggest that this was a neat structure with flowing movement from one to the other. It was not! In reality all these processes weaved in and out of each other in criss-cross fashion as the therapy went on.

Humanistic/existential aspects

As indicated above, the relationship that developed between us was central to the whole work. I believe it was a real relationship, within which it was safe enough to explore openly those relational processes that helped or hindered the work. It was of vital importance for Max to develop a real sense of himself, to be able to stand erect as a man and declare unequivocally in the face of annihilating anxiety 'I EXIST!' Such an 'I AM' experience of self comes, I believe, in the context of an 'I-THOU' encounter. In this respect, the core conditions of congruence, empathy and acceptance create the ethos within which such experience can happen. This, I believe, was the case in the work with Max.

Psychodynamic aspects

In the exploration that followed the first session Max made reference to his father, and the physical abuse that both he and his mother had suffered at his hands.

Although, before he died, the father had undergone a religious conversion that seemed to change his life, Max could never get close to him. The father's terminal illness involved some bleeding, and Max dated his obsessive-compulsive disorder from that time. In the early days the rituals were designed to cleanse Max from any contamination caused by contact with blood. By the time Max entered therapy this had become generalised to any form of possible contamination by anything he considered to be dirty. He found it almost impossible to go to his mother's house where his father had been ill, and even considered that mother herself was 'unclean', making contact with her highly problematic. Max's internal world was dominated by the drama being played out between him and his father. It was a drama involving love and hate – the desire of a young child to be loved and admired by his father, and the hatred that arose from being abused and humiliated by him in the presence of his mother. His self-boundaries had been violated, and he felt himself to be powerless to stop it. Internally, he was perpetually under threat of violation/contamination. In order to regain some sense of control he developed secret ways of protecting himself. His rituals were an indication of being stuck at a stage of development where life could be controlled by magic. However, the strategies that at first had held out the promise of liberty, had usurped the power and now held Max in a form of bondage that was progressively robbing him of his life.

Using whatever material that emerged in each session, as associations were made from current to previous experience, we worked together constructing, re-constructing and very tentatively interpreting Max's story in order to gain some sense of how the past was being played out symbolically in the present. As insight developed, we were able to gradually identify together a main task of the therapy, as indicated above – the development of a present sense of self that was strong enough to enable Max to take charge of his life as a man in his own right, without the need to resort to rituals that did not belong in his present.

Cognitive aspects

In the early sessions Max was prepared to acknowledge that his beliefs about contamination were faulty, even though he had had good reasons for developing them in the light of his previous experience. Nevertheless, he still held on to them. At first both Alicia and I sought to convince him of the irrationality of his arguments in support of his need to go through these elaborate cleansing procedures. However, whenever we embarked on this kind of process, we were always unsuccessful. Max had an ability to move rapidly through a maze of convoluted thinking, leaving me and Alicia feeling lost and bewildered. We came to the conclusion that reasoning with him in this kind of way was totally fruitless. Instead, we appealed to Max's rational mind to make a 'once and for all' statement of belief that these rituals were destructive rather than creative, binding rather than liberating, and life-denying rather than life-enhancing. We then insisted on a full-stop being placed behind the statement and refused to enter the maze of convoluted thinking. This was the second identified task of the therapy – to recognise that the rituals were backed up by a process of thinking that, once embarked upon, would take over and undermine the process of recovery. Max was to work hard at identifying the earliest stages of this convoluted thinking and refuse to go down that pathway. This was not a process of counter-reasoning but one akin to thought-stopping – refusing to go into the maze of convoluted thought that basically contradicted his statement of belief, heightened anxiety and weakened resolve.

Systemic and behavioural aspects

Together we 'deconstructed' the system that Alicia and Max had created between them that had maintained the disordered status quo. Alicia's collusion was a necessary part of the rituals and her own need to take care of the 'little boy', whose distressed face had such a powerful effect on her, helped to maintain the destructive process. This led to what we termed 'The Deal'. Max would make a comprehensive and detailed list of each of the steps of the rituals. He would then form a hierarchy by marking out those steps that were the easiest to tackle, and we would agree at each session which step was to be eliminated by the following session. Alicia's part of the deal was to agree to continue to assist with the rituals that were not targeted providing Max made good progress with those that were. Max worked hard at this, and for the first time we began to feel that he was genuinely on our side. Up to this point, there was a strong sense that whenever we agreed on a strategy, Max would rapidly work out a way of appearing to comply whilst at the same time secretly compensating for the progress on one front by increasing the strength of the cleansing rituals on another!

Max worked through the list remarkably well up to those steps that were of high difficulty. The list looked very impressive with a whole battery of ticks against items that had been successfully eliminated. Then we had a break of several weeks for the summer holidays. When we returned, Max reported with obvious delight that during the break he had worked through the entire list and was now able to begin to live life to the full. It was as though an oppressive regime had been challenged by a determined populace and had had to make concessions on a number of fronts. This led to the rapid collapse of the whole edifice, and the feared major confrontations on those items that were considered to be of high difficulty never actually materialised – they were simply swept away as unnecessary and outdated elements that belonged to a different period of life.

Conclusion

The above account cannot give any real sense of the ethos of the therapeutic encounter. The relationship between us was a massive part of the therapy and ran through all that we did together. I believe it was a genuine relationship, evoking real emotion in each of us – including much frustration, despair at times, deep empathy, occasional anger, some hurt, and, above all, deep affection. It also included elements of transference and counter-transference. After all, here was a therapist in his sixties working with a young couple in their twenties – one of whom had issues with his internalised father! How could the dramas of the internal world *not* get played out between us? When we were 'tuned-in' enough to recognise these often very subtle processes, we were able to work with them, I believe, to good effect.

There were also events that happened entirely outside of therapy that had a profound effect on the process – not least the impending marriage of Max and Alicia. These events were used in the therapy and, for the most part, were made to work in our favour.

The development of insight into inner processes still bound to past experience, the cognitive strategies that brought the undermining thought processes to heel, the development of a structure for behavioural change, and, through it all, the emergence of a sense of 'I am' in the context of an 'I-Thou' relationship, all played a part in the therapy. Whether or not any one of these elements would have been sufficient in itself, had the therapy been conducted in that way, it is impossible to say. I suspect not, but then I am an integrative therapist!

A follow-up phone call about five months after the conclusion of the therapy confirmed that the wedding had gone well and that life was, indeed, being lived to the full.

REFERENCES

Alexander, F. (1963) 'The dynamics of psychotherapy in the light of learning Theory', *American Journal of Psychiatry*, 120: 440–48.

Arkowitz, H. (1992) 'Integrative theories of therapy', in D.K. Freedheim (ed.), *History of Psychotherapy – A Century of Change*. Washington, DC: American Psychological Association.

Ayer, A.J. (1982) *Philosophy in the Twentieth Century*. London: Unwin.

BACP (2002) *Ethical Framework for Good Practice in Counselling and Psychotherapy*. British Association for Counselling and Psychotherapy: Rugby.

Bateman, A. (2002) 'Integrative therapy from an analytic perspective', in J. Holmes and A. Bateman (eds), *Integration in Psychotherapy*. Oxford : Oxford University Press.

Bergin, A.E. (1968) 'Technique for improving desensitization via warmth, empathy and emotional re-experiencing of hierarchy events', in R. Rubin and C.M. Franks (eds), *Advances in Behavior Therapy*. New York: Academic Press.

Caputo, J. D (1997): *Deconstruction in a Nutshell – A Conversation with Jacques Derrida*. New York: Fordham University Press.

Clarkson, P. (2003) *The Therapeutic Relationship*. London: Whurr Publishers.

Crossley, D. and Stowell-Smith, M. (2000) 'Cognitive analytic therapy', in S. Palmer and R. Woolfe (eds), *Integrative and Eclectic Counselling and Psychotherapy*. London: Sage.

Dollard, J. and Miller, N.E. (1950) *Personality and Psychotherapy: An analysis In terms of learning, thinking and culture*. New York: McGraw-Hill Book Company.

Dryden, W. (1984) 'Issues in the eclectic practice of individual therapy', in W Dryden, (ed.) *Individual Therapy in Britain*, London: Harper Row.

Dryden, W. (1991) *A Dialogue with John Norcross: Towards Integration*. Milton Keynes: Open University Press.

Egan, G. (2004) *The Skilled Helper* (7th edn.), Pacific Grove: Brooks/Cole Publishing Co.

Feltham, C. (ed.) (1999) *Understanding the Counselling Relationship*. London: Sage.

Frank, J.D. (1961) *Persuasion and Healing*. Baltimore: Johns Hopkins University Press.

French, T.M. (1933) 'Interrelations between psychoanalysis and the experimental work of Pavlov', *American Journal of Psychiatry*, 89: 1165–203.

Friedman, M.A., Cardemil, E.V., Ueblecker, L.A., Beevers, C.G., Chestnut, C. and Miller, I.W. (2005): 'The GIFT Program for major depression: integrating group, individual and family treatment', *Journal of Psychotherapy Integration, 15: 2.*

Garfield, S.L. and Kurtz, R. (1975): 'A Survey of clinical psychologists: characteristics, activities and orientations', *The Clinical Psychologist,* 28: 7–10.

Gergen, K.J. (1997) *Realities and Relationships.* Cambridge MA: Harvard University Press.

Gold, J.R. (1996) *Key Concepts in Psychotherapy Integration.* New York and London: Plenum Press.

Goldfried, M.R. and Davison, G.C. (1976) *Clinical Behavior Therapy.* New York: Holt, Rinehart & Winston.

Hinshelwood, R.D. (1985) 'Questions of training', *Free Associations,* 2: 7–18.

Hobson, R.F. (1985) *Forms of Feeling: The Heart of Psychotherapy.* London: Tavistock Publications.

Hollanders, H. E. (2000) 'Eclecticism/integration: historical developments', in S. Palmer and R. Woolfe (eds), *Integrative and Eclectic Counselling and Psychotherapy.* London: Sage.

Hollanders, H.E. and McLeod, J. (1999) 'Theoretical orientation and reported practice: a survey of eclecticism among counsellors in Britain', *British Journal of Guidance and Counselling,* 27(3): 405–414.

Jayaratne, S. (1978): 'Characteristics and theoretical orientations of Clinical Social Workers: A National Survey', *Journal of Social Service Research,* 4(2): 17–30.

Jenkins, P. (2000) 'Gerard Egan's skilled helper model', in S. Palmer and R. Woolfe (eds), *Integrative and Eclectic Counselling and Psychotherapy.* London: Sage.

Kahn, M. (1997) *Between Therapist and Client: The New Relationship.* New York: W.H. Freeman and Company.

Karasu, T.B. (1996) *The Deconstruction of Psychotherapy.* Northvale, NJ: Jason Aronson.

Kraft, T. (1969) 'Psychoanalysis and behaviorism: a false antithesis', *American Journal of Psychotherapy,* 23: 482–7.

Kuhn, T.S. (1970) *The Structure of Scientific Revolutions,* 2nd ed., enlarged. Chicago: University of Chicago Press.

Lapworth, P., Sills, C. and Fish, S. (2001) *Integration in Counselling and Psychotherapy: Developing a Personal Approach.* London: Sage.

Lazarus, A.A. (1967) 'In support of technical eclecticism', *Psychological Reports,* 21: 415–16

Lazarus, A.A. (1981). *The Practice of Multi-Modal Therapy.* New York: McGraw-Hill Book Company.

Lazarus, A.A. (1990) 'Why I am an eclectic (not an integrationist)', in W. Dryden and J.C. Norcross, *Eclecticism and Integration in Counselling and Psychotherapy.* Loughton: Gale Centre Publications.

Lazarus, A.A. (1992) 'Multimodal therapy: technical eclecticism with minimal integration', in J.C. Norcross and M.R. Goldfried (eds), *Handbook of Psychotherapy Integration.* New York: Basic Books.

Margison, F. (2002) 'Psychodynamic interpersonal therapy', in J. Holmes and A. Bateman (eds), *Integration in Psychotherapy.* Oxford: Oxford University Press.

Marks, I.M. and Gelder, M.G. (1966) 'Common ground between behaviour therapy and psychodynamic methods', *British Journal of Medical Psychology,* 39: 11–23.

Marmar, J. (1964) 'Psychoanalytic therapy and theories of learning', in J. Masserman (ed.), *Science and Psychoanalysis.* (vol. 7). New York: Grune and Stratlen.

Martin, J. and Margison, F. (2000) 'The Conversational Model', in S. Palmer and R. Woolfe (eds), *Integrative and Eclectic Counselling and Psychotherapy.* London: Sage.

Mearns, D. and Cooper, M. (2005) *Working at Relational Depth in Counselling and Psychotherapy.* London: Sage.

Messer, S.B. (ed.) (2001) 'Special Issue: assimilative integration', *Journal of Psychotherapy Integration,* 11(1).

Moodley, R. and West, W. (eds) (2005) *Integrating Traditional Healing Practices into Counselling and Psychotherapy.* Thousand Oaks and London: Sage Publications.

Norcross, J.C., Dryden, W. and Brust, A.M. (1992) British clinical psychologists: a national survey of the BPS clinical division', *Clinical Psychology Forum,* 40: 19–24.

Norcross, J.C. and Newman, C.F. (1992) 'Psychotherapy integration: setting the context', in J.C. Norcross and M.R. Goldfried (eds), *Handbook of Psychotherapy Integration*. New York: Basic Books.

O'Sullivan, K.R. and Dryden, W. (1990) 'A survey of clinical psychologists in the South East Thames health region: activities, role and theoretical orientation', *Clinical Psychology Forum,* October.

Orlinsky, D.E. and Rønnestad, M.H. (2005) *How Psychotherapists Develop: A Study of Therapeutic Work and Professional Growth*. Washington DC: American Psychological Association.

Palmer, S. (2000) 'Multimodal therapy' in S. Palmer and R. Woolfe (eds), *Integrative and Eclectic Counselling and Psychotherapy*. London: Sage.

Parker, I. (ed.) (1999) *Deconstructing Psychotherapy*. London: Sage.

Paul, G.L. (1966) *Insight versus Desensitization in Psychotherapy*. Stanford, CA: Stanford University Press.

Perry, W. (1970) *Forms of Intellectual and Ethical Development in the College Years: A Scheme*. New York: Holt, Rinehart & Winston.

Power M.J. (2002) 'Integrative therapy from a cognitive behavioural perspective', in J. Holmes and A. Bateman (eds), *Integration in Psychotherapy, Models and Methods*. Oxford: Oxford University Press.

Prochaska, J.O. (1984) *Systems of Psychotherapy: a Transtheoretical Analysis*, 2nd edn. Homewood, IL: Dorsey Press.

Rorty, R. (1989) *Contingency, Irony and Solidarity*. Cambridge: Cambridge University Press.

Rorty, R. (1999) *Philosophy and Social Hope*. London: Penguin Books.

Rosenzweig, S. (1936) 'Some implicit common factors in diverse methods in psychotherapy', *American Journal of Orthopsychiatry*, 6: 412–15.

Rubin and Franks, C.M. (eds) *Advances in Behavior Therapy*. New York: Academic Press.

Ryle, A. (1990) *Cognitive Analytical Therapy: Active Participation in Change – New Integration in Brief Psychotherapy*. Chichester: John Wiley & Sons.

Saffron, J.D. and Muran, J.C. (2000) *Negotiating The Therapeutic Alliance*. New York & London: The Guilford Press.

Samuels, A. (1989) *The Plural Psyche: Personality, Morality and the Father*. London and New York. Routledge.

Samuels, A. (1993) 'What is good training?', *British Journal of Psychotherapy*, 9(3): 317–23.

Schreurs, A. (2002*) Psychotherapy and Spirituality: Integrating the spiritual dimension into therapeutic practice*. London & Philadelphia: Jessica Kingsley.

Stern, D.N. (2004) *The Present Moment in Psychotherapy and Everyday Life*. New York & London: W.W. Norton.

Szasz, T.S. (1974) *The Ethics of Psycho-Analysis: The Theory and Method of Autonomous Psychotherapy*. London: Routledge & Kegan Paul.

Van Dyke, G.A.J. and Nefali, N.C. (2005) 'The split-ego experience of Africans:Ubuntu therapy as a healing alternative, *Journal of Psychotherapy Integration,* 15(1): 48–66

Wachtel, P.L. (1977) *Psychoanalysis and Behavior Therapy: Toward an Integration*. New York: Basic Books.

Wachtel. P.L. (1987) *Action and Insight*. New York: Guilford.

Wachtel, P.L. (2005) 'Anxiety, consciousness, and self-acceptance: placing the idea of making the unconscious conscious in an integrative framework',. *Journal of Psychotherapy Integration*, 15(3): 243–53.

Wachtel, P.L. and McKinney, M.K. (1992) *Handbook of Psychotherapy Integration*. New York: Basic Books.

Watson, G. (1940) 'Areas of agreement in psychotherapy', *American Journal of Orthopsychiatry*, 10: 698–709.

Weitzman, B. (1967) 'Behaviour, therapy and psychotherapy', *Psychological Review*, 74: 300–17.

West, W. (2000) *Psychotherapy and Spirituality: Crossing the Line Between Therapy and Religion.* London, Thousand Oaks, New Delhi: Sage Publications.

West, W. (2004) *Spiritual Issues in Therapy: Relating Experience to Practice.* Basingstoke and New York: Palgrave Macmillan.

Winston, A., Been, H. and Serby M. (2005) 'Psychotherapy and Psychopharmacology: Different universes or an integrated future?' *Journal of Psychotherapy Integration,* 15(2): 213–23.

Wosket, V.(1999) *The Therapeutic Use of Self.* London: Routledge.

Yalom, I.D.(1991) *Love's Executioner.* London: Penguin Books.

Yalom, I.D. (2001) *The Gift of Therapy.* London: Piatkus Ltd.

Zohar, D. and Marshal, I. (1993) *The Quantum Society.* London: Bloomsbury.

SUGGESTED FURTHER READING

Gold, J.R. (1996) *Key Concepts in Psychotherapy Integration.* New York and London: Plenum Press.

Holmes, J. and Bateman, A. (eds) (2002) *Integration in Psychotherapy.* Oxford : Oxford University Press.

Lapworth, P., Sills, C. and Fish, S. (2001) *Integration in Counselling and Psychotherapy: Developing a Personal Approach.* London: Sage.

O'Brien, M. and Houston, G. (2000) *Integrative Therapy: A Practitioner's Guide.* London: Sage.

Palmer, S. and Woolfe, R. (2000) *Integrative and Eclectic Counselling Psychotherapy.* London: Sage.

18

Methods, Outcomes and Processes in the Psychological Therapies across Four Successive Research Generations

Michael Barkham

The preceding chapters have documented a wide range of theoretical approaches to the practice of individual psychotherapy. Whilst interest in psychotherapy as a profession has never been greater, there exists a considerable gap between practice and research which is long-standing and has been repeatedly documented in the psychotherapy literature (e.g., Barlow et al., 1984; Chwalisz, 2003; Talley et al., 1994). Frustration at this gap arises because one of the central roles of psychotherapy research is to inform practice. However, it has tended to be the case that clinical insights have guided research. This situation is largely attributable to researchers and clinicians having different priorities and different paradigms within which they work. Research, as reported in the major international journals, tends to employ large-scale studies and focus on differences between group means representing the 'average' client. In contrast, practitioners work with individual clients and it is often difficult for practitioners to see the relevance of research findings to the clients seen in their practices. Hence, researchers and practitioners carry out their respective functions using different paradigms which, in themselves, define different approaches or methods to investigate the subject matter.

Set against this context of differing methods are the two broad domains or categories covered by psychotherapy research activity: outcome and process. Outcome research comprises making evaluative statements about the efficacy or effectiveness of particular interventions. Process research comprises attempts to explain why improvement or deterioration occurs. The knowledge that a particular therapy is effective together with an understanding of what makes it effective can then inform practitioners' decisions ranging from planning and implementing an effective psychotherapy service delivery system to informing the moment-to-moment interventions by therapists with individual clients. Attempts have been made to identify the practical implications of findings from psychotherapy research in the domains of outcome research (e.g. Whiston and Sexton, 1993) and process research (e.g. Dryden, 1996).

It is important at the outset to appreciate that, much like psychotherapeutic practice, the quality of process and outcome research varies considerably. In the same way that practitioners aim to learn and integrate into their practice those ingredients which enhance the effectiveness of psychotherapy (i.e. 'good practice'), so researchers seek to adopt those methods and procedures which lead to good research. Increasingly, guidelines are being disseminated which aim to enhance the implementation and reporting of research activity (e.g. Oxman and Guyatt, 1988; Elliott et al., 1999). However, the foundations for high-quality psychotherapy research rest upon 'method'. The skill of the psychotherapy researcher can be summarized by a five-stage model using the acronym DIARY: *d*esign, *i*mplementation, *a*nalysis, *r*eporting, and *y*ield. *Design* requires a substantive knowledge base of the range of possible designs and being able to select or generate one that is best suited to address the question being asked. *Implementation* requires the ability and resources to carry out the selected design. *Analysis* requires considerable knowledge and understanding of the multiple ways in which data can be analysed and, importantly, selecting procedures appropriate to the adopted design. *Reporting* – which also includes interpretation – focuses on conveying the results in a fair way and identifying the strengths and limitations of the work. *Yield* focuses on the utility of the research – how the findings inform practice. All these skills and activities make up the activity of research. Accordingly, it is not the result of any study *per se* which is important but the foundations upon which any research is built.

Texts which incorporate methodological issues include *Bergin and Garfield's Handbook of Psychotherapy and Behavior Change* (Lambert, 5th edition, 2004) which, in addition to reviewing specific content domains, contains chapters on methodology (Kendall et al., 2004) and process and outcome measurement (Hill and Lambert, 2004). There are also chapters on outcomes of efficacy and effectiveness studies (Lambert and Ogles, 2004) and the process of psychotherapy (Orlinsky et al., 2004). Kendall and colleagues (1999a) also provide a useful chapter on therapy outcome research methods. Greenberg and Pinsoff (1986) have produced a text on process research and, in addition, Hill (1991) has summarized a range of methodological issues relating to process research as well as a collection of work on methods and findings relating to process research (Hill, 2001). A key text emanating from Britain is Roth and Fonagy's *What Works for Whom? A Critical Review of Psychotherapy Research* (2005). In terms of designing and implementing research activity there is Aveline and Shapiro's *Research Foundations for Psychotherapy Practice* (1995) together with two excellent and complementary texts on research methods: Barker, Pistrang and Elliott's *Research Methods in Clinical Psychology* (2004) and McLeod's *Doing Counselling Research* (2003).

Against this background, the purpose of this chapter is twofold. First, to provide an overview of current international research on the psychological therapies focusing on one-to-one settings (i.e. individual therapy), and secondly, to provide a similar overview of research carried out in Britain. The framework for presenting this research is via successive research generations, each driven by a particular thematic question and each adopting different and developing research methods to address the questions. In so doing, this chapter charts the key questions that have been raised about the psychological therapies and the research yield arising from the subsequent effort over more than half a century – from 1950 to the present.

Focusing on the time frame from 1950 to the present is not meant to imply that there was no research activity prior to this time. Indeed, the equivalent time span from 1900 to 1950 saw considerable activity focusing on laying down the foundations for the empirical investigation of psychotherapy and this can be termed the 'pioneering generation'. During these years, a wealth of case material was documented. For example, Freud published many accounts of psychoanalytic therapy (e.g., the 'Rat Man', 1909: Freud, 1979) using qualitative and case study methods – methods which have once again come to the fore of psychotherapy research in recent years. Increasingly, research was influenced by developing ideas about science, in particular the notions of logical positivism (testing propositions against real world observations) and operationalism (defining how a concept is to be measured). In addition, developments in the domain of technology (e.g. audio-recordings) and further refinements in issues of design and analysis (e.g. null hypothesis) paved the way for the setting up of research programmes investigating the process of psychotherapy. The work of Rogers (1942), Porter (1943a, 1943b) and Robinson (1950) all used response mode codings (i.e. coding speech into a series of intentions – question, reflection, interpretation) to carry out investigations into the process of change. Similarly, there are early reports of work into psychotherapy outcomes. For example, Huddleson (1927) provided an account of psychoneurosis in war veterans suggesting that approaching 20 per cent of patients in his sample were either 'recovered' or 'much improved' at discharge and approaching 50 per cent at follow-up (albeit some time later). Thus, both outcome and process research were actively being carried out prior to the 1950s. However, there was no clear agenda to drive research activity. By contrast, the research from the 1950s onwards progressed in response to a range of issues driven by academia, government policies, economics and demand.

PART I: METHODS, OUTCOMES AND PROCESSES – INTERNATIONAL FINDINGS

The first part of this chapter presents findings from the international scientific community as a series of four successive but overlapping research generations initiated by Eysenck's (1952) landmark critique of psychotherapy. These research generations are set out briefly here and then explicated in greater detail throughout the chapter. However, although electronic searches have been used to identify relevant work, space does not permit comprehensive coverage.

Generation I research spans the period 1950s to 1970s and addresses the outcome question 'Is psychotherapy efficacious?' and the process question 'Are there objective methods for evaluating process?' Generation II research spans the period 1960s to 1980s and utilizes scientific rigour to address the outcome question 'Which psychotherapy is more effective?' and the process question 'What components are related to outcome?' Generation III research spans the period 1970s to the present and addresses the outcome question 'How can we make treatments more cost-effective?' and the process question 'How does change occur?' Generation IV research can be seen as originating in the mid-1980s and addresses the question 'How can we make outcome and process research clinically relevant to clients, practitioners and services?' The research generations as defined here should not, however, be seen to be carved in stone. Other writers have used slightly different time frames and emphases (e.g. see Russell and Orlinsky, 1996). Research addressing outcome and process domains is addressed under separate subheadings within each generation. More specific accounts of process and outcome research can be found in a number of texts: psychotherapy process research (e.g. Llewelyn and Hardy, 2001); efficacy and effectiveness in outcome research (e.g. Nathan et al., 2000); and a review of process and outcome issues (e.g. Kopta et al., 1999).

An outline of the research generations is presented in Table 18.1. This identifies the research questions relating to outcome and process work together with some of the key issues addressed and the methods used to investigate these issues. In addition, Table 18.1 sets out landmark texts which are associated with each generation. The term 'landmark' is not being used as synonymous with 'classic'. It is more that these texts define a particular time rather than that they are timeless.

Generation I

Efficacy of psychotherapy

Although psychotherapy research was being carried out well before the 1950s (see Orlinsky and Russell, 1994), it was the publication of Eysenck's (1952)

Table 18.1 Summary of research generations

		Research generations		
	I 1950s – 1970s onwards *Justification*	**II** 1960s – 1980s onwards *Specificity*	**III** 1970s – 2000 onwards *Efficacy/cost effectiveness*	**IV** 1984 – present *Effectiveness/clinical significance*
OUTCOME				
Thematic question	Is psychotherapy effective?	Which psychotherapy is more effective?	How can treatments be made more (cost) effective?	How can the quality of treatment delivery be improved?
Methodologies	Control group comparisons; effect sizes; meta-analysis;	Randomised control trial; factorial design; placebo group;	Probit analysis; growth curves; structural modelling;	Clinical significance; patient-focused research
Key issues	Efficacy; spontaneous remission;	What treatment, by whom, is most effective for this individual with that specific problem, and under which set of circumstances?	Dose-response; medical offset; health economics; evidence-based medicine; empirically validated treatments; practice guidelines	User perspectives; evidence-based practice; outcomes monitoring
Landmark texts	Eysenck (1952); Bergin & Garfield (1971); Sloane et al. (1975); Waskow & Parloff (1975) Smith & Glass (1977; 1980)	Paul (1967); Gurman & Razin (1977); Garfield & Bergin (1978); Stiles, Shapiro & Elliott (1986); Elkin et al. (1989)	Howard et al. (1986); Garfield & Bergin (1986); Bergin & Garfield (1994); Roth & Fonagy (1996); UK Department of Health (2001)	Jacobson et al. (1984; 1991); *Consumer Reports* (1995); Howard et al. (1996); Strupp et al. (1997); National Advisory Mental Health Council (1999)
PROCESS				
Thematic question	Are there objective methods for evaluating process?	What components are related to outcome?	How does change occur (via a quantitative approach)?	How does change occur (via a qualitative approach)?
Methodologies	Random sampling of sections of therapy; 'uniformity myth' assumed	Single-case methodologies; sampling 5-minute sections of therapy	Taxonomies; linking process to outcomes	Qualitative methods; narrative approach; discourse analysis; descriptive studies; theory development
Key issues	Verbal & speech behaviours;	Rogerian facilitative conditions (e.g. empathy)	Therapeutic alliance; verbal response modes	Events paradigm; single case approach; qualitative methods
Landmark texts	Rogers & Dymond (1954); Whitehorn & Betz (1954); Rogers et al. (1967)	Frank (1971); Bordin (1979); Strupp (1980a-d)	Russell & Stiles (1979); Greenberg & Pinsoff (1986); Orlinsky et al. (1994); Norcross (2002)	Rice & Greenberg (1984); Hill et al. (1997); Stiles et al. (1998); Elliott et al. (1999)

critique of the effectiveness of psychotherapy which marshalled activity leading to a generation of research focusing on the issue of the efficacy of psychotherapy. As such, the overarching theme of this generation is one of 'justification' for psychotherapy, with the central question 'Is psychotherapy efficacious?' and subsequently 'If so, how efficacious is it?' Eysenck (1952) claimed that approximately two-thirds of clients presenting with neurotic problems who received non-behavioural psychotherapy improved substantially within two years and that an equal proportion of people presenting with similar problems who had not received treatment also improved within the same time period. Bergin and Lambert (1978) made a number of observations about the way Eysenck had analysed his data. For example, they noted that the most stringent improvement percentage was used for psychotherapy while the most generous was used for calculating spontaneous remission rates. Also, differing rates could be deduced depending on the criterion used. In general, their view was that conclusions drawn from the studies used by Eysenck were suspect due to their inherent limitations (not surprising given the date when the data were collected). In looking at subsequent data, Bergin and Lambert (1978) found the rate for spontaneous remission to be 43 per cent rather than 67 per cent. Importantly, these authors also noted the finding from outcome studies that substantial change generally occurred within the initial 8–10 sessions, considerably quicker than the two-year time frame of spontaneous remission.

The response of researchers to Eysenck's critique was to incorporate a no-treatment control group into the research design and one exemplar design of Generation I is the study by Sloane, Staples, Cristol, Yorkston and Whipple (1975). They contrasted psychodynamic with behavioural treatments, each with an average 14-session duration of treatment, with a wait-list control group. The total sample size used for the analysis was 90 clients, with 30 clients randomly assigned to each of the three treatment conditions. The setting was a university psychiatric outpatient centre in which 54 per cent of the clients were students. The design used three experienced therapists in each of the two psychotherapy treatment conditions. The results used interview-based measures and showed improvement in all three conditions but with the two active treatments being broadly similar and both superior to the wait-list condition. These gains were maintained at various follow-up intervals.

The findings from the Sloane et al. (1975) study were 'confirmed' later by the publication of the original meta-analytic study of psychotherapy carried out by Smith and Glass (1977) and elaborated upon in their book *The Benefits of Psychotherapy* (Smith et al., 1980). The book provides a considered way through the claims and counterclaims of various researchers. Smith and Glass (1977) collated 475 controlled studies across 18 differing therapy types (including placebo treatment and undifferentiated counselling). The average effect size (ES) across all studies was 0.85, indicative of a large effect for psychotherapy over no psychotherapy, indicating that the average treated person was better off than 80 per cent of non-treated people. The effect sizes ranged from small (0.14

Table 18.2   Guide to interpreting between-group effect sizes

Cohen's guidelines for interpreting effect sizes	Effect size (d)	Proportion of people in control condition who are below the mean of people in the treated condition
No effect	0.0	.50
Small Effect	0.1	.54
	0.2	.58
Medium Effect	0.3	.62
	0.4	.66
	0.5	.69
	0.6	.73
	0.7	.76
Large Effect	0.8	.79
	0.9	.82
	1.0	.84

for reality therapy) to large (2.38 for cognitive therapies other than rational-emotive therapy). The authors found little evidence for negative effects, with only 9 per cent of the measures being negative (i.e. control groups were better than treated groups). In terms of overall effectiveness, the subsequent refinements of meta-analytic procedures and greater specificity, as well as the inclusion of more recent and more accomplished studies, have not delivered substantially different results, with the ESs remaining relatively stable. A guide for interpreting between-group effect sizes is presented in Table 18.2 in which an ES of 0.2 is deemed to be small, 0.5 is medium, and 0.8 or above is large (Cohen, 1977).

In subsequent years, beyond the time frame of Generation I, many further studies have been included in meta-analytic reviews addressing the issue of the efficacy of psychotherapy. Lambert and Bergin (1994: 144) have stated: 'There is now little doubt that psychological treatments are, overall and in general, beneficial, although it remains equally true that not everyone benefits to a satisfactory degree'. Meta-analytic studies provide the most concise summary of outcome findings. For example, in the area of depression, the number of studies (N) included in the meta-analysis and the effect sizes (ES) for three major meta-analytic reports are as follows: Nietzel, Russell, Hemmings and Gretter (1987), N = 28, ES = 0.71; Robinson, Berman and Neimeyer (1990), N = 29, ES = 0.84; and Steinbrueck, Maxwell and Howard (1983), N = 56, ES = 1.22. In terms of more diverse presenting problems, Lambert and Bergin (1994) have provided a summary table of 30 meta-analytic reviews covering a range of presenting problems and psychological interventions. Five studies (including that of Smith and

Glass) are defined as 'mixed' and result in a large average ES of 0.90. The range of other studies is so diverse as not to warrant categorization. However, they show the smallest and largest ESs (excluding control conditions) to range from 0.00 (schizophrenia; Quality Assurance Project, 1984) to 1.30 (stuttering; Andrews et al., 1980). Using only those studies (N = 25) which report effect sizes, the median ES was 0.76, which is approaching a large ES. In terms of comparisons, an ES of 0.67 is obtained from nine months of instruction in reading, while the ESs for antidepressants range from 0.40 to 0.81. Thus, as Lambert and Bergin (1994) argue, there appears to be evidence that psychological interventions are as effective, if not more effective, as medication. Apparently contrary to these substantial effects, it has been claimed that psychotherapy accounts for only 10 per cent of the outcome variance. This might appear small. However, it needs to be realized that 10 per cent variance arises from a correlation of 0.32 between psychotherapy and outcome. This is appreciably greater than other established correlations in the field: for example, correlations of 0.03 for the effect of aspirin on heart attacks, and 0.07 for service in Vietnam and alcohol consumption.

In relation to the psychodynamic therapies, randomized controlled trials are more rare. However, Shefler, Dasberg and Ben-Shakhar (1995) report on a randomized controlled trial of Mann's time-limited psychotherapy (TLP) in which 33 patients were randomly assigned to one of two conditions: three-months of TLP immediately (experimental group), or delay for three months and then receive TLP (control group). Whilst the study reflects the increased wisdom acquired over time of carrying out RCTs, this design essentially belongs to Generation I research in that it is comparing an active treatment against a wait-list control. No alternative therapy was involved in order to advance arguments of specificity, although measures of specific effects which would be predicted from the model of therapy were administered. Results showed the group receiving TLP immediately to have improved significantly more at end of treatment than the control group after the same elapsed time. The effect size for the treatment vs. no-treatment comparison (i.e. prior to the control group receiving therapy) was 0.99, which would be defined as a large effect size and is what would be expected when comparing an active treatment with a no-treatment condition.

An additional question which has been raised is whether psychotherapy is more efficacious than a placebo. In response, a critical point, well summarized by Lambert and Bergin, is worthy of reiteration: 'In interpreting this [placebo] research, it is important to keep in mind that failure to find incremental effects (effects beyond those attributable to common factors) for a specific therapy does not mean that psychotherapy is ineffective. Rather it means that no effect has been demonstrated beyond the effects of the common factors' (1994: 149). Lambert and Bergin provide a useful summary table of 15 meta-analytic studies whereby three two-way comparisons are made: psychotherapy vs. no-treatment; placebo vs. no-treatment; and psychotherapy vs. placebo. The first of these comparisons produced a mean/median ES of 0.82 (very similar to that stated previously). The placebo vs. no-treatment comparison produced a mean/median ES of 0.42, while the placebo vs. psychotherapy comparison produced a mean/median ES of 0.48. By way of comment on the use of placebo controls, Lambert and Bergin summarize: '... we have concluded that the typical placebo controls used in outcome studies are so conceptually and procedurally flawed that they have essentially failed in their purpose of helping to isolate the active therapeutic ingredients. It is time to discontinue placebo controls and design studies with more meaningful comparison groups' (1994: 152).

Measuring the process of therapy
Within the domain of psychotherapy process, the major thrust of this generation focused on the question 'Can the therapy process (e.g. facilitative conditions) be measured?' The influence of Rogers was profound in Generation I's development of objective procedures for measuring events of recorded therapy sessions. His influence has been noted as deriving from his 'respect for the scientific method and dedication to the objective study of the efficacy of his methods' (Hill and Corbett, 1993: 5). Although there was a great surge of activity in pursuit of establishing the effectiveness of psychotherapy, it was largely Rogers and his students who pursued research on the process of therapy. While the earlier process work had focused on verbal response modes as indicators of therapist techniques, process measures turned to the evaluation of Rogers's facilitative conditions.

Examples of research in this early phase include the work of Rogers and Dymond (1954) who found evidence supporting the view that good outcome was associated with improvements in self-perceptions. Other research drew on the work of Whitehorn and Betz (e.g. 1954) who found, via a retrospective study of psychiatrists, that those who were successful in working with schizophrenic patients were warm and communicated with their patients in a personal manner. Similar findings arose from the various reports of the classic study of the therapeutic conditions with a group of schizophrenic patients carried out at the University of Wisconsin (e.g. Rogers et al., 1967). This study arose following publication of Rogers's (1957) paper on the necessary and sufficient conditions for change. The Wisconsin project was a major empirical investigation undertaken with schizophrenic clients (Rogers et al., 1967). However, Truax and Mitchell (1971: 300), in a review of therapist variables, stated: 'it quickly became apparent to us that we were assuming that such variables are unitary when, in fact, they are not'. They went on: 'just as therapists are not unitary, neither are specific therapist variables'. They concluded: 'Therefore, in our opinion, most if not all the research dealing with therapist characteristics needs to be re-done.' This was the call for specificity.

Overall, Generation I research established the scientific foundations and methods for determining the efficacy of psychotherapy and delivered strong evidence that psychotherapy was efficacious. Similarly, the scientific foundations for process research were established although this line of research was not directly linked to the need to justify the activity of psychotherapy research. The procedures and techniques developed or espoused in this research generation (e.g. meta-analysis in outcome research and audio-recordings in process research) have become integral to subsequent research activities.

Generation II

Specificity in outcome research

Research characterizing Generation II began in large part as a search for greater specificity in response to what became known as the 'uniformity myth'. This myth reflected the held view that clients were thought to respond similarly to particular interventions. In other words, little attention had been paid to differences across clients, therapists, therapies, or across the course of therapy itself. In response to this situation, the archetypal question of Generation II research became encapsulated in Paul's litany: 'What treatment, by whom, is most effective for this individual with that specific problem, and under which set of circumstances?' (1967: 111). Clearly this was an important and logical step in research as it sought to address the issue of what was the most effective treatment. The question of whether psychotherapy was efficacious was seen as simplistic (Krumboltz, 1966) while process and outcome were increasingly viewed as differing across clients, therapists and therapies (Kiesler, 1966). Once the general theme of determining the overall efficacy of psychotherapy was instigated, Paul's matrix of specifying the various components led researchers to focus more on the differing types of intervention (e.g. Luborsky et al., 1975). In addition, the 1960s saw the rapid development of behaviour therapy within the domain of clinical psychology. The combination of seeking greater specificity together with the availability of contrasting treatments led researchers to question whether these newer therapies (or other brands of therapy) were more effective than, for example, the verbal (e.g. dynamically oriented) therapies.

Generation II research is best characterized by the randomized control trial (RCT). The most influential RCT to date has been the National Institute of Mental Health Treatment of Depression Collaborative Research Program (NIMH TDCRP; Elkin, 1994; Elkin et al., 1989). The design comprised three research sites in which 250 clients were randomly assigned to one of four treatment conditions. The four treatment conditions comprised the two psychotherapies which were of major interest, namely, cognitive-behaviour therapy (CBT) and interpersonal psychotherapy (IPT). In order to provide a standard reference condition, the third condition comprised imipramine plus clinical management (IMI-CM). Finally, a placebo condition (PLA-CM) was used primarily as a control for the drug condition and also as an imperfect control for the two psychotherapies. Among the features of the design, expert therapists were used in the two differing psychotherapies, and the particular treatments were documented in training manuals and the delivery of the treatments was investigated to check on therapists' adherence to the treatment protocols. Findings showed that clients in the IMI-CM condition improved most, clients in the PLA-CM condition improved least, and clients in the two psychotherapy conditions fared in between but were generally closer to the IMI-CM condition. However, differences were not large. Indeed, there were no significant differences between the two psychotherapies or between either of them and the IMI-CM. Differences between the psychotherapies and the placebo condition showed only one instance of a trend towards lower scores for clients in the IPT condition as compared with PLA-CM and no significant or trend advantage to CBT compared with PLA-CM.

A meta-analysis of 28 RCTs (US DHHS, 1993) found improvement rates for individual and group treatments for depression to be comparable: 50 per cent for cognitive therapy, 52 per cent for interpersonal therapy, and 55 per cent for behavioural therapy but 35 per cent for brief dynamic psychotherapy. However, the latter group may have been adversely affected by the proportionally higher number of studies investigating group rather than individual psychotherapy. Overall, these findings have confirmed the view that technically different therapies result in broadly similar outcomes, a conclusion referred to as the 'equivalence paradox' (Stiles et al., 1986). It is not disputed that there is often a reported advantage to one particular method of therapy (invariably cognitive-behavioural), but what is important is that the size of this advantage is relatively small. How such a small advantage translates into clinical status or psychological health is unclear. The most recent meta-analysis carried out by Wampold and colleagues (1997) reaffirmed the equivalence finding. Their study found that under the most liberal assumptions, the largest extent of any true difference in effect size was in the region of 0.20, which is viewed as a 'small' effect. One important point to keep in mind is that such a finding arose from applying more rigorous procedures than previously employed. For example, it only included studies making a direct within-study comparison between contrasting treatments and therapies that were deemed 'bona fide' (i.e. treatments had to be both credible and therapeutic).

The theme of Generation II's research is being extended in terms of evaluating therapies for more challenging patients. For example, recent research on psychotherapy with borderline personality disorders has focused on the efficacy of dialectical behaviour therapy (DBT) and psychodynamic psychotherapy (Koenigsberg, 1995). The former is associated with the work of Linehan (1993) who found DBT to be superior to treatment in the community in a randomized trial over one year as defined by having fewer days in hospital and fewer and less lethal parasuicidal acts (Linehan et al., 1991). These results were largely maintained one year after treatment although there was no difference in patients' levels of general satisfaction, hence suggesting that the effects of DBT are quite specific and do not address non-behavioural symptoms or overall personality functioning (Linehan et al., 1993). An interesting note has been made regarding the discrepancy between the high level of interest from clinicians and the still relatively small amount of research evidence regarding DBT (Scheel, 2000).

However, a standard RCT may not necessarily be the most appropriate research design for this particular patient population. Research on psychodynamic psychotherapy for borderlines has been carried out mainly on Kernberg's model (see Clarkin et al., 1992).

A review of the effectiveness of psychotherapy for personality disorders has been published (Perry et al., 1999). The review comprised 15 studies (although nine of these were uncontrolled observational studies). All studies showed improvements in personality disorders across a range of interventions (e.g. psychodynamic/interpersonal, cognitive-behavioural, and supportive therapies). The within-group ESs (i.e. pre-post change) were 1.11 for self-report measures and 1.29 for observational measures. Although the size of these changes may appear 'large', this within-condition ES is considerably more liberal than the traditional between-condition effect size reported in the literature (i.e. when an active treatment is compared with a control or comparison condition). The authors found evidence to suggest that psychotherapy for personality disorders may yield a recovery rate seven times faster than the natural history of borderline personality disorders. In addition to personality disorders, Generation II research is also being applied to the study of child and adolescent psychotherapy; for example, the special section in *Journal of Consulting and Clinical Psychology* (1995) on efficacy and effectiveness in studies of child and adolescent psychotherapy.

Generation II studies can be summarized by referring to Bergin and Garfield (1994: 822) who stated: 'We have to face the fact that in a majority of studies, different approaches to the same symptoms, (e.g. depression) show little difference in efficacy'. This is the view summarized by Stiles, Shapiro and Elliott (1986) in their question 'Are all psychotherapies equivalent?' They posited three ways of understanding the supposed equivalence of outcomes. The first was methodological in that equivalence could be achieved through lack of stringency in research methodology. The second argument concerned the possibility that differing therapies may be broadly equivalent due to the overriding effects of common factors. The third argument revolved around the implementation of new research strategies to detect differences. However, the one area where there has accumulated increasing evidence of non-equivalent treatment effects are the anxiety disorders. Here, the treatment of choice is cognitive therapy.

Specificity in process research

Process research built its base on the 'recorded' therapy session and in Generation II was dominated by the work carried out to investigate the 'facilitative' conditions (i.e. empathy, warmth and genuineness). This was a logical step deriving from a theoretical basis and employing observational and self-report measures. The core period for Generation II process research was the 1970s and there is a noticeable difference between Truax and Mitchell's review from the *Handbook of Psychotherapy and Behavior Change* (1971) reported above and the Mitchell, Bozarth, and Krauft's chapter published in *Effective*

Psychotherapy: A Handbook of Research (1977). The authors of the latter text acknowledged that the former had focused too much on gross outcome and not sufficiently on the potential correlates between, for example, empathy and out- come. Hence, they stated that 'demographic and process studies were ignored which might have answered the question: "Which therapists, under what condi- tions, with which clients in what kinds of specific predicaments, need to reach what levels of these interpersonal skills to effect what kinds of client changes?"' (1977: 482).

In contrast to the 1971 review which implied that the facilitative conditions were both necessary and sufficient, and that they were relatively invariant, Mitchell et al. stated that 'the mass of data neither supports nor rejects the over- riding influence of such variables as empathy' (1977: 483). They went on: 'their [the facilitative conditions] potency and generalizability are not as great as once thought' (p. 483). Hence, while the authors reported some studies which sup- ported to varying degrees the positive role of the facilitative conditions, the majority of studies they reported showed little or no direct relationship between the facilitative conditions and outcome (e.g. Sloane et al., 1975).

While process research focused largely on the facilitative conditions, which in itself became the basis for subsequent research on the therapeutic alliance, it was, as Orlinsky and Russell (1994) observe, 'peculiarly flawed' to the extent that it virtually ceased by the late 1970s. The 'conceptual critique', specifically in relation to the facilitative conditions, combined with the increasing search for psychologically appropriate methods for investigating aspects of the therapeutic process, led to the demise of research in this area. In historical terms, the absence of a research centre linked to Rogers assisted the demise. More generally, there was probably a move away from investigating 'common' factors towards deter- mining the more specific components of individual orientations. In addition, there was an increasing move towards a re-evaluation of the clinical utility of the single-case study (e.g. Strupp, 1980a, 1980b, 1980c, 1980d).

Overall, Generation II research moved the agenda on from general issues towards greater specificity in terms of one therapeutic approach versus another and in terms of the contribution of the facilitative conditions. Interestingly, although the call for specificity was a logical one, the general finding of outcome equivalence across different treatment approaches was somewhat problematic for the field. Similarly, the yield arising from the facilitative conditions fell short of expectations. However, specificity has become a major driver in both outcome and process research and set the foundations for the moves towards evidence- based practice.

Generation III

Cost-effectiveness and service delivery
The research included in Generation III spans the period from the 1970s through to the 1990s and incorporates what appear to be two quite diverse foci:

cost-effectiveness and change mechanisms. However, these two areas can be seen to be natural developments arising from the previous two generations of research. Cost-effectiveness has become a central concern, partly driven by research interest but also by the interest of a variety of stakeholders. As such, it is a natural extension of the outcome research carried out in Generation I. The focus on change mechanisms reflects an extension to the issue of 'specificity' which was a feature of Generation II process research, although it might equally be construed as a reaction to it. It is an extension in that it retains specificity as a hallmark but a reaction in terms of redirecting research on to the process of change. The focus on cost and economic aspects of psychotherapy has been reviewed by Gabbard, Lazar, Hornberger and Spiegel (1997). These authors reviewed a total of 18 studies published between 1984 and 1994 and concentrated on the impact of administering psychotherapy on the costs of care. Using actual cost accounting or data on medical care utilization or functioning at work, the data strongly indicated that psychotherapy reduces total costs. The main reductions in costs arose from decreases in work impairment.

Information on service delivery systems has been derived from the 1987 National Medical Expenditures Survey (Olfson and Pincus, 1994a, 1994b) which has provided comprehensive data on the use of services by over 38,000 individuals in the United States. The results (usefully summarized by Docherty and Streeter, 1995) suggest that 79.5 million outpatient psychotherapy visits were made by 7.3 million people (representing 3.1 per cent of the US population). Women used the service at 1.44 times the rate of men. In terms of patient characteristics, 90 per cent of patients were white with the majority being either separated or divorced, aged between 35 and 49, and having more than 16 years of education. Two-thirds of psychotherapy visits were made for a mental health reason (mainly depression, anxiety disorders and adjustment disorders). Outpatient psychotherapy accounted for 8 per cent of all expenditure on outpatient health care. The percentage of patients attending for specified numbers of sessions was as follows: 1–2 sessions, 33.9 per cent; 3–10 sessions, 37.0 per cent; 11–20 sessions, 13.4 per cent; and > 20 sessions, 15.7 per cent. This latter group accounted for 63 per cent of psychotherapy outcome expenditure. The issue of the cost-effectiveness of psychotherapy has been addressed by Krupnick and Pincus (1992), who have provided a strategy for including this aspect into research studies.

The debate concerning length of treatment ('How much is enough?') has come to the fore in Generation III research. The major finding relating to the dose-effect literature derives from a study carried out by Howard, Kopta, Krause and Orlinsky (1986) which combined 15 outcome studies over a period of 30 years. These authors found that the percentage of clients showing measurable improvement following specified numbers of sessions was as follows: 24 per cent after a single session, 30 per cent after two sessions, 41 per cent after 4 sessions, 53 per cent after 8 sessions, 62 per cent after 13 sessions, 74 per cent after 26 sessions, 83 per cent after 52 sessions, and 90 per cent after 104 sessions. This relationship between the number of sessions received by clients and the percentage of clients showing measurable improvement was best represented by a negatively accelerating curve. This means that while the curve 'accelerates' (i.e. the percentage of clients improving gets higher as a result of more sessions), it does so 'negatively' in that the greatest improvement occurs early in therapy and there are diminishing returns thereafter such that smaller and smaller gains are made later on in therapy in response to the provision of more sessions. However, it is worth noting that almost half of the studies reported by Howard et al. (i.e. seven) had a median of 15 or more sessions, considerably more than the often-quoted averages for attendance in service delivery systems (Taube et al., 1984). Further, the data set did not comprise cognitive-behavioural, behavioural or cognitive therapy orientations. The findings from Howard et al.'s (1986) work are interesting in terms of how they have been used by people espousing differing viewpoints. Howard et al. (1986) obtained two dose-effect curves: one based on therapist ratings and one on client ratings. Defence of longer-term therapy has utilized the former curve, which suggests that diminishing returns only occur after about six months of therapy. In contrast, data from the client ratings suggest that greatest improvements are derived from the initial 8–10 sessions. The dose-effect findings have given rise to a three-phase model of psychotherapy (Howard et al., 1993). This model proposes that the first few sessions of therapy are characterized by *remoralization*, which then leads on to a phase of *remediation* of symptoms occurring upwards of about the fifth session, which then leads on in later sessions to *rehabilitation* (i.e. improvement in life functioning).

Generation III outcome research has been marked by an increase in research on brief therapies which has been summarized by Koss and Shiang (1994). However, while findings indicate that for many clients the greater impact of counselling or therapy occurs during the initial time frame, with subsequent gains requiring more time, for many clients, especially those who have been severely damaged, effective therapeutic work may not be possible until considerable work has been carried out in establishing, for example, the therapeutic alliance. What this means is that there are clients for whom briefer therapies are appropriate and clients for whom longer therapies are appropriate. The issue is to determine what is best for each client. It is not necessarily true that more therapy is always the preferred option. Given limited resources, it is important to ensure that longer-term interventions are appropriately used and that they are evaluated in order to provide supporting evidence for their use.

The focus on brief therapies has continued, with researchers investigating and reviewing the components that make brief therapies effective. Messer (2001) has reviewed components that contribute to making brief psychodynamic therapy time efficient, while McGinn and Sanderson (2001) have done likewise for cognitive behavioural therapy. Of particular note is a review by Elliott (2001) of brief experiential therapy. What is of interest is that this review attempts to re-establish the research base for experiential therapies. Elliott (2001) identified a sample of 28 studies comprising both controlled and comparative studies. The pre-post change effect size (i.e. within group) was in the order of 1.1 with the effects consistent across the three main types of problems studied: neurotic problems (ES = 1.02), depression (ES = 1.61) and anxiety (ES = 1.16). When comparisons were made between treated and untreated clients, there was a large effect size difference (ES = 1.14). Comparisons between experiential and non-experiential therapies showed very little difference (ES = −0.04). These findings suggest there is increasing evidence for the efficacy of brief experiential thera-pies, which has particular significance in that the outcomes work on experiential therapies is closely linked with many of the principal process researchers ema-nating from Generation IV. It is interesting to note that the chapter focusing on research in brief psychotherapies which appeared in the 4th edition of the *Handbook of Psychotherapy and Behavior Change* was not retained for the 5th edition because brief psychotherapies was considered to be intrinsic to all other chapters. That is, most of the research now being reported utilizes brief psy-chotherapy models making a specific chapter on this topic redundant.

The culmination of Generations I, II and III can be seen in the activities center-ing around the broad development of the 'evidence-based practice' (EBP) para-digm. This movement grew in the early 1980s at McMasters University and arose from attempts to help readers appraise the existing research literature in medicine. This movement rapidly expanded to other disciplines such that texts can now be found on 'evidence-based psychotherapy' (e.g. Parry, 2000). The gold standard in terms of evidence within this paradigm consists of the randomized control trial and meta-analytic studies. This is the rationale for why the EBP movement is being placed in Generation III even though much of its impact is only becoming appar-ent in the 2000s. And as a result of, for example, the growing numbers of meta-analytic studies that have been published there are now reviews of meta-analytic studies (e.g., Butler et al., 2006). Clearly, methodologies have to be continually adapted in order to keep control of the amount of available information. The crit-ical point here is that the underlying themes (i.e. specificity, cost-effectiveness) and the methods (RCTs) are those of Generations II and III.

The EBP paradigm has also underpinned the identification and validation of what have been called 'empirically supported treatments' (ESTs; for a review see Chambless and Ollendick, 2001; DeRubeis and Crit-Christoph, 1998). The con-cerns within the US about the number of psychological treatments on offer led to initiatives to marshal the levels of existing evidence for particular therapies. Three levels of criteria were set by Division 12 (Clinical Psychology) Task Force: well-established treatments, probably efficacious treatments, and experi-mental treatments. These are set out below.

- *Well-established treatments*: At least two good between-group design experiments must demonstrate efficacy via superiority to pill or psychotherapy placebo (or to other treatment) or equivalence to already established treatment with adequate sample sizes. Or a large series of single-case design experiments must demonstrate efficacy with use of good experimental design and comparison of intervention to another treatment. Experiments must be conducted with treatment manuals or equivalent clear description of treatment. Characteristics of samples must be specified and effects must be demonstrated by at least two different investigators or teams.

- *Probably efficacious treatments*: Two experiments must show that the treatment is superior to waiting-list control group, or one or more experiments must meet well-established criteria. Or a small series of single-case design experiments must meet well-established-treatment criteria.
- *Experimental treatments*: Treatment not yet tested in trials meeting task force criteria for methodology.

However, a raft of criticisms have been leveled at the concept of ESTs (e.g. Wampold, 1997, 2001). These include the wholesale adoption of a 'medicalization' of psychotherapy, omitting quasi-experimental studies (which are more representative of psychotherapy as practised in routine settings), and premised on DSM-IV diagnostic categories. In terms of ecological validity, one dilemma is that many of the therapies used in routine clinical settings do not meet the EST criteria (e.g. eclectic therapy, long-term psychodynamic therapy). The concept and research evidence for ESTs build on the combined and developmental research traditions from Generations I, II and III and provide the most fully developed response to Eysenck's (1952) original critique of psychotherapy. Equally, they serve to draw a transition line between Generations I–III and Generation IV.

Change pathways

The review of process and outcome in psychotherapy by Orlinsky, Grawe and Parks (1994) summarized a wealth of material relating to possible effective pathways. They identified stability of treatment arrangements and counsellor adherence to a treatment model as showing promise. They identified 'patient suitability' and 'therapist skill' as particularly robust with over two-thirds of studies in each of these areas reporting significant findings. In terms of therapeutic operations, the authors summarised three areas: problem presentation; expert understanding; and therapist intervention. With regard to problem presentation, the cognitive and behavioural processes within the client's problem presentation are related to outcome. Findings on 'expert understanding' target client problems and client affective responses during sessions. In terms of therapist interventions, there appears to be substantial evidence supporting experiential confrontation as well as interpretations. In addition, paradoxical intention appears to show a consistent relationship with outcome. In terms of the therapeutic bond, this showed strong associations with outcome, especially when assessed from the client's perspective. This review of change pathways has been recently updated (see Orlinsky et al., 2004) but findings remain essentially the same.

Specific techniques

The use of verbal response modes (VRMs) in various research studies has shown that therapists use responses which are consistent with their theoretical orientation (Elliott et al., 1987). Relating VRMs to immediate outcomes (i.e. in-session), a range of studies have identified 'interpretation' (or responses closely allied to it) as being 'effective'. For example, O'Farrell, Hill and Patton (1986) found interpretation to be related to a decrease in client problem description and an increase in experiencing and insight. However, the role of therapist 'intentions' is just as important. Horvath, Marx and Kamann (1990) found clients' ability to identify the intention of the counsellor depended, in addition to other factors, upon the stage of therapy, with understanding increasing from initial to mid-therapy and then decreasing. Factors accounting for this may involve the intentions becoming more complex or tacit as therapy develops. The complex relationship between these factors (e.g. response modes and intentions) is summarized by Sexton and Whiston:

> Based on a variety of complex factors (experience, training, client behavior), counselors develop intentions or goals that guide their choices of intentions or response modes. After each counselor response, the client reacts (decodes, interprets, and experiences) and responds. In response, the counselor develops an adjusted intention and subsequent response mode. Over time these patterns become stabilized in client and counselor expectations. (1994: 21)

However, it has been found that response modes account for very little of the outcome variance, even for immediate outcome. Hill reports that 'therapist intentions and client experiencing in the turn preceding the therapist intervention each contributed more to the variance than did response modes' (1990: 289). She cites her intensive analyses of eight single cases (Hill, 1989) in which she found that 'client personality, therapist orientation and personality, and adequate therapeutic relationship, and events external to therapy all influenced whether or not clients incorporated changes begun in therapy' (1990: 289).

Research into the effectiveness of interpretations has been summarized by Orlinsky et al. (1994). These authors cited a total of 38 findings from 16 studies, of which 24 findings were positively related to overall outcome, 11 showed no association, and 3 showed negative associations. Hence, while two-thirds of the findings showed a positive association between interpretations and outcome, inspection of their data (Orlinsky et al., 1994: 303) in which 11 studies yielded sufficient information for the reviewers to determine effect sizes, showed the average size of this effect to be small (ES = 0.21). Although this summary has been recently revisited by Orlinsky et al. (2004), they did not update the table of findings relating to positive, nil, and negative associations, presumably due to the size of the task. However, they did argue that while the evidence for interpretations was generally positive, such a view did not extend to the use of transference interpretations in brief psychotherapies. Research into the accuracy of therapist interpretations has been carried out by Crits-Christoph, Cooper and Luborsky (1988) who found that accuracy of interpretation was the best predictor of outcome. However, rather surprisingly, it was not related to improvements in the therapeutic alliance. A useful summary of important domains related to change in psychotherapy is included in a special section of the *Journal of Consulting and Clinical Psychology* (1993) which is devoted to curative factors in dynamic psychotherapy. Areas include interpersonal problems and attachment styles, the therapeutic alliance, psychodynamic formulations, transference interpretations, and patients' representations of psychotherapy.

Generation III process research has combined much of the more 'technical' and quantitative research efforts. However, difficulties undoubtedly occur when evaluating specific techniques and many researchers within this domain have contrasting views. For example, Garfield has stated that there is 'no truly strong support for the accuracy of interpretation as a process variable of importance ... the interpretation of explanation that is accepted by the patient is the one that may have some positive therapeutic impact' (1990: 276). Others, for example Silberschatz and Curtis (1986), have argued that the interpretations which are important are those which are consistent with the client's unconscious plan for therapy rather than those relating, for example, to the transference.

The role of specific techniques in CBT has also been investigated. For example, patient change in the later stages of therapy has been linked specifically to the procedure of cognitive restructuring (DeRubeis et al., 1990). Further, evidence suggests certain cognitive techniques (e.g. logical analysis and hypothesis testing) are linked with amelioration of symptoms in the mid-to-later phases of therapy (Jarrett and Nelson, 1987). In addition, the potential prophylactic effect of CBT has been suggested by results showing that patients who have received CBT are less likely to relapse than patients receiving medication (Evans et al., 1992). Hence, patients who have learned cognitive techniques appear to be offered a degree of protection against subsequent depressive experiences by applying the learned techniques. These findings are congruent with the 'compensatory skills' model of change which suggests that CBT offers a set of effective coping strategies (i.e. compensatory skills) which are implemented by patients. This model appears to be more consistent with research evidence than that which suggests that CBT results in any permanent change in patients' schema. A review by Iliardi and Craighead (1994) suggested that non-specific factors may play a significant role in the early part of CBT. This suggestion arose from an analysis of a set of studies which showed that early response to CBT (i.e. symptomatic improvement) occurred prior to the formal introduction of cognitive restructuring techniques. The authors suggested that these findings are consistent with the three-phase model of therapy (see Howard et al., 1993) in which the early phase is characterized by remoralization (i.e. non-specific effects of expectancy and hope).

Common factors
Process research has often been viewed as a dichotomy comprising common factors and specific techniques. As indicated above, research interest has moved from the facilitative conditions to investigating the therapeutic alliance. While the facilitative conditions have been viewed as a possible mechanism of change, the therapeutic alliance is best viewed as a mechanism which enables the client to remain in and comply with treatment (Bordin, 1979). Sexton and Whiston

(1994) reviewed the research literature on the client–therapist relationship since 1985 using three domains: the 'real' relationship, the transference, and the working alliance. Findings summarized here focus on the last of these: the working alliance. A meta-analytic review of 24 studies (Horvath and Symonds, 1991) found that the working alliance was positively related to outcome and that client and observer ratings were better predictors of outcome than therapist ratings. However, the overall effect only approached medium size and it appears that findings from individual studies are affected by such factors as when the alliance was assessed and the particular outcome index used. Overall though, from the available evidence, it appears the therapeutic alliance might account for upwards of 45 per cent of outcome variance (Horvath and Greenberg, 1989).

The perspective taken by the rater influences the results and it is invariably the client's rating of the alliance that is most predictive of outcome. Further, if client change is the criterion for measuring outcome, then client ratings of process are the best judges. There is also evidence that clients have predispositions to the quality of the alliance they might develop. Horvath and Greenberg (1994) cite work suggesting that clients who have difficulty in maintaining their social relationships or have experienced relatively poor family relationships prior to therapy are less likely to develop strong alliances. However, severity of presenting symptoms did not appear to impact on the quality of the alliance. In terms of the temporal nature of the therapeutic alliance, research findings are equivocal with some researchers (e.g. Eaton et al., 1988) finding that it is constant while others (e.g. Klee et al., 1990) have suggested the opposite. This is an area requiring further research as it relates to the development and maintenance of the client–therapist relationship. While there has been considerable effort in the development of measures of the therapeutic alliance, there has been 'greater emphasis on inter-rater reliability and predictive validity and less emphasis on issues of dimensionality and convergent and discriminate validity' (Marmar, 1990). Thus, it is not clear that equivalent emphasis has been placed on furthering our understanding of what are the actual components of this 'umbrella' concept.

Nevertheless, it is clear that 'umbrella' or overarching models can be helpful in providing a framework for increasing our understanding of therapeutic processes. In an attempt to provide an overarching model for understanding the process of change through therapy, Stiles, Elliott, Llewelyn, Firth-Cozens, Margison, Shapiro and Hardy (1990) developed the assimilation model. This model presents change along a continuum comprising eight stages from 'warded off', through 'unwanted thoughts' and 'emerging awareness' and on to 'problem clarification' and 'insight/understanding'. Thereafter come the stages of 'application/ working through', 'problem solution' and 'mastery'. The model focuses on problematic experiences such that different problems can progress at a different pace. Evidence is encouraging (e.g. Stiles, 2002; Stiles et al., 1994) and further refinements have been made. The model requires considerably more rigorous testing, but it does have high face validity upon which to hang research questions (see Stiles, 2006).

The debate concerning the respective roles and contributions of specific and common factors is still as much an issue as ever and has been referred to as 'the great psychotherapy debate' (see Wampold, 2001). Ahn and Wampold (2001) carried out a meta-analytic study to determine the extent to which proven psychological therapies (i.e. those that had shown themselves to be efficacious) produce client change via specific mechanisms as opposed to common factors. Importantly, the studies used were 'component' studies which involved comparisons between the treatment package and the treatment package without a theoretically important component. A total of 27 studies met the criterion for inclusion in the study and the results showed that the effect size for the difference between the two conditions (with component versus without the component) was not significantly different from zero. Further, the authors suggested that because there was very little variance in the effect sizes, it was unlikely that important variables were moderating the effect sizes.

The focus in Generation III on evidence-based practice in outcomes research and on specific and common factors in process research was brought together in a major text which addressed the evidence base underpinning a range of areas that contribute to the therapeutic relationship (Norcross, 2002). This text arose from an APA Division of Psychotherapy Task Force which was commissioned to (a) identify elements of effective therapy relationships, and (b) establishing proven methods for tailoring therapy to individual clients based on their characteristics. In terms of the former, it considered elements that were deemed to be either 'effective' (e.g., the alliance, empathy, goal consensus) or 'promising' (e.g., congruence, feedback, repairing alliance ruptures), and for the latter it identified methods for customizing treatments to individual clients (e.g., stages of change model, assimilation of problematic experiences, attachment style). In effect, it brought together the approach of developing practice guidelines with the content area of the therapeutic relationship.

Overall, Generation III outcome research has built on the basis of Generation II research but advanced it by setting it in the context of service settings and costs. Hence, it can be viewed as an extension of Generation II research. The moves towards taking account of real world situations set the agenda for prioritizing the needs of clinicians and practitioners in routine service settings. Meanwhile, research on process issues built up a huge research base but was unable to resolve the debate on the contributions of specific and common factors in psychotherapy.

Generation IV

Towards a paradigm of clinically meaningful outcome research
Generation IV outcome research has developed both 'from' and 'in reaction to' the previous research generations. In the broadest sense, what is 'new' in Generation IV is the central focus on the user perspective and on prioritizing the external validity derived from studying routine settings. In terms of the former,

a landmark but controversial study of psychotherapy even at the time of its publication was the Consumer Report Survey (*Consumer Reports*, 1995). *Consumer Reports* – the equivalent of *Which?* magazine in the UK – carried out a survey of its readers who had experienced stress or other emotional problems at any time during the previous three years for which they had sought help from a range of support systems. Seligman (1995) reported the following key findings: (1) treatment by a health professional usually worked; (2) long-term therapy produced more improvement than short-term therapy; (3) there were no differences between psychotherapy alone and psychotherapy plus medication for any disorder; and (4) no specific modality of psychotherapy did any better than any other for any problem. His conclusions were that the findings confirmed the overall effectiveness of psychotherapy. However, there was widespread criticism of the Consumer Report because of the small sample who actually responded to the mental health questions (around 4 per cent of the original sample), lack of a control group, paucity of information on a range of client, therapist and treatment variables, and lack of a reliable metric for summarizing therapeutic change. Seligman viewed most of the criticisms as focusing on what the CR might have done rather than what it actually did within the financial and time constraints and stated that 'this was first-rate journalism and credible science as well' (1996: 1086). Yet some commentators have noted that the criticisms of the design noted above suggest that the CR survey is more akin to a consumer satisfaction survey and should not be held up as an exemplar of effectiveness research (Nathan et al., 2000).

Within mainstream outcome research, the momentum towards seeking a new paradigm has been driven by general disquiet at the ability of the research paradigms used in Generations I, II and III to increase our understanding of psychotherapy outcomes. For example, recent meta-analyses continue to report broadly similar outcomes for different therapies (Grissom, 1996; Wampold et al., 1997). However, as Kopta et al. state: 'It seems clear though that no one believes all psychotherapies are equally effective for all disorders' (1999: 444). One way forward suggested by Elliott, Stiles and Shapiro (1993) is that researchers should focus on the specific effects of specific psychotherapies on specific types of patients. At one level such an argument appears to hark back to the theme of Generation II research, but there is greater sophistication about this call which recognizes the considerable variation in the effect sizes obtained in earlier meta-analyses (e.g. the standard deviation of the 0.85 effect size was 1.25). The need to consider therapist effects is crucial as well as taking into account possible unwitting biases due to researcher allegiance. There is also the need to consider what criteria must be satisfied in order for two or more treatments to be deemed as having a differential impact.

In relation to this issue, a principal driver for Generation IV research has been the central issue of whether the way in which outcomes are measured is meaningful. Jacobson and colleagues (1984, 1986, 1991) devised a heuristic to address two key questions: (1) Is the extent of client change reliable given the change measure used?, and (2) What is the end state of the client in relation to any given population? Jacobson and Truax (1991) have summarized this work on determining reliable and clinically significant change and have provided three methods for calculating this index. The principle they use is movement by the client from one population (i.e. dysfunctional) to another population (e.g. general population, or non-distressed population). Of course, it is only possible to determine membership of the 'normal' population when normative data are available. In the absence of such data, movement to two standard deviations below the intake mean would signify 'clinical' change (i.e. belonging to a different population, although not necessarily a non-distressed population). This approach enables clinicians to identify individual clients who have met a specified criterion of improvement (e.g. Kendall et al., 1999b; Kendall and Sheldrick, 2000). A review of the history, definitions and applications of clinical significance is provided by Ogles, Lunnen and Bonesteel (2001).

Generation IV research has built on these methodological developments which have provided the means to achieve better outcomes monitoring in practice settings. One component to this has been the recognition of an agreed core outcome battery – that is, an attempt to standardize the selection of outcome measures in order to facilitate increased comparisons across treatments, settings and services (Strupp et al., 1997). Lest it be thought that this was a new development, the idea of a 'core outcome battery' was first developed at a landmark conference in the 1970s (see Waskow and Parloff, 1975). But whatever measure is selected, there is a considerable problem in collecting Time 2 data – that is, data at termination or discharge. Many clients terminate therapy unilaterally and it is difficult to obtain post-therapy data. Accordingly, monitoring outcomes is most likely to inform practice through the application of session-by-session tracking of individual patients in the context of empirically derived parameters that determine the range of response to particular interventions for particular diagnoses (e.g. Lutz et al., 1999). This 'patient-focused' outcome paradigm can provide individual dose response curves to help inform individual case management and support clinical decision-making in service of enhanced quality (e.g. Howard et al., 1996; Lambert et al., 2001a; Lueger et al., 2001). Systems have also been developed and validated for the early identification of 'signal' cases (e.g. Kordy et al., 2001). Evidence that outcomes monitoring enhances clients' outcomes has been shown in a study evaluating the effects of providing practitioners with feedback on their clients' progress (Lambert et al., 2001b). Clients who were deemed not to be 'on track' in terms of expected outcomes trajectories and whose therapists were provided with outcomes feedback yielded a treatment effect size advantage of 0.44 over an equivalent 'not on track' group whose therapists were not provided with outcome feedback. Although these results should be treated with caution – the authors note that the confidence intervals for the size of treatment effect ranged from 'just above zero to more than 0.80' – there is a clear indication of the potential for a direct impact on clinical practice. A meta-analytic review of three large scale studies using a therapist feedback system reported a reduction in client deterioration in the range of 4-8 per cent (Lambert et al., 2003).

A key concern for Generation IV research has been the clinical relevance of the body of efficacy research. Shadish and colleagues (1997, 2000) addressed the key question of whether the findings from psychotherapy outcome studies were different as a function of their clinical representativeness. That is, are there outcome differences from studies spanning the continuum from efficacy to effectiveness? If no substantive differences are found, then this might help to allay concerns that efficacy results are not transportable to routine clinical practice. And indeed, the findings reported by Shadish (Shadish et al., 1997, 2000) provide support for this argument. Effect sizes from 56 studies were categorized into three stages that increasingly represented routine clinical practice. There were no substantive differences in effect size as a function of clinical representativeness. This finding was replicated in a refinement of the earlier study (Shadish et al., 2000). Hence, this programme of work suggests that the concern about applying efficacy results to routine practice may be more apparent than real.

However, even if actual outcome results are similar, it still leaves the outcomes of routine settings as being determined by the results from efficacy studies. It is simply impossible for the efficacy paradigm to address the many questions that need to be asked and to deliver answers quickly enough in order to meet the needs of services and patients. Other outcome paradigms are needed regardless of the transportability of efficacy results. Indeed, there have been recent calls for some radical reappraisals of how outcome research is carried out. In response, the NIMH has been proposed an integration initiative in an attempt to bridge the gap between efficacy and effectiveness research (NAMHC, 1999; Norquist et al., 1999). In effect, a new paradigm is proposed that would be inclusive of both experimental and observational data and that would require development of existing methods and new statistical techniques.

Towards a paradigm of clinically meaningful process research
In the same way that the method of investigating reliable and clinically meaningful change employed a rigorous but clinically useful approach applicable to outcome research, so there is a range of methods adopted in psychotherapy process research which are rigorous but remain sufficiently close to the clinical material that they are seen to be clinically relevant to practitioners. The traditional model of investigating process–outcome correlations has been challenged (Stiles and Shapiro, 1989) and there has been a movement towards the adoption of newer styles of research aimed at focusing on the 'change process' (Greenberg, 1986, 1994). In this paradigm, 'the process of therapy can … be seen as a chain of patient states or suboutcomes that are linked together on a pathway toward ultimate outcome' (Safran et al., 1988). A hallmark of qualitative research is that the data comprise 'vivid, dense, and full descriptions in natural language of the phenomenon under study' (Polkinghorne, 1994).

Akin to the desire to make research relevant to the practitioner, process researchers adopted a particular paradigm – the events paradigm – to investigate the mechanisms of change. The logic was that in therapy, 'significant events' occur which initiate the change process. The logic of the events paradigm was to capture and study such events rather than using other sampling techniques. Hence, the 'events' paradigm assumes that the intensive study of significant moments occurring during therapy is more informative than aggregating within and across sessions whereby considerable 'noise' is included in the data. It is a substantially better informed strategy than sampling random segments of therapy sessions. The events paradigm emphasizes the experiences and perceptions of participating patients and therapists by focusing on a particular class of events (e.g. moments of perceived empathy, or insight). The events are usually derived from a variant of a procedure called interpersonal process recall (IPR; Elliott, 1984) which requires the patient, following a therapy session, to identify with an assessor a significant event that occurred during the session. This event then becomes the focus of subsequent intensive analysis. In order to make IPR less labour intensive, a brief format has been devised (see Elliott and Shapiro, 1988). The events paradigm aims to investigate change episodes in therapy and to develop 'micro-theories' to explain how change takes place. The focus is on 'providing causal explanations of therapeutic change and on making explanation rather than prediction the primary goal of psychotherapy research' (Greenberg, 1994: 115).

A related procedure, called task analysis, is uniquely suited to the analysis of the psychotherapeutic change process. It attempts to explicate a model of the information-processing activities which the patient and therapist perform across time which leads to the resolution of particular cognitive-affective tasks. The preliminary model, termed the rational model, can be developed by theoretical speculations and then its 'goodness of fit' verified against empirical examples of change processes occurring in psychotherapy. The result is a synthesis of the rational model and empirical examples termed the performance model. The rational model is then constantly revised in an iterative process between theoretical and performance models. The resulting model will potentially provide clinicians with information about the type of patient operations necessary for a therapeutic intervention to be effective or for a good outcome to be achieved. Further, such models have clear implications for training and the manualization of therapies. This overall research approach requires the intensive analysis of concrete change performances via two methods: first, the intensive observation and measurement of in-session behaviour, and secondly, accessing practitioner and client subjective recall of their experience (Greenberg, 1999).

A further initiative within Generation IV research has been the development of the concept of responsiveness. This initiative has been driven by the failure of previous research methods to confirm the importance of process variables that are self-evidently central to practitioners – and thereby perpetuating the divide between research and practice. The approach of responsiveness has been summarized as follows: 'We use the term *responsiveness* to describe behavior that is affected by emerging context, including emerging perceptions of others' characteristics and behavior. Insofar as therapist and client respond to each other, responsiveness implies a dynamic relationship between variables, involving bidirectional causation and feedback loops' (Stiles et al., 1998: 439). This approach is based on clinical experience which has assumed that it is not only an issue of *what* intervention a therapist makes but also a matter of *when* and *how* to offer an intervention. Accordingly, the therapist needs to be responsive to the individual client's needs at any given time in treatment within the broader context of the client's history and therapeutic progress. Hence, offering an interpretation may be helpful, but only in certain situations (influenced by history and progress). The concept of responsiveness has crucial methodological implications because it lays the basis for explanations as to why the research literature has failed to yield stable associations between outcome and apparently important process variables.

A key feature of Generation IV process research has been the investment in developing and disseminating qualitative methodologies that would underpin and serve the development of a knowledge base. Hill and colleagues have explicated the components, procedures and evaluation criteria for consensual qualitative research (CQR; Hill et al., 1997). They list the components as comprising the use of open-ended questions to collect data and using words to describe phenomena (i.e. as opposed to diagnostic labels). The approach invests in studying a small number of cases intensively and with an emphasis on the contribution of context. Decisions are made via consensus within a team and auditors are used to 'check' decisions which are verified against the raw data. The procedures comprise the developing and coding domains, constructing central themes, and then developing categories to reflect consistencies across cases. The results are evaluated against a range of criteria including the trustworthiness of the method, the coherence of results, representativeness of the results in relation to the sample, the utility of the results and their replicability across differing samples. Similarly, Elliott and colleagues have produced 'evolving guidelines' for the publication of qualitative research studies in psychology which are highly applicable to psychotherapy research (Elliott et al., 1999). A central aim of their work has been to legitimize qualitative research and generate more appropriate reviews of qualitative research and increase aspects of quality control.

Although outcomes research captures the attention of funding agencies and governments, practitioners will always be drawn to the richness of qualitative approaches which investigate the processes of therapy. This trend is evidenced by the appearance of substantial texts covering the domain of process work. Examples include texts on the contribution of narrative to psychotherapy (e.g., Angus and McLeod, 2004) and on the core processes in brief psychodynamic therapy (e.g., Charman, 2004).

Overall, Generation IV has moved outcome and process research in the direction of the practitioner and attempted to combine process and outcome work into a single activity. In this way, change is seen as the process of achieving small outcomes that in turn become processes working towards further outcomes. The process methods used to achieve this are increasingly drawing on qualitative approaches while outcomes work has prioritized the individual in the context of social norms.

PART II: METHODS, OUTCOMES AND PROCESSES – RESEARCH IN BRITAIN

It is clear from the work reported above that a considerable proportion of research has derived from the United States. In addition, there has always been a strong research tradition in continental Europe although it is only recently that this is becoming accessible through publications in the English language (see the journal *Psychotherapy Research*). Although it might be thought that research in Britain would be very much a poor relation, there is a wealth of high-quality research which has been, and currently is being, carried out. The aim of the second part of this chapter is to provide an overview of past and present work on individual psychotherapy research in Britain employing the same structure as in the first part of this chapter.

Generation I

Initial response to Eysenck
Generation I research began in Britain, as elsewhere, with Eysenck's (1952) critique of the effectiveness of psychotherapy. The response in Britain came from work by Malan and his colleagues based at the Tavistock Clinic who investigated rates of spontaneous remission in 45 cases of untreated people presenting with neurotic symptoms (Malan et al., 1968, 1975). Malan and his colleagues found that while 49 per cent of clients had improved using symptomatic criteria, only 24 per cent had done so when using dynamic criteria. However, the generalizability of these findings is compromised by the highly selective nature of the sample. Malan also carried out two series of studies on analytic psychotherapy (Malan, 1963, 1976). In the first of these, Malan (1963) investigated a sample of patients in which psychodynamic formulations were devised for all clients based on disturbances in their social relationships which required a resolution between the id and the superego. Malan assessed therapy according to whether patients improved in their social relations consequent on their symptom improvement. Of the 21 patients in the sample, five met the criterion for substantial improvement. In the second series of studies, Malan (1976) studied the outcome of a further 30 clients and found significant improvement in five. In particular, he found a

significant association between outcome and interpretations linking transference with patient or sibling. In reality, the value of these two studies lies more in their attempt to study the material of psychotherapy by keeping closely to the clinical material rather than as definitive studies of the effectiveness of psychoanalytic therapy. Ironically, therefore, they might almost be seen to have come full circle and sit within Generation IV research.

The advent of meta-analytic techniques provided the field with a much-needed procedure for summarizing findings in a quantitative and replicable fashion. Following Smith and Glass's (1977) meta-analytic publication, Shapiro and Shapiro (1982) replicated and refined the analysis. They analysed the effects of 143 outcome studies in which two or more treatments were compared with a control group. The mean effect size for treated versus untreated groups approached one standard deviation unit (slightly higher than the 0.85 effect size obtained by Smith and Glass). When they compared a smaller data set in which two active treatments were compared with each other, they found cognitive and certain multimodal behavioural treatments to be superior. However, they very clearly pointed out that much of this research was analogue and hence unrepresentative of clinical practice.

The extension of Generation I outcome research has been continued by its application in more clinically challenging problems. For example, the treatment versus no-treatment (i.e. wait-list) design has been used to evaluate the effect of CBT in the treatment of hypochondriasis. Warwick, Clark, Cobb and Salkovskis (1996) randomly assigned 32 patients to CBT or a no-treatment wait-list control. Results indicated that people receiving CBT showed significantly greater improvements than those in the wait-list control group on all therapist, assessor and patient – bar one – completed measures. These gains were maintained at three-month follow-up.

Generation II

Outcome research

The meta-analysis reported above (and limitations identified in it) led to a series of comparative studies evaluating different modes of therapies carried out by Shapiro and colleagues (see Shapiro et al., 1991). A programmatic series of studies was devised to evaluate both the outcome of these therapies as well as what was effective (i.e. processes) within each therapy. The first Sheffield Psychotherapy Project (Shapiro and Firth, 1987) compared eight-session phases of prescriptive (cognitive-behavioural) and exploratory (psychodynamic-interpersonal) therapy in which 40 professional and managerial workers diagnosed as depressed or anxious received either eight sessions of prescriptive followed by eight sessions of exploratory, or the same two therapies in the reverse order. All clients saw the same therapist throughout therapy. Findings showed a slight advantage to prescriptive therapy as well as an advantage to the initial phase (i.e. first eight sessions) of a 16-session therapy. This slight advantage to prescriptive over exploratory therapy was also obtained in the larger Second Sheffield Psychotherapy Project but only on one out of seven client self-report measures (SPP2; Shapiro et al., 1994). The design called for 120 white-collar workers, diagnosed as depressed, to be randomly assigned to one of the four treatment conditions: either psychodynamic-interpersonal (PI) or cognitive-behavioural (CB) therapy delivered in either eight- or 16-session durations. The study also found that 16 sessions was only superior to eight-sessions for those patients presenting with more severe levels of depression (as measured by the Beck Depression Inventory or BDI). Follow-up data at one year showed that patients in the 8PI condition were faring worse than those in the other three treatment conditions (Shapiro et al., 1995). It was also found that clients presenting with cluster C personality disorders had significantly poorer outcomes than clients without a cluster C personality disorder following PI therapy but not CB therapy (Hardy et al., 1995). The SPP2 has been extended to NHS settings in a Medical Research Council (MRC)/NHS collaborative study acting as a replication (Barkham et al., 1996). The effectiveness of treatments was found to be similar to that of SPP2 with the exception that patients had not maintained their gains at three-month follow-up. Scott and Watkins (2004) have provided an update on psychological treatments for depression and on cognitive therapy for the treatment of depression.

The effectiveness of psychotherapy has also been evaluated against other forms of clinical management. This applies particularly in clients diagnosed with anorexia nervosa or bulimia nervosa. In one study of severe anorexia nervosa, clients were randomly assigned to either 12 sessions of dietary advice or 12 sessions of combined individual and family psychotherapy (Hall and Crisp, 1987). At one-year follow-up, the dietary advice group showed significant weight gain. In contrast, while clients receiving the combined psychotherapy did not obtain a statistically significant improvement in weight gain, they did make significant improvements in their sexual and social adjustment. In another study of bulimia nervosa, 92 women diagnosed as bulimics were randomly assigned to one of three treatment conditions (cognitive-behavioural, behavioural, and group therapy) while a further 20 women were assigned to a waiting-list control group (Freeman et al., 1988). All three treatments were effective compared with the control group. The researchers predicted that cognitive-behavioural therapy would be superior to the other two active treatments. However, where differences did occur, they tended to favour behaviour therapy.

The efficacy of cognitive therapy has been extensively investigated. Teasdale has written extensively on a model of understanding depression within a cognitive-behavioural framework (Teasdale et al., 1984). Through both theoretical (Teasdale, 1985) and empirical (Fennell and Teasdale, 1987) work, Teasdale has developed a model of depression in which 'depression about depression' is a central component. Teasdale (1985) argues that depression about depression is best attacked by helping clients to view it as a problem to be solved rather than evidence of personal inadequacy. To test out this hypothesis, Fennell and

Teasdale (1987) investigated the process of change in outpatients with major depressive disorder. Cognitive therapy was compared to treatment as usual. Cognitive therapy produced marked improvement within the initial two-week period which was maintained through the course of treatment. The study showed that when fast responders were analysed between the two treatment groups (cognitive therapy vs. treatment as usual), only the good responders in the cognitive therapy group maintained their level of improvement. Establishing predictors of improvement is an important aim of psychotherapy research. By detailed session-by-session analysis, Fennell and Teasdale (1987) found the major differentiating factor between high and low responders to be clients' responsiveness to a booklet about depression. Clients who responded positively to the booklet improved most quickly. The authors argued that this was because the booklet addressed the issue of being 'depressed about their depression'.

Evaluations of the comparative effectiveness of cognitive therapy with pharmacotherapy have been carried out by Blackburn (for review, see Blackburn, 1995). Findings for hospital patients presenting with depression, although not statistically significant, tended to support the view that combined drug and cognitive therapy was more effective than cognitive therapy alone which was, in turn, more effective than drug treatment alone (e.g. Blackburn et al., 1981). However, this pattern of findings did not hold for general practice clients. Rather, patients receiving pharmacotherapy alone did significantly worse than the other two client groups, and further, there was little difference between the combined therapy and cognitive therapy groups. These findings suggested that drug and cognitive therapies failed to have the additive effect in the general practice group which occurred in the hospital patient group. Blackburn, Eunson and Bishop (1986) reported on the recurrence rate at two years for cognitive therapy, medication, and combined. Results showed appreciably lower rates of recurrence for cognitive therapy alone (23 per cent) and cognitive therapy/drug combination (21 per cent) as compared with medication alone (78 per cent).

A series of studies of cognitive therapy for anxiety have been carried out by Butler and colleagues. Butler, Cullington, Hibbert, Klimes and Gelder (1987a) treated a total of 45 clients meeting criteria for a diagnosis of generalised anxiety disorder (GAD), with 22 receiving anxiety management immediately while a further 23 received the same treatment after a three-month wait period. The results suggested that clients in the immediate treatment group improved significantly more than the matched group waiting for treatment. When the wait group received treatment, a similar improvement was obtained. A subsequent study treated 57 patients diagnosed with GAD and compared three treatment conditions: cognitive-behavioural therapy (CBT), behaviour therapy (BT), and a wait list (Butler et al., 1991). Results showed CBT to be superior to BT alone (relaxation training plus graded exposure), with both treatments superior to the wait-list control. Whilst the study had relatively low statistical power to detect differences between the two active treatments and the wait-list group (19 patients initially in each of the three conditions), the fact that differences were found for

CBT over BT attests to the robustness of the findings. Hence, addressing the cognitions of those patients presenting with GAD is clearly beneficial. The authors note that this is one of the few examples where one form of psychological treatment has been found to be more effective than another as a treatment for GAD. However, inspection of the pre-post change effect sizes on one of the criterion measures of anxiety, the Beck Anxiety Inventory, suggests that it may not be so much a story of CBT being superior (the pre-post ES of 1.35 is standard) but more a story of BT being inadequate (as indicated by the pre-post ES of 0.65) and hence not a treatment of choice with GAD.

Salkovskis (1995) provides a summary of how cognitive-behavioural therapy has advanced in the area of panic disorder together with a very useful 'hourglass' model of how psychotherapy research progresses through various stages. Following on from Butler et al.'s (1991) assertion of the non-equivalence of psychotherapies, Salkovskis states:

> The myth of psychotherapy equivalence is not helpful in the process of refinement. Like the idea that all swans are white, the range of exceptions is now too striking to be ignored. As more knowledge is acquired about maintaining factors involved in different types of psychological problems, the rate of progress increases. Of course, where research is not guided by attempts to understand the idiosyncratic nature of the factors involved in the maintenance of such problems, outcome studies may show that there is no difference between therapies. (1995: 224)

In a comparative trial, Blowers, Cobb and Mathews (1987) studied a sample of 66 clients diagnosed as suffering from generalized anxiety. Clients were randomly assigned to one of three conditions: wait list, non-directive counselling, or anxiety management training (combined relaxation and brief cognitive therapy). Surprisingly, perhaps, there were few significant differences in outcome between non-directive counselling and anxiety management training. Blowers et al. summarized their findings as follows: 'A reasonable conclusion would therefore be that anxiety management training is indeed effective, but that its superiority to a less structured and less directive alternative remains to be proven' (1987: 500). However, as Morley (1988) suggests, it can be no surprise that such studies find little differences between anxiety management training and non-directive counselling. These studies are not really evaluating cognitive therapy but rather cognitive components divorced from their behavioural concomitants.

The comparative effectiveness of cognitive therapy (CT) and other interventions has been investigated (Clark et al., 1994). A total of 64 patients were allocated (the report does not state that this was carried out randomly) to either CT, applied relaxation therapy, imipramine or a waiting list. Patients on the waiting list received no treatment for the initial three months and were then randomly allocated to one of the three treatment conditions. Patients in the CT or applied relaxation conditions received up to 12 sessions in the first three months and up to three booster sessions in the next three months. Results showed CT to be the most effective treatment. However, as with the Butler study, finding CT to be superior is less impressive when the 'competing' therapy may not be as powerful as it should. Blanes and Raven (1995), in a review of psychotherapy of panic disorder, questioned the findings from Clark et al. given that over 80 per cent of their sample had some degree of agoraphobia and that the treatment of choice for this problem is systematic self-exposure with homework diaries.

A multinational study investigating treatments for panic disorder with agoraphobia has been carried out (Marks et al., 1993). The study compared the combination of alprazolam and exposure to either treatment alone for patients with a diagnosis of panic disorder. A total of 154 patients were randomly allocated to one of four treatment conditions: alprazolam and exposure, alprazolam and relaxation, placebo and exposure, placebo and relaxation. Patients in all four treatment conditions improved when evaluation of panic was used as the single outcome indicator. In brief, the findings indicated that while alprazolam and exposure were more effective than placebo, the effect size for exposure was approximately twice that for alprazolam, with the gains from exposure being maintained whilst those for alprazolam were not.

In a development of the Generation I design reported earlier (see Warwick et al., 1996), Clark and colleagues extended their investigations into the effective treatment of hypochondriasis (Clark et al., 1998). The study comprised 48 patients randomly assigned to one of three groups: cognitive therapy, behavioural stress management (BSM), or no-treatment wait-list control group. Patients in the last group were subsequently assigned randomly to one of the treatment conditions at the end of the waiting period. Both active treatments were more effective than the waiting list – a finding derived from a Generation I comparison. However, comparisons between the two active treatments showed that CT was more effective than BSM on specific measures of hypochondriasis but not for comparisons of general mood disturbance either at mid- or end of treatment.

There is an increasing empirically based literature on treatments for people presenting with psychosis. Studies have developed cognitive-behavioural strategies for problem-solving and coping (Tarrier et al., 1990, 1993). Cognitive-behavioural principles have also been developed and applied to aspects of psychosis (Chadwick and Lowe, 1990; Kingdon and Turkington, 1991). CT has been evaluated in the acute phase of psychosis in a trial carried out by Drury and colleagues (Drury et al., 1996). A total of 40 clients were assigned to either a multi-component CBT programme or a social recreational programme with informal support, both conditions acting as an adjunct to standard care. The social recreational programme provided clients with access to the same therapists as the CT group, thereby going some way towards controlling for common factors. Clients in the CT condition showed a significantly faster rate of decline in symptoms over the initial 12 weeks of the intervention and significantly fewer symptoms at weeks 7 and 12 compared with clients in the alternative condition. At nine months, only 5 per cent of clients in the CT condition showed moderate or severe residual symptoms compared with 56 per cent of clients in the social recreational programme (Drury et al., 1996). A follow-up at five years showed no significant differences in relapse rate, symptoms or insight between the groups. However, clients in the CT group did show significantly greater perceived 'control over illness'. In addition, for those clients who had experienced no more than one relapse in the follow-up period, self-reported residual delusional beliefs and observer-rated hallucinations and delusions were significantly less for those people in the CT group (Drury et al., 2000).

A pilot control trial of CBT for drug-resistant psychosis has been reported by Garety, Kuipers, Fowler, Chamberlain and Dunn (1994). Patients meeting a diagnosis of schizophrenia or schizo-affective psychosis and who presented with unremitting (i.e. for a period of at least six months) drug-resistant positive psychotic symptoms were assigned (but not randomly) to either the treatment group or a wait-list control group. Patients in the treatment group received on average 16 weekly sessions of cognitive-behavioural therapy (Fowler et al., 1994) and were found to report significantly less intense conviction in the delusional thoughts than the control group at end of treatment. Overall, the treatment group fared better than the no-treatment control group. Given that this was obtained using very low statistical power (a maximum of 13 treated vs 7 no-treatment patients), it is likely that this low power masks differences which might actually be found to exist, given adequate statistical power.

The results of the full trial have been published in a series of articles (see Freeman et al., 1998; Garety et al., 1997; Kuipers et al., 1997, 1998). A total of 60 subjects presenting with at least one positive and distressing symptom of medication-resistant psychosis were randomly allocated to one of two conditions: cognitive-behaviour therapy plus standard care, or standard care only. Hence, the study investigated the added value of CBT as an adjunct to routine standard care. Therapy lasted nine months and was targeted to the presentation of each individual patient. Results indicated that significant improvements were found only in the combined treatment group, with a 25 per cent reduction in scores on the Brief Psychiatric Rating Scale. No other measures suggested any significant change. There was a comparatively low drop-out rate (11 per cent) and a majority (80 per cent) expressed satisfaction with the treatment they received. Some of the design and analysis features of this series reflect Generation III research, such as consideration of treatment responders and drop-out rates. An overview of individual CBT in the treatment of hallucinations and delusions has been carried out (see Haddock et al., 1998).

Fairburn and colleagues have carried out a series of studies on the effects of psychotherapy on bulimia nervosa (e.g. Fairburn et al., 1991). Fairburn, Jones, Peveler, Hope and O'Connor (1993) compared cognitive-behavioural therapy (CBT) with interpersonal therapy (IPT) and also with behaviour therapy (BT; construed as a simplified version of CBT): 25 patients were allocated to each treatment condition, with patients receiving 19 sessions over 18 weeks. The results indicated a high rate of attrition and withdrawal (48 per cent) among patients assigned to BT with few patients in this condition meeting the criteria for a good outcome. By contrast, patients in the CBT and IPT treatments made substantial, lasting, and broadly equivalent changes across the various domains measured. Interestingly, while IPT showed the lowest percentage of patients meeting criteria at the end of treatment, the rate increased monotonically across the three post-treatment assessments such that it was the highest (44 per cent) at one-year follow-up compared with 36 per cent and 20 per cent for CBT and BT respectively. A follow-up study of 89 patients, assessed on average just under six years following treatment, from two consecutive studies (Fairburn et al., 1986, 1993) found that patients who had received either CBT or interpersonal therapy (IPT or focal) had a better prognosis than patients receiving behaviour therapy (Fairburn et al., 1995).

Roth and Fonagy (1996) identified psychotherapeutic interventions that have demonstrable benefit to patients (i.e. an evidence base) and also attempted to draw implications for their delivery within the NHS. In drawing attention to a number of limitations in the available research literature, they identified systemic and psychodynamic models as requiring research effort. They also identified a number of methodological limitations which should be noted, including generalizing results from highly controlled randomized controlled trials, the ambiguity of findings from less well-controlled studies, the relative absence of long-term follow-up, statistical analyses, and most importantly in their view, the complexity of mental health problems and issues of classification raised by such complexity. They concluded that meta-analyses and qualitative reviews of psychological treatments for depression strongly support CBT even for severe depression, and that they were superior to alternative psychotherapeutic treatments. However, they added the observation that 'the range of contrast therapies is sometimes rather limited and rarely includes psychodynamic treatments'. This reiterates the point made previously that some of the advantages shown for CBT may arise as a function of the weaker alternative treatment selected rather than the superiority *per se* of CBT.

The research reported so far has been based within a 'pure' treatment method (either CBT or PI [psychodynamic-interpersonal], or BT). However, there has also been an increase in integrative therapies. For example, a comparison between more traditional 'interpretative' therapy versus cognitive-analytic therapy (CAT: Ryle, 1990) has been carried out (Brockman et al., 1987). Although the overall findings reported no difference, one aim of this study was to evaluate effectiveness as carried out by trainees. Accordingly, it could be argued that the finding of no difference is a function of inexperienced therapists rather than similarly effective treatments. It is still valid to conclude that the two treatments are equally effective with trainee therapists. However, as the authors acknowledge, an unequal attrition (i.e. dropout) rate led to the two groups differing in severity level at intake. Because the two groups were not equivalent in severity at intake, rigorous comparisons of the comparative effectiveness of conditions is problematic. Subsequent reports on CAT have comprised single case studies showing the impact of CAT on patients presenting with borderline personality disorders (e.g. Ryle, 1995; Ryle and Beard, 1993).

Shapiro, Barkham, Reynolds, Hardy and Stiles (1992) combined prescriptive (cognitive-behavioural) and exploratory (psychodynamic-interpersonal) therapies by administering them as 'pure' therapies within a session but alternating within certain constraints across the course of therapy in response to a match between client requirements and a particular overarching integrative model (the assimilation model). The outcome for this single case was successful but requires replication. Overall, there is a dearth of direct evidence for the equivalence in efficacy, let alone superiority, of integrative therapies. Much of the argument in support of their use derives indirectly from the equivalence of outcomes. In addition, it is not clear that skills and expertise gained in one particular method of delivery transfer to a more integrated method without additional training. The current interest in, and articles emanating from, this area is considerable and reflects the fact that integrative therapies are probably more palatable to practitioners than pure treatment methods. Following a major workshop which focused on the research required to move this area forward, little empirical work has been carried out (Wolfe and Goldfried, 1988). Indeed, considerably more work is needed in order to provide hard data on the comparative effectiveness of integrative therapies.

Fonagy (1995) has provided a very useful summary of problems emanating from outcome research but states that without them we would not know what the optimal effects of treatments would be. Taking this forward, he argues for outcome studies (i.e. research from Generations I and II) to be enhanced by clinical audit, thereby bringing it into the realm of every practitioner: 'outcome studies and clinical audit should be performed in tandem. The first will identify potentially useful interventions which may be adopted by clinicians for specific disorders, and the second will show clinicians how effective they are in implementing these procedures' (1995: 176). He continues: 'Without outcome studies, the design of clinical services will lack strategic direction; without clinical audit, services may be massively distorted in unknown ways based on findings of little relevance to work at ground level' (ibid.). The domain of clinical audit is very much to the fore at present and it makes eminent sense that this agenda be carried forward collaboratively in the context of rigorous research in the area of psychotherapy.

Process and therapist skills

Generation II process research differs appreciably in Britain from the United States where Carl Rogers acted as a central motivator for research activity. A series of studies carried out by Shapiro (1969, 1970, 1973, 1976) which investigated the role of the facilitative conditions in psychotherapy offered little support for the view that they played a central role in accounting for change. However, later work investigating the role of various verbal response modes found 'exploration' (a response between interpretation and reflection) to be associated with client and helper experiences of perceived empathy (Barkham and Shapiro, 1986).

An ongoing programme of psychotherapy teaching and training has been implemented and evaluated in Manchester, largely through the work of Goldberg, Hobson, Margison and colleagues. This work has arisen as a result of its being a regional centre for psychotherapy. Consistent with its teaching priority, there has been considerable research into teaching specific psychotherapeutic methods to other caregivers, in particular, the development of the Conversational Model of psychotherapy, together with a comprehensive teaching programme (Goldberg et al., 1984; Maguire et al., 1984). The Conversational Model of therapy has been developed over the past 30 years as a therapeutic method for dealing with people who have experienced difficulties in their interpersonal relationships. Hobson, in some ways reflecting the impact of Rogers, not only developed the model, but has also been central in advocating its investigation through video-recording and research. This method has been packaged for teaching purposes and has been shown to be transferable to junior doctors (Goldberg et al., 1984). The development of teaching methods was paralleled by the development of manuals for specified therapies (a defining hallmark of Generation II research). For example, Startup and Shapiro (1993) carried out an adherence study on the Second Sheffield Psychotherapy Project in which each of 220 sessions (110 sessions from each of CB and PI therapies) were coded by two people according to a rating manual. These authors found that 97 per cent of sessions were correctly assigned.

The extension of psychotherapy skills to people in a primary care setting emphasizes not only the increasing adoption of a psychosocial model of presenting problems but also the notion that providing primary caregivers with psychotherapeutic skills results in an increase in the detection of psychological illness. For example, Gask (Gask and McGrath, 1989) has worked extensively on the application of psychotherapeutic skills by general practitioners dealing with issues such as AIDS. Research has also focused on therapist difficulties (Davis et al., 1987). These authors devised a taxonomy of nine categories: using these they were able to classify reliably therapists' difficulties. The three most commonly occurring difficulties were therapists feeling *threatened* (i.e. the therapist feels a need to protect self against the client), feeling *puzzled* (i.e. the therapist cannot see how best to proceed), and *damaging* (i.e. the therapist feels that he or she may be injuring the client). Most interestingly, therapists showed internal consistency in the patterns of difficulties experienced. This led the authors to argue that these profiles would be highly related to therapists' personalities and consequently might help identify potential counter-transference problems for different therapists. This work is ongoing.

Generation III

Cost-effectiveness and service delivery

There is currently considerable interest, both economically and clinically, in evaluating the cost-effectiveness of the psychotherapies (e.g. Healey and Knapp,

1995). For example, McGrath and Lawson (1987) have argued for the legitimacy of assessing the benefits of psychotherapy from an economic standpoint and conclude that it is possible to justify the provision of psychotherapy within the NHS on economic grounds. At a broad level, Parry (1992) has identified a range of issues which are pertinent in devising cost-efficient psychotherapy services.

A major feature of the studies detailed in Generation II is their attempt to combine both internal validity (i.e. the attempt to minimize bias, usually through random assignment of clients to particular conditions) and extrinsic validity (i.e. sampling a clinical rather than a student population). Perhaps the best single indicator of such attempts is the use of random allocation of clients to treatment conditions (RCT). Often, however, it is not possible to do this either for ethical or for practical reasons. When it is not possible to incorporate high components of both forms of validity, researchers face a choice: they must either employ ana-logue studies (e.g. studying students with test anxiety) in which internal validity is high but which are problematic in relation to generalizing the findings to clin-ical populations, or use more naturalistic studies (describing and evaluating clients referred to outpatient settings) which do not permit the researcher to manipulate specific variables. Naturalistic designs have been used and are a logical means for evaluating service delivery systems. A study using naturalistic design and studying inpatients has been carried out by Denford, Schachter, Temple, Kind and Rosser (1983). These workers completed a retrospective study of 28 successive admissions for inpatient psychotherapy at the Cassel Hospital, a community using a combination of both individual and community psy-chotherapeutic methods. Their findings suggested that 'to maximise the propor-tion of patients who improve, the hospital should be inclined to accept patients who have neurotic rather than borderline or psychotic psychopathology, those who appear considerably depressed, those with a history of minimal out-patient psychiatric treatment, and possibly those judged to be of superior intelligence' (Denford et al., 1983: 235–6). An important difference between successful clients when compared with clients rated as failures and dropouts was that moti-vation for insight and change was high in 50 per cent of successful cases and lower in both failed (38 per cent) and dropout clients (13 per cent). Blind ratings of motivation tended to distinguish success and failed groups at triage, a finding consistent with the results obtained by Malan (1963, 1976).

Another retrospective study was carried out by Keller (1984) who investigated the applicability of brief psychotherapeutic methods developed at the Tavistock Clinic in NHS outpatient psychotherapy clinics. Fifteen clients in all were treated but results did not obtain statistical significance. At non-significant lev-els, however, the results indicated that outcome was better for those clients who experienced high levels of distress subjectively but who functioned well exter-nally. In addition, outcome was better for those clients who had a supportive relationship outside therapy and for whom a psychodynamic focus could be formulated. Keller argued that these findings generally substantiate Malan's (1976) work. Interestingly, this study exemplifies the difficulties of practitioners carrying out research. In their favour, these practitioners set up a workshop to provide a framework for the participating practitioners to adapt their methods to the clients they saw in their own practices as well as providing an environment for research to be implemented and carried out. However, from the researcher's viewpoint it is difficult to have much confidence in the findings: they are non-significant, based on a small sample, and contaminated by other influences (including rater bias). In addition, the finding that more distressed clients fare better (a finding also reported by Denford et al., 1983) may be a function of scores regressing to the mean. Accordingly, this phenomenon should always be borne in mind when considering improvement in high scorers.

Research has also occurred with specialized populations who are of particular concern to practitioners in service delivery settings. For example, the treatment of survivors of childhood sexual abuse (CSA) has been reviewed by Cahill et al. (1991), who concluded that virtually all publications in this area to date take the form of therapists' experience of treating patients. They conclude that what is needed is the application of empirical research methodology to establish the most effective treatments. In a study of six survivors of CSA, Clarke and Llewelyn (1994) report on the changes achieved by patients following cognitive-analytic therapy. Similarly, Birchwood (1992) has proposed practical intervention strategies to help reduce the occurrence of florid schizophrenic relapse where the emphasis is on providing an early intervention service.

The issue of cost-effectiveness has been addressed in several studies in which very brief interventions have been devised (i.e. therapy is construed as assessment). One model delivers therapy in the form of two sessions one week apart and a third session three months later. This generic model of therapy, termed two-plus-one therapy, has been evaluated in a large randomized controlled trial (Barkham et al., 1999). A total of 116 clients experiencing a range of subsyndromal depression received two-plus-one sessions of either CB or PI therapy either immediately or after a four-week delay (the latter acting as a control condition). The initial advantage for patients in the immediate group disappeared once clients in the delayed condition received treatment (i.e. offering treatment immediately relieved distress quicker but the other clients 'caught up'). In terms of the comparative treatments, there were no significant differences in outcomes between CB and PI therapies at the end of treatment. However, at one-year follow-up, there was a significant advantage to CBT on the Beck Depression Inventory. Other features of the reporting in this study – for example utilizing reliable and clinically significant methods to show that approximately two-thirds of clients met such stringent criteria for change – reflect Generation IV research.

Other clinicians have devised variants of the original model; for example, a model of intervention comprising a three-plus-one design for patients presenting with greater severity (Aveline, 1995). Preliminary results based on analyses midway through this latter study, which compared a brief intervention and follow-up with a standard assessment for psychotherapy procedure, suggest that there are more discharges in the brief intervention model than in the standard assessment, together with greater change at the four-month follow-up. One consequence of the higher rate of discharge arising from the brief intervention model is that if this were adopted, it would help decrease the waiting time for patients prior to starting therapy. However, as Aveline (1995) correctly cautions, care should be taken in analysing results midway through a trial, particularly if those results themselves are less than clear-cut. Such models are informed by the dose-effect curve which, for example, would predict 30 per cent of clients to show improvement after two sessions. Interests in cost-effectiveness are therefore focused on identifying, like Fennell and Teasdale (1987), those clients who are able to respond beneficially to such treatment models. This is consistent with attempts to match treatment-specific delivery models with clearly defined presenting problems.

There have also been examples of established CT interventions being adapted to make them briefer (more cost efficient). Clark and colleagues adapted CT for panic disorder – normally comprising 12–15 one-hour sessions – to be administered in five one-hour sessions by making extensive use of inter-session work and self-study modules (Clark et al., 1999). A total of 43 patients were randomly allocated to one of three conditions: full CT, brief CT, or a three-month wait list. Both full and brief interventions were superior to the wait list – in itself a Generation I comparison – but it is the comparison between the full and brief versions which is of importance here. Clark and his colleagues found no significant differences between the two versions, both of which had large and very similar effect sizes.

However, cost-effectiveness is not synonymous with brevity. For example, while Freeman et al. (1988) acknowledged that improvement rate for bulimics in their study (77 per cent) was marginally less than in other studies, they argued that the greater intensity offered by other treatments (e.g. being seen several times a week or for half a day at a time) for marginally greater improvement was not necessarily cost-effective. Similarly, Peveler and Fairburn (1989) argued that while their treatment for a case of anorexia nervosa with diabetes mellitus lasted one year, 'the treatment was of relatively low intensity, amounting to just under 40 hours of therapist time in total'. More salient, perhaps, was the fact that the diabetes required only routine specialist input and no hospital admission, making the treatment cost-effective when compared with the potential cost of a single hospital admission.

Guthrie, Moorey, Margison, Barker, Palmer, McGrath, Tomenson and Creed (1999) evaluated the cost-effectiveness of brief psychodynamic-interpersonal therapy in 110 high users of psychiatric services. The sample was defined as patients who had made no improvement in their psychological symptoms. Their results showed that brief PI therapy for this particular patient sample resulted in significant improvement in their psychological status as well as a reduction in health care utilization and health care costs in the six months following treatment. The issue of cost-effectiveness has become an increasingly central issue in the design and delivery of psychotherapy services.

The impetus behind establishing effective psychological interventions in primary care has seen several programmes of research. One programme combining the issues of brief interventions and cost issues set in primary care has been carried out by Mynors-Wallis and colleagues (Gath and Mynors-Wallis, 1997; Mynors-Wallis, 1996). A series of studies have been carried out on problem-solving treatment (PST) and observations include that PST can be effectively delivered in primary care by a range of professionals (e.g. psychiatrists, nurses) but that it may be more expensive than usual treatment (by GPs) in primary care as indicated by direct costs. However, when indirect savings are considered, then greater cost savings are likely. A Cochrane review carried out by Rowland and colleagues (Rowland et al., 2000, 2001) found four randomized and controlled patient preference trials comparing *bona fide* counselling in primary care with usual general practitioner care. Findings suggested that clients receiving counselling had significantly better psychological symptom levels after their counselling compared with those receiving standard GP care, as indicated by an ES difference of 0.30.

A large outcome study – the London–Manchester trial – has compared non-directive counselling, CBT, and usual general practitioner care for the presentation of depression in primary care and is an exemplar of the combination of efficacy (Ward et al., 2000) and cost-effectiveness (Bower et al., 2000) issues that is a hallmark of Generation III research. A total of 464 patients took part in this prospective controlled trial which utilized both randomized and patient preference allocation arms. Patients who had a preference as to which treatment they preferred selected that treatment condition; those who stated they had no preference were randomized to one of the three treatment conditions. A total of 137 patients selected their own treatment, 197 patients were randomly assigned to one of the three treatment conditions, and 130 were randomized to one of the two psychological therapies (in which patients received upwards of 12 sessions). At four months, patients in the two psychological therapies showed greater gains on the BDI than those randomized to usual GP care (even though all groups improved over time). But interestingly, there were no significant differences between the two psychological therapies (i.e. non-directive counselling and CBT) at four months and no significant differences between all three conditions at 12 months. The additional cost-effectiveness analysis (Bower et al., 2000) showed that there were no significant differences in direct costs, production losses or societal costs between the three treatment conditions at either four or 12 months. It was concluded that the two psychological interventions were significantly more cost-effective in the short term (at four months) as patients showed greater improvement at no additional cost. However, all cost and clinical differences disappeared at 12 months.

The evidence drawn from both Generation II and Generation III has provided the basis for the development of the evidence-based approach to the psychological therapies. Rowland and Goss (2000) have presented the multifaceted components of an evidence-based approach to counselling and the psychological therapies. The main drivers for evidence-based health care are presented (Baker and Kleijnen, 2000), together with reviews of policy (Ferguson and Russell, 2000), economic issues (Maynard, 2000), as well as an overview of evidence-based psychotherapy (Parry, 2000). Methodological issues are presented, including those pertaining to RCTs (Bower and King, 2000), efficacy versus effectiveness (Barkham and Mellor-Clark, 2000), and the contribution of qualitative research (McLeod, 2000). The approach to clinical practice guidelines has been addressed by Cape and Parry (2000) and draws on the publication by the Department of Health of the *Treatment Choice in Psychological Therapies and Counselling: Evidence Based Clinical Practice Guideline* (2001). The *Guideline* was based on a systematic review of the literature and made recommendations on treatment of choice in relation to the following presenting problems: depression, anxiety, panic disorder, social anxiety and phobias, post-traumatic disorders, eating disorders, obsessive-compulsive disorders, and personality disorders. It also included psychological approaches to chronic pain, chronic fatigue, gastrointestinal disorders, and gynaecological presentations. A series of recommendations were made comprising generic points focusing on general principles, and specific points relating to therapies for specific presenting problems. Each recommendation was annotated according to four levels of evidence supporting it: meta-analysis or RCT (Level A); controlled or quasi-experimental study, or extrapolated from level A evidence (Level B), descriptive studies or extrapolated from level B evidence (Level C), and expert committee/clinical experience of respected authority, or extrapolated from level C (Level D). Examples of each level of evidence are presented here.

In relation to the area of initial assessment, it was recommended that 'Psychological therapy should be routinely considered as a treatment option when assessing mental health problems' (Level B evidence 2001: 34). For patient preference, it was recommended that 'Patient preference should inform treatment choice, particularly where the research evidence does not indicate a clear choice of therapy' (Level D evidence: 36). For depressive disorder, it was recommended that 'Depressive disorders may be treated effectively with psychological therapy, with best evidence for cognitive behaviour therapy and interpersonal therapy, and some evidence for a number of other structured therapies, including short-term psychodynamic therapy' (Level A evidence: 37). For personality disorder, it was recommended that 'Structured psychological therapies delivered by skilled practitioners can contribute to the longer-term treatment of personality disorders' (Level C evidence: 38). Of course, setting out recommendations – however scientifically sound – does not guarantee that they will be implemented in all settings, nor that they will be adhered to. So while the aim is to provide guidelines based on the best available evidence in an attempt to ensure that people in need are allocated to appropriate psychological interventions, the whole process requires auditing, evaluation and constant updating. More importantly perhaps, it also requires an educational process at the point at which clients are first assessed and the resources to provide the very interventions that are recommended.

Change pathways

In the study of 'psychotherapeutic process', work on psychoanalytic therapy has been, traditionally, the most difficult to carry out. However, there are studies worthy of note. For example, Moran and Fonagy (1987) carried out a non-experimental single-case study of a diabetic teenager who received psychoanalysis five times weekly for three and a half years. They investigated the relationship between psychoanalytic themes and glycosuria (the presence of sugar in the client's urine). They found that the working through of psychic conflict predicted an improvement in diabetic control, both in the short and in the long term. Of particular importance to the authors were the findings occurring in the short term where, they argued, other common factors could not be viewed as competing explanations. This view appears to counter research evidence attesting to the potency of common factors irrespective of time. Importantly, however, an aim of this study was to attempt to apply scientific rigour to psychoanalytic processes. As the authors state: 'the present study is viewed as an initial step towards the increased systematization of the treatment of psychoanalytic data and ... other workers using similar methodologies may be able to explore psychoanalytic hypotheses which eluded the current authors' (Moran and Fonagy, 1987: 370).

In an attempt to ascertain how cognitive therapy works, Fennell (1983) drew together the purported mechanisms of change in cognitive therapy for depression. She asked three questions: How does cognitive therapy achieve its immediate effect? How does cognitive therapy affect depression over the course of the treatment as a whole? and How are treatment effects maintained over the longer term? In answer to the first question, Fennell (1983) concluded that active thought modification in itself can bring about significant change. In addition, where the intensity or frequency of depressive thinking is reduced, a reduction in severity of depression occurs. In answer to the second question, Fennell concluded that the most powerful strategy for achieving change is a 'close interweaving' of thought-change and behaviour-change. 'Thought-change allows behaviour-change to occur and behaviour-change in turn provides evidence to further counter distorted negative thinking' (1983: 102). The third question is answered by suggesting that long-term improvement will be most effectively achieved with the widest range of clients by training in generalized coping skills rather than modifying assumptions. This is because the modification of underlying assumptions is less easy to acquire and more difficult to implement when depressed. In a study of clients diagnosed as anxious, Butler, Gelder, Hibbert, Cullington and Klimes (1987b) attempted to determine the effective components of anxiety management. These researchers found evidence to suggest that treatment-specific components included the control of anxiety-related cognitions and the confronting of anxiety-provoking situations (as compared with the previous strategy of avoidance).

The attempt to discover the therapeutic ingredients responsible for the effectiveness of psychotherapy has been undertaken in a series of studies deriving from detailed analyses of the first Sheffield Psychotherapy Project (Shapiro and

Firth, 1987). For example, Stiles, Shapiro and Firth-Cozens (1988) investigated the impacts of exploratory and prescriptive sessions. Impacts refer to the participants' evaluations of the immediate effects of the therapy session (their evaluation of the session, how they feel immediately afterwards, etc.). Both therapists and clients rated prescriptive sessions as smoother (i.e. smooth, easy, pleasant, safe) than exploratory sessions. However, while both therapists and clients rated exploratory sessions as rougher, therapists but not clients rated exploratory sessions as deeper (e.g. deep, valuable, full and special). Taken together, these results show different therapies to have different impacts. When these results are combined with the findings that there is a general equivalence of outcome, the most parsimonious explanation is that equivalence 'occurs' after the differing therapies have had their impact. That is, there are different routes (i.e. processes) to achieving broadly similar outcomes with the processes differing as a function of the different goals of therapy.

Common factors and integration

The above sections have addressed particular therapies which are based upon the assumption that they comprise specific techniques which can, or will, account for effective change. By contrast, research into common factors has provided a vehicle for arguing that the effective ingredients of therapy tend to be shared factors (i.e. the therapeutic relationship). Murphy, Cramer and Lillie (1984) asked clients to describe curative factors following individual therapy. Findings showed 'advice' and 'talking to someone interested in my problems' to be elicited from more than half the clients. Further, the study found that 'receiving advice' and 'talking with someone who understands' were both moderately correlated with outcome. The relationship of each of these to outcome accounted for approaching 20 per cent of the outcome variance.

In a study of phobic clients, Bennun and Schindler (1988) investigated therapist and client factors operative within behavioural treatments. Ratings on these factors by clients and therapists were positively correlated with outcome, suggesting that interpersonal variables may contribute to treatment outcome. The results showed that the more positive the participants' ratings of each other after the second session, the greater the amount of change achieved at the end of therapy. Bennun and Schindler concluded: 'Researchers and clinicians should not be too preoccupied with technique; favourable interpersonal conditions are also essential for therapeutic change' (1988: 151). In a study of clients' and therapists' views of therapy, Llewelyn (1988) sampled 40 therapist–client dyads participating in psychological therapy in standard British clinical settings. During the course of therapy, the most frequently reported helpful events for clients were 'reassurance' and 'problem evaluation', while at termination 'problem solution' was the most frequently rated as helpful. By contrast, therapists rated 'insight' as the most common helpful event both during therapy and at termination. These findings suggest that clients and therapists have quite different perceptions of what is helpful during the course of therapy. Clients appeared to value the common ingredients of reassurance and relief. In contrast, therapists valued both the cognitive and affective insight felt to be attained by their clients during therapy. Of course, if insight 'leads' to problem solution, at least in the sense of preceding it, it may be that clients are focusing on the consequences of their insight while therapists value the more personal and dynamic component of insight itself rather than the action arising from it. In the final analysis, it is to be expected that two differing perspectives on the therapeutic process will provide two differing perceptions.

Ryle has carried out research spanning some two decades into psychotherapy. Underlying his work is the aim of establishing an understanding of psychotherapy based within a cognitive framework. This was apparent in his early work using repertory grids. Ryle has developed three important constructs relevant to understanding change (Ryle, 1979): 'dilemmas' (the narrow way in which a client will see the possible alternatives), 'traps' (patterns of behaviour which are based upon and also serve to reinforce negative assumptions about the self), and 'snags' (the avoidance of change due to its effects, real or imagined). Ryle (1980) studied 15 cases in which clients received focused integrated active psychotherapy. The aim was to define therapeutic goals which were specific and individual to clients and yet which referred to underlying cognitive processes as well as to overt symptoms. In general, clients reported improvements both in target complaints as well as in target dilemmas, traps and snags. Results showed that when a change in target dilemmas in the predicted direction occurred, this change was invariably accompanied by a change in the client's cognitive structure as well as in problems targeted at the beginning of therapy. This provided support for Ryle's view that, first, a cognitive framework for understanding psychotherapeutic change is both feasible and informative. Further, Ryle argued that his research counterbalances the more narrow approaches to psychotherapy, stating that attending to deeper cognitive structures enables questions to be answered which have long interested dynamic therapists but which have eluded researchers. It is certainly true that psychotherapy research 'should attend with adequate subtlety ... the fundamental but less easily demonstrated changes aimed for' (Ryle, 1980: 481). These findings have led to the formalization of Ryle's cognitive integration of theory and practice (Ryle, 1982), and more recently, to the development of a form of brief therapy termed cognitive-analytic therapy (CAT).

Generation IV

Clinically meaningful outcome research
In previous research generations, large-scale research studies addressed questions about the 'efficacy' of a particular intervention as delivered under optimal conditions. The results of such studies formed the basis for 'evidence-based practice' which is now required to substantiate the delivery of any psychological (or medical) intervention in service settings. As such, the evidence-based practice

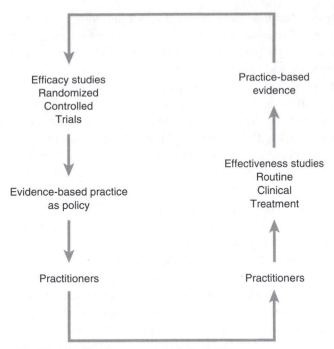

Figure 18.1   The efficacy-effectiveness research model

movement – which applies to all health-related professions – is now a central tenet in all health care delivery (see Parry, 2000). It is the basis upon which government health agencies make recommendations for treatment and is premised on the view that the gold standards of research methodology lie in randomized controlled trials (RCTs) and meta-analytic studies. The findings from these studies are then used to inform practice in routine settings. However, it is a questionable logic that findings derived from research studies carried out under optimal conditions should be adopted as policy and then directly transported 'down' into routine service settings. In contrast to the evidence-based paradigm, there has been an increased focus on developing an evidence base within routine practice. This focus has culminated in the development of a complementary paradigm for accumulating and presenting evidence: 'practice-based evidence'. In contrast to the 'top-down' paradigm of evidence-based practice in which RCTs inform policy, 'practice-based evidence' utilizes a 'bottom-up' paradigm in which 'routine clinical treatment' (RCT) is accumulated in practice settings to derive an evidence base in which practitioners are partners (see Barkham and Mellor-Clark, 2000; Margison et al., 2000). This process is summarized in Figure 18.1, which shows how these two paradigms can inform each other providing they are equally valued. Indeed, it has been argued that they are complementary to each other and that both are required in order to build a robust knowledge base for the psychological therapies (Barkham & Mellor-Clark, 2003). This can also be seen to apply to process research which is grounded in the day-to-day and moment-to-moment work of practitioners. Because each paradigm can be viewed as representing the constituencies of researcher and practitioners respectively, it is likely that it is the combination of the two paradigms which is most likely to form an effective bridge between practice and research in the future.

Within this practice-based paradigm, outcome research activity in the UK has been given real impetus from three differing perspectives. First, as with the field in general, there has been disquiet with the yield from the traditional outcome paradigm employing RCTs. Indeed, there are increasing criticisms of RCTs as the design of choice for investigating the psychological therapies (see Barkham and Mellor-Clark, 2000). Secondly, there are increasing directives from the Department of Health (DH) on monitoring outcomes as part of the broad agenda of clinical governance (e.g., NIMHE, 2005). And thirdly, there is a widening acceptance by practitioners of the potential utility of collecting routine outcome data to inform clinical practice and services.

The move towards adopting outcome measures in routine practice settings has grown from developmental work on a range of different but related instruments. These include the Health of the Nation Outcome Scales (HoNOS; Wing et al., 1998), the Functional Analysis of Care Environments (FACE; Clifford, 1999), and the Clinical Outcomes in Routine Evaluation (CORE) System (Mellor-Clark et al., 1999), the latter of which includes the CORE outcome measure (CORE-OM) (Barkham et al., 2001; Evans et al., 2002). Between them, these measures cover the range of people presenting from primary care settings through to those deemed to be experiencing severe and enduring mental illness. The availability of these measures provides a real incentive for services to generate data that will inform their service and will, in turn, increasingly generate large data sets that can be used to investigate variables associated with outcomes. However, the question as to whether routine outcome measurement is feasible in the broad domain of mental health (including psychotherapy) remains to be addressed. Three criteria have been identified that outcome measures would have to meet: (1) standardized, (2) acceptable to clinicians, and (3) feasible for routine use (Thornicroft and Slade, 2000). Hence, the agenda is very much that of determining the effectiveness of psychological therapies. Studies have reported falls in HoNOS scores of almost 50 per cent in people experiencing a range of mental illnesses (e.g. McClelland et al., 2000). Similarly, various studies using components of the CORE System have indicated that, for example, approximately 80 per cent of clients referred to secondary care services scored above a predetermined clinical cut-off point prior to therapy, a figure which halved to approximately 40 per cent at discharge (Barkham et al., 2001). Another study carried out in primary care settings reported that 58 per cent of clients showed both reliable and clinically significant change and a further 17 per cent achieved reliable change (Mellor-Clark et al., 2001).

A consequence of the widespread adoption of common outcome measurement in routine settings is that large databases can be built which can then be used to address key practice-based questions (see Mellor-Clark et al., 2006). Using this approach, comparisons have been made between CBT, psychodynamic therapy, and person-centred therapy as practised in routine NHS primary care settings. Results indicated all three approaches to be broadly equivalent (Stiles et al., 2006). Another approach is the establishment of benchmarks using anonymous data derived from multiple sites which can then be used by a single service as a point of reference or comparison (e.g., Mullin et al., 2006). Further research is required into determining the range of possible contextual factors that influence outcomes in routine settings.

One area of research which has grown rapidly in recent years is that of self-help interventions. Although self-help materials have long been available, it is the growth of IT developments and the possibility that self-help might make psychological support more widely available than ever before which has brought this area to the fore. And it is this combination of widespread access to a cost-efficient form of psychological help which has captured the attention of government. In relation to computerized cognitive behaviour therapy (CCBT) for depression and anxiety, the National Institute for Clinical Excellence (NICE) has published an appraisal of a range of technologies available (NICE, 2006). They have approved *Beating the Blues* for the management of mild and moderate depression, and *FearFighter* for the management of panic and phobia. As an example of the speed with which this area has moved, an appraisal just over three years earlier had failed to find sufficient evidence to support any of the technologies. A systematic review of CCBT has been carried out (Kaltanthaler et al., 2004).

Clinically meaningful process research
The procedures employed in Generation IV process research can be described as either descriptive/exploratory or as aiming to link specific processes to theories of change. These two types of process work have been reviewed by Llewelyn and Hardy (2001) but not specifically within a model of psychotherapy research generations. Evidence of Generation IV process research can be seen as arising from the work employing the 'events' paradigm which has yielded findings that bridge the use of quantitative and qualitative approaches. Central to this approach has been interpersonal process recall (IPR) and its variants which can be used as the method for obtaining events to carry out comprehensive process analysis (CPA; Elliott, 1989; Elliott et al., 2001; Rees et al., 2001), as can having patients complete the Helpful Aspects of Therapy Form (HAT; Llewelyn, 1988). Llewelyn, Elliott, Shapiro, Hardy and Firth-Cozens (1988) investigated client perceptions of helpful impacts occurring in prescriptive and exploratory therapy. The most common impacts reported by clients as helpful at the session and phase level (i.e. after eight sessions) were (a) 'awareness' (the client getting in touch with feelings that may previously have been warded off) and (b) 'problem solution' (possible ways of coping being worked out or rehearsed in the session). Not surprisingly, 'awareness' was largely attributable to exploratory therapy and 'problem solution' to prescriptive therapy. As Llewelyn et al. (1988) argue, these findings suggest that

clients are achieving the major types of therapeutic realization intended by the two different therapies. The least helpful was reported to be 'unwanted thoughts'. This latter finding raises the point that clients and therapists have differential perspectives, with the clients experiencing 'unwanted thoughts' as negative while therapists may well see this as a necessary stage for the client to progress through towards improved psychological health.

CPA was used to analyse six client-identified significant insight events in cognitive-behavioural (CB) and psychodynamic-interpersonal (PI) therapy (Elliott et al., 1994). Results suggested a general model of insight events which involved a 'meaning bridge' that linked the client's reaction to its context. Elliott et al. (1994) proposed the following five-stage sequential model: (1) contextual priming, (2) novel information, (3) initial distantiated processing, (4) insight, and (5) elaboration. However, the contents of the insight events from the contrasting therapies were very different. CB events were primarily reattributional while PI events involved connection to a conflict theme from a previous session. Two further single-case studies combining outcome and process components have been drawn from the Second Sheffield Psychotherapy Project. The first study tested the assimilation model using a very stringent procedure and found support for successful assimilation of a problematic experience to be associated with a positive outcome (Field et al., 1994). The second study reported a task analysis of a single case in which a rupture and subsequent resolution of the therapeutic alliance was investigated (Agnew et al., 1994). While it may appear that this new generation of research is more grounded in clinical material, and hence more appropriate to the concerns of practitioners, it is probably too early, historically, within this research generation to be able to evaluate fully whether or not it is successful.

The concept of responsiveness has been employed to advance our understanding of the process of change. Recall that this concept suggests that the therapist needs to be responsive to the requirements of the individual client at a particular moment in therapy within the wider context of the client's presenting history and therapeutic progress. Hardy and colleagues have carried out research in this area and shown that therapists offered different moment-by-moment interventions to clients as a function of clients' particular interpersonal style (Hardy et al., 1998a, 1998b). This approach was applied to a study of 10 significant therapy events in psychodynamic-interpersonal therapy (Hardy et al., 1999). It was proposed that responsiveness would occur when therapists provided clients with a sense of security by responding to the moment-by-moment attachment needs of the clients. Moreover, appropriate responsiveness would occur when working with the clients in the zone of 'proximal development' whereby clients would feel safe to explore potential threats and dangers without being overwhelmed by them. Therapist responsiveness was classified into three categories: containment (i.e. made to feel safe), reflection (i.e. to be understood), and interpretation (i.e. challenged). Results showed nine out of the 10 events included containment strategies.

As in the international arena, a major tool of Generation IV process research has been the application of qualitative methodologies. For example, McLeod has written texts (McLeod, 1997) and carried out research (Grafanaki and McLeod, 1999) on the use of narrative as a means of understanding the therapy process. Similarly, examples of the potential of conversational analysis (Madill et al., 2001) and discourse analysis (DA; Madill and Barkham, 1997) have been presented. The study using DA addressed the question of how therapeutic change was achieved in one specified problem area for a client receiving psychodynamic-interpersonal therapy. Whilst providing an overall heuristic for researchers, the analysis focused on how the available linguistic resources and cultural meanings were used in both the construction of the client's presenting problem and also its solution. Conversational analysis and discourse analysis provide a perspective from outside the 'institution' of psychotherapy that offers considerable potential for practitioners to gain insight into their own work. This, ultimately, may be one of the major contributions of process work – providing a proxy to clinical supervision whereby other experts come to clinical material and apply their models and approaches in order to challenge the assumptions held by practitioners.

CONCLUSION

Future directions

The focus of this chapter has been on face-to-face individual therapy. It has not included research on group approaches nor on the growing area of self-help with the exception of noting the recent NICE appraisal of two computerized CBT packages. Both these modalities have considerable potential in terms of the cost-effectiveness of delivering services to those who require them (Generation III research). The development of self-help interventions is also bolstered by the increased potential provided by computers. The ability to devise affordable computer-based packages (CD-Roms), easily updated, for individual use provides one means of ensuring widespread support of people in need. However, it might be argued that the voice and process of therapy is diminished in service of a more educational approach. Beyond the specific potential of computers, there is also the vast potential of the internet and what this might offer in terms of facilitating communication and data collection. Related to this, there is already a trend towards increasing the statistical power of studies by developing research networks that contribute data from local services to nationally co-ordinated studies. This approach applies equally to RCTs as it does to practice-based approaches.

Another perspective that has been increasingly heralded is that of the 'user' – the person receiving therapy. Researchers are now required to include the views of users, but much of this has been tokenism. While it appears absolutely right to incorporate users into the research domain, moving it to the point where they are equal partners in research activity requires considerable thought and effort.

In terms of outcome and process, outcomes research faces challenges to ensure that it does not become synonymous with generating league tables of therapies or services. Such procedures are ultimately divisive where so often like is not compared with like. This is a potential danger from, for example, establishing national outcome benchmarks against which local services are compared. Service delivery systems, like clients, have individual characteristics and features which need to be acknowledged and taken into account when making comparisons. But like many things, the danger is more in such procedures being misused than in the procedure itself. It is undoubtedly true that psychological therapy services will be increasingly performance managed and therefore it is important for research to provide an appropriately robust, rigorous, and relevant base upon which to build best practice.

Similarly, process research needs to ensure that it is seen to be central to the delivery of quality services through the mechanisms of training, supervision and continuing professional development. There remains a reluctance to focus on the practitioner. Studies are still designed and powered primarily according to client numbers rather than based on practitioners. Methodologically, ignoring therapist effects will inflate any estimate of treatment effects, so it is critical that the investigating of these effects becomes a central focus of research in the psychological therapies. Wampold (2001) has argued cogently for the case to replace the 'therapy' with the 'therapist' as the focus for future research.

TENSIONS AND DEVELOPMENTS

In reviewing psychotherapy research over the past 50 years, it is striking how the field and the phenomena investigated tend to be presented in a dichotomous fashion: outcome vs process; qualitative vs quantitative methods; evidence-based practice or practice-based paradigms; client or practitioner perceptions; efficacy vs effectiveness; cognitive-behavioural therapy vs psychodynamic-interpersonal therapies; statistically significant findings vs no statistically significant findings; and so on. It would appear that this propensity to dichotomize phenomena, processes and methods is done in service of making the subject matter easier to research and, therefore, understand. However, has such a meta-paradigm yielded sufficient for the scientific and practitioner communities?

Over the past half-century, psychotherapy research has moved from establishing the efficacy of therapy via increasing specificity towards grappling with issues of service delivery and clinical meaningfulness for clinicians and patients. Yet it is interesting to note that by far the largest section of this chapter has been taken up by Generation II research, which may reflect the currency of 'specificity' at this point in time – an issue which underpins the evidence-based practice movement. However, while these generations can be placed in broad chronological and linear order, for some areas of clinical practice there is a cyclical order, with some areas only now moving towards Generation I-type research. These generations are conceptual and thematic and do not appear to have a definitive sell-by date. The cyclical phenomenon in which early issues are revisited by a new research generation or in which some political or social movement gives renewed salience to a paradigm from a prior research generation may suggest that there is a limit to the actual number of research generations. The accumulated evidence drawn from Generations I, II and III has provided a robust base for the broad activity of psychotherapy – and the evidence base is still growing. The hallmark of Generation IV research has been to move towards clinically meaningful research (process) and effectiveness in the field (outcome). In many ways these hallmarks reflect reworkings of process work prior to Generation I (see pp. 454 and 477) and the outcome work comprising Generation I. It may be useful in the future to reflect on developments and trends in psychotherapy research equally as reworkings of earlier research generations rather than construing them as genuinely 'new' generations.

Some of the research strands reported in this chapter appear to be developmental (e.g. specificity leading on to empirically supported treatments) while others appear to reflect reactions to perceived past failures (e.g. the call for more qualitative research in response to the perceived failure of outcome research to identify significant differences between treatment approaches). In the efficacy versus effectiveness debate, there are developmental forces operating (e.g. the need to extend research from RCTs into field settings) as well as more reactionary forces (e.g. testing treatments in unrealistic conditions yields little for routine practice). The same tensions exist in relation to the debate concerning specific versus common factors in which some argue for increased efforts in the area of specificity whilst others argue that the influence of and evidence for common factors is so prevalent that this should be the focus of research efforts. Hence, while there is clearly a mounting knowledge base in the area of the psychological therapies, the products and positions taken reflect an art of science rather than any given single truth. In a personal reflection on the issues relating to psychotherapy research, Goldfried has argued that: 'In order for psychotherapy to mature, we need to make use of our creative research and clinical energies to build upon, rather than rediscover, what we already know' (2000: 13–14). And therein lies the challenge to us all.

AUTHOR NOTE

This chapter is dedicated to the memory of Kenneth I. Howard, a founding father of the Society for Psychotherapy Research.

REFERENCES

Agnew, R.M., Harper, H., Shapiro, D.A. and Barkham, M. (1994) 'Resolving a challenge to the thera-peutic relationship: a single case study', *British Journal of Medical Psychology*, 67: 155–70.

Ahn, H. and Wampold, B.E. (2001) 'Where oh where are the specific ingredients? A meta-analysis of components studies in counseling and psychotherapy', *Journal of Counseling Psychology*, 48: 251–7.

Andrews, G., Guitar, B. and Howie, P. (1980) 'Meta-analysis of the effects of stuttering treatment', *Journal of Speech and Hearing Disorders*, 45: 287–307.

Angus, L. and McLeod, J. (eds) (2004) *The Handbook of Narrative and Psychotherapy: Practice, Theory, and Research*. London: Sage Publications.

Aveline, M. (1995) 'Assessing the value of brief intervention at the time of assessment for dynamic psy-chotherapy', in M. Aveline and D.A. Shapiro (eds), *Research Foundations for Psychotherapy Practice*. Chichester: Wiley. pp. 129–49.

Aveline, M. and Shapiro, D.A. (eds) (1995) *Research Foundations for Psychotherapy Practice*. Chichester: Wiley.

Baker, M. and Kleijnen, J. (2000) 'The drive towards evidence-based health care', in N. Rowland and S. Goss (eds), *Evidence-based Counselling and Psychological Therapies*. London: Routledge. pp. 13–29.

Barker, C., Pistrang, N. and Elliott, R. (2004) *Research Methods in Clinical Psychology*, 2nd edn. Chichester: Wiley.

Barkham, M. and Mellor-Clark, J. (2000) 'Rigour and relevance: practice-based evidence in the psycho-logical therapies', in N. Rowland and S. Goss (eds), *Evidence-based Counselling and Psychological Therapies*. London: Routledge. pp. 127–44.

Barkham, M. and Mellor-Clark, J. (2003) 'Bridging evidence-based practice and practice-based evidence: developing a rigorous and relevant knowledge for the psychological therapies', *Clinical Psychology & Psychotherapy*, 10: 319–27.

Barkham, M. and Shapiro, D.A. (1986) 'Counselor verbal response modes and experienced empathy', *Journal of Counseling Psychology*, 33: 3–10.

Barkham, M., Rees, A., Shapiro, D.A., Stiles, W.B., Agnew, R.M., Halstead, J., Culverwell, A. and Harrington, V.M.G. (1996) 'Outcomes of time-limited psychotherapy in applied settings: replicating the Second Sheffield Psychotherapy Project', *Journal of Consulting and Clinical Psychology*, 64: 1079–85.

Barkham, M., Shapiro, D.A., Hardy, G.E. and Rees, A. (1999) 'Psychotherapy in two-plus-one sessions: outcomes of a randomized controlled trial of cognitive-behavioral and psychodynamic-interpersonal therapy for subsyndromal depression', *Journal of Consulting and Clinical Psychology*, 67: 201–11.

Barkham, M., Margison, F., Leach, C., Lucock, M., Mellor-Clark, J., Evans, C., Benson, L., Connell, J., Audin, K. and McGrath, G. (2001) 'Service profiling and outcomes benchmarking using the CORE-OM: towards practice-based evidence in the psychological therapies', *Journal of Consulting and Clinical Psychology*, 69: 184–96.

Barlow, D.H., Hayes, S.C. and Nelson, R.O. (1984) *The Scientist-Practitioner: Research and Accountability in Clinical and Educational Settings*. Oxford: Pergamon Press.

Bennun, I. and Schindler, L. (1988) 'Therapist and patient factors in the behavioural treatment of pho-bic patients', *British Journal of Clinical Psychology*, 27: 145–51.

Bergin, A.E. and Garfield, S.L. (eds) (1971) *Handbook of Psychotherapy and Behavior Change*. New York: Wiley.

Bergin, A.E. and Garfield, S.L. (1994) 'Overview, trends, and future issues', in A.E. Bergin and S.L. Garfield (eds), *Handbook of Psychotherapy and Behavior Change*, 4th edn. New York: Wiley. pp. 821–30.

Bergin, A.E. and Lambert, M.J. (1978) 'The evaluation of therapeutic outcome', in S.L. Garfield and A.E. Bergin (eds), *Handbook of Psychotherapy and Behavior Change*, 2nd edn. New York: Wiley. pp. 139–90.

Birchwood, M. (1992) 'Early intervention in schizophrenia: theoretical background and clinical strate-gies', *British Journal of Clinical Psychology*, 31: 257–78.

Blackburn, I-M. (1995) 'The relationship between drug and psychotherapy effects', in Aveline, M. and D.A. Shapiro (eds), *Research Foundations for Psychotherapy Practice*. Chichester: Wiley & Sons. pp. 231–45.

Blackburn, I-M., Bishop, S., Glen, A.I.M., Whalley, L.J. and Christie, J.E. (1981) 'The efficacy of cognitive therapy in depression: a treatment trial using cognitive therapy and pharmacotherapy, each alone and in combination', *British Journal of Psychiatry*, 139: 181–9.

Blackburn, I-M., Eunson, K.M. and Bishop, S. (1986) 'A two-year naturalistic follow-up of depressed patients treated with cognitive therapy, pharmacotherapy and a combination of both', *Journal of Affective Disorders*, 10: 67–75.

Blanes, T. and Raven, P. (1995) 'Psychotherapy of panic disorder', *Current Opinion in Psychiatry*, 8: 167–71.

Blowers, C., Cobb, J. and Mathews, A. (1987) 'Generalized anxiety: a controlled treatment study', *Behavior Research and Therapy*, 25: 493–502.

Bordin, E.S. (1979) 'The generalizability of the psychoanalytic concept of the working alliance', *Psychotherapy: Theory, Research and Practice*, 16: 252–60.

Bower, P. and King, M. (2000) 'Randomised controlled trials and the evaluation of psychological therapy', in N. Rowland and S. Goss (eds), *Evidence-based Counselling and Psychological Therapies*. London: Routledge. pp.79–110.

Bower, P., Byford, S., Sibbald, B., Ward, E., King, M., Lloyd, M. and Gabbay, M. (2000) 'Randomised controlled trial of non-directive counselling, cognitive-behavioural therapy, and usual general practitioner care for patients with depression. II: Cost effectiveness', *British Medical Journal*, 321: 1389–92.

Brockman, B., Poynton, A., Ryle, A. and Watson, J.P. (1987) 'Effectiveness of time-limited therapy carried out by trainees: comparison of two methods', *British Journal of Psychiatry*, 151: 602–10.

Butler, A.C., Chapman, J.E., Forman, E.M. and Beck, A.T. (2006) 'The empirical status of cognitive-behavioral therapy: a review of meta-analyses', *Clinical Psychology Review*, 26: 17–31.

Butler, G., Cullington, A., Hibbert, G., Klimes, I. and Gelder, M. (1987a) 'Anxiety management for persistent generalized anxiety', *British Journal of Psychiatry*, 151: 535–42.

Butler, G., Gelder, M., Hibbert, G., Cullington, A. and Klimes, I. (1987b) 'Anxiety management: developing effective strategies', *Behavior Research and Therapy*, 25: 517–22.

Butler, G., Fennell, M.J.V., Robson, P. and Gelder, M. (1991) 'Comparison of behavior therapy and cognitive behavior therapy in the treatment of generalized anxiety disorder', *Journal of Consulting and Clinical Psychology*, 59: 167–75.

Cahill, C., Llewelyn, S. and Pearson, C. (1991) 'Treatment of sexual abuse which occurred in childhood: a review', *British Journal of Clinical Psychology*, 30: 1–12.

Cape, J. and Parry, G. (2000) 'Clinical practice guideline development in evidence-based psychotherapy', in N. Rowland and S. Goss (eds), *Evidence-based Counselling and Psychological Therapies*. London: Routledge. pp. 171–90.

Chadwick, P. and Lowe, F. (1990) 'The measurement and modification of delusional beliefs', *Journal of Consulting and Clinical Psychology*, 58: 225–32.

Chambless, D.L. and Ollendick, T.H. (2001) 'Empirically supported psychological interventions: controversies and evidence', *Annual Review of Psychology*, 52: 685–716.

Charman, D.P. (2004) *Core Processes in Brief Psychodynamic Psychotherapy: Advancing Effective Practice*. Mahwah, NJ: Lawrence Erlbaum Associates.

Chwalisz, K. (2003) 'Evidence-based practice: a framework for twenty-first-century scientist-practitioner training', *The Counseling Psychologist*, 31: 497–528.

Clark, D.M., Salkovskis, P.M., Hackman, A., Middleton, H., Anatasiades, P. and Gelder, M. (1994) 'A comparison of cognitive therapy, applied relaxation and imipramine in the treatment of panic disorder', *British Journal of Psychiatry*, 164: 759–69.

Clark, D.M., Salkovskis, P.M., Hackman, A., Wells, A., Fennell, M., Ludgate, J., Ahmed, S., Richards, H.C. and Gelder, M. (1998) 'Two psychological treatments for hypochondriasis: a randomised controlled trial', *British Journal of Psychiatry*, 173: 218–25.

Clark, D.M., Salkovskis, P.M., Hackman, A., Wells, A., Ludgate, J. and Gelder, M. (1999) 'Brief cognitive therapy for panic disorder: a randomized controlled trial', *Journal of Consulting and Clinical Psychology*, 67: 583–9.

Clarke, S. and Llewelyn, S.P. (1994) 'Personal constructs of survivors of childhood sexual abuse receiving cognitive analytic therapy', *British Journal of Medical Psychology*, 67: 273–89.

Clarkin, J.K., Koenigsberg, H.W., Yeomans, F., Selzer, M., Kernberg, P. and Kernberg, O.F. (1992) 'Psychodynamic psychotherapy of the borderline patient', in J.F. Clarkin, E. Marziali and H. Munroe-Blum (eds), *Borderline Personality Disorder: Clinical and Empirical Perspectives*. New York: Guilford Press.

Clifford, P.I. (1999) 'The FACE Recording and Measurement System: a scientific approach to person-based information', *Bulletin of the Menninger Clinic*, 63: 305–31.

Cohen, J. (1977) *Statistical Power Analysis for the Behavioral Sciences*. New York: Academic Press.

Consumer Reports (1995, November) 'Mental health: does therapy help?', 734–9.

Crits-Christoph, P., Cooper, A. and Luborsky, L. (1988) 'The accuracy of therapists' interpretations and the outcome of dynamic psychotherapy', *Journal of Consulting and Clinical Psychology*, 56: 490–5.

Davis, J.D., Elliott, R., Davis, M.L., Binns, M., Francis, V.M., Kelman, J.E. and Schroder, T.A. (1987) 'Development of a taxonomy of therapist difficulties: initial report', *British Journal of Medical Psychology*, 60: 109–19.

Denford, J., Schachter, J., Temple, N., Kind, P. and Rosser, R. (1983) 'Selection and outcome in in-patient psychotherapy', *British Journal of Medical Psychology*, 56: 225–43.

Department of Health (2001) *Treatment Choice in Psychological Therapies and Counselling: Evidence Based Clinical Practice Guideline*. London: DH.

DeRubeis, R.J. and Crit-Christoph, P. (1998) 'Empirically supported individual and group psychological treatments for adult mental disorders', *Journal of Consulting and Clinical Psychology*, 66: 37–52.

DeRubeis, R.J., Evans, M.D., Hollon, S.D., Garvey, M.J., Grove, W.M. and Tuason, V.B. (1990) 'How does cognitive therapy work? Cognitive change and symptom change in cognitive therapy and pharmacotherapy for depression', *Journal of Consulting and Clinical Psychology*, 58: 862–9.

Docherty, J.P. and Streeter, M.J. (1995) 'Advances in psychotherapy research', *Current Opinion in Psychiatry*, 8: 145–9.

Drury, V., Birchwood, M., Cochrane, R. and MacMillan, F. (1996) 'Cognitive therapy and recovery from acute psychosis: a controlled trial. I: Impact on psychotic symptoms', *British Journal of Psychiatry*, 169: 593–601.

Drury, V., Birchwood, M. and Cochrane, R. (2000) 'Cognitive therapy and recovery from acute psychosis: a controlled trial. 3: Five year follow-up', *British Journal of Psychiatry*, 177: 8–14.

Dryden, W. (ed.) (1996) *Research in Counselling and Psychotherapy: Practical Applications*. London: Sage.

Eaton, T.T., Abeles, N. and Gutfreund, M.J. (1988) 'Therapeutic alliance and outcome: impact of treatment length and pretreatment symptomotology', *Psychotherapy*, 25: 536–42.

Elkin, I. (1994) 'The NIMH Treatment of Depression collaborative research study', in A.E. Bergin and S.L. Garfield, (eds), *Handbook of Psychotherapy and Behavior Change*, 4th edn. New York: Wiley. pp. 114–39.

Elkin, I., Shea, M.T., Watkins, J.T., Imber, S.D., Sotsky, S.M., Collins, J.F., Glass, D.R., Pilkonis, P.A., Leber, W.R., Docherty, J.P., Fiester, S.J. and Parloff, M.B. (1989) 'National Institute of Mental Health Treatment of Depression collaborative research program: general effectiveness of treatment', *Archives of General Psychiatry*, 46: 971–82.

Elliott, R. (1984) 'A discovery-oriented approach to significant events in psychotherapy: interpersonal process recall and comprehensive process analysis', in L.N. Rice and L.S. Greenberg (eds), *Patterns of Change*. New York: Guilford Press. pp. 249–86.

Elliott, R. (1989) 'Comprehensive process analysis: understanding the change process in significant therapy events', in M. Packer and R.B. Addison (eds), *Entering the Circle: Hermeneutic Investigation in Psychology*. Albany: State University of New York Press. pp. 165–84.

Elliott, R. (2001) 'Contemporary brief experiential psychotherapy', *Clinical Psychology: Science & Practice*, 8: 38–50.

Elliott, R. and Shapiro, D.A. (1988) 'Brief structured recall: a more efficient method for studying significant therapy events', *British Journal of Medical Psychology*, 61: 141–53.

Elliott, R., Hill, C.E., Stiles, W.B., Friedlander, M.L., Mahrer, A.R. and Margison, F.R. (1987) 'Primary therapist response modes: a comparison of six rating systems', *Journal of Consulting and Clinical Psychology*, 55: 218–23.

Elliott, R., Stiles, W.B. and Shapiro, D.A. (1993) '"Are some psychotherapies more equivalent than others?"', in T.R. Giles (ed.), *Handbook of Effective Psychotherapy*. New York: Plenum. pp. 455–79.

Elliott, R., Shapiro, D.A., Firth-Cozens, J., Stiles, W.B., Hardy, G.E., Llewelyn, S.P. and Margison, F.R. (1994) 'Comprehensive process analysis of insight events in cognitive-behavioral and psychodynamic-interpersonal psychotherapies', *Journal of Counseling Psychology*, 41: 449–63.

Elliott, R., Fischer, C. and Rennie, D.L. (1999) 'Evolving guidelines for publication of qualitative research studies in psychology and related fields', *British Journal of Clinical Psychology*, 38: 215–29.

Elliott, R., Shapiro, D.A., Firth-Cozens, J., Stiles, W.B., Hardy, G.E., Llewelyn, S.P. and Margison, F.R. (2001) 'Comprehensive process analysis of insight events in cognitive-behavioral and psychodynamic-interpersonal psychotherapies', in C.E. Hill (ed.), *Helping Skills: The Empirical Foundation*. Washington, DC: American Psychological Association. pp. 309–33.

Evans, C., Connell, J., Barkham, M., Margison, F., Mellor-Clark, J., McGrath, G. and Audin, K. (2002) 'Towards a standardised brief outcome measure: psychometric properties and utility of the CORE-OM', *British Journal of Psychiatry*, 180: 51–60.

Evans, M.D., Hollon, S.D., DeRubeis, R.J., Piasecki, J.M., Grove, W.M., Garvey, M.J. and Tuason, V.B. (1992) 'Differential relapse following cognitive therapy and pharmacotherapy for depression', *Archives of General Psychiatry*, 49: 802–8.

Eysenck, H.J. (1952) 'The effects of psychotherapy: an evaluation', *Journal of Consulting Psychology*, 16: 319–24.

Fairburn, C.G., Kirk, J., O'Connor, M. and Cooper, P.J. (1986) 'A comparison of two psychological treatments for bulimia nervosa', *Behavior Research and Therapy*, 24: 629–43.

Fairburn, C.G., Jones, R., Peveler, R.C., Carr, S.J., Solomon, R.A., O'Connor, M.E., Burton, J. and Hope, R.A. (1991) 'Three psychological treatments for bulimia nervosa: a comparative trial', *Archives of General Psychiatry*, 48: 463–9.

Fairburn, C.G., Jones, R., Peveler, R.C., Hope, R.A. and O'Connor, M. (1993) 'Psychotherapy and bulimia nervosa: the longer-term effects of interpersonal psychotherapy, behavior therapy, and cognitive behavior therapy', *Archives of General Psychiatry*, 50: 419–28.

Fairburn, C.G., Norman, P.A., Welch, S.L., O'Connor, M.E., Doll, H.A. and Peveler, R.C. (1995) 'A prospective study of outcome in bulimia nervosa and the longer-term effects of three psychological treatments', *Archives of General Psychiatry*, 52: 304–12.

Fennell, M.J.V. (1983) 'Cognitive therapy of depression: the mechanisms of change', *Behavioural Psychotherapy*, 11: 97–108.

Fennell, M.J.V. and Teasdale, J.D. (1987) 'Cognitive therapy for depression: individual differences and the process of change', *Cognitive Therapy and Research*, 11: 253–71.

Ferguson, B. and Russell, I. (2000) 'Towards evidence-based health care', in N. Rowland and S. Goss (eds), *Evidence-based Counselling and Psychological Therapies*. London: Routledge. pp. 30–43.

Field, S., Barkham, M., Shapiro, D.A. and Stiles, W.B. (1994) 'Assessment of assimilation in psychotherapy: a quantitative case study of problematic experiences with a significant other', *Journal of Counseling Psychology*, 41: 397–406.

Fonagy, P. (1995) 'Is there an answer to the outcome question? "… waiting for Godot"', *Changes*, 13: 168–77.

Fowler, D., Garety, P. and Kuipers, L. (1994) *Cognitive Behavioural Therapy for People with Psychosis: A Clinical Handbook*. Chichester: J. Wiley & Sons.

Frank, J.D. (1971) 'Therapeutic factors in psychotherapy', *American Journal of Psychotherapy*, 25: 350–61.

Freeman, C.P.L., Barry, F., Dunkeld-Turnbull, J. and Henderson, A. (1988) 'Controlled trial of psychotherapy for bulimia nervosa', *British Medical Journal*, 296: 521–5.

Freeman, D., Garety, P., Fowler, D., Kuipers, E., Dunn, G., Bebbington, P. and Hadley, C. (1998) 'The London–East Anglia randomized controlled trial of cognitive-behaviour therapy for psychosis IV: self esteem and persecutory delusions', *British Journal of Clinical Psychology*, 37: 415–30.

Freud, S. (1979) 'Notes upon a case of obsessional neurosis (the 'Rat Man')' (1909), *Pelican Freud Library*, Vol IX: *Case Histories II*. Harmondsworth: Penguin.

Gabbard, G.O., Lazar, S.G., Hornberger, J. and Spiegel, D. (1997) 'The economic impact of psychotherapy: a review', *American Journal of Psychiatry*, 154: 147–55.

Garety, P.A., Kuipers, L., Fowler, D., Chamberlain, F. and Dunn, G. (1994) 'Cognitive behavioural therapy for drug-resistant psychosis', *British Journal of Medical Psychology*, 67: 259–71.

Garety, P., Fowler, D., Kuipers, E., Freeman, D., Dunn, G., Bebbington, P., Hadley, C. and Jones, S. (1997) 'London–East Anglia randomised controlled trial of cognitive-behavioural therapy for psychosis. II: Predictors of outcome', *British Journal of Psychiatry*, 171: 420–6.

Garfield, S.L. (1990) 'Issues and methods in psychotherapy process research', *Journal of Consulting and Clinical Psychology*, 58: 273–80.

Garfield, S.L. and Bergin, A.E. (eds) (1978) *Handbook of Psychotherapy and Behavior Change*, 2nd edn. New York: Wiley.

Garfield, S.L. and Bergin, A.E. (eds) (1986) *Handbook of Psychotherapy and Behavior Change*, 3rd edn. New York: Wiley.

Gask, L. and McGrath, G. (1989) 'Psychotherapy and general practice', *British Journal of Psychiatry*, 154: 445–53.

Gath, D. and Mynors-Wallis, L. (1997) 'Problem-solving treatment in primary care', in D.M. Clark and C.G. Fairburn (eds), *Science and Practice of Cognitive Behaviour Therapy*. Oxford: Oxford University Press. pp. 415–31.

Goldberg, D.P., Hobson, R.F., Maguire, G.P., Margison, F.R., O'Dowd, T., Osborn, M.S. and Moss, S. (1984) 'The clarification and assessment of a method of psychotherapy', *British Journal of Psychiatry*, 14: 567–75.

Goldfried, M.R. (2000) 'Consensus in psychotherapy research and practice: where have all the findings gone?', *Psychotherapy Research*, 10: 1–16.

Grafanaki, S. and McLeod, J. (1999) 'Narrative processes in the construction of helpful and hindering events in experiential psychotherapy', *Psychotherapy Research*, 9: 289–303.

Greenberg, L.S. (1986) 'Change process research', *Journal of Consulting and Clinical Psychology*, 54: 4–9.

Greenberg, L.S. (1994) 'The investigation of change: its measurement and explanation', in R.L. Russell (ed.), *Reassessing Psychotherapy Research*. New York: Guilford Press. pp. 114–43.

Greenberg, L.S. (1999) 'Ideal psychotherapy research: a study of significant change processes', *Journal of Clinical Psychology*, 55: 1467–80.

Greenberg, L.S. and Pinsoff, W.M. (eds) (1986) *The Psychotherapeutic Process: A Research Handbook*. New York: Guilford.

Grissom, R.J. (1996) 'The magical number .7+ −.2: meta-meta-analysis of the probability of superior outcome in comparisons involving therapy, placebo, and control', *Journal of Consulting and Clinical Psychology*, 64: 973–82.

Gurman, A.S. and Razin, A.M. (eds) (1977) *Effective Psychotherapy: A Handbook of Research*. New York: Pergamon.

Guthrie, E., Moorey, J., Margison, F., Barker, H., Palmer, S., McGrath, G., Tomenson, B. and Creed, F. (1999) 'Cost-effectiveness of brief psychodynamic-interpersonal therapy in high utilizers of psychiatric services', *Archives of General Psychiatry*, 56: 519–26.

Haddock, G., Tarrier, N., Spaulding, W., Yusupoff, W., Kinney, C. and McCarthy, E. (1998) 'Individual cognitive-behaviour therapy in the treatment of hallucinations and delusions: a review', *Clinical Psychology Review*, 18: 821–38.

Hall, A. and Crisp, A.H. (1987) 'Brief psychotherapy in the treatment of anorexia nervosa: outcome at one year', *British Journal of Psychiatry*, 151: 185–91.

Hardy, G.E., Barkham, M., Shapiro, D.A., Stiles, W.B., Rees, A. and Reynolds, S. (1995) 'Impact of Cluster C personality disorders (Avoidant, Dependent, Obsessive-Compulsive) on outcomes of contrasting brief psychotherapies for depression', *Journal of Consulting and Clinical Psychology*, 63: 997–1004.

Hardy, G.E., Shapiro, D.A., Stiles, W.B. and Barkham, M. (1998a) 'When and why does cognitive-behavioural treatment appear more effective than psychodynamic-interpersonal treatment? Discussion of the findings from the Sheffield Psychotherapy Projects', *Journal of Mental Health*, 7: 179–90.

Hardy, G.E., Stiles, W.B., Barkham, M. and Startup, M. (1998b) 'Therapist responsiveness to client attachment issues during time-limited treatments for depression', *Journal of Consulting and Clinical Psychology*, 66: 304–14.

Hardy, G.E., Aldridge, J., Davidson, C., Reilly, S., Rowe, C. and Shapiro, D.A. (1999) 'Therapist responsiveness to client attachment styles and issues observed in client-identified significant events in psychodynamic-interpersonal psychotherapy', *Psychotherapy Research*, 9: 36–53.

Healey, A. and Knapp, M. (1995) 'Economic appraisal of psychotherapy', *Mental Health Research Review*, 2: 13–16.

Hill, C.E. (1989) *Therapist Techniques and Client Outcomes: Eight Cases of Brief Psychotherapy.* Newbury Park, CA: Sage.

Hill, C.E. (1990) 'Exploratory in session process research in individual psychotherapy: a review', *Journal of Consulting and Clinical Psychology*, 58: 288–94.

Hill, C.E. (1991) 'Almost everything you ever wanted to know about how to do process research on counseling and psychotherapy but didn't know who to ask', in C.E. Watkins, Jr. and L.J. Schneider (eds), *Research in Counseling.* Hillsdale, NJ: Lawrence Erlbaum Associates. pp. 85–118.

Hill, C.E. (ed.) (2001) *Helping Skills: The Empirical Foundation.* Washington, DC: American Psychological Association.

Hill, C.E. and Corbett, M. (1993) 'A perspective on the history of process and outcome research in counseling psychology', *Journal of Counseling Psychology*, 40: 3–24.

Hill, C.E., Thompson, B.J. and Williams, E.N. (1997) 'A guide to conducting consensual qualitative research', *Counseling Psychologist*, 25: 517–72.

Hill, C.E. and Lambert, M.J. (2004) 'Methodological issues in studying psychotherapy processes and outcomes', in M.J. Lambert (ed.), *Bergin and Garfield's Handbook of Psychotherapy and Behavior change,* 5th edn. New York: Wiley. pp. 84–135.

Horvath, A.O. and Greenberg, L.S. (1989) 'Development and validation of the Working Alliance Inventory', *Journal of Counseling Psychology*, 36: 223–33.

Horvath, A.O. and Greenberg, L.S. (eds) (1994). *The Working Alliance: Theory, Research, and Practice.* New York: Wiley.

Horvath, A.O. and Symonds, D.B. (1991) 'Relation between working alliance and outcome in psychotherapy', *Journal of Counseling Psychology*, 38: 139–49.

Horvath, A.O., Marx, R.W. and Kamann, A.M. (1990) 'Thinking about thinking in therapy: an examination of clients' understanding of their therapists' intentions', *Journal of Consulting and Clinical Psychology*, 58: 614–21.

Howard, K.I., Kopta, S.M., Krause, M.S. and Orlinsky, D.E. (1986) 'The dose–effect relationship in psychotherapy', *American Psychologist*, 41: 159–64.

Howard, K.I., Lueger, R., Maling, M. and Martinovitch, Z. (1993) 'A phase model of psychotherapy: causal mediation of outcome', *Journal of Consulting and Clinical Psychology*, 61: 678–85.

Howard, K.I., Moras, K., Brill, P. L., Martinovitch, Z. and Lutz, W. (1996) 'Evaluation of psychotherapy: efficacy, effectiveness, and patient progress', *American Psychologist*, 51: 1059–64.

Huddleson, J.H. (1927) 'Psychotherapy in two hundred cases of psychoneurosis', *The Military Surgeon*, 60: 161–70.

Iliardi, S.S. and Craighead, W.E. (1994) 'The role of nonspecific factors in cognitive-behavior therapy for depression', *Clinical Psychology: Science and Practice*, 1: 138–56.

Jacobson, N.S. and Truax, P. (1991) 'Clinical significance: a statistical approach to defining meaningful change in psychotherapy research', *Journal of Consulting and Clinical Psychology*, 59: 12–19.

Jacobson, N.S., Follette, W.C. and Revenstorf, D. (1984) 'Psychotherapy outcome research: methods for reporting variability and evaluating clinical significance', *Behavior Therapy*, 15: 336–52.

Jacobson, N.S., Follette, W.C. and Revenstorf, D. (1986) 'Toward a standard definition of clinically significant change', *Behavior Therapy*, 17: 308–11.

Jarrett, R.B. and Nelson, R.O. (1987) 'Mechanisms of change in cognitive therapy of depression', *Behavior Therapy*, 18: 227–41.

Journal of Consulting and Clinical Psychology (1993) Special Section: 'A briefing on curative factors in dynamic psychotherapy', 61: 539–610.

Journal of Consulting and Clinical Psychology (1995) Special Section: 'Efficacy and effectiveness in studies of child and adolescent psychotherapy', 63: 683–725.

Kaltenthaler, E., Parry, G., Beverley, C. (2004) 'Computerized cognitive behaviour therapy: a systematic review', *Behavioural and Cognitive Psychotherapy*, 32: 31–55.

Keller, A. (1984) 'Planned brief psychotherapy in clinical practice', *British Journal of Medical Psychology*, 57: 347–61.

Kendall, P.C. and Sheldrick, R.C. (2000) 'Normative data for normative comparisons', *Journal of Consulting and Clinical Psychology*, 68: 767–73.

Kendall, P.C., Flannery-Schroeder, E.C. and Ford, J.D. (1999a) 'Therapy outcome research methods', in P.C. Kendall, J.N. Butcher et al. (eds), *Handbook of Research Methods in Clinical Psychology*, 2nd edn. New York: Wiley. pp. 330–63.

Kendall, P.C., Marrs-Garcia, A., Nath, S.R. and Sheldrick, R.C. (1999b) 'Normative comparisons for the evaluation of clinical significance', *Journal of Consulting and Clinical Psychology*, 67: 285–99.

Kendall, P.C., Holmbeck, G. and Verduin, T. (2004) 'Methodology, design and evaluation in psychotherapy research', in M.J. Lambert (ed.), *Bergin and Garfield's Handbook of Psychotherapy and Behavior Change*, 5th edn. New York: Wiley. pp. 16–43.

Kiesler, D.J. (1966) 'Basic methodological issues implicit in psychotherapy research', *American Journal of Psychotherapy*, 20: 135–55.

Kingdon, D.G. and Turkington, D. (1991) 'Preliminary report: the use of cognitive behavior therapy with a normalizing rationale in schizophrenia', *Journal of Nervous and Mental Disease*, 179: 207–11.

Klee, M.R., Abeles, N. and Muller, R.T. (1990) 'Therapeutic alliance: early indicators, course, and outcome', *Psychotherapy*, 27: 166–74.

Koenigsberg, H.W. (1995) 'Psychotherapy of patients with borderline personality disorder', *Current Opinion in Psychiatry*, 8: 157–60.

Kopta, S.M., Lueger, R.J., Saunders, S.M. and Howard, K.I. (1999) 'Individual psychotherapy outcome and process research: challenges leading to greater turmoil or a position transition?', *Annual Review of Psychology*, 50: 441–69.

Kordy, H., Hannöver, W. and Richard, M. (2001) 'Computer-assisted feedback-driven quality management for psychotherapy: the Stuttgart-Heidelberg model', *Journal of Consulting and Clinical Psychology*, 69: 173–83.

Koss, M.P. and Shiang, J. (1994) 'Research on brief psychotherapy', in A.E. Bergin and S.L. Garfield (eds), *Handbook of Psychotherapy and Behavior Change*, 4th edn. New York: Wiley. pp. 664–700.

Krumboltz, J.D. (1966) *Revolution in Counseling: Implications of Behavioral Science*. Boston, MA: Houghton Mifflin.

Krupnick, J.L. and Pincus, H.A. (1992) 'The cost-effectiveness of psychotherapy: a plan for research', *American Journal of Psychotherapy*, 149: 1295–305.

Kuipers, E., Garety, P., Fowler, D., Dunn, G., Bebbington, P., Freeman, D. and Hadley, C. (1997) 'London–East Anglia randomised controlled trial of cognitive-behavioural therapy for psychosis I: Effects of the treatment phase', *British Journal of Psychiatry*, 171: 319–27.

Kuipers, E., Fowler, D., Garety, P., Chisholm, D., Freeman, D., Dunn, G., Bebbington, P. and Hadley, C. (1998) 'London–East Anglia randomised controlled trial of cognitive-behavioural therapy for psychosis III: Follow-up and economic evaluation at 18 months', *British Journal of Psychiatry*, 173: 61–8.

Lambert, M.J. (ed.) (2004) *Bergin and Garfield's Handbook of Psychotherapy and Behavior Change*, 5th edn. New York: Wiley.

Lambert, M.J. and Bergin, A.E. (1994) 'The effectiveness of psychotherapy', in A.E. Bergin and S.L. Garfield (eds), Bergin and Garfield's *Handbook of Psychotherapy and Behavior Change*, 4th edn. New York: Wiley. pp. 143–89.

Lambert, M.J. and Ogles, B.M. (in press) 'The efficacy and effectiveness of psychotherapy', in M.J. Lambert (ed.), *Bergin and Garfield's Handbook of Psychotherapy and Behavior Change*, 5th edn. New York: Wiley. pp. 139–93.

Lambert, M.J., Hansen, N.B. and Finch, A.E. (2001a) 'Patient-focused research: using patient outcome data to enhance treatment effects', *Journal of Consulting and Clinical Psychology*, 69: 159–72.

Lambert, M.J., Whipple, J.L., Hawkins, E.J., Vermeersch, D.A., Nielsen, S.L. and Smart, D.W. (2003) 'Is it time for clinicians to routinely track patient outcome? A meta-analysis', *Clinical Psychology: Science and Practice*, 10: 288–301.

Lambert, M.J., Whipple, J.L., Smart, D.W., Vermeersch, D.A., Nielsen, S.L. and Hawkins, E.J. (2001b) 'The effects of providing therapists with feedback on patient progress during psychotherapy: are outcomes enhanced?', *Psychotherapy Research*, 11: 49–68.

Linehan, M.M. (1993) *Cognitive-behavioral Treatment of Borderline Personality Disorder*. New York: Guilford.

Linehan, M.M., Armstrong, H.E., Suarez, A., Allmon, D. and Heard, H.L. (1991) 'Cognitive-behavioral treatment of chronically parasuicidal borderline patients', *Archives of General Psychiatry*, 48: 1060–4.

Linehan, M.M., Heard, H.L. and Armstrong, H.E. (1993) 'Naturalistic follow-up of a behavioral treatment for chronically suicidal borderline patients', *Archives of General Psychiatry*, 50: 971–4.

Llewelyn, S.P. (1988) 'Psychological therapy as viewed by clients and therapists', *British Journal of Clinical Psychology*, 27: 223–38.

Llewelyn, S.P. and Hardy, G. (2001) 'Process research in understanding and applying psychological therapies', *British Journal of Clinical Psychology*, 40: 1–21.

Llewelyn, S.P., Elliott, R., Shapiro, D.A., Hardy, G.E. and Firth-Cozens, J. (1988) 'Client perceptions of significant events in prescriptive and exploratory periods of individual therapy', *British Journal of Clinical Psychology*, 27: 105–14.

Luborsky, L., Singer, B. and Luborsky, L. (1975) 'Comparative studies of psychotherapies: is it true that "everyone has won and all must have prizes"?', *Archives of General Psychiatry*, 32: 995–1008.

Lueger, R.J., Howard, K.I., Martinovitch, Z., Lutz, W., Anderson, E.E. and Grissom, G. (2001) 'Assessing treatment progress of individual patients using expected treatment response models', *Journal of Consulting and Clinical Psychology*, 69: 150–8.

Lutz, W., Martinovitch, Z. and Howard, K.I. (1999) 'Patient profiling: an application of random coefficient regression models to depicting the response of a patient to outpatient psychotherapy', *Journal of Consulting and Clinical Psychology*, 67: 571–7.

McClelland, R., Trimble, P., Fox, M.L., Stevenson, M.R. and Bell, B. (2000) 'Validation of an outcome scale for use in adult psychiatric practice', *Quality in Healthcare*, 9: 98–105.

McGinn, L.K. and Sanderson, W. (2001) 'What allows cognitive behavioral therapy to be brief: overview, efficiency, and crucial factors facilitating brief treatment', *Clinical Psychology: Science and Practice*, 8: 23–37.

McGrath, G. and Lawson, K. (1987) 'Assessing the benefits of psychotherapy: the economic approach', *British Journal of Psychiatry*, 150: 65–71.

McLeod, J. (1997) *Narrative and Psychotherapy*. London: Sage.

McLeod, J. (2000) 'The contribution of qualitative research to evidence-based counselling and psychotherapy', in N. Rowland and S. Goss (eds), *Evidence-based Counselling and Psychological Therapies*. London: Routledge. pp. 111–26.

McLeod, J. (2003) *Doing Counselling Research*, 2nd edn. London: Sage.

Madill, A. and Barkham, M. (1997) 'Discourse analysis of a theme in one successful case of brief psychodynamic-interpersonal psychotherapy', *Journal of Counseling Psychology*, 44: 232–44.

Madill, A., Widdicombe, S. and Barkham, M. (2001) 'The potential of conversational analysis for psychotherapy research', *The Counseling Psychologist*, 29: 413–34.

Maguire, G.P., Goldberg, D.P., Hobson, R.F., Margison, F.R., Moss, S. and O'Dowd, T. (1984) 'Evaluating the teaching of a method of psychotherapy', *British Journal of Psychiatry*, 144: 576–80.

Malan, D.H. (1963) *A study of Brief Psychotherapy*. New York: Plenum Press.

Malan, D.H. (1976) *Toward the Validation of Dynamic Psychotherapy: A Replication*. New York: Plenum Press.

Malan, D.H., Bacal, H.A., Heath, E.S. and Balfour, F.H.G. (1968) 'A study of psychodynamic changes in untreated neurotic patients: I. Improvements that are questionable on dynamic criteria', *British Journal of Psychiatry*, 114: 525–51.

Malan, D.H., Heath, E.S., Bacal, H.A. and Balfour, F.H.G. (1975) 'Psychodynamic changes in untreated neurotic patients: II. Apparently genuine improvements', *Archives of General Psychiatry*, 32: 110–26.

Margison, F., Barkham, M., Evans, C., McGrath, G., Mellor-Clark, J., Audin, K. and Connell, J. (2000) 'Measurement and psychotherapy: evidence-based practice and practice-based evidence', *British Journal of Psychiatry*, 177: 123–30.

Marks, I.M., Swinson, R.P., Basoglu, M., Kuch, K., Noshirvani, H., O'Sullivan, G., Lelliott, P.T., Kirby, M., McNamee, G., Sengun, S. and Wickwire, K. (1993) 'Alprazolam and exposure alone and combined in panic disorder with agoraphobia', *British Journal of Psychiatry*, 162: 776–8.

Marmar, C.R. (1990) 'Psychotherapy process research: progress, dilemmas, and future directions', *Journal of Consulting and Clinical Psychology*, 58: 265–72.

Maynard, A. (2000) 'Economic issues', in N. Rowland and S. Goss (eds), *Evidence-based Counselling and Psychological Therapies*. London: Routledge. pp. 44–56.

Mellor-Clark, J., Barkham, M., Connell, J. and Evans, C. (1999) 'Practice-based evidence and need for a standardised evaluation system: informing the design of the CORE System', *European Journal of Psychotherapy, Counselling and Health*, 3: 357–74.

Mellor-Clark, J., Connell, J., Barkham, M. and Cummins, P. (2001) 'Counselling outcomes in primary health care: a CORE System data profile', *European Journal of Psychotherapy, Counselling and Health*, 4: 65–86.

Mellor-Clark, J., Curtis Jenkins, A., Evans, R., Mothersole, G. and McIness, B. (2006) 'Resourcing a CORE Network to develop a National Research Database to help enhance psychological therapy and counseling service provision', *Counselling and Psychotherapy Research*, 6: 16–22.

Messer, S.B. (2001) 'What makes brief psychodynamic therapy time efficient', *Clinical Psychology: Science and Practice*, 8: 5–22.

Mitchell, K., Bozarth, J. and Krauft, J. (1977) 'A reappraisal of the therapeutic effectiveness of accurate empathy, nonpossessive warmth, and genuineness', in A.S. Gurman and A. Razin (eds), *Effective Psychotherapy: A Handbook of Research*. Oxford: Pergamon Press. pp. 482–502.

Moran, G.S. and Fonagy, P. (1987) 'Psychoanalysis and diabetic control: a single case study', *British Journal of Medical Psychology*, 60: 357–72.

Morley, S. (1988) 'Status of cognitive therapies', *Current Opinion in Psychiatry*, 1: 725–8.

Mullin, T., Barkham, M., Mothersole, G., Bewick, B.M. and Kinder, A. (2006) 'Recovery and improvement benchmarks for counseling and the psychological therapies in routine primary care', *Counselling and Psychotherapy Research*, 6: 68–80.

Murphy, P.M., Cramer, D. and Lillie, F.J. (1984) 'The relationship between curative factors perceived by patients in their psychotherapy and treatment outcome: an exploratory study', *British Journal of Medical Psychology*, 57: 187–92.

Mynors-Wallis, L. (1996) 'Problem-solving treatment: evidence for effectiveness and feasibility in primary care', *International Journal of Psychiatry in Medicine*, 26: 249–62.

Nathan, P.E., Stuart, S.P. and Dolan, S.L. (2000) 'Research on psychotherapy efficacy and effectiveness: between Scylla and Charybdis?', *Psychological Bulletin*, 126: 964–81.

National Advisory Mental Health Council, National Institute of Mental Health (1999) *Bridging Science and Service: A Report by the National Advisory Mental Health Council's Clinical Treatment and Services Research Workshop* (NIH Publication no. 99–4353). Washington, DC.

National Institute for Clinical Excellence (2006) 'Computerised cognitive behaviour therapy for depression and anxiety', *Review of Technology Appraisal 51*. NICE.

National Institute for Mental Health in England (2005) *Outcomes Measures Implementation: Best Practice Guidance*, London: Department of Health.

Nietzel, M.T., Russell, R.L., Hemmings, K.A. and Gretter, M.L. (1987) 'Clinical significance of psychotherapy for unipolar depression: a meta-analytic approach to social comparison', *Journal of Consulting and Clinical Psychology*, 55: 156–61.

Norcross, J.C. (2002) *Psychotherapy Relationships that Work: Therapist Contributions and Responsiveness to Patients*. New York: Oxford University Press.

Norquist, G.S., Letowitz, B. and Hynam, S. (1999) 'Expanding the frontier of treatment research', *Prevention & Treatment*, 2: 1–10.

O'Farrell, M.K., Hill, C.E. and Patton, S. (1986) 'Comparison of two cases of counseling with the same counselor', *Journal of Counseling and Development*, 65: 141–5.

Ogles, M.M., Lunnen, K.M. and Bonesteel, K. (2001) 'Clinical significance: history, application, and current practice', *Clinical Psychology Review*, 21: 421–46.

Olfson, M. and Pincus, H.A. (1994a) 'Outpatient psychotherapy in the United States, I: Volume, costs, and user characteristics', *American Journal of Psychiatry*, 151: 1281–8.

Olfson, M. and Pincus, H.A. (1994b) 'Outpatient psychotherapy in the United States, II: Patterns of utilization', *American Journal of Psychiatry*, 151: 1289–94.

Orlinsky, D.E. and Howard, K.I. (1986) 'Process and outcome in psychotherapy', in S.L. Garfield and A.E. Bergin (eds), *Handbook of Psychotherapy and Behavior Change*, 3rd edn. New York: Wiley. pp. 311–81.

Orlinsky, D.E. and Russell, R.L. (1994) 'Tradition and change in psychotherapy research: notes on the fourth generation', in R.L. Russell (ed.), *Reassessing Psychotherapy Research*. New York: Guilford Press. pp. 185–214.

Orlinsky, D.E., Grawe, K. and Parks, B.K. (1994) 'Process and outcome in psychotherapy – *Noch einmal*', in A.E. Bergin and S.L. Garfield (eds), *Handbook of Psychotherapy and Behavior Change*, 4th edn. New York: Wiley. pp. 270–376.

Orlinsky, D.E., Rønnestad, M.H. and Willutzki, U. (2004) 'Fifty years of psychotherapy process-outcome research: continuity and change', in M.J. Lambert (ed.), *Bergin and Garfield's Handbook of Psychotherapy and Behavior Change,* 5th edn. New York: Wiley. pp. 307–89.

Oxman, A.D. and Guyatt, G.H. (1988) 'Guidelines for reading literature reviews', *Canadian Medical Association Journal*, 138: 697–703.

Parry, G. (1992) 'Improving psychotherapy services: application of research, audit and evaluation', *British Journal of Clinical Psychology*, 31: 3–19.

Parry, G. (2000) 'Evidence-based psychotherapy: an overview', in N. Rowland and S. Goss (eds), *Evidence-based Counselling and Psychological Therapies: Research and Applications*. London: Routledge. pp. 57–75.

Paul, G. (1967) 'Strategy in outcome research in psychotherapy', *Journal of Consulting Psychology*, 31: 109–18.

Perry, C.J., Banon, E. and Ianni, F. (1999) 'Effectiveness of psychotherapy for personality disorders', *American Journal of Psychiatry*, 156: 1312–21.

Peveler, R.C. and Fairburn, C.G. (1989) 'Anorexia nervosa in association with diabetes mellitus: a cognitive-behavioural approach to treatment', *Behavior Research and Therapy*, 27: 95–9.

Polkinghorne, D. E. (1994) 'Reaction to special section on qualitative research in counseling process and outcome', *Journal of Counseling Psychology*, 41: 510–12.

Porter, E.H. Jr. (1943a) 'The development and evaluation of a measure of counseling interview procedures: Part I', *Educational and Psychological Measurement*, 3: 105–25.

Porter, E.H. Jr. (1943b) 'The development and evaluation of a measure of counseling interview procedures: Part II', *Educational and Psychological Measurement*, 3: 215–38.

Quality Assurance Project (1984) 'Treatment outlines for the management of schizophrenia', *Australian and New Zealand Journal of Psychiatry*, 18: 19–38.

Rees, A., Hardy, G.E., Barkham, M., Elliott, R., Smith, J.A. and Reynolds, S. (2001) '"It's like catching a desire before it flied away": a comprehensive process analysis of a problem clarification event in cognitive-behavioral therapy for depression', *Psychotherapy Research*, 11: 331–51.

Rice, L.N. and Greenberg, L.S. (eds) (1984) *Patterns of Change*. New York: Guilford Press.

Robinson, F.R. (1950) *Principles and Procedures in Student Counseling*. New York: Harper.

Robinson, L.A., Berman, J.S. and Neimeyer, R.A. (1990) 'Psychotherapy for the treatment of depression: a comprehensive review of controlled outcome research', *Psychological Bulletin*, 108: 30–49.

Rogers, C.R. (1942) 'The use of electrically recorded interviews in improving psychotherapeutic techniques', *American Journal of Orthopsychiatry*, 12: 429–34.

Rogers, C.R. (1957) 'The necessary and sufficient conditions of therapeutic personality change', *Journal of Consulting Psychology*, 21: 95–103.

Rogers, C.R. and Dymond, R.F. (eds) (1954) *Psychotherapy and Personality Change*. Chicago: University of Chicago Press.

Rogers, C.R., Gendlin, E.T., Kiesler, D.J. and Truax, C.B. (1967) *The Therapeutic Relationship and its Impact: A Study of Psychotherapy with Schizophrenics*. Madison: University of Wisconsin Press.

Roth, A. and Fonagy, P. (2005) *What Works for Whom? A Critical Review of Psychotherapy Research*, 2nd edn. New York: Guilford Press. (First edition, 1996.)

Rowland, N. and Goss, S. (eds) (2000) *Evidence-based Counselling and Psychological Therapies*. London: Routledge.

Rowland, N., Godfrey, C., Bower, P., Mellor-Clark, J., Heywood, P. and Hardy, R. (2000) 'Counselling in primary care: a systematic review of the research evidence', *British Journal of Guidance and Counselling*, 28: 215–31.

Rowland, N., Bower, P., Mellor-Clark, J., Heywood, P. and Godfrey, C. (2001) 'Effectiveness and cost effectiveness of counselling in primary care (Cochrane Review)', in *The Cochrane Library*, issue 3. Oxford: Update Software.

Russell, R.L. and Orlinsky, D.E. (1996) 'Psychotherapy research in a historical perspective: implications for mental health care policy', *Archives of General Psychiatry*, 53: 708–15.

Russell, R.L. and Stiles, W.B. (1979) 'Categories for classifying language in psychotherapy', *Psychological Bulletin*, 86: 404–19.

Ryle, A. (1979) 'Focus on brief interpretative psychotherapy: dilemmas, traps, and snags as target problems', *British Journal of Psychiatry*, 134: 46–54.

Ryle, A. (1980) 'Some measures of goal attainment in focused integrated active psychotherapy: a study of fifteen cases', *British Journal of Psychiatry*, 137: 475–86.

Ryle, A. (1982) *Psychotherapy: A Cognitive Integration of Theory and Practice*. London: Academic Press.

Ryle, A. (1990) *Cognitive-analytic Therapy: Active Participation in Change*. Chichester: Wiley & Sons.

Ryle, A. (1995) 'Transference and counter-transference variations in the course of the cognitive-analytic therapy of two borderline patients: the relation to the diagrammatic reformulation of self-states', *British Journal of Medical Psychology*, 68: 109–24.

Ryle, A. and Beard, H. (1993) 'The integrative effect of reformulation: cognitive analytic therapy with a patient with borderline personality disorder', *British Journal of Medical Psychology*, 66: 249–58.

Safran, J.D., Greenberg, L.S. and Rice, L.N. (1988) 'Integrating psychotherapy research and practice: modeling the change process', *Psychotherapy*, 25: 1–17.

Salkovskis, P.M. (1995) 'Demonstrating specific effects in cognitive and behavioural therapy', in M. Aveline and D.A. Shapiro (eds), *Research Foundations for Psychotherapy Research*. Chichester: Wiley & Sons. pp. 191–228.

Scheel, K.R. (2000) 'The empirical basis of dialectical behaviour therapy: summary, critique, and implications', *Clinical Psychology: Science and Practice*, 7: 68–86.

Scott, J. and Watkins, E. (2004) 'Brief psychotherapies for depression: current status', *Current Opinion in Psychiatry*, 17: 3–7.

Scott, J. (2001) 'Cognitive therapy for depression', *British Medical Bulletin*, 57: 101–13.

Seligman, M.E.P. (1995) 'The effectiveness of psychotherapy: the Consumer Reports study', *American Psychologist*, 50: 965–74.

Seligman, M.E.P. (1996) 'A creditable beginning', *American Psychologist*, 51: 1086–8.

Sexton, T.L. and Whiston, S.C. (1994) 'The status of the counseling relationship: an empirical review, theoretical implications, and research directions', *The Counseling Psychologist*, 22: 6–78.

Shadish, W.R., Matt, G.E., Navarro, A.M., Siegle, G., Crits-Christoph, P., Hazelrigg, M.D., Jorm, A.F., Lyons, L.C., Nietzel, M.T., Prout, H.T., Robinson, L., Smoth, M.L., Svartberg, M. and Weiss, B. (1997) 'Evidence that therapy works in clinically representative conditions', *Journal of Consulting and Clinical Psychology*, 65: 355–65.

Shadish, W.R., Matt, G.E., Navarro, A.M. and Phillups, G. (2000) 'The effects of psychological therapies under clinically representative conditions: a meta-analysis', *Psychological Bulletin*, 126: 512–29.

Shapiro, D.A. (1969) 'Empathy, warmth and genuineness in psychotherapy', *British Journal of Social and Clinical Psychology*, 8: 350–61.

Shapiro, D.A. (1970) 'The rating of psychotherapeutic empathy: a preliminary study', *British Journal of Social and Clinical Psychology*, 9: 148–51.

Shapiro, D.A. (1973) 'Naive British judgements of therapeutic conditions', *British Journal of Social and Clinical Psychology*, 12: 289–94.

Shapiro, D.A. (1976) 'The effects of therapeutic conditions: positive results revisited', *British Journal of Medical Psychology*, 49: 315–23.

Shapiro, D.A. and Firth, J.A. (1987) 'Prescriptive vs. exploratory psychotherapy: outcomes of the Sheffield Psychotherapy Project', *British Journal of Psychiatry*, 151: 790–9.

Shapiro, D.A. and Shapiro, D. (1982) 'Meta-analysis of comparative therapy outcome studies: a replication and refinement', *Psychological Bulletin*, 92: 581–604.

Shapiro, D.A., Barkham, M., Hardy, G.E., Morrison, L.A., Reynolds, S., Startup, M. and Harper, H. (1991) 'Sheffield psychotherapy research program', in L.E. Butler (ed.), *Psychotherapy Research Programs: An International Review of Programmatic Studies*. Washington, DC: American Psychological Association.

Shapiro, D.A., Barkham, M., Reynolds, S., Hardy, G.E. and Stiles, W.B. (1992) 'Prescriptive and exploratory psychotherapies: toward an integration based on the assimilation model', *Journal of Psychotherapy Integration*, 2: 253–72.

Shapiro, D.A., Barkham, M., Rees, A., Hardy, G.E., Reynolds, S. and Startup, M. (1994) 'Effects of treatment duration and severity of depression on the effectiveness of cognitive-behavioral and psychodynamic-interpersonal psychotherapy', *Journal of Consulting and Clinical Psychology*, 62: 522–34.

Shapiro, D.A., Rees, A., Barkham, M., Hardy, G.E., Reynolds, S. and Startup, M. (1995) 'Effects of treatment duration and severity of depression on the maintenance of gains following cognitive-behavioral and psychodynamic-interpersonal psychotherapy', *Journal of Consulting and Clinical Psychology*, 63: 378–87.

Shefler, G., Dasberg, H. and Ben-Shakhar, G. (1995) 'A randomised controlled outcome and follow-up study of Mann's time-limited psychotherapy', *Journal of Consulting and Clinical Psychology*, 63: 585–93.

Silberschatz, G. and Curtis, J.T. (1986) 'Clinical implications of research on brief dynamic psychotherapy: 2. How the therapist helps or hinders therapeutic progress', *Psychoanalytic Psychology*, 3: 27–37.

Sloane, R.B., Staples, R.F., Cristol, A.H., Yorkston, N.J. and Whipple, K. (1975) *Psychotherapy versus Behavior Therapy*. Cambridge, MA: Harvard University Press.

Smith, M.L. and Glass, G.V. (1977) 'Meta-analysis of psychotherapy outcome studies', *American Psychologist*, 32: 752–60.

Smith, M.L., Glass, G.V. and Miller, T.I. (1980) *The Benefits of Psychotherapy*. Baltimore: Johns Hopkins University Press.

Startup, M. and Shapiro, D.A. (1993) 'Therapist treatment fidelity in prescriptive vs. exploratory psychotherapy', *British Journal of Clinical Psychology*, 32: 443–56.

Steinbrueck, S.M., Maxwell, S.E. and Howard, G.S. (1983) 'A meta-analysis of psychotherapy and drug therapy in the treatment of unipolar depression with adults', *Journal of Consulting and Clinical Psychology*, 51: 856–63.

Stiles, W.B. (2002) 'Assimilation of problematic experiences', in J.C. Norcross (ed.), *Psychotherapy Relationships That Work*. New York: Oxford University Press.

Stiles, W.B. (2006) 'Assimilation and the process of outcome: introduction to a special section', *Psychotherapy Research* (Special section).

Stiles, W.B. and Shapiro, D.A. (1989) 'Abuse of the drug metaphor in psychotherapy process-outcome research', *Clinical Psychology Review*, 9: 521–43.

Stiles, W.B., Shapiro, D.A. and Elliott, R. (1986) '"Are all psychotherapies equivalent?"', *American Psychologist*, 41: 165–80.

Stiles, W.B., Barkham, M., Twigg, E., Mellor-Clark, J. and Cooper, M. (2006) 'Effectiveness of cognitive-behavioural, person-centred, and psychodynamic therapies as practised in UK National Health Service settings', *Psychological Medicine*, 36: 555–66.

Stiles, W.B., Shapiro, D.A. and Firth-Cozens, J.A. (1988) 'Do sessions of different treatments have different impacts?', *Journal of Counseling Psychology*, 35: 391–6.

Stiles, W.B., Elliott, R., Llewelyn, S.P., Firth-Cozens, J.A., Margison, F.R., Shapiro, D.A. and Hardy, G.E. (1990) 'Assimilation of problematic experiences by clients in psychotherapy', *Psychotherapy*, 27: 411–20.

Stiles, W.B., Shapiro, D.A. and Harper, H. (1994) 'Finding the way from process to outcome: blind alleys and unmarked trails', in R.L. Russell (ed.), *Reassessing Psychotherapy Research*. New York: Guilford Press. pp. 36–64.

Stiles, W.B., Honos-Webb, L. and Surko, M. (1998) 'Responsiveness in psychotherapy', *Clinical Psychology: Science and Practice*, 5: 439–58.

Strupp, H.H. (1980a) 'Success and failure in time-limited psychotherapy. A systematic comparison of two cases: Comparison 1', *Archives of General Psychiatry*, 37: 595–604.

Strupp, H.H. (1980b) 'Success and failure in time-limited psychotherapy. A systematic comparison of two cases: Comparison 2', *Archives of General Psychiatry*, 37: 708–16.

Strupp, H.H. (1980c) 'Success and failure in time-limited psychotherapy. With special reference to the performance of a lay counselor', *Archives of General Psychiatry*, 37: 831–41.

Strupp, H.H. (1980d) 'Success and failure in time-limited psychotherapy. Further evidence (Comparison 4)', *Archives of General Psychiatry*, 37: 947–54.

Strupp, H.H., Horowitz, L.M. and Lambert, M.J. (1997) *Measuring Patient Changes in Mood, Anxiety, and Personality Disorders: Towards a Core Battery.* Washington, DC: American Psychological Association.

Talley, P.E., Strupp, H.H. and Butler, S.F. (eds) (1994) *Psychotherapy Research and Practice: Bridging the Gap.* New York: Basic Books.

Tarrier, N., Harwood, S., Yusopoff, L., Beckett, R. and Baker, A. (1990) 'Coping strategy enhancement (CSE): a method of treating residual schizophrenic symptoms', *Behavioural Psychotherapy*, 18: 283–93.

Tarrier, N., Beckett, R., Harwood, S., Baker, A., Yusopoff, L. and Ugarteburu, I. (1993) 'A trial of two cognitive behavioural methods of treating drug-resistant residual psychotic symptoms in schizophrenic patients: I Outcome', *British Journal of Psychiatry*, 162: 524–32.

Taube, C.A., Burns, B.J. and Kessler, L. (1984) 'Patients of psychiatrists and psychologists in office-based practice: 1980', *American Psychologist*, 39: 1435–7.

Teasdale, J.D. (1985) 'Psychological treatments for depression: how do they work?', *Behavior Research and Therapy*, 23: 157–65.

Teasdale, J.D., Fennell, M.J.V., Hibbert, G.A. and Amies, P.L. (1984) 'Cognitive therapy for major depressive disorder in primary care', *British Journal of Psychiatry*, 144: 400–6.

Thornicroft, G. and Slade, M. (2000) 'Are routine outcome measures feasible in mental health?' *Quality in Healthcare*, 9: 84.

Truax, C.B. and Mitchell, K.M. (1971) 'Research on certain therapist interpersonal skills in relation to process and outcome', in A.E. Bergin and S.L. Garfield (eds), *Handbook of Psychotherapy and Behavior Change*. New York. Wiley. pp. 299–344.

US Department of Health and Human Sciences (US DHHS) (1993) *Depression in Primary Care: Treatment of Major Depression*. Depression Guideline Panel. Rockville: AHCPR Publications. pp. 71–123.

Wampold, B.E. (1997) 'Methodological problems in identifying efficacious psychotherapies', *Psychotherapy Research*, 7: 21–43.

Wampold, B.E. (2001) *The Great Psychotherapy Debate: Models, Methods, and Findings*. Mahwah, NJ: Lawrence Erlbaum Associates.

Wampold, B.E., Mondin, G.W., Moody, M., Stich, F., Benson, K. and Ahn, H. (1997) 'A meta-analysis of outcome studies comparing bona fide psychotherapies: empirically, "all must have prizes"', *Psychological Bulletin*, 122: 203–15.

Ward, E., King, M., Lloyd, M., Bower, P., Sibbauld, B., Farrelly, S., Gabbay, M., Tarrier, N. and Addington-Hall, J. (2000) 'Randomised controlled trial of non-directive counselling, cognitive-behaviour therapy, and usual general practitioner care for patients with depression. I: Clinical effectiveness', *British Medical Journal*, 321: 1383–8.

Warwick, H.M.C., Clark, D.M., Cobb, A.M. and Salkovskis, P.M. (1996) 'A controlled trial of cognitive-behavioural treatment of hypochondriasis', *British Journal of Psychiatry*, 169: 189–95.

Waskow, I.E. and Parloff, M.B. (eds) (1975) *Psychotherapy Change Measures* (DHEW Pub. no. (ADM) 74–120). Washington, DC: US Government Printing Office. pp. 245–69.

Whiston, S.C. and Sexton, T.L. (1993) 'An overview of psychotherapy outcome research: implications for practice', *Professional Psychology: Research and Practice*, 24: 43–51.

Whitehorn, J.C. and Betz, B. (1954) 'A study of psychotherapeutic relationships between physicians and schizophrenic patients', *American Journal of Psychiatry*, 3: 321–31.

Wing, J.K., Beevor, A., Curtis, R.H., Park, S.B.G., Hadden, S. and Burns, A. (1998) 'Health of the Nation Outcome Scales (HoNOS): research and development', *British Journal of Psychiatry*, 172: 11–18.

Wolfe, B. and Goldfried, M.R. (1988) 'Research on psychotherapy integration: recommendation and conclusions from an NIMH workshop', *Journal of Consulting and Clinical Psychology*, 56: 448–51.

19

The Training and Supervision of Individual Therapists

Mark Aveline

The purpose of training in psychotherapy is to facilitate the exercise of natural abilities and acquired skills to best effect and for the patient's best interest.[1] This statement asserts several propositions in the service of a virtuous purpose. First, that therapists bring to their work a greater or lesser degree of natural talent for psychotherapy. Subsidiary propositions are that the possession of talent is an essential foundation on which expertise can be built in training and that the talent is not a unitary predisposition; it may be for one of the individual therapies or for some other form such as group or family therapy. Secondly, psychotherapy is a purposeful activity in which trainees and trainers share a professional and ethical commitment to evaluate and refine their work. Thoughtful therapists will ask themselves three questions again and again: (1) what in the therapy and this person's life actually helped the patient? (2) could the end have been achieved more expeditiously? and (3) was anything done that was to the patient's ultimate detriment? These build to the ultimate question: was the patient's best interest well served?

It is impossible to do justice in this chapter to the fine detail of training in each of the many forms of individual therapy. Instead, attention is drawn to important issues in each area of training. After the introduction, I present a checklist of training objectives, then explore motivating factors in therapists and selection for training before considering the universally important dimensions of counter-transference and the abuse of power. Discussion of the three cardinal elements of theoretical learning, supervised clinical work, and personal therapy follows.

The move towards statutory registration of psychotherapists and counsellors, and the need for continued education is then considered. A section on supportive therapy concludes the review.

INTRODUCTION

'In what is called "individual psychotherapy" two people meet and talk to each other with the intention and hope that one will learn to live more fruitfully'. This deceptively simple statement by Lomas (1981) encompasses the central dimensions in psychotherapy practice: meeting, talking (I prefer the form 'talking with' rather than 'talking to') in a hopeful spirit and the purposeful intention of achieving more fruitful living in the patient's everyday life. The definition sets out in ordinary language the parameters of a kind of psychotherapy with which I can identify, a rather ordinary encounter between two people but one of exceptional promise. However, as is often the case, the results of our intentions do not always measure up to our hopes. Training is intended to enhance the competence of the therapist but in itself is no guarantee of success. Please note that types of training that emphasise apparent substantial differences between therapies may obscure underlying, powerful similarities.

Luborsky and Singer (1975), in a survey of the effectiveness of different approaches to psychotherapy subtitled 'Is it true that "Everyone has won and all must have prizes"?', call attention to the fact that in research studies all the psychotherapies are similarly effective and none pre-eminent, a sobering conclusion for partisans of any school or faction. In other words, what effective therapies across schools have in common is more important than what divides them, a theme I return to later. This is not to deny that certain therapies are particularly suitable for a given person or problem, or that a therapist will function especially well in the approach that she finds most congenial. What are the best applications of the different therapies is a matter for research (Roth and Fonagy, 2004), while the natural affinity of a trainee for particular approaches is a key aspect to be identified in training.

The findings of Luborsky and other researchers certainly have not stilled debate about who is or is not a psychotherapist or which theoretical system, if any, approximates most closely to the complexity of being human. Or can one variant, for example psychoanalysis and psychoanalytic psychotherapy that share so many features, consistently and with enhanced therapeutic effect be distinguished from the other? Sandler (1988), a distinguished psychoanalyst, thinks not. In such debates, questions of power, prestige and authenticity lurk in the shadows and threaten to upstage the essential question of 'what treatment by whom is most effective for this individual with that specific problem and under which set of circumstances' (Paul, 1967). When, as all too often, the tribes in the psychotherapy nation go to war with one another, they yield to the temptation of vested interest in promoting ascendancy over competitors and, within their own ranks, in stilling dissident voices; in such struggles, the pursuit of truth may be neglected. They neglect the communality of interest on the larger stage of developing a profession of psychotherapy and counselling where effective practice may be refined through the opposite processes of differentiation and integration. In selecting a training programme, trainees need to bear these points in mind.

Given the wide range of approaches that may be gathered under the generic title of individual psychotherapy, and the partisanship that goes with differences that are often more apparent than real, I am mindful of the hazard of this chapter being dismissed by adherents of one approach on the grounds of irrelevance to their practice, ignorance of what they do or believe, and partiality to my own bias. In contrast, my intention is to address important issues for trainees and trainers which I hope will be heard across the spectrum. But first I must state what is central to my approach. I declare my bias and set out a synthesis, derived from my experience as therapist and trainer, with which readers may compare their own conclusions (Aveline, 1979, 2005a).

Psychotherapy attends both to the vital feelings of hope, despair, envy, hate, self-doubt, love and loss that exist between humans and to the repeated pattern of relationships that a person forms; in particular, to those aspects of the patterns for which that person has responsibility and over which they can come to exercise choice. As a therapist, I encourage my patient to take personally significant action in the form of new ways of relating, both in the consulting room and in his relationships outside, which, once succeeded in, will begin to rewrite the cramped fiction of his life. This therapeutic action challenges the determining myths that a person has learned or evolved to explain his actions; commonly, these myths are restrictive and self-limiting. I work with the psychological view that a person takes of himself, his situation and the possibilities open to him; essentially, this is the view that has been taken of him by important others and that he has taken of himself in the past, and it will go on being the determining view unless some corrective emotional experience occurs. The view that the person takes of himself is illuminated by the relationship patterns that form between the patient and the people in his life, including me; jointly, the patient and I examine the meaning of the patterns. Importantly, it is change in the external world of the patient, rather than inferred intra-psychic change, against which I judge the success of our mutual endeavour. Lest this sound too demanding, let me balance the statement by recognising the need of many patients with deep problems of self-doubt and negative world-view for sustained care in order to gather the courage to change.

On one level, I make no distinction between enlightened psychoanalytic and cognitive-behavioural theory and practice; both recognise and utilise the therapeutic factors they have in common; both offer encouragement, the one covertly, the other overtly. In psychoanalytic psychotherapy, intra-psychic terrors are faced and the treatment proceeds by analogy; if a new end to the old sad story can be written in the relationship with the therapist, the same new chapter can be written in the natural relationships outside the consulting room. In cognitive-behavioural therapy, direct action is taken in the patient's social world, perhaps after a period of rehearsal, often undertaken with the therapist. What characterises good psychotherapy of any sort is a sustained, affirmative stance on the part of an imaginative, seasoned therapist who respects and does not exploit (Schafer, 1983). I hope that my relationship with the patient is both passionate and ethical, for both these elements are necessary if personal change is to occur. In the interplay of therapy, I influence and am influenced by what passes between us. It is the other person's journey in life, but it is a journey for us both and one in which I may expect to change as well as the patient. It is a journey and not an aimless ramble: though the ultimate destination may be unknown, the way stations are known by the therapist and aimed for; the therapist has expertise in guiding the other through terrain which is new to them and has some responsibility for the choices made (Aveline, 2001). It is, also, a journey in which I do not expect to be the guide for the whole way; someone may enter therapy for a while, gain what they require to get their life moving, go away to try their modified approach and return later if they need; in this, I am a minimalist. I do not aim, even if it were possible as early psychoanalysts hoped, to exhaust through the psychotherapy the patient's potential for neurosis or, necessarily, to locate the locus of change wholly in the relationship with me.

Having offered these conclusions as points of reference for the following sections, let us begin by recognising the formidable task that awaits the trainee therapist.

WHAT THE INDIVIDUAL THERAPIST HAS TO LEARN

Despite the plethora of texts and manualised procedures whose clinical purpose is to lend assistance to both experienced and novice therapists, the practice of psychotherapy is challenging in its elusive complexity, ambiguity and frustratingly slow pace of change. Even in the more procedure-dominated cognitive and behavioural therapies, the ambiguous, uncertain reality of practice is disconcerting to those (and this includes many with medical, nursing and psychology backgrounds) who are used to the greater predicability in physical science of structure, intervention and consistent outcome. In physical science at a macro level, linearity is the rule. In psychotherapy, chaos theory is a more apt model; change being the product of a complex and uncertain interaction between the form and severity of problems, the patient's personality, developmental stage and motivation, the appropriateness, intrinsic power and dose of the therapy, the skill, motivation and healing capacity of the psychotherapist, the malleability of the life situation and the operation of chance and good or ill-fortune. In this maelstrom, change may be planned and incremental but, often, little changes trigger large unexpected effects or hard-won advances are swept away by the re-emergence of maladaptive patterns in response to stress.

Furthermore, what happens between therapist and patient is complicated by the often unrecognised involvement of the therapist in the patient's self-limiting fiction and the arousal of unresolved personal conflicts in the therapist; this phenomenon of transference and counter-transference has the central place in the psychoanalytic therapies (and, of course, is fostered by their techniques) but to a greater or lesser extent is also part of any human interaction and, certainly, of any therapy where the participants have a close relationship. Yet despite these caveats, I trust that for readers of this volume, the struggle to become proficient therapists is worthwhile, not least because psychotherapy is a fundamentally important activity in our technological and materialistic age: it attends to individual and shared experience and meaning and attests to the ability of people to support and help each other. But this practical discipline and creative art is not easily learnt.

What a therapist has to learn depends on the level and intensity at which she has to practise, be it at the level of beginner gaining a limited appreciation of what psychotherapy is or of qualified professional who needs psychotherapeutic skills as part of her generalist work, or of career psychotherapist and future trainer of therapists. The caveat is that, at all levels, the same lessons are repeated again and again. The individual therapies vary substantially in theory, focus and technique and there is much to be learned. However, the trainee who quite appropriately immerses herself in one approach risks being ignorant of others. The alternative, when faced with such variety, is to attempt to learn simultaneously two dissonant approaches, which may cause trainee confusion and a degree of trainer alienation. Yet not to look widely at the therapy spectrum during the formative period of training is to risk premature closure in thinking and mental ossification. I favour exposure to many approaches, especially early in training.

From the point of view of the trainee therapist, the objectives in training can be stated as follows:

General:

1   make progress towards the optimal use of natural ability and acquired skills;
2   identify the type(s) of therapy and range of patient problem and personality with which the therapist can work effectively.

Specific (in approximate order of priority):

1   learn to listen to what is said and not said by patients and to develop shared languages of personal meaning;
2   develop the capacity to stay in contact with patients in their emotionally painful explorations; create a safe psychological space;
3   learn to move between participation and observation while interacting with patients, thereby acquiring a sense of when and when not to intervene;
4   gain a coherent conceptual frame within which to understand what happens in therapy and is intended to happen;
5   study human development, the process of learning, and the functioning of both naturally occurring personal relationships between friends, couples and in families and the artificial, constructed relationships of psychotherapy where strangers are brought together;
6   understand and bring to bear both the therapeutic factors that types of therapy have in common (these, which are often referred to as non-specific or common factors, are detailed in the section on theoretical learning) and those that are approach specific;

7 gain confidence in the practice of the preferred type of therapy; make full use of the therapist's emotional responses, theoretical constructs and techniques in resolving the patients' problems; become competent in own way of working; become adept in working briefly and long-term, and at different frequencies;

8 commit to evidence-based practice;

9 increase self-awareness and work towards the resolution of personal conflicts that may interfere with therapy;

10 come to know personal limitations and be able to obtain and use supervision;

11 know the features of major psychiatric illness and the indications and contra-indications for psychotropic medication; make valid diagnostic assessments psychiatrically, psychologically and dynamically (Malan, 1995: Chapters 18–23; Aveline, 1997);

12 be sufficiently knowledgeable about other types of therapy so as to match therapy to patient need either by modifying technique or referring on; accept that individuals may need a variety of help, either concurrently or sequentially;

13 be aware of ethical dilemmas and internalise high ethical standards; cultivate humility, compassion and modesty as well as a proper degree of self-confidence;

14 be familiar with the chosen theoretical system and aware of its strengths and limitations; appreciate the significance of cultural and social factors and adjust therapy accordingly; evaluate critically what is enduring truth and what is mere habit or unsubstantiated dogma in the practice of psychotherapy through (a) the experience of clinical practice, (b) being supervised and (c) studying the research literature; be able to evaluate outcome; set standards of practice and systematically audit implementation;

15 understand the implications of the employment context in which practice is to occur (philosophical, political, institutional, economic and contractual);

16 commit to continuous professional development; at the level of career psychotherapist, acquire that professional identity.

For the trainer, the objectives are:

1 assess (a) the developmental stage of trainees and (b) identify their strengths and weaknesses. At different stages, this may involve the normative functions of selection for training and evaluation for graduation. (Educationally, 'normative' refers to entry/exit, pass/fail criteria, whereas 'formative' refers to non-examined elements that enrich the educational experience of training);

2 help trainees secure the formative learning experiences which will clarify and develop their natural affinity with particular types of therapy and problem;

3 hold the balance of interest between the learning needs of trainee therapists and the clinical needs of their patients until such time as the therapist can do this for herself.

This long list is not intended to be intimidating but it does serve to underline the seriousness of embarking on training to be a therapist. It provides a framework with which to assess training needs, progress and the suitability of training programme for a particular trainee.

Training has no endpoint or single path. Personal and occupational choices determine the form of an individual's training over time and may mark progression from the expertise needed by a generalist with an interest in the subject to that required by a career psychotherapist, and within psychotherapy from one type to another as the trainee's interest changes. Further training will be necessary to update the therapist with advances in practice and to maintain existing expertise at a good level. Just as therapy should meet the needs of the patient, so should training meet the requirements of the therapist's practice, both those that stem from the type of therapy practised and from the work setting. What a therapist working in brief therapy in a clinic with a long waiting list needs to know is very different from someone specialising in long-term therapy in independent practice who only takes on new work as vacancies occur.

The reader at this point may be eager to plunge into the detail of the three cardinal elements of training, namely theoretical learning, supervised clinical work and personal therapy. To accede to this wish would be premature. It would collude with the view that proficiency in psychotherapy is a simple, acquired technical skill. Instead, I argue that the wish to train in psychotherapy arises from events in the trainee's personal history and their consequent effect on character structure. The reflective therapist will want to take stock of what she brings from her inheritance and life experience to this work before she becomes deeply committed to it. Two things are certain. In the work of psychotherapy, whatever the type, the personal, unique reactions of the therapist will complicate and illuminate the relationship that she and the patient have, and being a therapist will expose her to the temptation of abusing that powerful position. What I mean by these strong statements is spelt out in the next four sections that deal with motivating factors in therapists, selection for training, counter-transference and the abuse of power.

Motivating factors in the therapist

The trainee therapist has been long in the making before he or she formally enters training. Family circumstance, life events, gender, race and culture combine with inherited predisposition to form a unique individual who may or may not be suited to the practice of some or all of the psychotherapies. Each potential therapist will be special in their values, expectations and sensitivities; each will have natural ability in different measure for the work and natural affinity with particular types of therapy and patient problems.

Being a psychotherapist offers many satisfactions: the opportunity to develop a unique personal style of practice with a substantial degree of professional independence, to share at close hand an endless variety of human activities far beyond that generally encountered in the therapist's own life, to satisfy the desire to help others, to be intellectually stimulated, to gain in emotional growth ... and to have prestige and be paid (Bugental, 1964; Burton, 1975; Greben, 1975; Farber and Heifetz, 1981; Farber, 1983; Yalom, 2002)!

Guy (1987) distinguishes between functional and dysfunctional motivators. In fact, his items encompass both motivating factors and functional attributes of effective therapists. Functional motivators include a natural interest in people, the ability to listen and talk, the psychological mindedness of being disposed to enter empathetically into the world of meaning and motivation of others, and the capacities of facilitating and tolerating the expression of feelings, being emotionally insightful, introspective and capable of self-denial, as well as being tolerant of ambiguity and intimacy and capable of warmth, caring and laughter (see also Greben's six functional attributes in the next section).

Dysfunctional motivators draw people to the role of therapist and may prove to be functional, but when excessive subvert the process for the therapist's own ends. There is a well-established tradition in dynamic psychotherapy, clearly articulated by Jung, that only the wounded healer can heal. Thus, Storr writes: 'Psychotherapists often have some personal knowledge of what it is like to feel insulted and injured, a kind of knowledge which they might rather be without, but which actually extends the range of their compassion' (Storr, 1979; 173). Guy (1987) lists six dysfunctional motivators, the first of which is the most common:

1   emotional distress: therapists may seek and gain self-healing through their work; the crucial question is one of magnitude. Some acquaintance with emotional pain is essential; an over-preoccupation with unresolved personal needs hinders the therapist from giving full attention to the patient;
2   vicarious coping as a life style which imparts a voyeuristic quality to the therapy relationship;
3   conducting psychotherapy as a means of compensating for an inner sense of loneliness and isolation; this is self-defeating as it is life lived at one remove;
4   fulfilling the desire for power and fostering a false sense of omnipotence and omniscience (Marmor, 1953; Guggenbuhl-Craig, 1979)
5   a messianic need to provide succour; one positive aspect of psychotherapy is that it is an acceptable way for a person to show their love and tenderness, but becomes dysfunctional when it is compulsive;
6   psychotherapy as a relatively safe way of expressing underlying rebellious feelings in the therapist through getting the patient to act them out.

These dysfunctional motivators give rise to counter-transference problems which are considered later (counter-transference means distortions derived from unresolved conflicts in the therapist's life which she unconsciously introduces into the therapy relationship).

The prevalence of dysfunctional motivators among psychotherapists is not known. In a major survey of 4,000 American psychotherapists (Henry, 1977), most reported good relationships with their families though 39 per cent said that their parents' marriage was not good. Childhood separations, deaths and incidence of mental illness were similar to that of other college educated populations. These global statistics doubtless conceal much individual variation. Thus Storr's (1979) impression may be true that many therapists (and here he means dynamically oriented therapists) had depressed mothers to whose feelings they may have developed special sensitivity, together with an urge not to upset or distress; their childhood experiences may well prompt them to seek out in adult life the role of therapist. In Kleinian terminology, the need to make reparation will be great in these therapists; they may be especially adept at making contact with timid and fearful patients. There is some evidence that within the occupation of psychotherapy a history of personal conflicts and a greater experience of mental illness in the family of origin inclines practitioners more towards dynamic rather than behavioural orientations (Rosin and Knudson, 1986). I know of no research that distinguishes between the personal backgrounds of therapists choosing to work in individual therapy and those choosing family and group therapy.

These factors and attributes constitute the natural ability for which selection has to be made and which is built on in training.

The selection of therapists for training

Trainers have a dual responsibility in selecting their trainees: to help that person avoid taking on work for which she is not suitable; and to ensure that patients from whom the trainee will learn have optimal care.

Selection is a matter for both the trainee and the trainer: the trainee will want to test out what is on offer and the trainer will test the trainee's readiness for each level of training. Brief introductory courses and workshops offer the trainee the opportunity to try different types of therapy and discover those for which she has natural affinity. Little or no attempt is made to select at this level. Another formative route into formal psychotherapy training is being supervised by therapists whose style and orientations vary and, either before or as a supplement, being in personal therapy; both experiences form and clarify aptitude. With advancing level, selection procedures become correspondingly complex. Commonly, for analytic training, a candidate will complete an autobiographical questionnaire and undergo two extended interviews with different assessors, one more factual and the other analytically explorative; to reduce bias, a panel of assessors considers the results. During training, progress has to be approved before entry to each stage, a meticulous and extended procedure. The first step is training therapy (five times a week); after at least a year and having secured satisfactory reports from her therapist, the analysand adds participation in theoretical seminars, and, yet later, embarks on training cases. Educationally having reports from the therapist helps exclude unsatisfactory trainees but may compromise the neutrality of the therapy and enhance its asymmetry (see the section on abuse of power). Some institutes attempt to mitigate negative effects by excluding personal details from the report.

Sadly, the correlation between length of training and effectiveness as a therapist is low (Auerbach and Johnson, 1977; Beutler et al., 2004). While this finding may reflect deficiencies in research methodology, it is probably a function of the relative unimportance of training in comparison with other therapeutic factors, namely the vital role of pre-existing therapist personality factors such as decency, respectful empathic concern with others, neutrality, persistence and optimism in promoting personal change ... and the even greater importance of patient motivation, ego-strength and favourable social context. In my experience as a trainer, a therapist's effectiveness over the years of her career often seems to follow a U-curve and is a function of different attributes. Early on, patients benefit especially from the therapist's energy and enthusiasm and later from her acquired wisdom and skill as a therapist. In the middle phase, as therapists become more self-conscious and aware of the complexity of the subject, performance may decline temporarily. Later, therapists may work with patients whose problems are more severe and entrenched; gains may be slow and hard-won albeit potentiated by the beneficial effect of training and experience. Trainees should not feel dismayed by feeling deskilled when they enter the next level of training. Information on the longitudinal development of psychotherapists can be found in Orlinsky and Rønnestad (2002).

The above should not be taken to imply that putting effort into selection is worthless. Personality is all important. 'The greatest technical skill can offer no substitute for nor will obviate the pre-eminent need for integrity, honesty, and dedication on the part of the therapist' (Strupp, 1960). As a selector, I look for the functional motivators listed by Guy (1987), and also the six qualities identified by Greben: empathic concern, respectfulness, realistic hopefulness, self-awareness, reliability and strength of character (Greben, 1984). These are the qualities that are necessary if the therapist is to win the patient's trust; they give him the sense of being tended to and valued. Women often seem to have these qualities in greater abundance than men. It must be stressed that no one is perfect: what is required for this work is a sufficiency of these qualities. In addition, I look for two markers of maturity: that the trainee has struggled with some personal emotional conflict and achieved a degree of resolution, and that she has enjoyed and sustained over years a loving, intimate relationship. The first may bring in its wake humility and compassion, the second an active commitment to and capacity for good relationships, so well summed up in Fairbairn's concept of mature dependence (Fairbairn, 1954). I am wary of aspiring therapists who have a scornful, rejecting or persecutory cast to their nature or who are not emotionally generous in their interaction.

My impression is that therapists who prefer to work in individual therapy rather than in, for example, group therapy have several characteristics. They seem to have a greater interest in the vertical or historical axis of there-and-then exploration into the childhood origins of adult problems and their recreation within the therapy relationship, as opposed to the horizontal axis of here-and-now interactions that is central to the focus of the group therapist (and increasingly of the modern psychodynamic therapist). They are more interested in fantasy, prefer a relatively passive role, like the immediacy of one-to-one relationships and the opportunity to work in depth. These impressions may help the trainee in the choice of which type of therapy to train in, though other factors will also be influential. Cognitive-behavioural therapy (CBT), which is mostly practised individually, has seized the high ground in the competition for legitimacy through research and is favoured by purchasers. While some CBT practitioners work in depth with complex personality problems, the emphasis on current life issues, action and symptomatic change (as well as being on the winning side for now) has particular appeal. In private practice, high patient demand for individual therapy boosts its economic viability and may reinforce natural affinity for individual work.

Should psychotherapists be qualified in one of the core health care professions as a prerequisite for this work? Generally, these are taken to be medicine, psychology, nursing and social work (all degree occupations) and occupational therapy and, perhaps, the new categories of art and drama therapy. Talent as a psychotherapist is not the exclusive preserve of any profession. The development in the UK within the National Health Service (NHS) of the *ad hoc* grade of Adult Psychotherapist, open to all with aptitude and training, testifies to the truth of this proposition. However, the possession of a core qualification indicates that the trainee has a certain level of intelligence and is familiar with the symptoms and signs of psychiatric illness; it is certainly advantageous for NHS practice. In qualifying, the trainee had the opportunity to internalise high ethical standards and, through membership of that professional group, will have access to continued professional development (CPD) and be subject to disciplinary procedures, provisions which help maintain good practice. Qualifications in literature, philosophy and religion are relevant but trainees with these backgrounds will need special training in the features of major psychiatric illness and in what may be gained from pharmacological treatments, especially if they intend to practise independently. I return to this question in the sections on theoretical learning, supervised clinical practice, and registration.

At the heart of individual therapy is a closed, intense, asymmetrical relationship between patient and therapist. The next two sections deal with potential consequences of that intensity: problematic counter-transference reactions and the temptation for the therapist to abuse her power.

Counter-transference

Unconsciously mediated transference and counter-transference reactions inevitably feature in any relationship and, especially, in the intimate relationship of prolonged individual therapy. These powerful distortions are present even in symptom-oriented cognitive and behaviour therapies. Increasingly, cognitive-behavioural training programmes recognise the importance of such processes.

The term counter-transference is used in two senses; feelings that are the counterpart of the patient's feelings and those that are counteractions to the patient's transference (Greenson, 1967). Counterpart feelings are part of empathy; they provide valuable information about the other, as when the therapist feels in herself the disowned, hidden sadness or anger of the other, technically a manifestation of projective identification (a Kleinian concept). Thus the therapist's unconscious mind understands that of her patient (Heimann, 1950). Counteractions are situations where the patient's communications stir up unresolved problems of the therapist. An example would be a therapist who fears her own aggression and placates the patient whenever she detects hostile feelings towards her. In addition, the patient, through some combination of age, gender or other characteristics, may be a transference figure for the therapist, perhaps a parent to be placated or rival to be undermined. Furthermore, dependence on the therapist and the intimacy of the role relationship will have personal meaning for the therapist for good or for ill, based on past and childhood experiences of psychologically similar situations.

Consider the following list of counter-transference reactions and their consequences (Bernstein and Bernstein, 1980: 48) and see how each limits the therapeutic potential of the encounter.

1   Do I require sympathy, protection and warmth so much myself that I err by being too sympathetic, too protective toward the patient?
2   Do I fear closeness so much that I err by being indifferent, rejecting and cold?
3   Do I need to feel important and therefore keep patients dependent on me, precluding their independence and assuming responsibility for their own welfare?
4   Do I cover feelings of inferiority with a front of superiority, thereby rejecting patients' need for acceptance?
5   Is my need to be liked so great that I become angry when a patient is rude, unappreciative or uncooperative?
6   Do I react to the patient as an individual human being or do I label him with the stereotype of a group? Are my prejudices justified?
7   Am I competing with other authority figures in the patient's life when I offer advice contrary to that of another health professional?
8   Does the patient remind me too much of my own problems when I find myself being overly ready with pseudo-optimism and facile reassurance?
9   Do I give uncalled for advice as a means of appearing all wise?
10 Do I talk more than listen to a patient in an effort to impress him with my knowledge?

Counter-transference problems are signalled by intensification or departures from the therapist's usual practice. At the time, the alterations seem plausible, even justified; yet, when considered in supervision or in the routine self-scrutiny ('internal supervision', Casement, 1985) that is the mark of responsible psychotherapy, their obstructive nature becomes apparent. Menninger (1958) lists among the items that he has 'probably experienced': repeatedly experiencing erotic feelings towards the patient, carelessness in regard to appointment arrangements, sadistic unnecessary sharpness in formulating interpretations, getting conscious satisfaction from the patient's praise or affection and sudden increase or decrease in interest in a certain case.

Items like the above serve as a checklist to identify habitual counter-transference problems that arise from the therapist's own conflicts. This is different from the equally problematic process that manifests the therapist's involvement in the patient's determining fiction or, in the language of psychoanalysis, transference and transference neurosis. An example is the way in which a patient who has been brought up in a persecutory environment expects others to persecute him, perceives the therapist as being persecutory (transference) and unconsciously prompts the therapist to act in a persecutory way (transference neurosis); another is when the therapist finds herself not respecting the boundaries of a patient whose boundaries as a child have been breached by a parent in incestuous acts. Counter-transference feelings are acted-out, thereby enacting formative events from the patient's past in the patient-therapist relationship. Being on the brink of acting-out is not without therapeutic value. Identifying these involvements, exploring their meaning, disentangling therapist and patient, and repairing ruptures in the relationship is an excellent way to work with interpersonal problems and promote change (Safran and Muran, 2000; Meares, 2001).

The abuse of power

All types of psychotherapy are vulnerable to abuse of power. Therapists are easily self-seduced into corrupting the therapy relationship; then, the relationship stops being therapeutic. Typically, the abusive process is set going by the conjunction of patient transference wishes and therapist dysfunctional motivators, potentiated by the inequality of power between the two. Trainees need to learn to anticipate the potential for abuse, recognise its phenomena and take corrective action; clinical supervision is particularly helpful in achieving this learning.

Crucially, the therapist constructs the therapy arena and, subject to some negotiation, decides the therapy's duration, frequency and form. Ultimately, beginning and ending are in her hands, ending being a powerful threat to a patient who is dependent or not coping. With rare exceptions, the meetings take place on the therapist's territory. The therapist, whether trainee or trained, is held to be expert in what goes on in the arena, certainly by the patient who is relatively a novice in this setting. Whatever procedures the therapist propounds, the patient is predisposed to accept. It is all too easy for eccentric, unsubstantiated beliefs to be peddled as truths by those with power and clung on to by vulnerable, uncertain patients who deserve better. Because the sessions take place in private, the therapy is not subject to the natural regulation of outsider scepticism and incredulity. All this gives the therapist great power and, consequently, exposes her to great temptation.

The conjunction of a patient's need for an ideal parent who will protect, guide and succour with a therapist's wish to be idealised is hazardous. What Ernest Jones (1913) termed the 'God complex' lies in wait for the unwary (Marmor, 1953). The therapist's ego is boosted by transference admiration; this seductive trap is compounded by the common tendency in psychotherapy and especially in individual therapy for therapists to mystify the process through the use of esoteric jargon and the adoption of an aloof, all-knowing stance. In the artificial, time-limited world of therapy sessions, the therapist may have the pretence of having all the answers. They run the risk of coming to feel superior, free of the struggles, conflicts and defeats of their patients. From a detached position – which may be bolstered by viewing all the patient's communications as manifestations of transference and, as such, only needing to be put back to the patient for his sole consideration – the therapist is tempted to be a bystander in life, vicariously involved but spared its pain and puffed up by the patient's dependent approval. Progress towards separation and individuation is obstructed.

Guggenbuhl-Craig (1979) asserts that within us all is the archetype of the patient and healer. In order to reduce ambivalence, the archetype may be split and either polarity projected on to others. But both are necessary for healing. The sick man needs an external healer, but also needs to find the healer in himself; otherwise he becomes passive through handing over his healing ability to the other. This is obviously antithetical to the spirit of good psychotherapy. For the healer, the danger is to locate the polarity of the 'patient in her' in her patients and not recognise it in her own self. Then, she will come to see herself more and more as the strong healer for whom weakness, illness and wounds do not exist. As a healer without wounds, she is less able to engage the healing factor in her patients.

The therapist who locates weakness in others becomes powerful through their failure. In some therapists, the split in the archetype is minimal; their own problems are illuminated by the patient's and consciously worked on; they remain a patient as well as a healer. The best way of reducing the split is through involvement in ordinary life in non-analytic, symmetrical relationships that have the power to touch deeply and throw off balance, and which are quite different from the asymmetrical ones of therapy. Loving, forceful encounters with equals develop the therapist as a whole person. What the therapist advocates for others is good for her.

Not surprisingly, given the intensity and privacy of individual therapy, some therapists become sexually involved with their patients. It is hard to conceive of circumstances when this is not abusive in its impact or a dereliction of therapist responsibilities. One can understand how it happens but it should not be condoned. Many more male therapists have sexual involvement with female patients than do female therapists with male patients but all combinations do occur, including with the same sex. Some sexually exploitative health care professionals show evidence of sexual addiction or other compulsive behaviour. A study of 88 severe cases showed several graphic patterns with three having high rates of addiction and, hence, of serious risk to patients: naive prince (7.9 per cent, no sex addicts), wounded warrior (21.6 per cent, 37 per cent sex addicts), self-serving martyr (23.9 per cent, 62 per cent sex addicts), false lover (19.3 per cent, 94 per cent sex addicts), dark king (12.5 per cent, 91 per cent sex addicts), wild card (14.8 per cent, 23 per cent sex addicts). The false lover enjoys living on the edge and the dark king is manipulative and sees sexual exploitation as an expression of power (Irons and Schneider, 1999). Eroticised transference and counter-transference are common in psychotherapy and may be acted out (Holroyd and Brodsky, 1977). In the transference, the patient may be looking for a loving parent. Their wish may connect with the therapist's need to be a helping figure but subsequent sexual action represents confusion of childhood wishes, albeit expressed by the patient in adult language, with mature intent; sexual action fractures the boundaries that are necessary if therapy is to be psychologically safe.

Lust is a relatively straightforward motivation in acting-out; its intensity depends on the urgency of the therapist's biological drive, age, state of health, recency of drive satisfaction, general satisfaction with personal life and, of course, the attractiveness of the patient. Darker motivations such as unconscious hostility to women or reaction formations against feared homosexuality or gender inadequacy may be present (Marmor, 1972). Sexual action may be rationalised as being for the patient's benefit but this self-deception should not survive the monitoring of self-scrutiny, clinical supervision and personal therapy.

Occasionally, therapist and patient fall in love and form a long-term relationship. Though one may wonder about the basis of a personal relationship founded in the strange circumstances of the therapy room, the ethically correct action is to suspend therapy and arrange for it to be continued by a colleague if necessary.

CARDINAL ELEMENTS IN TRAINING

Theoretical learning, supervised clinical practice and personal therapy are cardinal elements in training. As they are so interrelated, it is difficult to discuss one without making an artificial distinction from the others; thus, the following sections should be read with these elements in mind and the section on what individual therapists have to learn. The order of discussion reflects my priority. Many analytic therapists might wish to give primacy to personal therapy; many cognitive-behaviourists might dispute its relevance to their work. Academic courses awarding certificates, diplomas and Master's degrees are likely to emphasise theory and research, though this is a changing scene as universities realise that they have to incorporate supervised practice if their graduates are to be registered as practitioners by one of the national registering bodies. Many of the points made here are also relevant to training in other modalities of psychotherapy such as group therapy (Aveline and Ratigan, 1988).

Theoretical learning

Purpose and content
The purpose of training is to facilitate the exercise of natural abilities and acquired skills to the patient's best interest. To achieve this, the therapist needs to gain extensive experience in the type(s) of therapy required for her practice and for which affinity has been shown, e.g. individual therapy. To begin with, the trainee needs to acquire a conceptual framework of what therapy is about, how people mature and learn, and the role of the therapist. Later in training, theory will be critically examined to discover its areas of greatest applicability and limitations. Studying theory means that therapists do not reinvent the wheel. Assimilating theory into practice provides the therapist with an internalised rationale to understand clinical phenomena, derive technique and formulate testable, clinically relevant hypotheses.

Studying theory is part of a broad educational process, which, in enlightened trainings, encourages informed critical thinking. Theory often is taught in an approach-specific way but general, overlapping and complementary perspectives should also be addressed. Specific and general learning need to be presented in the quality and level appropriate to the trainee's need and ability. Ideally, theoretical learning would encompass the following:

Theory and techniques specific to the therapy approach being learned   In most types of training this is the major component but, as has been proposed, the well-educated therapist needs to consider the range of approaches.

The common therapeutic factors   Frank (1973) has argued convincingly that six influential factors operate in all effective therapies. Therapy provides (1) an explanatory rationale and (2) facilitates the exploration of traumas and conflictual issues in a state of emotional arousal. The effect is strengthened (3) when the therapist is sanctioned as a healer by the society. Responding to the patient's request for help (4) encourages that person to be hopeful about themselves and counters the demoralisation which typifies most patients' state. Therapy provides or prompts (5) success experiences, which enhance the sense of mastery. Finally psychotherapy provides (6) an intense confiding relationship with a helping person. These factors have a much greater influence on outcome than the contribution made by approach-specific theory and technique; in Lambert's review of empirical studies, common therapeutic factors accounted for 30 per cent of the therapeutic effect, technique 15 per cent, expectancy (placebo effect) 15 per cent and spontaneous remission 40 per cent (Lambert, 1986).

The necessary conditions   Rogers (1957) promoted research studies to test his proposition that three therapist conditions were necessary and sufficient for personality change: genuineness, unconditional positive regard and accurate empathy. The contention that these conditions are sufficient in themselves, are always helpful and should be taken as absolutes has been much investigated and caveats placed on the original proposition. However, a sufficiency of each constitutes the basis of a helpful relationship; a strong therapeutic alliance is essential to effective psychotherapy (Horvath and Luborsky, 1993). In passing, it should be noted that Freud took it as read that the analyst would be a decent, understanding, non-judgemental, respectful and neutral person. These qualities formed the basis of the therapeutic alliance and gave, in Sandor Ferenczi's word, 'stability' (Tragfestigheit) to the relationship (Strupp, 1977). In terms of therapeutic action, the person of the therapist is not all-important (contributing 10–20 per cent to the outcome variance (Beutler et al., 2004; Aveline, 2005a)) but, without the therapist, there would be no therapy.

Natural capacity for healing   Hubble and his colleagues see successful therapy as being that which assists the person's natural capacity for healing (Hubble et al., 1999). Each person has their own theory of change which is an emergent reality in the therapy, there to be prized and learnt from. The therapist has to be sufficiently flexible to work congruently and creatively with the patient's world-view.

Technique acts like a magnifying glass, focusing forces for change and causing them to ignite into action.

The evolution of psychotherapy ideas   How the concepts of psychoanalysis, analytical psychology, individual psychology, existentialism, humanism, Gestalt psychology, psychodrama, cognitive, learning and systems theory have developed, their interrelationship and the implications for practice. In the analytic tradition, how an instinct-based theory has evolved to ego-psychology and then to self-psychology with increasing emphasis on object relations (human relations) and, especially in North America, on cultural and interpersonal aspects.

Human development   How individuals develop over the life-span with particular reference to maturational tasks, attachment theory, and the elements that contribute to being able, in Freud's definition of maturity, to love and to work.

Mental mechanisms, character structure and the concept of conflict   How to make a dynamic formulation of the origin and meaning of the patient's problems (Aveline, 1980; Eells, 1997). The meaning and significance in clinical practice of the technical terms: process, content, therapeutic alliance, transference, counter-transference and resistance. When and how to make effective interpretations and other interventions. Good examples of the practical application of these concepts may be found in Malan (1995) and Casement (1985).

Learning and systems theory   The role of shaping, modelling, generalisation and *in vivo* learning and faulty cognitions in determining human behaviour. The importance of problem definition and behavioural analysis in making a diagnostic assessment. How behavioural, system and dynamic processes operate in marriage and families and result in disturbed functioning. The contribution to understanding psychological change and resistance of cognitive dissonance, attribution theory and crisis theory.

Ways in which therapists need to take account of linguistics, philosophy, religion and ethics in formulating a comprehensive model of human aspirations and functioning.

Cultural relativity   with special reference to race, gender, sexual orientation, age and culture itself. The specific contribution made by feminist psychology, understanding of role relationships and psychology in the 20th century.

Physical disease presenting as mental disorder   In addition, the signs and symptoms of major psychiatric illness, the likely benefits and side-effects of psychotropic medication and when and to whom to refer on. As a counterpart to this medical knowledge, the ways in which the sociological concepts of stigma and labelling further our understanding of alienation and isolation.

Indications and contraindications for different kinds of psychotherapy.

The vital role of support in psychotherapy.

Preparation for therapy and patient-therapist matching How to assess, anticipate duration and likely effects of therapy, and seek informed consent. How therapy can produce negative effects and may be minimised. Taking into account available alternatives, does the therapist have the necessary interest, skills and time to help this patient?

Research methodology and classic studies How to evaluate the research literature and derive implications for clinical practice (Aveline et al., 2005). See Roth and Fonagy (2004) and Parry (2001) for statements of evidence-based practice.

Clinical audit How to set standards for practice and monitor them systematically through audit reference.

Clinical governance the profession-long responsibility for the quality of one's work and the work of other psychotherapists (Department of Health, 1998). Identifying and implementing needs for continuing professional development (CPD). System errors and root causes.

Ethics Practice dilemmas, conflicts of interest, duty of care, informed consent and confidentiality including extended confidentiality in teamwork (Aveline, 2001), principle-based ethics i.e. non-maleficence, beneficence, respect for autonomy and justice (Bond et al., 2002). see Bloch and Green (2006) for a comparisan of ethical systems and the utility in clinical decision-making of a virtue-based approach.

Supervised clinical practice

Clinical practice

Appropriate supervised practice is the central learning experience in training. The trainee needs to learn what can be achieved in brief (up to 10 sessions), focal work (16/25 weekly sessions), medium (40–70 sessions) and long-term therapy (upwards of 2–3 years). Weekly therapy is the most common mode in National Health Service psychotherapy and in many other settings; this has its own rhythm and intensity and is different from more frequent therapy, whose intensity may accelerate change or be necessary in order to contain major personal disturbance. Weekly therapy tends to be more reality oriented; two, three or five times a week therapy affords greater scope for exploration and regression. Both ends of the spectrum need to be sampled.

The supervisor has a key role in ensuring that patients with a wide range of problems and character structure are worked with. Both breadth and depth of experience are important for development. Breadth develops flexibility and highlights problematic counter-transferences or personal limitations specific to the trainee that need to be worked on through more experience, supervision and personal therapy or, occasionally, avoided. Depth fosters stamina, the ability to contain intense feelings and the patience to work at a slow pace when the patient's sense of basic trust and confident autonomy is poorly developed; often the therapist will have to endure feeling powerless and helpless as she engages with the reality of the patient's inner world (Adler, 1972).

In intermediate and advanced training, the trainee should gain supervised experience in making assessments. While the thrust of this chapter is towards individual therapy, I strongly favour the conduct of therapy groups e.g. a small group over 18 months as a required element in training. A degree of competence in group therapy or, at the very least, a favourable familiarity with the approach should be part of the skills of an individual therapist. This can only be gained through direct experience.

What is judged to be an adequate training for a fully trained, autonomous practitioner in terms of duration, frequency and amount of clinical practice varies between the psychotherapies. At the level of career psychotherapy, it is hard to see that less than 900 hours of conducting therapy over three whole time equivalent years plus 300 hours of supervision divided between one main and two subsidiary supervisors could be sufficient, and this would need to be built on a foundation of less intensive, preliminary training in psychotherapy over two or more years; to learn well, one needs to immerse oneself in the subject. This is the standard set by the Royal College of Psychiatrists for the training of con-sultant medical psychotherapists. In addition, the College specifies that of the 900 hours, 700 should be in the main branch of psychotherapy being studied and 100 in each of the other two branches; currently, the branches recognised are psychodynamic/interpersonal, cognitive-behavioural and systemic (JCHPT, 1996). The British Association for Counselling and Psychotherapy specifies 450 hours of practice and 250 hours of supervision for accreditation as a counsellor. The United Kingdom Council for Psychotherapy requires a full programme of training over four years at degree level for registration and is moving towards objective-led training.

Format
Theory orders the mass of clinical information and helps orientate the therapist in finding a way forward. This useful function should not curtail curiosity and the spirit of enquiry that is necessary for the development of the profession and the professional. Theory should always be relevant and, congruent with the train-ing level, comprehensive in coverage.

How theory is presented varies greatly. Commonly the span of knowledge to be studied is set by the training organisers, which has the virtue of making it clear what is to be learnt. There may be set readings either by author or topic, an approach that specifies the route of study and makes it easy for trainer or trainee to spot omissions. Curriculums, while reassuringly solid for trainers and trainees, may not engage the student's active participation. An alternative, which we employed for a time in the South Trent Training in Dynamic Psychotherapy, a specialist NHS training, is to have a planning event each year where the trainees and seminar leaders jointly decide what is to be studied and how this is to be done. Instead of the conventional study of topics and authors, the question may be posed: 'What do I need to know in order to understand a specific psychotherapy process or problem?' This is the approach of researching a topic rather than simply reading someone else's selection of what is relevant. Another way is to specify learning objectives, and then pose practice-dilemmas for exploration and debate.

At the advanced level, when many topics will have to be studied, teacher enthusiasm may be retained by offering a menu of courses in the teachers' areas of expertise; the trainee may select from these, with the training committee having the responsibility of ensuring that a balanced choice has been made. Here, an over-inclusive curriculum can be helpful. When, manifestly, every subject listed cannot be studied formally within the time available, a trainee in conjunction with the personal tutor can plan a more personal course of learning that takes account of prior learning and present interest. Self-directed learning and discovery is the adult way of learning. Didactic teaching soothes curriculum anxiety but at the cost of regression and passivity.

Theory is not just to be found in textbooks. Novels, plays, films and poems portray the human condition more vividly, complexly and, often, more sensitively than do dry texts. Biographies and autobiographies trace individual lives (Holmes, 1986). All these should be studied.

Whatever the format, the trainee should return again and again to the fundamental, practical question: *what are the implications of this theory or portrayal of life for my practice in my working environment with the patients that I see?*

The same principle of breadth and depth in practice applies to supervision. To gain alternative perspectives against which the trainee's own view may develop, several supervisors need to be worked with for a year at a time. To know one perspective in depth and to feel safe enough to explore doubts and personal conflicts, one main supervisor needs to be engaged with over two or three years. The choice of main supervisor is a matter of great importance. Group supervision is also beneficial as it affords the great benefit of multiple perspective, peer support and morale-enhancing opportunities to be of assistance to colleagues.

In addition, trainees who are not qualified in one of the core mental health care professions should gain through clinical placements sufficient acquaintance with major psychiatric illnesses to recognise their presence; knowledge of the effects and likely benefits of pharmacological and physical treatments is also necessary. One example of why therapists need to be familiar with such matters is the high risk of suicide and depressive homicide in severe depressive illness; in such cases, antidepressants or ECT (electro-convulsive therapy) can be life-saving measures that restore normal functioning (Ebmeier et al., 2006). Psychotherapists should not persist in interpreting psychopathology when a speedier and more effective biological remedy is at hand. When the patient is once more accessible to verbal interaction and the risk of harm to himself and his family has receded, precipitants and psychological vulnerabilities can be explored in psychotherapy with the benefit of greater self-understanding and reduced likelihood of recurrence.

The role of the supervisor
The clinical supervisor has a privileged, responsible position as mentor, guide and, often, assessor; it is quite different from regulatory managerial supervision. From the clinically flattering position of hearing about therapy at second hand and generally after the event, the supervisor places her accumulated experience and knowledge at the service of the trainee. She helps the trainee work out with the patient the meaning and significance of that person's communications, the nature of the conflicts and, certainly in the more dynamic therapies, brings into focus ways in which patient and therapist engage and how the engagement may be turned to good account. In the beginning, the trainee may feel an ambivalent mixture of excitement and dread in taking on a new role. During this time of insecurity and fearing being inadequate, she will need the support of her supervisor. As training progresses, the supervisor has to encourage the trainee to let go of early, perhaps necessary, idealisation of the supervisor so that identification can be replaced by an internalisation of professional skills (Gosling, 1978). In successful training, the trainee moves through stages of inception, skills development and consolidation to mutuality of expertise with the trainer (Hess, 1986).

When patient and therapist concur in their appreciation of the aims of therapy and when there is clarity in accurately understanding the nature of patient conflicts and session processes, two major contributions have been made to the success of the endeavour. Many psychotherapy centres use a pre-assessment interview questionnaire to help clarify the patient's aims, test motivation and orientate to the perspective of therapy. In Nottingham, this has questions on what the problems are, how the patient thinks they have come about and in what ways have they been shaped in their life, their self-concept, the characteristic form of their relationships, what they have found helpful and unhelpful in the past, what has prompted them to seek help now, and what change they want to make through psychotherapy. Of course, in cognitive-behavioural therapy establishing a baseline for therapy through goal definition and quantifying problem severity is integral to the approach. In every type of individual therapy, formulation of the underlying dynamics is beneficial and, I argue, more useful than categorical diagnosis (Aveline, 1999). Though different approaches use their own vocabulary, content schemas are to be found in Aveline (1980), Cleghorn et al. (1983), Friedman and Lister (1987), Perry et al. (1987), Aveline (1995), Mace (1995) and Eells (1997). I favour an interpersonal formula that identifies a personally characteristic narrative of recurrent acts of self. In an adaptation of the 'dynamic focus' (Strupp and Binder, 1984) and 'CCRT' (Luborsky and Crits-Christoph, 1990), the Nottingham Core Conflicts Form records conscious and unconscious wishes, formative acts by others, and responses to self and to others are recorded as well as restorative actions, risk factors and prediction of clinically significant patterns in therapy (Aveline, 2002); though derived from analytic and cognitive approaches, the Core Conflicts formula is atheoretical and may be used by all.

Whichever conceptual schema is used, the supervisor helps the supervisee make more use of the session and, crucially in my view, see how she gets caught up in the patient's self-limiting relationship patterns. Getting caught up is inevitable; the skill in psychotherapy is in recognising what is happening and using the entanglement constructively (Aveline, 1989). In the phenomenon of 'negative fit', therapists act in ways that fit the patient's negative preconceptions, which have been formed by how important people in his past have responded to him. Analysis of tape recordings of experienced therapists demonstrated two major patterns of negative fit (Luborsky and Singer, 1974). In one, the patient's fear of rejection was confirmed by the therapist being critical, disapproving, cold, detached and indifferent; in the other, fear of being made weak by being too directive, controlling and domineering. Clearly every effort should be made in supervision to identify negative patterns and turn their deleterious impact to therapeutic effect. Often the supervisor is able to guide the trainee in selecting suitable patients for her stage in training. The supervisor may consider pairings that promise well e.g. when the therapist has successfully resolved in her life a similar conflict to the patient's or avoiding pairings where the therapist seems likely to reinforce the patient's maladaptive pattern (Aveline, 1992).

Ways of supervising

Pedder (1986) sees clinical supervision in three ways: (1) as being analogous to gardening, that is as a process of promoting growth, (2) as a place for creative play and (3) as being like therapy in that it provides a regular time and place for taking a second look at what is happening. Supervision aims to enhance the creative potential of the therapist. It should be noted that supervision is not – and should not be – therapy, though at times the distinction may blur.

Supervision may focus on any of four areas: the process and content of the patient's concerns and communications, theoretical understanding and technique, transference and counter-transference reactions between therapist and patient, and the supervisee-supervisor relationship. Doehrman's classic study (1976) provides some justification for the last; in what is called parallel-process, the dynamics between patient and therapist were recreated in the supervisee-supervisor relationship. Thus, comprehending and resolving supervision dynamics can undo blocks in the therapy relationship (for an example see Caligor, 1984). All these foci are useful though, in my practice, I incline towards the first, as it is the patient's life that is my primary concern.

Much debate rages in psychotherapy circles about how supervisory material should be presented. Classically in psychoanalytic training, a free-flowing account of the session is given with much attention being paid to what is said and not said and the elucidation of counter-transference and mental associations as ways of illuminating unconscious processes. This is listening with the third ear (Reik, 1949). That the report may correspond poorly to the observable events of the session is held to be of little importance; indeed some supervisors argue that factually precise reporting misses the point and, furthermore, may positively obscure it. I cannot accept this position. All ways of capturing the facts and essence of what went on are useful. Aids to supervision such as audio and video recordings are just that: servants, not masters. They can be adapted to meet the needs of the moment.

After each session, trainees write notes detailing content, process and feeling issues. It is advantageous to have audio or video recordings of the session, which may be viewed from the beginning, a point of difficulty or interest … or not at all. Recordings document the actual sequence of events and bring non-verbal, paralinguistic communication and emotional tone change dimensions into the arena of supervision (Aveline, 1997). Openness is served by the supervisor putting her own tapes forward occasionally for discussion. Other means may be utilised. Transcripts allow the leisurely study of process and form of verbal intervention; as a qualitative research exercise, the method of brief structured recall (Elliott and Shapiro, 1988) may be used to go over the most significant events in a session with the patient; the patient identifies significant events immediately after the session, then therapist and patient listen to the tape just before, during and after the event, and, through discussion, amplify associated feelings, meaning and impact of that interaction segment. Live supervision from behind a screen with either telephone contact or a 'bug in the ear' is common practice in family therapy and may be used in individual work. However, live supervision does reduce the scope for the therapist to grapple on her own with the patient's issues.

Being supervised is supposed to be helpful, but can be persecutory (Bruzzone et al., 1985) and intrusive (Betcher and Zinberg, 1988). The trainee's self-esteem is vulnerable; during training, there needs to be room for privacy and for mistakes to be made and discussed without dire penalty or excessive shame. Obstructive counter-transference reactions on the part of the supervisor must not be forgotten. The trainee may represent the coming generation who may equal or pass the supervisor in skill and knowledge. Rivalry and the struggle for professional power may add a subtext to supervision and, if not resolved, prove detrimental to professional development. Training for supervisors and a forum for them to discuss problems in supervision are beneficial (Hawkins and Shohet, 1989).

Skills development

While I favour weekly supervision over months and years as the best complement to the work of individual therapy, workshops and role-plays quickly lead to the acquisition of fundamental skills (structured examples of exercises are to be found in Egan (1982a and b); Jacobs (1985, 1991); Tolan and Lendrum (1995)). Without risking any harm to the patient, difficult situations that therapists commonly face can be practised, the effects of different interventions observed and the model presented by more experienced therapists evaluated. Microcounselling training courses, first described at the end of the 1960s, have retained their promise for the relatively inexperienced trainee; they provide structured, focused learning over periods of one, two or three days with a strong emphasis on skills acquisition through role-play. At the more advanced, approach-specific level, the use of detailed treatment manuals for such diverse approaches as supportive-expressive psychoanalytic psychotherapy, cognitive and interpersonal therapy of depression and short-term therapy continues to be an interesting, effective method of skill development (Matarazzo and Patterson, 1986).

Personal therapy

'The therapist can only go as far with the patient as she can go herself', so the maxim runs. What the therapist can bear to hear in herself, she can hear in the patient. What the therapist can find in herself, she can recognise in the other. In addition to the patient's resistance to free exploration and dismantling defensive, outmoded (but originally adaptive) patterns, the therapist contributes a resistance of her own. The resistance may take the form of avoidance or over-interest; the former limits opening up of areas of concern for the patient, the latter diverts the focus of the discourse to the therapist's conflictual issues; these processes largely take place out of consciousness. Examples have been given in the sections on counter-transference and the abuse of power of some common personal conflicts, which may limit or adversely distort the therapist's engagement. Many therapies at some stage confront the reflective therapist with the dilemmas in her own life and the partial solutions that she has adopted — as does life itself! Overlap of conflictual issue between therapist and patient often results in blocked therapy, but may generate a particularly fruitful dyad when the therapist's conflict is not too great and the overlap enhances empathic contact (Aveline, 1992).

Experiencing life and practising psychotherapy educate the therapist about herself. Self-scrutiny takes learning about personal conflicts and their resolution one step further but the therapist's own internal security measures maintain blind spots and protect self-esteem from sobering self-realisations; these defences limit what can be done alone. Personal therapy offers the therapist the same opportunity as the patient has to explore, understand and resolve inner conflicts. It brings together theoretical learning and psychotherapy practice in an experience that makes personal sense of the two. At a practical level, personal therapy provides a means through which sufficient self-understanding can be gained for the therapist to recognise how her personality and life experience affect her ability to be objective and to reduce her tendency to impose her own solutions on the life problems of the patient. The nature of the conflicts that interfere with the therapist's work predicate her requirement for therapy in terms of type, duration and frequency; an endpoint of personal therapy is achieving sufficient resolution to work more effectively.

At the next level, therapy aims to enhance the therapist's ability to relate empathically and creatively to her patients. One facilitator is knowing at first hand what it is like to be a patient; another is the loosening through therapy of the self-limiting grip of personal conflicts. Beyond that, as was detailed in the section on motivating factors in the therapist, therapy offers an opportunity for the therapist to heal herself, an unmet need which may have been of prime importance in the selection by the trainee therapist of this kind of work. At a sociological level, personal therapy functions as a rite of passage, forming and affirming her identity as a psychotherapist and member of her professional group.

Importantly, personal therapy offers support with difficult work. Therapy cannot be conducted at arm's length. The therapist opens herself to feeling what it is like to be the other, thereby experiencing to some degree their painful story and its effects. Moving between identification and reflective observation, the therapist puts aside many of the self-protective measures that help people get by in everyday life and engages with stories, feelings and enactments that are often disturbing, tragic and unpleasant. Letting other people's stories get inside you may be traumatic (as well as growth-promoting). Personal therapy, as well as supervision and leading a contented life, can help heal those wounds and assist the therapist in coping with demanding work.

Perhaps the most compelling argument in favour of personal therapy is that every therapist, like every patient, sees the world through the perspective of her guiding fictions and is impelled to impose that order, those patterns and her solutions on others. Thus, the more the therapist is aware of her personal determining fictions, the more likely she will be able to engage fully with the reality of the other.

Personal therapy in varying intensity and duration is a required component of most formal, advanced trainings in psychotherapy. In psychoanalysis, full personal analysis is mandatory: the training sequence is being in therapy, then adding theory seminars and finally conducting analyses. In Henry's (1977) survey of 4,000 North American psychotherapists 74 per cent had been in personal therapy and nearly 50 per cent had re-entered therapy for two to four periods; conversely, 26 per cent had chosen not to pursue that course. Similar rates are recorded in a recent international survey (Norcross and Guy, 2005; Orlinsky et al., 2005b). Despite the consensus in favour of personal therapy, especially at the psychodynamic end of the spectrum, there is little published evidence of its efficacy in enhancing therapeutic ability. Surveys of the literature (Greenberg and Staller, 1981; Macaskill, 1988; Macaskill and Macaskill, 1992) conclude that (a) 15–33 per cent of personal therapies have unsatisfactory consequences e.g. damage to marriage, destructive acting-out and excessive withdrawal from the outside world; (b) therapy early in the therapist's career may have deleterious effects on work with patients; and (c) there is no positive correlation between either the fact of having been in therapy or its duration on outcome of the therapist's professional work. The level of reported dissatisfaction is in line with that generally expected for negative effects in psychotherapy, and, as such, emphasises the importance of the trainee's making a sage choice of therapist.

More positively, there is some research evidence that therapy may enhance counter-transference awareness and containment; more rigourous studies are needed (Macran and Shapiro, 1998). Interestingly, 85 per cent of 3,600 therapists reported having had at least one personal therapy of great or very great value to them. This may be a crucial formative experience of the potency of therapy, which in turn can be conveyed to their patients (Orlinsky et al., 2005a).

When personal therapy is decided upon, its form, intensity and duration should parallel the form of psychotherapy that the therapist is going to practise. This follows the educational principle of congruence. Generally for training in individual therapy, this will be one or more times a week for three or more years. It is important that the therapist enters therapy not just because the training so requires but to resolve personal conflicts or difficulties that are being encountered in her work and life (as is the case with most psychotherapists entering therapy (Norcross and Connor, 2005)). Advice on whom to consult should be sought from an experienced adviser who can steer the trainee away from pairings that are less than optimal and towards those of greater promise (Coltart, 1987). A balance needs to be struck between comfortable similarity and challenging difference. Exploratory sessions should be held with several potential therapists before the choice is made. Over a lifetime, many therapists re-enter therapy for periods as their life and clinical practice throw up issues that they need to deal with. For the most part, this is an appropriate confirmation of the worth of therapy.

EVALUATION

During training, there should be opportunities for evaluation, both formative and normative. Educationally, 'formative' evaluation refers to non-examined elements that enrich the educational experience of training, whereas 'normative' refers to entry/exit, pass/fail criteria. The aims of the training should be clearly stated and be attainable within the learning experiences of the scheme. A system for monitoring progress both by self-assessment and by the trainers is necessary, as is the giving of feedback so as to help the trainee improve the quality of her psychotherapy.

Individual and psychometric assessments of patient problems' severity can form a baseline for the evaluation of the success of practice during training. Casebooks recording progress and any alteration in formulation of the patient's problems document the range of therapy experience and the lessons learnt from actual practice as opposed to the fine rhetoric of texts. Though case accounts are relatively weak base for evidence-based practice (Aveline, 2005b), detailed written case accounts of one or more psychotherapies carried out by the trainee are good ways to demonstrate trainee's development and illustrate how difficulties have been encountered and struggled with. The accounts should demonstrate how supervision has been used. Annual and summative reports by the personal tutor should appraise the trainee's strengths and weaknesses as a therapist and show how the tutor has helped the trainee find her way through the training. Ultimately, evaluation should address the difficult question of competence: how effective is this therapist in aiding the quest of her patients towards more fruitful living? Compliance can be demonstrated but this is only part of the competence story. It should also be noted that effective therapists are not universally effective; they are better with some patient problems while even poor therapists are effective sometimes (Luborsky et al., 1986).

National Vocational Qualifications

Since 1987, the British government has been committed to introducing National Vocational Qualifications (NVQs) for as many occupations as possible. NVQs are based on a functional analysis of what a competent worker does. They describe competencies at five levels of increasing complexity of activity. Level one describes routine and predictable tasks where the worker follows rules set by superiors, and level five the application of fundamental principles or complex techniques across a wide range of unpredictable contexts by someone operating with substantial, personal autonomy. Level five would equate to the standards of the established professions like law or medicine, though these occupations have yet to be mapped by this process. The declared purpose of NVQs is to provide an alternative pathway to qualification other than traditional university courses and to help employers judge that their employees have the competencies to discharge the duties of a specific post.

After much deliberation, the British Association for Counselling (BAC, now BACP see next section) joined with the Department of Employment in 1992 to map and devise standards in the fields of work covered by BAC. The organ for this project was the Lead Body for Advice, Guidance, Counselling and Psychotherapy. After an ambivalent period, the United Kingdom Council for Psychotherapy (see next section) voted to join the Lead Body in 1994. Competency statements were agreed for advice, guidance, and counselling and contracts placed with awarding bodies to turn these into NVQ qualifications for advice and guidance. Joint work began on mapping competencies for therapeutic counselling and psychotherapy but that concordat fell apart. The development of functional standards aroused many anxieties. Critics argued that the approach is atomistic, and risks losing the sum of the parts by splitting the whole into so many elements, slavishly to be checked off during training. They fear that it will emphasise action over reflection, 'doing to' over 'being with', and is all too cognitive, rather than emotional. They say that the method misses out synthesis and intuition, and suggests falsely that the practice of psychotherapy is algorithmic when, truly, it is heuristic. The participating sceptics, myself among them, value the healthy emphasis on outputs and anticipate that it will bring out commonalties and differences between the psychotherapies. It has the potential to clearly define the competencies to be developed through training and promote equivalence between trainings.

It now seems unlikely that NVQs will become another route to qualification for psychotherapists. This is partly because the last decade has seen a huge expansion of University Diplomas, MSc's and Doctorates that provide externally validated qualifications and have proved very popular. Educationally, these are objective-led and bring a welcome level of critical enquiry to the field. Sometimes they are light on clinical practice.

Registration

At present, any one in Britain may practise as a psychotherapist and advertise their services as such. Unlike the situation in North America and many European countries, psychotherapy is not a regulated profession. While some titles such as psychoanalyst and child psychotherapist are protected, no formal training or subscription to an ethical code is required by statute for psychotherapists or counsellors. Within institutions such as the NHS and university counselling services, the patient as consumer of psychotherapy is usefully protected by the therapist having been appointed to their post in open competition and being subject to the sanction of the institution's code of practice and complaints procedure. Membership of professions that are regulated by statutory body (as is medicine by the General Medical Council) or have chartered status, such as psychology, or of training institutes with regulatory powers affords some assurance that the professional standards of the therapist are adequate and will be maintained. But in the private sector, members of the public have little protection against misinformed or unethical therapists. This is bad for the consumer and bad for the profession.

The Foster Report (Foster, 1971), the result of a government appointed inquiry, recommended that the profession of psychotherapy be regulated by statute. Seven years later, the Sieghart Report (Sieghart, 1978) proposed the establishment of a council that would draw up and enforce a code of professional ethics and approve training courses. Registration of individuals as psychotherapists would be indicative rather than functional, that is, on the basis of titles associated with various forms of psychotherapy in which the therapist was qualified rather than the content of the work, the latter being a much more restrictive form of registration. The desirable goal of registration as some guarantee of integrity and competence, at present on a voluntary basis, has since made significant progress, especially in the last decade.

During the 1980s, psychotherapists and psychotherapy organisations from across the spectrum of practice met each year in Rugby (the Rugby Conference), initially under the auspices of the British Association for Counselling, and latterly in Canterbury. In 1989 the conference adopted a formal constitution as the United Kingdom Standing Conference for Psychotherapy (UKSCP), metamorphosing into the United Kingdom Council for Psychotherapy (UKCP) in 1993. UKCP is an organisation of organisations, grouped into eight sections: Analytical Psychology; Behavioural and Cognitive Psychotherapy (BABCP left UKCP in 2005 to return as an Institutional Member); Experiential Constructivist; Family,

Couple, Sexual and Systemic Therapy; Humanistic and Integrative Psychotherapy; Hypno-Psychotherapy; Psychoanalytic and Psychodynamic; and Psycho-analytically based Therapy with Children. In 1993 UKCP established a register of its qualified members, now some 5,200, grouped for competence by the title of the section in which they are registered. Registrants have to meet a common standard of training and ethics and are subject to disciplinary procedures (Pokorny, 1995).

UKCP is committed to seeking statutory registration. Achieving this goal depends on all the major psychotherapy organisations speaking with a common voice and showing evidence of being able to uphold high standards, investigate complaints and discipline registrants who malpractice. A Bill to regulate psychotherapy was introduced by Lord Alderdice in the House of Lords in 2000 but failed. For a time, it seemed likely the Government would regulate psychotherapy and a wide range of related therapies in the NHS alone through an Order in Council. This would have had the benefit of recognising the status and training of registered NHS therapists but missed the point that patients are more at risk in the unregulated private sector than in the public sector with all its in-built safeguards. The proposal then was to regulate psychotherapy and counselling in both the public and private sectors through the established mechanism of the Health Professions Council (HPC). This body already regulates professions such as art therapy, occupational therapy, physiotherapy and speech and language therapy. Going down this route would mean substantial loss of control over training and the handling of complaints by psychotherapists and counsellors (not necessarily a bad move but certainly a change), and moving towards being a graduate or post-graduate occupation with a core curriculum. At the time of writing, the Government appears to be having second thoughts about this route.

Just at the moment when UKSCP was preparing to vote UKCP into existence, a substantial proportion of the organisations from the psychoanalytic end of the spectrum withdrew from the conference. They were unhappy about the breadth of psychotherapy approach represented in UKSCP and, it would appear, about being one voice among many. They preferred to cluster round a psychoanalytic identity and formed the British Confederation of Psychotherapists (BCP) in 1992. In 1994, they launched their register of 1,200 practitioners (Balfour and Richards, 1995), now 1,400. I regret that they turned away from the greater good of a representative profession of psychotherapy. Doubtless, a rapprochement will be necessary if statutory registration for all is to be achieved. BCP changed its name in 2005 to the British Psychoanalytic Council.

For many years, the British Association for Counselling, a substantial organisation with 24,000 members, has operated a system of individual accreditation of counsellors. In 1996, the counselling organisations launched the United Kingdom Register of Counsellors; BAC holds the register. As well as individual registration, counsellors may be registered by sponsoring organisations that will guarantee the counselling that they do within that organisation. Thus, a counsellor might be registered for independent practice and/or for work in, for example,

Relate or Cruse. In 2000, BAC altered its name to include psychotherapy i.e. BACP.

These moves help identify areas of competence among practitioners of psychotherapy and therapeutic counselling and provide useful protection both for the public and employers of therapists.

Implicit in the above is the proposition that continued attention to maintaining and extending competence is part of the professional attitude of the psychotherapist. The rubric for this further education is continuing professional development (CPD); it can help guard against burnout (Grosch and Colsen, 1994). This is particularly important for the individual therapist, who tends to work in relative or absolute isolation and, in the absence of challenging opportunities for further learning, may develop poor working practices. Feedback from colleagues in peer group supervision of actual clinical work is especially helpful.

SUPPORTIVE PSYCHOTHERAPY

The rhetoric of psychotherapy is towards fundamental change in people's feelings, attitudes and interactions; this is the purpose of the training described in this chapter. The trainee therapist in her enthusiasm and inexperience of the struggle to survive that many patients face may be tempted to press for a pace and depth of change for which her patient is not ready. It is important to respect the compromises that people inevitably make to get by. Fundamental change will not be possible or desirable for all and, if possible, the patient may not have given authorisation for deep exploration that can profoundly challenge his self-view. Courses that recognise the validity of this principle will value support and teach it positively. Furthermore, all therapy has to contain sufficient support in order to help the patient contend with the upheaval of change: most therapies move between challenging and supportive phases. Supportive psychotherapy is a subject in its own right (Bloch, 2006). It is indicated for the many individuals who need sustained assistance in order to regain their optimal level of adjustment and maintain themselves there. It has its own complex skills and needs to be learned by even the most therapeutically ambitious therapist.

CONCLUSION

The current practice of psychotherapy distils what is known about human healing. In its practice, it is both an art and a science; both elements need to be borne in mind in training. Training may occur in phases but is a lifelong commitment. Competence is achievable but there is always more for the therapist to learn. No endpoint has been reached in the development of individual therapy as an agent of personal change or the way that therapy is delivered e.g. by e-mail, online and CD-Rom. Further refinement in theory, scope and practice can be expected, especially if the practitioners of the different individual psychotherapies learn to speak with one another in pursuit of the common goal of assisting their fellow human beings lead more fruitful lives.

NOTE

1. In this chapter, I use the word patient as a generic term for someone who suffers and is seeking help. Also, to avoid the cumbersome form of he/she, the male form is used unless a named authority is being referred to. The female form is used for the therapist and supervisor.

REFERENCES

Adler, G. (1972) 'Helplessness in the helpers', *British Journal of Medical Psychology* 45: 315–25.

Auerbach, A. A. and M. Johnson (1977) 'Research on the therapist's level of experience', in A.S. Gurman and A.M. Razin (eds), *Effective Psychotherapy*. Oxford: Pergamon Press. pp. 84–102.

Aveline, M. (1979) 'Towards a conceptual framework of psychotherapy - a personal view' *British Journal of Medical Psychology* 52: 271–5.

Aveline, M. (1980) 'Making a psychodynamic formulation.' *Bulletin, Royal College of Psychiatrists* (December): 192–3.

Aveline, M. (1989) 'The provision of illusion in psychotherapy', *Midland Journal of Psychotherapy* 1: 9–16.

Aveline, M. (1992) 'Parameters of danger: interactive elements in the therapy dyad', in M. Aveline, *From Medicine to Psychotherapy*. London: Whurr.

Aveline, M. (1995) 'Assessing for optimal therapeutic intervention', in S. Palmer and G. McMahon, *Client Assessment*. London: Sage. pp. 93–114.

Aveline, M. (1997) 'The use of audiotapes in supervision of psychotherapy', in G. Chapman, *Supervision of Psychotherapy and Counselling. Making a Place to Think*. Buckingham: Open University Press.

Aveline, M. (1999) 'The advantages of formulation over categorical diagnosis in explorative psychotherapy and psychodynamic management', *European Journal of Psychotherapy, Counselling and Health,* 2(2): 199–216.

Aveline, M. (2001) 'Complexities of practice: psychotherapy in the real world', in F. Palmer-Barnes and L. Murdin, *Values and Ethics in the Practice of Psychotherapy and Counselling*. Buckingham: Open University Press: 128–43.

Aveline, M. (2002) 'Focal therapy, a brief interpersonally-focussed psychotherapy', *Psychiatry,* 1: 2–9.

Aveline, M. (2005a) 'The person of the therapist', *Psychotherapy Research,* 15: 155–164.

Aveline, M. (2005b) 'Clinical case studies: their place in evidence-based practice', *Psychodynamic Practice,* 11: 133–52.

Aveline, M. O. and Ratigan, B. (1988) 'Issues in the training of group therapists', in M. O. Aveline and W. Dryden, *Group Therapy in Britain*. Milton Keynes: Open University Press. pp: 317–36.

Aveline, M., Strauss, B. M. and Stiles, W. B. (2005) 'Psychotherapy Research', in G. Gabbard, J. Beck, and J. Holmes, (eds), *Oxford Textbook of Psychotherapy*. Oxford: Oxford University Press. pp. 449–62.

Balfour, F. and Richards, J. (1995) 'History of the British Confederation of Psychotherapists', *British Journal of Psychotherapy,* 11: 422–6.

Bernstein, L. and Bernstein R. S. (1980) *Interviewing: a guide for health professionals*. New York: Appleton-Century-Crofts.

Betcher, R. W. and Zinberg, N. E. (1988) 'Supervision and privacy in psychotherapy training', *American Journal of Psychiatry,* 145: 796–803.

Beutler, L. E., Malik, M., Alimohamed, S., Harwood, T. M., Talebi, H., Noble, S. and Wong, E. (2004). 'Therapist variables', in M. Lambert (ed.), *Handbook of Psychotherapy and Behavior Change,* 5th ed., New York: John Wiley. pp. 227–306.

Bloch, S. (2006) 'Supportive Psychotherapy', in S. Bloch (ed.), *An Introduction to the Psychotherapies.* Oxford: Oxford University Press. pp. 215–36.

Bloch, S. and Green, S. A. (2006) 'An ethical framework for psychiatry', *British Journal of Psychiatry,* 188: 7–12.

Bond, T., Ashcroft, R., Casemore, R., Jamieson, A. and Lendrum, S. (2002) *Ethical Framework for Good Practice in Counselling and Psychotherapy.* Rugby:British Association for Counselling and Psychotherapy. p. 16.

Bruzzone, M., Casaula, E., Jimenz, J. P. and J. F., J. (1985) 'Regression and persecution in analytic training. Reflections on experience', *International Review of Psycho-Analysis,* 12: 411–15.

Bugental, J. F. T. (1964) 'The person who is the psychotherapist', *Journal of Counseling Psychology* 28: 272–7.

Burton, A. (1975) 'Therapist satisfaction', *American Journal of Psychoanalysis* 35: 115–22.

Caligor, L. (1984) *Parallel and Reciprocal Processes in Psychoanalytic Supervision.* New York, Plenum Press.

Casement, P. (1985) *On Learning from the Patient.* London: Tavistock Publications.

Cleghorn, J. M., Bellissimo, A. and Will, D. (1983) 'Teaching some principles of individual psychodynamics through an introductory guide to formulations', *Canadian Journal of Psychiatry* 28: 162–72.

Coltart, N. (1987) 'Diagnosis and assessment for suitability for psycho-analytical psychotherapy', *British Journal of Psychotherapy* 4: 127–34.

Department of Health (1998) *A First Class Service.* London: HMSO.

Doehrman, M. J. G. (1976) 'Parallel processes in supervision and psychotherapy.' *Bulletin of the Menninger Clinic,* 40: 1–104.

Ebmeier, K. P., Donaghey, C. and Steele, J. D. (2006) 'Recent developments and current controversies in depression', (Seminar), *Lancet,* 367: 153–68.

Eells, T. D. (ed.) (1997) *Handbook of Psychotherapy Case Formulation.* New York: Guilford Press.

Egan, G. (1982a) *Exercises in Helping Skills.* Wadsworth: Belmont.

Egan, G. (1982b) *The Skilled Helper.* Wadsworth: Belmont.

Elliott, R. and Shapiro D. A. (1988) 'Brief structured recall: a more efficient method for studying significant therapy moments', *British Journal of Medical Psychology,* 61: 141–53.

Fairbairn, W. R. D. (1954) *An Object-Relations Theory of the Personality.* New York: Basic Books.

Farber, B. A. (1983) 'The effects of psychotherapeutic practice upon psychotherapists', *Psychotherapy: Theory, Research and Practice,* 20: 174–82.

Farber, B. A. and Heifetz L. J. (1981) 'The satisfactions and stresses of psychotherapy work: a factor analytic study', *Professional Psychology,* 12: 621–30.

Foster, J. G. (1971) *Enquiry into the Practice and Effects of Scientology.* London: HMSO.

Frank, J. D. (1973) *Persuasion and Healing.* Baltimore: Johns Hopkins University Press.

Friedman, R. S. and Lister P. (1987) 'The current status of the psychodynamic formulation', *Psychiatry,* 50: 126–41.

Gosling, R. (1978) 'Internalization of the trainer's behaviour in professional training', *British Journal of Medical Psychology,* 51: 35–40.

Greben, S. E. (1975) 'Some difficulties and satisfactions inherent in the practice of psychoanalysis', *International Journal of Psycho-Analysis,* 56: 427–33.

Greben, S. E. (1984) *Love's Labor.* New York: Schocken Books.

Greenberg, R. P. and Staller, J. (1981) 'Personal therapy for therapists', *American Journal of Psychiatry,* 138: 1467–71.

Greenson, R. R. (1967) *The Technique and Practice of Psychoanalysis, Vol. 1.* New York: International Universities Press.

Grosch, W. N. and Colsen, D. (1994) *When Helping Starts to Hurt: A New Look at Burn Out among Psychotherapists.* New York: W W Norton & Company.

Guggenbuhl-Craig, A. (1979) *Power in the Helping Professions.* Irving, TX: Spring Publications.

Guy, J. D. (1987) *The Personal Life of the Psychotherapist.* New York: John Wiley and Sons.

Hawkins, P. and Shohet, R. (1989) *Supervision in the Helping Professions.* Oxford University Press: Oxford.

Heimann, P. (1950) 'On counter-transference', *International Journal of Psychoanalysis,* 31: 81–4.

Henry, W. A. (1977) 'Personal and social identities of psychotherapists', in A. S. Gurman and A. M. Razin, *Effective Psychotherapy.* Oxford: Pergamon Press.

Hess, A. K. (1986) 'Growth in supervision: stages of supervisee and supervisor development', in F. W. Kaslow, *Supervision and Training: Models, Dilemmas, Challenges.* New York: Haworth Press.

Holmes, J. (1986) 'Teaching the psychotherapeutic method: some literary parallels', *British Journal of Medical Psychology,* 59: 113–21.

Holroyd, J. C. and. Brodsky, A. M. (1977) 'Psychologists' attitudes and practices regarding erotic and non-erotic physical contact with patients', *American Psychologist,* 32: 843–9.

Horvath, A. O. and Luborsky, L. (1993) 'The role of the therapeutic alliance in psychotherapy', *Journal of Consulting and Clinical Psychology,* 61: 561–73.

Hubble, M. A., Duncan, B. L. and Miller, S. D. (1999) *The Heart and Soul of Change: What Works in Therapy.* Washington DC: American Psychological Association.

Irons, R. and Schneider, J. (1999) *The Wounded Healer; An Addiction-sensitive Approach to the Sexually Exploitative Professional.* Northvale, NJ: Aronson.

JCHPT (Joint Committee on Higher Psychiatric Training) (1996) *Requirements for Specialist Training in Psychotherapy.* London: Royal College of Psychiatrists.

Jacobs, M. (1985) *Swift to Hear. Facilitating Skills in Listening and Responding.* London: SPCK.

Jacobs, M. (1991) *Insight and Experience.* Milton Keynes: Open University Press.

Jones, E. (1913) 'The god complex', *in Essays in Applied Psychoanalysis, Vol. 2.* London: Hogarth Press.

Lambert, M. J. (1986) 'Implications of psychotherapy outcome research for eclectic psychotherapy', in J. C. Norcross, *Handbook of Eclectic Psychotherapy.* New York: Brunner Mazel.

Lomas, P. (1981) *The Case for a Personal Psychotherapy.* Oxford: Oxford University Press.

Luborsky, E., Crits-Christoph, P., McLellan, A. T., Woody, G. E., Piper, W. E., Lieberman, D. M. et al. (1986) 'Do therapists vary much in their success? Findings from four outcome studies', *American Journal of Orthopsychiatry,* 51: 501–12.

Luborsky, L. and Crits-Christoph P. (1990) *Understanding Transference. The Core Conflictual Relationship Theme Method.* New York: Basic Books.

Luborsky, L. and. Singer, B. (1974) 'The fit of therapists' behavior into patients' negative expectations: a study of transference-countertransference contagion', University of Pennsylvania.

Luborsky, L. and Singer, B. (1975) 'Comparative studies of psychotherapies. Is it true that "Everyone has won and all must have prizes?"', *Archives of General Psychiatry,* 32: 995–1008.

Macaskill, N. D. (1988) 'Personal therapy in the training of a psychotherapist: is it effective?', *British Journal of Psychotherapy,* 4: 219–26.

Macaskill, N. D. and Macaskill, A. (1992) 'Psychotherapists in training evaluate their personal therapy: results of a UK survey', *British Journal of Psychotherapy,* 9(2): 133–8.

Mace, C. (1995) *The Art and Science of Assessment in Psychotherapy.* London: Routledge.

Macran, S. and Shapiro, D. A. (1998) 'The role of personal therapy for therapists: a revew', *British Journal of Medical Psychology,* 71: 13–25.

Malan, D. H. (1995) *Individual Psychotherapy and the Science of Psychodynamics.* Oxford: Butterworth Heinemann.

Marmor, J. (1953) 'The feeling of superiority: an occupational hazard in the practice of psychotherapy', *American Journal of Psychiatry,* 110: 370–3.

Marmor, J. (1972) 'Sexual acting-out in psychotherapy', *American Journal of Psycho-Analysis,* 22: 3–8.

Matarazzo, R. G. and. Patterson, D. R. (1986) 'Methods of teaching therapeutic skill', in S. L. Garfield and A. L. Bergin, *Handsbook of psychotherapy and behavior change.* New York: John Wiley and Sons.

Meares, R. (2001) *Intimacy and Alienation: Memory, Trauma and Personal Being.* Hove: Brunner-Routledge.

Menninger, K. (1958) *Theory of Psychoanalytic Technique.* New York: Basic Books.

Norcross, J. C. and Connor, K. L. (2005) 'Psychotherapists entering personal therapy', in J. D. Geller, J. C. Norcross and D. E. Orlinsky (eds.), *The Psychotherapist's Own Psychotherapy*. Oxford: Oxford University Press. pp. 192–200.

Norcross, J. C. and Guy, J. D. (2005) 'The prevalence and parameters of personal therapy in the United States' in J. D. Geller, J. C. Norcross, and D. E. Orlinsky (eds), *The Psychotherapist's Own Psychotherapy*. Oxford: Oxford University Press. pp. 165–176.

Orlinsky, D. E. and Rønnestad, M. H. (2002) *The Psychotherapist's Perspective: Therapeutic Work, Professional Development, and Personal Life*. Washington, DC: APA.

Orlinsky, D. E., Norcross, J. C., Rønnestad, M. H. and Wiseman, H. (2005a) Outcomes and impacts of the psychotherapist's own psychotherapy', in J. D. Geller, J. C. Norcross and D. E. Orlinsky (eds), *The Psychotherapist's Own Psychotherapy*. Oxford: Oxford University Press, pp. 214–30.

Orlinsky, D. E., Rønnestad, M. H., Willutze, U., Wiseman, H., Botermans, J. -F. and Network SPR (2005b) The prevalence and parameters of personal therapy in Europe and elsewhere', in J. D. Geller, J. C. Norcross and D. E. Orlinsky (eds), *The Psychotherapist's Own Psychotherapy*. Oxford: Oxford University Press. pp. 177–91.

Parry, G. (2001) *Treatment Choice in Psychological Therapies and Counselling*. London: Department of Health.

Paul, J. L. (1967) 'Strategy of outcome research in psychotherapy', *Journal of Consulting Psychology*, 31: 109–18.

Pedder, J. (1986) 'Reflections on the theory and practice of supervision', *Psychoanalytic Psychotherapy*, 2: 1–12.

Perry, S., Cooper, A. M. and Michels, R. (1987) 'The psychodynamic formulation: its purpose, structure, and clinical application', *American Journal of Psychiatry*, 144: 543–50.

Pokorny, M. R. (1995) 'History of the United Kingdom Council for Psychotherapy', *British Journal of Psychotherapy*, 11(3): 415–21.

Reik, T. (1949) *Listening with the Third Ear*. New York: Farrer & Straus.

Rogers, C. R. (1957) 'The necessary and sufficient conditions of therapeutic personality change', *Journal of Consulting Psychology*, 21: 95–103.

Rosin, S. A. and Knudson, R. M. (1986) 'Perceived influence of life experiences on clinical psychologists' selection and development of theoretical orientations', *Psychotherapy*, 23: 357–63.

Roth, A. and Fonagy, P. (2004) *What Works for Whom? A Critical Review of Psychotherapy Research*, 2nd edn. New York: Guilford Publications.

Safran, J. D. and Muran, J. C. (2000) *Negotiating the Therapeutic Alliance: A Relational Treatment Guide*. New York: Guilford.

Sandler, J. (1988) *Psychoanalysis and Psychoanalytic Psychotherapy: Problems of Differentiation*. Psychoanalysis and Psychoanalytic Psychotherapy (Association of Psychoanalytic Psychotherapy in the NHS), London, 22–23 April.

Schafer, R. (1983) *The Analytic Attitude*. London: Hogarth Press.

Sieghart, P. (1978) *Statutory Registration of Psychotherapists*. London: Tavistock Clinic.

Storr, A. (1979) *The Art of Psychotherapy*. London: Secker & Warburg.

Strupp, H. H. (1960) *Psychotherapists in Action*. New York: Grune & Stratton.

Strupp, H. H. (1977) 'A reformulation of the dynamics of the therapist's contribution', in A. S. Gurman and A. M. Razin, *Effective Psychotherapy*. Oxford: Pergamon Press.

Strupp, H. H. and Binder J. L. (1984) *Psychotherapy in a New Key*. New York: Basic Books.

Tolan, J. and Lendrum, S. (1995) *Case Material and Role Play in Counselling Training*. London: Routledge.

Yalom, I. D. (2002) *The Gift of Therapy*. New York: Harper Collins Publishers.

Appendix 1: Chapter Structure (for Authors of Chapters 2–17)

1 HISTORICAL CONTEXT AND DEVELOPMENT IN BRITAIN (1,000 WORDS)

1.1 Historical context

Your aim here should be briefly to acquaint the reader unfamiliar with your approach with its *historical context*. Examine its historical origins, its intellectual roots and explain why it is called what it is.

1.2 Development in Britain

Your aim here should be to treat briefly the development of the approach in Britain (where this is different from 1.1 up to the time of writing).

2 THEORETICAL ASSUMPTIONS (2,500 WORDS)

2.1 Image of the person

Outline the basic assumptions made by the approach about the person and human nature.

2.2 Conceptualization of psychological disturbance and health

Outline how the approach conceptualizes both psychological disturbance and psychological health. Explain in detail the *major concepts* utilized by the approach in accounting for psychological disturbance and health.

2.3 Acquisition of psychological disturbance

Explain the approach's view on how psychological disturbance is acquired.

2.4 Perpetuation of psychological disturbance

Explain the approach's position on how psychological disturbance is perpetu-ated. What *intrapersonal mechanisms* are utilized by individuals to perpetuate their own psychological disturbance; what *interpersonal mechanisms* are recog-nized as important in the perpetuation process; what is the role of the *environ-ment* in the perpetuation process?

2.5 Change

You should use this section to outline briefly the approach's view on how humans change with respect to movement from psychological disturbance to psychologi-cal health. This section should orient the reader to what follows under 'Practice' but should not be limited to the change process in therapy (i.e. it should not dupli-cate section 3.6). Thus it should both complete the 'Acquisition–Perpetuation–Change' cycle and orient the reader to what follows.

3 PRACTICE (5,500 WORDS)

3.1 Goals of therapy

Your aim here is to set out the goals of the approach.

3.2 Selection criteria

What selection criteria are used to determine whether or not clients will benefit from the approach in its *individual therapy format*? There are two issues here: first, what clients (if any) are deemed unsuitable for the particular approach under consideration (refer back to 3.1 here where relevant), and secondly, what criteria are employed in deciding whether or not clients who are suitable for the approach would benefit from individual therapy (as opposed to couples, family and group therapy) at the outset. What criteria are employed when decisions concerning transfer from one modality (e.g. individual therapy) to another (e.g. group therapy) become salient? Indeed when do these issues become salient? What are the approach's views on the use of concurrent therapeutic modalities (e.g. where the client is seen in both individual and group therapy)?

3.3 Qualities of effective therapists

From the point of view of the approach under consideration, what qualities do effective therapists have? Focus on both personal qualities and skill variables. In writing this section what is the relative importance of personal characteristics vs skill factors here?

3.4 Therapeutic relationship and style

Here you should outline the type of therapeutic relationship that therapists of your orientation seek to establish with their clients. You should also characterize the interactive style of the therapist in the conduct of the approach in action. (While you will no doubt use your own dimensions, the following might be kept in mind: action–passive; formal–informal; self-disclosing–non-self-disclosing; humorous– serious.) How does the interactive style of the therapist change during the therapeutic process?

3.5 Major therapeutic strategies and techniques

List and describe the major strategies and techniques advocated as therapeutic by the approach. According to Marvin Goldfried, strategies lie at a level of abstraction between theory and techniques, so techniques are more *specific* than strategies. Please use this formulation in preparing this section and list the strategies first, showing how the techniques are specific ways of operationalizing the strategies. I am quite aware that some approaches cannot easily be described in these terms. Contact me if this is the case and we'll discuss how best to write this section.

3.6 The change process in therapy

Here outline the process of therapeutic change from beginning to end. What reliable patterns of change can be discerned in successful cases? Outline the major sources of lack of therapeutic progress and how these are addressed in the approach.

3.7 Limitations of the approach

Here describe the limitations of the approach. Where is there room for improvement? How should the approach develop in the future to rectify such deficiencies?

4 Case example (1,500 words)

Fully describe a case (a British client) which shows the approach in action, referring whenever possible to the above framework and dividing the section thus:

4.1 THE CLIENT

Briefly describe the client and his/her presenting concerns.

4.2 The therapy

Here the emphasis should be on describing the process of change (i.e. how the therapy unfolded over time). Speculate on the sources of the therapeutic change. What, with hindsight, might you have done differently?

Please resist the temptation to select a 'brilliant success'. Choose a case that readers can relate to, i.e. one that had its difficulties and where the client had a realistic (not an idealistic) outcome.

NB: Those of you who contributed a chapter to *Handbook of Individual Therapy* should present a *new* case.

Index